More praise for *Alexis de Tocqueville: A Life*

"Hugh Brogan is a British scholar richly specialized in French as well as American history. No one is better qualified to write this first exhaustive biography in English, and Brogan does not disappoint." — Michael Kammen, *Boston Sunday Globe*

"One of the greatest virtues of this book is the fact that the author pulls no punches. . . . This is a book that the reader wants never to end." — Alan Ryan, *The New York Review of Books*

"A welcome addition. Brogan writes with intelligence and style entertaining to a serious reader, and instructive to students of biography." — Harvey Mansfield, *New Criterion*

"Brogan's book will have to be reckoned with by all Anglophone students of Tocqueville. It is lively, comprehensive, well-researched, and exceedingly well-written." — Daniel J. Mahoney, *Claremont Review of Books*

"This is a magnificent biography. Hugh Brogan's knowledge of the details of Tocqueville's life is extraordinary, as is his erudite account of his family life and of French politics and society in the first half of the nineteenth century. And how splendidly the book is written! Tocqueville's life was marked by a triumph of character; Hugh Brogan's biography is a triumph of history and letters." — John Lukacs

"Brogan has written the definitive English language biography of the best known and most perceptive foreign interpreter of the American experience. The work's major achievement, however, is its lucid presentation of Tocqueville in the French contexts of monarchy and revolution that shaped his perceptions of the emerging democracy across the Atlantic." — Dennis Showalter, Colorado College

"One of the delights of this remarkable biography is to . . . see the past as if it were the present. . . . A biography as humane, learned, humorous, and perceptive as this extends our understanding of ourselves and where we came from." — Hilary Spurling, *The Observer*

ALEXIS DE TOCQUEVILLE

A LIFE

HUGH BROGAN

Yale University Press
New Haven and London

Published with assistance from the Annie Burr Lewis Fund.

First published in the United States in 2007 by Yale University Press.
First published in Great Britain in 2006 by Profile Books Ltd.

Designed by Geoff Green Book Design, Cambridge.

Set in Fournier by MacGuru Ltd.

Printed in the United States of America.

Library of Congress Control Number: 2006934482

ISBN 978-0-300-13625-8 (pbk. : alk. paper)

A catalogue record for this book is available from the British Library.

The paper in this book meets the guidelines for permanence and durability of the Committee
on Production Guidelines for Book Longevity of the Council on Library Resources.

10 9 8 7 6 5 4 3 2 1

Dedicated to the Memory of

SIR DENIS BROGAN
(1900–1974)

My Father – Teacher – and Inspiration

CONTENTS

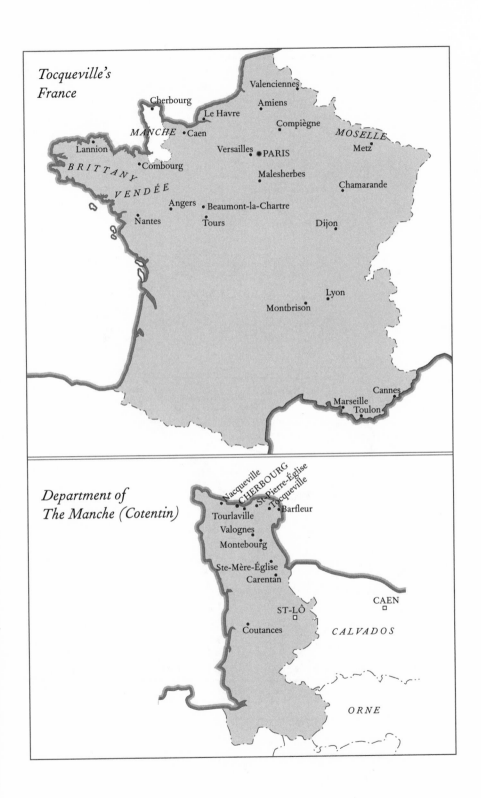

Tocqueville's
France

Cherbourg
Valenciennes
Amiens
Le Havre
MANCHE • Caen
Compiègne
MOSELLE
Lannion
Versailles • PARIS
Metz
BRITTANY
• Combourg
Malesherbes
VENDÉE
Chamarande
Angers • Beaumont-la-Chartre
Nantes
Tours
Dijon
Lyon
Montbrison
Cannes
Marseille
Toulon

Department of
The Manche (Cotentin)

Nacqueville
CHERBOURG
St-Pierre-Église
Tocqueville
Tourlaville
Barfleur
Valognes
Montebourg
Ste-Mère-Église
Carentan
CAEN
ST-LÔ
CALVADOS
Coutances

ORNE

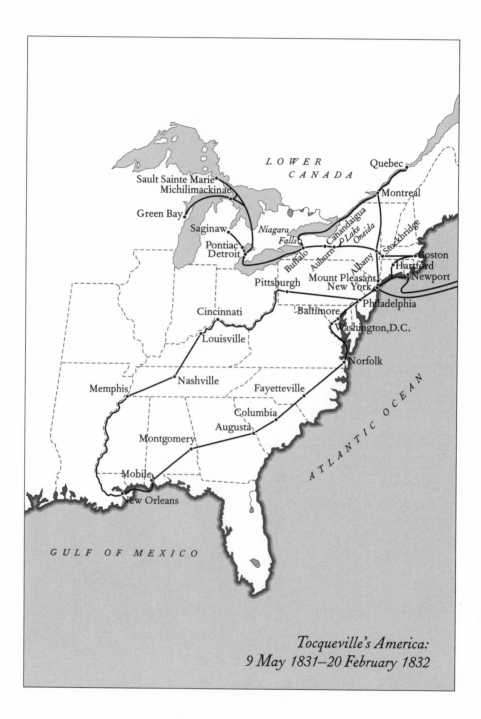

LOWER
CANADA

Quebec

Sault Sainte Marie
Michilimackinac

Montreal

Green Bay

Saginaw

Niagara
Falls

Canandaigua
Lake
Oneida

Stockbridge

Pontiac
Detroit

Buffalo

Auburn

Albany

Boston
Hartford
Newport

Pittsburgh

Mount Pleasant
New York

Cincinnati

Baltimore

Philadelphia

Louisville

Washington, D.C.

Nashville

Norfolk

Memphis

Fayetteville

Columbia

Montgomery

Augusta

ATLANTIC OCEAN

Mobile

New Orleans

GULF OF MEXICO

Tocqueville's America:
9 May 1831–20 February 1832

BOOK ONE

✦

Young Tocqueville

CHAPTER ONE

NOBLESSE

1773–1794

*Titles count for little with the French, and mere wealth is
not respected. Blood they understand.*

HILAIRE BELLOC

IT IS NO PARADOX to say that the greatest event of Tocqueville's
life occurred before he was born: the French Revolution, which decisively influenced almost everything that ever happened to him.

But behind and beyond that transforming convulsion there lay
another France – the France for which we still use the revolutionary
term, *l'ancien régime*, or old order. This played an equally important
part in shaping him. Tocqueville's families, paternal and maternal,
nobles of the sword and the robe, were distinguished in that lost world,
and he took a proper pride in their achievements, however remote.
Thus, late in life, he was enchanted to learn for certain that one of his
ancestors had sailed with Normandy's greatest hero, 'William Bastard
de graunt vigour', to the conquest of England in 1066.[1] He had been
almost equally delighted some years earlier when his wife discovered a mass of ancient parchment in a worm-eaten cupboard which
seemed to show that the Clérels (the original family name) had been
noble since at least 1425.[2] Yet nothing could more precisely illustrate
one of the main changes brought about in France by the Revolution
than the fate of those documents; for what Marie de Tocqueville had

almost certainly found was the once-cherished dossier of proofs of the family's ancient nobility, to be used if their status was ever challenged. In the new France such muniments were of little more than antiquarian interest.

Nevertheless, the Clérels were indeed an ancient noble family, Norman of the Normans, even before they acquired the manor-house of Tocqueville in the mid seventeenth century. It lies in the Cotentin,* a few miles east of Cherbourg, near the sea. In the middle of the eighteenth century it was occupied by the second Comte de Tocqueville, Bernard (1730–76), and his wife Catherine, the grandparents of Alexis. His story begins with them, for some of their traits, both social and individual, were to mark their descendants for the next hundred years.

Bernard was a soldier, and took his profession seriously – he had a portable military library of fifty-one volumes, ranging from the 1741 edition of the *Code militaire* to a work on *La Nouvelle Artillerie*, published four years before his death.[3] He had an exemplary career and was made a Chevalier of the military order of Saint-Louis. He was a younger son, but inherited the house and estates of Tocqueville when his brother, also a soldier, was killed in the Seven Years War and his nephew died at school in a playground accident. Bernard had never expected to be rich enough to marry, but that now became his duty if the family were not to die out. A comrade told him of Comte Étienne de Damas-Crux, who had several unmarried sisters. This was promising: the Damas were a numerous family which combined great landed wealth with Court favour and a firm commitment, like that of the Tocquevilles, to the duty and privilege of bearing arms for the King. Bernard was found acceptable, and was paired off with Catherine-Antoinette de Damas-Crux. His family had a record of making 'good' marriages, but this was better than usual: it marked the beginning of a great rise in the world. It is to be presumed that Catherine's dowry helped to finance Bernard's decision to rebuild his manor-house, enlarging it and giving it an elegant modern façade: the pediment of the garden-front was emblazoned with both the Tocqueville and the Damas-Crux coats-of-arms. The *manoir*, from now on, was unequivocally a *château*.[4]

---

* Best known in English as the Cherbourg Peninsula.

The alliance with the Damas was to be of great importance to the next two generations of Tocquevilles, for good and ill, but not exactly as was expected.[5] Great change was at hand, although its coming was probably not very visible from the Cotentin. There, life for the provincial *noblesse* went on in the manner that had long since become traditional. The Tocquevilles were not among the families which in the previous century had heeded the Sun King's invitation and gone to Versailles, there (after showing the necessary proofs) to become *noblesse de Cour* and join the perpetual competition for perquisites by which Louis XIV kept his *grands* docile and politically impotent. Like their neighbours they continued to be what they had always been – rustic Norman gentry, who spent their time farming or squeezing money out of the peasantry when they were not fighting in the King's wars. The Tocquevilles had long been in the middle rank of Norman *noblesse – nobles de race*, patrons of churches (*gentilshommes seigneurs de paroisse*) as well as fiefholders. They enjoyed the usual privileges of their order, among which were exemption from the *taille* (general tax) and the *gabelle* (salt tax), and the right to bypass the lower courts in any cases which involved them, going instead, in the first instance, to the higher royal courts. Only nobles were allowed to wear swords in public and to put battlements on their houses. They took precedence of lesser beings in public gatherings, and had a specially lofty pew in each parish church to which they had the presentation – Alexis eventually inherited the pew at Tocqueville, one of the few privileges to survive the Revolution. Although the soldierly tradition of the Tocquevilles forbade it, they could, as nobles, have claimed exemption (except in great emergencies) from all forms, physical or financial, of military service. Above all, they had various 'feudal dues' enabling them to tax, as it were, the land and business of their neighbours: dues which, in the days of serfdom, may possibly have had some functional justification, but which by the eighteenth century had become merely sources of income, as Alexis de Tocqueville, taking the peasants' side, indignantly demonstrated in his *Ancien Régime*. Some of their other privileges were surely more trouble than they were worth. They had the sole right to hunt and to trample down the peasants' crops in pursuit of their quarry. And in one of the three round towers of Tocqueville Comte Bernard kept 3,000 pigeons, another standing cause of peasant resentment, since the birds despoiled the harvest (in an epoch when famines were all too frequent). It is hard to see the point of this abuse, even if Bernard was fond of pigeon pie, unless it was intended as a ruthless display of his power and standing. Otherwise he, like his forebears, seems to have been a responsible landlord to the peasantry – 'We have lived among them as protectors and friends for centuries,' said his grandson,[6] not quite credibly. But the Tocquevilles did not mingle with their inferiors. There was no need. Social and intellectual life in the French provinces was remarkably vigorous and varied in the eighteenth century. Every local capital seems to have aspired to be a little Paris: Valognes, the capital of the Cotentin, was proud to be known as a little Versailles. The Tocquevilles had a town-house there to which they went every winter, to escape the mud of their estate and the chill of their damp chateau and to enjoy the company of their equals.

Forty years later, when Alexis de Tocqueville was born, this noble way of life had largely been destroyed. But it still had enough vitality to leave a permanent mark on his attitudes, particularly towards his countrymen. 'When I talk to a *gentilhomme*, though we have not two ideas in common, though all his opinions, wishes, and thoughts are opposed to mine, yet I feel at once that we belong to the same family, that we speak the same language, that we understand one another. I may like a *bourgeois* better, but he is a stranger.'[7] First and foremost he was a noble, to the end of his days, and cannot be understood unless this is recognized.

Tocqueville was never able entirely to shake off nostalgia for this lost world. In his first publication on the *ancien régime* he wrote:

> Anyone who wished to paint an accurate picture of the order of the *noblesse* would have to resort to many and various classifications, distinguishing nobles of the sword from nobles of the robe, nobles of the Court from nobles of the country, the most ancient families from the most recent; he would discover in this small society as many nuances and classes as in the greater society of which it was only a part. However, he would also have found that a certain homogeneous spirit guided the whole body; as a whole it obeyed certain fixed rules, governed itself according to certain invariable customs, and all its members had certain ideas in common.[8]

But by the mid eighteenth century the bonds of caste were stretched to breaking-point. By immemorial tradition the people of the kingdom of France were divided into three estates, but the division no longer made sense. The position of the Church (the First Estate) was coming under ferocious attack from the philosophers of the Enlightenment. In a nation rapidly growing from 20 million towards 30 million the privileges of a few hundred thousand nobles (the Second Estate) were more and more anomalous. And as Tocqueville hints, the *noblesse* was far from united. The greatest nobles – the richest, best educated, best connected – took advantage of France's material progress to further their own interests; they plunged into high finance and industrial investment, and eagerly married into rich *roturier* (commoner, Third Estate) families, which in their turn were easily ennobled; they were charmed and excited by the limitless possibilities opening to European civilization, and began to regard the prospect of social and political reform with eagerness, not apprehension: they were even prepared, in principle, to sacrifice their privileges if it meant that they could merge with the far more numerous leaders of the Third Estate in a new governing class of notables,* an ambition which was largely to be achieved, thanks to the Revolution. But at the other end of their order were the rural squireens, the *hobereaux*, families with nothing to live on but their feudal dues and the produce of their ill-managed lands, often no larger than peasant smallholdings: ill-educated, provincial, struggling, often unsuccessfully, to cling to their noble status. They had less and less in common with the polished ladies and gentlemen of the Parisian *salons*.

If there was ever any doubt as to which end of the scale the Tocquevilles would move towards, the Damas marriage settled it.

Not that Bernard and Catherine were particularly worldly, in the English sense of the word. Besides the military library the chateau contained eighty-four volumes of religious devotion. The Tocqueville family's way of life was permeated, and in their eyes justified, by Catholicism. They were devout in the Jesuit, rather than the Jansenist tradition† (although, in the next century, Alexis de Tocqueville deeply

---

* In French, *Notables*. There is no good equivalent for this word in day-to-day English, so 'notable' will have to do.

† The Jansenists were a party in the French Church which in the name of Divine grace resisted

admired the greatest Jansenist writer, Blaise Pascal). The quality of their religion emerges in Catherine's account of the birth of her son, which took place at her mother's family home in 1772.

> Hardly had this child been born [she writes] than my husband offered him to God and consecrated him to Him. He [her husband] was present at the christening ceremony, *pénétré* with faith and religion. Several persons have told me that nothing in the world could be more touching or more edifying than the sight of him at that moment. When he came back to my side he told me that he had been extremely moved, and that he had asked God with all his heart to remove the child from the world if he should prove to be *un mauvais sujet* [black sheep]. ... He often said to me that it was necessary to offer this little treasure to God every day, and to be ready to sacrifice it to Him, because it had belonged to Him before it was ours.[9]

So pious a man could not be a follower of the *philosophes*; but he had picked up some of Rousseau's ideas about the rearing of children (he owned several books on education). He thought he could make his little boy hardy by dressing him in nothing but a linen shirt, whatever the weather, without shoes or stockings. Before long the child was seriously ill, but before he was quite at the point of death the father himself died, urging his son at all times to love and respect his mother, and to take her advice even if he lived to be fifty.

The boy was named Hervé Louis François Bonaventure; he was always known as Hervé (although his name-day feast was that of St Louis, which eventually he shared with his wife, Louise). For a few years after his father's death he was extremely happy: he loved Tocqueville and the country round; we do not hear of any playmates. At the age of eight he was sent to the Collège d'Harcourt in Paris, a school favoured by pious noble families: it was extremely expensive.[10] Unluckily Hervé was given in charge to a priest who was both cruel and an unbeliever. He gave the boy too little to eat, and whipped him when, as was inevitable, he stole an apple. He was so regularly brutal that Hervé, according to himself, suffered from constant terror; he became both timid and sneaking. Then, one day, one of his Damas uncles noticed works by

---

the orthodox alliance of the Church hierarchy with the monarchy. Louis XIV regarded them as no better than Huguenots and republicans.

Voltaire and Rousseau on the tutor's bookshelves. This was serious: the tutor was quickly dismissed and a substitute found, the Abbé Louis Le Sueur, who won Hervé's heart at their first meeting by giving him a hunk of bread, which the boy immediately wolfed down. Le Sueur was a man of simple religious faith, witty, urbane and cultivated, but it was his immense kindliness which won the lifelong devotion of Hervé de Tocqueville, as of his sons afterwards. Before long he had taken the place of a father in his pupil's life. It was just as well, for when Hervé was thirteen his mother contracted a fatal case of smallpox. He was not allowed to enter her bedroom, for fear of infection; but he stayed the other side of her door, and heard her death-cries. 'Forty-nine years later they still echo in my heart.' It did not matter to him particularly that in spite of all precautions he caught the disease, fortunately only a mild infection. He felt appallingly lonely: his aunts and uncles and grandmother could not fill the void. Rather the reverse: he was very shy, and one of his aunts, thinking him a dolt, made him the regular butt of her wit. It was just as well that he had the abbé to love him.*

He left school almost at the very moment that the Revolution broke out.

Like every other Frenchman he was confronted with the immediate, inescapable need to make painful choices. He discovered that neither the traditions of his family nor the tumultuous experiences of the time were much help to him in working out a course that was both honourable and safe.

> I have often heard that my grandmother, a woman of great piety, [said Alexis de Tocqueville in the 1850s] after having urged her young son to exercise the virtues of a private life, never failed to add – 'And then, my child, never forget that a man belongs, above all, to his country; that there is no sacrifice which he must not make to it; and that God requires him to be ready to devote, on every occasion, his time, his fortune, and his life, to the service of the State and the King.'[11]

It is unmistakably the voice of Catherine de Tocqueville, and it is the creed by which all her immediate descendants tried to live, but it was not applicable in 1789. For one thing, most of her family, the Damas,

---

* 'Abbé' is the colloquial designation of a priest; cf. 'Father' in English.

left France for Brussels in the grotesquely named *émigration joyeuse* which followed the fall of the Bastille, and they summoned young Hervé to join them as of right: had they not previously obtained for him a reserve commission in the Vexin regiment, of which his uncle Charles was colonel? But Hervé, who had grown up an earnest, even priggish young man, had already formed an aversion to what he saw as the frivolity and immorality of the great nobles, which he was inclined to blame for the fall of the King's government. Besides, the advantage of the commission in his eyes was that it expressly allowed him to stay in Paris and continue his education. He disapproved of the emigration, thinking that it was largely inspired by mere fashion, and was a desertion of king and country. He was not yet without hope that a liberal, reforming government would emerge. He had lodged for some time with the son of General de La Fayette, who was also a victim of the Rousseau treatment, so that he became feeble in both body and mind; but Hervé thought that 'the hero of two worlds' might gain power and exercise it wisely, so he stayed where he was. Madame de La Fayette began to disillusion him. She did not share her husband's enthusiasm for the Revolution: on one occasion, when she was collecting alms for penniless 'conquerors of the Bastille' (leaders of the crowd which had stormed the prison on 14 July) she pushed her collector's bag disdainfully at Hervé, remarking, 'Do admit that I look a fool.'

He stayed in Paris until after the royal family's flight to Varennes in 1791, in which his uncle Louis de Damas figured ingloriously; then at last he went to Brussels. The Damas got him a commission in an *émigré* regiment, but things were just as bad as he had feared: money which should have been husbanded against hard times was flung away on 'senseless luxury' because the refugees were sure that it could only be a matter of months before they returned to France in triumph; every hopeful rumour, and there were many, was believed. Hervé did not share these illusions and saw no point in staying. He went back to Paris and enlisted as an ordinary soldier in the King's Guard. 'I wanted to prove to the King that my devotion was untainted by personal ambition.' But then the National Assembly forced Louis XVI to disband the Guard.

Hervé witnessed the successful attack on the Tuileries of 10 August 1792. Like many others he tried in vain to save the king, and was lucky to get home unscathed and unsuspected (he hid his sabre and his gun in the room of the Abbé Le Sueur). As he crossed the Place Louis XV (soon to be the place de la Révolution) he saw that it was heaped with the decapitated bodies of the Swiss Guards: 'Women and children stripped the bodies, and fought each other, their feet covered in blood, for rags of clothes torn off the victims. The rage and cupidity were even more horrible than the murders.' That evening the city was covered by a black and stinking cloud of smoke: the revolutionaries had piled up the bodies and burnt them. Hervé's preoccupation now was to save Le Sueur. He contrived to send the abbé out of Paris to his family in Picardy, and followed him next day. In this way they escaped the September massacres. Six months later Hervé married.

This event was in part an attempt by all concerned to keep some sort of normal life going even in desperate times. Louise Le Peletier de Rosanbo (1771–1836) was the second of three sisters; Hervé, who met her at a party, seems to have known no more of her than that she was pretty, and she knew as little of him.[12] Both came from good families and in ordinary times would have been accounted well-off, even rich. They would make a good match, so the usual negotiations went ahead. It was all according to custom – a custom of which Alexis de Tocqueville was to express almost violent disapproval. Attaching enormous importance to successful marriages, he denounced the fact that in France a young man and woman could marry while knowing nothing essential about each other. Can he have been thinking of his parents? In France, he grumbled, the choice of a wife was taken less seriously than the choice of a pair of gloves.[13] He advised his nephew Hubert to make every effort to know any prospective bride's family, if he could not get to know her: 'few good trees produce bad fruit.'[14] This maxim would have given Hervé no trouble, had it come his way, for Mlle de Rosanbo was a granddaughter of Chrétien-Guillaume Lamoignon de Malesherbes.

At this point we encounter the second strain in Alexis de Tocqueville's ancestry: it was possibly even more important than that of his father's family. The Lamoignon were one of the greatest clans of the *noblesse de robe*. Malesherbes was First President of the Cour des Aides, the body which administered the tax laws. Nevertheless, he had been a thorn in the side of French government ever since his youth, when because he was a Lamoignon and his father was chancellor he had been appointed director of the Librairie – that is, censor of publications. In that post he had fostered freedom of the press, protecting the *philosophes* (he was one himself), ensuring the continued publication of the *Encyclopédie* after the Church tried to suppress it, and helping Jean-Jacques Rousseau so tactfully that he kept the respect of that paranoid genius. As First President he was one of the leaders in the struggle of the *parlements* against the measures of Louis XV which in 1771 resulted in the abolition of the old courts and the exile of their members to their estates. Malesherbes did not mind: his fall meant that he could devote himself to his real passion, botany. But Louis XVI not only recalled the *parlements* on his accession in 1774: he appointed Malesherbes a minister at the same time that Malesherbes's friend Turgot was made controller-general of finance. Neither man was enough of a courtier to succeed at Versailles: they were soon ousted. Nevertheless, Malesherbes now felt himself entitled to send the king memoranda whenever he wished on whatever subject seemed to him to be urgent. He recommended the abolition of *lettres de cachet* and the fiscal privileges of the nobility; he advocated toleration for Protestants and citizenship for Jews; he wanted expenditure on the splendours of the Court to be ruthlessly cut, urged the summoning of a National Assembly and, just before the Estates-General were convened in 1789, advised the king to remember the fate of Charles I and take thought to avoid it (Louis later avowed his regret for not having followed this advice). He helped to draw up several of the *cahiers de doléances** (presumably of the nobility) in 1788–9,[15] those same *cahiers* which one day Alexis de Tocqueville would analyse in his *Ancien Régime*. Tocqueville does not mention his great-grandfather in that connection, but quotes substantially from one of his protests to Louis XV: 'You hold your crown, sire, from God alone; but you are not going to deny yourself the satisfaction of believing that you also owe your power to the voluntary submission of your subjects. In France certain inviolable rights belong to the nation; your ministers will not be bold enough to deny it to you ... No, sire, in spite of much effort, no-one has yet persuaded you

---

* Petitions of grievances. Each election district of each of the three orders which made up the Estates-General drew up such a *cahier*.

that there is no difference between the French nation and a people enslaved.'[16] Tocqueville's point was that Malesherbes both expressed and shaped the pre-revolutionary climate of opinion.

Malesherbes briefly served again as a minister in 1786–87, but declined to serve in the Estates-General of 1789, although at first he strongly approved of what was going on. He was content, at this moment, to enjoy private life. In 1787 his eldest granddaughter had married the young Jean-Baptiste, comte de Chateaubriand, head of a Breton family of much the same standing as the Norman Tocqueville. This union brought the comte's younger brother into the Malesherbes circle: François-René de Chateaubriand, destined to be the greatest French writer of his generation and eventually a decisive influence on Alexis de Tocqueville. He was warmly welcomed, and in his memoirs has much to say of Malesherbes and his family:

> M. de Malesherbes had three daughters, Mesdames de Rosanbo, d'Aunay, de Montboissier: Mme de Rosanbo was his favourite, because she shared his opinions. [She and her husband] Président de Rosanbo also had three daughters, Mesdames de Chateaubriand, d'Aunay and de Tocqueville, and a son [Louis] whose brilliant intelligence was veiled by his perfect Christianity. M. de Malesherbes delighted in the company of his children, grandchildren, and great-grandchildren. Many times, at the beginning of the Revolution, I saw him arrive at Mme de Rosanbo's, hot and bothered by politics, and throw off his wig, lie on my sister-in-law's carpet, and let himself be swarmed over by a mob of shrieking infants. ... He was a man of science, integrity and courage, but always on the boil, impassioned to the point that one day, when talking to me about Condorcet, he said, 'That man was once my friend; today, I would have no scruple about killing him like a dog.'[17]

(Since the Revolution was going to murder both Malesherbes and Condorcet this remark seems unfortunate.)

Malesherbes was otherwise a kindly man, and seems to have noticed that François-René was someone quite out of the common. He took the boy under his wing. They were both becoming disillusioned and alarmed about the Revolution. Chateaubriand had long wanted to go to America; now that he knew he was a writer he desired it more than ever: he wanted authentic experience of unknown lands and noble savages to give power to his work. But not expecting his relations (who would have to pay for the trip) to sympathize with such a project, he gave out that he would go on foot to discover the North-West Passage – 'a scheme so staggeringly impractical', says George D. Painter, 'that it could not but appeal to the hardest heads in that enterprising age'.[18] Malesherbes was especially enthusiastic: 'If I were younger I'd go with you ... But at my age a man must die where he is.' The scheme was a fantasy: apart from anything else, the North-West Passage did not exist, as Malesherbes, a student of geography, should have guessed. But Chateaubriand, the penniless child of a social order that was collapsing round him, his head whirling with notions of virtuous farmers, Red Indians and a communion with Nature in vast solitudes, had every motive to seek his fortunes elsewhere, and anyway all young men like to travel. His voyage would be one, not of geographical, but of self discovery. To Malesherbes the *philosophe* and botanist, on the other hand, the allure of a new country was enormous. 'Do not forget to write to me by every ship ... It is a pity that you know no botany.' Chateaubriand sailed for America in January 1791.[19]

He returned exactly a year later, after numerous adventures which had given him a huge literary capital that in a few years he would use to launch the Romantic age (the North-West Passage remained undisturbed). As soon as he got back his family married him to a young woman whom he had never met and would never much like, but who was supposed (incorrectly) to be rich. Chateaubriand soon left her in Paris and went off to join the army of the emigration ('No royalist could stay at home without being considered a coward') more or less as Hervé de Tocqueville was deserting it. Malesherbes thoroughly approved of this new adventure, and urged François-René to take his brother with him, which, fatally for Jean-Baptiste, he did.[20]

Malesherbes soon met his destiny. The monarchy fell, the King was to be put on trial; the former magistrate and minister volunteered to be his chief counsel. He told the President of the Convention: 'I was twice called to the Council of him who was my master, at a time when that employment was the object of everyone's ambition: I owe him the same service when such employment has become, in the judgement of many men, dangerous.' Louis XVI gladly accepted the offer, and there followed the most touching passage of both men's lives, as they conferred on the King's defence and talked about the past. Louis had two other counsel, able and devoted, but he regarded Malesherbes as an old friend, the last left to him. Malesherbes, cheerful and optimistic by nature, at first supposed he could win the king an acquittal, or at least save his life, but by the end of the trial he knew that such hope was vain. He broke down in tears when he tried to give a closing speech to the Convention. 'Robespierre rose and said that he forgave Malesherbes the tears he had just shed for Louis,' but the king must die.[21]

After the execution Malesherbes felt that he was a marked man. 'Robespierre's eye is on me everywhere,' he said. '… That man must hate me, for he wishes to pass for virtuous.'[22] * He and his family left Paris for their estate at Malesherbes in the Orléannais. And then Hervé de Tocqueville turned up to marry Louise de Rosanbo.

'I arrived at Malesherbes on 30 January 1793; as I got out of the coach I saw M. de Malesherbes under the peristyle. The venerable old man, whom I was meeting for the first time, opened his arms to me as if I were already his son, and thereafter the closest confidence was united in me with the respect that he inspired.' Hervé fell as completely under Malesherbes's generous spell as had Chateaubriand: they were both fatherless boys, and Malesherbes's ready kindness and interest were irresistible. Lonely, anxious and shy, Hervé suddenly found that he had a large and lively family to call his own. He fell in love with everyone at Malesherbes, including his *fiancée*. The wooing was not without its difficulties. Louise de Rosanbo was as pretty as ever, and Hervé began to find her charming; but before he succumbed he thought they should have a private and frank conversation about what marriage would entail. This was unconventional, especially if Hervé raised the matter of sex; Mlle de Rosanbo responded so coldly that Hervé wondered if it would not be best to withdraw; but a second conversation (no doubt the young lady's mother had advised her) went much better. All seemed well. 'Confidence was not slow to grow and was soon followed by a lively and tender affection.' They were married on 12 March 1793 in some secrecy by the local *curé*, who, being a refractory priest (that

---

* In fairness to Robespierre it should be said that there is no evidence that he had a hand in the destruction of Malesherbes. Nor did he try to prevent it.

is, one who refused to accept the 'constitutional' Church set up by the National Assembly), had gone into hiding.

'The day after my wedding I went with my wife to make a call in Malesherbes town; there she was seized with a nervous attack.* I had never seen anything like it, I was extremely frightened. I thought she was going to die. Her parents reassured me, but the fact was that she was already liable to that nervous affliction which has got worse since and which has thrown a sombre pall over her existence and mine, but I had never been warned.'

It is difficult to acquit the Rosanbos of irresponsibility, to say the least. Hervé was diffident and inexperienced, but he was not a man who would ever flinch from a duty, and he had the intelligence and character to bear up under any such burden. He never failed his wife. She caused him much unhappiness, nevertheless, and he should at least have been given the opportunity of walking into the trap with open eyes. But beyond setting out the tale in his memoirs, he never seems to have complained.

For the time being he consoled himself with the company at Malesherbes. There was Jean-Baptiste de Chateaubriand, returned from emigration to look after his wife Aline and their two small sons, Louis and Christian; there was the youngest Rosanbo daughter, Suzanne-Guillemette, who had recently married her first cousin, Charles Le Peletier d'Aunay; there were M. and Mme de Rosanbo and their son Louis, aged fifteen. Malesherbes' youngest daughter, Marie de Montboissier, had emigrated to Switzerland, from where she wrote indiscreet letters to her sisters. It seems that in spite of all that had happened these royalists had not yet grasped the nature and the extremity of their danger. The family could not believe that the Jacobins would try to kill Malesherbes, and although he himself had no such illusion he did not think that any move would be made against the others. He was resolved to stay in France in case he could help Marie-Antoinette or the King's sister, Madame Elisabeth, if they were put on trial; besides, he wanted to testify to the glorious memory of Louis XVI (much more reverenced in death than he had ever been in life) and believed that he could not do so effectively if he emigrated. He even went back to

* Exactly what this means is not clear.

Paris for a few weeks in the summer of 1793, until he received a secret warning from the Committee of General Security to make himself scarce. He took the hint.[23]

Spring, summer, autumn: in spite of everything the family was happy. 'The life we led was very agreeable,' Hervé was to record.

> At nine o'clock every evening everybody gathered in the *salon*. M. de Malesherbes would arrive and seize on one of us for a talk which went on until midnight. While talking he never failed to undo the buttons, of coat and waistcoat, of his interlocutor. [We are not told how he treated ladies.] At midnight he went to bed fully clothed, and slept for several hours; he was made to keep his clothes on because he had the habit, when an idea struck him in the middle of the night, of getting up to write it down. At such moments he never thought of getting dressed, and several times he had suffered badly from cold.

They were left unmolested until the winter, but eventually the authorities searched the Rosanbo mansion in Paris and there found, along with such incriminating evidence as a bust of Louis XIV given by that monarch to one of Rosanbo's ancestors, a manuscript dating from 1790 in which Rosanbo, who had then been a President of the Paris *parlement*, and his fellow magistrates had formally protested against the abolition of that body, just as they had protested against its abolition under Louis XV. There was also a vast amount of compromising correspondence: sixty letters from François-René de Chateaubriand, for example. The head of the Revolutionary Tribunal, Fouquier-Tinville, himself scrutinized all the evidence, and then a warrant was issued for Rosanbo's arrest.[24]

> On 17 December we were at table [says Hervé de Tocqueville] when the *concierge* of the château came in with consternation on his face and, employing unusual language, said: 'Citizen Rosanbo, outside are some citizens from Paris asking for you.' We all turned pale. M. de Rosanbo left the room at once, and our anxiety was extreme when it became clear that he was not coming back.

Early next morning the Parisians (two workers from the Bondy Section) carried him off to prison as a conspirator against the security of the republic, one and indivisible. Two days later Malesherbes and the rest followed. The house had been searched and more compromising letters had been found (those of Mme de Montboissier in particular), though nothing which directly inculpated Malesherbes, the Chateaubriands, or the Tocquevilles.* It hardly mattered. All were incarcerated. Hervé: 'I had never seen a prison. I don't know how to express what I felt when I had to crawl through a door only three feet high and heard the great key turn in the locks behind us.'

The *sans-culottes* were delighted with the arrests; not so the people of Malesherbes. One tradition affirms that when the prisoners were carried off on 20 December some of the villagers ran after their carriages, shouting angry protests and trying to free them. It is at least certain that the officers of the commune sent an attestation of the old nobleman's good citizenship to Paris, and displayed a copy in the office of the *maire* for three days without provoking any opposition. 'We certify and attest that Citizen Chrétien-Guillaume de Lamoignon has at all times shown himself to be the most zealous possible defender of the rights of the people ...' It did no good.[25]

The Reign of Terror was in full swing: the war must be won and the Revolution saved, and judicial murder was one of the means employed. It could be delayed, but not finally averted. Rosanbo was executed on 20 April 1794; Mme de Rosanbo on the 21st, for being his wife, and on the same day Jean-Baptiste de Chateaubriand, for having been an *émigré* and for corresponding with *émigrés*; Mme de Chateaubriand, for the same, although she had never emigrated; and Malesherbes himself. He made a worthy exit. His hands tied, he was being led from the court-room to the tumbril when he stumbled on the threshold. 'Mauvais présage,' said he. 'Un Romain ne serait pas allé plus avant.'[26†]

As Jean-Baptiste was led away to the Revolutionary Tribunal, Hervé asked his permission to take charge of his sons, who were being sheltered by a peasant family at Malesherbes. Jean-Baptiste willingly agreed, but his brother-in-law must have wondered if he would live to take up his obligation. In June the Convention passed the notorious law of 22 Prairial, which stripped accused prisoners of

---

* According to HT, what upset the noble inhabitants of the chateau more than anything else was that the intruders used the *tutoyer* to them all, even the ladies. The suspects would not reciprocate, which was in turn resented.

† 'A bad omen. A Roman would travel no further.'

all legal or judicial protections and, in Norman Hampson's phrase, 'was little more than a formal way of clearing the gaols'.[27] Fortunately the prison of Port-Libre [sic], where the Tocquevilles were confined, was not immediately selected for one of the resultant repetitions of the September Massacres. Prisoners were taken away to die in handfuls rather than wholesale. Every afternoon a grim little ritual occurred: a jailer would approach five or six prisoners with the words, 'Citizens, you are wanted at the office.' Sometimes he added, 'You won't need to take anything with you.' There would follow heartrending scenes of farewell. To avoid witnessing them (he sorrowed enough anyway) Hervé made a habit of taking a nap at that hour. One day he woke up to find that his hair had gone white from the strain. He was twenty-one years old, and as he says in his memoirs, his responsibilities were crushing, even apart from the constant threat of the guillotine: he had to look after his brother-in-law, Louis de Rosanbo, now seventeen, and two young women, his wife and her surviving sister, Mme d'Aunay; and their health was collapsing from grief and fear.

The terms of their imprisonment deteriorated. Prisoners were no longer allowed to prepare their own meals and eat them in privacy, they had to share a common table and eat the common food, which was very bad though not actually poisonous ('le cuisinier de notre prison était honnête homme'*). No-one dared complain, lest spies report an attempt to spread dissaffection; they even had to pretend to like the food, to prove their patriotic devotion: 'One day we were reproached by one of those shameless scoundrels, smiling hellishly, for not having a good appetite.' This moral sadism reached its climax on the Feast of the Supreme Being (8 June 1794). Executions went on as usual, but the prisoners who were spared that day were herded into the common room of the jail for a patriotic concert, men on one side, women on the other. Larive, once a tragedian at the Théâtre Français, was obliged to declaim suitable verses, and one of the ladies, Mlle de Béthisy, 'who had a superb voice', was forced to sing the 'Marseillaise':

Marchons, marchons, qu'un sang impur
Abreuve nos sillons!

---

* 'The cook in our prison was one of us.'

17

This was too much for Suzanne d'Aunay: she had a hysterical attack and began to cry, 'Oh! the monsters! The monsters!' This might get them all guillotined. Hervé rushed over, caught her in his arms, and repressed her cries, which fortunately none of the jailers noticed.

Some days later Hervé was trapped into paying a bribe to the prison-keepers, for which, he subsequently discovered, he would have been sent to the scaffold on XII Thermidor; but on the afternoon of the IX (27 July), as he was looking out of his window, he saw a cripple being carried into the prison by a *gendarme*. It was Couthon, one of Robespierre's closest associates. Newsboys' cries in the street announced the arrest of Robespierre. Then came word that he had been rescued and taken to the Hôtel de Ville. Through the night and day following the prisoners of Port-Libre waited in the sharpest anxiety. But for them it all ended happily. The Tocquevilles had to wait until October to be liberated, but on the 20th – ten months to the day since their arrest – they were set free; and Abbé Le Sueur was at the door to welcome them. 'How cloudless the sky looked! How fresh the air seemed! How vast was the horizon!' They hired a *fiacre* and drove about Paris all day 'to feel their liberty'.[28] But as Hervé later remarked, grief still threatened their joy: 'Nine of us had entered the house of grief, only four came out. Our parents,* our friends had disappeared, and the wreckage of two families had no one to rely on except a young man of twenty-two who knew little of the world and whose only experience was of misfortune.'† Nevertheless, he was alive, and free.

* Note how completely HT identifies himself with his wife's family.
† HT somewhat understates the disaster which befell Malesherbes, his family and household. As well as the Rosanbos, the Chateaubriands and Malesherbes himself, his sister, Mme de Senozan (whose letters, which showed her to be actively plotting with the *émigrés*, precipitated the investigation and arrests), was executed three weeks after her brother. Malesherbes's two secretaries were guillotined; only his *valet-de-chambre* was spared.

CHAPTER TWO

ROYALISTS

1794–1814

Un troubadour béarnais
Les yeux inondés de larmes
A ses montagnards chantait
Ce refrain, source d'alarmes:
Louis, le fils d'Henri
Est prisonnier dans Paris. *

RELEASE FROM PRISON put an end to danger but not to difficulty. Hardly had the last prisoners been freed than the Convention ordered that all nobles must leave Paris.[1] The Tocquevilles found refuge at Saint-Mandé, just outside the city, and there spent the frightful winter of 1794–5, the coldest, hungriest and most deadly of the Revolution. In Paris, starvation was followed by an epidemic of dysentery. In Saint-Mandé, 'Mme de Tocqueville was dangerously ill with a nervous fever.' Towards winter's end the Convention relented, and allowed the nobles to return; the Tocquevilles settled for a time in the Hôtel de Rosanbo, where everything easily portable had been stolen. Bread was still in short supply and they often had to eat cakes of rice instead, but Hervé noted sardonically that there was plenty of meat in the restaurants,

---

* 'A Pyrenean troubadour / Whose eyes were drowned in tears / Sang to his fellow-mountaineers / This burthen, breeding fears: / *The son of Henry of Navarre / In Paris lies a prisoner.*' This was the song which AT's mother sang. See *below*, p. 25.

where the profiteers of the Revolution were spending their gains. In the summer of 1796 the Tocquevilles returned at last to Malesherbes, which had also been comprehensively looted.

Hervé wasted no time after his release. A family council confirmed his position as guardian of the two Chateaubriand boys (who had been sheltered by their old nurse). He set to work to restore the income from the Chateaubriand estates, though it was a slow business. It was not so difficult to rescue his own estates, since he had neither emigrated nor been convicted by the Revolutionary Tribunal, but he had at least one narrow escape. During the Revolution the peasants had burned the roof off the detested pigeon-tower at Tocqueville and killed all the birds, but had otherwise left the chateau alone. Some of them, however, cast covetous eyes on its land. They went to the local administration and claimed the right to buy it, or some of it: if the comte de Tocqueville was not an *émigré*, he ought to have been, and anyway it would be easy and risk-free to add his name to the list of the proscribed, whose property could be sequestrated. Fortunately Hervé's devoted man of business was able to frustrate this initiative.

By now Hervé himself was emerging as man of real practical ability, utterly dependable. Even the Damas (somewhat to their surprise) came to acknowledge it. In 1802 he travelled into Germany as escort to his cousin, Elisabeth-Charlotte de Damas, when she needed her still-exiled father Comte Étienne's consent to her marriage (which was not forthcoming: he persuaded her to marry someone else). Hervé also rescued the Malesherbes inheritance and protected the rights of Mme de Montboissier. In 1800 or thereabouts he and Louis de Rosanbo successfully approached Mme Bonaparte, the wife of the First Consul, to get Mme de Montboissier's sentence of exile lifted. (Thirty years later he still remembered Josephine fondly: 'she had already lost her looks, but she kept that incomparable grace which was to distinguish her on the Throne ...'). And he managed to arrive at a satisfactory agreement with the numerous creditors who had large claims on the Rosanbo estates.[2]

This was of immediate importance to him. His wife was one of the principal Rosanbo heirs, and the Chateaubriand boys, who were effectively being brought up as his sons, were two more. The ménage needed a settled home, all the more because, in 1797, Mme de Tocqueville bore a son, Hippolyte (nursing him, her husband tells us proudly in his memoirs, with her own milk). In 1800 a second son, Édouard, was born. Malesherbes was now Louis de Chateaubriand's property, and perhaps for this reason (Louis would one day want it for himself) or because it was not close enough to Paris, Hervé decided to move. (Tocqueville, of course, was even farther, and anyway, in view of the renewed war with Britain, may have been deemed dangerously close to the coast.) At any rate, in 1802 the Tocquevilles settled at the *château* of Verneuil-sur-Seine, a property which had belonged to Mme de Senozan, M. de Malesherbes' guillotined sister. At first it was rented, but in 1807 the large white house and its park became the property of the Tocquevilles when the Lamoignon estate was finally distributed among the inheritors.

Until then the comte and comtesse also maintained a house in Paris, at 987 rue de la Ville-l'Évêque, and it was there, at two in the afternoon, XI Thermidor An XIII (29 July 1805) that Mme de Tocqueville gave birth to her third and last son, Alexis-Charles-Henri Clérel.* Mme de Tocqueville was desolated by the appearance of another boy: she had badly wanted a girl. But Hervé said that the baby's face was so individual and expressive that he was sure to be a great man: 'I added, as a joke, that he would become Emperor one day.' We are not told if this cheered up the mother at all.

During the following winter Mme de Tocqueville's health took 'a convulsive turn' (*une tour convulsive*) which never slackened for three months. The doctors said that winter in a warmer climate was essential for her, so in November 1806 the whole family (including the young Chateaubriands, removed discontentedly from their school and their friends) set off for Italy. But in the Alps Édouard had the first of the dangerous asthma attacks which were to afflict him throughout life, and in Turin Hervé was warned (rather late in the day) that in view of the continuing war Naples, his destination, was dangerous. So he retreated to Nice, where Mme de Tocqueville's health greatly improved, and where the Chateaubriands, pious youths, were shocked at being taken to the opera. Christian, the younger, sat in the back of the box throughout the performance, with his eyes shut.

---

* The name 'Tocqueville' does not appear on the birth-certificate; the father simply signs himself 'Clérel'. Revolutionary orthodoxy was not quite dead. One of the witnesses signing the document was the Abbé Le Sueur.

After a leisurely journey home they were back in Verneuil in May 1807. Life began to resume something of the old *plaisir*. Hervé might have been prepared to serve the state had the Republic lasted; but he could not and would not abandon the Bourbons for the new dynasty of Bonaparte. He devoted himself instead to improving his property. The Tocquevilles became part of one of the little groups which formed all over France under the Napoleonic Empire; groups of passive, tacit dissent from the assumptions of the time. As members of such a group they acknowledged the ideals which kept it together, and were loyal to the individuals who composed it, but the circumstances which led to its formation militated against any particular activity. To intervene in public affairs would be to risk renewed disaster. Under the Bonapartist regime conformity to the master's slightest wish was the order of the day. Those who, admiring the genius of the Emperor and acknowledging the achievements of France since the Revolution, tried to co-operate with Napoleon while keeping faith with their own principles always got into difficulties. For instance, François-René de Chateaubriand, who was struck off the list of proscribed *émigrés* by Napoleon's sister Elisa, and who returned to France in 1800, was winning fame as an author. He dedicated the second edition of his *Génie du Christianisme* to the First Consul, and was eventually rewarded with a diplomatic post. But the kidnapping and murder of the duc d'Enghien in 1804 revolted him: he resigned, and rejoined his relations in private life. Mme de Staël, Pius VII, Alexander I of Russia, Louis of Holland – these are only some other conspicuous names on the list of those who in the last resort could not pay the price of complete submission. Yet the price of active resistance was fearfully high. To lie low and wait for better days was, many thought, the course of prudence. Something could thus be conserved. So reasoned Talleyrand. So, on the whole, reasoned Hervé de Tocqueville.

Yet in 1810 he became *maire* (the same word as 'mayor', but differing from the English office as a French commune differs from an English town) of Verneuil, which entailed taking an oath of loyalty to the imperial regime. The reasons he gives for this action are significant. He acknowledges that loyalty to his family and to the memory of 'the defender of Louis XVI' obliged him to keep his distance from any government which was not that of a Bourbon; but being *maire* would shield him from the plots of envious and ill-intentioned peasants, and give him the chance of acquiring some patronage which would be useful to others and himself. In other words, Hervé wanted to increase and consolidate his local influence. André Jardin detects in this a 'quasi-feudal' sense of *noblesse oblige*: he behaved as if the commune was an extension of his personal estate, and had to be reminded that it was his official deputy, not his steward, who was supposed to run Verneuil during the *maire*'s absences (which were frequent: the Tocquevilles passed their winters in Paris). Either way, he had seen his opportunity and taken it: it was available to him because the régime was always short of qualified men to fill the positions which it created. And although Hervé would never have admitted it (he prided himself on having always served the same master, the true king of France) it was in fact a first step towards endorsing the Empire. 'The Emperor was then at the apogee of his glory'; there was no premonition of the prodigious events to come.[3]

Hervé was now in his late thirties; he had good abilities, and so far had had no chance to employ them in public life. As *maire* he could at least keep a strict (perhaps an over-strict) eye on his subordinates. His energy and ambition demanded an outlet as would, one day, those of Alexis, who felt that he inherited his father's temperament:

> this unquiet mind, this consuming impatience, this need for acute and repeated excitement [which] characterize our father to an almost childish degree. This disposition can give great *élan* at certain moments. But more often it torments one for no cause, agitates fruitlessly, and makes those who possess it very unhappy. Such, I see plainly, is often my condition ...[4]

It is difficult to know exactly what to make of this passage. Tocqueville gives a recognizable likeness of himself. Such a life as his father was obliged to lead while youth slipped away would have been intolerable to him: he complained bitterly of far milder restrictions under the Second Empire. But nothing in what we know of Hervé from his life, his writings, or his portraits, which seem to show a cheerful, shrewd, energetic and self-confident man – above all, a man at ease with himself – fits with his son's remarks. In his memoirs he emerges as warmhearted, sensitive, and frequently ironical. On the other hand, Alexis would be most unlikely to make unrecognizable statements about their father when writing to his brother Édouard, as he was here. Perhaps it would be wisest to reflect that all human beings are bundles of inconsistencies and leave it at that; or perhaps the truth is that their common restlessness operated differently in father and son. It gave Hervé *élan*, which at times his less vigorous children may have found hard to bear; but it tormented Alexis, whose temperament in other respects seems closely to resemble his mother's.

Hervé could and did count his blessings. He enjoyed 'cette bonne vie de château', even though little worth recording ever happened. Louis de Rosanbo and his wife had settled nearby, and visits were constantly exchanged. He studied law as part of his job as *maire*, and was to reap the benefit in a few years. But most of his time was spent on the education of his children, and the cultivation of his land, and on hunting, 'for which I had a great liking'. (In these respects his sons were to be very like him.) The rest of his time was devoted to the pleasures of society – too much so, he sometimes thought. Verneuil was so near to Paris, and he had so many relations, friends and acquaintances, that he and his family were seldom alone. But then, the visitors were all agreeable. In fact, the only real cloud on life, until the war took a bad turn, was the continuing ill-health of his wife.

Madame de Tocqueville's infirmities had certainly not been helped by her experience of prison and Terror. Jardin describes her as capricious, impatient, even extravagant, and at bottom always melancholy, 'which was nothing exceptional among those who escaped the Terror. The family atmosphere during Alexis de Tocqueville's young years must have been greatly darkened by it.' Rédier is more sympathetic, yet says that she was often cross and discontented, and suffered perpetually from migraine. Abbé Le Sueur mentions her great irritability. But the language which Alexis uses to her in his letters is always respectfully affectionate, and his young cousin Louis de Kergorlay seems genuinely to have liked her: he called on her regularly after he grew up, telling Alexis that he was touched by the kindness that, in spite of her troubles, she showed to him; he thought her lovable.[5] She remains a shadowy figure. Her wish for a daughter suggests that she felt herself unlucky, her immediate family being entirely masculine: the business of her life for more than twenty years was to bring up five boys; by 1800 her mother and both her sisters were dead. Her one surviving letter to Alexis is lively and affectionate (perhaps that is why it was kept) though chiefly concerned with how ill she has been made by a thunderstorm. In his letters to her there is a certain reserve – even when, writing from America, he admits to homesickness. The American letters were certainly meant to be handed round the family circle and read aloud, yet those addressed to his father, his brothers and even his sisters-in-law always contain touches particular to each correspondent. All he can find to talk about to his mother is her health, which he is careful to mention every single time he writes. In a letter written just after her death he remarks that she had endured twenty years of misery.[6] Sad to say, her only immaterial legacies to her son seem to have been her uncertain temper and her sickliness, whereas he found in his father the best of companions and the most reliable of friends. When at length Hervé died, Alexis wrote:

> You saw how friendly and gentle he was; these qualities, which even foreigners noticed, showed themselves to his sons in a limitless indulgence and the tenderness of a mother; in an unwearying but never intrusive interest in all our affairs. This sensibility, instead of weakening, grew steadily more marked with the years, which I have never seen in anyone else. He had always been good-hearted; but as he aged he became the kindest of men.[7]

It is perhaps just to infer that if the family atmosphere was indeed darkened, Mme de Tocqueville lost most by it. Yet she is at the centre of her son's earliest recorded memory.

> At this day I remember, as if it were still before me, an evening in my father's château, when some family rejoicing had brought together a large number of our near relations. The servants were gone, and we sat round the fire. My mother, whose voice was sweet and touching, began to sing a well-known royalist song, of which the sorrows of Louis XVI and his death were the subject. When she ended, we were all in tears; not for our own misfortunes, not even for the loss of so many of our own blood, who had perished on the field of civil war and on the scaffold, but for the fate of a single man, who had died fifteen years before, and whom few of us who wept for him had ever seen. But this man had been our king.[8]

This is a significant anecdote in several ways. Tocqueville is precise about when the incident occurred: fifteen years after the King's death, therefore in 1808, when Alexis can have been, at the very most, three years and a few months old. If he is right about the date, the story is evidence of his precocity; but even if he is wrong by a year or two it is no wonder that the episode affected him deeply. The cousins gathered round the fire – Tocqueville, Rosanbo, Chateaubriand – had particular reasons for mourning the King's death. It had entailed so much loss and suffering for their families; the martyrdom of Louis XVI was the idea that gave meaning and dignity to their sorrows. Tocqueville was to forsake this family creed in his early twenties, but he could never entirely put loyalty from him, as his references to the House of Bourbon – even when he had despaired of it – so different from what he said about the House of Orleans, let alone the Bonapartes – amply illustrate; and he is noticeably reticent, almost tender, in his references to Louis in the *Ancien Régime* (he may even have agreed with the regicide Barbaroux that bad causes have their martyrs as well as good ones). He does not say, or want us to think, that his family had forgotten the sufferings which they and their order had endured. The death of the King and the ruin of his *noblesse* were far too closely intertwined for that, and between them had put an end to the *frondeur* tradition by which the nobles had felt free to go to almost any lengths in opposing and sabotaging royal policy when they saw fit. Every adult in the room at Verneuil knew what it was to be murderously persecuted, not for actions, not for thoughts, but merely for identity, for being noble. Saint-Just's vicious remark 'One cannot reign innocently'[9] had been extended to them, and like the surviving victims of the death camps and the labour camps in the twentieth century many of the traumatized survivors could never free themselves of the nightmare. The cost to themselves and to France was huge. For nearly two hundred years French conservatives were convinced that persons on the Left were all assassins at heart;* the Left believed that all royalists were traitors. All events were interpreted to reinforce these beliefs, and the weakness they induced in the body politic had much to do with the

* Such a conservative once assured me that I had taken my life in my hands by dining in a restaurant near the place de la Bastille. By a curious irony, he was a direct descendant of the terrorist Bertrand Barère.

catastrophes of 1848, 1870–71, and 1940 (to mention only the worst). This was the first and heaviest of the ideological chains which Alexis de Tocqueville was to spend his life trying to break.

Not that he had any such ideas in his childhood. 'The whole object of those among whom I was brought up, was to amuse, and be amused. Politics was never talked of, and I believe very little thought of.'[10] That is, it was never talked of until the servants had left the room and bright little boys were in bed: Napoleonic France was a police state. Besides, the extended family was not at one on political issues. If Le Peletier de Rosanbo had died for the *parlement*, Le Peletier de Saint-Fargeau (*ci-devant* marquis) had been a leading Jacobin, had voted in the Convention for the death of Louis XVI, and had been stabbed to death on that account the day before the King's execution. The Jacobins honoured him as the first martyr of the Revolution. His widow tried to atone for his apostasy by serving as a royalist courier up and down France for the rest of her life.[11] His daughter was more distressed that her father had been a regicide than that he had been murdered, whereas his brother adopted Babeuf's children after their father's execution. Félix Le Peletier d'Aunay went into the civil service under Napoleon; so did a more distant cousin, the young Comte Molé. Young Alexis was apparently oblivious of these divisions.

> Literature was one of the standing subjects of conversation. Every new book of any merit was read aloud, and canvassed and criticized with an attention and a detail which we should now think a deplorable waste of time. I recollect how everybody used to be in ecstasy about things of Delille's,* which nothing would tempt me now to look at. Every considerable country house had its theatre, and its society often furnished admirable actors. I remember my father returning after a short absence to a large party in his house. We amused ourselves by receiving him in disguise. Chateaubriand was an old woman ... Every incident was matter for a little poem.[12]

Chateaubriand ... Alexis de Tocqueville was not the only immortal in the group. The great writer had in 1807 bought a house near Verneuil, the Vallée-aux-Loups, where he endured the pains of living with his

---

* The Abbé Delille, a member of the Académie Française, was an ardent royalist. He once astonished Chateaubriand by offering to turn some pages of what became the *Mémoires d'outre-tombe* into verse. HT admired Delille all his life: see his *Louis XVI*, p. 243n.

wife and of being in disgrace at Court (he could never keep out of hot water for long). It was, quite possibly, the happiest period of his life: anyway, he planned that it should be. He had recently made a much-publicized pilgrimage to Jerusalem, which he entered on what he thought was his birthday, thereby bettering Jesus Christ. In his garden he planted exotic trees which he had brought back from the East (Malesherbes would have been pleased) and looked forward to enjoying their shade in his old age. He wrote copiously, and presented himself as living in a kind of hermitage: 'I may be a knight-errant, but I have the sedentary tastes of a monk: since I settled in this retreat, I doubt if I have stepped out of its enclosure as much as three times.'[13] This was not exact: in 1811 he took refuge at Verneuil after once more incurring the wrath of Napoleon. Their first breach had occurred in 1807, when Chateaubriand's journal, the *Mercure de France*, was suppressed for threatening the new Nero with a new Tacitus:* this was what drove the writer to the Vallée-aux-Loups. In 1809 a Chateaubriand cousin, Armand, an *émigré*, was shot for carrying letters from the Bourbon princes into France: pleas for mercy by François-René were in vain. Napoleon next made the conciliatory gesture of forcing the Institut's 'class of language and literature' (the *ci-devant* Académie Française) to elect him to membership, but blue-pencilled the speech which he proposed to give at his reception: as a result Chateaubriand refused to take his *fauteuil* until the Restoration.† Napoleon made dreadful threats, which the marquise de Fontanes persuaded him to forget; but Chateaubriand thought he would be less conspicuous at Verneuil than at the Vallée-aux-Loups. He and Mme de Chateaubriand stayed there for several months. Hervé de Tocqueville recalls:

> Seated in a corner of the room, while others played cards or conversed, he would be seen, pensive and silent, withdrawn from all that surrounded him. Thus he composed whole rants [*tirades entières*]

---

* It tells a great deal about conditions in Napoleonic Europe that when the young Guizot arrived for his first visit to Mme de Staël in Switzerland and was asked for news of Paris, he enraptured her simply by reciting Chateaubriand's inflammatory paragraph (Guizot, *Mémoires*, vol I, 11–12).

† Chateaubriand's predecessor, Marie-Joseph Chénier, had been, among other things, a regicide. The Emperor was displeased by Chateaubriand's animadversions on the fact. 'How dare the Académie prate of regicides when I, crowned as I am, who should hate them much more, dine with them and sit next to Cambacérès?' (Clément, *Chateaubriand*, 234).

of his tragedy [*Moïse*] which he next wrote down. For the rest of the time, he was always in a gay humour ...*

By the time he wrote his memoirs Hervé's attitude to his illustrious kinsman had become infinitely ironical. He did him the justice to remark that when he returned from exile Chateaubriand was simple and modest and lacking confidence in his literary powers. This was quickly put right when the *Génie du Christianisme* went into sixteen editions in no time at all. 'Words flowed from his pen which moved the soul profoundly. The author seemed to know the heart's most delicate strings; he could touch each one as he would, when he would.' But Hervé noticed that he never found time to visit his nephews at school, however often he was reminded. 'M. de Chateaubriand is certainly not sensitive.' But they were friends, and such reflections did not stop Hervé from subscribing when, in 1812, the duchesse de Duras (one of the devoted ladies whom Mme de Chateaubriand derisively referred to as 'les Madames') hit on a scheme, later revived by Mme Récamier, to pay the writer's debts by selling shares in a company whose assets were to consist of the copyright of Chateaubriand's next book. It did not solve his financial problems (nothing could) but he did not foresee that.[14]

Curiously, François-René, never less than entirely self-preoccupied, is the only person known to have recorded an impression of the child Alexis de Tocqueville. It is a very characteristic effusion:

> M. de Tocqueville, my brother's brother-in-law and the guardian of my two orphaned nephews, was living in the château that had belonged to Madame de Senozan: such legacies of the scaffold were everywhere. There I saw my nephews growing up with their three Tocqueville cousins, among whom Alexis, future author of *De la démocratie en Amérique*, stood out. He was more spoiled at Verneuil than I ever was at Combourg. Is he the last celebrity whom I shall have seen unknown in swaddling-clothes? Alexis de Tocqueville has explored the cities of America, I its wilderness.[15]

It would be easy but ill-advised to discount this passage. Chateaubriand was not a man for unambiguous statements, but he does commit

---

* Rédier (p. 33) comments: '*Sur la gaieté de Chateaubriand, il n'y a beaucoup de documents.*'

himself to the observation that Tocqueville was spoiled or pampered (*gâté*). He was self-centred but not malicious, except when in a rage: we may believe him. Besides, André Jardin also feels that Tocqueville was spoiled, and that it explains certain features of his adult character.[16]

Alexis was so very much younger than his company. His cousin Louis de Kergorlay (1804–80) was of much the same age, and the Kergorlays lived in the same Parisian street as the Tocquevilles during the winter (rue Saint-Dominique, seventh *arrondissement*) and, in summer, at their chateau of Fosseuse in the Oise – not very far from Verneuil. Kergorlay would become the closest friend of Tocqueville's adolescence, but that was in the future. Meanwhile Alexis (we may guess) was the sort of child that adults like to indulge: delicate, pretty, intelligent, eager. The tradition by which French nobles were cold, if not cruel, to their children seems to have died with the eighteenth century. Finally and most important, we have the direct testimony of Tocqueville himself. His remarks about his father's boundless indulgence have already been quoted; the death of the Abbé Le Sueur in 1831 – Le Sueur taught the sons as he had the father – elicited a similar eulogy, which confirms the impression of an almost suffocating intensity of affection. The boys had nicknamed him 'Bébé' – no doubt a corruption of 'Abbé', but the name would never have stuck to a grimmer man. He taught them, ate with them at table, tucked them into bed at night and blew out their candle.[17] They rewarded him with absolute devotion. When, in America, Alexis learned of his death, he wrote to Édouard: 'we have lost what neither time nor friendship nor the future, whatever it may be, can restore to us, something given to few people in this world: a being whose every thought, every affection, belonged to us alone; who lived only for us. I have never seen or heard of a like devotion.'[18] Tocqueville rebelled passionately against Fate when it dealt him such blows, and never tried to disguise his feelings. It was just the same when his father died in June 1856. *L'Ancien Régime et la Révolution* was on the very point of publication; Tocqueville would have stopped it, to mark his grief, had he been able to.[19] Anyone who has loved and lost will sympathize with this extravagance, but it must be seen as one of a series of occasions on which Tocqueville allowed unchecked instinct to carry him away. He rebelled against human destiny, and it is surely likely that one reason was that too-happy, too-secure childhood which he regretted so deeply (nostalgia brims through his letters), when he was carefully sheltered from all anxiety, when every incident was matter for a poem, and when Bébé taught him simple distinctions between right and wrong.

Most details of the Verneuil days have vanished beyond conjecture. Alexis was fond of both his brothers, though as he grew up he came to think that Hippolyte was more headstrong than sensible; Édouard was much more sympathetic. At the New Year the children would be given presents, in the old French style, and the adults would write letters full of news and greeting to their friends. Tocqueville never forgot the tradition, although it occasionally slipped his mind, as on New Year's Day, 1832, in New Orleans, when he and Gustave de Beaumont intruded on a family party in that still largely French city:

> The Eagle of the New Orleans Bar [Étienne Mazureau], wrapped in a dressing-gown, and sitting in the corner by what is called a French fireplace in Louisiana and a rustic one in France, was at that very moment receiving the best wishes of the family gathered about him. There were his children, grandchildren, nephews, first cousins, second cousins even, sugar-plums, toys and pots of jam – the family picture was complete. It was only left for us to be moved, even to tears of joy, like any eighteenth-century philosopher in a book. Joy reigned on every face, harmony in every heart. We are such good friends on New Year's Day!
>
> As for the two of us, we stood as if struck dumb by the spectacle. At length light broke in, even on us. Now we understood the astonishment of the Negro servants, those good Negroes whom we had treated as churls. To present a letter of introduction on New Year's Day! What unseemliness!
>
> Alas, where now is the happy time when I would sooner have forgotten my name than the coming of the first of January![20]

We surely learn a great deal about Tocqueville's earliest years from this passage.

Great events suddenly destroyed the idyll.

By 1812 the Napoleonic régime was gravely weakened, as was clearly demonstrated by the nearly successful conspiracy of General Malet, who attempted to seize Paris during the Emperor's absence in Russia. Napoleon was trying his countrymen too high. The perpetual war, bringing with it appalling casualties, savage taxation, economic ruin, the ever more hateful conscription, and little gain for anybody, was more than they could bear: everyone yearned for peace. One consequence of this state of mind was a revival of royalism; the organization known as the Chevaliers de la Foi was founded, ostensibly as a nationwide Catholic charity, but really as a secret society to further the interests of the Bourbons and seize any opportunity which arose.[21] Chateaubriand, probably, was a member, but it seems that Hervé de Tocqueville was not.[22] A marked strain of prudence runs throughout Hervé's career, though he was heroic when necessary. Then the defeats began. 1812 was the year of the retreat from Moscow; 1813, of the Battle of the Nations at Leipzig; winter brought the enemy to the very gates of France. This might not have meant the end for Napoleon had he not been blinded by the furious arrogance of his character and his faith in his military genius. Again and again his enemies offered him generous terms; again and again he spurned them, preferring to gamble everything on another battle, and not choosing to see that even victories could not now do him much good, so vast were the armies arrayed against him and so diminished his resources. The Austrians were in the Franche-Comté, the Russians in Lorraine, Wellington had crossed the Pyrenees into Gascony. Napoleon did not relent. The terrible conscription went on.

This created difficulties for the *maire* of Verneuil. His office was lowly, but part nevertheless of the Napoleonic machine, the purpose of which was to grind out tax receipts and soldiers. Comte Hervé had no sympathy with either aim; he seems to have shared the views of Chateaubriand, who in his famous pamphlet *De Buonaparte et des Bourbons* would soon be denouncing the conscription as homicidal and hellish: 'Each French generation was cut down systematically like trees in a forest: each year eighty thousand young men were slaughtered.' Hervé did his best to sabotage the process. 'It was held that the notice of conscription was a sentence of death and I exerted myself to rescue the young men of my commune. The law exempted married men and I encouraged marriages by all the means in my power. When the emergency grew too pressing I sometimes published the banns and held the wedding on the same day, thus exposing myself with more zeal than prudence to grave penalties for saving that young generation confided to my care.' He was not alone: in the royalist Vendée, for instance, the authorities abandoned the attempt to enforce the conscription, so great was the resistance.[23]

At this time Alexis de Tocqueville was in his eighth and ninth years. It is worth dwelling on this episode because it helps to explain his unrelenting, lifelong opposition to military dictatorship and the Bonapartes. If not at the time, then later, he will have learned of his father's actions; if not in 1814, then before long, he will have read Chateaubriand. And he can hardly have been unaware of the *maire*'s vigorous response when hospital ships, carrying the wounded down the Seine to Normandy, brought typhus with them, creating dreadful mortality in the riverside villages. Hervé fumigated every house in Verneuil with vinegar, and burned the straw mattresses on which the sick had lain, measures which seem to have been effective, for there were only two deaths, one of them that of the Tocquevilles' cook who had rashly taken some soup to the sufferers.

France, which had embraced the Consulate and the Empire as a chance to rest from the tumult, fear and exhaustion of the Revolution and its wars, was stirring again. Even the Corps Législatif, previously always so docile, demanded peace, liberty and political rights, for which impertinence its master summarily dissolved it on 31 December 1813. Chateaubriand, tiring of the distant sound of artillery, dared to leave the Vallée-aux-Loups for the rue de Rivoli, taking with him the unfinished *De Buonaparte et des Bourbons*, on which he was working in secret.* Paris sensed that something fundamental was changing. Its temper is perhaps best conveyed by that most delightful of memoir-writers, the comtesse de Boigne:

> I remember that M. de Châteauvieux ... who was absent from Paris for two years, arrived at the beginning of 1814. His first visit when he reached town was to my house. There he heard speeches of such hostility that, as he has since told me, his chief desire was to get away. Throughout the night he dreamt of nothing but dungeons and Vincennes, although he had made a firm resolve never again to visit so imprudent a society. The next day he continued his round of visits,

---

* Or so he supposed, but whenever he went out during the day he casually left the document among the litter on his desk. Mme de Chateaubriand charged herself with looking after it. At night Chateaubriand hid it under his pillow.

and was astonished to find the same attitude and the same freedom of speech everywhere, even among the middle classes and in the shops. We were not struck by the fact, because the change had been gradual and general. It was apparent even at the table of the Minister of Police, where the Abbé de Pradt said that there was one émigré whom it was time to recall to France, and that was common sense. M. de Châteauvieux was petrified ...[24]

Refugees began to pour into Paris. The Seine filled with the bodies of dead soldiers. On 12 March a detachment of Wellington's army occupied Bordeaux; the *maire* immediately donned the white cockade of the Bourbons, and that afternoon Louis XVI's nephew, the duc d'Angoulême, entered the city amid frantic enthusiasm.* It was a crucial episode in the Restoration: nowhere else had the returning princes met any real welcome, and the Allied commanders had kept the comte d'Artois, Angoulême's father, under virtual house arrest. But news of the duc's triumph reached Paris and the North just as the last conference, the last serious attempt to make peace with Napoleon, was collapsing because of the Emperor's incorrigibility: it broke up on 19 March. Castlereagh and Metternich now saw that the return of the Bourbons was inevitable, Napoleon being impossible and nobody but the Tsar supporting the ambitions of Bernadotte. Events moved with great speed. On 28 March Napoleon, whose political judgement seems at this time to have deserted him completely, began to execute a brilliant military manoeuvre which had the sole inconvenience of leaving Paris open to the invaders. The Emperor had forgotten the law so repeatedly demonstrated during the Revolution (it was not to be revoked until 1871) that the master of Paris was the master of France. The Allies marched, and on the 29th Marie Louise, obeying her husband's order (another disastrous misjudgement) fled to the Loire with the entire imperial government: Hervé de Tocqueville saw her cortège set off from the Tuileries. Next day, the 30th, Chateaubriand finished his pamphlet and the Allied armies fought their way to the suburbs, at the cost of 9,000 casualties. The French commanders asked for terms.

It was the moment that the Chevaliers de la Foi had been waiting

---

* This enthusiasm owed much to the fact that Wellington kept his troops in hand, whereas the imperial army, under Soult, plundered and ravaged the countryside as it was used to doing in Spain, Portugal, Russia, etc.

for. On the morning of 31 March their young men staged a demonstration: sporting the white cockade they paraded through the streets
shouting 'Vive le Roi!' But there were not very many of them, and
nobody joined in. Mme de Boigne saw them pass her window five
times, never increasing in number. It scarcely mattered. At eleven that
morning the Allied sovereigns entered Paris and were enthusiastically
welcomed by the people. They behaved perfectly. The Tsar was taken
on a tour of the city and shown the column in the place Vendôme
with Napoleon's statue on top. He said only, 'If I were raised so high I
would be afraid of getting dizzy.' Some of the Chevaliers seem to have
thought this was a hint: a few days later they pulled down the statue
with a rope. Mme de Boigne did not approve: she thought the action
entirely foolish and unnecessary. Like Chateaubriand, and no doubt
like thousands of other Parisians, she was divided between anger at
Napoleon and patriotic resentment of the conquerors. No foreign
army had entered Paris for nearly four hundred years.[25]

That same day Hervé de Tocqueville packed his wife, his youngest
son and some servants into two carriages and set off from Verneuil to
Paris: presumably he could no longer bear to be absent from the centre
of action. In spite of alarms about Cossacks and the retreating French
army they arrived safely, if circuitously, in the rue Saint-Dominique
that evening. Le Sueur and the two elder boys were left behind. Hervé
may have hoped to do something for the royalist cause, which seemed
to be on a knife-edge. By 1 April the royalists controlled the press and
Paris was placarded with announcements that a work by Chateaubri-
and was about to appear. It was the secret pamphlet, and came out
on 4 April, just in time (according to the author) to sway the Tsar in
favour of Louis XVIII, which if true explains why the King said later
that *De Buonaparte* was worth more to him than an army;[26] but Louis
was a master of gracious insincerities. Perhaps the real importance
of the pamphlet lay in its huge popular success, the most sensational
since 1789, for it legitimized the Restoration in the eyes of the French.
On the day it was ready the Madames and other noble ladies, Mme
de Tocqueville quite possibly among them, undertook to distribute it
through all Paris.

At this point a child's voice comes clearly and suddenly through the
clamour. Alexis de Tocqueville was much excited by the goings-on,

even if he did not entirely understand them, but he missed Verneuil and all the people there, and wrote four letters in less than three weeks to say so:

[*Early April*]. Good morning, dear little Bébé, I love you a lot. I will be so happy to see you again, and my brothers too, I kiss them with all my heart. I am having a fine time here with my dear Mamma and we are very well. Goodbye, little Bébé, I kiss the tip of your nose. Remember me to Nurse. Alexis.

Paris, 4 April. Good morning, little Bébé, I hope you are very well. Why didn't you come with us? How you would have shouted 'Vive le roi!' I must tell you something, yesterday Mamma, just after breakfast, went out visiting, and left me behind and did not come back until after half past five; then we had dinner. And do you know, after dinner she said she was going off again to bring back my brothers.

Goodbye. I hope you will come back soon. While I'm waiting, I kiss you with all my heart. Say to Alain, when you see him, that I wish him a very good day. Alexis.

Alain seems to have been a gardener at Verneuil.

[*Paris,*] *9 April*. Dear little Bébé, I wish you good day, I am going to tell you something. It is this, Papa, three days ago, bought Hippolyte and Édouard a dappled grey horse. ... Mamma has had a migraine since the day before yesterday. They have put leeches under her shoulders.

The statue on the column in the place Vendôme has just been knocked down and they have put in its place a white flag with *fleur de lys* on it.

Goodbye, please tell me if Alain has finished the pea-patch that we started. Try and come soon. Hugs and kisses. Alexis.

Paris, 22 April. My dear Bébé, please tell me if they have put in sticks to prop up my peas.

I am certainly going to surprise you, I have done my exercises, which I have sent you by Édouard.

Goodbye, little Bébe, I kiss you with all my heart and also Louis and Auguste.

Give Alain lots of best wishes from me.[27]

In this way Alexis de Tocqueville went through his first revolution.

CHAPTER THREE

A SENTIMENTAL EDUCATION
1814–1829

A man succeeds at nothing, especially in his youth, if he
does not have a trace of le diable au corps. *At your age*
I would have been ready to leap over the towers of Notre-
Dame if I had known I would find what I was seeking on
the other side.
> ALEXIS DE TOCQUEVILLE TO ALEXIS STOFFELS,
> 4 JANUARY 1856[1]

EVENTS HAD NOW AN IRRESISTIBLE MOMENTUM. On 6 April Napoleon abdicated at Fontainebleau; on the 12th the comte d'Artois entered Paris as the lieutenant-general of the kingdom, and was greeted with extravagant delight by an enormous crowd; Hervé and Hippolyte de Tocqueville (the latter no doubt riding the dappled horse) were part of his ceremonial cavalry escort. Artois reviewed them near a spot where the dead of the battle of 30 March had only just been buried; war had battered the nearby houses, which were now without doors, windows or occupants; Hervé thought it a dolorous sight for the returning princes. On the other hand, he noticed that they were welcomed most enthusiastically by women. 'The first restoration was the counter-revolution of the women. Robespierre perished because the nation could no longer tolerate the blood shed on the scaffolds. Napoleon fell because the nation was weary of the blood shed in the battles' – and the women most of all.[2]

On 23 April the provisional government signed an armistice with the Allies and on 3 May King Louis XVIII arrived, having just issued the celebrated Declaration of Saint-Ouen in which he conferred on his subjects the Charter of their rights and the new order of government. He was welcomed perhaps with as much joy as his brother, only less delirium. On 4 June the Charter was presented to the Senate and the Corps Législatif in a joint session, and adopted in another wave of enthusiasm. It was probably the greatest moment of the Bourbon dynasty since the days of Henri IV; certainly the greatest moment of the Restoration.[3]

The King had a most delicate task, of maintaining the support given to him by the men of the Napoleonic régime – the new nobility, the administrators, the members of the two chambers – while rewarding the royalists *purs*,* who had always been loyal to their rightful sovereign and had suffered so greatly in his cause. (The Bourbons hoped also to conciliate the army, but that, fatally, proved to be beyond them.) Continuity in government must be preserved as much as possible, to minimize dislocating effects on the French people, already the victims of invasion, defeat, unemployment and uncertainty; but irreconcilable opponents must be weeded out and, within government, a cadre of reliable supporters must be established. And a tidal wave of applications for posts washed over the princes and the ministers; it was difficult for them to keep their long-term objectives in view while dealing with so many claimants.

The descendants of Malesherbes did exceedingly well. Neither the King nor the duchesse d'Angoulême, Louis XVI's daughter, needed to be reminded of what was due to the memory of the late King's defender (but it did not hurt that the duchesse had so many of Hervé's relations, the Damas, about her that an untranslatable pun of the time said: 'sa maison était meublée en damas et doublée de même'[†]).[4] So Louis de Rosanbo was made a *pair de France*, meaning that he would sit in the Chamber of Peers which replaced the imperial Senate. Hippolyte and Édouard de Tocqueville were given commissions in the King's Guard (a new, or rather a revived, corps which, like so much

* uncompromising.
† *damas* means 'damask': 'her household was furnished and lined with damask.'

in the first Restoration, reflected Louis XVIII's deep desire to bring back the *ancien régime* as much as possible);* and Comte Hervé was appointed prefect of the department of the Maine-et-Loire on 18 June. He was slightly disappointed: he had hoped to be made a peer, like Rosanbo, but ministers felt that that would be doing too much for one family. Given his complete inexperience in senior administration, his failure to emigrate more than briefly, and that he had done nothing for the royalist cause thereafter, and that he had not been a person of the slightest distinction before 1789, he should have thought himself lucky.

Otherwise his attitude was straightforward. As a man of the same stripe, the baron de Frénilly, observed, 'All the loyal men who had lain low under Bonaparte now wanted prefectures.' Half a lifetime had passed without giving him a chance to prove himself publicly; he was a man of robust health and abounding self-confidence (he still felt shy before entering a drawing-room, but otherwise the diffident youth of 1793 was only a memory). His study of municipal law had been an excellent training, he felt, for the larger administrative duties of a prefect. Here at last was an opportunity to realize his ambition, to serve his king, his country and himself, an opportunity which would probably never recur. He seized it with both hands, and quickly established himself, his wife and his family at Angers, the administrative centre of the Maine-et-Loire. In this way emerged the pattern of their lives which was to endure, though not without modifications, for the next thirteen years.

Before they left Paris the King invited the family of Malesherbes to a private audience at the Tuileries. It must have been an educational experience for the youngest member. 'I shall never forget,' said his father, 'the impression which Louis XVIII made when he came out to receive us; we saw an enormous mass emerge from the King's study shuffling and waddling; this mass was topped by a fine and noble head, but the expression of the features was entirely theatrical; the King came forward with his hand on his heart, his eyes raised to Heaven. He said a few perfectly well-judged words to us, delivered in the most

---

* As Édouard was barely fourteen years old, this must have been a nominal commission, like his father's twenty-five years previously, which would permit him to continue his education.

sentimental manner. It was clear that he had rehearsed his performance. We retired from his presence with gratitude for the special kindness that he had showed us, and with the conviction that as King he would make an excellent actor.'

In the Maine-et-Loire, Comte Hervé found himself confronted with a political problem that was to vex the Restoration government throughout its existence. His department was essentially a somewhat shrunken version of the old province of Anjou, and Anjou was sharply divided between its royalist west and its imperialist east. Hervé had a duty to govern impartially, but first he had to get his authority accepted, and the royalist leaders, each supreme in his own neighbourhood, were fiercely reluctant to acknowledge him. Their royalism, ever since 1789, had always been anti-Parisian, anti-revolutionary, rather than pro-Bourbon.* To curry favour with them the prefect pointed out that he too came from the *bocage* – the countryside of small woods, small fields, unkempt hedgerows and isolated farms which stretches from Cherbourg to the lower reaches of the Loire – which had been the main theatre of counter-revolution in 1793 and 1794. This enraged the men of the east, already suspicious of such a palpable royalist, and they complained to Paris. At one moment the two parties nearly came to blows. How matters might have been resolved cannot be known, for Napoleon's return from Elba rendered the quarrel moot; but it is almost sufficient by itself to explain Hervé's emphatic preference for administration over politics.[5]

The adventure of the Hundred Days ranks among the most selfish of Napoleon's various discreditable actions. Almost nobody wanted him any more, except the army. France was slowly settling down as she learned painfully how to make a constitutional monarchy work. The Allies had been extraordinarily generous to their defeated enemy: no indemnity was exacted, and much of the territory annexed by the Revolution was left to the French, who were also allowed to keep the loot which filled the Louvre. At the Congress of Vienna Talleyrand had successfully reasserted France's position as one of the Great Powers, and split the coalition against her. As a result of Napoleon's escapade all this was jeopardized or undone. Once more, France

---

* The new, Bourbon-appointed prefect of Toulouse had even more trouble of this kind.

had to endure terrible defeat in battle. The prestige of the Bourbons suffered an irreparable blow, for they fled the country ignominiously, and only returned as the clients of the Duke of Wellington. All this, to amuse the Emperor. The only good to come of the affair was his final disappearance and the elimination of the army as an independent political power.

According to Hervé de Tocqueville, he foresaw many of these consequences when the news of Napoleon's *coup* reached Angers. There could be, for him, no question of acquiescence. Rather he saw a wonderful chance to play a heroic part. Angers, with the royalist west at its back, would be an excellent centre for resistance to Napoleon. With speed and energy, guns and soldiers could be brought in from Rennes and Nantes, and the Vendée* could become a Bourbon redoubt: Hervé even hoped that the King would take refuge there. Such a strategy could not defeat Napoleon, but it could keep the Bourbon cause alive, weaken the Emperor when he again fought all Europe, and earn for France some respect and mercy from the Allies when they were again victorious (as Hervé was sure they would be). It was all sound enough in theory, but the prefect quickly found that it was impracticable. While Bonaparte hastened to Paris the servants of the Bourbons seemed to lack all sense of urgency. Hervé met sloth, stupidity and (he came to suspect) treachery at every turn.[6] He was embarrassed when Louis de Rosanbo and the comte d'Orglandes (Louis de Chateaubriand's father-in-law) turned up to join the resistance: there was no resistance. Soon there was nothing for it: it was necessary to leave Angers and find a refuge. Hervé chose Lannion, near the north coast of Brittany: he had visited it with Mme de Tocqueville (who had a large property there) in 1810, and been impressed by the social harmony in the place.† But times had changed: the town was now furiously revolutionary – there were tricolours everywhere – and the countryside, because of the threat of conscription, was as furiously royalist. Luckily the *maire*, M. Guermarquer, was the Tocqueville agent, and his son-in-law was the sub-prefect. They were all that was helpful, but Comte Hervé thought it best to move on: for one thing, he did not see himself

---

* HT used this term to encompass the whole *bocage*, not just the department of the Vendée.
† It was on this journey that Mme la Comtesse paid her one and only visit to the château de Tocqueville.

as a royalist guerrilla. He and his family travelled to Caen, where the atmosphere was less frantic and where it would be easier to slip away by sea to join Louis XVIII in Ghent. This scheme was soon well in hand, but one morning, before it could be carried out, Hervé and Rosanbo saw a stage-coach arrive, and from it tumbled little old Mme de Saint Fargeau with the news of Waterloo. With indescribable feelings (at any rate, he does not describe them) Hervé immediately took the road to Paris.

He was just in time for the return of the King and the reconstruction of the government. He learned to his disgust that he was not to be sent back to the Maine-et-Loire. Chateaubriand, much too confident of his influence (he had loyally gone with the King into exile) promised him the prefecture of the Seine-et-Oise, where Verneuil lay, but in the event Chateaubriand was not made a minister and Comte Hervé was sent to the Oise (13 July 1815). Perhaps for this reason Hervé now disposed of the Verneuil chateau. Maintaining it if he was not going to live in it may have been too expensive.

Soon afterwards he was transferred to the Côte-d'Or (31 January 1816) and then to the Moselle (19 February 1817).

This constant shifting about was not unusual under the Restoration, though Comte Hervé never liked it. It reflected a certain tension between the administration and the government: like other prefects, Tocqueville was moved when it suited ministers, whether he was at fault or not.[7] There is little point in repeating Andé Jardin's admirable account of his career. One aspect of the matter, however, demands attention. After accompanying her husband to Angers, Lannion, Beauvais and Dijon, Mme de Tocqueville went on strike, so to say. Her health finally collapsed. It is impossible not to suspect that there was a neurotic or hysterical element in her malady, but mental suffering can be as real to a patient as physical. At any rate, when Hervé was appointed to the Moselle, Mme de Tocqueville refused to go with him to Metz.[8] She stayed, for months, prostrated in Dijon, leaving it only in October, for Paris. This set the stage for the first crises in the life of Alexis de Tocqueville.

He was twelve in July 1817, and it was high time that he began to receive a more advanced education than Abbé Le Sueur could provide. Metz was an excellent place in which to make this step.

Metz aux campagnes magnifiques,
Rivière aux ondes prolifiques,
Coteaux boisés, vignes de feu,
Cathédrale toute en volute,
Où le vent chante sur la flûte
Et qui lui répond par la Mute
Cette grosse voix du bon Dieu!

(La Mute, usually called La Muette, is the great bell of the cathedral.)
Even today, after three great wars and a long German occupation;
today, when an extremely noisy motor-road has been run across the
campagnes magnifiques, Verlaine's evocation still seems accurate. The
Gothic cathedral, built, like much of the rest of the city, of honey-
coloured Jaumont stone, still lifts its pinnacles on the ridge above the
river, the Moselle, that flows in half a dozen separate channels where
herons and small boys fish. During the eighteenth century the town had
spread onto the islands thus formed in the valley, and on the smallest
of them stood the prefecture, almost palatial in scale: it had formerly
been the *hôtel* of the intendant of the Three Bishoprics (Metz, Toul
and Verdun) and although it had suffered a bad fire in 1805 it was quite
habitable again by 1817 (Mme de Tocqueville may not have thought
so). Behind the *hôtel* ran the Moselle; the front enjoyed a glorious view
of the cathedral; on its east side was a large garden, sheltered from
the world by high walls and the river; on its west stood an elegant
theatre. Just round the corner, across a bridge, were the almost equally
elegant buildings of a former convent which had been turned into a
lycée (then the Collège Royale, now the Lycée Fabert): very convenient, if Alexis were enrolled there. Across the main channel of the river
lay the old town. It had formerly been predominantly ecclesiastical,
but the Revolution had changed all that: a school for artillery officers
had been installed in another ex-convent. The place was full of architectural and historical interest, as well as the usual bustle of a French
market-town.

None of this weighed sufficiently with Mme de Tocqueville to affect
her immediate plans: she retired to the rue Saint-Dominique, where
Alexis joined her. Before that, he had apparently attended classes at
the *lycée*: he reported his progress to Bébé;[9] but the experiment was not

deemed a success. Perhaps the boy's health suffered; perhaps his father thought it would be imprudent to establish Alexis definitely at a Metz institution when he might soon and suddenly have to be removed if Comte Hervé were shifted again (as it turned out, the Metz assignment was to last for six years, much the longest of the prefect's postings). Perhaps the comtesse insisted on having her child with her in Paris. Whatever the reasons, Alexis was for the next two and a half years confined to the household of a chronic invalid and a sexagenarian priest (Le Sueur was now combining the duties of tutor with those of domestic chaplain to the comtesse). It can hardly have forwarded his intellectual development, but he was saved from becoming any sort of muff by his friendship with his cousin, Louis de Kergorlay.

He was unquestionably fortunate in having someone in the family so near to him in age and tastes. It was a good fortune which followed him through life, reflecting the fact that he shaped his friends besides enjoying them. He gave as well as took, and such was the strength of his mind and personality that he was the dominant partner in these relationships: they assumed his colouring. But in youth there seems to have been an even balance.

Kergorlay's father was a leading Ultra (that is, an extreme royalist) in the celebrated Chambre Introuvable which, elected immediately after the Hundred Days, was dominated by that party (eventually Louis XVIII found it too much of a good thing and dissolved it). Unlike many Ultras he was respected even by his opponents: Guizot in his memoirs mentions him as one of the most honourable of all the deputies.[10] He was a man of the same type as Hervé de Tocqueville (also an Ultra) though politically more inflexible. His wife was related to the Tocquevilles through the Lamoignons: as events were to show, she had her share of the courage and gallantry of the line. Alexis called her 'ma chère cousine', but to him she was really more of an aunt, or even a deputy mother. He was devoted to all the Kergorlays, and seems to have spent many holidays at their chateau. There he could swim, learn to shoot, and acquire all the other skills and tastes of a country gentleman; there he and Louis de Kergorlay could explore and discuss the world as it unfolded for them, and share their thoughts and feelings. If Tocqueville ever had a secret from Kergorlay, posterity will never know what it was.

Le Sueur did not entirely approve. Perhaps he recognized a rival. The boys' frank devotion to each other may have suggested certain dangers; at any rate, when in 1821 Alexis was at last committed to the *lycée* at Metz the old priest sent him a letter full of advice and warning:

> Your Papa, my dear child, must have recommended that you should be upright in your dealings with all your comrades, but that you should not form any special friendships. I know better than anybody how dangerous they are, especially today when manners are so abandoned. Young people show by such practices that they may be outwardly fine and fair but that inwardly they are rotten.[11]

Bébé need not have worried: Tocqueville's temptations lay wholly and vigorously in the opposite direction. The tone of his letters to Kergorlay, while full of affectionate friendship, is devoid of passion. The same cannot quite be said of Kergorlay. Alexis was never in love with him, but it is not so clear that he was never in love with Alexis: to judge by his tone, he may have felt more than he could avow. But then, his youthful temperament was even more highly strung and self-tormenting than his friend's. This was a relationship in which Tocqueville was for long the more level-headed participant. Its value to each of them can only be appreciated by following the course of their lives; Tocqueville states plainly what it meant to him in his youth:

> [Friendship] cannot come to birth at all ages; yet once born, I don't see why age should weaken it or even make it change its nature, above all between those who, knowing its full value, cultivate it ceaselessly, and make sure that its essential prop does not weaken, which is, mutual confidence about big things as well as lesser ones.[12]

Tocqueville was given to making such affirmations to his closest friends, but we need not doubt his sincerity: he was a warm-hearted young man.

The education of Alexis was not Le Sueur's only preoccupation during the Metz years. His central task was somehow to keep the Tocqueville family together. It was not easy. Hippolyte and Édouard were fairly launched on their military careers (but Édouard was still asthmatic and in 1822 he had to resign his commission). Comte Hervé, isolated at Metz, threw himself into his work, but missed his family; and the ladies of Metz criticized his parties because there was no hostess to preside. Mme de Tocqueville became so tiresome that the abbé, while striving all the time to make her happier, felt free to be absolutely frank behind her back. In August 1821 he wrote to Édouard:

> Our celebration of St Louis' Day was cheerless. It was lucky for me that Christian [de Chateaubriand] was here. The two of us presented your Mamma with a wreath of roses and another of myrtle; nor was that all; she clings to the old customs, and would have detested the very scent of the bouquets had they not been accompanied by some poetry. So it had to be concocted as of yore. Christian luckily gave birth to a quatrain and I to a long disquisition on patience under the ills that afflict poor human beings. You know of course that for a pill to be swallowed it must first he gilded, which is what I did. It stuck in her throat for a while, but St Louis made it go down. ... I was indeed rather rash to praise patience to a woman who always loses her temper at the least jar and who breaks windows with her least explosion. What contributed more than anything else to getting my moral accepted was the arrival of the good Abbé Ronsin, who doubtless came to preach her the same sermon ...[13]

As Alexis grew up he was probably relieved when he could escape to Kergorlay from such a household, but he was still devoted to Bébé, and when in 1820 his father summoned him to live in Metz he was passionately distressed at parting from his old tutor. Le Sueur tried to console him:

> I wish that the happiness of living with a father who loves you and whom you love was a happiness without blemish. For our consolation, we must tell each other that Providence will perhaps reunite us sooner than we hope ... Ponder, my friend, on the motive which has separated us. With all your strength put away lost time by making good use of the present. It is the only way of securing you a happy future. Above all, put God at the forefront of your work and all your notions ...[14]

It seems clear that although Hervé probably welcomed company in the prefecture, the chief reason for returning Alexis to Metz was the need to educate him properly. 'At Metz you have found a better master than I,' wrote Le Sueur, after hearing that one of the teachers at the *lycée* was to become a tutor to Alexis; ' ... it was time. ... With the best will in the world, I would have let you waste the best years of your life. The natural talent which God has given you would have remained buried, and France would have been deprived of an enlightened judge or a distinguished orator or a celebrated diplomat.'[15] Two things stand out from this letter: that the boy's remarkable gifts were already apparent, and that for the time being he found them little consolation for being uprooted. The abbé is trying to awaken his ambition.

Yet he was not entered at the *lycée* for another eighteen months – not until November 1821, by which time he was sixteen. The delay in enrolling him must have had a cause – perhaps he was thought too delicate, too immature, or simply too ill-prepared academically – but it may have been unfortunate. It did nothing for his sociability. He seems to have been a solitary child: during his early adolescence his only friends were Bébé, Kergorlay, who was not always available, and Édouard, who was not always available either. When at last he became a *lycéen* he made friends quickly (later he was to write affectionately of 'my old friends in the rhetoric class'), and one of them, Eugène Stoffels, of an undistinguished middle-class family, soon became nearly as dear to him as Kergorlay himself: he was almost the only person outside his own family with whom Tocqueville used the *tutoyer*. He and Tocqueville sat together on the rough-hewn benches in class and learned simultaneously how to turn a phrase and how to bite their nails.[16] But his schooldays did not last long enough (less than two years)* to accustom him to middle-class manners and middle-class company. This seriously hampered him when he became a politician and had to rub shoulders with a great many people whose good will he needed but whom he regarded as coarse and vulgar.

Meanwhile, he had come to a decisive moment in his life; in fact, to several. For instance, as his intellectual brilliance became clearer and clearer – he walked off with an armful of prizes at the end of his first year in the *lycée* – Kergorlay and Le Sueur began to quarrel

---

* Nevertheless, the Lycée Fabert is proud of him. Its newest building (2004) is named in his honour.

over his future. Kergorlay was already committed to the army, and wanted Tocqueville to join him, putting his arguments in a series of lively letters written, it must he said, with a routine elegance that no eighteen-year-old in modern Britain could approach. The abbé and the Tocqueville parents thought the idea preposterous. Le Sueur mustered all his resources to stop it; we find him writing to Édouard in September 1822, after the younger brother's academic triumph:

> *Mon petit Édouard*, you have got to persuade him not to become a soldier. You know the drawbacks of that trade better than any of us and I am sure that he will listen to his brothers more than to his father on the point. It was that mad boy Louis Kergorlay who put the idea into his head. They are about to get together again and I am much inclined to ask M. Loulou to leave us in peace and mind his own business.[17]

And a few days later, reporting that Mme de Tocqueville has given Alexis a gold watch in recognition of his achievement ('he was in transports of joy'), the abbé adds, 'what a shame it would be to snuff out such a talent under a helmet when it has made its *début* with such distinction!' Bébé was particularly impressed by his former pupil's prize-winning essay, *Discours sur le progrès des arts dans la Grèce* (now missing). He must have been relieved when Alexis decided upon a civilian career, in spite of all his cousin's eloquence, and in spite of a Norman neighbour's disapproval of his choice of the law: 'Remember, Sir, that your family have always been *noblesse de l'épée*,' said Mme de Blangy of Saint-Pierre-Église.[18] (She chose to forget the maternal line.)

The abbé might be pleased, but he did not yet know that Tocqueville had been struggling for the past two years with two other problems which seemed to him quite as important as the question of his career; the outcome was very different from anything that Le Sueur could have wished.

In the years at Metz Hervé and Alexis de Tocqueville developed a new relationship with each other, in which mutual respect and sympathy were as important as simple affection. In 1822 the prefect had his portrait painted, a work in which Alexis also appeared, sitting behind his father, apparently taking notes or dictation (an implausible occupation, given the young man's already atrocious handwriting, about which Abbé Le Sueur often scolded him). The picture gives a happy sense of partnership, though Le Sueur had several objections to it, among them a complaint that it made Alexis look like a mulatto. But if the portrait is essentially truthful, it does not tell the whole truth. The prefect was a busy man, and all too often left his son to himself while he went about his business in the department – everything from fixing elections to building bridges to acting as chief of police; never before or afterwards did the prefects have quite so much autonomous responsibility as they were given under the Restoration. Teachers kept Alexis applied to his studies for most of the year, and the boy probably paid visits to his mother in Paris and to Kergorlay in the Oise; but during the summer vacation of 1821* he was on his own, loitering about the prefecture, and naturally found his way to the library, full of his father's books. Thirty-five years later he wrote to the devout Mme Sophie Swetchine:

Have I ever told you about an incident of my youth, one which has deeply marked my entire life? Withdrawn into a kind of solitude during the years which immediately followed my childhood, and given over to an insatiable curiosity which had nothing but the books of a large library to turn to for satisfaction, I stuffed my mind pell-mell with all sorts of notions and ideas that usually come at a later age. Until that time my days had passed in a home full of a faith which had not let my soul be so much as brushed by doubt. Now doubt entered, or rather rushed upon me with unheard-of violence, not just doubt of this or that proposition, but doubt of everything. Suddenly I felt a sensation like that reported by those who have been through an earthquake, when the ground has shaken beneath their feet, the walls around them, the ceiling overhead, the objects in their hands, and all Nature before their eyes. I was overcome by the blackest melancholy, seized by an extreme disgust for the life which I had not even begun, and crushed, as it were, by distress and terror at the sight of the road through the world which lay before me. Violent passions drew me out of this state of despair; they distracted me from the contemplation of

* AT is precise about his age when this incident occurred. His sixteenth birthday was on 29 July 1821; he entered the Collège Royal in November; study must have kept him busy throughout most of 1821–22, not to mention other distractions which will be mentioned. Late summer, 1821, seems, then, much the likeliest period; for one thing, it needs time and perhaps leisure to get through a number of demanding books, however brilliantly written.

intellectual ruin towards the life of the senses; but from time to time these impressions of first youth (I was then sixteen years old) again possess me; once more my intellectual world totters and I am again lost and desperate in a powerful tide which shakes or inverts every truth on which I have based my beliefs and conduct ...[19]

There is no reason to question the sincerity and accuracy of this account. It squares exactly with everything else that Tocqueville ever said about his religious and philosophical views. For instance, in 1831 he wrote from America to Charles Stoffels, Eugène's brother, who was suffering from an attack of intellectual anxiety like his own:

> When I first began to think, I supposed that the world was full of demonstrated truths; that it was only necessary to look hard to see them. But when I applied myself to considering them, I perceived nothing but inescapable doubts. I can't well tell you, my dear Charles, what a horrible state this discovery left me in. It was the unhappiest time of my life; I can only compare myself to a man suffering from giddiness who thinks the floor is shaking beneath him and sees the walls moving round him; even today, I remember that moment with horror.[20]

Evidently it was the moment that he was to describe to Mme Swetchine decades later.

It is impossible to understand Tocqueville or his thought without giving careful consideration to his religious ideas in general and this crisis in particular. For one thing, it exemplifies the lifelong predicament in which he found himself: caught between two worlds, unable to repose in the one where he was born, unable to go forward confidently into the one he saw rising inexorably before him. The dilemma was one which tormented all too many of his contemporaries. He might have resolved it had it been simply intellectual, but it was also, perhaps most of all, a question of the emotions, of his innermost being. It was not and is not something to be treated lightly.[21]

'If I were required to classify human miseries, I would put them in this order: 1. Illness. 2. Death. 3. Doubt.' He made this remark several times while he was in America,[22] but it was doubt which he was driven to discuss: he was too much of a stoic to waste time lamenting his poor health or whining about the inevitable, though he dreaded it. He was also courageous in facing doubt. Very little could be known (he had read Descartes) but to despair for that reason was to despair of existence, since uncertainty was one of the inflexible laws of human nature. It was not a reason for spiritual paralysis, for feeble inaction. 'When I have to take a decision, I weigh up the pros and cons with great care, and instead of despairing because I can't attain complete conviction, I set out for the goal that seems to me the likeliest, and do so as if I had never had any qualms.' We must not expect too much or too little from life. Life is 'a serious task allotted to us, which it is our duty to execute as well as possible.' This thought consoled and strengthened him, and enabled him to put up with the troubles, the tedium, the vulgarity of modern times. Writing to another friend, Ernest de Chabrol, on the same subject, Tocqueville admitted that while others were happy to live in the perpetual half-light of uncertainty, it wearied and demoralized him; but on the whole his determination to defy doubt, to live and to act, fortified him throughout his days.[23]

But if such were the maxims with which Tocqueville comforted himself in his maturity, it was several years before he could get over his first distress. We must not forget the boy in the library. The nature and consequences of his intellectual crisis must be carefully examined.

André Jardin has little doubt that Abbé Le Sueur exposed his pupil to religious works and doctrines that were, if not Jansenist, at least *jansenisant*. But it is doubtful how much this meant in the early nineteenth century. The great seventeenth-century battles over the doctrine of grace, the eighteenth-century struggle between Jansenists and Jesuits, between King and *parlements* (which lay in the background of the coming of the French Revolution) were issues of the past, interesting only because they eventually inspired Sainte-Beuve to write his masterpiece, *Port-Royal*. But as Jardin points out, the gloomy morality of the Jansenists, their insistence on original sin (Anglo-Saxons will notice a strong resemblance to the Evangelical party) were still current, and may well have affected Tocqueville for life. It is much more certain that Le Sueur brought up his charge in simple faith and loyalty to Throne and Altar, a faith and loyalty which almost everything in Tocqueville's world reinforced, until those summer days in Metz.[24]

In his letter to Mme Swetchine, Tocqueville says that he turned to the library because he was consumed by insatiable curiosity. He had reached puberty, his mind was awake, and nobody will be surprised that he began to find the simple piety of his childhood inadequate: as manhood approached, he was bound to start thinking for himself. Nor is it surprising that a budding writer should be forced by words on the page (possibly those of Descartes, probably those of Voltaire and Rousseau) to face for the first time the great problems of belief and unbelief. That the scale should tip so quickly on the side of unbelief suggests that he was already having doubts; or, at the very least, that he felt it necessary to apply himself to considering religious fundamentals, as he says in his letter to Charles Stoffels. The creed he had learned from Le Sueur was not such as to resist criticism very effectively. Had he previously read Pascal (eventually a favourite author) or encountered the Catholic revival of the Restoration as embodied in the figure of Lamennais, with his insistence on the inadequacy of human reason and on the wisdom of God as revealed in the life of Christ, in history and in the infallible papacy, he might have held out longer – but not very much longer.

Le Sueur was to worry that at school Alexis might read bad books ('like swallowing poison') or fall into bad company, which was perceptive of him, but ineffective.[25] Tocqueville could not have preserved his intellectual virginity: he was about to enter one of those *lycées* which Lamennais denounced as 'seminaries of atheism and vestibules of hell', where, inevitably, he discussed with his comrades the problem of faith* (and also, Jardin suggests, politics).[26] But the damage had been done before then.

We must not exaggerate the reach of Tocqueville's doubt: he became a deist, not an atheist, believing firmly in the existence and providence of God, and in an afterlife, on the curious if Cartesian grounds that God would not have been so unjust as to implant the idea in men if it were not true.[27] What he rejected was the entire apparatus of organized Christianity, especially the dogmas and authority of the Catholic Church: they might do for the poor and ignorant, but not for him. After 1821 he never again received communion until he was on

---

* According to Denis Brogan, 'It took far more courage than was needed in Tom Brown's Rugby for a boy to practise faith and chastity in the state schools' (*The French Nation*, London, 1957, 31).

his death-bed, and his motives for doing so then are much debated.[28]*
What needs explanation is that this shedding of obsolete mental
baggage caused him not relief but extreme distress; and what needs
exploration is his final view of the place of religion in human life and
society. The two topics are closely intertwined.

More than twelve years after the Metz episode, when, in his first
great work, Tocqueville was discussing the place of religion in modern
democracies, he composed a deeply pondered and heartfelt passage
which, in the light of the Swetchine letter, must be read as personal.
Religion, he says, is a permanent aspect of human life.

> The short space of sixty years will never close off Man's imagination;
> his heart will never find sufficiency in the incomplete joys of this
> life. Alone among living things, Man experiences both a spontaneous
> disgust for existence and an immense desire to exist: he despises life
> and fears unbeing. These contradictory instincts drive his soul inces-
> santly towards the contemplation of another world, and it is religion
> which will take him there. Religion, then, is only a particular kind of
> hope, and it is also as natural to the human heart as hope itself.

Unbelief, however brought about, is unnatural, an accident: 'faith
alone is the permanent condition of humanity.' Unbelief, he sadly
concedes, nowadays exists. 'What I will call negative doctrines' silently
undermine faith. 'Men there are who, as if through forgetfulness,
allow the goal of their dearest hopes to elude them. Carried away by an
invisible current which they lack the courage to struggle against, while
regretting their surrender, they abandon the faith which they love to
follow the doubt which leads them to despair.' But while ceasing to
accept religion as true, the doubter continues to find it useful. Considering religious belief in its human aspect, he acknowledges its empire
over morals, its influence on law. He understands how it can make men
live in peace and prepare them to die quietly. So he regrets the faith
which he has lost and, deprived of a good whose value he knows, he
fears to snatch it from those who possess it still.[29]

Nothing could make Tocqueville's painful position clearer. His
distress was very much one of his period, culture and class: it was widely

* See below, ch. 24, pp. 637–38.

felt all over the West – we may think of Matthew Arnold's 'Dover Beach'. Philosophy, history and science had combined to destroy for ever, for those with ears to hear, the framework of Christian, and even pre-Christian belief which had for so long given meaning and comfort to existence. Its loss was an agony of rage, fear and denial – at the least, of sorrow and anxiety – like that which is tearing at the Islamic world today. For behind the loss of traditional faith lay a deeper possibility: the discovery of the abyss, the absurd, the Universe's unawareness of our sufferings, which seems so cruel:

> ... *the crack in the tea-cup opens*
> *A lane to the land of the dead.*

For Tocqueville there seem to have been special emotions to deepen his anguish.

Whatever his feelings about his mother (and it cannot be stated too emphatically that any opinion must largely be conjecture) he might well feel guilt about repudiating the religion which was a central concern of her existence, the more so if the repudiation was in any respect an act of rebellion (he certainly did not like her way of life: during the vacation of 1822, writing from Paris, he complained to Eugène Stoffels that 'since I came here I have led a monotonous, tranquil existence which hardly suits my character and tastes ...').[30] We know that he loved Le Sueur, and that the abbé was deeply upset by Tocqueville's apostasy when he found out about it. His father was less likely to be shocked – there is reason to believe that where his youngest son was concerned he was more or less unshockable – but although he may not have been particularly devout (nowhere in his memoirs does he say anything about his personal religious convictions, and his parents' prayers for him seem to have been thrown away: who owned the dangerous books, after all?), he scrupulously carried out the public observances required of a Restoration prefect. On the other hand, he disliked the aggressive religious policy of the Restoration, which may be summed up as an attempt to restore the Church to something like its position under the *ancien régime* by means of energetic proselytizing and the activities of the so-called Congregation, which combined the attributes of a pressure-group and a semi-secret society – a kind of Catholic Freemasonry, in fact (Louis de Rosanbo was a member). The activities of the Congregation continually irritated the prefect: his strong common sense feared the consequences of stirring up Catholic zeal, and he disliked being compelled to lend his presence to missionary processions (on one occasion he feigned illness in order to avoid such a participation).[31] Here was common ground with Alexis; but Hervé, ambitious for himself and for his son, might well fear the worldly consequences of disaffiliation from the Church. There would eventually be a powerful anti-clerical reaction, one of the causes of the 1830 Revolution – Alexis once asserted that it was the chief cause.[32] Meanwhile, religion was a matter of politics; to lapse from Catholicism might well be seen as disloyalty (although as things turned out it freed Alexis to set his own political course). Such considerations might well weigh with the prefect, if not his son, who became a deist because he could not help it, and throughout his life showed clear hostility to all attempts by the Church to recapture a privileged position (whereas he was sympathetic to similar efforts by the legal profession).

Yet none of these points touches the heart of the matter, which is the intensity of Tocqueville's anguish. For as he said to Mme Swetchine, his pain recurred at intervals throughout his life, and as his entire story shows, he was always vulnerable to feelings of anxiety and loss. We are confronting a psychological pattern, and must look for a cause. In the background was the appalling upheaval of the French Revolution, which might well predispose a mind to anxiety, to doubt of everything, to finding all assurances fragile. The loss of Verneuil should perhaps be mentioned. It was the only home which Tocqueville had ever known, and he lost it when he was barely nine years old. There followed the years of traipsing round France, and then the separation of his parents. To lose his mother's faith may have felt like cutting the last cord binding him to his past. He had once been the young darling of a large and lively household; by 1821 he may at times have felt that now nobody really wanted him, perhaps through his own fault – a fault that he was deepening by abandoning Christian belief. If so, he might well feel guilty.

So much is speculation; what is not in doubt is that this episode is important not just because religion was important to Tocqueville, but because it brings out a particular pattern. One of the main themes of his life was the unremitting struggle of his brilliant, sensitive mind to shake free of the mental trammels of his upbringing, however painful the process, and to confront the realities of a new age. As he wrestled with the problem of Church and faith so he would later wrestle with those of politics and history. The drama would characterize all his best work.

Meanwhile he was a boy, and miserable – but only intermittently. 'Violent passions,' he says, rescued him from despair, only to plunge him into other difficulties. He made the experiment of visiting a brothel, where he was overcome by self-disgust.[33] Unconfirmed rumour says that André Jardin found in the Tocqueville archives the birth-certificate of a child born at about this time to Tocqueville and one of the prefecture's maid-servants, and we know that he had a summer-house built for his use in the big garden. Jardin has no doubt as to what it was for,* and gently mocks Abbé Le Sueur for not understanding that Alexis had grown too old for childish games, and now wanted a *garçon-nière*.[34] If he entertained many young women there it is hardly surprising that one of them was impregnated. Nor is his success with girls difficult to understand. He was short and slight, even after his growth was complete, with narrow, sloping shoulders and a narrow chest, but he had thick, wavy black hair, tending to curl, an open countenance, lively and expressive brown eyes. The face which appears in the likenesses of his youth is bright and smiling; indeed, his smile lurks even in the gravest portraits of his maturity. He had a winning tongue, energy, determination and the manners of a patrician. No wonder he was found attractive, but he could be hot-tempered and cross-grained. In 1823 he involved himself in an affair of honour. On 16 May Kergorlay wrote to him in astonishment: 'You tell me in a mere four words that you are perhaps going to have to fight a duel! With anyone other than your closest friend such brevity would be a case of truly Spartan self-control, if anything ever is. But how could you think that I would take the news as calmly? You worry me deeply, and I burn to know how matters stand. Write to me at once.'[35] That is all. We do not know the cause of the fight, or the date of its occurrence, or even if it actually

---

* In almost the same year, in Villers-Cotterets (Aisne), a young woman persuaded her mother to let her sleep in their summer-house, to which she then secretly admitted her lover, Alexandre Dumas, aged eighteen.

happened. The prefect either stopped it or hushed it up: Jardin suggests that he was careful to keep this and other of his son's indiscretions from the ears of the rest of the family.[36] Tocqueville's opponent appears to have been one Henrion, a *protégé* of Comte Hervé. Eugène Stoffels asserted that Tocqueville was entirely in the wrong; apart from that, all is obscure about the affair.

Perhaps a girl was the cause, for Tocqueville had now fallen seriously in love for the first time. The young lady's name was Rosalie Malye. Ten months his senior, she was one of the two daughters of a retired army officer who was employed as the archivist of Metz – as such, he might have made a most suitable father-in-law to the future historian. However, it is unlikely that marriage was ever a possibility. The Tocqueville parents would have considered it a dreadful *mésalliance* – Mlle Malye was neither well-born nor rich – and the lovers were very young. Unfortunately all their letters to each other are lost, and so are most of Tocqueville's letters about the business to Kergorlay and Stoffels. On the whole it is probable that Comte Hervé regarded the matter as just the latest of his son's scrapes. In the summer of 1822, rather to his displeasure, he was appointed prefect of the Somme and had to move his household from Metz to Amiens; he may have hoped that this would disengage Alexis from Rosalie. If so, he was to be disappointed.

Meanwhile Tocqueville had been unburdening himself to Kergorlay about the two great subjects, religion and sex. To judge by Kergorlay's side of the correspondence (all that survives until 1824) they had for some time been shaking their heads over the godlessness and immorality of modern youth;[37] but now Tocqueville dropped pretences, and did so in the same letter in which he announced his duel. In his reply Kergorlay showed himself much too astute to tackle unbelief head on, but he did express surprise that Tocqueville should let himself be influenced by the example of the thoughtless and ignorant, by whom Kergorlay probably meant his friend's schoolfellows. As to the other matter:

> I also wanted to speak of your temperament. But I see that we are too different on that point. I see that you catch fire as quick as gunpowder and that the important thing is not to put a match to you. With me it

is quite different. The feeling is secret, confused and habitual, never leaving me alone, tickling me on its own independently of any objects to excite it, that's to say, this or that woman. I feel less unbridled lust than you do and more love. I love, in the true sense of the word, without loving anybody; I just feel the need. But since the soul is more involved and the body less so than they are with you, I am much harder to please; I am waiting for the woman who suits me, as the Jews wait for the Messiah. Heaven grant that I don't have to wait so long.[38]

Much can be inferred about both young men from these remarks.

It was now time to make definite decisions about Tocqueville's career: what profession should he train for? Kergorlay's influence was strong enough to make him persist with mathematics, necessary for entry to Saint-Cyr, the military academy, but other influences prevailed, or perhaps Tocqueville himself recognized that, as the abbé had put it, he would be wasted under a helmet. He also rejected his father's profession, civil administration. In a letter written years later, to his nephew Hubert, he tried to explain his aversion to that career; it seems he may have been influenced by his father's indignation at repeatedly having to move to a new department to suit the political convenience of ministers: 'In France, administrators seldom operate in the general interest of the country, but almost always in the particular interest of the current government; and any man who isn't ready incessantly to sacrifice the one interest to the other has no hope of promotion. So it was under the Restoration, so it was under the government of July, and it is, if possible, even more the case under our present régime.'* He settled on law and the magistracy, 'of all civil careers ... the only one which allows a man to be a functionary and at the same time to remain true to himself'.[39] To the descendant of Rosanbo and Malesherbes it was no vast sacrifice. In the autumn of 1823 he began to study law.

This meant living with his mother in Paris; perhaps it was a relief to get away, next summer, to his father in Amiens. But he had by no means forgotten Metz. He had written to Eugène Stoffels the year before that 'Metz and some of its inhabitants will long haunt my memory, perhaps

* This is very much the author of the *Ancien Régime* talking: AT was then writing it. Readers of that work will remember its unvarying tone of hostility to 'the public administration' – the intendants, and the bureaucrats of the council of state.

more than I like ... Tell me something about Metz, what's going on there, what people are saying; you know that I am fairly inquisitive.' This meant, of course, that he wanted news of Rosalie, though it is not clear how fully Stoffels was in his confidence at this stage: that young man's reply was mostly concerned with his own amorous pangs at a ball given in the prefecture by Hervé de Tocqueville's successor.[40] But by April 1824 Stoffels was fully *au courant*, visiting Rosalie for the purpose of talking about her admirer and reporting to him afterwards.[41] And Kergorlay's letters demonstrate beyond argument that for several years more the lovers were intensely important to each other; Tocqueville visited Metz more than once, and once at least Rosalie visited Paris. This visit, his own sexual shyness, and perhaps his complicated feelings for Alexis, caused Kergorlay real distress:

> [*2 June 1825*] I was quite aware, yesterday, of your chilliness to me when we left the rue de Grenelle and I know that it arose from the ridiculous and inconvenient *froideur* which I myself showed to the ladies.* If you thought I wasn't extremely embarrassed the whole time you were much mistaken ... Men whose entire youth has been, like mine, drawn away from natural feelings and shut up far from everybody always lack tact for this sort of thing ... They probably took me for a carefree type who could pay such a visit without bother because he felt no embarrassment. And that is precisely what irritates me because I neither am nor could be careless concerning the regard of the only woman in whom up to the present I have seen tenderness and sincerity. That's what she is for me and it is much indeed for someone who has never seen anything like it, at home or abroad. I am writing all this because although you said nothing, I am very sure that you noticed my cold behaviour and you know very well that we two write a thousand things to each other that we could never bring ourselves to say; all I want is that since I couldn't show them what I felt it shan't be hidden from you. ... Adieu. I love you and yours.

> [*4 June 1825*] Your letter came at a moment when it made a more particular effect than it could have at any other, for I was full of the other day's visit and the sight of Rosalie, the few words she spoke, and besides her figure had finally made me understand how a great desire could have such an object. At the first moment when we saw each other, turning into the street, my salutation made her smile while

---

* Presumably Rosalie and her sister Amélie were staying at a house in the rue de Grenelle.

embarrassing her and if you had been standing in front of her you would have seen that she had an air of defying me by holding your arm as if to tell me that you were hers, and mine no more. ... At that moment your fate seemed to me to be such a happy one that I came home quite depressed at having had before my eyes something which perhaps I myself will never be granted.

Fortunately for all concerned Kergorlay did not quite lose his head. After Rosalie returned to Metz Tocqueville showed his friend a letter from her which, in Kergorlay's opinion, proved that she loved him as much as he did her; if he followed her to Metz she would deny him nothing; but what then? The two young men took it for granted that marriage was out of the question, so Kergorlay exerted all his eloquence, his knowledge of Tocqueville and his affection in urging that something else was also out of the question. It was time to break off.

> You will be guided in your decision either by your conscience or by the advantages stemming from your choice; if conscience guides you it will not leave you in any doubt. If you think only of Rosalie's interest and your own, be sure that there will be fewest evils in not seeing her again. If you go to Metz I am *certain* that you will consummate her ruin;* her happiness and her honour will be lost lifelong. She will only be made more unhappy, and you, you will be very guilty. If you do not go to Metz, you will be unhappy for some time and so will she; but, as she said, your consciences will sustain you and her life will not end in disgrace. Who knows what might happen to a woman sunk in the disgrace which you would bring about by seeing her again?

And then an almost comically qualified avowal:

> As to any remaining hope of happiness for you, a friend is nothing besides that which I want you to give up; but if ever a friend can be a consolation to anyone, believe that I will. From this moment I promise to do anything to lessen your pain which will be neither sinful in itself nor likely to impede my career ...[42]

Tocqueville did not go to Metz. So the gods amused themselves by sending Kergorlay there instead.

---

* *Sic*: 'tu consommeras sa perte'.

For he was to be an artillery officer, and after passing through the École Polytechnique in Paris entered the artillery school in Metz, arriving there in December 1826. He was soon very thick with Stoffels, and became the go-between for Tocqueville and Rosalie. But for this the affair would probably have died away (at her first meeting with Kergorlay Rosalie complained that she had had only two letters from Tocqueville since his last departure from Metz); instead it revived.[43] A few months later Rosalie married prosperously, but that did not deter her lover, who may, in the tradition of his order, have regarded a married woman as a more legitimate prey than a respectable young virgin. At any rate, he besieged her with letters, with the assistance of Kergorlay and Stoffels. Her sister Amélie was enlisted in the intrigue, with whom, to make matters still more farcical, Kergorlay fell in love, or thought he did (he found that he much enjoyed the attentions of pretty young women). Sometimes Rosalie wrote back. The letters being lost, it is impossible to say what she and Tocqueville hoped to gain from this correspondence, and her character is a mystery – even Kergorlay, who covered pages and pages reporting to Tocqueville, confessed himself baffled by her. All that is certain is that she liked receiving the letters, and did not discourage Tocqueville even when, after she became Mme Bergin, he had to write to her using lemon juice for invisible ink. Her husband intercepted one of these notes, but he did not guess at the lemon juice trick, though he was suspicious. At this point we must think of *Madame Bovary*, if not of *Les Liaisons dangereuses*, and it is sadly clear that Kergorlay and Stoffels, without realizing it, were beginning to act as a pair of pandars. The only excuse to be made for all concerned is that they were still very young. Then in 1829 Kergorlay graduated and left Metz, and the affair ended definitively. Its most palpable consequence was the consolidation of friendship between Stoffels and Kergorlay. The latter wrote to Tocqueville in 1828 that Stoffels was a man of the first order for good sense, judgement, and 'the tact which can read in what one says that which one does not say'.[44] He worried about Stoffels's health, describing symptoms which perhaps were the first sign of the tuberculosis that eventually killed him.

Tocqueville's part remains almost as mysterious as Rosalie's, but his constancy is striking: he courted her steadily, with steadily worsening prospects, for six years. Both his friends took him seriously, or they would not have been so active on his behalf. Their devotion deepened his belief in friendship: 'Decidedly, *mon cher ami*, only friendship means anything in this world. The more I try other feelings, the more I am sure of it. I still can't imagine how a man can live without a single friend ... such men can't be worth much.'[45] And it is possible that, circumstances having denied him the fulfilment of his first love, he determined that nothing and nobody should defeat him next time.

The memory of Rosalie was still vivid to him when he revisited Metz in 1836 with his new wife. In fact he was so moved that only the hospitality of Stoffels and his own agreeable wife made the town bearable to him.

> I experienced very strange emotions on revisiting the places which had witnessed so much passion, now dead, and so many storms, now calmed. I felt differently from what I had expected. I had no regret for time past, but an appalling sense of the weakness of the human heart, which lets go so quickly what it thought to hold so fast, of the flight of Time, of man's mutability and his inconsistency, of the void and nothingness of life. These thoughts, and a thousand more which I can no longer recall, but which crowded my brain, made Metz seem suffocating. So I was most willing to leave it. But one morning, very early, I made my way to the prefecture and asked for leave to visit the garden. I can't convey to you the impression made on me by seeing again, after thirteen years, a place which had remained so well graven on my memory that I noticed at once every small change which had occurred during those years. In your eyes, nothing would have seemed different, but in mine Time had made a thousand destructions; and each one plunged me into deep melancholy.[46]

He learned that Amélie had recently died during a pregnancy, and wrote a last short letter of sympathy to Rosalie, such a letter as could be safely read either by his wife or her husband. And that was that.

CHAPTER FOUR

FIRST FLIGHT
1824–1827

Édouard is making a copy of his Travels in Switzerland.
*The job will be done in a fortnight. Isn't it glorious to have
an author in the family?*

ABBÉ LE SUEUR TO ALEXIS DE TOCQUEVILLE,
1 JANUARY 1823[1]

AT SOME POINT in the summer of 1824 Tocqueville wrote ebulliently to Kergorlay about a splendid new scheme: the two of them should go together on a short journey to England and back.

> We will sail up the Thames between the two rows of vessels which line it and see all the wealth of England displayed. We will stay in London for two days. Williams* assures me that he would give us a detailed guide-book so that we could see everything in that time, and on the third day we would be back in France. What a pity that it is barely practicable.[2]

It is a little difficult, in the twenty-first century, to grasp what was impracticable in the idea of two young men travelling to England and back on a short holiday. Gustave de Beaumont comments: 'There were a number of difficulties about this project, among them (1): they did

---

* Unidentified.

not know how to get passports. (2) they had no money. (3) they did not see how they could get their parents' approval, or how to do without it.'³ Probably the expense of the journey was the crucial factor: the parents had no objection to a tour in France, indeed Mme de Kergorlay was positively helpful. But Tocqueville takes boyish pleasure in considering how he might pull the wool over his father's eyes, and how to get passports. Does Kergorlay have one? Could Tocqueville pass as his servant? Or should he borrow Williams's ('we are the same height and appearance')?

> Once in England we would not need passports; the difficulty is getting in and out of France. We might be arrested ... but one has to risk something. I admit that I would be more than pleased to travel fifteen leagues with you and [take] a look at those rascally English who, we are told, are so strong and prosperous.

And they would see the sea, 'of all sights that which most impressed and exalted me during my childhood ... I am curious what it will do to me nowadays.' He makes earnest calculations ('On my trips to Metz I have realized that it is impossible to feed a horse for less than thirty *sous* a day') and concludes that the English journey would cost 298 francs (say, twelve guineas).⁴

In a lost letter Kergorlay raised certain doubts. Replying, Tocqueville admits their sense ('you say that I would find it hard to pass for an Englishman, and you are perfectly right; I would not find it easy to pass for a servant either'). He wonders how to get help from his father: 'with him, you have to hide everything or tell him everything frankly and honestly. That's his character. If I didn't he would see at once what I was up to and [scold?] me for not being frank.' He urges Kergorlay in Paris to buy an up-to-date guide to London: 'Buy it even if it is in English, so long as you are sure that it is a good one; I will undertake to interpret it, well or ill.' (This is the first sure sign that Tocqueville has been learning English.) And he speaks out again in favour of a voyage to the Thames on a steam-ship: 'the passage being longer [than that to Dover] there would be more hope of adventures ... How exciting it would be to lose sight of land altogether!'

Tocqueville the traveller – bold, energetic, enthusiastic, and anxious not to waste his time through ignorance or inadequate preparation

– has begun to make his appearance; it is even possible to see what Beaumont meant when he said of him, 'it is impossible to conceive how far, when he wanted something, he could go in proving ingeniously to others and in demonstrating to himself that it was the most reasonable idea in the world.'[5] But in this instance it would not do; the scheme had to be given up. He went to Metz instead.

For the next two years (that is, until 1826) he *faisait son droit* (read law) in Paris, living with his mother at 77, rue Saint-Dominique in the west of the faubourg Saint-Germain – 'the noble faubourg'. His time was divided between his studies and his affair with Rosalie Malye, although his studies also led him to join a student debating society where current politics and legal matters were discussed. It was an exciting period in the history of the city: Louis XVIII died, an anticlerical (or, more precisely, an anti-Jesuit) agitation erupted, and the battle between the Romantics and the Classicists burst out. But the law course was exceedingly dull, and Tocqueville turned to M. Mougin, his old rhetoric teacher at Metz, for advice on intellectual stimulus. Mougin had much approved his decision to devote himself to law; it was not an agreeable study, but 'to till arid soil, perhaps bristling with thorns, is useful in a different way; and a difficulty conquered also has its pleasure.' Nevertheless, Mougin quite understood Tocqueville's problem, and approved something he said about English poetry. He went on:

> The genius of a language harmonizes with its manner of thinking, as the character of a nation is the effect of its morals and its political habits. For a long time the English character has been shaped by the form of its government, by its various pursuits, even by its geographical position and its laws which drive off foreigners and make these kings of the ocean a homogeneous and *autochthonous* people. No-one, in my opinion, can ... write or speak any language as a Great Briton can his own.

These remarks, although decidedly tinged with Romanticism, would be of very little interest were they not the first to show Tocqueville encountering the kind of study which he would eventually make his own. Later, Mougin did him another service by recommending that he start going to the various lecture courses open to the public which dealt with literature and history – 'history, of all your studies the most necessary and the most difficult'.[6] But it is doubtful if Tocqueville, wrestling with his legal studies, found time to take this good advice just yet. He graduated on 29 August 1826 by successfully defending his two theses, one in Latin, one in French. Under the ever more reactionary regime of the Restoration he was not expected to show the slightest originality, and did not: I cannot judge the Latin thesis, but the French one is stupefyingly dull, the only boring thing he ever wrote; at least it proves that he had worked very hard.[7] Beaumont was to remark that he thus finished brilliantly studies which he often regretted ever having begun; 'and then he went on his travels.'[8]

His yearning to see the world, so palpable two years previously, seems to have grown stronger in the interval, and was, if anything, strengthened by the journey to Italy and Sicily which he now undertook. No doubt his father paid for the voyage as a reward for his success; Édouard, unemployed and by now an experienced traveller, went with him as a companion and bear-leader (it should be borne in mind that foreign travel was then far more difficult than as a rule it is today). The two brothers were on good terms, and their six months' companionship strengthened their friendship, although after their return Alexis had to confess, 'I was often wrong with respect to you. In our petty quarrels you were almost always in the right. That is the sort of thing that one does not admit to oneself at the time but which you come to see quite clearly later on.'[9] Alexis kept a travel-diary, perhaps following Édouard's example. It was extant in 1861, when Gustave de Beaumont published extracts from it; but like so much else it has since disappeared.[10]

Perhaps no other lacuna in the archives is so lamentable. It is possible to sketch the development of the young Tocqueville's character and opinions from the materials available (though not without conjecture); his emergence as a writer is hidden in darkness.

He became one of the most distinguished French authors of his day, but his output is strikingly uniform. Even in his letters and his reported conversation the utterance is predominantly that of a publicist concerned with history, politics and society; in his writing for publication the preoccupation is total. Sainte-Beuve, discussing the second part of the *Démocratie*, remarked that while Tocqueville never read a book without digging out its heart and meditating upon it, he had not done enough casual, random reading. Tocqueville himself rather confirms this observation in remarks made to Nassau Senior. Apart from Racine, he said, the only French poetry worth reading was the light verse. 'I do not think that I could now read Lamartine, though thirty years ago he delighted me.' He said that he read no novels that ended ill: 'Why should one voluntarily subject oneself to painful emotions?' During his childhood his family had read Richardson and Fielding aloud, and Alexis had wept for Lady Clementina in *Sir Charles Grandison*, but the only novelist he mentions having read as an adult is George Sand, whom he dismissed, though he admired her style, because 'her plots and her characters are so exaggerated and unnatural, and her morality is so perverted.' At some stage in his youth he read Scott, and succumbed to his spell like everyone else in the 1820s. He read *Madame Bovary* while he was dying, and according to Beaumont thought it interesting, talented, and the incarnation of immorality.[11]

We are all more or less the prisoners of our tastes and circumstances, and sooner or later get to know what they allow and what they do not. But many of us like to splash in the bath. Tocqueville seldom did. He lived through one of the greatest epochs of French literature, art and music, but seems to have been unable to enjoy any of it much, except perhaps the art.

We know little of what may be called his educational reading. André Jardin mentions Horace, Racine, Cicero, Demosthenes and Quintilian (he might have added Tacitus), and, in his father's library, eighteenth-century travel-writers and such authors as Voltaire, Montesquieu and Rousseau.[12] We know nothing of his early writing, except for a few school essays. Yet a born writer, which Tocqueville certainly was, is a slave of the pen, cannot help scribbling, and in youth is likely to be an eager emulator. So where, then, are the experiments that one would expect to find – the epic (incomplete) on William the Conqueror, the novel à la Scott (unfinished), *The Lovers of Tourlaville*, the tragedy à la Corneille on his collateral ancestress, Jeanne d'Arc, the projected history of the world in nine volumes, the biography of Cicero, even the light verse which other members of his family turned out fluently? If anything like them ever existed, it has been completely lost.

Just possibly he was a late developer, though that is not the impression left by his first letters: there are no anecdotes of childish precocity, and he does not seem to have spread his wings until he went to school. Very probably he did not expect to turn author, and when he did, his *milieu* (except for his immediate family and closest friends) was discouraging: 'I was thought of as a poor eccentric, who, robbed of his career, wrote in order to kill time, admittedly a tolerable occupation since at any rate it is better to write a bad book than to go whoring.'[13] The tradition of his family required him to enter the service of the King, and his father, like many others, believed that the Restoration had brought back the *noblesse* as well as the legitimate monarch. Shorn of its unjust privileges by the Revolution, the nobility yet retained its most important assets: wealth, education and access to the government. Comte Hervé wanted the *noblesse* to be defined in future by its duty to the state, and in carrying out that duty to demonstrate its right to its pre-eminent position in society. The tradition of both sword and robe was to be modernized. (The idea was Napoleonic, although the comte would not have admitted the fact: the British peerage was the avowed model.) The future of the Tocqueville children, then, seemed unproblematic: Hippolyte and Édouard, as we have seen, were supposed to be soldiers, and Alexis, once his special gifts were recognized, was to be groomed for a career in politics. He did not want to be an administrator, but he was allured by the idea of political leadership, of oratory (one of his essays at the *lycée* was on the topic of eloquence, and another, in Latin, was a eulogy of Demosthenes). Unfortunately, under the laws of the Restoration, he would not be entitled to vote before the age of thirty, or to enter the Chamber of Deputies before he was forty. Yet all his studies before that rather remote period, all his writing, and whatever job he took, would be by way of preparing him for that particular destiny.

This interpretation is certainly valid, up to a point; but no young man of talent could confine himself to such a programme. As will be shown, the influence on Tocqueville of Chateaubriand was profound, and it drove him to experimentation. Tocqueville was a man of his time, which meant that although he might prefer classicism he could not help being a Romantic. Classicism, once it was no longer universally accepted as authoritative (and how could it be? This was the era when Népomucène Lemercier, as absurd as his name, laid down twenty-six rules for writing a perfect tragedy, all derived from *Athalie*),[14] became simply one mode among others which an author might choose for purposes of self-expression – a form of Romanticism, in short. In his mature work Tocqueville writes in the tradition of Montesquieu, Pascal and Rousseau; but in the *Voyage en Sicile*, which is, if not juvenile, at any rate youthful, we can glimpse him exploring literary possibilities, and must regret that glimpses are all that we will ever have.

Beaumont says that the manuscript of the *Voyage* was a quarto-sized volume of 350 pages, so what we have can only be a tithe of what was written. Tocqueville wrote on the cover 'very mediocre', which shows that he was a stern judge of his own productions, but he did not destroy it, and nor did Beaumont (it may yet turn up), who remarks that even were Tocqueville's verdict just, 'it would still be interesting to study in these first attempts of a great writer the direction of his spirit, his fumblings, his mistakes, his retreats, and the winding tracks by which he found his way to his right road.'[15] Very true, even of the mere fragment left to us – which is much better than mediocre.

The *Voyage* was written up in Sicily as a complete account of the brothers' journey, mostly as a literary exercise, but also, no doubt, for the entertainment of their family. Unhappily the fragment does not tell us how or when or where the travellers reached Italy; we first meet them in Rome, in January 1827. Until then, according to Beaumont, the journal had been the usual sort of thing: a young man's conscientious account of all the palaces and museums that he visited, of the paintings and medallions that he inspected. In Rome he abandons this sterile occupation, and tries his hand at something more fanciful: he falls asleep in the Campo Vaccino (the Forum) and has a vision of ancient Rome, 'her heroes, her glory, her power, above all her liberty'; all the great events and great men of antiquity parade before him, 'from the first Brutus to the coming of Augustus'. Then suddenly he is woken by a procession of bare-footed monks going up the steps of the Capitol, while a cowherd tinkles a bell to summon his beasts. 'I arose and slowly took my way to my lodging, looking back from time to time, and saying to myself, "Poor humanity, what art thou after all?"'[16]

This passage may well startle a British reader, but it is not a plagiarism: Tocqueville read Gibbon's *Autobiography* for the first time in the last weeks of his life.[17] Both men play with what must have been a frequent, even trite experience of visitors to papal Rome (and something very similar happened to Heine, or so he said, in the amphitheatre at Verona); but Gibbon made it matter, for it gave him the idea of writing the history of the city.* Tocqueville, by contrast, is banal and pretentious, and matters are not mended by the surviving fragment of a letter to Kergorlay in which he palpably steals from a well-known passage by Chateaubriand on the same subject.† He redeems himself only by a tart remark that the modern buildings planted among the ruins make Rome look like an old man wearing rouge.[18]

These Roman passages, insignificant in themselves, nevertheless embody the literary pattern of the entire *Voyage en Sicile*, as we have it. The young author, as Beaumont indicates, is trying to find his voice. Much of the time he writes in a faded, sentimental, eighteenth-century vein of Classical commonplaces; he also works hard to make the *chateaubrianesque* sublime his own, with only partial success; occasionally, almost without realizing it, he achieves his own authentic note, when his flair for observing and analysing foreign societies emerges. Throughout, some important aspects of his personality, which were not exhibited in his career as a young lover, are revealed.

From a letter written to Édouard three years later, not from the journal, we learn how much Tocqueville liked Naples when he got there: 'Nothing else in my travels ever gave me the sweet and agreeable sensations that I got from the sky and shores of Naples. The impression is still vivid, and I would be vexed to die without having gone back.'[19]‡ He climbed Vesuvius. But the *Voyage* as we have it starts only with the departure of his ship from Naples, bound for Sicily. He seizes the opportunity to show that he has read Tacitus, favourite historian of the French opposition under Napoleon: he gazes up at the horrid rocks

---

* Why is there not a statute of Gibbon on the slopes of the Capitol?

† A year later Chateaubriand himself came to Rome as French ambassador; in his memoirs he gives an unintentionally distressing account of his nephew Christian, who after seeing service as an army officer went to Rome as a Jesuit novice. Presumably the Tocqueville brothers enjoyed their cousin's company during their visit.

‡ Perhaps that is why in 1850 he did go back, when he may well have feared that he was dying. His wife feared it.

of Capri and decides that they were a fitting perch for such a bird of prey as Tiberius. Then a storm blows up. Three years before, at the time of the English scheme, Tocqueville wrote longingly of the sea; now his enthusiasm is to be rigorously tested. Huge waves arise, sea-spray covers the decks. Thunder and lightning. Tocqueville has always found night-storms, and the calm which proceeds them, sublime: 'but those who have not gone through the same spectacle far out at sea have missed the most terrible scene which nature can present ... the waves boiled around us with an energy of which I had had no idea.' Some poor passengers begin to chant a psalm, which moves him greatly: 'what philosopher was ever so sure of his system as not to do likewise when faced with this terrible manifestation of divine omnipotence?' The ship is laid on her beam-ends, waves pour into the cabins, passengers shriek and a dog howls, but the vessel rights herself. Rain pours down and the night seems endless; with dawn Tocqueville is happy to think that the danger is over and pokes a cheerful head out of his cabin, but the sailors are staring in alarm at the west, where a new storm is rapidly developing, likely to drive them onto the lee-shore straight ahead. Tocqueville crawls along the deck from handhold to handhold ('no living creature could have walked a step without instantly being thrown into the sea') to ask the captain if they are really in danger; the captain replies only, 'Credo così' ('I should say so'). Tocqueville crawls back to the cabin, but before he gets there an old sailor grabs him by the sleeve and says, grinding his teeth, 'It was your urgency to be off which made us leave port. Any moment now you'll see what that means for you and for us.' Tocqueville thinks this unfair, as before he and Édouard boarded they were assured that there was nothing to fear but 'una burasca' (a squall). He gets back to his brother and they try to prepare for shipwreck. A sailor comes by, collecting alms for souls in Purgatory.

> That made us think of the religion into which we had been born and to which our earliest thoughts had been guided; we prayed briefly and then sat beside the cabin door. I folded my arms across my chest and put myself to reviewing the few years that I had lived so far. I admit frankly that in that moment, when I believed myself about to appear before the Supreme Judge, the object of human existence seemed altogether different from what I had judged it until that moment.

Matters that I had considered very important until then appeared
infinitely petty ... the worst moment came when I fell to thinking
of those we would leave behind. When I imagined the way in which
news of the event would reach them, by purely public channels, I
felt that tears were pricking my eyes, and I hastened to busy myself
about something else, so as not to waste the strength which I thought
I would soon need.

Fortunately the ship survived the second storm, though she was blown
far off her course, and because of contrary winds landed them not at
Palermo but at Oliveri, a tiny place 150 kilometres to the east. It was 12
March. They were delighted by the green grass and flowering shrubs,
the aloes and the figtrees ('we had left winter in Italy') but they soon
noticed that there was not a single glass window in the village. The
next day they set off for Palermo, escorted by a soldier, gun in his
hand, dagger in his belt, riding on a vigorous horse, and three bare-
footed young peasants whose business it was to keep the mule-train
moving. There seem to have been more travellers than just the two
brothers: some had saddles, but others had to sit precariously perched
on top of the baggage.

Beaumont has not preserved any remarks about Palermo except
that it was believed by the people that if Napoleon had conquered
Sicily he would have thrown Monte Pelligrino into the sea: 'Nothing
in the world could better suggest the supernatural power over the
minds of his contemporaries which that man acquired.' They left on
17 March, and crossed the island from one antique site to another:
Segesta, Selinus, Agrigentum. At every spot Tocqueville records
suitable thoughts about Classical history and Classical architecture.
But it is modern Sicily that stimulates him to be himself, or rather, the
man he is becoming:

> There are no villages in Sicily, only towns, and not a few of those.
> After having gone eight or ten leagues, crossing an almost completely
> empty country, it is surprising suddenly to enter a town of 20,000
> souls, which no highway, no street hubbub, has announced from afar.
> What little there is of industry and well-being has retreated to these
> places, as warmth in a paralytic body retires little by little towards the
> heart. The cause of this singular state of affairs is not hard to find.
> The only great landlords of Sicily are the nobles and the monasteries

... The nobles dissipate their revenues in Palermo or Naples, giving no thought to their holdings in Sicily except for the rents they receive. Many of them, we were told, have never even visited their lands. As to the monks, a race eminently given over by nature to routine, they tranquilly eat up their customary revenues, without thinking how they might be increased. However, the people, who have little or no stake in the land and whose harvests can find no market, are little by little abandoning the fields.

A day or two later he indulges in another bout of political economy, trying to arrive at the truth about large estates and peasant smallholdings: which makes for greater prosperity? He arrives at the rather unsatisfactory conclusion that the former suit the north, the latter the south: 'If I were king of England I would favour great estates, if master of Sicily I would do all I could to encourage small ones; but being neither the one nor the other, I return quickly to my journal.' He had perhaps been alerted to the question of landholdings (it would long preoccupy him) by the fierce debates of a year or two back in the French parliament; he was feeing his way towards what today we would call topics in social science; but what is most striking in these passages is their liberalism. Reacting to a specimen of the *ancien régime* at its very worst, he writes like a man of 1789; which, considering what he actually was, may in retrospect be seen as ominous for the restored French monarchy.

Next, the ascent of Etna. Tocqueville exerted all his powers to pull off a truly *chateaubrianesque* effusion, but he had to get Édouard and himself to the top first:

We crossed the latest hillock formed by the repeated falls of ash, of which the slope is, therefore, very steep. On this shifting soil, as steep as a roof, we could not take a step without sinking in deep and often slipped back by more than a fathom. I had already experienced the unpleasantness of a similar path when I visited Vesuvius. But here was something more: to the difficulty of getting along such a road was added that of breathing at such a height. We were then about 1,700 fathoms [more than 10,000 feet] above Catania. The air was thin but however not pure. Volcanic seepings filled it with sulphurous fumes. We had to halt every ten or fifteen paces. When we did, we collapsed on the ash and for several seconds felt extraordinary thumpings in our chests. My head ached as if it were clamped into an iron bonnet. Édouard admitted that he was not sure that he could get to the top.

It will be remembered that Édouard was asthmatic. Nevertheless he did get to the top, inspired perhaps by his dauntless younger brother; and together they saw the sun come up over Sicily.

> We were making one of our forced halts when the guide, clapping his hands, cried out in a voice that I still seem to hear, 'Il sole, il sole!' We turned immediately to face east; the sky was thick with clouds; nevertheless the sun, looking like a red-hot iron millstone, in spite of all obstacles brought up day, and showed half himself above the sea of Greece. A reddish, violet shade spilt over the waves and bloodied the mountains of Calabria that stretched before us. It was a sight such as one sees only once in a lifetime, one of those severe and terrible beauties of Nature that drive you in on yourself and crush you with a sense of your littleness. There mingled with this splendour something sad, something strangely gloomy. The immense star shed but a doubtful light. He seemed to drag himself up the heights of heaven rather than climb. That, we said to ourselves, is how he will rise on the world's last day.

Then he spoils it all by evoking Pluto, Proserpine, Ceres, Pan, *et cetera*, a mythological list 'such as a College easily supplies', and concludes, almost lapsing into verse, 'Terre de dieux et des héros! Pauvre Sicile! que sont devenues tes brillantes chimères!'* His inability to maintain a consistent language suggests very strongly that whether he realized it or not he was writing against the grain; but it was several years yet before he abandoned his attempts at Romantic rhapsody (the Classical gods vanished much sooner).

After Etna came Stromboli (his third volcano) and a bad attack of homesickness; then a final literary experiment, an imaginary conversation between a Sicilian nobleman, Don Ambrosio, and one from Naples, Don Carlo, in which the political and moral weaknesses of both types were ruthlessly depicted.

Don Carlo (laughing bitterly): Very well, if our yoke weighs so

---

* 'Land of gods and heroes! Poor Sicily! Where now are your brilliant fantasies?'

heavily upon you, why not break it? Why is the tocsin not ringing over your fields? What are you waiting for? Are you gathering, are you marching? No! You will never decide that oppression has gone too far, and, down to your latest descendants, you will always defer vengeance to tomorrow. But should you ever be bold enough to raise the banner of revolt, how easily Naples will pulverize your weakness! Search your memory; remember 1820.* Where are your ships, your soldiers? Your young men hate the trade of arms. There are no Sicilians in the army.

Don Ambrosio (in a constrained and altered voice): It is true; all that is too true: what good to hide it? And yet, we were not born for slavery …

(These words were first published in 1861, the year after Garibaldi landed at Marsala.)

The dialogue is a great success. It seems a pity that Tocqueville never did such a thing again (although, significantly, some of his writing about Ireland resembles it). Taken as a whole, the *Voyage en Sicile* is full of achievement, as well as promise: there ought to be a modern English translation. It shows that intellectually Tocqueville was maturing fast, which was just as well: for on 6 April 1827, even before he got home from Italy, he was appointed *juge-auditeur* at the law-courts of Versailles.

---

* In 1820 a sudden rebellion forced Ferdinand I of the Two Sicilies to grant his subjects a constitution, but the prompt arrival of an Austrian army enabled him to withdraw this concession.

CHAPTER FIVE

PUPILLAGE

1827–1830

He thought about himself and the whole earth,
Of man the wonderful and of the stars
And how the deuce they ever could have birth,
And then he thought of earthquakes and of wars,
How many miles the moon might have in girth,
Of air balloons and of the many bars
To perfect knowledge of the boundless skies,
And then he thought of Donna Julia's eyes.

LORD BYRON, *DON JUAN*

IT WAS HIS FATHER'S doing.

In June 1826, Comte Hervé had achieved a long-standing ambition: he was appointed prefect of the Seine-et-Oise, of which Versailles was the *chef-lieu*. In 1815 Chateaubriand had presumptuously promised him the job, and when, in 1823, he entered the Villèle ministry as foreign minister, Hervé again cherished high hopes; but as he afterwards remarked bitterly, he should have realized that M. de Chateaubriand never thought of anyone but himself.[1] When, soon afterwards, Chateaubriand went into opposition, Hervé stuck to Villèle; perhaps the Seine-et-Oise was his belated reward. Placed between Normandy and Paris, the department permitted Hervé to keep in touch easily with his estates and his wife (though she still refused to live in a prefecture),

and he knew it well from his Verneuil days. In another respect it was
a suitable posting for a *verdet,* a long-standing follower of the comte
d'Artois, for Artois was now King Charles X and resided in summer at
Saint-Cloud, where he required the prefect to pay his court. The château
at Versailles was too dilapidated for occupation, but the king made a
point of visiting the town from time to time and dining in public at the
Grand Trianon.[2] The prefect had to be in attendance; nor was that all.
He was appointed gentleman of the bed-chamber and in his memoirs
has left a faintly ironical account of the last Bourbons' attempts to
emulate Louis XIV in an age of greatly reduced resources:

> There was nothing burdensome about my service. It consisted of
> an obligation to accompany the King to mass. On his return, we
> assembled briefly in the drawing-room. The King said something
> polite to each of us. The Dauphin and the Princesses formally bowed
> and curtsied to him, and then retired. He himself returned to his
> apartments and I would be free until eight in the evening, when I had
> to reappear, by standing order. My task was thus complete.
>
> My privileges consisted in partaking, if I liked, of an excellent
> *déjeuner* and a very good dinner at the table of the *premier maître
> d'hôtel* and then staying to play cards with the King, an exceedingly
> tedious honour.
>
> The King played whist every evening, the only moment in his
> life when he shed his usual urbanity. He would scold his partner and
> even his opponents. M. le Dauphin* would play a game of chess and
> then retire at nine o'clock. Those of us who were not required by the
> one or the other party played *écarté.* Madame la Dauphine worked at
> her tapestry until she put down her canvas in order to take her turn at
> *écarté.* The atmosphere was cold as ice. Respect prevented any sort of
> relaxation and imposed boredom instead. At half past ten the evening
> would end.[3]

The prefect had come a long way from his dungeon in Port-Libre;
nevertheless, he probably preferred the meetings of his departmental
conseil général, which, as André Jardin remarks, served also as a family
reunion, for there he would meet his relations Louis de Rosanbo,
Comte Molé and Félix Le Peletier d'Aunay, all of whom had estates
in the Seine-et-Oise. The *conseil* was divided between liberals and

* The eldest son of Charles X, better known as the duc d'Angoulême.

conservatives, and from 1827 onwards d'Aunay sat in the Chamber of Deputies as deputy from the Seine-et-Oise and a leading member of the opposition; but they all agreed in praising their prefect.[4] Nobody made any objection to the installation of his youngest son as a *juge-auditeur* and resident of the Versailles prefecture. Questions of a conflict of interest simply did not arise. The young man, at twenty-one, was old enough to qualify as a magistrate, and he was the *arrière-petit-fils* of M. de Malesherbes. Under the Bourbons the *noblesse de robe* regrouped, like the *noblesse d'épée*. There could be no question of reviving the old *parlements*, but by accepting only candidates of good family for legal posts the courthouses of the new France could be made into fairly satisfactory substitutes. It could all be justified in the name of creating a *noblesse* of service.[5] As such it was a renewed denial of the cherished Revolutionary principle, that all careers should be equally open to talent.

There is no reason to suppose that Alexis de Tocqueville saw anything wrong with his father's plan. It was an excellent way to launch his legal career. French tribunals, including that at Versailles, were each organized into two chambers, one for hearing and deciding cases, the other for investigating them and, if necessary, prosecuting – the *parquet*. *Juges-auditeurs* were the lowliest members of the *parquet* – unsalaried young gentlemen learning their trade who, it seems, could work as much or as little as they pleased. Tocqueville, full of ambition, was determined to learn and work as hard as possible.

He entered on his duties in June 1827, and felt the emotions usual to those starting their first job. He told Édouard that it was not life as he had envisaged it at sixteen, but his comrades were welcoming, and the work, though dull in itself, was interesting as a challenge. 'Although I know moments of deep boredom and even disgust, I would for many reasons like to see you occupied as I am.' (Édouard had still not found any career.) Two weeks later he wrote in more detail and with greater frankness to Kergorlay:

> beforehand, I thought myself fairly good at law, but I was greatly deceived. I was, as to law, as someone just out of school is to science. My head was full of unshaped material, that was all. When I have to apply it, I am lost, and my inadequacy makes me despair; I am by far the feeblest of us all, and though vanity, which is as much part of me

as it is of everyone else, whispers that when I have worked as long as the others I will be as advanced as they are, I still feel crushed. For generally speaking, as I feel every day, I have a craving to excel which will make my life a torment ... I find it hard to get used to speaking in public; I grope for words and cut my arguments too short. Beside me are men who reason ill and speak well; that puts me in a continual rage. It seems to me that I am their superior, but when I want to make an effect, I know I am inferior. On the other hand ... I am not bored; you can't imagine what it is like to think seriously about a point of law. The work in the end forces me to find it interesting. So law which disgusted me in theory doesn't produce the same effect in practice. All my abilities come together to find a solution or method; I feel that my mind is active, and developing in every way, and the result is the same well-being that I knew in my heart when I was in love ... my companions all seem to be prigs, more or less, but there is more to them than I thought at first. Almost all of them now show me a friendship and a good fellowship which is agreeable enough, ... and on close examination I have found among them one or two truly honourable young men full of good feeling and integrity. This discovery has enabled me to overcome the natural disgust I feel at legal minds and manners. To sum up, *mon cher ami*, I begin to think that I will enter into the spirit of my calling ...

His only anxiety was that he might turn into a mere legal drudge.[6]

He was saved from any such fate, if it ever truly threatened, by one of the honourable young men, Gustave de Beaumont (1802–66). Tocqueville had to get over his shyness and the attitude of disdain with which he compensated for his insecurity, but a year and a half later he would be invoking a friendship which, 'I don't know how, was born *old*', and was to continue almost unclouded to life's end.[7] André Jardin has listed all the ways in which they were suited to each other. Their backgrounds were almost identical. Beaumont came from a large noble family – almost a clan – which had spread all over the *bocage*; his father lived on the estate of Beaumont-la-Chartre in the Sarthe; his uncle Armand was a prefect, and both were strict Ultras. Gustave was three years older than Tocqueville, but it may be significant that he too was a youngest son with a pair of older brothers. He began his legal career in 1824 or thereabouts, and advanced rapidly. He had been *substitut* (deputy prosecutor) at Bar-sur-Aube and transferred to the same job at Versailles in 1826; it carried a salary. According to Jardin, Beaumont was soon regarded as the young eagle of the Versailles *parquet,* yet he did not allow his success to swell his head. He was Tocqueville's immediate superior and won the novice's liking at once by proposing that they share equally the work of preparing cases. This gesture of trust and thoughtfulness was typical of Beaumont's large friendliness; he was a good speaker, a genial partner, and highly intelligent; very much a countryman, with a touch of peasant cunning (says Jardin) that did not affect his perfect honesty.[8] In any circumstances Tocqueville would have found him an excellent colleague.

But there was more to it than that. Partly it was the attraction of opposites: Beaumont had the sunny solidity of a man at ease with himself, which Tocqueville, always a prey to self-doubt and, as he well knew, of an uncertain temper, was naturally drawn to. Beaumont, on the other hand, found in Tocqueville an intellectual brilliance which he himself could not quite match; a little, eager, highly strung man of reserved manners who yet, once his interest or affection was engaged, held nothing back. In his 'Notice' Beaumont recalls the impression which Tocqueville made on his colleagues:

> As soon as Alexis de Tocqueville had appeared a few times for the public prosecutor before the court of assize at Versailles, his grave utterance, his serious turn of thought, the maturity of his judgement and the superiority of his intelligence marked him out as exceptional. He had no great success with the crowd, but never failed with the elite; no-one doubted that a brilliant future was his, and more than one president of assize prophesied a high destiny for him. I need only add that in these prognostications they mentioned Malesherbes rather than Montesquieu.[9]

It is a mark of Beaumont's excellent character that he never seems to have felt jealous of this rising star; perhaps he was a follower rather than a leader; but analysis must not end there. The fact was that if the characters of the two friends differed, their intellects were profoundly alike. They had the same interests, the same concerns, the same tastes, the same ambitions; their abilities were strikingly similar; they were in all ways compatible. Perhaps no-one who has not known such a meeting of minds can really understand how precious it is, especially in early youth; but Tocqueville has done his best to enlighten us. In a letter of 8 May 1830 we find him writing to Beaumont, whom by then he had known for nearly three years:

> The fact is that you are the only man in the world on whose judgement I can rely with confidence. Kergorlay is a good judge, but he is not of our profession. You alone have both intelligence and appropriate experience. When I think it over, *mon cher ami*, it seems to me that we are not grateful enough for our good luck in finding and binding each other among the crowd. It was especially lucky for me; not that I am putting on false modesty and saying that I am worth less than you, although I do think that in several respects, I mean only that you have more chance of being appreciated and noticed than I, whose character seems so icy and unforthcoming. You have already made some good friends, sooner or later you would have met a man you could love as much as you do me; but among the circumspect and shrivelled souls of those who wear the black robe I don't know where I would have found a second *you* if you had never crossed my path.

(Here Tocqueville was doing himself an injustice. Throughout his life, he was good at forming friendships, and nothing is more striking about his Versailles years than the speed with which he gathered round himself a circle of like-minded young men.)

> Anyway, however it came about, the deed is done, here we are united, and to my mind it is clearly for life. The same studies, the same projects, the same locations bring us together and may well do so during the whole course of our existence. What a rare and priceless circumstance![10]

Once more the characteristically frank avowal of strong feelings; and an admission of his own stiffness among strangers. Both themes will recur.

In the autumn of 1827 Hervé de Tocqueville was appointed a member of the Chamber of Peers. His family was not much pleased with the honour. On 23 November Alexis wrote to Kergorlay with the news: 'Behold my father arrived at a peerage. He really wanted it four years ago, and asked for it too. Today, when he neither asked nor wished for it he is swept up among the new creations. Such is the world. He made plain his disapproval of the measure before they took it, he has not changed his mind since, and I am certain that he is right.'

At this stage Tocqueville wanted the Chamber of Peers to be taken seriously as the only aristocratic element in the Constitution, and this was impossible if the government of the day felt free to pack it when desirable and to bestow peerages as rewards on reliable backbenchers from the lower house. And he was furious with those extreme royalists who, in the recent general election, had preferred to vote for liberals rather than for supporters of the Villèle ministry. It struck him as crazy: it was merely helping men who, if they got their chance, would not only throw out Villèle but would crush all royalists like flies.[11]

This letter to Kergorlay, the first to survive in which Tocqueville discusses politics, is interesting on several counts. For one thing, it is the first in which he uses the word 'aristocratic'. It shows that he was not yet in the least a democrat – not even, in party terms, a liberal. Like his father, he was a ministerialist, as he well might be, for not only had Villèle appointed Hervé de Tocqueville to his favourite prefecture, he had shown himself the ablest, as well as the longest-serving, of all the prime ministers of the Restoration. France had prospered under Villèle; in the early twenties he had seen off a rash of ill-managed republican conspiracies; Chateaubriand's expedition to Spain in 1823, which restored Ferdinand VII to power, had demonstrated that France was once again a country to be reckoned with (even if Ferdinand was a most discreditable client); and by some judicious measures Villèle had resolved several of the disputes, most notably that over the compensation due to former *émigrés* for their confiscated property, which had bedevilled and weakened the Restoration settlement. But by 1827 he had made too many enemies: the Ultra party, steadily gaining in arrogance and extremism, found him too moderate; neither the election of 1827 nor the creation of peers helped him; on 4 January 1828 he resigned. Hervé de Tocqueville, the new peer, who had that quality of common sense so conspicuously lacking in most Ultras, decided to vote with the moderates in the Chamber of Peers.[12]

As a peer Comte Hervé was debarred from continuing as a prefect: for this reason he left Versailles in January 1828. This furthered the friendship of Alexis and Beaumont. They set up house together at 66, rue d'Anjou, Versailles: a quiet, grey, dignified street near the cathedral of St Louis, and within a few minutes' walk of the royal park. It was the first time that Tocqueville had lived in a house of his own, and he found the experience delightful. He was a frequent visitor to his parents, now living together again in Paris (many of his letters were written there at this period) but to be a householder increased his sense of maturity and independence. He was not, in fact, financially independent, having no salary and, no doubt, tending to exceed his allowance. Once his father offered to pay his tailor's bill, and he wrote to Beaumont: 'I want to present him with it as soon as possible; as you know, one must never let such paternal impulses cool,'[13] but he was tasting autonomy for the first time and enjoying it.

On at least one occasion autonomy brought with it a real test of judgement. In the summer of 1829, while Tocqueville was in Normandy, the landlord wrote to Beaumont to complain angrily that Madeleine, their servant, who ran their household with admirable economy, had in their absence taken to entertaining men and women in such a way that the house was becoming notorious as little better than a brothel. Beaumont wanted to dismiss her at once, but being absent himself was content to leave the matter for Tocqueville to deal with on his imminent return. Tocqueville arrived and found that matters were even worse than he had supposed: some of the 'canaille' whom Madeleine had admitted to the house had stolen the silver spoons and forks. One of her lovers had drunk a great deal of the best wine. According to a neighbour, *la mère* Gérard, Madeleine went about the streets with soldiers and whores, stayed out late (especially when her employers were away) and had once been seen climbing up a ladder to her bedroom window, presumably when the front door was locked and she did not want to rouse Tocqueville and Beaumont (and their suspicions). She would have to go when in two or three weeks her term of employment was up; or sooner.

The episode reads like something in the Goncourt journals. Its interest today is the light which it throws on young Tocqueville's character. He sifts the evidence and assesses the witnesses like the experienced magistrate he has become; he is sorry for Madeleine, who having been caught is trying hard to show herself reformed; and he blames both Beaumont and himself for having let things come to such a pass. They must exert themselves in future to maintain order in the house, or do without a servant, as formerly, 'which I must admit would be for me a painful remedy'. Their next housekeeper must not only be ugly, like Madeleine, but old: ugly young women are the worst of all, since they want to carry on as if they were pretty, and only the vilest men will take them up.[14]

The *parquet* taught him more than how to test the evidence of servant-girls. In his years at Versailles he prepared reports on some sixty cases; it was the sort of technical training from which any potential scholar would benefit. He learned how to ascertain and apply laws, and not to be satisfied with superficial research: at the end of one 5,000-word report he apologizes because 'a fairly serious illness did not allow us to study [the matter] as much as it undoubtedly deserved.'[15] More than that, the work continued his political and historical education. Like Daumier, he noted the weaknesses of the great magistrates: they could be offhand with litigants, make jokes at their expense, shrug their shoulders in contempt while lawyers for the defence were speaking, or smile their approval of the prosecutors when proceedings had got no further than the reading out of the charges (years later, after his visit to America, he thought it would do these judges good to be stripped of their robes and official pomp).[16] Several of the cases which he investigated concerned lawsuits brought by former *émigrés*, or their families, for the restitution of property lost during the Revolution, and although Tocqueville sympathized with the claimants he was forced to recognize that neither the law nor lawyers could nullify the events of thirty years: the Revolution was a fact to which everyone had to adjust. Its effects could be mitigated in some cases but not reversed.[17] This was not a thought with which his upbringing had made him familiar.

The profound effect of these discoveries may be inferred from the course of some of his private studies. As has already been recorded, he was advised by M. Mougin to read history.[18] (This recommendation suggests great insight in Mougin, but we must remember that in the Romantic Age history was universally fascinating.) Tocqueville took the advice and began on the *Histoire de la Révolution* of Adolphe Thiers, which came out in several volumes between 1823 and 1828. The author's name can have meant little or nothing to him (Thiers was only beginning to be known as a liberal journalist) but the subject was absorbing and so far unchronicled, except in memoirs. Tocqueville at twenty was utterly unprepared for what he found. Ten or eleven years later he wrote to a friend:

I was ablaze with the loyal simplicities natural to youth; besides, the traditions of my family still kept their primal power over my imagination. So the *Histoire de la Révolution* was peculiarly horrifying and caused a violent hatred of the author. I regarded M. Thiers as the most perverse and dangerous of men …[19]

It was the encounter with the *philosophes* all over again, only this time intellectual surrender was delayed. More was not possible. A man so acute and mentally honest as Tocqueville could not defer it indefinitely, especially as his professional work was pulling him in the same direction. Thiers put into his head the dismaying notions that the Revolution was not just the outcome of a treacherous plot by the Freemasons or the duc d'Orléans; that it had been brought on by noble selfishness and royal incompetence; that its work was essentially valuable and necessary; and that even the Convention might be exonerated; that in short, as Clemenceau was to say fifty years later, the Revolution must be accepted *en bloc* or not at all. Tocqueville never agreed; he spent the rest of his life looking for an alternative interpretation; but it was Thiers who first forced him to realize that the debate was not so one-sided as he had been brought up to believe, and that it could be won only by the party with the best arguments and information.* How soon this sort of exposure began to affect his political principles cannot be discovered; but as we have seen he was already (perhaps unconsciously) a man of 1789 when he went to Sicily. And when in 1828 Thiers brought out a revised edition of his first two volumes Tocqueville bought them and coolly began to take notes. In 1787–8, he observed, politics was in such a state of confusion that revolution was both imminent and necessary. He distinguished emphatically between the underlying cause of the Revolution and accidental circumstances, and that cause he identified as the obsolete privileges of the *noblesse* and the clergy. 'So a revolution was inevitable. It was easy.' He listed the accidental circumstances, including

---

* Not that he ever forgave Thiers. He regarded him as one of those writers of democratic times who preached a kind of blind surrender to historical inevitability (see OC I ii 91–2) and blamed the *Histoire de la Révolution*, along with Lamartine's *Girondins*, for helping to bring on the 1848 Revolution (OX VII 94–5).

contact with 'the American republics',* and began to compile an outline of events.

He had come a long way in a fairly short time. A few years later he recorded in a letter to a kinsman that it was about now that he began to think that the triumph of egalitarianism – which he called democracy – was inevitable, because ordained by God: the road was opening which led to *De la démocratie en Amérique*; and the notes on Thiers show that he was beginning to think along the lines which eventually led him to *L'Ancien Régime et la Révolution*. They also show that he had no suspicion that in a few months there would be another revolution in France.[20]

Any such anticipation would have seemed far-fetched to all the Tocquevilles in 1828, which may be called the last normal year of the Restoration. The new ministry, led by Jean-Baptiste de Martignac, was weak in parliament, but its moderation made it acceptable to the country at large; had the King given it his support it might well have grown stronger, but he only tolerated it: he would not even make Martignac *président du conseil*. However there was no immediate cause for anxiety, and Comte Hervé tranquilly devoted himself to his political duties, which had changed rather than disappeared when he ceased to be a prefect. As André Jardin puts it, he remained a faithful vassal of the Crown, in the family tradition;[21] it was now his business to maximize his local influence and use it in the interest of the King's party. Consequently he began to show a closer interest in the Cotentin, where his chief estates lay, than ever before. He spoke up for Cherbourg in the Chamber of Peers and took to visiting the region more frequently. His son Hippolyte had recently married Émilie Evrard de Belisle de Saint-Rémy, daughter of a noble family from Coutances, and although Hippolyte's military duties kept the young couple away for most of the time they spent the autumn of 1828 in Normandy. Alexis joined them there for his own vacation. He had written to Kergorlay that he was feeling restless: 'I feel as if I could undertake a long and adventurous journey with more pleasure than ever.' On the other hand, he admitted, after such an excursion he would want to settle down again. 'I

---

* At this stage of his development AT thought that the American example was thoroughly unsuitable for France.

need movement, I need rest – such are the alternatives between which I have been tossing these six or seven years.'[22] Perhaps Normandy could satisfy both impulses. Furthermore, although the comtesse de Tocqueville and her new daughter-in-law were already on bad terms, Alexis hoped to remain friends with Hippolyte and Émilie. He stayed with them at Saint-Rémy and at Saint-Blaise near Valognes, where he may have met Émilie's Bonapartist brother-in-law, Armand, comte de Bricqueville, who was the deputy for Cherbourg; finally he arrived at Tocqueville itself, accompanied by Hippolyte. While there, on 6 October, he started to write an enormous letter to Beaumont – perhaps the longest he ever wrote. After detailing his journey he went on:

> Here I am at last at Tocqueville, in my family's ancient ruins. I can see three miles away the port where William embarked for the conquest of England. I am surrounded by Normans whose names appear in the roll of the conquerors. I must admit that all that *chatouille de mon coeur l'orgeuilleuse faiblesse* *and rouses in me a puerile enthusiasm of which I will soon be ashamed.[23]

(He did not yet suspect that one day his fondness for Tocqueville and its neighbourhood would develop into a passion.) He began to pour out to Beaumont the results of his study of English history. He had just finished reading a translation of John Lingard's *History of England*, or as much of it as had been published: the final volume was not to appear until 1830. He had much to say – 10,000 words or so.

He and Beaumont had already agreed to study together, but it is not clear how they planned to do so, or what exactly they read. They were certainly not systematic, but then why should they be? – they were not reading for a degree. If they regularly wrote book reports for each other, then the Lingard letter is the only one to survive. But it reads as something spontaneous. Tocqueville is bursting with enthusiasm and ideas, and is evidently quite sure that Beaumont will respond suitably. The letter is thus an early and impressive testimony to their friendship.

Tocqueville had been interested in England for some years – England, the ancient enemy, who had beaten France in war and

---

* 'rouses vain weakness in my heart'

outstripped her in peace; M. Mougin had encouraged him to study French and English history in tandem.[24] He had not yet learned to like the islanders, and his blood boiled with patriotic rage when he came to Lingard's account of Edward III, 'who waged in France a war of devastation, he who wanted to reign there'. He even gloated a little when he read of the barbarian invasions by Scots, Saxons, Danes and Normans – 'successive revolutions besides which ours have been jokes'. But he did not allow such feelings to impede his analysis. He wanted to understand why France had failed where England had succeeded, and had no doubt about the answer, which every page of Lingard confirmed. England was and had been strong because of her liberty; France had been weakened, not exactly by despotism, but by a tangled social and political system which made the growth of liberty desperately difficult.[25]

It would be profitless to follow Tocqueville through every page of his précis. John Lingard was a Catholic priest who astonished Protestant bigots by his honest scholarship; but it would be absurd to pretend that his views and information can be of any weight today. He was neither a Gibbon nor a Macaulay, and as to his style, Tocqueville called him a *pisse-froid*. Furthermore, Tocqueville was writing without the book in front of him: he had apparently sent it back to Paris.[26] This no doubt explains some of the oddities of his summary, but anyway he was writing as a complete novice in his subject. On the whole the Lingard letter, as a discussion of English history, reads like an undergraduate's brilliant but over-long essay.

Regarded as a document of Tocqueville's intellectual development, it is much more impressive. Since the *Voyage en Sicile* he has reached maturity. He has found his themes and his style – that classical French style in which the unanswerable aphorism plays so essential a part. 'La rage des historiens est de vouloir des événements decisifs.' It is not wholly unlike some English authors – in a heavier manner, Samuel Johnson had the trick of it ('Where there is leisure for fiction there is little grief') – but in French writing it is swifter, more luminous, and far more common. The language exacts it of its votaries. It had come to Tocqueville, and was never to leave him: except for his youthful élan and cheerful inaccuracy, the Lingard letter might have been written twenty or thirty years later. Mme Françoise Mélonio writing of this period (not of this document) alludes to Tocqueville's precocity.[27] It is clear what she means, but precocity does not seem to be the right word. Many and many a talent has announced itself at the age of twenty-three. The vigour of manhood is suddenly at the flood, tutelage and self-doubt are shaken off, and a Byron, an Hugo, a Picasso appears. At twenty-four Pitt was Prime Minister; at twenty-five Bonaparte captured Toulon. Tocqueville's time had come (even if he did not shake off all self-doubt); it must be added that it was almost certainly the stimulus of Beaumont which made him take to the air.

The appearance of many of the chief Tocquevillean themes is even more striking, and yet is indistinguishable from the emergence of the style. At the end of a long passage comparing the struggles of king, nobles and commons in France and England, and emphasizing their differences, he points out that they ended in the same way: 'after all, a reasonable equality must be the sole condition natural to Man, since all nations come to it though they depart from such different points and travel by such diverse routes.'[28] Equality! – one of his three perennial preoccupations; and the reader does not have to look far in the Lingard letter for the other two, revolution and liberty.

He cannot yet systematize his insights; indeed, for all his decisive manner, he is putting questions and advancing hypotheses rather than fully thought-out conclusions; but his political concerns and opinions give his approach a certain consistency. On the whole it is remarkable how few are his sidelong glances at the current state of France, but it would have been beyond human strength to eschew them altogether. Nothing remains of the lively debates that must have gone on between Tocqueville and his friends, Tocqueville and his family; but perhaps we may catch some echoes. He was still clinging to the cherished myth that the *noblesse* were and ought to be the true guarantors of French liberty. André Jardin detected the influence of Montesquieu, Boulain-villers and Augustin Thierry* in this doctrine, which had formerly been dear to the *noblesse de robe*, but the facts of life were beginning to refute it. By 1828 it was clear that the great question of the day was whether the returned *émigrés* would succeed in their attempt to

---

* The influence of Montesquieu seems clear in an essay on duelling which AT presented to the *parquet* of Versailles that autumn, in which the practice is linked to the sentiment of honour, 'so precious in our monarchies' (OXC XVI 63).

establish a permanent ascendancy over the French state and French society, and that liberty was no part of their programme. Tocqueville is still unaware that a decisive crisis is approaching, but his intuition seems to be working against his consciousness. He observes of the Plantagenets' loss of Normandy that 'it did not diminish the tyranny of John, for it is the rule with all such dominions, past, present and future, that pretensions increase as power diminishes.' He points out that Magna Carta was at first not in the least what its modern partisans think it, 'the two Houses, ministerial responsibility, voted taxation and a thousand other things …' It had been drawn up simply in the interest of the nobility. But it gave a precise shape to opposition. 'That is all a revolution needs. Magna Carta became the standard thenceforward under which marched a host of men for whom its details were unknown or unimportant.' Henry III was a decent enough king, but so null that he let the country drift into revolution.[29] Can a young man of Tocqueville's lively intelligence, writing to another such, have possibly said these things without having in mind the incursions of Charles X on the chambers, the struggle over the Charter of 1814, and the failure of Louis XVI? Professor Douglas Johnson would think not. He wrote: 'The crowds of young people who applauded Guizot at the Sorbonne, or who applauded Amédée Thierry at Besançon, or who were later to applaud Michelet, were enthusiastic for their liberal opinions as much as for their eloquence and erudition. In nineteenth-century France it was never possible to leave politics behind. Every form of thought was charged with politics. A comment on the ambition of Clovis, on the government of Charlemagne … was taken to be an allusion to the contemporary scene.'[30]

At the very least we can say that history had justified itself as a subject of study. That winter (1828–9) Tocqueville and Beaumont started to read the economist J.B. Say (they do not appear to have got very far); and they were learning English. But in the spring they began to go to François Guizot's celebrated historical lectures at the Sorbonne, and another epoch in Tocqueville's education opened.

Guizot was more than halfway through his course on the history of civilization in France when Tocqueville, who had been laid up with what sounds like a ferocious bout of influenza, but may have been measles, began to attend (Beaumont got there sooner);[31] and even then he did not go to every session. Yet the importance of the experience can hardly be overstated, whether we are considering him as a future writer or as a future politician.

For one thing, Guizot was to him a new type socially and intellectually. 'I am one of those whom the *élan* of 1789 raised up and who will never consent to descend again,' said the veteran in his memoirs, and he might equally well have said it in 1829.[32] Born in Nîmes in 1787, he had been brought up as a Protestant of the straitest sect, and would have had few career opportunities under the *ancien régime*. The Revolution did indeed change all that, but his father was guillotined in April 1794 (the same month as Malesherbes). Guizot was taken to say good-bye to him in prison. The family was stripped of all its property and after some years migrated to Geneva, temporarily annexed to France. Guizot never forgot the Midi, but he could never again bear to live there. In Geneva he received an excellent education, learning English and German among other things. He arrived in Paris in 1806, with a letter of introduction and without a *sou*. He found work as a literary journalist and in an astonishingly short time established himself in the heart of philosophical Paris: even Chateaubriand was, briefly, a friend (politics soon divided them). He was appointed professor of history at the Sorbonne in 1812; in 1814, at the first Restoration, he became Secretary-General of the Ministry of the Interior, thanks to his friend Royer-Collard, leader of those who would soon be called the Doctrinaires – the first liberals. He stuck to the Bourbons during the Hundred Days; afterwards, so great and evident was his ability that he exercised vast political influence during the liberal phase of the Restoration, though he was still too young to be a deputy. All this changed with the coming to power of Villèle: in 1822 Guizot, with several colleagues, was forbidden to lecture any more; he had already been dismissed from the Conseil d'État. He returned to full-time historical research and part-time journalism, but also displayed remarkable skill as a political organizer: he was the mainspring of the association *Aide-toi, le Ciel t'Aidera* ('God helps those who help themselves'), which organized the liberals' first great victory, in the parliamentary election of 1827, when they captured some 180 seats, having previously only held fifty. The result was the fall of Villèle and the formation of the Martignac ministry, which immediately lifted the ban on Guizot's lectures. In short, it was not merely a professor whom Tocqueville and Beaumont went to hear, but a party leader.

Guizot was a speaker and teacher of outstanding talent. As a lecturer, he sacrificed everything for the sake of lucidity. No fascinating but incidental facts, no jokes, no sudden thoughts were allowed to interrupt the course of his limpid exposition. He meant, above all, to be understood and to be remembered. He succeeded almost perfectly, as Tocqueville's surviving notes amply demonstrate. Guizot on the rostrum was irresistible. He spoke distinctly in a sonorous voice, and subdued any restlessness in his audience by the power of his huge sombre eyes. He even dressed up to his role: the high black stock which he always wore made him seem the embodiment of stern Calvinist integrity. No wonder his hearers were transfixed.[33]

At one level his lectures imparted basic information. Like so many in his time Tocqueville had succumbed to the fascination of medieval history, but his ignorance was still immense. Thus we find him writing to Beaumont in the summer of 1829, concerning Guizot's lectures of the previous year, which he had not heard* but was now reading, '[They have] given me some fairly vast insights into the IVth century, which was totally unknown to me.'[34] With fourteen centuries to cover in twenty-four lectures Guizot could only articulate the bare bones of history; he frequently reminded his listeners that he was making huge omissions; but he could not omit everything, and as every experienced lecturer knows, student audiences are always hungry for facts to write down. Hence Tocqueville's careful enumeration of Charlemagne's fifty-three wars ('18 v. the Saxons').[35]

It was also possible to take the lectures as political allegories. Guizot was well aware of this, but as he was a serious *érudit* he did his best to evade the tendency. One of his few references to the nineteenth century was a comparison of Napoleon's successes and failures with those of Charlemagne, which nobody could object to except those who thought it was unfair to Charlemagne. Tocqueville took no interest in cheap political points, though he cannot have failed to notice that Guizot's

---

* Both André Jardin and Larry Siedentop state that Tocqueville began to attend Guizot's lectures (on the history of civilization in Europe) in 1828. They give no authority, I have found absolutely no confirmation of the statement, and the letter which I cite (30 August 1829) seems conclusive that AT first heard Guizot in 1829.

depiction of feudalism and the Middle Ages was quite incompatible with the Ultra myth of a golden age when king, *noblesse* and peasants lived harmoniously together under the pastoral care of a benevolent Church. He carefully copied the lecturer's words:

> The Middle Ages, in short, were the heroic age of France, the age of poetry and romance, the true realm of fancy, when fancy was stronger than we may think possible in the lives of men. On the other hand, gentlemen, the hatred that the Middle Ages have aroused is even easier to explain: the common people were so unhappy during that period of their existence, they emerged so damaged and with so much effort from the condition into which it plunged them, that a deep instinct makes its memory agonizing … The French Revolution, gentlemen, was no more than a defining explosion of hatred against the ideas, the manners and the laws which were bequeathed to us by the Middle Ages.

Yet it was at the end of this very passage that Guizot threw off the aphorism 'A people with no memory of its past is like a mature man who has lost all recollection of his youth.' This thought too was faithfully copied down.[36]

For what most fascinated Tocqueville about Guizot's lectures was their ambition, their profundity, their scope. They were so immensely suggestive – or, as he would have put it, so full of *idées mères*. They were the inspiration which he needed; they showed him his own way forward. They were no mere chronicles, like the work of Thiers and Lingard. 'I am not writing [*sic*] of history properly so-called, but of the development of French civilization.' 'The history of civilization, in my view, has two purposes: it combines the history of society and that of human intelligence, it pursues both the march of events and that of ideas.' History must cease to be a narrow specialism, it must be comprehensive: 'It must trace [Man's] mental developments through events, manners, opinions, laws, intellectual monuments, it must condescend to self-examination, even to measuring the foreign influences to which Man finds himself subjected.'[37] Nowadays these observations do not seem at all startling, but they were highly original in their day. It was through Guizot that Tocqueville realized he must study not events ('*faits*') but their significance.

Guizot's analysis of feudalism made a deep impression. This word (in French *féodalité*) was an eighteenth-century, if not Revolutionary, coinage, which was destined for a long life as a thought-suppressing cliché of Marxism, an unanalytical term of abuse. Guizot was absolutely removed from such usage. He identified the essence of feudalism as a system of land tenure, and carefully described how it worked. From there he moved on to discuss the labour force, the towns, and the rise of royal government; by the time that he had finished he had made a complete and intelligible sketch of a society in all its workings, and the dates which he gave for its duration (roughly from the reign of Hugues Capet to that of Philippe le Bel) seemed almost self-evident; from the beginning of the fourteenth century onwards feudalism (he said) was merely one obsolete element in an altered society. Tocqueville learned from Guizot how important it was to use archival sources, and how to do so, how to reason historically (in terms of social forces, not the divine will)* and how to relate institutions to one another and to society as a whole. Eventually he would see that Guizot's methods could be applied to the present, as well as to the past – that one could be a political scientist or a sociologist as well as a historian. The results would be displayed in *De la démocratie en Amérique*.

But not yet. He had not yet discovered his subject. In October 1829, in a letter in which he poured out his soul on many matters to Beaumont, he lamented his ignorance. He knew more than Beaumont about historical events, no doubt:

> but as to what brought them about, what support men have given to those who have moved them during the last two centuries, the condition to which revolutions had borne the nations by the end of that period, that in which they left them, their classification, their manners, their instincts, their current resources, the division and disposition of those resources, I am ignorant of all that to which, in my opinion, all other studies can serve only as an introduction.

Perhaps they should take up geography.[38]

The Lingard letter shows that another study was as important as ever. On the opening page we learn that one of Tocqueville's motives

---

* The references to Providence in DA I, 'Introduction', are a sad, but not inexplicable, backsliding.

for travelling to the Cotentin in 1828 was to pursue Mademoiselle X (as he discreetly calls her – her pseudonymity is never breached), a young lady of Valognes; he analyses his feelings for her in the best French psychological style:

Mlle X. gains enormously from being seen regularly and I never felt more like falling in love with her than now. But let us understand each other on this point. You will say that there can be no question of love, which is not a child of time but comes to one at a stroke, full-blown, but only of a real friendship. M., for her Christian name also begins with M., has decidedly the most frank and open character, the freest from petty passions that I have ever seen in a woman. She is so spontaneously vivacious and she has such a good heart that you get attached in spite of yourself. She is a complete original and in her way unique. Add that she is very pretty, which for a long time I was not sure of, but I am now certain about it since my brother [Hippolyte] has said she is. This last remark will make you laugh, but investigate yourself, my dear philosopher, and see if by chance it may not be confirmed at the bottom of the human heart ... I am not in love ... but I am at the point of wanting to be able to tell her that I love another and to ask her to keep a corner for me in her affections to which, in truth, I begin seriously to aspire.[39]

Meanwhile he is consoling himself with another woman of Valognes: 'I went to bed, you know where, not without difficulty but not with any adventure worth the trouble of telling.'[40]

It was 1828, the year of the lemon-juice letters to Rosalie Malye, and Kergorlay was still faithfully sending reports about her from Metz (the last surviving is dated 1 November). But however hard he found it to let go, it must have become obvious to Tocqueville that the affair had no future, and it is not surprising that such a highly sexed young man sought pleasure elsewhere. He continued to do so for the next two years: a letter of May 1830 shows that he and Beaumont were involving themselves with two sisters, Amélie and Sidonie d'Aumont, who lodged in the château of Versailles.[41] We hear no more of Mlle X. There remains the question of the other young woman whose name began with M.

The likeliest guess is that she was Mary Mottley. The story goes that she met Tocqueville because she was his neighbour in the rue d'Anjou (when writing about her from America he archly refers to her as 'la voisine').[42]

Since the disappearance of the Court, Versailles had been a dull little town, and Tocqueville, at least when he was alone there, took small advantage of it; he writes to Beaumont:

> I die of boredom here: the evenings seem endless, I drift about the woods of the neighbourhood until after night has fallen. Then I come home and start taking off my frock-coat so as to change my clothes and go into society. And then when I am in my shirt-sleeves I can't resist the opportunity to go to bed. Such is my life. For the rest, I work like the devil at the *parquet*.[43]

Things were livelier when Beaumont was at home, and Paris was always close at hand; Tocqueville was not always a hermit; but his world was not Miss Mottley's.

She was an Englishwoman. Sheila Le Sueur has established that she was born on 2 March 1801 or thereabouts, at Gosport. The Mottleys were an emphatically naval family: her father was the bursar of the seamen's hospital at Gosport, one of her uncles was an admiral, and her three brothers were all officers in the Royal Navy. She had four sisters.[44] Readers of *Mansfield Park* will understand what happened. At the age of four Mary was handed over to her father's rich sister for her upbringing, like Fanny Price in the novel: one less mouth for her parents to feed. But this aunt was no baronet's lady. She was Elizabeth Belam, the widow of a man who made and sold 'pills and remedies' and had, apparently, prospered. Born in 1769, she was comparatively young when she adopted Mary. She seems to have made an excellent mother-substitute: she and Mary might occasionally quarrel, but they were devoted to each other.

Why and when did they move to France? They cannot have done so before the fall of Napoleon, which the British celebrated by pouring over the Channel in vast numbers to a Continent which they had not seen for a decade or more. Most went as tourists, but more and more settled, for all sorts of reasons: Beau Brummell fled to Boulogne-sur-Mer to escape his creditors. It is unlikely that Mrs Belam had serious money problems; still, she may have had reason to economize, and living in France was notoriously cheaper than living in England.

Versailles was notoriously cheaper than Paris. As a result houses left empty by the departure of courtiers and government officials began to fill with English and Irish people of modest means, who were sneered at as less than genteel by their snobbish compatriots, while the French welcomed all agreeable company. The poet Tom Moore used the phrase 'Versailles English' as shorthand for second-rate, though he himself was another refugee from creditors. At any rate, by 1828 Mrs Belam and her niece were established at Versailles, and Mary had learned to speak fluent French.[45]

She was pretty, or Tocqueville would probably never have noticed her. Rédier has ungallantly preserved a tradition that she had unattractively long yellow teeth but the likeness taken of her in 1831 by Candide Blaize does not support it. No doubt the artist felt obliged to flatter his sitter where necessary, but the face as he drew it is far too individual to be disbelieved: for one thing, it is much more vividly precise than the only other likenesses.[46] In it Miss Mottley is dressed to kill, her thick and lustrous dark curls crowned fashionably with a tortoiseshell comb, her face framed by pearl ear-rings, her dress a frothy confection of lace and silk. She has a tiny waist (this, perhaps, is painter's licence). Her look is patient, modest, even a little anxious, as if she does not like sitting and will be glad when the ordeal is over; but her large eyes are alert, her mouth is firm: this is a woman of courage and intelligence. The overall impression is of a woman not to be taken lightly and, surprisingly, a slightly sad one.

Tocqueville needed women for much more than sex; or perhaps it would be more accurate to say that for him sex could comprehend much more than eager physical pleasure. He wanted mothering. Perpetually anxious about his talents, his health, his worldly prospects, he needed tenderness and reassurance. He also needed forgiveness and patience: he was well aware of his faults. He needed companionship. Perhaps his effusive expressions of devotion to Kergorlay and Beaumont were in part attempts to get something from men that women had not yet offered him; certainly no woman would permanently succeed with him who could not enter into his ambitions, his intellectual life, his political preoccupations. To a lesser, but still great extent, he needed someone who needed him: someone he could cherish and protect. In Mary Mottley he found it all.

She was not perfect, even for him. She was something of a hypo-chondriac, perhaps because of her background in quack medicine. She had little humour and no wit, although she enjoyed good conversation. She was tenacious in her grudges. But for the most part these traits were inconsequential.

We do not know what first drew her to Tocqueville; indeed we know nothing at all about their courtship. It is only certain that by the summer of 1830 their affair was solidly established, which makes it all the more curious that Tocqueville should at that time (as he wrote to Beaumont) have prowled after Sidonie d'Aumont through the Versailles fair, making 'carp's eyes' and shooting 'Assassin glances' at her and doing his best to win an assignation. Perhaps he reflected that Marie, as he called her (and as I will from this point), having moved to Saint-Cloud, could not easily detect his goings-on – which included a brief fling with an unnamed woman at Caen. He was always an unre-strained, or shall we say a selfish, lover, which was to cause Marie much unhappiness; but that did not diminish his permanent commit-ment to his *maîtresse en titre*.[47]

None of his friends seems to have had the least doubt as to what was going on, but there are various mysteries. While Tocqueville was in America (1831–2) he sent his letters to Marie under cover to his friend Ernest de Chabrol; the explanation is presumably that Mrs Belam had still to be kept in the dark. As a respectable Englishwoman she could only approve of Tocqueville if he offered honourable marriage, and whatever he and Marie hoped for he was not yet in a position to do anything of the kind. He was still entirely reliant on his father for money, and Marie was conspicuously unsuitable by the standards of the comte and comtesse, even if they knew of her existence (which they probably did – Comte Hervé's Versailles connections were excellent). She was English, Protestant and middle-class: Rédier goes so far as to say that if Alexis married her he would violently overturn the preju-dices of his race (meaning the whole extended family of the French *noblesse*).[48] The post-revolutionary nobility felt that it was hanging on to its identity with its fingernails. The Second Estate was no longer recognized in law; the reduced monarch in the Tuileries was never in a position to restore the hierarchies of Versailles; wealth and social position – even noble titles – were now also enjoyed by bankers and

Bonapartists; the old *noblesse* could only maintain itself by insisting on the importance of birth. Unless she was very rich (like Édouard de Tocqueville's wife) a bride had to be *née*, and Marie Mottley was neither. It was probably years before Alexis dared to mention the possibility of this marriage to his parents. It is not even certain that at this stage he was sleeping with Marie. She may have held back; besides, Versailles was the epitome of those small French towns which were, as Richard Cobb repeatedly insists, close, cruelly observant, and very hierarchical neighbourhoods.[49] As a foreigner, Mrs Belam was presumably not fully integrated into the network of gossip and spying, but it would have been difficult to hide a sexual liaison from her (we may remember Tocqueville's poor servant, Madeleine). Then there was the possibility of pregnancy: the consequences of that would be ruinous to them all.

If Tocqueville and Marie did indeed at first refrain from coupling, it helps us to understand why he continued to pursue other women. But whatever the facts, he loved Marie, and was firmly loyal (if not constant) to her; and there was something else. He was bored, almost disgusted, by the sort of young woman whom men of his breeding were expected to marry. A noble young lady, brought up in the utmost seclusion and educated, if that was the word, only by nuns, was carefully drilled in all the insipidities of correct behaviour and then launched into 'the world', where her reputation as a *jeune fille bien élevée* was promoted by her family; sometimes she was encouraged to be ostentatiously pious. After marriage she showed her true colours, either by becoming implacably frivolous, living only for pleasure, or implacably religious and domesticated. In neither incarnation was she the sort of wife that Tocqueville desired. Kergorlay too was emphatic on the point: on a visit to Germany in 1837 he was disgusted at the hypocritical prudery of German ladies who when suffering from sore throats said that they had 'pains in their necks', and, if pregnant, that they were 'expecting'. He put it down to Protestantism, and asked Tocqueville if English-women and Americans were not just as bad? Tocqueville, though by now married to Marie, gave modified assent to this suggestion. There was much pretence of virtue in England, he said, so that it was actually easier to get into an Englishwoman's bedroom to sleep with her than for any other purpose (how did he know?), but at the same time there was more genuine virtue and self-respect among women in London than in Paris.[50] Since he held such views it is not surprising that he married an Englishwoman, or that he opposed arranged marriages, or that the list of his women friends – Mme Swetchine, Mme Ancelot, Mrs Grote, Mrs Child, Mme Mohl, for instance – does not contain the name of a single Frenchwoman of his own age, outside his family, except those whom his male friends married. During the 1848 revolution he met George Sand at a party and to his surprise got on very well with her, but Mme Sand was not in the least typical of her countrywomen.[51] He delighted in the company of women of an older generation – Mme Récamier, Mme de Kergorlay, Mme de Dino – but they had no successors. He never lapsed into misogyny, unlike Kergorlay, but it can hardly be denied that his attitude to Frenchwomen would tend to isolate him in his own country; and from the point of view of his parents, it made him a most intractable son.

His love of Marie was the strongest and deepest emotion of his life. Their relationship grew and changed over time, but perhaps this is as good a point as any to quote a letter which he wrote to her after some years of marriage: it goes to the heart of the matter in every sense.

Apparently Marie had been doubting her success as a wife.

... Must I reproach you? What for? For having given me the only real happiness I have felt in life, and a great zest for existence, and for having endured without complaint my violent and despotic character, for subduing me by your sweetness and tenderness? To my knowledge these are the only complaints I have to make. You have done yet more for me, *mon amie chérie,* and I have kept that service for mention in the final place. You have diverted me from a course in which perhaps without you I would have been lost. You have shown me for the first time all the nobility, generosity and, let me add, the virtue of true love. I swear that I believe my love for you has made me a better man. I love the good more because I love you than for any other reason. When I think of you I feel my soul ascend; I want to make you proud of me and to prove every day to you that you did not make a mistake when you chose me. Lastly, I never feel more inclined to think about God, more convinced of the reality of the other life, than when I think of you ... You are *without exception* the only person in the world who knows the bottom of my soul in these matters; you alone see my instincts, my hopes, my doubts. If ever I become a Christian, I will owe it, I think, to you … I love you as a sixteen-year-old never could, but in thinking of you I feel all the generous passions, all the noble instincts, the complete surrender of oneself, that as a rule lovers feel only at that age …[52]

It was a betrothal, it would one day be a match; and meanwhile it was already a spur to ambition.

It may be said in conclusion to this chapter that by 1830 Tocqueville had rejected his family traditions in religion, history and love.

There remained politics.

CHAPTER SIX

JULY
1829–1830

Once, the Italian went on, once only in his life, and that
in his early manhood, had his grandfather known what
it was to feel profound joy. That was at the time of the
Paris July Revolution. He had gone about proclaiming to
all and sundry that some day men would place those three
days alongside the six days of creation, and reverence
them alike. Hans Castorp felt utterly dumbfounded
– involuntarily he slapped the table with his hand.

THOMAS MANN, *THE MAGIC MOUNTAIN*,

TR. H. T. LOWE-PORTER

ON 2 MAY 1829 there was a public disturbance at Saint-Germain-en-Laye. Some thirty young workingmen who had been drinking outside the town in one of the *cabarets* which were a well-known feature of the district, on returning to Saint-Germain were challenged when they reached the gate: '*Qui vive?*' They were in a jolly mood: it was a spring evening, and a Monday (perhaps they were prolonging Sunday); two or three of them were even in fancy dress. At any rate, a voice called out in reply, '*Troupe de Napoléon! Vive l'Empéreur!*' They entered Saint-Germain, refreshed themselves further at another *cabaret*, and eventually arrived at the place de l'Église. There one of them, who was carrying a long branch of birch, became the centre of the group, which danced round him crying '*Vive l'Empéreur, à bas Charles X, vive la République,*' and, some of them, '*Le pain à 24 sous les huit livres!*'* They found their way to yet another *cabaret* and drank some more, and then began to feel the need for cockades. So they tied a red and blue handkerchief and a white one to the branch of birch, and lo! – a tricolour. By 10 p.m. they were ready to go home, and the streets were quiet again. But the authorities could not overlook such a shocking business. Twenty arrests were made, and Tocqueville, with a colleague, was sent from Versailles to investigate the incident. His report was as temperate as possible: he said everything he could to minimize the affair, though he had to report that one of the men arrested had said that 'he didn't love Charles X more than he did Napoleon and if he supported the latter he was fully entitled to shout *Vive l'Empéreur* now that there was freedom of the press.' But the tribunal was severe: eventually seventeen of the twenty were found guilty and sent to prison for terms ranging from five days to six months.[1]

In this nutshell may be seen the causes of the July Revolution: the failure of the Bourbon Restoration to win any solid support among the labouring people of Paris and its immediate hinterland; popular nostalgia for the age of the tricolour, whether republican or (which they preferred) imperial; the dangerous threat of hard times – a crisis had begun in 1827 which was not going to abate until 1832, and meanwhile the price of bread was twenty-one sous for a four-pound loaf;[2] the stupid rigidity of an insecure regime.

Apparently Tocqueville was not yet much interested in questions of penal policy; it may or may not have struck him that prison was an absurd and cruel punishment for an evening's revel. But he was certainly much concerned about a quite different display of the Ultras' heavy-handedness that followed hard upon: the dismissal of the Martignac ministry and its replacement by that of Polignac on 8 August. Next day Tocqueville wrote to his brother Édouard, who was honeymooning in Italy:

> It seems that they want to begin by working with the present Chamber [i.e. of Deputies]; but it is most unlikely that they will find common ground; and if they summon another it will make no difference while

* 'Bread at twenty-four pence for eight pounds!'

the electoral law remains the same. So there they are, committed to a system of *coups d'état*, of governing by proclamation, that is to say; the issue is drawn between royal power and popular power, a fight engaged at close quarters, a gamble in which, in my opinion, the people risk only their present, whereas royal authority risks both its present and its future. If this ministry collapses, royalty will lose a great deal in its fall, for the ministry is its own creation and the victors will want guarantees that will reduce still further a power already too much enfeebled. God grant that the House of Bourbon may never have to repent what it has just done![3]

This prediction, which within twelve months would be vindicated in every detail, would be even more impressive evidence than it is of Tocqueville's ripening powers if almost everybody else had not been saying the same. In his memoirs Guizot, discussing the new cabinet, remarks with a shrug of his shoulders, 'What was it proposing? What would it do? Nobody knew, M. de Polignac and the King himself as little as the public. But Charles X had raised the flag of counter-revolution over the Tuileries.'[4] 'Here comes the Court again,' said the *Journal des débats*, 'with its ancient grudges, the emigration with its prejudices, the priesthood with its hatred of liberty, all throwing themselves between France and her king.' 'Coblenz, Waterloo, 1815 – these are the three principles of the ministry.'[5] These sentiments got Louis-François Bertin, the editor, a six-month jail sentence. Chateaubriand, who had been greatly enjoying himself as ambassador to Rome (the Vatican had already complained) foresaw disaster and resigned his post. After a farewell interview with Polignac he concluded that the new minister's imperturbable confidence 'made him a mute conspicuously suited to strangle an empire'.[6] Many nervous months lay ahead, while France waited for the King to drop the other shoe.

Charles briefly thought of making Comte Hervé minister for the navy. Nothing came of this, but as a precaution Alexis made his father promise to lie low politically until the outlook was clearer.[7] Excellent counsel, though it is doubtful if the comte, with all his experience, needed it; but it is agreeable to see father and son taking heed for each other. They would do so again the following year.

Meanwhile a young man had his career to think of. Tocqueville enjoyed his work and his friends of the *parquet*, but he had now been a *juge-auditeur* for more than two years; he had worked hard, mastered his job, and won golden opinions. Quite reasonably he began to feel strongly that he was entitled to promotion and a salary. His father agreed (perhaps hoping to be spared any more tailors' bills). Besides, Beaumont was clearly going to be promoted immediately – who better than Alexis to succeed him as *substitut* at Versailles? Comte Hervé went to work. Great-uncle Damas put in a word. There were two moderate men left in the ministry and fortunately one of them, M. Courvoisier, was the Garde des Sceaux. Unfortunately the other, the comte de Chabrol, the minister of finance, also had a hopeful great-nephew, Ernest. The comte de Tocqueville called on M. Courvoisier; they exchanged political views, and Comte Hervé made his request. But the minister thought it more important to support his colleague than yet again to acknowledge the heirs of Malesherbes; young Chabrol got the job.[8]

The news reached Alexis in the autumn while he was on a walking tour of Switzerland with Kergorlay. It did not please him. He poured out his thoughts to Beaumont in what turned into a kind of intellectual love-letter, for Tocqueville was much more upset by the thought that his friend would have to leave the rue d'Anjou (apparently the possibility had not previously crossed his mind) than by the fact that his own career was stalled. 'Allow me *not* to congratulate you, *mon bon ami*, on what has just happened ... We are now bound intimates, bound for life, I think ... you have done things for me which can't be forgotten: from the first you treated me in a way that I couldn't forget even if I wanted to; it was you who got my career going: it won't be your fault if I don't get on. So we will always be one. But our true friendship, my dear Beaumont, that intimacy of every hour and minute, that mutual confidence without any limit whatever, everything which, in short, makes up the charm of our life together – all that is finished.' Beaumont was now fairly launched on the world; Tocqueville, robbed of both his friend and his promotion, would have to make the best of lodgings where he was always bored without Beaumont; would have to go for walks and to work alone; would have no-one with whom even to share his grumbles. It was awful. But they must fight against fate, and see as much of each other as possible, dine once a week in Paris and go on reading Guizot together. Tocqueville had written to young Chabrol, whom he had known for years (he too was the son of a prefect, the prefect of Paris, no less) to ask if he would like to take Beaumont's place in the rue d'Anjou; Chabrol was a good enough fellow, and might help with work and study.[9]

As this piece of magnanimity shows, Tocqueville's youthful warmth of heart soon enabled him to overcome his panic at losing Beaumont, and as it turned out they saw almost as much of each other as ever, Chabrol making an agreeable third to their association: in fact he soon became another intimate friend. But the actual check to Tocqueville's career could not so easily be overlooked or overcome. Three weeks after his letter to Beaumont from Switzerland he wrote to him again, from Gray (Haute-Saône), where he was staying with Hippolyte and Émilie. His news was bad. We know almost nothing of his Swiss tour, but in spite of assurances to his mother ('We wanted to climb the high valleys, but there was too much snow'[10]), it is probable that he overdid things. At any rate, after parting from Kergorlay he arrived at Gray on 21 October and collapsed with 'une indigestion' and a fever which required that he be bled ('say nothing of my fever if you see my family'). By the 25th he was better, although his stomach was still troublesome, and he was afraid of catching a *grippe* because the wind blew under his bedroom door and the chimney smoked. (This seems to contradict the statement in a letter to his mother that apart from one in Émilie's bedroom the only fire in the house was in the kitchen, where he had taken refuge, writing, reading such books as he could find among Hippolyte's boots and bridles, and discussing morality with the cook – also religion, politics and cookery.)[11]

> My health seems to get no better with the years, and physical exertion seems to take more out of me than it used to. I fear that this ill dispos-ition, made worse by my way of life, may turn me into an invalid. And besides – it's all so difficult to understand – I'm afraid of being afraid. That is, it seems that my moral being, which is *not* animal, Beaumont, whatever they say, gets too preoccupied by my physical condition, and enormously exaggerates its infirmity. I am appalled by how much my imagination dwells on my stomach aches, and how it takes away all taste for study, all hope for the future, all ambition, in other words life itself, as I can tell you, *mon cher ami*, because somehow the veil between us is rent and we see each other face to face. What I fear more

than anything else is this sort of moral enfeeblement which so easily diminishes the only human quality that I really respect, energy.[12]

This is the first letter in which Tocqueville's lifelong ill-health comes clearly into view, and it is necessary to ask what was wrong with him. In prescientific terms it might be said that he inherited his mother's poor constitution, but that explains nothing. The 'gastritis' which afflicted him from his boyhood onwards was probably what would nowadays be termed functional dyspepsia; it could prostrate him with agonizing stomach pains for days, and remissions were to become rarer and rarer. He himself blamed his malady on irregular hours and unsuitable food; but it is also the case that stress brings on dyspepsia and dyspepsia brings on stress. The correlation between the state of his mind and that of his body is always striking. He was by nature mercurial (in medical terms, cyclothymic), a creature of violent mood swings: perhaps they were the origin of his dyspepsia. Full of eager vitality, he seems to have taken early to living on his nerves – to driving himself forward by sheer will. None of these traits helped his quest for physical and psychological stability. He asked too much of himself: as he wrote to Eugène Stoffels in 1839, 'too much activity wears me out, and rest kills me.'[13] However, it seems certain that his trouble was basically physical rather than psychological, and it grew worse as he left youth behind. As George Pierson has remarked, his life became one long unceasing silent struggle against illness. It is not surprising that he was occasionally, as in 1829, alarmed and depressed. But as Pierson also says, 'his relentless, unquenchable spirit only spurred him to try to forget his bodily sufferings, too, in feverish activity.'[14]

There was more to life than illness. He had had a letter from Beaumont (now missing) in which his friend showed that his feelings had been hurt by some of the things said in Tocqueville's own letter of 4 October; Tocqueville now poured out reassurance, and began to discuss plans for the future. These took a significant new turn. Tocqueville was now perforce a convert to the doctrine of *la carrière ouverte aux talents* (nowadays we would call it equal access), and he was no longer afraid of competition: he knew that he was a better speaker than Chabrol. But he was not so eloquent as Beaumont. He could argue well when he had had time to arrange his ideas, but he was not good at improvising and at best he was a chilly orator. 'I may perhaps be able to move my hearers on political topics, because political passions move me so powerfully that I feel a different man, literally, when I experience them; but in the ordinary course of life it is not at all the same thing, I swear.' Besides, though he did not say so to Beaumont, he recognized that his career had been checked, and there was no knowing when it would start moving again. In the circumstances it is not surprising that he raised the possibility of collaborating with Beaumont on some work of history, even though he could not specify a subject.

Meanwhile it was back to life and work at Versailles, and back to Guizot's lectures. It seems that Tocqueville's attitude to these had slightly changed: he now went less for the sake of his general historical and political education than for training as a scholar; at any rate he was much more assiduous in his attendance. Guizot's own position had altered. He was now old enough (forty) to enter the Chamber of Deputies, and in January 1830 came in through a by-election in the Calvados. When he arrived at the Sorbonne to give his next lecture his audience, including Tocqueville, rose to its feet as one man and cheered. Guizot calmed the demonstration – politics, he said, had no place in an academic lecture-hall – but the incident, like the by-election itself, showed the way that events were tending.[15]

There was nothing to make the Revolution of 1830 inevitable – nothing, that is, except the blind folly of the King and his cherished minister. Both had succumbed to the unreal romanticism which was to be such a feature of post-1830 legitimism.[16] Polignac had spent ten years in a Napoleonic prison, which had fatally weakened his never strong sense of French realities. Half a decade as French ambassador in London had not improved matters: as Guizot was to say, he lived in England without understanding it, any more than he did France. 'He believed that the Charter could be reconciled with the political preponderance of the ancient nobility and with the definitive supremacy of the ancient monarchy.'[17] These were his principles, but he had no programme for realizing them: he was inert. His master, who was just as much of a noodle, cherished him because he was perhaps even more reactionary than himself. Charles was King, and owed a duty to all France, but he behaved as if he were only a party leader. He professed loyalty to the Charter, but like Polignac interpreted it as re-establishing the monarchy of Louis XV. He was convinced that he, his supporters and their power were mortally threatened by the rising strength of the Liberals. Had he been merely a conservative he could not have made this mistake, for Guizot, Casimir Périer, Royer-Collard and the rest were themselves profoundly conservative, as the history of the July Monarchy was to demonstrate. A statesmanlike king would have let them form a government, confident that they would do little harm and would, after a few years, again lose support to the Ultras, as they had in 1824. But Charles X was not a statesman. He could not accept the nineteenth century. The question before the country in early 1830 was how far he would go in trying to enforce his unworkable vision.

Spring came on. Édouard and Alexandrine were still in Italy, and at their request Alexis undertook to keep them informed about politics. The result was a series of five letters, written between March and May, which demonstrate the increasing sharpness of Tocqueville's political insight.

He states the plain truth of the problem in his first letter, of 18 March: 'I confess that I can't foresee what is going to happen. The King and the ministry are confronted by a united and violent majority in the Chamber of Deputies, and the Chamber of Peers seems disinclined to get involved in the quarrel.' As for the Peers, Chateaubriand had opened the debate on their address to the Crown with a speech savagely attacking the ministers. Some of the points he made were good, but on the whole he exhibited such overweening conceit, such insupportable vanity, that no-one was satisfied. 'Not a single voice was raised to propose that the speech be printed, which greatly mortified the noble peer.' Things were even worse in the Chamber of Deputies. After postponing its meeting as long as possible the King greeted it on 2 March with what Tocqueville called a 'haughty' speech in the course of which his hat fell off and was picked up by the duc d'Orléans, who was standing next to him. The onlookers knew an omen when they saw it, but possibly the King's actual words were of more significance: 'Were guilty manoeuvrings to raise obstacles in the path of my government that I do not wish to predict, I would summon the strength to overcome them from my resolve to maintain public peace, from the well-judged support of the French people, and from the love which they have always shown to their king.' Coming from the brother of Louis

XVI this remark was preposterous, though it is possible that Charles had in mind the warm welcome which his subjects had given him at his accession and during a recent tour of the provinces. Whatever he meant, his threat to use force against parliament if necessary deeply angered the deputies; they promptly elected Royer-Collard president of their Chamber, and on 18 March presented an address to the Crown, voted by 221 to 181, which politely but firmly reasserted the principles of parliamentary government and affirmed the liberal interpretation of the Charter:

> [The Charter] requires a permanent acquiescence of your govern-
> ment in the wishes of the people as the indispensable condition for
> the regular conduct of public affairs. Sire, our loyalty, our devotion,
> compel us to point out to you that this acquiescence does not exist. An
> unwarranted mistrust of the feelings and opinions of France is now
> the fundamental attitude of your administration; this distresses your
> people because it insults them; it worries them because it is a threat
> to their liberties.

This address in turn angered Charles X; the day after he received it parliament was prorogued; before long a general election would be called.[18]

Tocqueville wrote again a week later, with further details of what was happening. Many of the debates were closed to the public, but he had excellent contacts, so he could report that Polignac had been 'pitiful' in the debate; the new royalist deputy, Pierre-Antoine Berryer, admirable. Considering what he called the violent language of the address, Tocqueville thought it immensely significant that it had been passed, even if only by forty votes. People were saying that:

> the nation, which was calm, has been roused by the coming of the new
> ministry, that a spirit of defiance against the nation rules the cabinet,
> and that the King must choose between the nation and those who
> slander it ... The King received the address with the greatest *hauteur*.
> He said that he had hoped for the support of the two Chambers, but
> that the Chamber of Deputies had refused him, and so tomorrow he
> would make his wishes known through his ministers. All that smacks
> of Louis XIV, as you can see, but it may be that the Frenchmen of
> Louis XIV's day died with him.[19]

Tocqueville blamed the gathering storm partly on the press, which had thrown off all restraint, Ultra papers even more than Liberal ones. 'Every day sprouts a newspaper article or a pamphlet urging the King to abolish the Charter and govern by decree ... if the government lends itself to such proposals I really don't know what will happen. All in all, the moment is critical.'[20] The King was playing double or quits; he hoped that by taking such a risky course he would force his quarrelling supporters to unite behind him, and the ministers boldly asserted that they would win an election. Tocqueville did not think so, though he expected the royalists, united, to do better than they had in 1827; but 'I can't believe that from a nation so profoundly irritated against the ministry there can ever come a majority of deputies favourable to it.'[21]

In pursuit of a quarrel that had been simmering for some years between France and the Dey of Algiers a vast military expedition was preparing, commanded by Marshal de Bourmont. Ministers hoped that its success would help them in the election, and indeed everyone was rallying to their support in the matter. But Tocqueville was more interested in Hippolyte's desperate attempts to get taken on to Bourmont's staff (he had left it too late: even the Dauphine could not help him) and in the fact that Kergorlay was going with the advance guard: 'We are all anxious for him, because everyone says that the landing will be difficult.'[22]

Kergorlay was setting out on the great adventure of his life, in ever-rising spirits, reeling off letters to Tocqueville describing it all with what to the modern eye seems breathtaking disregard of military security and an equally blithe unsuspicion of what the involvement in Algeria was going to mean for the two countries. Going on campaign, he felt, was bringing him to life again; it was even making him more confident about women.[23] Tocqueville's replies are lost, but as yet he does not seem to be very interested in Algeria; in his letters to Édouard and Alexandrine his preoccupations are profoundly political, and not just because that is what Édouard wants. Apart from small items of family news (the comte and comtesse have moved to the rue de Verneuil, Bébé is well and exercising regularly in the Tuileries gardens) he concentrates exclusively on the crisis. His remarks are always lucid and intelligent, and cannot really be described as inconsistent; but they seem to embody a certain tension. Much of what he says seems to reflect his father's attitude (which was possibly also Édouard's) but he seems to know that it is untenable: he is struggling, as yet without success, to find a position of his own. He does not yet identify himself with the Liberals.

Parliament being prorogued until 1 September everybody at first supposed that they had a breathing-space: calm reigned, and the Bourse rose remarkably. On 24 March Tocqueville did not think that anything would happen before Édouard's return to France.[24] Twelve days later he thanks his brother, with apparent sincerity, for a long letter on the Neapolitan constitution: how could he and Édouard (he asks) have spent so long in Italy in 1827 without studying this important subject? The French ministry is moving steadily to the Right: Chabrol and Courvoisier are thought to be on the point of resignation. 'The King talks only of force, the ministers of firmness, wise royalists are worried about the future, the madmen, much the greatest number, are *aux anges*. Among themselves they talk of nothing but *coups d'état* and changing the electoral law by edict ... In the midst of all this the French people are perfectly calm.' The courts are coming down heavily on journalists of both parties, which pleases neither side, and in the process are establishing the right of resistance to all extra-constitutional undertakings. 'In my opinion the judges are only doing their duty.' (In all these letters Tocqueville shows himself proud of his profession.) Tocqueville is anxious about the future of the ministry because of the mediocrity of its members ('there is only one opinion as to its leader'), because of the number and zeal of its enemies and the lukewarmness of most of its friends, and because of the over-confidence of its most ardent supporters: 'It's like a perpetual Coblenz.' The most conspicuous royalists are only a handful, so they spend all their time quarrelling with everyone else in a way that would be funny were it not so deplorable. They seem to think that they have nothing to do but dispute over the spoils of their impending triumph. The Villèlist paper and the Polignac paper attack each other every morning, for which they are much mocked by the Liberals. Six prefects have been dismissed for their constitutionalism, and replaced, by two men notorious for their part in the electoral frauds of 1827, and by four fools, among them the *sous-préfet* of Cherbourg. God knows

how it will all end, but at the moment everything looks both lamentable and frightening.[25]

Three weeks later he takes advantage of a tedious half-hour in
court to scribble another letter: he now thinks that there may not, after
all, be an election, since it would be imprudent to dissolve the present
Chamber, even though it is so refractory, while the royalists continue
so divided and incapable: 'For a party in such a state to carry the day
would be something new and astonishing.'[26] But on 6 May his tone is
even gloomier. He finds from Édouard's last letter that they take the
same view of the situation: they see the evil but not the remedy. At
least Alexis is now quite clear about the nature of the evil.

We are in fact caught in a vicious circle. If it sticks to legality I don't
see how the ministry can survive … Its chief is over-confident and
exceedingly mediocre, inspiring confidence in no-one. The royalists
are uncertain, divided, without enthusiasm and, worse still, unafraid
of the future because they think that anger is aimed only at the House
of Bourbon and not at royalty itself and that a revolution would be
trouble-free [by a revolution, here, Tocqueville probably only means
a change to a Liberal ministry]. So if the ministry follows the rules
laid down by the Charter, it is most unlikely that it can survive. If
the King abandons it there will be a reaction and royal power will be
much reduced.

However, that would still be the safest course, for to nullify the
Charter would infallibly drive the King from his throne. Such, at
least, is my conviction. For example, *mon cher ami*, let us consider
cold-bloodedly what a labyrinth he would find himself in if he put
aside the law. What would support him? Certainly not public opinion;
almost nobody would approve the measure, I might even say that
it would unite the nation against anyone who tried it. The courts
perhaps? On the day that the King sets out to rule by decrees the
courts would refuse to apply them; I know them and can answer for
it.

So it would be necessary to turn to the army, to have soldiers
incessantly in arms. 'But are we sure that they would like this rôle for
very long? that, finally, is the determining consideration: a King of
seventy-two, so easy-going and so very kind in character, Charles X,
is not the man to accept in cold blood such consequences, or to follow
resolutely such a plan.'

Tocqueville seems to have the XVIII Brumaire in mind, and understands that Charles is no Bonaparte. Nor did he have anyone at his disposal bold or cunning enough to act successfully as his minister in the affair – no Talleyrand, no Siéyès.* So what would result from a coup?

> Perhaps the fall of the ruling house and, quite certainly, an extreme enfeeblement of the royal authority, which would have been uselessly compromised. Nobody in France wants to be ruled by decree, that is the first point to grasp. It is in nobody's interest. The judiciary would lose its importance, the peers their rank, most men of talent their hopes, the lower classes their rights, most officers their chance of promotion. What can be done against such massed determination?[27]

As an explanation of the Revolution of 1830 these remarks are excellent, as far as they go, but they do not go quite all the way. No more than anybody else did Tocqueville foresee the part that would be played by the people of Paris, which gave the revolution its distinctive, indeed heroic character. He was concerned almost solely with the grievances and anxieties of the notables – the Liberals, bankers, officials, journalists and so on whom the King was almost systematically alienating. It is harder to explain another omission. Some years later, writing to an Englishman, Lord Radnor, he said flatly that the religious hatreds stirred up under the Restoration were the principal cause of the Bourbons' fall. 'Left to themselves, the princes of the senior line would have had difficulty in surviving; united with the clergy and exposed to the burning enmities which the political power of the priests provoked, they were bound to succumb.'[28] Perhaps he exaggerated after the event, but the unpopularity of the almost mythical Congregation, the Jesuits, the Catholic missions and royalist bishops was no illusion, as all readers of *Le Rouge et le Noir* are aware. Tocqueville in 1830 may have thought that the religious issue was not strictly relevant to his theme, although without it the obstinate folly of Charles X cannot be entirely explained; or he may have been sparing the feelings of his pious relatives.

Events took their course: Chabrol and Courvoisier resigned, as

---

* In 1830 Talleyrand was on the other side, financing Thiers's paper, *Le National*.

expected, when Polignac started talking about declaring a state of emergency under Article 14 of the Charter; elections were called for 27 June and (under the two-tier system then current, which gave rich landholders two votes each) 3 July; Tocqueville filled in his time by going every Saturday to hear Guizot.

It was by now impossible, even for the lecturer, to ignore the political subtext of his lectures. For instance, on 1 May his subject was the rise of the French monarchy. In the reign of St Louis, he said (ignoring Ultra nostalgia and myth-making) the King was not absolute; he did not pretend to incarnate either the state (no doubt everyone at this point remembered Louis XIV's most famous remark) or the will of God. The change came in the reign of Philippe le Bel. 'I am aware, gentlemen, that many people still insist on seeing nothing in human affairs but the results of pre-existing necessity, which sweeps men along unknowingly to an end of which they are ignorant. But in my opinion, if things act upon men, men have more often greatly influenced things.' So it was with Philippe, 'a despot in the fullest sense of the word'. It was he who began the perversion of the French monarchy; but even in his own time, there was resistance. Towards the end of his reign the *noblesse* began to form associations which success-fully opposed his aggrandizement. The march towards absolutism was checked for a long time.[29]

This was highly flammable material, and Guizot heaped plenty more on the pile during the rest of the month (he gave his last lecture on 29 May). Tocqueville missed none of the implications. But in spite of himself, perhaps, he remained less concerned with the politics of the lectures than with the method and substance of the historical analysis. It was his intellect which was catching fire. Guizot's practice was to enunciate a general proposition (for example, that Philippe le Bel began to meddle, through his tame lawyers, in all sorts of matters that had never before concerned the French kings); give two or three unanswerable demonstrations of the fact, drawn from his mastery of the archives; and then restate the proposition in a more challenging form: 'Here, gentlemen, we have the earliest examples of that regu-latory mania which has always been the distinctive character of the French monarchy.' Any reader of the *Ancien Régime* will recognize the doctrine. On 8 May Guizot began to recount the rise of the Third

Estate. 'Once born, it never ceased to grow for a single moment. Born feeble, it ended by destroying everything round it. It lay lowest in the hierarchy of social powers but all classes were eventually lost in it, it absorbed them all, it became *la nation toute entière*.' First, in alliance with the Crown, the Third little by little undermined and destroyed the feudal nobility, supporting absolutism 'so that at least all would be equal under one master.' (Tocqueville underlined this remark in his notes.) Then it turned against the monarchy which, without its support, could easily be destroyed. And then it modified that monarchy 'in our own time'. The rise of the Third Estate was unique – there was nothing like it in Asiatic or Roman history; it was something especially French. The Third must not be confused with the *bourgeoisie*, that is, the inhabitants of the medieval towns. The Third made great strides in the later Middle Ages, while the towns, in the same period, lost their political autonomy. And while they were declining, small noble fiefs were being absorbed into larger ones – duchies, counties, etc. – which in turn came to be dominated by the kings. The tide of centralization had set in. Theoretically, the towns might have saved themselves by federating, but:

> federal government, gentlemen, is the most difficult of all forms. The mass of the people have to be very intelligent to understand and submit to it and few except those nations which have attained a high degree of civilization can manage it. No political system requires more real enlightenment, more devotion to the public interest and a smaller amount of that often blind egoism which is the ordinary impulse of societies as of individuals.

Anyway, Guizot, reflecting on the record of Holland, Belgium and Italy, did not think much of communal self-government. Its disappearance was good for France. Centralization had been necessary to create the nation, 'striving towards the same end, moved by the same ideas, shaken by the same passions, marching, in short, like one man to overcome the same difficulties.'[30]

Here, indeed, was matter for reflection. Here was a frontal challenge to the political creed in which Tocqueville had been reared. Even Guizot's incidental or merely illustrative remarks were striking: for example, how over time words stay the same but their meaning changes – there was as much difference between the Roman republic and the republic of the United States as there was between the US and a representative monarchy. And, commenting on the fact that slavery existed in some French medieval towns and not in others, he said that to understand the importance of this fact one should look at the state of affairs in contemporary America. 'Everyone knows that the spirit and opinions of the northern and southern provinces of the Union [differ] ... the ideas, the habits of the latter are infinitely more aristocratic than those of the former, and yet both live under the same manners, the same way of life.' Medieval communes, he said, were dominated by *l'esprit démocratique* – 'that is, by the will to rise socially, by the taste for equality, by turbulence and envy ... But it is not enough to evoke the existence of these two attitudes [the other being aristocratic] ... it is also necessary to discover their traces in both institutions and facts.' As if all this were not enough, Tocqueville had also to contemplate the supreme discovery, governing all Guizot's observations, that for hundreds of years there had been a levelling tendency in history, and that it was still going on. If Guizot was right there could be no hope for the idea of a renewed noblesse governing France under the King; and what was the alternative?[31]

Tocqueville was never to accept all these Guizotin doctrines, but he agreed with many of them, and saw that anyway they all required logical and well-informed – the French would say, scientific – discussion. With this in mind, as well as the political situation, he and Beaumont went to see Guizot, rather as modern graduate students seek out professors to help them find research topics. Guizot received them most graciously, but 'with remarkable affectation' evaded all discussion of their studies, 'no doubt in order to drive home to us the idea that he was not just a professor.' So they talked of politics, and Guizot was confident both that the Liberals would carry the forthcoming elections (as indeed they did, with an increased majority) and that the King would invite them to form a government, which they would do, dropping their more radical supporters.[32] Tocqueville came away rather disillusioned, and it was at about this time (that is, in June) that he wrote a bitter little essay, 'Truth, 1830', the main purpose of which was to relieve his feelings about the parliamentary politicians. Tocqueville still clung sincerely to the Charter of 1814, but he now thought that few others did so. All the Liberals professed the utmost loyalty to the King whom they had chased into exile twice already and were quite prepared to drive out yet again; they also professed loyalty to the Charter; they lied, and everyone knew that they lied. The only way to get ahead in politics, especially during a time of crisis, was to choose your party and stick to it (a lesson, we may add, that Tocqueville could never quite accept). Truthfulness, he concluded cynically, was a private, not a public virtue.[33]

Yet he was beginning to reach out to the Liberals, as the visit to Guizot suggests. He formed an acquaintance with E.-E. Forestier-Boinvilliers, a barrister and follower of La Fayette. Boinvilliers was a habitual conspirator, yet as indiscreet as Kergorlay himself. Tocqueville was impressed by his ardour and also, we may think, taken in by it: this devoted republican was to accept Louis-Philippe and serve Louis-Napoleon, who made him an imperial Senator. Tocqueville thought him 'an impassioned soul, capable of everything energetic and generous; I find his intelligence to be inferior to his soul ... He seems in general to be ruled rather by his passions than by his ideas.' He and Tocqueville did not obviously have much in common, but they were both young and ill-suited to dissimulation and craft; besides, Boinvilliers wanted to convert Tocqueville to republicanism. So he boasted that he had been involved in every republican plot of the previous fifteen years, and was ashamed that his party had taken up the cry of the Charter, when they really wanted to get rid of it as well as the Bourbons; but it was a regrettable necessity – if the majority knew where the republicans were going it would never follow. As it was, there was a nationwide network of 'correspondents', controlled centrally by the *Aide-toi*. 'He also said to me, I don't know why the nation dislikes the Bourbons so much. All in all, they are decent people, they have given us more liberty than we ever had before. I think it is because they were imposed on us by foreigners. A great nation can never pardon its princes for that.' Tocqueville was not converted, but as with Guizot, he saw sense in much of what Boinvilliers had to say.[34]

The election carried Comte Hervé into Normandy, both as a voter and as president of the electoral college of the department of the Manche (the Cotentin under another name). He took Alexis with him and they electioneered together: it was perhaps now that Alexis discovered that, as a noble, he was unpopular in the department (as he was to recall in 1848).* He described his doings in a lively letter to his mother on 29 June. Letters to the comtesse always had to be cheerful, but there is no reason to be sceptical about Tocqueville's high spirits as he and his father spent two days riding round the countryside to canvass farmers and then stayed at Hippolyte's chateau of Nacqueville, where Émilie was energetically planning all sorts of improvements. There was much anxiety about the rural incendiarism which broke out all across northern France that summer: even the old curé at Tocqueville kept a gun in his parlour. But the only cloud on Tocqueville's personal horizon at the moment was his anxiety about Kergorlay.[35] He need not have worried: on 2 July a letter arrived at Versailles joyously describing Kergorlay's first battle, on 19 June, which he had gone through without a scratch:

> As soon as our howitzers began to fire they concentrated all their efforts upon us. In a short time six men of our company were wounded, one of them fatally. Bullets whistled about us and I was unsure if that was what is called *feu vif* or nothing much. That evening I learned by talking to fellow officers that it had been very heavy. Being under fire affected me as everything does of which one makes a monster: it was unimpressive. From time to time I felt somewhat inclined to take cover, but that soon passed off ... I assure you that cuts from a sabre or a battle-axe or a bayonet frighten me much more than cannon balls or bullets because with them you have to take action to parry and I don't think I am a more skilful swordsman than the usual run of men. This discovery has cured me of any taste for battles featuring *l'arme blanche*.[36]

On 8 July he wrote to announce the fall of Algiers and to discuss the benefits of founding a French colony in Algeria. The letter arrived at Versailles on 26 July, the day that the Revolution of 1830 broke out.[37]

The elections had turned out disastrously for the Ultras, and left the King with no sensible alternative to dismissing Polignac and sending for the Liberals. But he did not see it like that; rather, he thought the time had come to assert his royal right once for all and stage the *coup d'état* which had been rumoured for months. He was one of those returned

---

* Nassau Senior, *Journal*, 26 May 1848.

émigrés of whom Talleyrand said so accurately that they had learned nothing and forgotten nothing. He had the professional deformation of a pre-Revolutionary king: he hated to relinquish power as old men (he was that too) hate the loss of sexual potency. So it is not surprising that he wanted to reduce the free institutions of the new France to mere façades, as Nicholas II, another stupid monarch, gradually emptied the 1905 Russian constitution of its meaning, with even more disastrous results. Then, as leader of the Ultra party, Charles could not contemplate sharing power with another faction. As both King and party chieftain, his motives were so mixed together as to be inseparable. At any rate, on Sunday, 25 June 1830, saying, 'the more I think about it, the more I remain convinced that it is impossible to act otherwise,' he signed the famous *ordonnances*, the four decrees which led directly and almost immediately to the collapse of his monarchy.[38]

The *ordonnances* were, respectively, a decree dissolving the newly elected Chamber of Deputies before it had ever met; a second, reducing the already tiny electorate by 75 per cent, thus weighting it even further in favour of the rich, and by various devices weighting it still more in favour of landed wealth as opposed to urban, industrial, commercial or financial varieties; a third, calling new elections for September; and finally, most explosive of all, a decree abolishing freedom of the press – in future no periodical and no pamphlet of less than twenty pages might be published without authorization, which might be withdrawn at any time and anyway had to be renewed every three months. This *ordonnance* supplemented the already severe press law of 1826, which provided for the suppression of books deemed dangerous. When published in the *Moniteur*, the official newspaper, the decrees would be accompanied by a long official document almost entirely given over to abusing the opposition newspapers, which had had the impudence to carry elections against the Crown: 'We no longer enjoy the ordinary conditions of representative government ... A turbulent democracy is tending to substitute itself for legitimate authority.' It was therefore only right that the King had invoked Article 14 of the Charter and its emergency powers: by this means the Charter and its institutions could not only be saved, but strengthened. As David Pinkney comments, 'In the usual manner of makers of coups d'état the ministers justified violation of the constitution by an appeal to the constitution.' All these documents were to appear in the *Moniteur* on Monday, 26 July. When asked by one of the ministers what he thought of them the paper's editor replied, 'God save the King and France! Gentlemen, I am fifty-seven, I saw all the *journées* of the Revolution and I am absolutely terrified.' But the prefect of police swore by his head that Paris would not stir.[39]

The *ordonnances* were a deliberate attempt to undo some of the most important work of the Revolution. July 1830 was like 1789 all over again; it was like Louis XVI's clash with the Estates-General that led to the Oath of the Tennis-Court, the creation of the National Assembly and the attack on the Bastille. Ministers did not expect such resolute and successful opposition this time, and made no preparations to deal with any at all. All they could think about was keeping the *ordonnances* secret until the last minute. They did not even forewarn Marshal Marmont, whom they relied on to keep order in Paris: he learnt the news only by borrowing a copy of the *Moniteur* from the Dutch ambassador. The decrees became public knowledge during Monday morning. Alexis de Tocqueville, who had spent Sunday and Sunday night with his parents in the rue de Verneuil, had already left for Versailles when the *Moniteur* appeared. As the news spread the implications of the press decree were immediately obvious: apart from silencing political debate, it would put a great many journalists and printers out of work, and times were hard. Groups of workers and students began to form in the streets, particularly in and round the Palais-Royal; they shouted '*Vive la Charte! A bas les ministres!*' The Liberal opposition was taken entirely by surprise: many of the newly elected deputies had not yet got back to Paris from electioneering in their constituencies. The leaders could not think what to do, and were afraid of the government. The *Constitutionnel* and the *Journal des débats* decided to take no risks and to forgo publication next day. But the radicals gathered at the offices of *Le National* and put out a protest, written by Thiers, against the illegality of the *ordonnances*. It was immediately printed and distributed throughout Paris. In the evening, after the police had seized a print-shop in the Palais-Royal, the crowd grew riotous, breaking the windows of the ministry of finance and stoning Polignac's carriage as the *président du conseil* went to his office. The prefect of police reported to the minister of the interior that tranquillity reigned in all parts of the capital. 'No event worthy of attention is recorded in the reports that have come to me.' Government stocks fell four points on the Bourse (and would fall eight points on Tuesday).[40]

The King spent the day hunting at Rambouillet, like Louis XVI on 14 July 1789.

Madame de Boigne was less complacent. She was employing thirty workmen on alterations to her house, and on Tuesday morning (27 July) they told her that ferment was beginning to spread all over Paris. She had already been impressed by their intelligence, their politeness, and their skill; now, 'I was still more struck by their arguments concerning the danger of these fatal ordinances, of which they understood the range and also the probable results. If our governors had been half as foresighted and prudent, King Charles X would still be living quietly at the Tuileries.'* None of her workmen appeared next day, Wednesday.[41]

For the ferment was indeed spreading. On the Monday a meeting of employers at the Hôtel de Ville had decided to shut their businesses, in protest against the *ordonnances*, which among other things were a direct attack on the political aspirations of men of their type. So on Tuesday the streets of Paris were full of men unable to work: men angry, if not yet anxious, though most of them lived close to the subsistence level; men hot and thirsty (there was a heatwave all week); men idle: ripe for mischief. Among them were many printers, for the prefect of police had forbidden the publication of any newspaper without previous authorization, which none had yet received. Not all journals obeyed this injunction (*Le Temps* and *Le National* did not) but whether at work that day or not, all printers had reason for anxiety. The walls of the city were plastered with copies of Thiers's protest. The police provoked trouble by seizing presses which had been used to defy the new regulations: there was a barricade and a scuffle at the office of *Le Temps*. Crowds began to mill about the streets, tearing down royal coats-of-arms; there was some pillaging of gunshops. By mid-morning the King was sufficiently alarmed to send Marmont to restore order, but the marshal found, on arriving at the Tuileries, that Polignac, as acting minister of war, had done nothing to get a body

---

* She was writing in 1832.

of troops together, and it took hours to assemble one. Meanwhile a meeting of thirty of the newly elected deputies commissioned Guizot to draw up another protest. At much the same moment the first death occurred: a demonstrator at the Palais-Royal was shot by the police. Later, as Marmont's men seized such strategic points as the Pont-Neuf and the place Louis XVI,* there were more casualties. The guardhouse at the Bourse was set on fire. Nevertheless, by nightfall quiet seemed to be returning, and Marmont sent a reassuring message to the King at Saint-Cloud. Unknown to him, twelve revolutionary committees were being formed for the various districts of Paris.[42]

Wednesday, 28 July, was the decisive *journée*. At dawn the *quartiers populaires* rose in insurrection. A crowd of workers, former National Guards, students and ex-soldiers marched through the streets, cutting down trees to build barricades (the great revolutionary innovation of 1830), waving the tricolour and shouting '*A bas les Bourbons! Vive la République! Vive l'Empéreur!*' It was indeed 1789 all over again, but this time the royal forces were at an even greater disadvantage than formerly. In 1827 Charles X had petulantly dissolved the National Guard, the militia, but its members had kept their weapons and uniforms, and now it was re-forming – but not to defend the King. The long years of war had given a great many Frenchmen military training, including thousands of Parisians. The École Polytechnique, as Kergorlay had found, was full of young middle-class liberals, and trained them also in military science. There were many arsenals and gunshops in Paris: there would have been no need to loot the Bastille this time if it had been still standing. The women of Paris sat on their doorsteps moulding bullets for the insurrectionists; bands of men went from door to door borrowing weapons (which, according to Mme de Boigne, were scrupulously returned afterwards).[43] Nor were targets of decisive importance lacking. The government was no longer remote at Versailles: its offices were in central Paris, all too close to the revolutionary districts. Finally, the troops of Charles X, besides being too few for their task, were even less reliable than those of Louis XVI had been: they showed a marked tendency to fraternize with the rebels, and even to desert. In the circumstances the crowd had a fairly easy job.

---

* Now the place de la Concorde.

Marmont's men soon had to abandon the streets and retreat to the Louvre and the Tuileries. The crowd seized the Arsenal, the gunpowder stores at La Salpetrière, the Hôtel de Ville and Notre-Dame, where the *polytechniciens* quickly ran up a tricolour: anxious courtiers at Saint-Cloud could see its flutterings through telescopes (they could also hear the gunfire). The Banque de France was stormed. The great bell of Notre-Dame rang an incessant tocsin. By the end of the day Marmont had lost 2,500 men, 'killed, wounded, captured, and above all deserters'.[44] Reinforcements were ordered up from outside Paris, but they were to prove even less loyal than the soldiers already in combat, who were bitter because neither the King nor the Dauphin had come to join them. Instead the King played his usual evening game of whist, to a background of cannon-fire.

His ministers continued to exhibit their incompetence. They encouraged Charles to refuse all concessions, and Polignac refused to meet the Liberal leaders bearing Guizot's petition. As a result the Liberals, slowly mustering their courage, their wits and their convictions, began to see that the Bourbons would have to go. But who, or what, would replace them? The banker Lafitte was the first to mention the duc d'Orléans; but as yet the other Liberal deputies, still afraid that Polignac would win, could agree on nothing but the publication of Guizot's protest; and the Parisians were growing angry and impatient at the failure of the deputies to offer any effective leadership.[45]

During Wednesday night the insurgents continued to erect barricades (in the end there were 4,000). Early on Thursday morning (29 July) Marmont disposed his troops for the defence of the Louvre and the Tuileries: many of them were Swiss Guards, who uneasily remembered the massacre of 1792. Brisk fusillades from the palace windows kept the insurgents at a distance for a while, but the position of the Bourbon monarchy was worsening all the time. Mail-coaches flaunting tricolour flags were carrying the news to the provinces, which in response prevented effective reinforcements being sent to the garrison in Paris. At Saint-Cloud the King was vehemently urged by some of his supporters to withdraw the *ordonnances* and dismiss his ministers, but he had still not brought himself to do so when the news arrived that Marmont had been driven from the Tuileries. Finally, at 4 p.m., Polignac announced that a new ministry would be formed, pledged to withdraw the *ordonnances*, but it was too late. The Prince de Talleyrand, who from his windows had watched the royal troops fleeing the Tuileries gardens, had long since taken out his watch and observed, 'Five past twelve. The elder line of the House of Bourbon has ceased to reign.'[46] The prefect of the Seine (the comte de Chabrol, father of Tocqueville's house-mate) was replaced at the Hôtel de Ville by General de La Fayette, now commander of the revived National Guard and the most popular man in Paris, and a so-called Municipal Commission, which was really a provisional government appointed by the Liberal deputies. Behind the scenes, intense pressure was mounted to induce the duc d'Orléans to assume the Crown – or, we may say, to pick it up on the point of his soon-to-be-famous green umbrella. Next day Mme de Boigne's workmen came back to her, and 'with an heroic simplicity' told her of their exploits in the rising. Paris was papered with a fresh poster, beginning 'Charles X can never return to Paris. He has caused the blood of the people to be shed.' (The fact that this proclamation was drafted by Thiers is an irony too painful, in view of 1871, to contemplate for long.) 'A republic would expose us to terrible divisions; it would embroil us with Europe. The duc d'Orléans is a prince devoted to the cause of the Revolution ... It will be from the people of France that he will hold his crown.'[47] That evening the duc, who had been nervously hiding in the suburbs for the past four days, returned to the Palais-Royal, and next day went to the Hôtel de Ville to accept the lieutenancy-general of the realm – an interim step towards kingship. He and La Fayette appeared together on the balcony, wrapped in a tricolour flag, and were greeted with thunderous applause. On 1 August they met again, at the Palais-Royal, and there a conversation took place of such importance, not only to France, but to the story of Alexis de Tocqueville, that it must be recorded in full:

> LA FAYETTE: You know I am a republican and that I regard the consti-
> tution of the United States as the most perfect that ever existed.
>
> ORLÉANS: I think as you do; it is impossible to have spent two years
> in America* and not to be of that opinion; but do you believe that in

* Orléans had lived in the United States from 1796 to 1798, as a refugee from the great Revolution.

France's situation, in the present state of opinion, it would be proper for us to adopt that constitution?

LA FAYETTE: No, what the French people must have today is a popular throne surrounded by republican institutions, completely republican.

ORLÉANS: That is precisely what I think.[48]

Ten days later everything had been settled: the chambers had met, the Charter had been revised (not very drastically) and Orléans was on the throne as King Louis-Philippe I. On 16 August Charles X and his family sailed from Cherbourg into permanent exile.

And Tocqueville? There are only glimpses of him during the July Days, but together they tell a story. When the news of the *ordonnances* reached Versailles on the Monday (26 July) he apparently denounced them in public before the *parquet*, saying that they were illegal and should not, would not be enforced. It is a pity that we do not know more about this, his first political action, but it was sufficiently dramatic to alarm his father when he heard of it. On Tuesday morning he wrote a hasty note to Alexis: 'Whatever you may think of the measures taken, I engage you to express yourself with restraint and moderation. You will easily realize that both sides will be much exasperated, and that the government, having taken such a decision, will have to break all opposition.' (The comte did not yet believe that the Bourbons would fall.) 'Young people, above all, must be prudent so as not to compromise their position, especially those who having most talent can excite most envy. For the rest, we will talk it over on Thursday. Until then, *je t'embrasse bien tendrement.*' But when Thursday came Tocqueville, after writing a hasty note of reassurance to Marie ('we can be sure that, a week from now, calm will certainly have returned to Paris'), had to escort his parents from the rue de Verneuil to Saint-Germain-en-Laye, where they took refuge with Édouard's in-laws. It was a wise precaution, if only for the sake of Mme de Tocqueville's nerves: that day the barracks of the Swiss Guard, on the nearby rue de Babylone, was attacked; but it was probably not an easy journey, for the revolutionary struggle was moving westward, and the area between the wall of Paris and Saint-Cloud was swarming with militants. And there was trouble at Versailles: the people had seized arms from the barracks of the royal bodyguard and invaded the town hall. The local National Guard was hastily resuscitated and Tocqueville enlisted in it. He had no intention of standing by to let royalists be massacred, or of being massacred himself. But what he had seen of events in Paris had already changed his political views quite radically. On Friday (30 July) he wrote to Marie that the Bourbons, not one of whom had gone out to lead or encourage the soldiers who were being killed in their service, were cowards, 'and don't deserve a thousandth part of the blood which has just been shed in their defence'. At dawn the next day (Saturday, 31 July) he was on guard on the outer boulevards of Versailles and saw the royal family go by on the first stage of their long retreat. The sad procession of coaches, in single file, reminded him of a funeral, and he wept to see them: 'for I felt, even to the last, a residual, hereditary affection for Charles X.'

Men are we, and must grieve when even the Shade
Of that which once was great is passed away.

He returned to the National Guard headquarters and handed in his gun and ammunition, exclaiming to one of his comrades of the *parquet*, 'There is nothing more to do, it's all over ... I have just seen the hearse of the monarchy go by, the King, the House of France, the ministers ... would you believe it, the escutcheons on the royal coaches had been hidden with coats of mud.'* He was much moved, but he had finally made his choice: as he wrote twenty years later, 'that king fell because he had violated rights which were dear to me, and I hoped that my country's liberty would be revived rather than destroyed by his disappearance.' He decided to take the oath of loyalty to Louis-Philippe.[49]

---

* It is perhaps necessary to remark, in fairness to Charles X, that the precaution was not pointless: before he got to Cherbourg he had to pass through some very hostile country, and one night the escutcheon was torn from his carriage.

CHAPTER SEVEN

UPHEAVAL

1830–1831

*Soyez l'esclave de votre propre opinion et le serviteur de
personne. D'ailleurs, dans le temps de pitoyable confusion
dans lequel nous vivons, rien ne presse de prendre un
cocarde.* *

ALEXIS DE TOCQUEVILLE TO BEAUMONT,
4 OCTOBER 1829[1]

IN JANUARY 1830 few in France had particularly desired, and
none had expected, the immediate fall of the Bourbons; by the end of
July few desired or expected their survival. They had disgusted and
disappointed even their most faithful supporters.

No Tocqueville, it seems, journeyed with the fallen King on his
dismal trek towards exile, although it took him eventually to Cherbourg
by way of Saint-Lô (where he heard that Louis-Philippe had accepted
the throne) and Valognes – right through the Tocquevilles' own
country. Louis de Rosanbo accompanied his wife, one of the duchesse
de Berry's ladies-in-waiting, and according to Mme de Boigne (but
she was a malicious Orleanist) was rewarded by unwelcome amorous
advances from the duchesse herself. Colonel Louis de Chateaubriand,

---

* 'Be the slave of your own opinions and nobody's servant. Besides, in the time of pitiful
confusion in which we live, there is no hurry to adopt a cockade.'

whose regiment had deserted him and the Bourbon cause, went all the way with his King to Cherbourg, on a pony – the only mount he could find.[2] His uncle François-René stayed in Paris to give his last political speech in the Chamber of Peers in support of the duc de Bordeaux, the grandson in favour of whom Charles had abdicated. Hervé de Tocqueville did not even attend the session.

In his memoirs he makes it plain that he had lost all faith in the judgement and leadership of the King and the Dauphin: in his opinion they should have stayed near Paris and called the revolutionaries' bluff. He supported the duc de Bordeaux, but knew that the issue was settled. He despised the Chamber of Peers ('when the Gauls took Rome, the Senate did not offer the crown to Brennus'); he believed that it would have been right and politically profitable to go down in defence of principle. Matters were not helped when the same session, having accepted Louis-Philippe as King, excluded all peers created by Charles X – Hervé, of course, being one of them. He decided that his political career was over. He had always supported the elder branch of the Bourbons, and received many honours and benefits at their hands. He felt no temptation to rally to their supplanters: he wanted to keep the respect of his friends. Besides, he had seen so many revolutions and so much social upheaval, 'my life had been shaken so often by events, that my soul was weary. After so many disappointed hopes, so many changes in my life, so many illusions destroyed, I felt the need to rest in the happy bosom of my family from the deceptive spectacle of human passions.' His sons would be his consolation, his grandchildren his hope (he does not mention his wife). And compared to some more illustrious persons he thought himself lucky.

His sons were variously affected by the disaster. Édouard, leading the life of a rich country gentleman, suffered least. Hippolyte did not at once resign his army commission, as many of his fellow officers did; he took the oath to Louis-Philippe, for it seemed quite possible that the revolution would provoke a European war, and he did not wish to desert his country; but by January 1831 the emergency was over, and he too resigned.

Alexis was hit hardest. He was doubly afflicted, as a Frenchman and as a magistrate with a career at stake. The street-fighting which he had witnessed in Paris had shocked him deeply. He wrote to Marie

Mottley on 30 July of how horrible it was 'to see Frenchmen cutting each other's throats for fun, to hear such cries of fury and despair all in the same language, and those poor, unlucky soldiers who gave their lives for an opinion which was certainly not theirs and for a man who should have died fighting at their head ... we ought to be ashamed to be alive!' He was also ashamed to be a bystander; he ought to be marching in the van of those confronting the armed populace. The thought of the bloodshed in Paris and the din of the tocsin haunted him. He would never forget the experience; it would shape much of his thought in later years, but for the time being (once the fighting stopped) he was more concerned with the political consequences of the revolution, in both the short and the long terms.[3]

He had shed tears of sorrow for the Bourbons, but they might just as sincerely have been tears of rage. Charles X, in his obstinate folly, had not only thrown away his crown and wrecked his dynasty, he had destroyed nineteenth-century France's best chance of political stability. The constitutional question was not the only problem facing the country, but it was one which the French might have been spared had Charles X been a wiser man; then they could have devoted themselves to husbanding their strength and modernizing their society – in short, to preparing themselves for the challenges of the next 130 years. Instead, what was probably the most brilliant period of French civilization was marked by chronic political debility characterized by incipient or actual civil war, growing weakness relative to the other Great Powers, and three wars with Germany, each marked by disasters which ultimately came near to destroying the very nation. Charles X does not deserve all the blame for this state of affairs, but his fall, which was entirely his own doing, opened a new era of instability in which Tocqueville was destined to struggle all his life. If nothing else, the July Days had revived the Parisians' taste for revolution; and since each convulsion ended, inevitably, in disappointment (for which the people blamed anything and anybody rather than their own unrealistic expectations), its principal achievement was to make a repeat performance likely.

Tocqueville understood much of this in 1830: as Beaumont was to remark, he already had the gift of seeing more quickly, and further, than other people. The enthusiasm of July did not deceive him for a moment; he was chiefly afraid that Louis-Philippe, having come to the throne so dubiously, would either turn to military adventures to make himself feared at home and abroad, or meekly submit to every bully (such as the Tsar) to win pardon for his seizure of power.[4] (In due course Louis Napoleon was to justify one of these apprehensions, Louis-Philippe the other.) Had he fully known what was to happen he might well have despaired and turned to farming, like so many of his fellow nobles (and like Beaumont after 1851). As it was, he hoped, in spite of all difficulties, to see a revival of liberty and rallied to the new régime, seeing in it the last chance for constitutional monarchy.

This requires some explanation. In retrospect, it is difficult to believe that a republic headed by General de La Fayette would have been less liberal and constitutional than a monarchy headed by Louis-Philippe. The drift of French history from the Hundred Days onwards was towards some sort of republic; in 1848 Tocqueville himself became a republican of a kind. But such considerations are beside the point. As we have seen, La Fayette himself did not believe that in the conditions of 1830 a republic was possible or, at least, could be permanent. European opinion, not unjustly, identified the French Republic with war and invasion. It proved difficult enough to induce the Tsar, Nicholas I, to accept Louis-Philippe; confronted with a republic he might well have revived the Holy Alliance, tried to restore the Bourbons yet again, and precipitated a European war. Furthermore, in 1830 republicanism was the creed of only a handful of Frenchmen. Had there been a suitable mature Bonaparte available an imperial resurrection might have been popular, although just as alarming to Europe; but since Napoleon II was only a youth dying in Vienna, the Bonapartists had to compromise. Many of them had been willing to make the Restoration work, if possible; when it failed, they flocked to Louis-Philippe, who was in several ways the successor not of Charles X but of Napoleon. Bonapartism would not become a viable alternative to Orleanism until 1848, as Louis Napoleon's failed *coups d'état* in 1836 and 1840 were to demonstrate (Louis Napoleon was the Emperor's eldest surviving nephew). The Bourbon cause would take even longer to revive. Tocqueville in 1830 was right to feel that his choice lay between Orleanism and abandoning politics. His only mistake was his failure to foresee that Orleanism would soon become unpopular and that republicanism would gain enormous strength as the only immediately practicable alternative.

Personal interest, he was uneasily aware, pointed in the same direction as patriotism. His judicial career had been getting nowhere under the Bourbons; it would probably do no better under Louis-Philippe, but if he took the oath he would at least keep his job. It gave him a certain standing and, as he was soon to discover, certain opportunities. But his decision to support the new monarch was sincere, if unenthusiastic; to take the oath of allegiance was his only means of affecting the situation, however marginally. And he would have to act soon. Guizot, now the minister of the interior, was ruthlessly purging the administrative and judicial corps: there was already a new prefect at Versailles. Tocqueville and his colleagues took the oath on 16 August.[5] He wrote to Marie immediately:

> My conscience is absolutely clear, but nonetheless I am deeply upset, and I count this day as among the unluckiest of my life. Marie, this is the first time, since I entered society, that I have had to avoid the company of people I admire while disapproving of them. Oh! ... the thought tears me to pieces; my native share of pride is in revolt against me, and yet I have not failed in my duty, rather I have done what I should for my country which can find salvation only in the dominion now arising to save us from anarchy. But have I done my duty to myself, to my family, to those who once died for the cause which I am ceasing to serve just as everything turns against it? I am not a child, Marie, I am not giving way to some trivial grief, but I feel the blow I have just received acutely, I feel it more than I can say. I am at war with myself, a new sensation, horrible.[6]

His voice had changed pitch as he uttered the fatal words, he felt his heart beating as if to break.

This moment of agony must be respected. As Tocqueville knew perfectly well, he was being both sensible and patriotic in taking the oath, and the Bourbons simply did not deserve that he should abandon all his prospects for their sake. His strongly emotional reaction to the crisis was characteristic: we will see him responding to later events in the same way, and calming down afterwards. But it cannot be truthfully said that on this occasion he over-reacted. He was making a decisive, public break with everything that he had been brought up to believe in and act upon, and it would have been strange had he not felt like a traitor. He might not have been able to bring himself to act in time had there not been a family council over the weekend to strengthen his resolve. Beaumont, who was in exactly the same position (and who, as a member of the *parquet* of Paris, had perhaps taken the oath already), joined in the discussion. Comte Hervé, an admirable father, not only supported his sons in whatever they chose to do (Hippolyte's course was also debated) but gave them the benefit of his advice as to how their decisions might be carried out, and used such influence as he retained to help them. He went to the war ministry to make sure that Hippolyte's oath was accepted, and he joined Édouard and Beaumont in urging Alexis to act in unison with his colleagues.

Alexis was already calmer when he wrote to Hippolyte two days later (or perhaps he was not ready to be as open with his brother as he was with Marie). His pride, he now said, was affronted by the idea that some people would think that he was acting against his principles for selfish reasons. He was not sure how long he would stay in the magistracy, which, like the army, had found taking the oath humiliating. If he had another profession to turn to he would resign; as it was, he thought he would stay on until he was dismissed, as he certainly would have been by the Polignac ministry, for resisting the *ordonnances*, had it triumphed. The thought was a small consolation.[7]

He had agonized, he had acted, and his situation was still extremely uncomfortable. Kergorlay was in the same straits. Writing to Tocqueville from Algiers during August, and from the ship which carried him back to France in early September, he was far from sure about his course. He did not at all want to give up his military career, and like Hippolyte felt that his country might soon need him. He might or might not take the oath, and expected to discuss the matter with Tocqueville when he got to Paris (he would be on sick-leave, having caught what was probably dysentery during the campaign). His situation was complicated by his father, who, as a peer appointed by Louis XVIII, could have stayed in the Chamber, but instead resigned, taking a very public stance in favour of the Bourbons, claiming that they had been deposed unlawfully; which meant that, legally, Louis, his son and heir, could have entered the Chamber himself had he so wished; but Louis would not, and came to feel that having refused to take the oath as a peer he could not logically do differently as an army officer. He sent his colonel a letter of resignation on 7 October.

So far as we know, Tocqueville and Kergorlay accepted each other's different decisions without acrimony. Another young man of their circle was not so tactful. Tocqueville's former antagonist, Henrion, was told by Eugène Stoffels that Alexis and Hippolyte had taken the oath, but affected not to believe it. He wrote to Tocqueville praising Louis de Rosanbo, who had published a letter affirming his loyalty to the fallen dynasty:

> there spoke the true grandson of Malesherbes, but of a Malesherbes cursing the philosophy that he had unluckily protected, and listening only to the religion which made him die a hero's death. When one is lucky enough to be M. de Rosanbo's nephew one cannot take a chance on the party which controls events. I am sure, my dear Alexis, that you have sacrificed your place to your conscience, that Hippolyte has resigned, and that your father rejoices in a proscription which proclaims him to Europe a faithful [vassal?]

He feared that he insulted Alexis by supposing for a moment that the alternative was possible.

Tocqueville was furious. Henrion, he wrote back, had lectured him like an usher in school. 'Yet I think you know that while I always take pleasure in my friends' advice, I have never had the habit of submitting my conduct to their control.' How dare Henrion insinuate that he had acted basely?

> Since I became old enough to exhibit them, my opinions have been manifest. On the day of the *ordonnances* I declared before the session of the tribunal that henceforth resistance seemed legitimate to me and that I would resist in my narrow sphere. When the movement went so far as to overthrow the dynasty I did not conceal my opposition to that measure. I said that I would fight in the civil war if it came about. But when the matter was settled I continued to believe, as I have always believed, that my strictest duty was owed not to a man or a family, but to the country. The salvation of France, as things stood, seemed to me to lie in sustaining the new King. So I promised to support him, without hiding that it was not for his sake that I did so ...

Finally, to save you in future from wasting your eloquence on the subject of my grandfather [*sic*], I will tell you that, rightly or wrongly, I am deeply convinced that he would have acted in my place exactly as I have done, just as I have the presumption to hope that I would have acted like him in his.

Tocqueville has changed his tune since his letter to Marie, and he meant every word of this thunderbolt. When Henrion called at the rue de Verneuil, hoping to be reconciled, he was told that M. Alexis was not at home.[8]

This explosion of wrath may have relieved Tocqueville's feelings, but the quarrel was one more reminder of how far he was moving from his accustomed moorings. Life was also becoming awkward at Versailles: elite society there had split into two camps, legitimist and Orleanist, and it was impossible to be on friendly terms with both, or indeed with either: the legitimists regarded Tocqueville as a traitor, while the Orleanists despised him as a time-server.[9]

His professional prospects were as bad as ever. The familial network of distinguished connections was now worse than useless: it made him an object of suspicion to the government. At that very moment his distant cousin Maxence de Damas was serving as governor to the duc de Bordeaux. As Beaumont was to say, 'what chance did the Restoration prefect's son have of receiving from the July government the promotion which the Restoration government had not given to the grandson of Malesherbes?'[10] He was so far from being in favour that in October he was made to take the oath a second time. Besides, the general political outlook was highly uncertain. As Pamela Pilbeam stresses in all her work, the July Revolution did not end with the installation of Louis-Philippe; France would not really settle down again until 1834–5, if then. There might be a war, there might be a restoration, there might be a republican *coup*. Tocqueville could not see his way. The one thing that became clear was that it would be a good thing to disappear for a while, evading hostile observation and the necessity for any more unpleasant choices. By late August he had made up his mind: he would go on a journey to the United States.

By most measures, this was the most important decision of his life, but its origins are frustratingly obscure (which may remind us how much of a human life will always be hidden from observers).

Tocqueville had long been aware of America. At some time in his boyhood he had read a sentimental novel, *Voyage au Lac Oneida*, which told a touching tale of a French noble and his wife who had fled from the Revolution to an island in Lake Oneida in the Iroquois country and lived there happily ever after, in a kind of Rousseauian rhapsody. This story had extraordinary power over its reader. In the first place, he took it for fact, though its relation to history was somewhat remote: the noble from whose story it was derived was not a refugee, for instance, and lived on the island for only two years; he had two children before he went there, and in the end returned to France, having inherited a fortune. Tocqueville himself did not understand why he was so moved by the legend: 'Whether this effect on me was worked by the talent of the author, by the real charm of the adventure, or by the influence of my age, I cannot say; but the memory of the two French lovers of Lake Oneida was never effaced from my memory.'[11] He may have first read it at a lonely moment of his adolescence, when feeling more than usually misunderstood, and have savoured the idea of flight with his Rosalie to a woodland refuge where they could create a new Garden of Eden. Eventually he shared the dream with Beaumont, and it became a proverb between them: 'No happiness in this world save on the shores of Lake Oneida.'[12] But this fantasy can have had little to do with his decision in 1830, except perhaps that it had established America in his mind as a place of refuge.

Further conjectures are possible. News out of the United States was scarce, but there was some in the French press. For instance, the election of General Andrew Jackson to the presidency in 1828 occasioned many worried comments about America's alleged lapse into demagoguery and barbarism. And as René Rémond has shown in an admirable treatise, under the Restoration there was always, in France, a lively concern with the United States, both as a new political experiment and as a new sort of society.[13] Unfortunately Rémond also shows that it was on the whole a minority concern, a matter for discrete groups, and it cannot be shown that Tocqueville belonged to any of them. And with a single exception, none of Tocqueville's family and friends can be shown to have had any particular interest in America or any reason for developing one.

The exception was mighty: Chateaubriand. 'It would be interesting to know what Tocqueville and Beaumont had read about the United States before their departure,' sighs André Jardin; but at least he is sure about Chateaubriand (Tocqueville himself adds the name of Fenimore Cooper).[14] In the archives at the château de Tocqueville Antoine Rédier once found the draft of an article, written by Tocqueville in his law-student days but never published, quarrelling with views of America expressed by Chateaubriand in the *Journal des débats* of October 1825. Chateaubriand had celebrated American democracy and commended its example to France. Lamentably, this draft – the earliest writing by Alexis de Tocqueville on the United States – has been lost, like too many of the papers which passed through Rédier's hands. Rédier thought of publishing it but decided not to, respecting the opinion of the author who at a later date had characteristically written 'très médiocre' on the manuscript, but this detail is less interesting than the grounds on which Tocqueville attacked his illustrious relation.[15]

He wrote, apparently, as a convinced monarchist and French nation-alist. He denounced Chateaubriand's opinions as those of a genius who had lost his way and was devoting his heaven-sent talent to the ruin of his fellow citizens and his country. Chateaubriand, he said, was wholly wrong in arguing that France had anything to learn from what he called 'the American republics': 'I only see one Republic in America, that of the United States. The only task worthy of such genius would have been that of demonstrating to us the difference between us and the Americans, and not to cozen us by illusory parallels.' Coming from the future author of *De la démocratie en Amérique*, this opinion is suffi-ciently striking, and it must be added that it was long before Tocqueville swerved from it: during his first weeks in the United States he was to insist repeatedly that conditions in America were so different from those in France as to make its political example worthless.

Tocqueville's attitude to Chateaubriand, at least during his youth, always had a sour streak in it; perhaps he was repelled by François-René's theatrical personality, or resented his treatment of Comte Hervé; but he was much too sensitive to language and ideas to resist the enchanter's spell. And as René Rémond affirms, Chateaubriand, although the least scientific, was by far the most influential of pre-1835 French interpreters of the United States.[16] Tocqueville's minor writings about America, such as 'Quinze jours dans le désert', are so many exercises in the *chateaubrianesque*, of which traces can be found even in the *Démocratie* itself. During the last years of the Restoration, Chateaubriand, in the intervals of his assault on his enemy Villèle, published *Les Natchez* (1826) and *Voyage en Amérique* (1827). If, as is almost certain, Tocqueville read the *Voyage*, he found there a few pages on the present and future prospects of the United States which might well make him think:

> The establishment of a representative republic in the United States was one of the greatest political events in the history of the world: an event which proved, as I have said elsewhere, that there are two kinds of practicable liberty: one, belonging to the childhood of nations, is the daughter of manners* and virtue; the ancient Greeks and Romans possessed it, so did the savages of America; the other is born in the old age of a people, the daughter of enlightenment and reason; it is the liberty which, in the United States, has replaced that of the Indians. That happy land has passed in less than three centuries from the one liberty to the other, almost without effort, and by a struggle which did not last for more than eight years![17]

Here was a phenomenon which might well seem worth investigating to a young man already committed to an ideal of enlightened freedom; and this 'Conclusion' to the *Voyage* – only eight pages long in a modern edition – was full of other suggestive thoughts. Chateaubriand throws off remarks about American roads, railways and postal services which seem to anticipate not only Michel Chevalier but George R. Taylor; and at one point he definitely anticipates the celebrated frontier theory of F. J. Turner: 'The United States have one more safeguard [of their freedom]: their population only occupies one eighteenth of their territory. America still lives in a solitude; for a long time yet her wilderness will be her way of life, and its wisdom her liberty.'[18] Chateaubriand had not been to America for thirty-five years, but he had done his best to update his information, and the result was a sketch of a dynamic society, thrusting westwards, its population rapidly

* *Moeurs.*

138

growing, wedded to republicanism ('useless to discuss the constitutions of the various States: it is enough to know that they are all free') and to complete religious liberty, which seemed to encourage Christianity: every citizen belonged to some sect or other, and the Catholic faith was making considerable progress in the western states. There, in America, was the last domain of freedom; but would it survive? Could the Union endure? The states were already quarrelling over the issue of slavery.[19]

Readers of the *Démocratie* today may well see in Chateaubriand's brief musings the germ of Tocqueville's masterpiece; here, the younger man may have thought, was just the topic he needed for the application of the techniques and theories which he had learned from Guizot. Assuming that Tocqueville read the *Voyage*, we may be struck by what may nevertheless have been a coincidence. Perhaps Chateaubriand was simply moving with the times. Earlier, in *Atala* and his other famous works on America, he, like Fenimore Cooper (whose novels enjoyed an enormous vogue in Restoration France), had promulgated what René Rémond calls 'the primitivist mirage'[20] – a vision of America rather than of the United States, in which noble savages and dauntless backwoodsmen lived in harmony with the Nature of river, forest and dusky maidens. Tocqueville was not immune to the charms of this vision, but his intellect inclined in a quite different direction, which helped to make him the man for his time.

But even if Chateaubriand's writings were to some extent a cause of Tocqueville's burgeoning interest in the United States, it is likely that it was Chateaubriand the man whose influence and example struck the spark, igniting the sudden decision, not only to make the journey, but to make it as soon as possible. The 'noble peer' was much in the public eye in 1830. At one point during the July crisis he had been recognized by the crowd and carried in triumph, as an opposition leader and a supporter of press freedom, to the Palais du Luxembourg, where the Chamber of Peers sat. Had he chosen he could have become a leading figure in the new régime. He did not so choose. On 7 August he opposed the transfer of the crown in the speech already mentioned. He argued with logic, passion and good sense against both a republic and what he called an 'elective monarchy'; but although the speech was one of the best that he ever gave, and created a stir, his cause was lost, and he knew it. The peers voted for Louis-Philippe, 89–10 (fourteen fainthearts abstained).

The speech marked the end of Chateaubriand's political career. It could not fail to please his relations, yet it was not based on romantic loyalty. 'I do not believe in the divine right of royalty, and I do believe in the power of revolution and of facts.' It was on severely practical grounds that Chateaubriand advocated the Bourbon cause and predicted the failure of the Orleanist experiment. His speech was a genuine prophecy. 'The representative republic is undoubtedly the future state of the world, but its time has not yet arrived.' He disliked the elective monarchy partly on the grounds which induced La Fayette to support it: it would be a republic in all but name, a monarchy overwhelmed by democratic laws, or by the struggle of factions. Even the liberties claimed by the July insurgents, for instance freedom of the press, would be no safer under Orleans than they had been under Bourbon: new challenges would arise, and seem to necessitate the old oppression. Initial self-confidence and enthusiasm would soon be disproved by events.[21]

A new vision of French history was emerging, one which was at the very least a corrective to Guizot's ideas; Tocqueville, who would reflect on these questions almost to his dying day, must have been impressed. And as he contemplated Chateaubriand resigning his peerage and membership of the Conseil d'État, and renouncing all his official emoluments (except that his friends persuaded him to remain in the Académie Française) he might well be moved, as by an intuition, to identify himself with his quasi-uncle. If he did, he could easily have remembered the story of Chateaubriand's youth: how, caught between his liberalism and his loyalty in the early days of the great Revolution, uncertain of his career, he had sought to solve his dilemma by a journey to North America, with the encouragement of Malesherbes. The experiment had succeeded: it had eventually brought great fame to Chateaubriand. Why should not Alexis de Tocqueville, facing the same dilemma a generation later, try the same solution?

Much of this is guesswork, though not without value. At least we know that almost as soon as Tocqueville conceived his notion he took it to Beaumont, whom he wanted as his travelling-companion. Beaumont jumped at the idea.[22] His own position was even more uncomfortable than Tocqueville's since not only were his parents legitimists, but La

Fayette was a cousin – and La Fayette was as suspect as any Ultra to the new government, which jockeyed him out of the command of the National Guard as soon as it could. Personally, Beaumont was much approved by the Orleanists, but he knew that it could not last. The American scheme was attractive in itself: it was another project, the boldest so far, in their enterprise of joint education, and Beaumont shared Tocqueville's belief, originating in the events of July, that France was becoming a democracy. It made sense to study the system in the only great nation which had adopted equality while apparently preserving liberty, even if the lessons could not be wholly, or even partially, applied elsewhere. The journey might further their long-standing but so far ineffective dreams of collaboration. The die was cast: America it was to be, as soon as possible.

Their families made no difficulty, agreeing to pay for the trip. Nor did Marie Mottley. She may simply have accepted that she was in no position to stop the adventure, but more likely she recognized its importance to Tocqueville. He showered her with love that summer (and it was about now that Blaize drew their portraits). On 20 August he wrote to her:

> Do you know what my first thought was this morning, Marie? I thought that today was a happy day for me since it was the anniversary of your birth. Oh, I will never forget the 20 August! ... I will always remember, Marie, that on this day of days she was born who would show herself so tender a friend, so sweet a consolation for all the sorrows and all the annoyances which arise to torment a man's life. Oh, I will always thank God for at least one thing, I am sure, that he caused you to be born.[23]

During the judicial vacation that autumn he paid a visit to Le Ménil, his uncle Rosanbo's estate in the Cotentin, and wrote to her in such a way as to show how close they had grown, and how much closer he wanted her to be:

> I am very glad that I came on this trip. My great scheme is approved by the members of my family that I care most about, and my mother, who I was afraid I would find somewhat upset by my long silence, received me on the contrary with an affection which really moved me ... I work in the morning and go hunting in the afternoon. Above all

I enjoy that good which, as you know, I put above all others, liberty. I am at leisure to be as stupid as I please, speaking whenever I like, being silent when I want, snoozing in the salon without anyone saying a word. Short of doing without trousers and living in a forest, I couldn't be more my own master. Marie, I wish you could see the master of this *château*, if only for an hour. I am sure you would venerate him. He is virtue incarnate, virtue without show or haughtiness ... If you could see him, relieving the poor of the neighbourhood, or playing with his grandchildren, always surrounded by the almost religious devotion of his family and servants, I am sure you would be touched. As for me, my uncle has always been the most conclusive argument in favour of religion.[24]

This was surely a love Marie could trust. She resigned herself to doing without him for a year. Ernest de Chabrol agreed to act as their go-between, and to give her moral support during Tocqueville's absence. (Like Tocqueville and Beaumont he had taken the oath, and continued to live and work at Versailles.)[25]

But since neither Tocqueville nor Beaumont wished to resign his post, even though, as Beaumont says, Tocqueville's judicial career no longer meant anything to him,[26] they would have to persuade their superiors to give them leave of absence, which would not be possible unless they could show that their proposed journey was a mission of public utility. Fortunately or unfortunately, the perfect rationale lay ready at hand.

As magistrates, they had necessarily become somewhat acquainted with the French prison system, and in 1828 or 1829 Tocqueville had read an English work on penal reform.[27] He and Beaumont knew of *Du système pénitentiaire en Europe et aux États-Unis*, by Charles Lucas, which had created a stir in 1827 and been awarded the Monthyon prize by the Académie des Sciences Morales et Politiques. Prison reform had been an important issue since before the fall of that model establishment, the Bastille, and in 1791 Tocqueville's black sheep cousin, Le Peletier de Saint-Fargeau, had brought in a bill which, when passed by the Constituent Assembly, became the foundation for all subsequent penal legislation. The duc d'Angoulême patronized a prison reform society during the Restoration. In 1830, under pressure of the faltering economy, crime rates – the number of offences, of convicts, of recidivists – were all rising, and Montalivet, the minister of the interior appointed to succeed Guizot in November,* was well aware of the problem. (The last revision of the penal code had been undertaken in 1810 by his father, then minister.) The July Revolution had given a slight but perceptible impulse to all reform politics, which did not immediately fade. Tocqueville and Beaumont rightly felt that if they proposed a fact-finding mission to study at first hand the new prisons of the United States, which were supposed to be the best in the world, they would have an excellent chance of official approval. And such a mission would open many doors to them in the United States. They went seriously to work on preparing a memoir for the minister.

Their *modus operandi* was thoroughness itself, and one which Tocqueville was to employ on his writing projects ever after. Their legal work had taught them the importance of well-prepared briefs. There were several categories of French jails: in August Tocqueville seized a chance to visit a *maison d'arrêt*, or remand prison, at Versailles, and on 26 September he and Beaumont together inspected the *centre nationale* nearby, at Poissy, one of the prisons where convicts sentenced to more than a year served their time.† They devoured all available statistics on crime and punishment, which enabled them to make a convincing case that there was a crisis in French jails. They read everything that they could find on American prisons, including the newly published reports of the Prison Discipline Society of Boston, and together they composed a 'Note on the Penitentiary System' which consisted of a vigorous denunciation of the current state of French prisons and a justification of the proposed mission to see how things were done in the United States, 'the classical land of penitentiaries'.[28] It was ready by the end of October and at once sent to Montalivet; it was so effective, especially when endorsed by Félix Le Peletier d'Aunay, still the deputy from the Seine-et-Oise (the resources of cousinhood were not quite exhausted), that on 6 February 1831 they were given

---

* Camille, comte de Montalivet (1801–80), son of a Napoleonic official, was one of Louis-Philippe's most trusted advisers and was semi-permanent minister of the interior during the 1830s; but he refused to join Guizot's ministry in the 1840s, thinking it altogether too reactionary.

† It is worth remarking that neither in 1830 nor at any later date did the young reformers inspect Saint-Pélagie, where political prisoners were confined; nor did they ever mention it in their writings.

formal permission to make the journey, and eighteen months' leave of absence: but they would have to pay all expenses themselves.

It is tempting to linger on the 'Note on the Penitentiary System'. It contains a clear exposition of the penological principles which Tocqueville had adopted and of which he was always to be an adherent.[29] But these will be more conveniently examined in later chapters; only one point needs to be made clear at this stage.

Tocqueville was not the first of his family to visit Poissy: his father had done so in the course of his duty as prefect of the Seine-et-Oise, and, as his report makes plain, had been shocked by what he found. The reek of neglected latrines could be smelt everywhere; the windows in the workshops were never opened; the prison doctor was notoriously incapable; the prisoners' summer clothing was made of shoddy and harboured both vermin and 'deleterious miasmas'; the food was frightful: 'I tasted the bread and found it soggy, heavy, half-baked and containing more rye than the rules permit.' Above all, the convicts were grossly over-worked by the businessman to whom their labour had been contracted. The prefect said nothing about the purposes of imprisonment: he was only concerned that the state should not, by its neglect, degrade and even kill its prisoners (the mortality rate at Poissy in 1827 was unnecessarily high). Hervé de Tocqueville had not forgotten what it was like to be a captive.[30]

The response of his son, a prosecutor by trade, who would not be sent to jail for years yet (and then was not detained long enough for it to do him any good) could not have been more different. The prison had perhaps changed somewhat in three years,* but even if it had that cannot account for the horror with which Tocqueville and Beaumont saw the prisoners making the most of Sunday:

> Some smoked their pipes, others played draughts; we heard laughter and shouting; most were eating; next to one prisoner eating dry bread another was *carving a chicken* in a bowl of salad; wine flowed in torrents and every face was bright with cynical gaiety. It could have been taken for a feast given by Satan to his friends.[31]

---

* Mme. Perrot thinks not: '... it was not the prison which had changed, but the nature of the observation directed at it. The prisoners had ceased to be "unlucky", they were now "guilty". The time of rigour in the prison system had arrived' (OC IV i 10).

Elsewhere those who care to do so may find evidence of Oedipal conflict:

> Everywhere in France we see a strict and scrupulous philanthropy concerning itself with the material lot of prisoners. The report of the minister which we have just cited goes on at length about the quality of the soup served to inmates, about the stove-pipes by which the dormitories are kept warm in winter, and the footwear given to the inmates to keep them from the cold: important details, no doubt, but surely the concern of charitable organizations rather than that of a statesman?

Such was the spirit in which Tocqueville and Beaumont set out for America. They were not going to let philanthropy mar their prison investigations. They intended to be thoroughly statesmanlike observers.

For Tocqueville, whether at this date or years later, prison reform was never to be more than a secondary concern, a means to an end. In 1830–31 he knew exactly what he was up to. Charles Stoffels apparently expressed doubts about the wisdom of going to America, so Tocqueville explained himself in letters to both brothers:

> [*26 August.*] If I am forced to give up my career and if nothing requires me to stay in France, I have decided that I shall flee the idleness of private life and take up again for several years a traveller's restless existence. I have long wanted to visit North America. I shall go there to see what a great republic is like.

> [*4 October.*] Suppose that, without ceasing to be a magistrate and losing my rights of seniority, I go to America; fifteen months elapse. In France, meanwhile, parties will be articulating themselves; I will be able to see clearly which one is incompatible with the peace and greatness of the country; I shall come back with clear and settled opinions and free of all commitments to anybody. Only this journey can draw one up out of the common herd.

> [*21 February.*] Merely as a voyage, nothing could be more agreeable than the one we want to make. Bearing a public character, we will have the right to enquire into everything, and the *entrée* to all the best society. Furthermore, it's not just a matter of seeing big towns and beautiful rivers. We are going with the intention of examining in detail

and as scientifically as possible the entire scope of that vast American society which everybody talks about and nobody knows. And if our adventures leave us enough time, we rely on putting together the makings of a fine work, or of a new one at least – nothing has been published of this type.[32,33]

As the moment of departure drew near he began to wonder nervously if he was really doing the right thing, but as he wrote to Beaumont, who was down in the Sarthe saying goodbye to his family, 'When I calculate how unlikely are the dangers we fear [shipwreck? Indians?] and factor in our delicate position in France, where it is impossible for us to play any part whatever, it seems to me that we should applaud our decision and regret only that we did not carry it out sooner.'[34]

The ambition displayed in these remarks is no more striking than the acute judgement, and both are surpassed by the precision of Tocqueville's aim. Without having ever spoken to an American* or set foot on American soil he already begins to glimpse and sketch the masterpiece that was to be; and his self-confidence is equally evident – as Pierson has pointed out, it did not occur either to him or to Beaumont that such a work as they planned might be beyond their powers.[35] Finally, it is very evident that the prison investigation was indeed not Tocqueville's main preoccupation.

February and March 1831 were mostly given over to hectic preparations for the great journey. Tocqueville went shopping. Among other things he bought five pairs of boots and shoes: perhaps, like Mrs Trollope planning her 'bazaar' in Cincinnati, he underestimated the progress of American civilization.[36] He and Beaumont flew round Paris scrounging letters of introduction: they secured seventy in the end, although the biggest name of all, La Fayette, eluded them: he was never in when they called. We do not know the names of all the letter-writers. It is unlikely that Chateaubriand was one of them: his contacts with the US were too ancient to be useful.[37] Charles Lucas, the newly appointed inspector of prisons, sent them an official letter, decidedly cool in tone, making a long list of suggestions as to what

---

* In his old age, after Tocqueville's death, Jared Sparks wrote of having met him in Paris in 1828; but there is absolutely no corroboration for this statement anywhere, and it is intrinsically unlikely.

they should investigate, most of which they would ignore, but one of which anticipated what became one of Tocqueville's chief preoccupations: 'One thing which it is important to study and record is the development of the spirit of association for the improvement of prisons. This spirit does not exist in France, yet it is a necessary auxiliary for the Government; it must be organized and propagated here.'[38] Perhaps because they already distrusted Lucas, Tocqueville and Beaumont had their 'Note' on penitentiaries printed: it was a useful piece of advertising, would help their friends to defend their interests while they were away, and may have helped to elicit some of the letters of introduction. Abbé Le Sueur, who knew that he had not long to live and would probably never see Alexis again, gave him a little book of prayers and a last letter of good counsel: he had never abandoned the hope of reconciling his pupil to the Church. After warning him against the *philosophes* for the last time, he wrote: 'Adieu once more. I commit you and your kind companion to the care of Divine Providence. My wishes, my prayers and my blessing will go with you, everywhere.'[39] Tocqueville was painfully moved, although the citadel of his doubt remained unshaken.

Then it was time to be off. After an affectionate farewell to Kergorlay they left Paris for Le Havre on 29 March, accompanied by Tocqueville's father and brothers. They boarded ship on 2 April. Their vessel, *Le Havre*, missed the tide and hit a sandbank: they had to disembark and hang about the waterside all afternoon. *Mauvais présage*, but false. In the evening they went on board again, and soon after midnight Tocqueville went on deck to find that the ship was hurrying down-Channel, all sails stretched, and a fair wind at her back.[40]

CHAPTER EIGHT

A VOYAGE OUT

1831

Heureux qui comme Ulysse a fait un beau voyage.
JOACHIM DU BELLAY

TOCQUEVILLE WENT TO BED to be sea-sick, as he expected, for two days, while the east wind carried *Le Havre* out of the Channel, into the ocean. On the third day he felt better, and on the fourth was quite himself again. He was pleased to find that his fellow-passengers could not say the same: none of them emerged until the sixth day. The one exception was Beaumont, who was never sick at all; 'the natural order of things,' sighed his friend.[1] On the whole it was as good a start as might reasonably have been expected to a sea-journey which they greatly enjoyed. For one thing, it was fairly swift, by the standards of the day: they landed in the United States on 9 May, after thirty-seven days at sea. Other ships had been known to take a full two months, or even more. *Le Havre* – an American vessel, in spite of her name – was as stout as she was speedy: Tocqueville congratulated himself that there was no danger that she would capsize, as had so nearly happened to the ship on his Sicilian voyage, although at times they met weather that was just as rough: one storm blew for thirty-six hours. Real privacy was impossible on board: when Tocqueville and Beaumont went to bed while the other passengers were at supper, as they usually did, they fell asleep to the music of clashing cutlery and in all but full view of the diners. Meal times were enlivened by plates flying off the table, bottles and glasses smashing, and the constant danger of getting gravy poured down your neck. Our travellers rose cheerfully above all these inconveniences. Their one serious complaint was that though the food was good the cooking was atrocious, and by the last day of the voyage supplies were running dangerously low, the captain having apparently miscalculated his needs.

They enjoyed their company, partly on principle ('at sea, if you don't want to fight, you must be the best of friends'), partly out of natural amiability and high spirits. They were occasionally homesick, and would be from time to time throughout the rest of their journey; but the affliction, though acute (and Tocqueville pined for Marie) was intermittent. The chief note of all their letters home is an unmistakable gusto. So it was easy for them to like their fellow passengers; indeed, at times they seem to have been the life and soul of the passenger-deck. Beaumont, an enthusiastic musician, had brought his flute with him, and on one occasion played it to the young people on board (including Tocqueville) so that they could dance a quadrille. On another day a barrel was noticed floating on the sea and immediately became a target for pistol-practice: Tocqueville, though short-sighted, was the champion marksman who hit it. And one evening he straddled the bowsprit to enjoy the sensation of rushing and plunging through phosphorescent waves, 'a sight more wonderful, more sublime than I can describe'.[2]

A charming young American, Miss Edwards, gave them English lessons, for they had quickly discovered that they knew the language much less well than they had supposed. They made special friends of Charles Palmer, MP (a Whig, owner of the celebrated Bordeaux vineyard), and of the Schermerhorn family, rich New Yorkers: these new acquaintances took the greatest interest in the prison mission and were to be very useful to Tocqueville and Beaumont in New York. Tocqueville made his first notes about America: according to Mr Schermerhorn no-one there cared about anything but getting rich, and he thought that crime was increasing. He also made some surprising remarks about the economics of the American merchant marine.[3] One reason for all this friendliness was undoubtedly the extreme tedium of shipboard life: according to Tocqueville, most of the passengers distilled boredom drop by drop, as in an alembic. Tocqueville and Beaumont were immune to this complaint. They had work to do. They got up soon after five every morning and read together until breakfast, as they had at Versailles. They translated an English work on American prisons, read a history of the United States and studied Jean-Baptiste Say's *Cours d'économie politique*. As they worked, Beaumont's opinion of his friend rose higher and higher: 'Tocqueville is a really outstanding man; he is great in the loftiness of his ideas and in the nobility of his soul. The more I know him the more I love him.'[4] Their confidence about being able to produce a valuable book steadily increased.

Yet the difficulties of their project made themselves felt, if not apparent, as soon as they landed. Because of the contrary winds and the shortage of food *Le Havre* first docked at Newport, Rhode Island, instead of New York, on the afternoon of 9 May. Next day Tocqueville and Beaumont, weary of the vagaries of sail, trans-shipped to the *President*, a huge steamboat which took them down Long Island Sound to Manhattan. They did not spend many hours in Newport, though Beaumont, whose accomplishments included sketching, did a nice little drawing of the church tower; but he saw fit to write to his mother that the women were amazingly ugly and that the Americans were a wholly commercial people: 'in the little town of Newport alone there are four or five banks. It is the same in all the towns of the Union.'[5] He had yet to learn not to jump to conclusions.

Tocqueville was vastly impressed by the size and speed of the *President*, but not by the Connecticut shore, wholly deforested at that period. In the early morning, however, they entered the East River and he was as delighted, even in that age before skyscrapers, as all must be who approach New York by sea:

> we cried out in admiration on seeing the outskirts of the town. Imagine shapely banks, their slopes covered with lawns, flowers and trees right to the water's edge; and more than that, countless country-houses, no bigger than chocolate-boxes [*bonbonnières*] but excellently crafted. Further imagine, if you can, a sea covered with sails, and you have the entry to New York from the Sound.[6]

He thought he might get the plan of a chocolate-box for his sister-in-law Émilie: she might like to build one on the Nacqueville estate.

They reached the Battery, the southern tip of Manhattan, at about noon, and with some difficulty found a suitable boarding-house, at 66 Broadway: it happened that Mr Palmer was staying there too. They went to bed, exhausted, at four in the afternoon, and slept until eight o'clock in the morning; and then the fun began.

It immensely flattered the New Yorkers to learn from their morning papers that the French government had sent an official mission to study their famous prison system with a view to improving its own. The American character was then an all-too-human mixture of conceit (which Tocqueville immediately detected) and anxiety. Americans were equally sensitive to praise and blame, which latter was and would be heaped upon them by the British, who were always hinting (if that is the word) that the ex-colonists were, alas, mere insignificant provincials: 'Who reads an American book?' asked Sydney Smith. The arrival of Tocqueville and Beaumont was therefore amazingly welcome. Mr Schermerhorn and his family vouched for the good character of the visitors and led the way in offering them all possible help, especially in the matter of dinner invitations. Mr Palmer was equally assiduous. They were the sensation of the hour, and Beaumont foresaw that soon they would have to deny their door to eager visitors. Somewhat to their surprise (it was one of the things they had not thought of) New York had a smart society which took them up enthusiastically; Tocqueville tried to persuade himself that this was a good way of learning about the country. However, he had not come well-equipped for balls, routs and evening parties: he wrote to his brother Édouard asking urgently for silk stockings, cravats, and two dozen pairs of kid gloves – indispensable for evening wear (American ones were far too expensive and ill-made).[7]

They tried to keep their heads, but it was a fearful struggle. The danger was not that they would become conceited and believe their own publicity, but that their success would make serious observation and reflection impossible. During the first fortnight they poured out their thoughts in their letters home, and in a few scribbled notes, and it is easy to see, in what has survived,* that they were thoroughly bewildered.

---

* One of AT's notebooks and all of Beaumont's are lost, except for fragments; the same is true of most of AT's letters to Marie and Kergorlay.

One of their problems was that America seemed even less like France than they had expected; another was that the differences often lay in surprising areas. Thus, it was astonishing that neither citizens nor public officials seemed to have any idea of the deference due to rank: on their third day in New York they were presented to the governor of the state, Enos Throop, who was staying in a boarding-house just as they were themselves, and thought it quite natural to receive the foreigners in the parlour; he would shake hands with anyone, they were told.[8] (They were not told that Mr Throop was in the city to attend the annual banquet of Tammany Hall, or that he was a member of the Albany Regency: these redolent names as yet meant nothing to them.) A Bostonian wrote to President Andrew Jackson, offering him a tortoiseshell comb of American manufacture: his letter was printed in a newspaper, and began simply 'Dear Sir', to Tocqueville's astonishment.[9] American national vanity was also disconcerting. In a desperate attempt to make some sort of sense of their impressions, they filled their letters with rash generalizations based on little evidence and no experience (a trait which Tocqueville was never entirely to throw off). American Protestants, they said, well understood the 'necessity' of religious dogma. American women were all chaste, partly because American men were too busy for sex. Americans on the whole were disagreeably vulgar, but they were all well-educated and hard-working: there were no idle 'fashionables' (Tocqueville used the English word). Political parties were unknown in the United States. Gastronomy was in its infancy; so were the fine arts.[10]

They did better when they recorded the incidents of their life in New York. One evening they found a church open, but there was nobody in it except a few people praying. The door to the tower was also open, so up they climbed:

> At last, after much trouble, we arrived at the top and enjoyed a wonderful sight: that of a town of 240,000 inhabitants built on an island bordered on one side by the Ocean, on the other by vast rivers on which could be seen a multitude of ships and barges. The port is of an immense size. The public buildings are few and on the whole unimpressive.[11]

One day the mayor, the aldermen, and, it seemed, every public official in New York turned up in five carriages to take them on a tour of the city's prisons, workhouse, deaf-and-dumb asylum and madhouse, with a banquet halfway through. At the banquet Beaumont was chiefly alarmed lest he be compelled to drink a toast to La Fayette, the Hero of Two Worlds, whom his young cousin regarded as a dangerous revolutionary (he did not foresee that one day he would marry one of La Fayette's granddaughters).[12] Tocqueville was distressed at the idea of drinking toasts at all, for everyone present (some two dozen officials) wanted to take a glass of wine with the Frenchmen:

> We were just like hares with a pack of hounds at their heels ... But at the third glass I decided never to take more than a sip, and so I got successfully enough to what we in France call the end of the meal but which here is merely the end of the first act; most of the plates having been removed lighted candles are brought and you are offered suitably enough a clean plate bearing cigars. Each of us took one,* the party enveloped itself in a cloud of smoke, the toasts began, muscles relaxed somewhat, and we gave ourselves up to the heaviest merriment possible.

He could not help smiling to himself when he remembered how insignificant the guests of honour were in their own country. But renown had its downside. Even ladies at the dinner-table thought it their duty to make suitable remarks about hangings and lock-ups before allowing the conversation to turn to more commonplace subjects.[13]

None of this contributed much to their purposes in America. As time would show, they were excellently equipped to interpret the country (their English rapidly improved) but at first they could not make head or tail of it. They did not know where to begin, and clutched desperately at any clue – for instance, the notion which Mr Schermerhorn first put into their heads, that the Americans were no more than a nation of shopkeepers. Tocqueville grumbled to his father that there was far more in the newspapers about the price of cotton than about great political questions.[14] He could not have chosen a worse example. Though he did not yet see it, the price of cotton was itself a great political question. Cotton was far and away America's greatest export, underpinning its prosperity and earning the credit and hard

---

* AT had not yet developed the allergy to tobacco which afflicted him in middle age.

currency which, reinvested, financed the industrial revolution that would one day make the United States the world's greatest power. Meanwhile cotton sustained the regime of plantation slavery that in exactly thirty years' time would plunge America into civil war. Cotton made a mockery of the country's claims to liberty and democracy, and among the merchants of New York there were men who would have insisted on this to Tocqueville, had he met them: the Tappan brothers, for example, the bankers of the reviving abolitionist movement.* And cotton, by stimulating an intense political battle over the tariff, played its part in establishing the two-party system.

There was wisdom in Kergorlay's observation, made in the first letter which Tocqueville in America received from him, that to understand a place you had to live in it for at least two months.[15] Instead, during his first two and a half weeks in New York, Tocqueville clung to his stereotype, in which there was not a little snobbery. He did not even recognize that he was also stereotyping his own country. Lurking behind his generalizations at this stage, one might say, was the implication that in France everyone spent the nights in adultery and the days in revolutionary politics, and no-one cared about money. He would have been furious had anyone pointed this out, but it was implicit in what he was saying – he, the countryman of Balzac! He and Beaumont were at risk of succumbing to a version of the prejudices which did so much to injure the observations that English writers made of America – Mrs Trollope, Basil Hall, Charles Dickens.

They were saved from superficiality by the prison mission. It required them to make systematic investigations, which was excellent training for their larger enquiry; and it kept their attention firmly directed to American actualities. They spent long mornings at a public library wrestling with statistics of all kinds, which furthered both investigations,[16] and on 26 May they set out on a visit to the celebrated penitentiary at Sing-Sing, thirty miles up the Hudson. The trip lasted for ten days, and proved extremely useful. Not only did they make a thorough study of one of America's most famous jails, but they escaped from the incessant socializing which overwhelmed them in New York, and found time to think systematically. They were

* Eventually AT and GB met two of the Tappans in Boston.

in holiday mood. The Hudson valley was extremely beautiful, rural and peaceful; though perhaps too civilized: Tocqueville wished that he could have arrived with the first Europeans, when the shores were covered with wild forest. The American family with whom they lodged were as friendly and hospitable as everyone else. They visited the prison by day and lounged on the river-bank in the evening until it was cool enough to go indoors (by now they had discovered how appalling the heat and humidity of an American summer can be). Tocqueville took the opportunity to give Beaumont swimming lessons: it would never do if Gustave fell off a steamboat into one of the dangerous American rivers and was unable to help himself. Beaumont wrote a mock diploma congratulating Tocqueville on the improvement of his manners: he was now polite to old women as well as young ones, and prepared to pretend pleasure in the piano-playing of ladies who had neither looks nor skill nor talent. Beaumont certified all this, and then, giving in to one of the sentimental impulses that recurred throughout his life, added: 'since I am by way of handing out certificates, I further attest that the said Alexis is the best friend that Earth can furnish; and, he being mine, I am very happy to have him.'[17]

Their most practical concern was the penitentiary. They were well-prepared for this, having read Basil Hall's description, and much documentation. What they found was what they expected: a grim prison where a regime of hard labour and absolute silence was imposed on the prisoners by the free use of whips. The commissioners were deeply impressed by the experiment: 900 hardened villains were controlled by a mere thirty men; the convicts were trusted with tools, such as pick-axes, that could easily become weapons, yet they were not even chained while they laboured (their labour consisted of extracting stone from a quarry and using it to build their own prison). But Tocqueville was not convinced that the experiment was as yet proved a success. It had only been going for a few years, and might suddenly blow up at any moment, like one of those other wonderful American machines, the river steamboats. He noticed the apprehensiveness of the guards – 'Their eyes never stopped moving.' And he could get no confident affirmation that Sing-Sing contributed to the moral reform of the prisoners, which was the main point so far as he was concerned. He and Beaumont reserved their judgement until they had seen other

examples of 'the Auburn system', as it was called after the penitentiary at Auburn in western New York state where the system was first
installed.[18] They would be going there by and by.

Sing-Sing gave them a wonderful opportunity to take stock, as
was highly necessary: it was now two full months since they had left
France. Tocqueville seized his chance, both in his notebook and in a
letter home to his father; but although it cannot be proved, probably
it was in his conversations with Beaumont that he did the hard work
of clarifying his ideas. The friends were together every hour of the
twenty-four, fascinated by all they saw, sharing the same particular
interests, and (so far as we can judge) invariably coming to the same
conclusions. What they wrote down was simply the outcome of their
discussions.

Read in this light, their papers show that they were slowly getting
to grips with the dimensions of their task. Tocqueville wrote to his
father:

> Since arriving, we have had only one idea: that is, to understand the
> country that we are visiting. To do that, we find ourselves forced to
> deconstruct [*decomposer*] society *a priori*, to investigate the elements
> which make it up at home in France, so that we can ask useful
> questions here and overlook nothing. This study, very difficult but
> very attractive, shows us a host of details which would be hidden
> in the mass, failing such analysis, and suggests a host of questions
> which would otherwise never have occurred to us. This our labour
> has already resulted in a series of questions to which we ceaselessly
> search for answers. Knowing precisely what we want to find out, our
> least conversation is instructive, and we can affirm that no man, at
> any level of society, can't teach us something.[19]

Tocqueville is becoming a true sociologist, and the method he sketches
here was to be applied throughout the rest of his journey through
America.

It got its first airing during their return journey to New York. They
paid a courtesy call on a member of the Livingston family (research
has failed to decide which) in his country-house on the banks of the
Hudson, and while they waited for the steamboat which was to take
them down river Tocqueville raised a question arising from his observations: 'To my mind, one of the drawbacks of American society is the

general lack of intellectual activity.' Mr Livingston quite agreed, and put this deficiency down to the post-Revolutionary laws of inheritance, which by abolishing entail and primogeniture were destroying the upper class, especially the gentry of the Hudson valley to which he belonged. Tocqueville was familiar with this idea, which he had already met in Basil Hall, who may have got it from the same Mr Livingston;[20] since he was well aware how important primogeniture had been to the French *noblesse* before 1789 it was very attractive to him, and would one day find its way into *De la démocratie en Amérique*; but for the present it is more important to register the fact that this was the first extensive conversation with an American that he felt confident enough to record at length; he got up early next day in order to do so.[21]

They passed three more weeks in New York city, devoting their working hours chiefly to the House of Refuge, a detention centre for young offenders, and their evenings to high society. This was a mixed blessing, had they but known it. Their youth, their charm, their important mission and, not least, their noble status* made them exceedingly welcome to the old elite of New York, the Knickerbocker families; so they were invited to dinner parties, and picnics, and a night-time wedding-reception in the open air where Tocqueville was delighted by the fireflies and Beaumont made up to the beautiful daughter of Robert Fulton, the inventor of the steamboat.[22] These activities provided plenty of material for lively letters home (Tocqueville devoted much paper to denouncing what he called the *musique miaulante* played at these parties: unfortunately he gives no indication of what it was and who wrote it)[23] but they were dangerously misleading for serious students of the United States. Peter Schermerhorn and his friends were Federalists: relics, that is to say, of America's first conservative party, which had disintegrated and disappeared after the War of 1812. They had given up the competition for political power in the raw and raucous America of the early nineteenth century; in fact they were, as Denis Brogan once pointed out, *émigrés de l'intérieur*, like Tocqueville and Beaumont's relations and friends in France after 1830. They retained and vigorously expressed their anti-democratic opinions,

---

* Americans were so impressed by the noble *particule* and so unaware of French usage that they almost invariably referred to AT as 'De Tocqueville' until after the Second World War; and the practice has not entirely died out, even today.

which the commissioners eagerly solicited and carefully recorded – for example, the view that while republicanism was the only possible form of government for America, it would never do for a great European country such as France. This chimed with Tocqueville and Beaumont's prejudices, as did Mr Livingston's remarks about the inheritance laws, and they were not yet in a position to see that the views of, say, James Kent, the great Federalist lawyer, were as partial a guide to Jacksonian America as the views of the comte de Kergorlay or Beaumont's father would have been to the France of Louis-Philippe.

One of their blunders was entirely self-inflicted. When planning their journey they had resolved to have nothing to do with women in the way of sex (polite or even flattering attention at dances was another matter). This was not easy for either of them, but they were proud of their success in keeping their vow: Tocqueville wrote to Édouard, 'Can you believe, *mon cher ami*, that since our arrival in America we have practised *the austerest virtue*. Not the slightest swerve. Monks – I ought to say, good monks – could not have done more.' They meant to keep to the rule for the rest of their journey, since American married women were so virtuous that complete ruin would punish them if they fell, and seducing young girls was more trouble than it was worth; anyway the pressure of work was such as to make the commissioners less inclined than usual to fall into sin.[24] It will be seen that Tocqueville is here applying to himself his contention that in America men were too busy for love; but the best comment is that of Jardin and Pierson, who remark that the resolution to live like monks 'perhaps entailed a lacuna in their study of American manners'.[25] Indeed it did: if Tocqueville and Beaumont ever had a serious conversation with an American woman, no record of it survives. Jardin and Pierson also point out that prostitution throve in the cities of Jacksonian America, including New York, which makes Tocqueville's obstinate belief in the chastity of American women, and for that matter in the sexual apathy of American men, all the more bizarre (but he was evidently thinking of women of his own social class).

It would be easy to go through Tocqueville's other observations at this point of his travels and demonstrate his mistakes, but the impression left by his letters and notes of June 1831 is rather of brilliant insight. Perhaps none of the particular points he makes is original in itself, but he makes of them altogether something startlingly new and suggestive, and by the time he writes to Kergorlay, on the day of his departure from New York city, he has found, and knows he has found, what will be the theme of his book:

> We are travelling towards unlimited democracy, I don't say that this is a good thing, what I see in this country convinces me on the contrary that it won't suit France; but we are driven by an irresistible force. No effort made to stop this movement will do more than bring about brief halts.[26]

This is the grand Tocquevillean doctrine. It is significant that he discovered it while again reflecting on the consequences of abolishing primogeniture and entail.

On 30 June he and Beaumont left New York, having spent nearly seven weeks there (except for the excursion to Sing-Sing). It had been an excellent introduction to the United States, and even Kergorlay might have thought it long enough; it was time to move on. The commonplace that New York isn't America has never been true, but the city is only part of the country and to understand its position in the United States it is necessary to explore the hinterland. Besides, the commissioners had exhausted New York's resources as a place for prison research; now they headed for Auburn, the first and most famous American penitentiary. They did not hurry: they meant to savour the beauties of the Hudson, look in at the spa of Saratoga Springs where some of their smart friends threatened to join them, and then go to Albany to study the state government. None of these plans turned out quite as they expected. They missed Saratoga altogether, for after a pleasant day at Yonkers (where Tocqueville took out his gun and slaughtered birds, while Beaumont sketched) and another at a tiny place called Colwells (or Colwell's)[27] they boarded a steamboat in the evening which, they found, was racing another one to Albany and would stop nowhere on the way, not even at West Point, which they had much wanted to see. At Albany they were warmly welcomed in the usual way and were made to take a prominent part in a grand parade on the Fourth of July; they were given all the official papers which they asked for (Tocqueville told his father that he would have to buy a trunk to get his documents home) but they were baffled in their researches by the unexpected fact that the state government seemed hardly to exist. They had letters of introduction to the local Congressman, Churchill C. Cambreleng, and although no conversation is recorded, it seems unlikely that they were unaware that in the House of Representatives he was a leading supporter of the Jackson administration. Beaumont found him 'positive and practical', and he introduced them to Azariah C. Flagg, the Secretary of State at Albany. Perhaps the encounter with Cambreleng made them aware for the first time that there was an active national government in this strange country; and they had seen for themselves the vigorous municipal administration of New York city. But in spite of Mr Flagg's best efforts they could not see that there was anything in between. Governor Throop was so badly paid that he had to spend half the year working his farm;* there did not seem to be much for him to do in the other six months, and soon they would be told that no able men wanted to go into the state government since it was so easy to make a fortune by other means.[28]

From the scientific point of view it was an unlucky visit. One of the weaknesses of *De la démocratie en Amérique* is its inadequate treatment of political parties, and this blemish might have been avoided had Tocqueville realized that a great discovery was waiting to be made at Albany. The so-called Albany Regency was at its height. The Regency was the name given in derision to the faction led by Martin Van Buren which dominated the politics of New York for twenty years or so. Not only that, but Van Buren had successfully applied his influence and organizational skills to the project of electing Andrew Jackson President of the United States, and in the process had in partnership with Jackson founded what soon became the Democratic party. American society had been pregnant with mass party politics almost since the ratification of the Constitution; Van Buren had been one of the chief midwives at the birth, and during his travels Tocqueville met several men – Throop, Cambreleng, Flagg, eventually Jackson himself – who could have shown him what was going on had he happened to ask the right questions. He did not do so, being blinded by his French and elitist preconceptions, which had been reinforced by what his New

---

* This, according to Tocqueville. He was apparently unaware that Throop was also a successful lawyer.

York friends had told him: that party politics was at an end, having been replaced by a mere vulgar scramble for office.[29] So he missed one of the universally important innovations which the America of his age was making.

The commissioners continued to do best as witnesses and recorders of the American scene. Almost against their will they were deeply impressed by the Fourth of July ceremonies. 'I would like to give you a precise idea of this spectacle,' Tocqueville wrote to Chabrol:

> in which vulgar, even burlesque details were mixed with a noble theme and managed to touch the heart. In the front row marched the militia: that is, the National Guard of this country, a country where the military spirit is absolutely unknown; you can imagine what a goose each honest citizen made of himself: the martial turnout was really ridiculous. Then came several carriages, bearing veterans who had served in the war of independence and seen the triumph of the American cause. The notion of associating with the ceremony these witnesses of the great events of which it was evoking the memory was an extremely good one.

Then the workingmen and their trade associations marched past, and the whole company assembled in a church, where a platform had been set up.

> With my French notions I expected that the Governor of the State, or the municipal officers, would sit there. Instead, they set up the banners of the trades and the standard of the County, which had been carried in the war of the Revolution, and in the middle of it all were the old officers I mentioned previously.[30]

Beaumont put a comic emphasis on the fact that two very distinguished visitors marched at the head of the procession between the governor and the chancellor ('*Tocqueville et moi*'). He went on:

> There was nothing brilliant about the occasion; for splendour it could not have borne the slightest comparison with the least of our political or religious solemnities. But there was something great in its simplicity … Nothing could be easier than to make fun of the standards we saw inscribed *Associated Butchers, Association of Apprentices*, etc.*But if you

* The last act of *Die Meistersinger* comes to mind.

stop to think about it, what could be more natural than these emblems among a people who owe their prosperity to trade and industry?

He reported the speeches in the church and the reading out of the Declaration of Independence, but he was most impressed by the fact that the first item on the programme was a prayer: 'I mention this, because it is characteristic of this country where nothing is done without religious assistance. I don't think that things go the worse for it.' He was more impressed by the whole than by any ceremony he had ever seen in France.[31]

Religion was much in the commissioners' minds. The day before (3 July) they had visited the Shakers, whose oldest settlement was nearby. The ceremony they watched seemed to them utterly bizarre, and they both wrote long letters home describing it, too long, unfortunately, to be extensively quoted. The Shakers danced, the Shakers preached, then after two hours formed a single circle, men and women together:

> They tucked their elbows into their sides while sticking out their forearms and dangling their hands, so that they looked like dogs trained to walk on their hind-legs. Thus prepared, they intoned an air more lamentable than any before and began to revolve round the room, an exercise which lasted for a good quarter of an hour ... do you see, my dear Mamma, into what aberrations the human soul can fall when it is left to itself? We had a young American Protestant with us, and he said as we came out, 'Two more such displays and I'll become a Catholic.'[32]

This was the most formidable challenge yet posed by American Protestantism, and Tocqueville's sympathies were not equal to it, as is shown by, among other things, his disdain of the music, which may have included the famous Shaker hymn ('To turn, turn, will be our delight, Till by turning, turning, we come round right.') The fact is that Tocqueville had spent all his life in Catholic countries, and did not realize how profoundly Catholic he was himself, and what that could mean, until he went to America. The shock was enormous, for until then his knowledge of Protestantism was almost wholly theoretical. In New York he went to Protestant churches and discovered to his horror that the preachers dealt only with morality and said nothing about dogma. He was glad to hear, and eager to believe, that Catholicism was rapidly gaining ground in the United States, as indeed it was; he was not so pleased to discover that Unitarianism was also advancing strongly. Unitarians were theists, like himself, but his creed had a strong Catholic colouring; Unitarians seemed to him nothing but atheists in disguise, and deplorably unsentimental. At least they were logical. He could not see the logic of ordinary Protestantism at all, and felt this so strongly that he committed himself to the view that Protestantism was dying out, and in so doing was preparing the ground for a final collision between unbelief and Catholicism.[33] On the other hand, he and Beaumont were both deeply impressed by the fact that American republicans saw religion as an essential support to democracy and liberty.

They left Albany on the evening of 4 July and two days later reached Syracuse. It was their first American journey by land of any length, and entailed vile roads, worse inns and bone-shaking vehicles. They noted the discomfort, but no more: they were falling under the enchantment of the forest, which hemmed the road in on either side, and which they were now experiencing for the first time:

> I think that in one of my letters I complained that there were no more woods in America; I must now make the *amende honorable*. Not only do we see one wood after another in America, the whole country is nothing but one vast forest, in the middle of which they have made clearings. If you climb a church-tower you see nothing up to the edge of sight but tree-tops bending in the wind like waves of the sea; everything attests a new country. What they call *défricher* in this country [it is not clear what English term Tocqueville had in mind] is to cut off a tree three feet from the ground. Once this operation is complete, you till and sow alongside. The result is that in the midst of the finest crops you see hundreds of dead trunks of old trees encumbering the soil ... But if the country is new, one observes at every step that the people which is settling it is old. When, by a frightful road across a sort of wilderness, you arrive at a cabin, you are astonished to find a civilization more advanced than in any French village. The attire of the farmer is trim; his cabin is perfectly clean; usually you see at his side his newspaper, and his first wish is to talk politics with you.[34]

This is a striking passage, and is not less interesting when compared with one in Basil Hall's book, published two years previously, which we know that Tocqueville read:

> ... an Englishman might fancy himself in the vale of Stroud. But, mark the difference: at the next crack of the whip ... he is again in the depths of the wood at the other extremity of civilized society, with the world just beginning to bud, in the shape of a smoky log-hut, ten feet by twelve, filled with dirty-faced children, squatted round a hardy-looking female, cooking victuals for a tired woodsman seated at his door, reading with suitable glee in the *Democratic Journal of New York*, an account of Mr Canning's campaign against the Ultra Tories of the old country.

The question of plagiarism does not arise: Tocqueville was writing a letter to his mother. We can make a good guess as to what happened. Tocqueville read Hall, who alerted him to what he should look out for. (Something of the same sort may have happened in his conversation with Mr Livingston.) The significant thing is what Hall notices and Tocqueville does not, and the two men's contradicting attitudes. Hall was not a lively writer, but he was a capable draughtsman, who carried a *camera lucida* with him and put it to good use in his sketching; he had a painter's eye. So did Beaumont. As a result their reports of America contain somewhat more striking detail than Tocqueville's. Tocqueville was certainly observant, but, more than the others, he was always more interested in analysis than in reportage.

He was consciously using his letters home as notes towards a book. He put into them whatever he found interesting or important, whether he discovered it himself or took it from someone else, even from Basil Hall, of whose intense unpopularity in the United States he was probably aware.* Hall's Tory opinions and, still more, that painter's eye for squalid detail infuriated his American readers and former hosts, who felt that they had been betrayed. So Tocqueville, while he appropriated Hall, took care to correct him where he saw cause: for instance, the log-cabins which he saw were clean and their inhabitants decent; he took pains to say so. Where Hall thought that the settlers in the forest were the dregs of civilization, Tocqueville

---

* AT got to know Hall in person after his return to Europe. Hall eventually published a deeply respectful review of the *Démocratie*.

thought that they embodied its triumph, and it can hardly be disputed that in this he showed superior insight. Here is an early example of the qualities which were to make the *Démocratie* so unusual among European commentaries on pre-Civil War America.

He and Beaumont arrived at Syracuse on 6 July. They had important business there – interviewing Elam Lynds, formerly governor of the Auburn and Sing-Sing prisons – and undertook it as conscientiously as usual; but only a few hours' ride to the north lay Lake Oneida, and it was simply impossible for Tocqueville to leave that sacred spot unvisited. So on their journey from Syracuse to Auburn (which they began on 7 July) they made a detour.

The forest, the lake, the island all lived up to Tocqueville's most romantic expectations, but as he was still under the delusion that the refugee tale was history, not fiction, he saw what he wanted to see, not what was in front of him: a desolate refuge of love, not a failed homestead which the settler family had abandoned after two years for a profitable market-garden near Albany:

> Left Syracuse at 2. Horseback. Umbrella, gun, game-bag ... Reached Fort Brewerton at six o'clock. Had a look round. The forest wars for ever against Man. Shot some birds. View of Lake Oneida. It stretches out of sight eastward between low wooded hills. Not a house or a clearing to be seen. Lonely, monotonous scenery. We slept in a detestable inn. Left at 6 in the morning. We plunged into an immense forest where the path was hard to follow. Delicious coolness. A wonderful sight, impossible to describe. Astonishing vegetation. Enormous trees of every kind. A *jungle*, grasses, plants, bushes. America in all her glory.[35]

Presently they reached a fisherman's cabin on the lakeside, in full view of the Frenchman's Island (still so called today). There was no-one at home but an old woman. She was the first of the common people of America, *les petits gens*, and the first woman, that Tocqueville talked to, or at any rate the first whose remarks he thought worth writing down. She answered his questions politely, but unintentionally fed his misapprehensions (never having met a tourist before, she could not imagine why he was interested in Frenchman's Island). Yes, a Frenchman once lived there – thirty-one or thirty-five years ago – before her time. Yes, he had had a wife – but she had died there (this was incorrect). It was all quite enough for Tocqueville and Beaumont. They borrowed a boat, rowed to the island, and spent some happy hours exploring it, looking in vain for traces of the refuge of their 'unhappy compatriots', such as the exiled lady's tomb. The best they could find was a half-dead apple-tree and a vine run wild. They wrote their names on the trunk of a pine-tree and came away; that evening Tocqueville confided to his notebook, 'this excursion has moved and interested me more powerfully, not merely than anything since I came to America, but anything since I first went travelling.'[36] Later he worked up his rough notes into an elegant piece of travel-writing like his Sicilian journal. It is somewhat *larmoyant* in style, and of psychological interest only: 'Not without regret I saw fall behind that vast rampart of leaves which had for so many years defended two exiles against the bullet of the European and the arrow of the savage, but which had not been able to hide their cottage from the invisible attack of Death.'[37]

Next day they reached Auburn, and immediately got back to their business. Their meeting with Elam Lynds in Syracuse had profoundly impressed them. Lynds, not to mince words, was a sadistic bully, of an American type all too familiar today from films and novels about the US Marines in the Second World War, and recent outrages in the prisons at Guantanamo and Abu Ghraib. He was the effective midwife of the Auburn system, which had emerged by trial and error after the founding of the prison in 1817. He was three times driven from the governorships of Auburn and Sing-Sing for gross cruelty.[38] When Tocqueville and Beaumont met him he was between engagements and running a hardware shop. They were somewhat wary of him, for they knew that he had enemies, and must have known why. Tocqueville, characteristically, observed that he had a common appearance, used vulgar language and couldn't spell. Lynds, he thought, had a markedly despotic streak. But the commissioners were won over by his intelligence and energy (so much so that they eventually published their conversation with him in the *Système pénitentiaire*).[39] Besides, he told them what they wanted to hear: that the penitentiary system could work anywhere, including France; that plentiful use of the whip was in the end the most humane form of discipline ('it is necessary to be pitiless and just'); that prisoners were cowards, over whom a determined warder could establish irresistible authority; and that prison labour was, or could be made, valuable to the convicts and to society, and could bring in enough money to make an important contribution to meeting the costs of the prison system. Furthermore, Lynds had limited but apparently realistic expectations of the degree to which penitentiaries could reform characters and reduce recidivism; he poured scorn on theorists and mere philanthropists. Lynds, in fact, was the complete representative of the Auburn system, whose philosophy was that 'The great end and design of the criminal law, is the prevention of crimes, through fear of punishment; the reformation of offenders being a minor consideration.'[40] These ends were to be attained, under the Auburn system, by isolating the prisoners from each other at night and whipping them to work in absolute silence, as at Sing-Sing, during the day. Tocqueville and Beaumont were not prepared to give up all hope of turning criminals into honest citizens in prison, but it is easy to see why Lynds had such an effect on them.[41]

Yet they arrived at Auburn determined to test his ideas thoroughly, and did so successfully by, for example interrogating the supervisors of the comb-shop, the stone-cutting shop, the tool-shop, the shoemaking shop, the cooper shop, the weavers' shop and the blacksmith's shop. As a result they finally decided, as Tocqueville told Chabrol, that the penitentiary system was indeed practicable in France – 'but keep that to yourself; we don't want to seem to have made up our minds.'[42] They had thus completed an important stage in their prison mission. Their next encounter would be an equally important incident in their political investigations. They travelled on westward to visit John Spencer of Canandaigua.

Spencer was the most congenial American they had met so far. He was the sort of man they both wanted to be: the most eminent lawyer in western New York, a leading politician (eventually he was to serve in President Tyler's cabinet, first as Secretary of War and then as Secretary of the Treasury) and a distinguished legal writer. He lived in a comfortable house on a beautiful lake, and he had a pair of blue-eyed daughters who were beautiful too. By this time Tocqueville and Beaumont were feeling the strain of their monastic resolve: 'our virtue is still intact,' Tocqueville told Chabrol, 'but we are beginning to stare at women with an impudence which hardly suits representatives of the Penitentiary System.' Beaumont was particularly taken with Mary

Spencer, and being unable to have any secrets from his family told his mother that Miss Spencer had 'that pink and white complexion that you sometimes see in Englishwomen and that is almost unknown in France'; but he made haste to add reassuringly that they were about to leave Canandaigua and would never return. The long morning conversations with their host had much more permanent consequences. They ranged over American state legislatures, the utility of two chambers rather than one, American lawyers, American press freedom, religious toleration, the poor laws, education and universal suffrage. On all these matters Spencer was as judicious as he was well-informed, and his influence was to leave deep traces on the *Démocratie* (of which he would be the first American publisher). He was even able to suggest fruitful comparisons between conditions in America and in France. Tocqueville was delighted.[43]

They left Canandaigua on 19 July, intending to travel to Buffalo, Niagara Falls and thence, by way of Lake Ontario, to Canada. It was a regular tourist trip, as they had discovered,[44] and the fact that they intended to take it suggests that they felt a need for rest from penitentiaries and politics: they were ready for a lark. And the further west they went in New York state the more conscious they became that they had a wonderful opportunity to experience and study a great historical movement, quite as interesting as anything else which they were likely to encounter. America (to use M. Rémond's useful distinction) was beginning to thrust the United States somewhat into the shade.

Ever since the end of the War of 1812 hundreds of thousands of emigrants from New England had been pouring into and across the Burned-Over District. Tocqueville and Beaumont were too intelligent not to notice the great movement going on all round them, and they wanted to understand it. Besides, it impinged directly on two of their preoccupations: Indians and wilderness. Like all Europeans, they were fascinated by the idea of Indians, and were agog for their first sight of them. When it came it was shocking. Just before they reached Syracuse they saw a knot of the once-proud Oneida nation begging in the dirt; and when they came to Buffalo they saw a young Indian man lying dead drunk in the road, being kicked by his woman in an angry attempt to wake him up or, if that failed, to punish him. Tocqueville and Beaumont were afraid he might die of drink or exposure, but nobody, Indian or American, would do anything for him, so reluctantly they left him to his fate. 'I don't think I have ever been more disappointed,' wrote Tocqueville next day (he was now beginning to keep a sort of journal). 'I was full of memories of M. de Chateaubriand and of Cooper, and in the natives of America I expected to see savages in whose faces Nature had nevertheless left the mark of some of those lofty virtues which beget the spirit of liberty.' He thought to see bodies developed in hunting and warfare 'which would lose nothing by nakedness'. Instead they were ugly, dirty and drunk.[45]

On the next day the commissioners walked about Buffalo ('Pretty shops. French goods') and slightly modified their first impressions of the Indians: 'Some of them have a look of our peasants – with a savage tint however – a Sicilian tint. Not an Indian woman tolerable.'[46] Their curiosity revived. Their first plan had been to go from Buffalo to Niagara, but they had a hankering for the wild, the untamed West, which had receded before them ever since they left Albany; and now on the dockside at Buffalo they found a small steamboat, the *Ohio*, bound for Detroit. Obeying an impulse which they had previously acknowledged to nobody but themselves, they booked a passage on her: it would only take a day or two, they were told.

It was an uncomfortable voyage. Nobody knew who they were, so for the first time in America they were treated with no more consideration than anyone else, let alone deference. It rained all the time, and Lake Erie was so large and turbulent that Tocqueville was seasick again. The journey took twice the time they had been promised ('Quarrel with the captain'), but at last the weather cleared, and they approached Detroit in the afternoon of 22 July. Nearby, across the narrow eastern channel of the river, was the Canadian shore and the settlement of Fort Malden, looking, in Tocqueville's opinion, like a Norman village. On the bank stood a British soldier, 'in that uniform which the field of Waterloo has made so famous' – a Scottish Highlander, kilt and all. On the water, to the left of the ship, was a birch-bark canoe with two naked Indians aboard, fishing; their skins were gaudily painted, and they had rings through their noses.[47]

Tocqueville was enchanted by this contrast between savagery and civilization, but he was not yet in a position to understand its tragic symbolism. The Indians and the Highlander were the doorkeepers of a ghost world, once living; what Richard White has taught us to call the Middle Ground.[48] Its fate had been settled in the long wars waged in the forty years between the outbreak of the American Revolution and the battle of New Orleans; like its great forests it was condemned, and waiting for execution at the hands of the Yankee pioneers; but for a moment it could still be discovered, and Tocqueville had arrived at that moment. Detroit was the heart of the *pays d'en haut*, the back country of the former colony of New France; the region where, for nearly two centuries, empires, tribes and villages had bloodily rivalled each other for control of the trade in beaver fur; where peoples mingled and cultures changed each other; the domain of Onontio, as the Indians named the French governor of Quebec (they called themselves his children). In the next three weeks Tocqueville and Beaumont would visit some of the domain's most important places: Saginaw, Sault Sainte-Marie, Michilimackinac, Green Bay; they travelled deep into the past, but they never lost the sense that they would soon return to the present, where the Middle Ground was doomed.

'We were curious to see entirely savage country,' said Beaumont, 'to reach the farthest limits of civilization. We thought that there we could find some entirely barbarous Indian tribes.' He did not yet realize that the influence of the Middle Ground, which was both an epoch and a region, had by now reached and transformed almost all the nations of North America, certainly all those which he had time to meet. 'Furthermore, we wanted to see how newcomers in these very remote lands went about establishing themselves.'[49] To themselves (and to us) their aspiration seems reasonable enough, but once again they discovered that on the frontier of settlement no-one could enter into the fine feelings of Romantic tourists. 'You wanna see the woods? They're right in front of you.'* To get the information they needed, they went to the land-office and pretended to be prospective settlers, or at least land-speculators.[50] This created no surprise: more than 5,000 pioneers had already come through Detroit that summer, mostly heading westward towards the St Joseph river, which debouches into Lake Michigan. Few or none of them were yet heading northwards; so

---

* 'Vous voulez voir des bois, nous disaient en souriant nos hôtes, allez tout droit devant vous
...'

northwards Tocqueville and Beaumont would go. They decided to aim at Saginaw, some eighty miles north-by-north-west of Detroit, and on 23 July, having hired two horses and added very necessary mosquito nets and a compass to their other equipment, they set off. (Beaumont drew a spirited sketch of Tocqueville mounted, wearing a large straw hat and holding an Indian pipe – possibly a calumet.)[51]

They were away for a week. They broke their journey at Pontiac and Flint River (now the city of Flint), spent two nights at Saginaw, and returned as they came. During that time they saw plenty of the wild, wet woods; of settlers, of Indians, and of the prairie; but such a bald statement gives no idea of the significance of the trip to Tocqueville. For that we have to turn to his own account, *Quinze Jours dans le Désert*,* which he began to write up from his rough notes as soon as he could. Incomplete, and never finally revised, it is nevertheless the strongest expression of his Romanticism, and decisive evidence of his continuing development as a writer. Like the *Voyage au Lac Oneida* it is the same sort of thing as the *Voyage en Sicile*, but all superfluities have been dropped, the material is more tightly organized and, above all, the literary design is stronger and simpler. When it was finally published, after Tocqueville's death, Sainte-Beuve commended it as, among other things, a corrective to the *chateaubrianesque*, 'giving us, in very good prose, what Chateaubriand first rendered, in bold, sublime strokes, as poetry',[52] and that is certainly true: Tocqueville himself felt that Chateaubriand had painted the American forest in false colours, and tried to correct him;[53] but today a reader is more likely to be struck by the degree to which Tocqueville himself attempts the sublime.

His central purpose, absolutely characteristic of his mind, is to describe and explain the three social groups that he encountered on the journey – Indians, traders and settlers, which he does with the precision, detail and quiet humour of a born observer; but the dominant trait of the piece is the travellers' wonderment as they venture further and further into the forest. It is like the story of a dream, the more so as much of the description concerns travel at night. On the second day an Indian appeared from nowhere and loped along the trail at their heels, easily keeping up with the horses and never speaking, though

* The title is an aspiration. AT did not manage to describe more than one bare week.

sometimes smiling brilliantly. What on earth was he doing? He was carrying a fine gun; eventually a stray settler in the woods explained to them that it had probably been given to him by the English, for use against the Americans, and that the Indian was returning from the annual ceremony where such presents were bestowed, like the drunken Iroquois they had seen at Buffalo (in this way, it may be observed, the customs of the Middle Ground were still maintained). Night fell, 'serene but freezing'. Tocqueville and Beaumont briefly lost each other, because Tocqueville could not help lingering beside a stream for a few minutes to enjoy the 'sublime horror' of the silent night-wood. Presently they came to a log-cabin where, instead of a watchdog, there was a bear on a chain; when they asked the settler for forage for their horses he went out and started mowing his grass by moonlight. Next day, as the faint trail plunged into the ever more silent and tangled forest, Tocqueville felt awed, as he had during a calm in mid-Atlantic. As the noonday sun shone down he heard a long sigh from deep among the trees, a distant, drawn-out, plaintive cry, the last effort of a dying wind. Afterwards everything round him sank back into a silence so deep, an immobility so complete, that he had to use one of his favourite phrases to describe its effect: his soul was pierced 'by a kind of religious terror'. The dreamlike feeling is even more marked in the description of their arrival at Saginaw. At about midnight they emerged from the forest onto a wide dim prairie. Their Indian guide, whom they had taken on at Flint River, announced them with a wild howl, which was answered from a distance; five minutes later they found themselves on the banks of a river. Presently the silence was broken by a slight noise, and a dug-out canoe grounded at their feet, paddled by, it appeared, another Indian; but as Tocqueville stepped into the canoe the boatman warned him to be careful – not only speaking in French, but with a Norman accent. Tocqueville could hardly believe his ears, and the effect was even odder when, as the pirogue moved back across the water (Tocqueville's tired horse swimming behind) Charon began to sing:

Entre Paris et Saint-Denis
Il était une fille ...

The boatman was a *bois-brûlé*, a half-breed: Tocqueville had met his first child of the *pays d'en haut*. As he waited for Beaumont the full moon began to rise, the waters of the river sparkled, and he could not see the paddle of the black canoe as it approached again: it suggested a Mississippi alligator coming to seize its prey.[54]

It was all deeply thrilling, to be cherished as a lifelong memory. They were back in Detroit by 31 July, oppressed by the thought that it was now exactly a year since the revolution which had uprooted them. They remembered the din and smoke of the street-fighting; as a result the forest seemed more silent and sombre than ever. They could not help wanting to explore further. They discovered that a pleasure-steamer, the *Superior*, was about to set off for Lake Michigan and that there were still a couple of berths which they might occupy. Appeasing their consciences by a hasty visit to the local jail, where they found nothing of interest, they booked themselves aboard and were off on another excursion. This one lasted for nearly a fortnight.

The *Superior* was enormous, carrying 200 passengers. It is possible to think that, up to this point, Beaumont and Tocqueville had been rather casual about the new technology which was bearing them so rapidly about so much of America, but such an attitude was no longer possible when the *Superior*, with them on board, became the first steamboat to reach the gate of the upper lakes, Sault Sainte-Marie and Michilimackinac. The Indians were stupefied when they saw her, their canoes swarmed about her sides on the water. Beaumont sympathized: 'even for a European these great steam-driven vessels are undeniably among the marvels of modern industry.'[55] The Frenchmen found their company somewhat mixed, but their charm and good manners veiled their reserve: they were thought delightful, especially by the ladies, whom Beaumont deemed unenticing. Miss Clemens, at forty, was too old, Miss Thomson too silly, and Miss Macomb was in the charge of an uncle who took against our friends. Nevertheless, when the *Superior* got to Sault Sainte-Marie, Tocqueville, Beaumont and the ladies ventured in a canoe onto Lake Superior, and no-one was too proud to dance on deck when the ship's band struck up in the evenings. In this way Beaumont came to hear the 'Marseillaise' for only the second time in his life – the first had been during the July Days. For the oddity of the thing he got out his flute and played variations on an air by

Rossini against the background of a beautiful starry night, the vast silent forest, and the fires of an Indian encampment ashore.[56]

It will be seen that the atmosphere on the *Superior* was not that of Saginaw, but still there were plenty of opportunities for serious study. A Catholic priest, Father Mullon, on his way to controvert the Presbyterians at Michilimackinac ('All the sects agree in hating Catholics, but the Presbyterians are the only ones who are violent') poured forth his pride in the Indians he had converted, but his most important contribution to the commissioners' education was his insistence on the value of completely disentangling the Church from the State. He conceded that Catholic priests in Europe thought differently, but if they came to America, he said, they would soon change their minds. The less that priests had to do with politics, the greater was the power of religious ideas. This chimed with what they had been told by every other priest they had met in America, and Beaumont, remembering the disastrous results of the alliance between throne and altar in France, was tempted to agree with them.[57]

The friends were penetrating deeper and deeper into Indian country, and at every port of call learned something more about the natives. Their respect, liking and pity for the Indians steadily increased. At Fort Gratiot on the Saint Claire river Tocqueville witnessed a war-dance, and was rather shocked: 'Handsome men. Dancing to pass the time and earn some money. We gave them a shilling [*sic*]* ... Horrible to see. What degradation'; but a few days later he was on the easiest terms with a Chippewa chief who greatly admired Tocqueville's waterproof gun: 'The fathers of the Canadians [i.e. the French] are great warriors!' Tocqueville in return admired two feathers which the chief wore in his hair: when he was told with a smile that they had been won for killing two Sioux he begged that he might be given one to show in the country of the great warriors, a request immediately granted with a mighty handshake.[58] Tocqueville and Beaumont sadly gave up any idea of reaching a country untouched by European civilization, though they snatched eagerly at rumours of happy hunting-grounds in the far West, where the Indians still used bows and arrows and where there

---

* It took half a century or more for Americans to get used to the new currency of dollars and cents.

was an extraordinary abundance of game, and of Prairie du Chien on the Mississippi, 'a place considered as neutral territory where the different nations meet in peace' (a last relic of the Middle Ground). But although the tribes did not, apparently, foresee their ruin, it was inevitable.[59] Something else was inevitable too. Tocqueville wrote to his father:

> The immense stretch of country which we have just travelled through offers no remarkable sights, mere plains covered with forest. This lake without a single sail upon it, its shore as yet showing no trace of human presence, the eternal forest which surrounds it, all that, I assure you, is not just great in poetry. It is the most extraordinary sight I have ever seen in my life. These lands which are, as yet, nothing but one immense wood, will become one of the richest and most powerful countries in the world. I can say so without being in the least a prophet. Nature has done everything ... Nothing is lacking but civilized man; and he is at the door.[60]

It was a visionary moment, but yet again Tocqueville succumbed to distraction. Among the fascinating details that he and Beaumont learned about the *pays d'en haut* was the story that still, even in the most distant wildernesses, Indians automatically greeted Europeans by saying *Bonjour*.[61] The friends were overwhelmed by this and all the other traces they were encountering of the former French empire in North America. It was something quite unexpected. Since 1763, when the treaty of Paris ceded Canada to the British, the metropolitan French had known nothing and wanted to know nothing of the colonists whom they had abandoned. Tocqueville and Beaumont had been no different from anyone else. But ever since they reached Saginaw they had been coming across evidence of what had been – and they were beginning to feel the pull of what still was – the thriving French community of Lower Canada. They became ever more eager to go there.

First they had to return via Detroit to Buffalo, where on 17 August they found letters waiting for them; then they set out again immediately for Niagara, with somewhat impaired enthusiasm. Tocqueville, replying to his mother, assured her that he was delighted to hear from her so often; writing tired her, so 'your letters are doubly dear to me, knowing what they cost you.' But at Buffalo they had also found European newspapers, from which they gathered that civil war was perhaps about to erupt in France, or at least a pro-Bourbon rising in the Vendée; as if that were not bad enough in itself, there was a personal anxiety as to what such young hotheads as Kergorlay and Hippolyte de Tocqueville might be up to.[62] Tocqueville was somewhat distressed and ashamed to be admiring a waterfall in America when so many of his friends might be running into trouble at home. On the other hand, what a waterfall! They reached Niagara at night, and though they could see nothing, they had heard its thunder from miles away. And when on the morrow, a day of fine weather, they went to look, they were, said Tocqueville, at a loss for words, though like everyone who says that they poured out their descriptions. The falls, said Tocqueville, surpassed everything that Europeans had written about them. This was another hit at Chateaubriand: Beaumont explicitly dismissed François-René's description as inadequate, except for his assertion that the great fall was 'une colonne de l'eau du déluge'. Tocqueville was especially struck by the great rainbow in the spray over the Horseshoe Falls, and still more by its appearance at night, in the light of the moon. He stood on a pinnacle above the chasm, water roaring all round him, and reached the highest point of his Romanticism: 'Nothing can equal the sublimity of the view from that point' except possibly the dangerous venture behind the fall, when the whole river seemed to be plunging down onto his head. But his peculiar angle of observation did not desert him. He wrote to his friend Dalmassy, another colleague of the Versailles *parquet*, that if he wanted to see Niagara in its glory he must hurry: in less than ten years the Americans would be putting a sawmill at its foot.* For his part, Beaumont was called back to earth by the unwelcome attentions of Miss Clemens, their companion of the *Superior*: she dogged his footsteps until he was driven into actual incivility in a vain attempt to get rid of her. He thought she should be called 'la folle de Niagara'.[63]

On to Canada, where they spent some ten days. This visit was the last and most complete distraction from the purposes of their journey, whether penitentiary or political. In the end it never yielded more than a note to the *Ancien Régime*,[64] and need not be chronicled at any length;

---

* And indeed, Niagara Falls are nowadays chiefly used for hydro-electric power; they are turned off at night, and the flow by day (maintained to please tourists) is much reduced.

but it vividly illustrated one aspect of Tocqueville and Beaumont's characters. They were delighted to find French people doing so well in the New World, even if they were burdened by a foreign yoke; and they did all they could to unearth evidence that one day soon the *Canadiens* would rise up successfully against British rule. By now they were practised observers, and the account of Canada in their letters and notes is full of life and interest; but the predominant impression left is that they had fallen in love with the country and made sure of seeing everything in the light that best supported their infatuation.

It is not hard to see why they fell in love. The country between Montreal and Quebec was more like Europe, and particularly France, than anywhere else they had so far seen in North America. All traces of the wilderness had vanished; from the deck of the steamboat which carried them down the St Lawrence, Tocqueville and Beaumont admired the landscape of tilled earth, church belfries and an abundant population which had replaced it. Montreal looked exactly like a French provincial town, and everybody spoke French. It was natural to feel indignant that such a thriving colony lay under British rule; Beaumont denounced 'the shameful treaty of 1763' to his father. Then, the people were so charming, gayer than the metropolitan French had been since the Revolution, and much more so than the gloomy, restless, money-mad Americans: Beaumont went so far as to say that it was not until he got to Canada that he heard anyone in North America laugh.

Tocqueville was tempted to conclude that a nation's character was hereditary, or at least derived far more from its blood than from its political institutions and physical geography. The *Canadiens* called their country New France, but it was really the Old France, France of the *ancien régime* purged of its faults, and not having endured a revolution. Equality was advancing in Canada as in the United States, and people complained of the remaining feudal dues, but those were so trifling! The clergy was enlightened, pious, democratic, and still French in character – 'gay, lively, mocking, lovers of glory and fame …' The peasants were just like French ones – they took pride in their independence and detested the memory of feudalism. They grew their own food and made their own clothes; every village was a family, and there was no sexual misbehaviour. Their religion was much superior to that of France – no statues of the Virgin on the streets or *ex-votos* in the churches: 'here, catholicism excites neither the hate nor the sarcasm of Protestants,' said Tocqueville. 'I admit that, so far as I am concerned, it is more spiritually satisfying than the Protestantism of the United States. Here, the *curé* is indeed the shepherd of his flock; there is nothing here of the industrial religion of most American ministers.' Priests, in fact, were useless if they were not like those of Canada.[65]

It was Utopia for the two young nobles, seeming to show that the ideals with which they had grown up were not, after all, totally illusory, and rousing all their eager patriotism (never very far from the surface). But in terms of their mission they had been wasting their time, and Tocqueville would soon get a letter from Le Peletier d'Aunay warning him to report to his superiors more frequently if he did not want his leave to be curtailed.[66] As it turned out, half their time in North America was almost gone, and it was nearly two months since they had done any serious prison study, let alone investigated democracy in the United States. To be sure, they had always planned to head for New England after their Canadian visit; but though they may not immediately have realized it, they were turning their backs on more than mosquitoes when they headed south on 2 September. On 3 September they travelled down Lake Champlain, and on the 5th were back in Albany, which they had left on the Fourth of July. The most intense and serious phase of their pilgrimage was about to begin.

CHAPTER NINE

A REPUBLIC OBSERVED
1831–1832

*Sir, a foreigner, when he sends his work from the press,
ought to be on his guard against catching the error and
mistaken enthusiasm of the people among whom he
happens to be.*

SAMUEL JOHNSON, 1773

THEY REACHED BOSTON on 9 September and found a packet
of letters waiting for them; as he sorted out his share Tocqueville
noticed apprehensively that there was nothing from Abbé Le Sueur.
He soon found his fears justified by what his family wrote. Bébé was
dead. Tocqueville poured out his grief in the passionate letter to
Édouard already quoted.* 'Yesterday evening, I prayed to him as a
saint.' He could hardly see what he wrote for tears.[1] His grief must
inspire respect and sympathy, but it is notable that the personality of
the shrewd and witty priest is lost to view in Tocqueville's lamentations for someone who was, to him, primarily a source of love and
reassurance, of the ostensibly uncritical tenderness which the mourner
needed so much and valued so highly. An oddity of the episode is that
he did not immediately tell Beaumont what had happened. Beaumont
would not have been anything other than warmly sympathetic; but in

---

* See above, p.30.

speaking to him Tocqueville would have had to confront his own guilt. 'It would have been the greatest of all consolations for me to have been able to place myself at his side and receive his final blessing,' he wrote to his mother;[2] but he had known before he left France that Bébé was rapidly failing. He had sailed just the same. No-one had refused him the consolation of watching at Le Sueur's death-bed: he himself had made it impossible. Nor did he allow his loss to deflect him from his American investigations, though for the time being it much diminished his pleasure in them: 'I turn to the work which interests me most like a convict to the treadmill.'[3]

His sorrow haunted him, though with healthily diminishing intensity, for the rest of his American journey; but his work was restorative and distracting, and so was the place where he now found himself. Years and years later he wrote to an American friend that if he had to live in America, it would be in Boston, where there were so many cultivated and friendly people; and it is easy to see why the town impressed him so favourably. Coming fresh from the wild, he and Beaumont were as delighted with Massachusetts as they had been with Canada. Massachusetts too was an old country, according to Beaumont: 'I call any country old which has existed for two hundred years ... You don't see tree-stumps in Massachusetts fields, or log huts serving as houses.' Tocqueville wrote a few days later that:

> Boston is a pretty town, sited picturesquely on several hills surrounded by water. From what we have seen of the inhabitants so far, they differ completely from the people we met in New York. Their society, at least that into which we have been introduced, and I think it is the best, is almost exactly like the upper classes of Europe. Luxury and refinement reign. Almost all the women speak French well, and all the men we have met so far have been to Europe. Their manners are distinguished, their conversation is intellectual; one feels free of the commercial habits and financier's outlook which make New York society so vulgar. At Boston there already exists a certain number of people who, having nothing to do, pursue the pleasures of the intellect. Some of them are writers ...

True, they mostly wrote on religious matters, but Tocqueville forgave them. He felt at home in America for the first time.[4]

They were given their usual warm welcome, once the Bostonians discovered that the famous French commissioners had arrived. The familiar routine resumed: when they were not dining out, they were dancing. They pursued their prison investigations: 'We're incontrovertibly going to be the *premiers pénitenciers* of the whole word,' Beaumont boasted.[5] But the heart of their Boston experience was to be their daily or twice-daily conversations with the city's politically sagacious *savants*. So far their investigations into democracy had been somewhat impressionistic and haphazard. Now, under the stimulus of so much intelligent discourse, they became systematic.

The most useful man they met was Jared Sparks, sometime editor of the *North American Review*, future president of Harvard (in which capacity he would confer an honorary degree on Tocqueville), first editor and publisher of the papers of George Washington. As a historical scholar, he was in a way the American equivalent of Guizot – they were nearly the same age – except that he had no wish to enter politics, and turned down the opportunity to become a Congressman. On 17 September he showed Tocqueville his vast collection of Washington's papers. Tocqueville was amazed at the beautiful regular handwriting and the hundreds of signatures, each of which might have been a facsimile of any of the others. The documents he was shown were business papers, dealing with military administration and Washington's private affairs; they would have done credit to a clerk. How could so large-minded a man have condescended to such details? Two days later Sparks, who if not a participant was a most intelligent observer of politics, gave his views on Andrew Jackson. Most educated men agreed that the general was not fit to be President, he said, but he would be re-elected because the people were slow to change their ideas: they had been taught for years that Jackson was a great man, and there was no time before the 1832 election to re-educate them. Tocqueville had once more fallen among Federalists: he wrote down what he was told without comment, but with all too much credulity.[6]

The trouble was that the Bostonians, though opening many fresh windows, all tended to say the same thing. Thus on 29 September a third conversation with Sparks took place, of which, fortunately and unusually, we have Beaumont's account in a surviving fragment of journal, as well as Tocqueville's. Sparks spoke good French, and the commissioners appear to have encouraged him to hold forth at length.

Much ground was covered: New England town meetings, democracy in Connecticut where Sparks had been born, the rivalry between Jackson and Henry Clay, American newspapers, decentralization … many topics were laid out, and Sparks's views on them would eventually reappear, undiluted if uncredited, in *De la démocratie en Amérique*. But he was not the first to expound them; rather, it is as if Tocqueville and Beaumont were using this particularly intelligent and well-informed friend to test views that they had already been exposed to. Thus, Sparks insisted on the importance of 'the point of departure': New England owed her freedom to the circumstances of her original foundation, to her colonial past. 'We arrived here as republicans and religious enthusiasts … Those who want to imitate us should consider that our history is unprecedented.' This was an idea which Tocqueville promptly laid before Alexander Everett, a former US minister at the Spanish court, and Everett at once endorsed it, if with a slightly different twist: 'A people's *point de départ* is an immense thing. Its consequences for good or ill are perpetually surprising in their scope.' He instanced the practice of imprisonment for debt, inherited from England, that was only slowly being abolished in the various states. Sparks also let fall the remark that in the United States it was dogma that the majority was always right; he added, almost in passing, that 'sometimes the majority has oppressed the minority. Fortunately we have in the governor's veto power and above all in the judges' right to refuse to apply an unconstitutional law a guarantee against democracy's passions and mistakes.' The grandson of *le président* Rosanbo simply could not resist this suggestion, particularly as he was already exploring the political aspect of the US legal system, especially the jury (which in the end was to be perhaps the most original part of his work). Unhappily the more seriously Tocqueville took Sparks's notion the more he tended to exaggerate the danger which it was supposed to counteract, the abuse of majority power, as Sparks found to his dismay when the *Démocratie* was published. He had little else to complain of: Tocqueville drew on him so exhaustively (not least by inducing him to write a valuable essay on 'The Government of Towns in Massachusetts') as almost to entitle him to be named as co-author. Nevertheless, his casual remark was the seed from which gradually developed Tocqueville's most serious mistake.[7]

Tocqueville found it difficult to let go any notion once formed. Thus, he clung to his Livingston-inspired idea about the laws of inheritance. He still thought that they explained the emergence of democracy in America and the decline of civilization. In Boston, Beaumont came to understand the truth: that the post-revolutionary laws of inheritance were much more democratic, in the sense of equalizing, in France than in the United States. In France, which was still a monarchy, entail and primogeniture had been abolished to secure the interests of families as such: every heir was to enjoy equal rights. The testator could only make a will within strict limits. An attempt by the Ultras in 1826 to restore some measure of primogeniture had led to one of the first great battles of the reign of Charles X. This incident may well have shaped Tocqueville's views, which in this instance were absolutely typical of his caste. In republican America, on the other hand, the testator could do as he liked: entail and primogeniture had been abolished to secure the interest of the individual property-holder. Unfortunately Beaumont never did anything with this discovery, and it was long before Tocqueville acknowledged it.[8]

Yet after a week in Boston he found himself forced to contemplate intellectual, or one might even say logical difficulties which would have to be resolved if his political investigations were to have a successful outcome. The first, if not the most important, was the fact that American democracy was a success. It contradicted everything which in Europe he had thought normal and natural, and yet it worked.

> An incredible *outward* equality reigns in America. All classes mingle incessantly, and there is not the least indication of their different social positions. Everyone shakes hands. At Canandaigua I saw a district attorney shake hands with a prisoner ... I don't think that there is any trade which in itself demeans the person who practises it. You are constantly reading in the newspapers in praise of a man that 'he keeps a respectable tavern in such [a] place'. It is palpable that white servants see themselves as their masters' equals. They chat with them familiarly. Aboard the steamboats we at first tried to tip the steward. People stopped us from doing so on the grounds that it would humiliate him. In taverns, I have seen the waiter sit down next to us at table once everyone had been served ...

It was not even considered shameful to be a hangman. And no fuss was made of great men. When they met John Quincy Adams, former President of the United States, at dinner, he was received very politely, as a distinguished guest, but that was all. Most of those present simply addressed him as 'Sir', though a few said 'Mr President'; either way it was quite unlike Versailles or Saint-Cloud. Women seemed to cope successfully without the personal maids and heaps of luggage that ladies in Europe found necessary when travelling.[9] And the political system which sustained, or was sustained by, this remarkably egalitarian society was just as surprising. Foiled at Albany, in Boston Tocqueville got a secure grasp of the way in which American government worked. He talked to Josiah Quincy, the current president of Harvard,* who besides emphasizing the *point de départ* – Massachusetts, he said, was almost as free before the Revolution as she was in 1831: 'We put the name of the people where formerly was that of the king. Otherwise nothing changed among us' – stressed the importance of local government and, as a consequence, the weakness of the central authority: 'The state of Massachusetts is an association of little republics which name their own magistrates and manage their own affairs.' The state legislature dealt only with statewide business. Much impressed by these remarks, Tocqueville reflected that one of the happiest consequences of such absence of government was the development of individual initiative and self-reliance. When an American projected some public benefit ('a school, a hospital, a road'), he relied, often successfully, only on his own efforts. The outcome might be less satisfactory than that of official activity, 'but altogether, the general result of all these individual undertakings surpasses by much that which a bureaucracy could undertake' and the moral and political benefits were more than enough to counterbalance any falling short. It was deeply impressive, and led Tocqueville to write that 'a good government's greatest care should be to accustom the people, little by little, to do without it' (which is like the famous American slogan 'That government is best which governs least'). By the end of September he felt able to tell himself that there were two great social principles which ruled American society, and to

---

* One of the curiosities of AT's visit to Boston is that he never saw fit to visit Harvard; indeed, he never visited any American university, not even Yale.

which it was always necessary to turn to explain the laws and habits which governed it:

1. The majority can err on some points, but on the whole it is always right and there is no moral power superior to it.

2. Every individual, private person, society, township or nation,* is the sole legitimate judge of its own interest, and so long as it does not damage the interests of anybody else, nobody has the right to interfere.

I think that I must never lose sight of this note.

He never did.[10]

But on the same day he wrote: 'An entirely democratic government is a machine so dangerous, *even in America*, that it has been necessary to take a host of precautions against the mistakes and passions of Democracy.' He lists the bicameral legislature, the governor's veto and judicial independence as among these precautions; he seems to be elaborating what Sparks told him, or what he thinks Sparks told him. But he does not yet see, and never will, that the American constitutions, from the state to the federal, rely principally on elections to control majorities, by converting them into minorities if necessary; this, no doubt, partly because, visiting the land of elections, he contrived, in the course of nine months, not to witness a single one. Nor does he see that the chief concern of the constitution-makers, at any rate from 1789 onwards, was to use the majority to check abusive minorities. They did not (and do not) always succeed, but that hardly excuses Tocqueville's blindness to the dangers of special interests.[11]

Even if his observations are disputable, they encompass much truth, and in logic there seemed to be no reason why they should not be applied to France. The difficulty was the *point de départ*. Contemplating the American system of as little government as possible, and perhaps remembering Chateaubriand's *Voyage*, Tocqueville wrote:

few are the peoples who can thus do without government. Such a state of things has never lasted except at the two extremes of civilization. The savage, who has only his physical needs to satisfy, relies only on

* A French usage: here (and in many other places) AT means 'state', in the US sense.

himself. For the civilized man to do the same he must have attained that condition of society in which his enlightenment allows him to perceive clearly what is useful to him, and in which his passions won't prevent him from carrying it out.

The French were in neither condition, and were therefore unpromising material for democracy *à l'américaine*. Tocqueville knew it, and if he had not, his Boston friends would have told him. For instance, Francis Lieber, a German immigrant who was the editor of the *Encyclopaedia Americana*, said that Europeans' great mistake was in supposing that a republic could be created simply by calling a constituent assembly. A people had to have republicanism in its bones – look at America! 'The republic is everywhere, in the streets as much as in Congress.' Tocqueville could not deny it; and Francis C. Gray, state senator and inspector of prisons, emphasized how early in life democratic attitudes were formed: 'there's not a boy of fifteen among us who hasn't acted as a juror a hundred times. I suspect that the humblest citizen of Boston had a more truly parliamentary outlook and is more accustomed to political debate than most of your deputies.' But Tocqueville could not entirely accept a theory which seemed to hold out so little hope for his own country. After all, one of his interlocutors, Mr Clay of Georgia,* thought that all nations, even the great powers of Europe, might one day become democratic. This astonished Tocqueville, as well it might, since Mr Clay thought that Protestantism was a necessary precondition; but waiving that, suppose he was right? A republican people, Tocqueville was told, had to be 'steady, religious and very enlightened'. It also had to be prosperous. Was all this beyond French capacity? 'In America a free society has created free political institutions; in France, free political institutions will have to create a free society. That is the end towards which we must work, without forgetting the *point de départ*.' It was simply a matter of defining the problem correctly, rather than dismissing it in advance as insoluble.[12] .

But during his visit to Boston another matter began to obtrude, which suggested very different thoughts about the future of the American republic. 'In Massachusetts blacks have the rights of citizens. They can

---

* Otherwise unidentified. Not to be confused with Henry Clay of Kentucky.

vote in elections ... but prejudice is so strong that their children are not admitted to the schools.'[13]

The fact that slavery created great problems for the United States was no secret in Europe: as we have seen, both Guizot and Chateaubriand alluded to it, and the British, whether through their diplomatic campaign against the slave trade, or through the anti-slavery agitation at home, kept the subject in the news. But largely by accident it had not previously forced itself on the attention of Tocqueville and Beaumont during their journey. Now, in Boston, soon to be the capital of abolitionism (William Lloyd Garrison had just started to publish the *Liberator*), the topic, in all its painful complexity, could not be missed. Sitting next to John Quincy Adams at dinner Tocqueville listened while the ex-President, in fluent and elegant French, held forth on slavery and its consequences for Southern society.

> Whites there make up a class which has all the passions and prejudices of an aristocracy, but make no mistake, equality, among whites, is nowhere greater than it is in the South. Here we have complete equality before the law, but it does not apply at all in daily life.* There are upper classes and working classes. In the South, every white man is an equally privileged being, whose destiny is to make Negroes work without working himself. You can't imagine how far the idea that labour is shameful has come to dominate the mind of the South ... They give themselves over to sports, to hunting, to racing. They are physically vigorous, brave, honourable; what is called 'the point of honour' is a much bigger issue there than anywhere else; duels are frequent.

Tocqueville saw that all this had ominous implications for the future of the Union, though Mr Adams refused to be drawn on the point (it was hardly a tactful question to raise with a former head of state); he also recorded certain remarks which showed that Adams was not altogether a believer in racial equality: 'the Negresses very frequently abuse the goodness of their mistresses. They know it is not the custom to inflict corporal punishment on them.'[14]

Then there was Mr Clay, the planter. He was Tocqueville's first

---

* This remark is the direct opposite of AT's own observations; but then AT's point of view, that of a noble from an intensely hierarchical society, was very different from Adams's. The two men contradicted each other, but both were right.

Southerner: 'I have rarely met a more amiable and well-educated man.' He thought that emancipation would come, and be followed by a separation of the two races. Whites and blacks could never merge into a single people. 'The importation of this foreign race is, moreover, the great, the unique plague of America.'[15] Here was another big theme for meditation: it fascinated Beaumont particularly.

Their time in Boston was up. It had been extremely valuable: Tocqueville now saw more clearly than ever before what his book might be; and he seems to have begun to understand that it could not be a work of collaboration. But could he manage it? He was afraid that his family might expect too much of his journey. It had given him experience, and ideas on political questions which might one day be of practical use to him. But he was far from sure that he could write anything about America. 'It would be a huge task to paint a picture of a society so vast and varied as this one.' However, he continued to collect documents assiduously.[16]

Meanwhile, the prison mission reclaimed his attention. He and Beaumont had not altogether neglected it during their stay in Boston. They had visited the Auburn-style penitentiary at Charlestown, and the very impressive 'House of Reformation' for young offenders. They had heeded the hint given them by d'Aunay and reported at length to Paris – indeed, this last precaution was more necessary than ever, for the authorities seemed bent on curtailing their leave of absence. Beaumont had been promoted again, and was badly needed at the *parquet*, and it was suspected that eighteen months were far more time than was needed to assess the American prison system. Besides, though the Garde des Sceaux did not know what the commissioners were really up to, the most basic acquaintance with human nature must have suggested a suspicion that they were devoting an undue amount of time to enjoying themselves. From now on Tocqueville and Beaumont felt themselves to be under a pending sentence of execution; it was eventually to play havoc with their plans, and if it was not to defeat them entirely they would have to intensify their application to their mission, even though Beaumont, at least, was very bored with it.[17] So on 3 October they tore themselves away from Boston and headed for Philadelphia by way of Hartford in Connecticut and New York. At Hartford, where they stayed for some days, they visited Wethersfield penitentiary, another new prison on the Auburn plan, and formed a very positive impression of it, for they did not discern that under the surface was brewing another of those scandals which the Auburn system seemed to invite: the governor was embezzling money and food intended for the prisoners, who as a result were half-starved.[18] In New York they shed half their baggage. By now, as a result of their own assiduity and the enthusiasm of the Americans, they were lugging a small library about with them. There was no point in continuing to do so since they could leave it to be called for when they embarked for home (but they continued to accumulate documents wherever they went in the meantime). They got to Philadelphia on 12 October.

They were eagerly awaited there; indeed, a small committee had been formed to assist them. For Philadelphia was the American city which had prison reform most at heart. The Quakers, who had founded it, no longer ruled it, but they were still the dominant social group, and the combination of their prestige with their religiously tended conscience made them amazingly effective agitators. They had embraced pacifism, and declared war on slavery, and assiduously pursued the dream of a rational and effective penology. Their first effort at reform had been the Walnut Street prison, an older establishment overhauled, somewhat on Auburn lines, in 1790. This had not answered (and by the time that Tocqueville and Beaumont arrived, Walnut Street had become the plaything of the spoils system),[19] so in 1829 they had opened the Eastern State Penitentiary (known familiarly as Cherry Hill), in which the inexorable logic of the penitentiary philosophy was most completely expressed in the building itself and in the regime adopted there. All other objects of incarceration – punishment, prevention, deterrence – were discarded:[20] once a convict entered Cherry Hill his guardians' sole concern was to be his moral reformation. Since prisoners corrupted each other, or at least hindered each other's reclamation if they were allowed to meet, each was now to be kept in solitary confinement, in a specially designed cell with a little exercise yard attached, talking to no-one except the prison chaplain, and warding off insanity by daily labour. The Quakers were confident (their faith in a man's inner light was boundless) that in these circumstances not the most hardened soul could fail to soften, repent and be transformed, to his own lasting benefit and that of society.

Not surprisingly, then, Tocqueville and Beaumont were overwhelmed with attention when they reached Philadelphia, and before long the Quakers had convinced themselves that they had won over the commissioners to their way of thinking.[21] They were wrong: Beaumont, in particular, found the Cherry Hill experiment impossibly expensive, at least for France, where there were currently no fewer than 32,000 prisoners; and they were both still uncertain that the penitentiaries (whether the Auburn or the Quaker model) actually induced penitence. But today the great interest of their encounter with Cherry Hill lies in the way that Tocqueville on this occasion went about his investigations.

It occurred to him and to Beaumont (as, surely, it ought to have occurred to them before) that in studying a prison – Cherry Hill, in this instance – it would be a good idea to talk to the prisoners. They got permission to interview each prisoner singly, without the presence of any warder; not wanting to intimidate the captives, they further decided that only one of them would conduct each interview, and in the end Tocqueville did them all – apparently because of Beaumont's hopeless boredom with his mission. So for the best part of a fortnight Tocqueville went daily to gather what he rightly guessed could be invaluable testimony. He interviewed sixty-three prisoners in all.[22]

It should have been the high point of the enquiry; that it was not tells us a great deal about Tocqueville. As he got into his stride his notes on each prisoner became extremely businesslike, almost stereotyped:

No. 15 – This inmate is twenty-eight years old; he has been found guilty of manslaughter; he has been in the penitentiary for nearly two years; his health is excellent; he has learned the trade of a weaver in his cell. His solitude, he said, seemed at first unbearable; but later he got used to it.

No. 1 – This inmate, the first to be sent to this penitentiary, is a Negro. He has lived in the prison for more than two years. His health is very good.

    This man works zealously: he makes ten pairs of shoes a week. His mind seems tranquil and his disposition excellent. He seems to look on his coming to the penitentiary as a signal blessing of Providence. In general, his thoughts are religious. He read to us from the Gospel the parable of the good shepherd, of which the meaning, which he had grasped, greatly touched him, he who was born of a degraded and oppressed race, and who had never experienced anything from his fellow men but indifference or hostility.[23]

Such were most of the interviews, and from them Tocqueville could gather, reassuringly, that the mental and physical health of the prisoners seemed good, that they welcomed the chance to work at a trade, if only to keep off despair, and that they knew how to sound pious. But all this was no more than the managers of Cherry Hill could and did tell him, and proved nothing except, perhaps, that it was better to be a prisoner in Philadelphia than in Sing-Sing. Yet it is possible to be absolutely certain that had Tocqueville asked different questions he could have got much more illuminating answers. 'No. 35. – This inmate is more than eighty years old. At the moment that we entered his cell, he was engaged in reading the Bible.'[24] Nothing more was recorded, yet how could Tocqueville have failed to ask why a man of such an age was a prisoner, and what the management hoped to achieve by keeping him locked up? (Had he done so he would surely have written down the answers.)

> No. 65. – This inmate is thirty years old, without a family, condemned for forgery; in prison these seven months; feels very well. This convict is uncommunicative; he complains of the evils caused by solitary confinement, of which labour, he says, is the sole alleviation. He seems little concerned with religious ideas.[25]

Above all, there was prisoner oo (one of several to whom Tocqueville gave this number), 'forty years old; condemned for armed robbery on the public highway', who, without much prompting, poured out the story of his life: of how, as a boy, he left the family farm and came to Philadelphia; how he was sent to prison for a month for vagabondage; how he fell in there with hardened young rogues and became one of them; how he was eventually sentenced to nine years in the Walnut Street prison (reduced to seven for good behaviour) for robbery; how, on his release, he tried, successfully at first, to earn an honest living as a tailor, and married; but how his criminal record lost him his job. How he fell ill; how in despair and anger he turned to robbery again; and how he was sent to Cherry Hill for ten years.

Tocqueville: What are your plans for the future?

oo: I don't feel inclined to blame myself for what I did, frankly, or to become a good Christian; but I am determined to steal no more, and I see a chance of succeeding. When, in nine years' time, I get out of here, no-one in the world will recognize me; no-one will know that I've been in prison; I won't have made any dangerous acquaintances. I will be free to earn my living in peace. That's what I see as the great advantage of this penitentiary ...[26]

Tocqueville recorded oo's narrative with the greatest care, and it remains one of the saddest and most touching pages in all his work; but he does not seem to have tried to elicit life-stories from any of the other prisoners. Yet perhaps they would have confirmed the palpable lesson implied by oo's tale: that in American cities, at least, it was all too easy to fall into a life of crime, and immensely difficult to escape it, and that savagely long prison sentences were of little use except as deterrents: what induced oo to renounce crime the first time was his observation that not even the cleverest criminals could for long evade arrest and punishment. Tocqueville, who had been startled to be told by a lawyer in Connecticut that the crime rate went up as prosperity increased ('This observation requires confirmation')[27] was near to discovering that the origins and nature of criminality were far more complex than enthusiastic reformers supposed, but, obsessed with comparing Auburn and Cherry Hill, he missed this crucial lesson.

And this in part was the outcome of his personal conditioning, which did not blind him only to the point of view of convicts. Wherever they went, he and Beaumont sought out '*les gens éclairés*' and were at a loss unless they made close contact with them. By this term they did not just mean the educated or enlightened. They meant the 'upper class' – 'those who have something to live on and have received a good education.'[28] They equated these fortunate beings with their own country's *hautes classes*. Worse, within the upper class they felt most at home with lawyers – at times the reader of Tocqueville's journal is bound to form the impression that they talked to no-one but *avocats distingués*. They thus forfeited one of the chief advantages of foreign travel, and of travel to the United States above all, the opportunity to shed the burden and trap of their own social identity.

Inescapably *noble* in France, they could have been whatever they liked in America, but instead of embracing this freedom they seized every chance of asserting their original status, since they would have felt lost without it. This was not, in either of them, a mere personal quirk. Their upbringing and the recent history of France made a different attitude impossible.

The loss to their investigation was immense. Tocqueville sometimes dimly sensed this, as when he noticed, as he did frequently, how different America was from France, or when, on the brink of returning home, he commented that it would take two years really to understand the United States.[29] Perhaps if he had been able to stay longer he would have broken through. As it was, he saw no problem in eschewing serious conversation with most Americans. It is futile to blame him for what was inevitable, but it is perhaps just to remark that a man who was so convinced that democracy was on the march and that America was ruled by 'the majority' (i.e. white adult males) should have sought out more democrats. His failure to do so meant that he came to build some of his most characteristic edifices of theory on sand, and vitiates the inferences he made from them.

To put it another way: when Tocqueville and Beaumont followed their fancy in the West they made great discoveries. They were almost participant-observers (it will be remembered that at one point they pretended to be land-speculators) and the informed understanding which they acquired enriches their books still. Even in Canada, where their desire to encourage sedition against King William IV misled them, they learned much and mis-learned little. But in New England and Pennsylvania the grid of their preoccupations once more locked them in, and seriously impeded their studies. The prison mission, which necessarily entailed constant contact with and reliance upon the elite and the expert, reinforced this tendency.

Yet when Tocqueville detected a weakness in his investigations, he was always most anxious to put it right. For example, his visit to Boston had shown him a great opportunity. If his business was to tell Europe how democracy in America worked, then he must make a thorough study of American governmental machinery, and publish the results: an added inducement was that, as Jared Sparks told him, there was no existing book on the subject.[30] Tocqueville resolved to fill this gap, and laboured mightily to do so; but he soon found that he needed help. Hence his applications to Sparks, Senator Gray and others. And mere information about political machinery was not enough; if his work was to be as valuable as he hoped, it would have to be comparative: he would have to show how American government differed from the French – and on reflection he and Beaumont realized that they were lamentably ignorant of how their own country was administered. So application was made to Chabrol, to Blosseville, and above all to Hervé de Tocqueville for enlightenment on this all-important matter:

> You could do me a great service, my dear Papa, which wouldn't cost you very much, now that you are enjoying your leisure. [Was this a quite tactful remark?] In judging America, nothing would be more useful to me than a knowledge of France. But that is exactly what is lacking. I know in general that with us the government meddles in almost everything; the word 'centralization' has been dinned into my ears a hundred times – without any explanation. I have never had the time or the occasion to study the various administrative machines which cover France. You have acquired this diverse knowledge, my dear Papa, by reflection and necessity. You have seen the administration operating in both big things and small, and I think that the matter is so familiar to you that you can, without any trouble, supply me with the documents I need … If, my dear Papa, you could deconstruct the word 'centralization' for me, you would do a great service not only for the present but for the future.[31]

Hervé splendidly responded: the subject was of real interest to him, as he had been involved in official discussions of it in 1828, when the Martignac ministry had tried in vain to get a timidly decentralizing law passed.[32] He sent his son a short essay in which he insisted that the vital principle of French government was centralization:

> Royalty exercises a general tutelage over all branches of the administration. It names, it directs, it approves, it prevents. … Without it the intimate union of all parts of the State would soon be replaced … [by a mass?] of small republics. … In a Monarchy surrounded by powerful and jealous States, a centre of unity is necessary.[33]

The contrast with what Alexis was learning about the American republic could hardly be starker, and did indeed give him matter for reflection for the rest of his life.

Prisons and parties: to start with, their life in Philadelphia was much the same as in Boston. They found the city to be clean and convenient, but too geometrical to be beautiful: Tocqueville did not think much of the practice of giving streets numbers rather than names: 'only a people whose fancy was frozen could have invented such a system.'[34] He let himself be somewhat distracted from his study of American state and local government by the equally important topic of the American legal system, especially the jury, which he investigated with professional insight and exactitude. But Philadelphia confronted him, and Beaumont still more, with a fundamental problem which, thus far, they had known about only by hearsay. The city had a sizeable black population, and wherever the commissioners turned they found that rigid racial segregation was enforced, although slavery had been abolished for fifty years. John Jay Smith, 'a very well-informed and capable Quaker', affirmed the full humanity and equal ability of African-Americans – 'a black cow is of the same race as a white one' – and asserted, from his experience as a Sunday school teacher, that their children did as well as or better than white children in school. But although the law gave them equal civil rights, they were not allowed to vote in Pennsylvania.

Tocqueville: What becomes of the rule of law in such cases?

Smith: Law with us is nothing unless it is supported by public opinion.

The conversation turned naturally to slavery and its prospects. Mr Smith thought that the slaves should be promoted to serfdom on the way to becoming free men, 'but I am perfectly certain that the Americans of the South, like all despots, will never consent to cede the least part of their power; they will wait until it is torn from them.'[35]

Next day Beaumont wrote to his sister-in-law: 'It is strange to see what aristocratic pride can exist among *free men* whose government is founded on the principle of absolute equality. Here the colour white is a patent of nobility and the colour black a mark of slavery.' But it could not last. 'The ignorance of the blacks is diminishing daily and, when they are fully enlightened, there is much reason to fear that they will take violent revenge for the contempt shown them.'[36]

These observations were soon tested: on 28 October they travelled to Baltimore, thereby entering a slave state (Maryland) for the first time. That evening they went to a grand public ball marking the start of the horse-races; as distinguished visitors the commissioners did not have to pay the entrance fee of $5 per person, but Tocqueville wrote in his notebook, 'In France they would hardly dare to charge so much for entry to a public occasion; it would be said that the rich were insolently presuming to separate themselves from everybody else.' Perhaps Tocqueville was more of a Jacobin than he realized. Next day they went to the races and saw another manifestation of Maryland society: 'A Negro having dared to enter the enclosure with some whites was by one of them showered with blows from a walking-stick, which did not appear to surprise either the crowd or the Negro himself.'[37]

This was not the only proof to Tocqueville that African-Americans were treated badly in Maryland. The sympathetic Mr Latrobe, son of the famous architect (who among other works had built a penitentiary at Richmond, Virginia), and a leader of the colonization movement which sought to settle free African-Americans in Liberia, remarked that the state legislature wanted to make Maryland intolerable for them: 'It can't be hidden, the white and black populations are in a state of war. They will never mingle. One of the two must give way to the other.' The day before, Tocqueville recorded: 'The law lends its power to the master of the slave. He is able to imprison his slave as long as he pleases provided that he pays the running costs.'[38]

But what most shocked the commissioners was the mad slave they were shown in the Baltimore alms-house:

> There is in Baltimore a famous slave-trader who is, I gather, much feared by the black population. The Negro I am describing thinks he sees this man, day and night, haunting his steps and tearing off parts of his flesh. When we entered his cell, he was sleeping on the floor rolled up in the blanket which was his only attire. His eyes rolled in their sockets and the look on his face was simultaneously one of terror and rage. From time to time he threw off his blanket and raised himself on his hands, crying: 'Get out, get out, don't come near me!' It

was an appalling sight. The man was one of the handsomest Negroes I have seen, he was in the prime of life.[39]

So by the time they returned to Philadelphia on 6 November, or thereabouts, Beaumont had apparently made a great decision (it is impossible to be more definite because of the disappearance of so many of his papers). The prison mission was substantially complete, though they had not told the Garde des Sceaux. Tocqueville was driving ahead with his political and administrative studies, always with his friend's help, but now, essentially, independently. It is likely that by the time they went to Baltimore the idea of a fully collaborative work on America had been given up: it had become an inconvenience. But Beaumont's literary ambition was still alight, and the discovery of American racism had given him a fresh subject. Besides, he and Tocqueville had realized that the American scene was too vast to be portrayed complete in one work. From now on they divided the labour. Tocqueville would tackle American government, Beaumont, American society – in particular, race relations. The categories were not watertight: one of the most valuable chapters of *De la démocratie en Amérique* would discuss race relations, for Tocqueville had been as deeply shocked as Beaumont by the horrors of slavery, which lurked so near the brilliant surface of Baltimore society. But one more barrier in his way to achievement had been removed.[40]

More decisions had to be taken in Philadelphia. On 2 September the Garde des Sceaux had written asking Beaumont to cut short his leave and return to France when it was convenient. 'His letter is very amiable' and left Beaumont free to decide what to do; however, the minister's request was so urgent that Beaumont felt it would be singularly ungracious not to comply as best he could. Tocqueville concurred, and they planned to leave on 1 April 1832. But there were more reasons than one for this decision. Mme de Kergorlay had written to say that the cholera pandemic which had been moving across Asia for years was now threatening France and Paris. So Tocqueville and Beaumont found themselves worrying less about their official careers than about the fate of their families, friends and loves. Tocqueville wrote to Chabrol:

If cholera comes to France, Marie must leave our country. To you I admit that it would be a frightful sorrow to see her depart, perhaps for ever, for I love her more than I can say. But her life is still more precious to me; her health is delicate; like me, she has for long had acute pains in the bowels; she would be more vulnerable than other women and the thought makes me despair. So act for the best; advise her and take what measures you think most advisable. Understand, for me this isn't a matter of pleasure or vanity, but of a real, vast concern, of a deep feeling which fills all my heart.

Not surprisingly, he and Beaumont, after reflection, decided to bring forward the date of their return: they now planned to sail on 16 February. And they went to considerable trouble to send home bottles of cajeput oil, an oriental remedy said to be effective against cholera (but Tocqueville did not believe in it, and nor does modern medicine).[41]

They felt that they ought to be with their families in this time of danger, but it would be absurd to leave America with their researches incomplete. So they stuck to their plans for the immediate future, even though from now on they would be living under a cloud of anxiety, and the prospect of their homeward journey would increasingly dominate the horizon. They had earlier settled that they ought to go to Washington for the opening of the Congressional session in January, in order to see the federal government in action. Before then they would make an extensive visit to the South, if only because of Beaumont's new interest in race and slavery. They would visit James Madison, they would go to Charleston, for they were now well aware of the political importance of the tariff question and of the impending contest between South Carolina and Washington. So far, so rational; what is less easy to understand, and is nowhere explained, is why they did not go by a coastal steamboat from Philadelphia to Charleston. Perhaps they could not bear the idea of having to spend a whole month or more in the heart of the slavery kingdom. Or perhaps they felt that they could not leave America without having seen the Mississippi. At any rate, they decided to get to Charleston by way of Pittsburgh, the Ohio river, the Mississippi, New Orleans, and from there across country to Savannah and their destination. 'It will be an immense journey,' Tocqueville wrote complacently to Eugène Stoffels, 'more than fifteen hundred

French leagues'. But even this itinerary was not expected to quench their thirst for instructive travel. They thought they might sail from New York to Liverpool, and spend three weeks getting to know Britain before, at last, re-entering France: Tocqueville's curiosity about that other country was longstanding, and the best way in which he could explain the fascination of America to his mother was by saying that 'with England, this country is the most interesting and instructive that one could possibly visit.'[42]

In the same letter of 24 October Tocqueville praised the Pennsylvania fall: 'America appears in all her glory'; but a month later, when they set out for Pittsburgh, things were very different. Beaumont said that the journey was one of the worst he had ever made: the roads were frightful, the carriages worse. When they reached the Alleghenies they were gripped by a terrible cold. 'For almost all the rest of the journey we travelled through the middle of a perpetual hurricane of snow, such as has not been seen for a very long time, least of all at this season.' After three days on the road they reached Pittsburgh, 'the Birmingham of America', but they had no time to look round, or visit the important penitentiary there, if they were to catch the next steamboat to Cincinnati. They boarded the *Fourth of July* on 25 November, very conscious that they were now to descend the Ohio as Chateaubriand had done (in a canoe) forty years earlier. But that had been in summer. Tocqueville, standing on the deck, admired the mountains, but lamented that they were covered in snow. Winter had caught him. He comforted himself with the thought that in a week he would have escaped southwards to the sun.[43] That night he was shipwrecked.

Towards midnight the *Fourth of July* hit Burlington Bar, a notorious reef in the Ohio, a little above Wheeling. The ship had been going fast, propelled by steam and the current, and the crash of her wreck was heard for a mile round. Water poured in: 'I have never heard an uglier sound,' Tocqueville was to report to Chabrol. The dark river was a mile wide and full of floating ice; water was filling the cabins; Tocqueville and Beaumont, giving themselves up for lost, shook hands in farewell. (Even at that moment they were impressed by the self-control of the Americans: not one woman screamed.) But then the water stopped rising: the ship had impaled herself so firmly that as she settled on the rock it acted as a plug of the hole it had made. Another steamer came by and took aboard the crew and passengers of the wreck, which had to be left eventually to sink to the bottom with all the cargo. On 1 December they at last reached Cincinnati.[44]

Tocqueville's substantial dossier of notes on Cincinnati and Ohio requires careful interpretation. He started to make sweeping generalizations about the state in not much more than twenty-four hours after arriving, and soon had to retract or modify them. He interviewed four lawyers and a doctor, and led all but one of them into anti-democratic remarks, even Salmon P. Chase, destined to be Lincoln's Secretary of the Treasury (and Chief Justice of the United States afterwards). The hold-out was Mr Justice McLean, who was instead induced to criticize the mounting campaign against the Bank of the United States: 'partisans are exploiting for their own ends the instinctive hate to which the idea of privilege and monopoly always gives birth.'[45] Chase, even younger than Tocqueville (he was born in 1808), was led to shake his head over the length to which democracy had gone in Ohio. The voters kept on making bad choices, especially in towns. Unworthy men won by flattery, which distinguished candidates would never stoop to. The unworthy had even been known to take drinks with voters![46] In all this, whether they knew it or not, Tocqueville's informants were responding to his anxious concern about the feasibility of democratic government, and he perhaps led them into saying more than they meant. As Donald Ratcliffe has pointed out in his study of Ohio politics at this period, three of them (including Chase) came from New England and had Federalist backgrounds, not to mention their native region's emphatic self-esteem; they were thus not entirely representative of Ohio; but all of them, as practical men, accepted the permanence and workability of democracy: the point was not to fight it, but to win democratic elections. 'In spite of everything,' said Chase, 'it is the influence of men of talent which governs us.' McLean emphasized the excellence of the federal system as a way of distributing power between the centre and the locality. Even Mr Walker ('a very distinguished young lawyer'), who expressed the most serious doubts, was full of confidence in the future of his region and his country, and so was Dr Drake ('Cincinnati's leading physician').[47] Tocqueville himself was not so much making a fresh investigation or pursuing an old one as testing an immensely important conclusion to which he had committed himself even before reaching Cincinnati. While still on the river he had written in one of his notebooks:

> One thing is incontrovertibly demonstrated by America which I doubted until now: it is, that the middle classes can govern a State. I do not know if they could emerge with honour from really difficult political situations. But they are equal to the everyday business of society. In spite of their petty passions, their incomplete education, their vulgarity, they can demonstrably supply practical intelligence, and that is enough.[48]

He had crossed a watershed.

Once this is understood, it becomes clear that his real preoccupations in Cincinnati were with two other matters: the Westward movement and slavery. As to the first, he had already discovered it and begun to investigate it during his travels on the Great Lakes. During his last days in Philadelphia he had met Joel Poinsett, who was accurately described to him as a very remarkable man.* Poinsett was warmly encouraging about the Mississippi journey ('It's in Kentucky and Tennessee that you can judge the character of Southerners') and made further remarks which confirmed the observations of the Westward movement which Tocqueville had made in Michigan. Here was another set of hypotheses to check by further enquiry, and consequently Tocqueville's notes on Ohio are full of the theme. As to slavery, he imbibed the notions of his informants. He had already been told by John Quincy Adams that in the South work was regarded as dishonourable; now he discovered that there were absolutely no idlers in Cincinnati, there was no leisure class; Mr Walker said that he knew no-one who did not have a profession and practise it; he also asserted that Kentucky was falling far behind Ohio, although it was by twenty years the older state. 'The sole discoverable reason for this difference is that slavery is established in Kentucky, and not in Ohio. There, work is despised, here it is honoured. There, idleness; here, endless bustle.'† Tocqueville listened

---

* Joel Poinsett (1779–1851), a South Carolinian, had been US minister to Mexico and was to be Secretary of War under President Van Buren. He was a close associate of Andrew Jackson, and led the resistance to nullification in his native state. For good or ill, it was he who introduced the poinsettia to the United States.

† We see here the germs of the free soil ideology (see Eric Foner, *Free Soil, Free Labor, Free Men*, New York, 1970) which contributed to the inter-sectional hostility which brought on the

to it all and elaborated it in his notebook, concluding: 'Man is not made for servitude; *this truth is perhaps still better demonstrated by the master than by the slave.*'[49]

Tocqueville and Beaumont left Cincinnati on 4 December. They took a steamboat for Louisville, and Beaumont, in excellent spirits, wrote a lively description of life aboard for his brother Jules. But two days later Tocqueville was writing to Chabrol:

> Decidedly, journeys by water do not suit us. Although we are on the latitude of Palermo and it is only 6 December, the cold has become so intense that this morning the Ohio froze … As I write, we are trying painstakingly to open a way through the ice; thanks to the river-current and to steam we are still making way, but we are afraid of dislocating our ship through the exertions exacted of her. I must add that the ears freeze if one pokes one's head outside: this is a Russian cold. Nobody remembers seeing its equal in this part of the world.

Beaumont was at first sceptical of this claim: 'That is what one-time visitors are always told'; but the winter of 1831–2 was indeed the most terrible that America had known for half a century. At Westport, twenty-five miles short of Louisville, the captain gave up the struggle and put his passengers ashore. Tocqueville and Beaumont had to hire a hand-cart for their luggage and a strong man to push it, and trudge through the snow, up to their knees, all the way to Louisville, where they arrived at nine in the evening. Next day they found that the river was as impassable below Louisville as above it.[50]

They refused to be trapped, and having been told that the Mississippi never froze below Memphis, 'we did not hesitate.' On 9 December they boarded a stagecoach for Nashville in Tennessee, which they reached the next day.[51] The Cumberland river was frozen, but if they could only get to Memphis they should be all right. So off they went across country on 11 December. It was the worst part of all their journey. Instead of a stagecoach they had to travel in what Beaumont called an open charabanc. The road was no more than a narrow, sometimes precipitous track through dense woods ('America is as yet no more

American Civil War. But it must be added that Mr Walker much exaggerated the difference between Ohio and Kentucky, and seriously misled Tocqueville.

than a forest'); the charabanc kept banging against tree-trunks on either side, and breaking down. They complained, and were told in true American fashion, 'Go ahead, moan: the other day one of our passengers broke an arm, and another a leg.' They travelled no more than ten leagues a day. One of their fellow travellers asked if there weren't very bad roads in France? 'Yes, sir,' said Beaumont, relieving his feelings, 'and you have such good ones in America, don't you?' But the shot did not seem to go home.[52]

Worst of all was that the cold was becoming too much for Tocqueville. He shivered all over, he lost his appetite, his head ached, he could not go much further. They were forced to take refuge in a log-cabin at Sandy Bridge about halfway (say, 100 miles) between Nashville and Memphis: it had three beds for hire to travellers. In spite of an immense fire which Beaumont lit in a huge fireplace it was desperately cold: the ill-built cabin let in icy draughts through every joint – Beaumont poured himself a glass of water, but it froze before he could drink it. He put Tocqueville to bed, and heaped him with every sort of cover he could find, but his friend only gradually began to get warmer. Beaumont seems to have sat up all night, keeping the fire going, watching the moonlight shine through the gaps in the walls and worrying about what would happen the next day: there was no doctor nearer than thirty miles away. The owners of the cabin offered no help at all.

Fortunately, the next day (14 December) Tocqueville felt somewhat better, though Beaumont had a hard time coaxing him to eat some stewed rabbit 'as a change from the eternal *beacon* [*sic*]'. For two days he gained strength, and on the sixteenth was more or less himself again – still feeble, but he had got his appetite back. The next day the stage-coach for Memphis came by, and the travellers were able to escape from Sandy Bridge; but when they got to Memphis, after another awful journey, they found that the Mississippi had frozen after all, and navigation was suspended. They were stuck in Memphis for a week. They thought the place dreary, but amused themselves trying for game in the forest: they were joined by some Chickasaw Indians. Tocqueville bagged two parrots. They found volumes of Shakespeare and Milton in the latest log-cabin where they had taken refuge; Tocqueville read what he later called 'that old feudal play', *Henry V*.[53]

On 24 December (Tocqueville makes absolutely no allusion to Christmas) a steamboat came up from the south *en route* for Louisville. She halted at Memphis, and the stranded travellers – there were fifteen besides Tocqueville and Beaumont – did their best to persuade the captain that, all the waters to the north being frozen, he should, in his own interest, return to New Orleans. They might not have succeeded; but suddenly out of the forest came a sad, extraordinary procession. Drums beat, horses whinnied, dogs barked, and at last a large band of Indians appeared – old men carried in their sons' arms, babies on their mothers' backs – making for Memphis on their way into exile. For these were Choctaw, victims of the notorious Indian Removal Act of 1830. Under that act the Five Civilized Tribes of the South-West – Creeks, Cherokee, Choctaw, Chickasaw, Seminole – were condemned to lose their lands and be removed to Indian Territory, what is now eastern Oklahoma. Tocqueville and Beaumont gazed at them with compassion and indignation. Tocqueville, indeed, was to become quite Voltairean when he described the incident to his mother. The Americans, he said, having discovered that one square mile could feed ten times more civilized men than savages, reasoned that wherever civilized men could settle, the savages should give way: 'see what a fine thing logic is.' So the Choctaw would have to give up lands which they had lived in for perhaps a thousand years, and, rewarded with rich gifts ('flasks of brandy, glass necklaces, earrings and mirrors'), intimidated by the hint of force, had to trudge 300 miles, without even being allowed to wait until spring. And Tocqueville was sure that within a century they would all have died out.[54]

The government agent who was escorting them offered the steamboat captain a handsome price for carrying the Choctaw downriver to the place on the Arkansas shore chosen for their disembarkation, so Tocqueville and Beaumont were at last to be free of Tennessee. They watched the pitiful spectacle of the Indians boarding the ship: the dogs howled and refused to go until their masters dragged them on. Tocqueville found one old man who spoke English. Why were the Choctaw leaving their lands, he was asked. 'To be free,' was the only answer they could get out of him.[55]

Even now their journey was not without incident. The *Louisville* hit a sandbar on the night of 26 December and remained stuck there for two days, to the great exasperation of our travellers, who were, however, calmly informed by the pilot that there was nothing to be done, and it was not his fault, since the sands of the Mississippi never stayed in the same place for a year – like Frenchmen. The insult had to be swallowed, but it may have given Tocqueville a dislike for the river. It did not deserve its fame, he wrote to his mother: 'It is just a great yellow flood ... On the horizon not a hill to be seen, just trees, more trees, and trees again; reeds and creepers; deep silence; not a trace of humanity, not even the smoke of an Indian camp.' His Romanticism was at a low ebb. The Choctaw were landed in Arkansas. On the last day of the voyage Tocqueville and Beaumont had a long and interesting conversation about Indians with a fellow-passenger, none other than Sam Houston, the future victor of San Jacinto and president of the republic of Texas. They visited a sugar plantation in Louisiana, presumably while the *Louisville* refuelled. Then on New Year's Day they saw a forest of masts ahead. They had reached New Orleans.[56]

It was now more than a month since they had left Philadelphia; they were at least two weeks behind schedule. After so long a time in the wild their sense of time was disoriented: their tactlessness in calling on Étienne Mazureau on New Year's Day has already been described.* But it was clear that some hard choices must be made if they were to get to Washington in time for the meeting of Congress, and then catch the packet sailing for France in early February. They found it difficult to tear themselves away from New Orleans once having got there: they had meant to spend one night there, but ended in spending three. This was no help to their schedule. They left on 4 January and arrived in Mobile the same day: no doubt they went by coastal steamer. At Mobile they made their final calculations. Not the most optimistic estimate of time and distance could blur the truth. They would have to give up Charleston. They would have to give up their proposed visit to James Madison at his Virginian plantation (which posterity must think was the greatest loss of their entire journey). They must go as straight and fast as they could to Washington, which meant crossing Alabama, Georgia and North Carolina until they reached the sea, when they could take to the water again and approach Washington by steam and

* See above, p. 31.

Chesapeake Bay. In any circumstances it would have been a demanding journey, and, as G. W. Pierson remarks, it was made worse because the bad luck which had dogged them since they left Philadelphia did not desert them now.[57] Tocqueville wrote to Chabrol of:

> carriages broken and overturned, bridges carried away, rivers swollen [there must have been a sudden thaw], no room in the stage ... The fact is that to traverse the immense stretch of country that we have just covered, and to do it in so little time and in winter, was hardly practicable. But we were right because we succeeded.

And his health had been equal to the strain; in fact he boasted of it to Alexandrine:

> If ever I write a book on medicine, I guarantee that it won't be like the usual ones that are brought out every day. I will maintain and will prove that, to be well, it is necessary, first, to live off maize and pork, to dine scantily, enormously, or not at all, according to circumstances; to make your bed on the floor and sleep fully clothed; to travel, in a week, from frost to heat and from heat to frost; to put your shoulder to a wheel or wake up in a ditch: above all, not to *think* ...[58]

In reality, it was impossible not to think, as the stagecoach jogged and lumbered slowly over the bad roads of Alabama. Tocqueville found himself going over and over all he had seen and heard and thought in the past nine months; conclusions welled up and, either in the coach itself, with great difficulty, or at whatever wayside tavern at which they stopped to pass the night, he wrote them down in his notebook. It was the intellectual climax of his voyage.

For instance, 'the jury' (by which he meant both grand and petty). He clung to his perception that it was 'the most direct application of the principle of the sovereignty of the people'. His thoughts turning to France, as they were now doing more and more, he added that wherever a power other than the people established the jury system in good faith (he was thinking of the Restoration)* it brought about its

---

* AT is largely repeating some thoughts on the Restoration and the jury which he had first written down on 11 October (OC V i 181–2). There, he had identified the Restoration's fatal mistake as its attempt to combine the principle of popular sovereignty with that of divine right.

own destruction. Perhaps an aristocracy might successfully manipulate it (he must have had England in mind); and it could be a mighty weapon in the hands of a tyrant. Bonaparte knew what he was doing when he made the jury dependent on the Crown. It was a mistake to think that Bonaparte had been the enemy of all liberty. His great, enlightened intelligence had clearly shown him the benefits to his regime of generously fostering civil liberty. But at the same time he hated political liberty. Even that was the hatred of an ambitious and masterful genius, not the blind antipathy of a clan leader (here, perhaps, Tocqueville was thinking of Charles X, but more likely of the usual reputation of Napoleon, who certainly acted as clan leader of the Bonapartes).[59]

Liberty. Tocqueville began to set down what his American experiences had taught him as to the meaning of that word, and of the word 'republic'. In doing so he reached not only the essence, the kernel, of his impending masterpiece, but the heart of his attitude to his country's recent history, and to his own times.

If our royalists could see the domestic progress of a well-ordered republic, its deep respect for vested interests, the power of those interests over the mob, law as a religion, the real and effective liberty which everyone there enjoys, the real power of the majority, the easy and natural progress in everything, they would see that they had been confounding under one label differing systems which have no real likeness. On their side, our republicans would feel that what we have called the republic has been only an unclassifiable monster, a [word missing in the MS] covered in blood and muck, clinging to the rags of classical names and quarrels. And what does it matter to me whether tyranny wears a royal mantle or a tribune's toga if I feel its hand weighing on me? When Danton strangled unhappy prisoners whose sole crime was not to think as he did, was that liberty? When Robespierre later sent Danton to the scaffold for daring to be his rival, it was justice no doubt, but was it liberty? When the majority in the Convention proscribed the minority, when the arbitrary power of the proconsuls deprived citizens of their goods and their children, of their lives, when an opinion was a crime, and when a thought uttered in the sanctuary of the domestic hearth incurred death, was that liberty?

And so on with regard to the Directory and Bonaparte, concluding: 'we in France have seen anarchy and despotism under all their forms but nothing which resembles a republic.' He immediately added:

If I ever write anything on America, it will be extremely important to devote a chapter, of which the foregoing is a rough sketch, to bringing out the difference between anarchy and a real republic so that it can also be shown where the great principles of liberty are practised ...

That chapter might be very interesting by reason of its novelty.[60]

This passage is immensely important partly because it sets out the core of Tocqueville's lifelong attitudes and opinions as to the historical and ideological questions which were to be the matter of all his work, and partly because it shows what effect the journey to the United States had had on his views. It had radicalized him. He had conceived a deep admiration for the American system as he had observed it; he had become, in principle, a republican, and although he was still well aware of the great differences between America and France, he had come to see how the American example could form the substance of a critique of French politics. His trenchant sketch of France's revolutionary past (clearly informed by what had happened to his family and so many others) makes plain why he was so afraid of a relapse into despotism or anarchy – it had happened before, and not long ago: 'vested interests' had been destroyed (here Tocqueville unequivocally identifies himself with the propertied classes). Finally, the passage clearly indicates what he meant by liberty and why he loved it – the main note being his cult of the rule of law; and of course it shows that he knew that what he had to say would seem quite startling in France and might well make his reputation.

The masterpiece was forming in his mind, but it would be a long time before he could get down to writing it. The journey was still unfinished, and still producing new experiences. On 13 January, probably at Columbia, South Carolina, who should board the coach but that remarkable Mr Poinsett? They remembered him well from their last days in Philadelphia, and he may have been as glad of their company on the coach as they were of his. He did not tell them much, if anything, of his most recent activities: that as a leading Unionist he had been trying in vain to get the South Carolina legislature to endorse Andrew Jackson for a second term, and that he was now going to Washington to report to the President and to try for a compromise on the great tariff issue.[61] He was quite willing to answer the

Frenchmen's questions, and indeed seems to have talked non-stop until they reached Washington, on topics as varied as nullification, Mexico, Indians, banks, roads, penitentiaries and the presidency of the United States. This last was a topic which Tocqueville had not yet studied, and he was certain to look into it after he reached the federal capital. Unfortunately Poinsett got him off to a poor start by informing him (bizarrely for a Jacksonian) that the President had no power, that it was Congress which governed.[62]

They arrived in Washington on 18 January in what, years later, Tocqueville remembered as extremely hot weather; but that night the Potomac froze.[63] Nevertheless, winter was not seriously to inconvenience them again. They went to call on the French minister, Baron Sérurier, who welcomed them warmly. A veteran diplomatist, Sérurier had served as minister to the US under Napoleon, whom he had indiscreetly supported during the Hundred Days; dismissed from the public service after the return of the Bourbons, he had been recalled by Louis-Philippe, who had made him a peer of France. He was thus a typical Orleanist. He was also a sincere patriot, and had supported Tocqueville and Beaumont's mission from the moment that he heard of it: he had written to all the French consuls in the United States telling them to give the commissioners every help with their 'honourable mission'; and now that he had met them he was charmed and delighted by the good impression they had made wherever they went. They were just the sort of young Frenchmen who ought to see and be seen by America.[64] The day after their arrival he took them to the White House to meet the President.

Tocqueville, by now, had come to understand the vivacity and energy of party politics in the United States, and (thanks to such informants as Joel Poinsett) realized that the current struggle over the tariff, which set South against North, might determine the future of the Union itself. But he did not understand the essential role of party competition in making the constitutional system workable, and still less did he understand the function, power and influence of the president within it. On both these points Andrew Jackson, party leader and imperious Executive, might have greatly enlightened him, but the opportunity was missed – if, given the circumstances of their meeting, it can be said to have existed. It was not merely that Jackson's visitors had been taught to think meanly of him, whether as a general or a politician ('formerly he was known chiefly as a duellist and a brawler,' said Beaumont), nor even that Jackson was not yet fully embarked on the great campaigns, against the Bank of the United States and the nullification movement, which were to stamp his mark indelibly on his age and dramatically increase the authority of the presidency. Receiving distinguished visitors was part of his routine; he would give them half an hour of his time, offer them refreshment, and say good-bye. So Tocqueville and Beaumont might enter the White House but were not likely to be shown any of the inner workings of American politics and government. They were not impressed by Jackson, a vigorous sixty-six, who uttered only commonplaces in their presence, but they were vastly impressed by the occasion itself. America could still surprise them:

> The President of the United States occupies a palace which in Paris would be spoken of only as a handsome private mansion; its interior is decorated in good taste, but plainly; the salon in which he receives visitors is infinitely less magnificent than those of our ministers; he has no guards watching at his door and, if he has courtiers, they are not very assiduous in their attentions, for when we entered the room he was alone, although it was the day he devotes to receiving the public, and during the whole of our visit only two or three other people came in ... he gave us each a glass of Madeira for which we thanked him, calling him 'Sir' like the first visitor.

Tocqueville was struck by the fact that Jackson shook hands with everyone. It was all a long way from the Tuileries.[65]

Tocqueville, like so many other visitors to Washington in the early nineteenth century, allowed himself to be ironical at the failed pretensions of the place: he told his father:

> If anyone wants to estimate humanity's power to calculate the future, he must visit Washington ... Today [it] displays an arid, sun-burned plain, on which are scattered two or three magnificent buildings and the five or six villages which make up the town. Unless you are Alexander or Peter the Great, at least, you should have nothing to do with creating the capital of an empire.

All the same, he enjoyed himself there. They were welcomed as warmly as ever, by old friends and new.

Washington at this moment contains the most important men of the whole Union. For us it is no longer a question of obtaining from them suggestions about topics we are ignorant of, but of re-examining, in conversation with them, almost everything we already know. We are settling the doubtful points.

Tocqueville conceded to Édouard that he had only a superficial impression of the South, and (as I have mentioned) that two years would be needed to compose a complete and exact picture of the United States; still, he thought that his time in America had been usefully and agreeably spent, not wasted; at the very least he had piled up documents, talked much and thought much. He modestly hoped that he would be able to write a useful book on his return to France.[66]

The prospect of that return now dominated everything he wrote and thought. Beaumont had been more or less homesick throughout the journey, constantly demanding longer and more frequent letters from the members of his family, and scolding them when they failed him. Now his one idea was that they should all gather at Beaumont-la-Chartre to welcome him back. Tocqueville's outlook was much more complicated. He still had grave doubts about the stability of the July Monarchy: news had reached him of a revolt in Lyon; strangely, this made him think that 'the wind ... begins to blow hard from the side of Royalism'.* But as to French politics, he said, he wrote like a blind man. The uncertainty he was in made it impossible to foresee what he would do on his return. Should he resign his post, as he often felt like doing, or try once more for promotion? 'At least I see clearly that I won't resume the robe of a *juge suppléant*'† – Versailles would know him no more, unless under another title. He wrote to Chabrol:

> That matter is settled (but don't mention it to anyone). I think I would make myself ridiculous if I acted otherwise. When I say that I will be seen no more at Versailles, I certainly go too far. I will probably show myself there two days after I get to Paris. But the visit will be incognito and I will not have come to deal with either political or judicial business. I hope that you will be able to let me have a bed

---

* He meant legitimism; he had forgotten, or in his heart did not believe, that the Orleanists were also royalists.
† The title which the Orleanists had substituted for *juge auditeur*.

in your apartment for one night. Perhaps I won't make much use of it, but appearances must be respected. You know my main reason for visiting you so promptly, and I would be a humbug to deny it; but I want you to know that the pleasure I expect from my return to Versailles is doubled by the thought that I will find you there too.[67]

He and Beaumont had given up the idea of returning by way of Liverpool. Tocqueville had heard rumours that cholera had reached England even before he got to Washington; he wrote to Chabrol:

> I see from her letters that your neighbour is very frightened. Use all your influence, *mon cher ami*, to calm her. During epidemics extreme terror sometimes makes one susceptible to infection. Besides, however rapid the march of the malady may be, I sincerely hope to get to France before it. If that actually happens and Marie is still there, I will almost answer for it that I can restore her habitual tranquillity.[68]

In Washington the rumours were confirmed: cholera had reached Sunderland (in February it would reach London). 'We have no wish to make its acquaintance,' said Beaumont, nor did they wish to be detained in quarantine on arriving in France. So they decided to sail directly from New York to Le Havre, and after some difficulty in finding a boat booked a passage on the same ship, *Le Havre*, that had carried them to America nearly a year previously. Tocqueville was bitterly disappointed at hitches which delayed their departure by ten days, the more so as his impatience to be in France killed his interest in America and Americans: after his return he was to remark to Beaumont that he seemed to have been reduced to imbecility during his last month in the United States. He wrote to Joel Poinsett from New York that:

> we are already living more in France than in America. Hitherto the friendly hospitality that we have found among your countrymen has almost made us forget that we were far from our native land. We still meet with the same kindness, and feel it with the same gratitude, but it is no longer enough, and we realize for the first time that we are only foreigners here.

Another irritation was the necessity of reassuring his family that he was not going to be wrecked by the equinoctial gales. He pooh-poohed the danger:

> We ran a hundred times more risks on the steamboats, but you were never anxious. Yet thirty of them blew up or were wrecked during our first six weeks in the US. We left one of them three hours before the explosion; another time, we split like a nutshell on a rock.

The Atlantic was harmless in comparison. 'I have seen enough of waves and sailors not to worry.' He and Beaumont were also kept busy to the last by the need to write letters of farewell, and letters acknowledging the various documents which Jared Sparks and others continued to heap upon them.[69]

Le Havre sailed on 20 February. Neither of the commissioners ever recorded his thoughts and feelings as America slipped behind them for ever.

CHAPTER TEN

WRITING PRISONS

1832

J'aurais pu voler, moi, pauvre homme;
Mais non: mieux vaut tendre la main.
Au plus, j'ai dérobé la pomme
Qui mûrit au bord du chemin.
Vingt fois pourtant on me verrouille
Dans les cachots de par le roi.
De mon seul bien on me dépouille.
*Vieux vagabonde, le soleil est à moi.**

JEAN-PIERRE DE BÉRANGER

IT SHOULD HAVE BEEN a purely triumphal re-entry. In spite of various difficulties and some danger, they had achieved all their purposes and nearly completed their prison investigations. There were various loose ends to tie in; otherwise there seemed to be nothing to stop them writing their report speedily and thereby achieving recognition as leading authorities on penology and as potential statesmen. And so indeed it proved. Their families were delighted to welcome them home, as were Marie Mottley and, no doubt, the faithful Chabrol.

---

* Poor man that I am, I could have robbed; / But no: better to hold out a beggar's hand. / At most, I helped myself to an apple / Ripening beside the road. Yet twenty times / I was locked in a cell by order of the King. / He robbed me of my only good / For, tramp that I am, the sun is mine.

But in all too many other ways they found themselves perplexed, obstructed and disappointed.

They got a hint of what to expect almost at once. It is unknown exactly when they reached Le Havre, but they were probably back in Paris by 24 March. They asked for an immediate interview with the Minister of the Interior, but their request was not even acknowledged. After waiting impatiently for a week Beaumont left for Beaumont-la-Chartre and the family reunion which he had talked about so much in his letters.

His collaborator sat in Paris, prostrate. Tocqueville had been living on his nerves for a year, perpetually driving himself to prodigies of exertion, and now Nature rebelled. Symptoms of what was to come may perhaps be discerned in the record of his last weeks in America. Neither he nor Beaumont ever wrote a word about their homeward voyage. Pierson says baldly, 'They were suddenly so tired.'[1] Certainly Tocqueville was, and his cross-grained temperament made it impossible for him to be patient while his energy renewed itself. He sat slumped in a huge armchair which his father had given him, his eyes half-shut, waiting, he said, for the genius of the penitentiary system to appear; which it didn't.[2] Charles Stoffels came to call and told his brother afterwards that Tocqueville was suffering from an attack of spleen. Tocqueville agreed, admitting to *ennui*, melancholy, and a sort of moral exhaustion 'which are, I think, the ingredients of spleen'. He put it down to the sudden change in his occupations. He was delighted to be home again, and yet he did not know how to cope with idleness after his year of almost feverish agitation. 'I was weary of tranquillity even before my body had recovered from its fatigue.' So he reported to Eugène Stoffels in late April; he added the news that he was not yet dead. This was barely a joke.[3]

For cholera had reached the Channel coast at much the same time as Tocqueville and Beaumont. It appeared at Calais on 15 March and in Paris ten days later; by the end of the month ninety persons had died of this agonizing and filthy disease in the capital alone.[4] The pandemic found the French as ill-prepared as every other nation. Professional medicine had no understanding of what was happening (the cholera bacillus was not identified until 1883)[5] so the public authorities were unable to devise any effective sanitary measures: the best they could do was to spray the gutters of the boulevards with chloride.[6]* The political as well as the medical results of the epidemic were disastrous. Ignoring the fact that the outbreak was worldwide, the rich blamed it on the poor for their squalid way of life and the poor said that the rich were trying to exterminate them by poisoning the water-supply. Class antipathy, already much heightened by the July Revolution, was exacerbated again: class war began to be a real possibility. The Orleanist monarchy, which had long outlived its brief initial flush of popularity, began to find it impossible to reach out to new supporters so as to be seen as a national rather than a factional regime. This was to do much to frustrate Tocqueville's political aspirations.

He did not foresee it, and seems also to have been a little slow to grasp the full scale of the horror now visiting Paris. Beaumont in the country had begun to draft the prison report, since there was no telling when Tocqueville would feel equal to doing so, but he needed help, and sent a long list of penitentiary questions, which Tocqueville discussed on 4 April. He complained that he was still in a state of imbecility, and that Beaumont's questions were too vague to be answered; then he gave a cheerful account of a pleasant chat which he had had with their patron, *le cousin* Le Peletier d'Aunay, who had given plenty of advice, much of it good; but in retrospect the really significant passages in this letter were the exordium and the postscript. He began on 4 April by assuring Beaumont (as he would Stoffels) that he was not dead, although fifty new cases of cholera had broken out in his district – *le quartier Saint-Thomas-d'Aquin* – since yesterday; the postscript was written on 6 April, from Saint-Germain-en-Laye, where he had gone to arrange a refuge for his parents with the Ollivier family, as in 1830. Between the two dates the upper class in Paris had panicked as they suddenly realized that they were no safer than anyone else. Casimir Périer, the head of the government, had contracted cholera when visiting the sick in a hospital: he was to die in May. Comte Molé's only child, Mme de Champlâtreux, and yet another Tocqueville cousin, the

---

* AT, who was inclined to exaggerate the improvements made in the material conditions of French prisons in the recent past, might with advantage have noted the fact that, nevertheless, the cholera induced the authorities to take hurried action about them. Warmer clothes and better food were given to prisoners, internal walls were whitewashed, dormitories were ventilated, and disinfectant was sprayed liberally through the bath-houses and latrines (Chevalier, *Le Choléra*, 16).

marquis de Chauvelin,* caught the disease and died almost at once; and Saint-Thomas-d'Aquin, in the heart of the noble faubourg, had one of the highest mortality rates in the city. A flight out of town began. Tocqueville urged Beaumont on no account to return to Paris for the time being.[7]

The Tocquevilles felt safe once ensconced at Saint-Germain, but Beaumont had set off for Paris before the letter from Alexis arrived. He sent a line ahead to forewarn of his arrival. So Tocqueville wrote another letter, anxiously inscribed on the envelope, 'The hotel porter is entreated to give this letter to M. de Beaumont as soon as he arrives', insisting that Beaumont not spend a night in Paris but come at once to Saint-Germain. Apart from many other considerations, it would be a splendid place in which to work on the prison report. Hervé de Tocqueville added a friendly postscript in the same sense. Beaumont does not seem to have paid much attention to these pleas: on 12 April he was in Paris trying once more to get an interview with the minister of public works. He still did not succeed: the minister (comte d'Argout) was too ill with cholera to receive him.[8]

So far as can be judged (documentation is lacking) the collaborators did thereafter set to work, probably at Saint-Germain, where Tocqueville remained well into May; but both had their troubles. They had left France for a year in the hope that things would have settled down politically by the time they got back, but this had not happened. Some young legitimist hotheads had in February devised a ridiculous plot to kidnap or even murder the royal family during a ball at the Tuileries (Chateaubriand, whom they tried to draw into the scheme, advised against it in vain); it failed, but another conspiracy was hatched immediately. It involved Kergorlay. He and his father had disappeared from France during the winter (it is clear from Tocqueville's letters to Mme de Kergorlay that he had a rough idea why)[9] and at the end of April everything became painfully public. The duchesse de Berry, who regarded herself as the rightful Regent of France (since Charles X had abdicated, Louis-Philippe was a usurper, and her son, 'Henri V', was a minor), had hired a Sardinian steamer, the *Carlo Alberto*, and landed

---

* British readers may like to be told that this was indeed the man whose name and history were so scandalously misappropriated by the Baroness Orczy when she needed a villain for her Scarlet Pimpernel stories.

in Provence, expecting to raise Marseille in the name of legitimacy. (It was like a parody of the Hundred Days.) But the people did not stir; so then, instead of returning to Italy as her more sensible counsellors advised, she travelled incognita through France to start a rising in the Vendée. The Kergorlays were part of her original band, but after the Marseille fiasco they stayed aboard the *Carlo Alberto*, meaning to sail to Spain. On 29 April a shortage of coal forced them to put in at Toulon, where they were immediately arrested.

Kergorlay was a young idiot ('*ce fou de Kergorlay*,' says Mme Perrot)[10] but Tocqueville was not going to leave him in the lurch. As soon as it could be arranged he travelled to Marseille, where the Kergorlays *père et fils* were jailed, acting as an escort to the comtesse de Kergorlay and her daughters, who were hurrying to the prisoners' side. It was not inconvenient: while in the south he could visit the *bagne* (convict prison) at Toulon. He and Beaumont were well aware that they knew less than was necessary, if they were to make convincing arguments, about French prisons. In fact Beaumont suggested that, after inspecting Toulon, Tocqueville should meet him in Geneva, so that together they could visit the penitentiaries of Switzerland.

The travellers reached Marseille on 17 May, and Tocqueville went at once to the prison, claiming admission as Kergorlay's cousin. It was a painful experience. As he sat waiting he remembered that the last time he had seen his friend was just before he left for America, and though on that occasion he had worried about possible future misfortunes he had never anticipated that they would next meet in jail, of all places. Louis's great joy at seeing Alexis dispersed Tocqueville's gloom, but although they were allowed to talk for half an hour they could not say anything serious in the warder's presence. Tocqueville came on a second visit two days later.[11]

All seemed to be going as well as might be, although Tocqueville was afraid that the duchesse de Berry's activities in the *bocage* (rumours were flying about) would complicate matters. He decided that now was the moment to go to Toulon and inspect the *bagne*. He arrived there on 20 May, and the next day read in a week-old *Moniteur* which had just arrived on the coast that Gustave de Beaumont had been dismissed from his post as *substitut* in Paris.[12]

The announcement seems to have come as a total surprise, though

Tocqueville must have known that Beaumont was in trouble. The issue was the first of the unpleasant scandals which afflicted the July Monarchy throughout its existence. The last prince de Condé had been found hanged (with two cravats) in his bedroom, and although he may have committed suicide or may have had an accident while trying for a sexual thrill, a great many people believed that he had been murdered by his mistress, Sophie Dawes, baronne de Feuchères, an English adventuress. She had been barred from court by Louis XVIII when he discovered that her marriage to the baron de Feuchères was a sham; under Charles X she was readmitted in return for bullying Condé into leaving most of his vast fortune to the duc d'Aumale, a younger son of Louis-Philippe (Mme de Feuchères got the residue). Then came the July Revolution: Condé began to think of emigrating and changing his will; Sophie Dawes felt her hold on him slackening, Louis-Philippe saw the great chateau of Chantilly slipping out of his grasp. The prince died on the night of 26–7 August 1830. A court brought in a verdict of suicide, but the incredulous reaction of public opinion is understandable. Mme de Feuchères, with the all-too-evident backing of the King, brought a suit for criminal libel against the Rohan family, whom the will had robbed of what would otherwise have been their inheritance, and who had spoken their minds much too freely (eventually Louis de Rohan was fined and sent to jail for three months). Beaumont was ordered to act as prosecutor in the case, and when he refused was summarily dismissed.[13]

Tocqueville was outraged. The attempt to force Beaumont into public association with Sophie Dawes seemed like a crude attempt to dishonour him for ever in the eyes of the legitimist party, which largely consisted of his friends and relations. Beaumont had argued in vain that he was still on leave and that anyway he was professionally ignorant of the case, which had been prepared in his absence; his real reason was that although he accepted the July Monarchy he wanted no part of its squalid intrigues. His attitude was an implied rebuke to the King himself. He had to go. His friend wrote as follows to the Procureur Général:

Being in Toulon at the moment, where I am inspecting the *bagne* and the other prisons of the town, I only learned today, from the *Moniteur* of 16 April, of the harsh and, I may say, supremely unjust decision with which *M. le garde des sceaux* has favoured M. de Beaumont.

Long bound in intimate friendship with the man just struck down by dismissal in this way, whose principles I share and whose conduct I approve, I think it my duty to share his fate of my own accord, and with him to abandon a profession in which neither a clear conscience nor services performed can guarantee a man against undeserved disgrace.

M. *le procureur général*, I have the honour to request you to bring to the attention of *M. le garde des sceaux* my resignation as *juge suppléant* at the Versailles tribunal.[14]

It was another splendid affirmation of friendship, even if Tocqueville sacrificed little by it (whereas Beaumont had lost a highly promising career).[15] As he had told Chabrol, he had not intended to continue as *juge suppléant*: promotion or resignation was his plan, and it was perhaps only his bout of spleen which had prevented him from doing anything about it before. Anyway, he had still been on leave, and there was the prison report to complete. But he had not intended to resign with such *éclat*, and was blazingly sincere in his indignation. It was a sorry ending to what had once seemed so bright a prospect, and might well have made him regret again the painful decision to take the oath in 1830, which had done him no good, except – a large exception – to make the American mission possible.

At any rate the episode dissipated the last traces of his lethargy. His report on the *bagne* of Toulon is briskness itself. He was by then a thoroughly seasoned inspector of prisons, as he showed in every sentence. Toulon was the first jail which he had visited since his return from America, and he knew exactly what he wanted to find out and how to assess his findings. The *bagne* was notoriously brutal, and at the back of his mind he was always comparing it with Sing-Sing. By that standard it failed badly: not the least attempt was made to reform the convicts, they corrupted each other (of the hundred patients in the hospital ward twenty-six were there because of venereal infections which they had caught from one another, 'the shameful consequence of the most infamous of vices') and the warders were terrified of the prisoners: 'the governor admitted to me that since the July Revolution a spirit of independence has gained ground among the convicts and that authority is obliged to shut its eyes to many small abuses in order to avoid great evils.' On the other hand, Toulon was preferable to the *maisons centrales* of France. Discipline was better. The work was healthier, and punishment by whipping was healthier than by the *cachot*, the punishment cell. A *bagne* was cheaper to build and run than a *maison centrale*, and there were fewer recidivists, such was the salutary terror which it inspired ('there are only two ways in which to influence the will of man: persuasion and fear'). The 'bastard charity' known as modern philanthropy had so softened the regime in the *maisons centrales* that they had become mere schools of corruption. At least the *bagne* did not make its inmates worse. (This observation does not seem quite consistent with some of Tocqueville's other comments.) Nevertheless, Tocqueville had various suggestions for reform. For instance, he thought that if proper workshops were organized (here he probably had the example of Auburn in mind) the use of leg-irons might be discontinued, which would eliminate the prison's most hideous aspect, 'deeply touch' the despised philanthropists, and diminish the prison's undeservedly black reputation.[16]

After drafting this document Tocqueville returned to Marseille on 25 May, and found that Kergorlay's position had worsened, no doubt, as foreseen, because of the duchesse de Berry's activities. He was allowed no visitors, not even his mother, and certainly not Tocqueville. This produced a day of collisions, as Tocqueville was sent from the pillar of the police chief at Marseille to the post of the chief magistrate and back again. He gave rather better than he got: he who had associated so long and on such equal terms with the great men of America was not going to tolerate nonsense from minor French officials. He said to the magistrate, president of the Aix tribunal, that he too had been a magistrate, he knew that prisoners could be held *incommunicado* only in the most special circumstances, and that an official who ignored this rule risked being held to account; but even that threat did not shake M. Pataille, who, when he had run out of lies, evasions and weak pleasantries, simply refused to receive Tocqueville again. It is possible to sympathize with him somewhat. He knew that Louis de Kergorlay, directly or indirectly, had been involved in a plot to overthrow the government of France by force; he had to be held until trial, and he had to be prevented from treasonable communications. How could

Pataille be sure that his imperious visitor was not another conspirator? So Tocqueville eventually gave up, and wrote a coldly exact narration of his encounter for Mme de Kergorlay's use. She continued the fight for access, and got a furious account of her wrongs, including Tocqueville's exclusion, into the *Ga₹ette du Midi*, a strongly legitimist newspaper; but Tocqueville left Marseille for Geneva on 21 May.[17]

He took what seems a somewhat leisurely and circuitous route, by way of Gap, Grenoble and Lyon; he may have been amusing himself by following Napoleon's route of 1815, and there was no hurry, since Beaumont was not planning to arrive in Geneva until 1 June. He had written to Tocqueville, taking his dismissal tranquilly, though complaining of the government's ingratitude; but he could not hide that it left him once again dependent on his father financially, and presumably that was why, in the end, he did not go to Geneva. Tocqueville's spirits sank, and his movements became still slower. Another of his friends, Blosseville, had published a book on the British penal colonies in Australia; Tocqueville, who was no friend to transportation, wrote a severe review of it, for his own use, in Gap on 31 May. The news from the West was distressing. On 3 June, from Lyon, he wrote to Marie:

> The royalists [again that curious usage] will perhaps have some transient success, but I still predict to you that they will be crushed. How much loyal and honourable blood will flow! I have already seen in the paper the name of a brave young man I knew. He has just been wretchedly killed. Explain to me why in every age honour and incompetence go hand in hand? Who were braver, more loyal and, at the same time, more maladroit and unlucky than your Jacobites? Our French royalists are following just the same path.

He went on to Geneva, and again wrote trenchant reports, on the penitentiaries there and at Lausanne. The prisoners were made far too comfortable, he said: at Geneva they even got baths once a month. The management had forgotten that 'the goal of real philanthropy is not to make prisoners happy, but to make them better.' Geneva was a *bonbonnière* of a prison – the same word which he had used to describe the houses on Long Island a year previously: perhaps it was put into his head by the penitentiary at Lausanne, a fine, arcaded building placed on a height next to the great lake ('*luxe extraordinaire*'). But he was pleased to find that Christianity was an important part of the discipline at both establishments. Then on 7 June he heard that serious revolutionary disturbances had broken out in Paris, and at once left for home.[18]

The Orleanist regime was under fierce attack from two sides, largely because of the cholera epidemic. The duchesse de Berry hoped that the suffering caused by the epidemic, and by the long economic recession which had started in 1828, would be her recruiting officer in the west. Much more dangerous was the rising in Paris which followed the death from cholera of the Bonapartist general Lamarque. The young republican conspirators of the secret societies (honour and incompetence can go hand in hand on the Left as well as the Right) made the funeral into a demonstration and the demonstration into an attempt to overthrow the monarchy. But the government was well-prepared and the King showed remarkable personal courage, which inspired the National Guard; on 6 June the rising was crushed. It had been a furious and dangerous affair, and the barricades had risen most thickly in the streets where cholera had been most murderous.[19]

By the time Tocqueville reached Saint-Germain the tragic business was finished. The alarm over, he was able to devote himself partly to the prison report and partly to *l'affaire Kergorlay*. He is not very visible to posterity, because although he wrote to Louis regularly, Kergorlay kept none of his letters, and Marie preserved only fragments of two letters written to her in July. But we know that, singly or together, Tocqueville and Beaumont continued their inspections, visiting at least four prisons and a *maison de refuge* in Paris during August. It is clear from the *Système pénitentiaire* itself that they both worked extremely hard on the text of their report throughout the summer, wanting to finish it as soon as possible.[20]

It was trouble enough, but Kergorlay gave more. He took to writing enormous letters on every subject that crossed his mind, full of touching avowals ('I love you with all my heart, more than ever, I need you, I need only you, I would be so happy if we were together ...') but also full of urgent demands, of which the largest concerned a pamphlet written by the prisoner which proved, to its author's satisfaction, that the seizure of the *Carlo Alberto* and her passengers was illegal. Tocqueville was required to undertake what must have been the extremely onerous task of distributing the thousand or so copies printed ('You told me in your last letter that you would love to be of use to me in some way; I know that what I now ask is not exactly what you had in mind, but ...') to various booksellers and legitimist journals, and to some of the most notorious legitimist plotters in France, including a young man who had tried to run down Louis-Philippe with his carriage as the King was crossing the place Vendôme on foot.* Other requests were not quite so troublesome; Tocqueville seems to have carried out all of them without complaint.[21]

In this way he passed the summer and early autumn. In October the penitentiary report was sent to the minister of the interior with six folio volumes of printed and manuscript documents as *pièces justificatives*, being the whole of the vast dossier which Tocqueville and Beaumont had amassed in America and which, it will be remembered, they had had to buy a trunk to contain. (Unfortunately this valuable archive, along with the original report, has long since disappeared.) The authors had always intended to publish their report as well as presenting it, and it came out a few weeks later. Without being a great success in the bookshops (as Mme Perrot puts it) it was as much a *succès d'estime* as Tocqueville and Beaumont could possibly have wished in both official and *savant* circles. It was favourably reviewed everywhere and awarded the Prix Monthyon by the Académie des Sciences Morales et Politiques. There was hardly a dissenting voice (at first) and the *Constitutionnel* may be taken as representative in hailing 'the work of our young and courageous compatriots'. They had made their mark.[22]

Le Système pénitentiaire aux États-Unis et son application en France is indeed a remarkable book, and remains a classic of penology. If for nothing else, it would deserve to be honoured still for setting new standards of research and assessment in the study of prisons. It is also one of the most valuable documents to have come out of Jacksonian America, and should be read by all who seek to understand that epoch in the history of the United States. But any adequate discussion of the book in these respects lies beyond a biography's scope. Comment must be restricted to what the work tells us about Alexis de Tocqueville.

* The recipients did not include Chateaubriand and Berryer, perhaps because they too had just been arrested and imprisoned on account of the duchesse de Berry's adventure, though the government was well aware that they had opposed it strongly (they were soon released).

No reader of the travel notes will be much surprised by anything in the treatise. The heart of the *Système pénitentiaire* is a comparison of the three prisons of Sing-Sing, Auburn and Cherry Hill (with frequent reference to other American jails) and a consideration of how applicable their example is to the prison system of France. These themes appear continuously in the surviving letters, diary notes and memoranda that Tocqueville and Beaumont made between May 1831 and August 1832. What does catch the eye freshly is the clarity, simplicity and logic with which a vast body of material has been reduced to literary form. The *Système pénitentiaire* is, above all, a limpid book. Most of the credit for that belongs to Beaumont.

Tocqueville was the first to say so. Although, or perhaps because, he became separately famous after the publication of his *Démocratie*, he was always anxious to do whatever he could to further Beaumont's reputation as a valuable author. When he was about to publish the second part of the *Démocratie* (in 1840) he thought of printing 'Quinze jours dans le désert' as an appendix; but 'according to his customary practice' he first read it aloud to Beaumont; who, hearing it with great admiration, remarked that it cast his own descriptive passages in his novel *Marie* into the shade. That was enough for Tocqueville: he put the manuscript away, and it was never published in his lifetime (however, Beaumont made sure that it appeared in the first volume of his edition of the *Oeuvres*).[23] And when he was pushing Beaumont's candidature for the Académie des Sciences Morales et Politiques he wrote to the historian François Mignet, the secretary:

> *Mon cher confrère* ... You know M. de Beaumont's claims, but there is one detail that perhaps you do not know. The first work that we published jointly, M. de Beaumont and I, on American prisons, was put together by the energy of M. de Beaumont. I only supplied my observations and some notes. I have never hidden from my friends the fact that although our two names were attached to the book, which I may now boast had a great success, M. de Beaumont was, so to say, the sole author. I am happy to have a chance to make these facts public ...[24]

These incidents are further illustrations of Tocqueville's devotion as a friend, but as to the *Système pénitentiaire* the documents show that he was greatly understating his contribution. According to Mme Perrot, he was responsible for about a third of the text as published, including the all-important 'Notes alphabétiques' and 'Notes statistiques'.[25] Yet he was truthful in calling Beaumont 'the author', as he did to his friend himself, because of the structure of the book. Nearly half of it consists of appendices and end notes, in writing which Tocqueville had a big, perhaps even a predominant part; but the main text, consisting of a foreword and three sections – on the American penitentiary system, on its possible application to France, and on American *maisons de refuge*, respectively – were written entirely by Beaumont. Not that that ended Tocqueville's contributions: in the intervals of attending to Kergorlay's affairs he spent the summer of 1832 visiting prisons, as we have seen, and going over every page of the work, making comments and suggestions which Beaumont frequently adopted, even if in modified form (thus, he rewrote, abridged and included a typically Tocquevillean outburst against Napoleon).[26] More fundamental than any of these considerations is the fact that during their American sojourn Tocqueville and Beaumont had agreed about almost everything, and on prison matters they always thought and spoke as one. It is impossible to say who formed which ideas first, and it does not matter anyway. The *Système pénitentiaire* was in the profoundest sense a truly collaborative work.

It is also a work to which it is difficult to be fair. Its merits, though undeniable, seem in certain lights to be inconsequential. The prison mission, however demanding and valuable, was of its nature strictly limited. The commissioners' job was to study the American penitentiaries and report on their possible applicability. The object of a penitentiary was to redeem the character of each prisoner so that he (or, in a few cases, she) would behave, after release, as a law-abiding citizen: 'Go, and sin no more.' The Tocqueville–Beaumont investigation was amazingly thorough, intelligent and conscientious, and their conclusions, modestly argued, were numerous and shrewd. But the investigators were haunted by the spectre of expense: could the money be found, in any minister's budget, to build penitentiaries in any adequate number in France, and how were the running costs to be met? (They were impressed by the number of American prisons which actually made a profit out of their inmates' labour, but had good reason to suspect that this reflected conditions – particularly the high cost of

free labour – which did not exist in France.) Their central preoccupation was the rate of recidivism, and as good servants of the French
state they were scandalized by the lack of official statistics in America:
again and again they had had to compile their own tables out of the
prison registers. In the end they were moderately optimistic about the
possibility of reforming criminals, in spite of the rooted scepticism of
Elam Lynds and others. But a reformed prisoner, in the very nature
of the case, had previously been convicted of a crime. Penitentiaries, therefore, on the best possible reading, could only have a modest
impact on the crime rate, and none at all on the conditions which led
to crime, as a social phenomenon, in the first place.

Tocqueville and Beaumont were well aware of such limitations,
and tried not to claim too much. But inevitably, in spite of all their
precautions, their views on the larger questions became apparent in
their discussion of penitentiaries, and influenced their conclusions. As
we have seen, Tocqueville was startled to be told that as Connecticut
grew more prosperous its crime rate rose.* He and Beaumont had not
failed to follow up this observation; indeed, their pages on the causes
of crime, in this context, are some of the best in the *Système Pénitentiaire*.[27] They concede that it is 'institutions, manners, political circumstances which influence the morality of free men; prisons only operate
on the morality of prisoners.' But even in that formulation they betray
their ineradicable confusion between the concepts of sin and crime.
Over and over again they write as if the purpose of a penitentiary
was and ought to be the reclamation of a soul, its restoration to its
'primitive purity', not the mere changing of behaviour. The idea does
cross their minds that society's only right and interest is to require not
that a former prisoner shall have saved his soul, but that he obey the
laws; but the implications of this observation are nowhere explored.[28]
Much more characteristically, the authors devote many pages to emphasizing that convicts, 'gangrened' members of society by definition,
will corrupt each other unless strictly separated and kept under a rule
of silence; the idea that they might comfort each other never appears.
Kind treatment of any sort is regarded with the utmost suspicion: it
is conceded that Mr Welles, of the house of refuge in Boston, does a

* See above, p. 192.

wonderful job with his young delinquents, whom he governs with the lightest of touches, but his success is attributed to his own remarkable qualities, not to his system.[29] In general, Tocqueville and Beaumont are hostile to what they think of as pampering prisoners. Tocqueville's views on bathing have already been indicated,* and his attitude to food and clothing was equally robust. Both he and Beaumont deplored 'the mania to erect architectural monuments' instead of strictly utilitarian prisons, wherever they found it.[30] They did not share the arch-utilitarian Bentham's belief that a well-planned building could help in a prison's work of redemption, for instance by looking suitably Gothic and terrifying. Tocqueville dismissed all music as unnecessary, while Bentham thought that good music would make prison chapel services more enjoyable, and therefore beneficial – but then, Bentham was a musician himself.[31] (We wonder what Beaumont the flute-player thought.) Only very occasionally do Tocqueville and Beaumont show any sympathy for the prisoners' plight, as when they discovered that at Philadelphia released prisoners were given nothing but a few coins to help them start again in life: 'this system seems to us to be excessively severe.' They pointed out that 'the most dangerous moment for released convicts is that in which they leave prison ...'[32]†

They thought themselves to be realistically humane and enlightened men, but the limitations of Tocqueville's humanity, at least, are precisely displayed in a report which he sent to Paris from Philadelphia describing the condition of one of the prisoners in solitary confinement whom he interviewed. The man, he said, was healthy, well-clothed, well-fed, well-bedded; 'however, he is deeply unhappy; the wholly mental punishment inflicted on him fills his soul with a fear far deeper than that of whips and chains. *Is it not thus that an enlightened and humane society should wish to punish* [my emphasis]?'[33]

The work of Michel Foucault suggests a terrible indictment of this sort of thing, and of more than Tocqueville's penal philosophy. No reader of *Discipline and Punish* can fail to recognize that Foucault was right to place Tocqueville and Beaumont, as prison reformers, in the

* See above, p. 222.
† This sentence strikingly anticipates one of the most famous pronouncements of the *Ancien Régime*: 'the most dangerous moment for a bad government is that in which it begins to reform' (OC II i 223).

movement that he describes; a movement, he declares, to reshape the world so that 'prisons resemble factories, schools, barracks, hospitals, which all resemble prisons.'[34] He finds the origins of that movement in the rise, during the seventeenth and eighteenth centuries, of new ideas of property which consolidated *noblesse*, peasants, bourgeoisie (both *grande* and *petite*) into a new class, determined to defend its interests against those it saw only as vagabonds and criminals: 'beggars, vagabonds, paupers, and all the freed prisoners,' said Tocqueville and Beaumont, 'whose ever-increasing numbers threaten the safety of private citizens and even the tranquillity of the State ...'[35]

According to Foucault, the required reforms were the particular concern of a continuous line of magistrates, from the *parlementaires* of the *ancien régime*, the legislators of the Constituent Assembly, the officials of the Napoleonic state, to the administrators of the Restoration and the July Monarchy. All were lawyers, members of a profession which, in France, never ceased to try to maintain or reconstitute itself as a privileged order, as it was under the *ancien régime*. They had no doubt whatever of their right, duty and ability to order and defend society through laws and law-courts. 'We believe that society has the right to do all that is necessary for its preservation and for the good of the established order ...' is how Tocqueville and Beaumont put it (so anything might be done with convicts, whose leanings were all corrupt and whose instincts were vicious).[36] Foucault quotes Rousseau:

> Every malefactor, by attacking social rights, becomes, by his crimes, a rebel and traitor to his country; by violating its laws he ceases to be a member of it; he even makes war upon it. In such a case the preservation of the state is inconsistent with his own, and one or other must perish; in putting the guilty to death we slay not so much the citizen as the enemy.'[37]

This piece of eloquence comes from *The Social Contract*, but it might as well be Robespierre, or Bonaparte, or Tocqueville's cousin, Le Peletier de Saint-Fargeau; and except that the reformers soon came to prefer imprisonment to execution as punishment for most crimes, it expresses the conviction which guided them from before the Revolution until the Second Empire – and beyond.

Saint-Fargeau is, for our purposes, the key figure, since it was he who laid before the Constituent Assembly the law which for the first time made the penal recommendations of the *philosophes* a matter of public policy. It was Saint-Fargeau who first suggested the *cachot* ('manacles on hands and feet, darkness, solitude, bread and water'), the prison cell and the labour regime. [38] Subsequent deliberations, in the assemblies or out of them, merely discussed variations or elaborations on Saint-Fargeau's themes, and the protests of the *cahiers* of 1789 against the very existence of state prisons were forgotten. [39] The Napoleonic regime, in what may be regarded as an ironic comment on the system where the very notion of the cell originated, converted many of the confiscated monasteries of France into prisons,* and regarded the attempt to control crime as an internal war, the equivalent of the international war in which it so constantly engaged – a metaphor which had the advantage of dehumanizing the criminal, and which has had far too long an innings ever since, not just in France. 'A great prison structure was planned, whose different levels would correspond exactly to the levels of the centralized administration.' [40] The Restoration and the July Monarchy, although a high proportion of their ruling elite had, like Hervé de Tocqueville, discovered the realities of prison at first hand (probably a higher proportion than of any other regime in history until the Bolsheviks seized control in Russia), carried on the Napoleonic programme with its attendant problems – which is where Gustave de Beaumont and Alexis de Tocqueville came in.

They fitted exactly into the prevailing orthodoxy by background, upbringing and training, and it was natural that their American journey reinforced the notions which they carried with them (however formed), since the penitentiary doctrines of the United States, particularly those of the Quakers, had been formed in step with those of Europe as developed by (for instance) John Howard and Jeremy Bentham. [41] It was the application, not the penitentiary theory itself, which was new. Perhaps it was not quite inevitable that Tocqueville and Beaumont should adopt mainstream views, which were always controverted. [42] Opposition to the new vogue for imprisonment was expressed in the Constituent Assembly by a deputy who objected that 'every imaginable

---

* Including St Bernard's Clairvaux, one of the greatest names in the history of Western monasticism, which today is still France's highest-security jail.

offence is punished in the same uniform way; one might as well see a physician who has the same remedy for all ills.' The Italian *idéologue* Sismonde de Sismondi denounced Tocqueville's cherished rule of silence to the Council of Geneva: 'It is absurd to pretend to reform men by taking from them the prerogative which distinguishes them from animals, speech.' As Tocqueville and Beaumont had to admit. La Fayette had declared himself a strong opponent of solitary confinement: 'That punishment', he said, 'does nothing to reform the guilty. I was held in solitary confinement for several years at Olmutz, where I was sent to prison for having launched a revolution; in my prison I dreamed only of new ones.' Charles Dickens, who visited Cherry Hill eleven years after Tocqueville did, and interviewed the prisoners to much greater effect, denounced solitary confinement as torture and agony, such as no man had a right to inflict on his fellow creatures, and declared that the benevolent Quakers did not know what they were doing.[43] But Tocqueville and Beaumont, as we have seen, formed very different views.

They were anxious never to appear sentimental. 'Philanthropist', as by now should be clear, was for them a term of contempt: it denoted a meddler who was more concerned with the comfort and happiness of prisoners than with their redemption. Philanthropists who made a career out of being prison-reformers were the worst of all. In particular, Charles Lucas became their *bête noire*, since he did not admit that the chief purpose of punishment was to hold up a useful moral example to society, not to reform the convict. Considering how much stress Tocqueville himself laid on personal redemption this accusation seems disingenuous, but he could never be fair to Lucas. In private he made no attempt to conceal his disdain: writing to Chabrol from Philadelphia he gloated that the success of the Beaumont–Tocqueville mission would turn Lucas yellow with envy and anxiety: 'For us, investigation of the Penitentiary System is like the *hors d'oeuvres* of our lives; for him, it's a business; he lives off philanthropy as off a landed estate; he draws a large rent from it every year, and is terrified when he sees anyone else settling on the same ground.'[44] It is difficult to acquit Tocqueville of odious snobbery in these remarks and others like them. But his attitude to the treatment of prisoners was closer to the outlook of his time, as it was developing, than was that of the philanthropists.

Indeed, it can be no wonder that the *Système pénitentiaire* was a success in its time, for the time had written it, faults and all. To judge from the reviews excerpted and included in the later editions of the book, readers were chiefly impressed by the authors' rigorous empiricism, their dazzling display of facts and documents. This was, after all, the age of the parliamentary blue book: the *Gazette de Normandie*, which proudly pointed out that one of the authors was 'a son of our province', also asserted that the book eclipsed 'those parliamentary enquiries of which they make so much fuss across the Channel'. Tocqueville's statistics were particularly enthralling: as Louis Chevalier told us long ago, the early nineteenth century was fascinated by this new art, which, as if by magic, gave solidity to what previously had been mere guesswork about society. Reviewers also took pains to praise the authors' style and presentation. 'What one finds in these pages above all are facts observed with impartial and philosophical intelligence, and presented with candour, in a clear style, appropriate to the subject' (*Le National*). And several of them endorsed the programmatic thrust of the book: MM. de Beaumont and Tocqueville, said the *Courrier de France*, were not to be counted among the 'monomaniacs of the penitentiary system' who thought it was a remedy for every evil; rather, they accurately stigmatized those unenlightened humanitarians who only concerned themselves with material conditions, and made loving mankind into a profession. *La France nouvelle* commended them for recollecting the duties which society owed to convicts while not belonging to that sect of 'exaggerated philanthropists' who blamed society for fostering crime and sided exclusively with the victims of punishment.[45]

For good and ill, the book was a success; yet one of Cicero's epigrams comes to mind. The younger Cato, he said, spoke in the Senate 'as if he were living in Plato's Republic instead of the cesspit of Romulus'. Kergorlay made much the same point after reading the book: 'It's well done, very well, if all your readers are really worthy citizens, bringing to it the will to hard study and the public good ... but three-quarters of your readers will dislike the lack of charlatanism or brilliance or whatever you call it which might stimulate minds sated and jaded by the vulgarity of the daily press.'[46] Beaumont and Tocqueville took the utmost pains to write a report which would be acceptable, by its scholarship and reasonableness, to any French party or government (though one or two references to 'un pays libre' show where their hearts lay).[47] They tried for a tone of dispassionate social science, and largely achieved it. Given the state of French politics and society in their lifetime this did little for French prisons and prisoners, though it worked wonders for the reputation of the authors, who showed that they were not only scientific, but statesmanlike. Their anxiety to be practical informed all their comments on the present state of affairs:

> We have never supposed that France could suddenly undertake a general revolution in its prison system, demolishing ancient establishments and suddenly building new ones, and devoting to this one object, in a single moment, enormous sums on which concerns of another kind make their claim. But one may reasonably ask for step-by-step reforms in our prison system ...[48]

They did not call for radical reform because they knew that it was unattainable and might even be thought undesirable: 'An institution can only succeed politically if it is undertaken for the benefit of the many; it will fail if it only profits a small number' – such as repentant convicts. They recognized that even the essential (in their eyes) element of reform, the installation of active and zealous chaplains in every prison, was probably not possible in France: even if French Catholic priests were enthusiastic about penal reform, which they were not, French anti-clericalism would be deeply suspicious of anything which looked like increasing their influence.[49] Beaumont and Tocqueville's pages on conditions in France were their most judicious and realistic, and were likely to increase their influence with all who read them – except the administrators of the prisons, who thought them deeply unfair. Laville de Miremont, inspector-general of *maisons centrales*, brought out a pamphlet defending every aspect of the French prison system which Beaumont and Tocqueville had attacked; he thereby heralded a controversy which was to involve the two friends for the whole duration of the July Monarchy, and make even their hopes for step-by-step reform seem Utopian.[50]

For this reason posterity may see fit to pass over the *Système pénitentiaire* as being no more than a dusty relic of a forgotten debate. This would not be fair: the issues that Beaumont and Tocqueville wrestled with are still very much alive. Anyone reading the book today is forced to reflect on current conditions in American and European prisons, with no very cheerful result. But what, in the end, must most impress such a reader is what may be called the subtext. For instance, Beaumont and Tocqueville took care to explain American federalism and how it shaped the prison system. This is a precise measure of how much they had learned in the United States, for when they first reached New York they apparently expected to find a centralized prison administration run *à la française* by a minister in Washington, and it took a letter from Baron Sérurier to set them right.[51] In turn, Beaumont and Tocqueville not only enlightened their readers as to federalism, which they rightly discerned was the embodiment of decentralization, but discussed its advantages and disadvantages, pointing out, among other things, that there was a certain healthy rivalry between the states, so that they vied to have the best prisons.* They also emphasized the principle of free association in the United States (following the hint given them by the despised Charles Lucas):[52] the excellent *maison de refuge* in New York had not been built by the state government, but by committees of private citizens formed for the purpose. They said further that associations, in the form of business corporations, were the engines of American economic growth; they were the means by which, in politics, 'minorities succeed in resisting oppression by the majority', and, in social life, the means to pleasure, education, science, religion and temperance.[53] Beaumont and Tocqueville also found it necessary to discuss race, slavery and the slave states; the role of public opinion; the press; the separation of Church and state; the school system; and American religion. A careful reader of the *Système pénitentiaire* can still learn much about how American society and government were organized and how they operated in the 1830s; and will also be exposed to what may be called a trailer for the two works which were to follow – Beaumont's *Marie, ou l'esclavage aux États-Unis*, and Tocqueville's *De la démocratie en Amérique*. Indeed, the *Système pénitentiaire* may be classified as a case-study of Jacksonian democracy in action; it remained for Tocqueville to expound at full length the general system and its principles.

* Nowadays they vie to have the worst.

CHAPTER ELEVEN

BETWEEN BOOKS
1833

'I want to introduce two very clever people to each other,'
said Mrs. Leo Hunter. 'Mr. Pickwick, I have great
pleasure in introducing you to Count Smorltork.' She
added in a hurried whisper to Mr. Pickwick – 'The famous
foreigner – gathering materials for his great work on
England – hem! – Count Smorltork, Mr. Pickwick.' Mr.
Pickwick saluted the Count with all the reverence due to so
great a man, and the Count drew forth a set of tablets.
CHARLES DICKENS, 1836

HE DID NOT GET DOWN TO WORK at once, or indeed
for months to come. No doubt he needed a rest after the effort
of bringing out the *Système pénitentiaire*; and then there was the
Kergorlay affair to conclude. In December Louis and his fellow
prisoners were transferred to Montbrison, *chef-lieu* of the Loire,
where their trial was to take place in March. Meanwhile the political
context was rapidly changing. The Orleanist government had had
no difficulty in brutally suppressing the duchesse de Berry's feeble
uprising in the West; everyone hoped that as a result she would leave
France. Instead she went into hiding, and at length the government
felt that it had no choice but to track her down and arrest her; Thiers,
the new and. energetic minister of the interior, caught her in Nantes

in November. She was imprisoned at Blaye, in the Gironde, but the government was utterly perplexed as to what should next be done with her. To put her on trial would be to create a legitimist martyr, and anyway she was the Queen's niece; but to keep her in prison without a trial would be equally provocative, since illegal. To send her back into exile, when she had raised a rebellion, however ineffectively, and when so many of her followers were going to be tried, was clearly anomalous, and would enrage the liberals. The legitimists took full advantage of the Orleanists' embarrassment. Chateaubriand, invoking the memory of his brother and of Malesherbes, 'defender of Louis XVI, who died on the same day, at the same hour, for the same cause and on the same scaffold', publicly volunteered to act as her counsel if she was tried, and published a pamphlet, *Mémoire sur la captivité de Madame la duchesse de Berry*, which got him put on trial himself (he was acquitted). The Tocquevilles too rushed into the limelight: Comte Hervé sent a petition to the two Chambers demanding the release of the duchesse and Hippolyte published a legitimist pamphlet, *Lettres aux Normands*. Much more surprisingly, Alexis, in his character as a lawyer, sent a letter to *La Quotidienne*, the leading legitimist newspaper, arguing the illegality of Mme de Berry's captivity. Beaumont did the same. The two ex-magistrates had no love for the July regime, and no doubt believed what they said; Tocqueville may have been carried away by family feeling; but the incident is probably best regarded as one more demonstration that although his head had renounced the Bourbon cause, his heart found it very difficult to do the same. Still, it was an indiscretion: the duchesse was for a moment the great legitimist heroine, and to support her publicly could only have one meaning. Kergorlay saw the point: although he thought that Tocqueville's protest lacked fervour, the great thing was that it associated him with all those who resented the ignominious government of Louis-Philippe.

But the questions raised by this lapse into legitimism were rendered moot when in February it emerged that the martyr-princess, rightful Regent of France, mother of the true King and chaste widow of his murdered father, had somehow become pregnant: a fact that she herself thought of little importance and did not try to keep secret for very long (she was one of the silliest princesses in all European history). She thus made the legitimists ridiculous.* The exiled Charles X cast her off, and when Mme de Boigne asked Chateaubriand (who had previously written 'A Hymn to the Maternal Virtues of Marie-Caroline') who he thought was the father of the child, he replied only, 'How do you suppose anyone can tell what she does not know herself?'[1] The duchesse coyly referred to the baby as 'the child of the Vendée', and one angry legitimist lady commented that 'in a sense, she is right.' The legitimists washed their hands of her, but that could not undo the fact that she had for the time being almost destroyed them as a serious political force. They were not to have another chance of power for forty years, although they were to make an endless nuisance of themselves. The government was rescued from its difficulty. The duchesse was sent back into exile as soon as the child was born: it turned out to be a girl, whom the duchesse turned over to a foster-mother as soon as she could; before long the baby died.

All this meant that Kergorlay would almost certainly be freed after his trial, even if he were found guilty: it would be too much to punish the follower, while the leader was let off. But Kergorlay was taking no chances. In October Tocqueville had volunteered to act as his counsel, and Louis was charmed by the idea: it would be as if they were comrades in battle, 'it would realize something of the dreams of our youth.' But legal tactics forced him to reject the offer; in the end Tocqueville appeared only as a character witness. Even that entailed minute preparation: Tocqueville was told to be sure to bring his lawyer's gown and diploma to Montbrison so that he could take his place with the other barristers in the section of the courtroom reserved for them; and two days before the trial Kergorlay anxiously urged his friend to say something forceful about his father, the comte de Kergorlay.[2]

The trial was held on 9 March 1833. Tocqueville spoke towards the end of the proceedings. His oration reads oddly. It has no bearing on the facts of the case, and is simply a long eulogy of Kergorlay and his father, lovers of liberty and souls of honour, their home a sanctuary of antique virtue. He stressed Louis's exemplary service in the army, his love of his country and, touchingly, their devoted friendship.

* The absurdity was not all on one side. When the *Carlo Alberto* was seized, a black ship's boy was found aboard. The local authorities were sure that he was the duc de Bordeaux in disguise, and the wretched child was scrubbed hard to make the colour come off (Jardin, 189).

Whatever we may think today of the performance, it was admirably suited to the tastes of the jury – landed gentry, provincial lawyers and physicians – local notables, some or all of them probably legitimists. They would perhaps have acquitted the defendants anyway – the July Monarchy always found it difficult to get 'guilty' verdicts in political trials – but Tocqueville's allocution did no harm. It went pretty far. Today, he said, seeing Kergorlay threatened with shaming punishment, he thought it necessary to assert that his friend had never stood higher in his esteem, never been truer to the oaths of their youth – 'I have never felt prouder of the sacred friendship which binds us.' It was no moment for half-measures, but once more Tocqueville was recklessly aligning himself with legitimism, and immoderate legitimism at that.[3]

Otherwise the speech is notable because it opens with a disquisition on the rights and duties of a jury which clearly shows the enthusiasm for that institution which Tocqueville brought back from America, and because, in its remarks about the comte de Kergorlay, it suggests the real nature of Louis's misfortunes. His father had flung himself into conspicuous opposition to the July Monarchy from the first (in November 1830 he had been tried and sentenced for seditiously publishing in the *Quotidienne* his speech of resignation from the Chambre des Pairs) and he dragged his son with him. It seems unlikely that Louis would have resigned from the army but for his father's influence, or that he would have involved himself with the duchesse de Berry; and in all his letters to Tocqueville from jail he seems much more anxious on his father's behalf than on his own. Filial devotion can be ruinously expensive. It is to be hoped that M. de Kergorlay suffered at least a few sleepless nights over the manner in which he had wrecked his son's career.

Tocqueville was luckier in his father, but he had his own family preoccupations. Documents are lacking (none is extant for the period between March and July 1833, no doubt chiefly because he and all his regular correspondents, except Eugène Stoffels, were now living in or near Paris); but even the most cautious scrutiny of the evidence must suggest that there was now a decisive turn in his relations with Marie Mottley, a turn which clarified matters in the most important respect, but still left him with a host of difficulties.

The journey to America had done nothing to weaken his attachment; rather, it had strengthened it, or strengthened Tocqueville's awareness of it. He had not been in the United States a month when he wrote to Chabrol: 'I never loved her so much as now when I see her no longer. Absence, so far, acts on me contrariwise. The fact is, I didn't think I was so bound to her ... Does she sometimes seem to remember me?' Every mail brought letters from her; getting them was the greatest pleasure that he had in America; he told her so, but he asked Chabrol to tell her so too. As we have seen, he worried that she might catch cholera. Of his letters from America to Marie herself not one survives, although he probably wrote to her more often than to anyone else, but we can be sure that they were full of serious devotion; how serious may be gauged from the fact that whereas he was careful to hide the tale of his various dangerous adventures from his family until he got safely home, we learn from a letter to Chabrol that he kept Marie informed. Presumably he knew that her nerves were stronger than his mother's; but perhaps he also felt that she was entitled to be told everything. And as we have seen, he flew to her arms as soon as he returned to Paris. [4]

While Tocqueville was in America a cousin (probably Louis de Chateaubriand) wrote to him proposing an arranged marriage to a noble and well-dowered young lady. The proposal was rejected, not, strikingly, on the grounds of an existing pledge, but because Tocqueville had never met Mlle de L. and did not know if they could love each other; as to her fortune (he said) the longer he lived the more clearly he saw that money was not particularly important to him: he could adjust easily to a modest income if it was matched with domestic happiness. This, as we have seen, was his consistent attitude to arranged marriages, but the fact that he does not even hint at Marie, indeed the fact that Louis de Chateaubriand made the proposal at all, suggests that before Tocqueville went to America her importance to him was not understood by his family (he did not wholly understand it himself) and is certainly consistent with other evidence that there was as yet no actual betrothal. Yet it seems clear that Tocqueville had resolved on marriage by the time he returned to Paris, and soon overcame the first obstacle, Marie's own doubts. His letters to her in the summer of 1832 are those of a man writing to his second self, to someone of whose interest in his thoughts and doings he is utterly confident, in short, of someone in a permanent union. But an actual wedding was not yet any closer. There was trouble with Mrs Belam. Whether or not Tocqueville and Marie had become lovers before the journey to America, they certainly were after his return, and this perhaps caused the 'great storm' between aunt and niece in the spring of 1832 to which Tocqueville alludes in a much later letter. And there was no movement on the side of the Tocqueville family. The comte and comtesse may well have come to realize that Marie was a permanent part of their son's life, but she was still Protestant, English and not rich.* At least Tocqueville was able to confide in his friends. Chabrol, of course, had known about the affair from the start; now Kergorlay, from prison, was inspired by Tocqueville's rhapsodies to compose a page of appalling misogyny, but he allowed that Marie must be an exceptional woman and urged Tocqueville to write letters about her whenever he felt like it. [5]

The indications of what happened next are extremely scanty. It was not until the spring of 1833, if then, that Tocqueville adopted the way of life which was to last until his wedding in 1835: living officially, and by day, with his parents in the rue de Verneuil, while spending his evenings, if not his nights, with Marie. It was hardly satisfactory, but no doubt his parents could not yet agree conscientiously to the marriage, and under the civil code as amended by the Bourbons he could not marry without their consent until he was thirty. He was still entirely dependent on his father for an income. According to that same code, he could not be disinherited: the famous law of inheritance guaranteed his equal share, with his brothers, in the family estate; but that had little bearing on his current difficulties. The only other visible factor which may explain his arrangements is that the death of the Abbé Le Sueur and the marriage of her two elder sons had left Madame de Tocqueville, always ailing, in need of Alexis's company.[6] There was no quarrel, no attempt at coercion or revolt; but there was deadlock.

One difference was resolved: by the early summer of 1833 Tocqueville was on excellent terms with Mrs Belam, and took pains to

---

* She was not poor, either. André Jardin points out that at the time of her marriage she had an annual income of 8,000 to 10,000 francs – say £800 (Jardin, 49).

remain so. This was doubly important: we know little about Marie's relations with her family in England, but it is clear that they were still on close terms, and if Mrs Belam had been hostile it might have created difficulties with the Mottley parents. As it was, the only fresh problem was with Kergorlay, who was probably suffering from the after-shock (so to say) of his prison ordeal. At any rate he felt so much adrift that he started to learn German, for occupation, and in the feeble hope that it would lead to something; he allowed himself to be appropriated by his parents for the management of the family estate at Fosseuse; and he told Tocqueville plainly that he did not approve of the proposed marriage – it is not clear on what grounds. His attitude annoyed and distressed Tocqueville, but changed nothing: it cast no more than a transient shadow over their friendship, and certainly did not cause second thoughts about Marie.[7]

Nor did it affect Tocqueville's general outlook. He was in high spirits that summer, perhaps because he had not yet begun work on his next book. Instead he travelled to England, where he stayed for five weeks (he did not turn to the book until the autumn).[8]

The decision to travel again has caused various scholars unnecessary perplexity.[9] Except in 1830, the revolutionary year, Tocqueville had gone abroad annually since 1826. It assuaged his self-acknowledged restlessness. He explained his motives for this particular trip when he wrote to his cousin, Mme de Pisieux, asking her for a letter of introduction to Lady Stuart de Rothesay, wife of the man who had been British ambassador to France from 1815 to 1830:

> I am already acquainted with her husband; the work which M. de Beaumont and I have published recently has put us in touch; but you are bound to feel that I cannot decently present myself in a lady's boudoir with the *Système pénitentiaire* for a visiting-card ... by going to England I hope to escape for a while from the insipid spectacle that our country presents just now. I want to go and feel slightly less bored among our neighbours. And then, I am told that they are definitely beginning a revolution and that I will have to hurry if I am to see them as they are. So I am making haste to go to England as to the last night of a great play.[10]

He left Paris on 15 July, and travelled leisurely to Cherbourg, stopping a few nights at the chateau of Tocqueville on the way: there he made himself agreeable to the neighbours, thinking ahead to the day when, as a candidate for the Chamber of Deputies, he would need their votes. (At about the same time Marie and Mrs Belam set off for a seaside holiday at Étretat in Upper Normandy.) He hung about Cherbourg for a day or two, trying for a passage to Southampton. On 5 August an Englishman with a yacht carried him as far as Guernsey, from where, next day, he went by steamer to Weymouth, 'a pretty little place'. On 7 August he travelled by stagecoach to Southampton, through country which impressed him less by its scenery than by its osten-tatious wealth: 'nothing but parks, country-houses, retinues, lackeys, horses: universal luxury which, they say, conceals poverty, but which, at least to a stranger's eye, conceals it marvellously well.' Southamp-ton, though only a small town, had shops as good as those in Paris ... his education in yet another country had begun.[11]

He took with him to England a string of preconceptions, some useful, some misleading.[12] French, and perhaps American newspapers, reporting the struggle over the Great Reform Bill and its attendant riots, public meetings, strikes and rick-burnings, had convinced him that England was on the brink of another 1789, as the letter to Mme de Pisieux shows. In this he was only slightly out of date: the year before, as the battle over the Reform Bill rose to its height, many intelligent English people feared that a revolution was imminent, but things had quietened down once the Bill became law. He was also convinced that England was as yet a purely aristocratic polity: he concentrated on this idea so emphatically in his note-taking that one might think that his next book was going to be *De l'aristocratie en Angleterre*. He did not forget America – indeed, the English journey seems to have reanimated his enthusiasm for writing on the subject: he was sure that investigat-ing the old country would throw necessary light on the new. But these interests by no means comprised the whole of his approach to England. He felt some of the excitement that a young man of the twentieth century felt on making his first visit to the United States. Although the Anglophilia which had characterized the era of the Restoration was past its peak, and was soon to turn into Anglophobia, Britain's prestige in France was still immense. Not only was this the country which had inspired and sustained the alliance that finally defeated Napoleon, it was also the monarchy whose history and institutions seemed to have most to teach France: Louis-Philippe had been brought to the throne in large part because it was hoped that he would prove to be another William III. It was the country whose mechanical inventions and new economic organizations were transforming the fundamental conditions of human life and generating new riches on a staggering scale: before long the French would coin the phrase the Industrial Revolution. It had also been one of the chief sources of the Romanticism which was flooding over Europe, and to which Tocqueville, in spite of his upbringing, was extremely susceptible. Sicily had been for him the land of Greek mythology; America was that of Fenimore Cooper and Chateaubriand; Britain was that of Walter Scott. It was also Marie Mottley's homeland. All in all, it is no wonder that Tocqueville was an eager visitor.

He reached London on 10 August, and stayed until the 26th. From first to last the city disconcerted him. It was so enormous, he told Beaumont, that he felt as insignificant as a gnat at harvest-time. The air was perpetually smoky, 'but it isn't raining, which, they say, is unusual', so he was able to walk everywhere, which was just as well: 'I've never been in a town so terribly expensive.' And for his purposes he had arrived at the wrong moment of the year: 'the world' was leaving for the country, and those great persons who still remained did not receive him as he wished, in spite of his letters of introduction. Perhaps Mme de Pisieux had done her work too thoroughly; at any rate Tocqueville complained that the aristocrats could not get it out of their heads that he was a mere Parisian *élégant*, and they only talked to him of balls and evening parties which anyway would not be given before the winter. Much to his surprise, it was the *Système pénitentiaire* which opened doors for him. Tocqueville was vastly pleased to find that it was the best passport that he could have asked for – politicians and *savants* had read and admired it and were delighted to meet one of its authors and to help him in any way he wanted.[13]

On 13 August he was taken to witness a debate in the House of Lords. It served to confirm all his first impressions. The peers met in a large room hung with scarlet cloth, and either sat round a table or lounged casually on cushioned benches. About fifty of them were present, dressed informally (except for the bishops), many of them in riding clothes and boots (in Paris, we must remember, the peers wore uniform). Many kept their hats on. There was no ceremony, but a general air of good fellowship, 'a certain *perfume* of aristocracy'. Tocqueville was enchanted, but his French good sense was astonished by the appearance of the Lord Chancellor, Brougham, in an enormous powdered wig. The clerks were also bewigged. Then the Duke of Wellington rose to open the debate. Tocqueville shuddered with excitement. There below him was the amazing man who had conquered France and Napoleon. No doubt he would say something extraordinary.

Alas, the Duke was no great speaker (as his followers knew all too well). He could hardly get through his remarks. He seemed as nervous as a child reciting its lesson before a harsh schoolmaster.

> The hero of Waterloo didn't know exactly where to put his arms and legs or how to balance his long body. He kept picking up and putting down his hat, fidgeting to left and right, buttoning and unbuttoning his breeches pocket, as if he might find there the words which were certainly not coming easily from his brain ...

Then the Lord Chancellor spoke, and immediately showed himself a first-rate orator, though he did not speak at any length.[14] Tocqueville much enjoyed his evening, but it is striking that in his account of it he scarcely mentions the topic of debate, although it was one of the greatest measures ever passed by Parliament: the bill to abolish slavery in the British Empire, which would become law on 29 August. At this stage of his development (and, we may add, of the development of parliamentary government in France) Tocqueville did not understand, and was certainly not interested in, the real work of a legislature. He hungered only for the dramatic and picturesque. He did not bother to visit the House of Commons, although the Reform Act had so enormously increased its power and significance. He had shown as little interest in the House of Representatives when he visited Washington.

Two days later he went to study the electoral process, as he had signally failed to do in the United States. There was a by-election in the City of London, and Tocqueville was present for the last of the polling in Guildhall. He arrived in the afternoon, and had to make his way through a crowd in the streets waving placards scrawled with slogans: 'Kemble for Ever' (Kemble was the Tory candidate), 'Crawford and Reform'. Some of the Crawford placards called for 'Poor Laws in Ireland!', 'Better Wages in England!' Tocqueville rather sniffily dismissed these demands as gross bribes offered to popular passions. He counted fifty placards waving in front of Guildhall itself, and saw that all the walls round were plastered with similar posters. Inside the hall he found a crowd which 'contrasted grotesquely with the feudal majesty of the place that held it'. Most of those present evidently belonged to the lowest classes: 'they even had impressed on their faces that degraded character which one only comes across in the people of great cities … It was, in short, both a very tumultuous spectacle and a somewhat disgusting one.' Cheers, hisses and catcalls as the voting went forward until four o'clock, when Crawford was declared the winner. Thunderous cheers, for the crowd was Whig. Crawford spoke, in what Tocqueville thought was a manner as vulgar as the crowd of his listeners, who constantly interrupted him: 'it was a kind of colloquy between them and him.' Kemble spoke, bravely restating his principles in defiance of the crowd. 'I couldn't help thinking of the savages of North America who delight in insulting their enemies while being burnt by them.' Then Crawford and the Whigs went off to celebrate in a tavern while the rest dispersed. There was not a soldier in sight, though many policemen.[15]

Tocqueville was unimpressed by what he called 'this electoral farce'. He commended the 'manly habits' which sustained Kemble in his defiance, but on the whole 'this Saturnalia of English liberty' filled him with disgust rather than fear; in fact he speculated that this sort of thing contributed to maintaining aristocracy by filling the middle classes with a horror of democracy, as the ancient Spartans used to get slaves drunk to give citizens a horror of wine. A few days later he was taken by Mr Bulwer,* a Radical MP, to a public meeting in support of the rebel Poles exiled to Switzerland (two years previously he and Beaumont had attended a similar meeting in Boston). On this occasion Tocqueville was much impressed by a man called Duffy, a much better speaker than the Duke of Wellington: 'we had laid eyes on an orator.' He denounced mere charity to the Poles and demanded a resort to

* Probably Edward Lytton-Bulwer, MP and popular novelist; later the first Lord Lytton.

arms, amid frantic cheering. 'Rarely, in all my life, have I been as much carried away by a speech as I was this evening listening to this man of the people,' wrote Tocqueville. '... In him, I saw the precursor of those revolutionaries who are destined, at no distant date, to change the face of England.' What did it matter that the lord presiding over the meeting was addressed by Duffy in respectful terms? Duffy had proclaimed himself 'a workingman belonging to the lowest ranks of industry', and been cheered for it. 'When men appear so content in and proud of their lowliness, let those placed above them tremble.'[16]

These two incidents show how firmly Tocqueville could cling to his preconceptions, and how little his tour of America had widened his social sympathies. He could not enjoy a crowd, and as to Duffy, he was indeed a portent, but not of revolution. Tocqueville should have reflected on how extraordinary it was, in French terms, that a public meeting could unite the upper, middle and working classes of England in a good cause – or at any rate a bellicose one.

The fact was that although he boasted to his father that he preferred to travel alone and would never again go on a long journey with a companion, he missed Beaumont. In England there was so much to discover and think about, he found it difficult to decide what to concentrate on, he needed Beaumont's advice: 'Try to get my intelligence moving: you know that that is what matters. Left to myself I slumber and can't get going until I clearly see where I want to arrive ... so I need your practical sense to give me a shove.' Beaumont was very willing to help. He would have liked to be with Tocqueville (it is not apparent why he was not) but, failing that, he made good use of the post:

> try to direct your attention to roads, canals, railways. When a canal or a railway is built, what part does the government play? What part private enterprise? Is government authorization *necessary* for such undertakings? is it ever *in fact* refused? Or is the application for such authorization a mere form?

And so on for a full page.

It is doubtful if his advice was of the slightest use to his friend. Beaumont's head was full of a project for launching a new magazine to deal with political and economic subjects in partnership with a country neighbour, André-Michel Guerry, who happened to be France's leading statistician. Naturally Tocqueville was to be involved: Beaumont's idea was that they should invest the Monthyon prize-money in the scheme, and he hoped that Tocqueville could find some contributors in London. Tocqueville was quite willing to try, though he could not promise to contribute himself until his book on America was finished (this remark is the only indication we have that it may have been begun).[17]

He continued his English investigations. On Sunday, 18 August, he was the guest of honour at what he called 'a penitentiary dinner', where one of the diners was Richard Whately, the archbishop of Dublin, who was also a political economist, a prison reformer and, Tocqueville was told, the only Whig on the bench of bishops. 'He was very civil to me, but I could not get used either to the *bizarrerie* of his attire [powdered wig and lawn sleeves, no doubt] or to seeing him accompanied by his wife and several tall pretty daughters, whom I couldn't match with my idea of a bishop.' Yet it was probably this encounter which emboldened Tocqueville to introduce himself to Whately's close friend, Nassau Senior, a distinguished economist,* who was hard at work with Edwin Chadwick preparing their famous report on the reform of the Poor Law. Perhaps Tocqueville had hopes of securing a contributor to Beaumont's review. At any rate he bounced into Senior's chambers in Lincoln's Inn one day with the announcement, 'Je suis Alexis de Tocqueville, et je viens faire votre connaissance.' The two men took to each other at first sight, and a lifelong friendship began. Unfortunately it did not start to leave a paper trail until the following year.[18]

Tocqueville had long and stimulating conversations with Mr Bulwer and John Bowring, a leading Benthamite, and in his usual fashion began to make notes, on such topics as religion (by which he meant the Church of England, which he thought was endangered as the French Church had been in 1789), aristocracy and decentralization. As to the last subject, Bowring told him that 'England is the country of decentralization', and Tocqueville, most unusually, felt that the principle had been carried too far, especially when it came to law enforcement.

* Nassau William Senior (1790–1864) was the son of a country clergyman. Trained as a lawyer, he practised successfully as a conveyancer for many years, but it was work as an economist and governmental adviser that made him eminent.

However, he pointed out to himself that a federal government could adjust to social diversity better than a unitary one: 'note for my book on America'. But for the time being his observations on aristocracy went further and left more of a mark, not only on his own thought but on that of later writers. The English aristocracy, nobles and gentry, was distinguished from all others by the ease with which inferiors, if rich enough, could enter its ranks. Everybody could hope to rise to the enjoyment of noble privileges, so the privileges themselves were not hated but valued, and served to make the aristocracy cherished. Aristocracy in England was not founded on birth but on wealth, 'and this single distinction has enabled it to survive when all others have succumbed, either to the commons or to kings.' Tocqueville did not expect this state of affairs to last much longer: economic distress was too great. Nevertheless, aristocratic ideas and instincts ran deep. 'I have not yet met a single Englishman who realized that a law of inheritance, dividing up property, might be passed, so natural does inequality of fortune appear and so customary has it become.'[19]

After a fortnight in London it was time to see the country. One of Tocqueville's letters of introduction had brought him an invitation to visit the Earl of Radnor at his country-house, Longford Castle near Salisbury. This was attractive: Radnor was a staunch Whig and as a boy had witnessed the early stages of the revolution of 1789; and Tocqueville very much wanted to see how a great English lord lived on his estate. He left London on 26 August, planning to fill in the time before he was expected at Longford with a ramble in search of the picturesque, or at least the Gothic.[20]

First stop, Oxford. He travelled by stagecoach, sitting on the roof with an iron bar for back support and his feet dangling in mid-air: it was an exception to the otherwise universal rule of English comfort (which always evoked Tocqueville's warm enthusiasm). It was a relief to get out of London and see the sun again: he thought that it must have been Milton's long residence in the city which gave him the idea of 'darkness visible'. As to Oxford, he fell in love with the place on sight: its Gothic lay-out and architecture made it the most interesting city in Europe. He roved through its alleys by moonlight, and was reminded of Pompeii, for the city seemed as if it had been disinterred to show him what medieval towns had been like – towns such as Victor Hugo had described in *Notre-Dame de Paris*. He was less impressed by the university as an educational or scholarly establishment. He dined with the fellows of Queen's College, and was appalled at the amount which he was expected to eat and drink: 'you know that overdoing it doesn't agree with me.' He thought he got off lightly by having a restless night as a result. The fellows lived on the revenues of the monks whom they had replaced, and gorged as if they were monks themselves: 'It is only the name of the abuse which has changed.'[21] Nor was that all. The curriculum centred on Greek and Latin, which Tocqueville would have approved if to these fourteenth-century studies they had added some nineteenth-century ones, but science was almost unknown and modern languages were not taught at all. The colleges seemed to exist solely for the benefit of the fellows, most of whom took their share of the revenue without doing any teaching. 'It's exactly like the abbeys of the *ancien régime*, of which the heads were often not even priests.' There were only 1,500 undergraduates in the twenty-two colleges, who lived in luxury and had six months of vacation annually! The chief beneficiaries of the system were the younger sons of the aristocracy. The only justification offered for this state of affairs was the will of the founders; but in that case, asked Tocqueville unkindly, should not the fellows have stuck to Catholicism? 'It is true that by a *mezzo termine* which is typically English, the monks having been expelled, the fellows were forbidden to marry.'[22] Oxford, in short, illustrated all too completely Tocqueville's reasons for thinking that England was an aristocratic society on the brink of collapse.

He was both an acute and, by now, a thoroughly trained observer; fortunately Warwick, his next port of call, was not in the least a place to excite his scorn. After dinner at his inn he walked out to see the castle and was overcome by Romantic admiration: 'We have nothing in France which so recalls the feudal age, those centuries of liberty and oppression, of great crimes and sublime virtues, of enthusiasm and energy, which will live in men's imagination as long as there is any poetry in the world.' He plunged into a detailed description of the castle which no doubt interested Marie, but need not be quoted. When he left he was still excited, and although night was falling decided to hire a horse and visit the ruins of Kenilworth castle, a few miles down the road.

Imagine an Italian night: not a breath of wind; the sky cloudless, the Moon full; add to this an eager, speedy horse between my legs, all the centuries of chivalry whirling in my head and the remains of youthful fire still pulsing in my blood; and you will realize that I rode, as it were, without touching the ground.

Everyone was in bed when he got to Kenilworth, but his shouts finally brought a young woman to her window ('very pretty, so far as the Moon and my eyes allowed me to judge') and she told him the way to the castle. He wandered about the ruins in a state of high *chateaubrianesque* rapture ('was I not, as a matter of fact, in Death's domain?'), sat on a stone and evoked the wraith of Amy Robsart, 'that delicious creation of Walter Scott's genius'. He seemed to hear the echo of her last cry as she fell from the precipice prepared for her, and might have stayed at Kenilworth all night if his horse had not begun to kick the fence to which it was tied. He jogged back to Warwick reflecting on the strange power of fiction.* It started to rain.[23]

He travelled from Warwick by way of Bath, and arrived at Longford on 31 August. Again he was in raptures: 'I have seen and lived in several of the finest chateaux in France, but this decidedly surpasses them all in the art of combining the small agreeabilities of life.' His bedroom was as big as a ballroom, and if he had wanted to he could easily have drowned himself in the smallest of the four or five washbasins provided.[24]

Besides all its comforts, Longford castle was as striking, architecturally, as Warwick, although it was not Tocqueville's favourite Gothic, but Tudor. On 1 September the pheasant season began, and we may assume that he went out with a gun (he had looked forward eagerly to the treat, only regretting that the fox-hunting season had not started). Lord Radnor was a gracious host, but Tocqueville's usual preoccupations now reasserted themselves. He can hardly have failed to talk about the Poor Law when he was with Senior, and on 3 September Lord Radnor, acting as a JP, had to go to Salisbury for the petty sessions. He took his guest with him. Tocqueville and Beaumont

* Scott had not been dead a year. It may be necessary to add that Amy Robsart, both in fact and fiction, died at Cumnor not Kenilworth, of falling (or being pushed) downstairs.

had long been aware of the links between penal policy and the problem of poverty; now, watching the Old Poor Law operating in all the glory of its abuses, Tocqueville realized that he had come across another major social problem, one, as it turned out, that was to preoccupy him for years to come. On this occasion he was chiefly struck by the way in which old and young men, single and married mothers, claimed public assistance even when they had no moral, as opposed to legal, right to it, or even economic need for it. Some young men complained that their village vestry would give them neither work nor charity; Lord Radnor growled to Tocqueville that he knew them, they were young scoundrels who were always ready to drink away their wages in taverns because they knew that the parish was obliged to support them. Young women, he said, did not mind having illegitimate children because they could always name rich men as fathers, or if that failed depend on the Poor Law. The law was undermining morality. Tocqueville decided that there was something to be said for the French law forbidding enquiry into paternity: it taught young women to look after themselves, which was very necessary, because nothing would stop young men from attempting seduction (*experto crede*). He pumped Lord Radnor on the subject, and also on several others, including his usual warhorse, the inheritance laws ('What happens to younger sons under your current laws of succession?').[25]

It was time to go home, and he was missing Marie; but as he wrote to Mrs Belam, in slightly peculiar English, his tour had been a great success. 'The country is generally very pretty, and the inhabitants receive the foreigners with the greatest ease and attention ... I have not been called a single time *chien de français*. You see that I must be full of gratitude, so I am.'[26] He was back in London by 7 September, when he wrote a substantial essay, 'Last Impressions of England'. It was his attempt to distil the lessons he had learned from his journey, and repays close reading.[27] Much of what he says is a repetition, or slight elaboration, of points already made (about the open elite, for instance, and pauperism – 'the condition of the poor is England's worst affliction'), but much the most interesting observation is his conclusion that there is not going to be a violent revolution after all. (This may put the reader in mind of the moment in America when he at last committed himself to the proposition that the middle class could govern a state.)

He admits that he has changed his mind, and wrestles with the question of why he did so and what he now expects. His most important point is that the English are a people seasoned by liberty. They have enjoyed freedom of the press for a century, and have thoroughly tested all ideas by debate, even the most extreme. They are ill-content with the present and hate the past, but they will rush into nothing. He contrasts this state of mind with that of the French in 1789, and thereby launches a train of thought which in due course would leave its mark on *L'Ancien Régime*. He does not waver from his opinion that the political ascendancy of the British aristocracy is doomed, but its fall will take a long time, if only because the English are all snobs: 'The whole of English society still runs on aristocratic lines and has contracted habits which only a violent revolution or the slow and continual pressure of new laws can destroy.'[28]*

The essay is a splendid illustration of Tocqueville's penetrating intelligence, and a good example of how much he could infer from the scantiest evidence. It would have made a good article for Beaumont's review, had that ever materialized. But another country now at last reclaimed his attention. Tocqueville left England on 7 September, and as soon as he got back to Paris began to work full time on his book about America.

---

* These observations exemplify Tocqueville's theory about manners. It is experience which has fitted the English for their kind of liberty, as it has fitted the Americans for theirs. Marx was recognizing the same reality when he burst out to Engels that England was cursed with a bourgeois aristocracy, a bourgeois proletariat and a bourgeois bourgeoisie.

CHAPTER TWELVE

WRITING AMERICA
1833–1834

*J'avoue que dans l'Amérique j'ai vu plus que l'Amérique;
j'y ai cherché une image de la démocratie elle-même, de ses
penchants, de son caractère, de ses préjugés, de ses passions;
j'ai voulu la connaître, ne fût-ce que pour savoir du moins
ce que nous devions espérer ou craindre d'elle.* *

ALEXIS DE TOCQUEVILLE,
DE LA DÉMOCRATIE EN AMÉRIQUE[1]

'WHEN I GOT HERE, I threw myself upon America in a kind of
frenzy,' wrote Tocqueville in Paris to Beaumont in the Sarthe on 1
November.

> The fit persists still, although through lapse of time it may seem to
> be ending. I think my work will be the better for it, though not my
> health, which suffers from the extreme preoccupation of my mind;
> for I think of hardly anything else, even when handling my cock. My
> ideas are enlarged and generalized. Is that good or bad? I am waiting
> for you to tell me. I expect to have finished with the *institutions* by the
> 1st of January next and I have a good mind to issue this first volume
> before the second.[2]

---

* I admit that in America I saw more than America; I sought an image of democracy itself there,
of its leanings, its character, its prejudices, its passions; I wanted to understand it, if only so as
to know at least what we ought to hope or fear concerning it.

Years later Beaumont held up this moment of Tocqueville's life as almost idyllic:

> Exempt from all professional duties, not yet married but already in love with his future wife, his mind tranquil and his heart full, he was in that situation, so rare in life and always so short, when a man, free from all obligations ... only seeing as much of his family and society as he chooses, takes full possession of his intellectual independence.[3]

The letter just quoted is not quite consistent with this agreeable picture. Beaumont did not take full account of his friend's character and emotions, and of how they led him to perceive his position. He might feel that he had paid for his freedom with his once-promising career; that if he had not yet married, it was because he was not allowed to; and he had just passed his twenty-eighth birthday, that terrible moment when a man realizes that he will one day be thirty.

He was passionately ambitious politically, but was deeply at odds with the three main parties of his day, the legitimist, Orleanist and republican. His success with the *Système pénitentiaire* had confirmed his belief in his abilities, but the book had exhibited them insufficiently. The other book on America which he had planned for so long must now be written, must be a masterpiece and must be his unburdening: in it he would hurl his convictions at the world. He had delayed long enough. His trip to England had not been a waste of time, but when he came back he found that Beaumont was at work on his own second book, the novel *Marie* – slowly, as yet, but nevertheless at work. And the topic itself, America, was returning to his mind ever more insistently. It is no wonder, given his temperament, that he set to work so furiously.

Throughout his life he needed solitude and silence for serious labour. So now every morning he left his parents' house in the rue de Verneuil (although it was then, as now, what passes for a quiet street in Paris) to climb up to what Beaumont describes as a '*mansarde mystérieuse*' nearby – an attic room, of which very few people knew the secret. By mid-November he was writing to Kergorlay:

My life is as regular as a monk's. From morning to dinner my existence is *toute de tête*, and in the evening I go to Marie's.* And with the utmost pleasure I rediscover the tenderest, sweetest intimacy and have long chats by the fireside that I never tire of. Next day I start all over again ...

His days were not entirely disengaged: Beaumont was still hoping to launch his review, and Kergorlay wanted to interest him in an investment in Algeria, but on the whole he was wonderfully undisturbed. Beaumont returned to Paris at the end of November, and thereafter they conferred on the progress and problems of their books; otherwise he probably had no visitors at all. In these circumstances *De la démocratie en Amérique* went ahead with speed.[4]

Tocqueville had a vast accumulation of papers and books to sort through and digest; James Schleifer thinks that he may have started this necessary work before he went to England, but there is nothing to confirm or refute the suggestion.[5] Dr Schleifer gives a splendidly lucid account of how Tocqueville reduced his materials to order and began to devise a scheme for his book. At one early moment, for example, he thought of dividing his exposition into three parts: political society, civil society and religious society. Soon afterwards he decided to drop the third section, although religion was to figure largely throughout the *Démocratie*, both in the 1835 volumes and those published in 1840. But he stuck, in a rough-and-ready way, to the distinction between political and civil society ('never entirely satisfactory,' says Dr Schleifer, with reason[6]) and they accordingly are the topics of what became volumes 1 and 2 respectively. He discovered that yet more research was needed, and enlisted two young Americans, Theodore Sedgwick III and Francis J. Lippitt, to find, read and summarize books and arguments for him. Most of this donkey-work was performed by Lippitt, who has left a nice description of Tocqueville's appearance at that time:

---

* By now she had apparently moved from Versailles to central Paris. Three years later, on the occasion of her marriage, she gives her address as the rue de Belle Chasse, no distance from the rue de Verneuil.

His physique was not at all striking. He was slightly built, and his height did not exceed 5 feet 6 inches ... There was certainly nothing about the contour of his head or the expression of his face that indicated him to be a man of more than ordinary intelligence. His manner was quiet and dignified, but somewhat cold.

He did not tell Lippitt what he was up to.[7]

He was more forthcoming with Sedgwick, whom he found to be a valuable intellectual stimulus: they became, and remained for life, warm friends. Sedgwick kept a journal, and was the first person ever to record Tocqueville's conversation properly:

> *Saturday 4th Jan'y [1834]* about 12 called on M. Tocqueville he says the Administration of France is a chaos & that the Ordre Justiciaire is the most remarkable part of the whole Administrative System, that he says is in high order – He said that all the Administrative System was founded under Napoleon & that it is essentially inconsistent with the representative and free order of things ... to the Legation to look for some Books about the Indians which Tocqueville wanted ...

> *Monday 20 Jan 1834* ... Tocqueville came about ½ past 11* and staid till 1 – Talking partly about the work he is to publish on our Country & partly about France –

> He says that as regards the religious spirit – Paris is an exception to the rest of France where in certain parts they are profoundly religious – that in Paris les classes moyennes les Boutiquiers, les Marchands, les Gardes Nationales have not the slightest religious principle while the upper classes who were first irreligious – are now generally the contrary – He says that the *manners* of the nation have changed entirely within 50 years – (the same thing is remarked with us) the suavity, the amenity of the men of the anterevolutionary period is exchanged for a brusquerie which is bourgeois.[8]

The book made extraordinarily rapid progress. Relying on various indications in the working manuscript and in the letters, Dr Schleifer has concluded that Tocqueville began to draft it in November 1834,

---

* AT's monastic regime seems by now to have lightened somewhat.

and it was apparently ready for the copyist by mid-August 1835.[9] *De la démocratie en Amérique* is not particularly long, but it is detailed and complex, covering a vast range of topics, and it is astonishing that Tocqueville could polish it off so fast: perhaps his training in preparing legal papers for the *parquet* helped him. Once he had decided on a list of possible chapters, his method of composition was to write in a column down the right-hand side of a page, leaving a column of blank paper of equal size to the left. He wrote second thoughts of all kinds in this left-hand column, crossed out discarded sentences and paragraphs in both columns, and sometimes inserted or pasted in bits of paper with yet more versions – all in his excruciating handwriting. How his copyists succeeded in producing a correct and coherent manuscript from this scrawling and patchwork remains a mystery: presumably they were professionals. How Tocqueville himself got it all into order is just as baffling. On 5 July 1834 he wrote to Beaumont: 'this second section [i.e. what became volume 2] makes my head spin. Almost everything is yet to do or must be done over again. What I have so far is only an incomplete sketch and sometimes not one page in three of my original manuscript survives.' Yet he was already negotiating with a publisher, Charles Gosselin, and we learn from his next letter, of 14 July, that he had been getting advice from Virginie Ancelot (whose salon he had begun to visit after his return from America) on how to puff his book in the press.* Mme Ancelot was well-acquainted with the world of letters: she and her husband wrote light comedies (*vaudevilles*) for the theatres. She tells us in her memoirs that Tocqueville read 'fragments' of his work to her before publication – presumably at this time, the summer of 1834. Tocqueville was probably seeking reassurance, but he had great confidence in his powers, as is shown by a buoyant letter which he wrote to Charles Stoffels on 31 July. Stoffels wanted to improve his literary style, and Tocqueville, warmly approving, did not hesitate to offer advice:

> I don't myself have a style that satisfies me in the least; however, I
> have much studied and long meditated on the style of others, and
> I am convinced of what I now tell you: in the great French writers

---

* Virginie Chardon (1792–1875) married J.A. Ancelot (who became a member of the Académie Française). She published memoirs entitled *Un salon de Paris*.

of whatever epoch you like there is a certain characteristic turn of thought, a certain manner of getting the reader's attention which is personal to each of them. I think that we are born with this individual stamp; or at least I confess that I don't see any other way of acquiring it, for if you try to imitate an author's particularity you fall into what painters call *pastiche*, while if you try not to imitate anybody, you become colourless.

The underlying characteristic of all the great French writers, from the time of Louis XIV to that of Mme de Staël and M. de Chateaubriand, is, he says, good sense. It would take a long time to define good sense in writing, but at least it is:

> care to present ideas in the simplest order, the easiest to grasp ... care to employ words in their true meaning, and as much as possible in their narrowest and most certain sense, so that the reader always knows precisely what object or image you wish to lay before him.

This is not the language of a man with serious doubts about the enterprise he was completing, though he did not always live up to his own precepts. In mid-August, as planned, he went off to the Sarthe to show his manuscript to Beaumont.[10]

Corrections and revisions were made in the light of second thoughts and of criticisms received from Beaumont and other friends, and from relations; but the impression is irresistible that the *Démocratie* was poured out rather than coolly composed, an impression strongly reinforced by a careful scrutiny of the published work.

At first reading it leaves nothing to be desired, nothing to be explained. It sweeps you away. Its programme is boldly stated in the Introduction, and the author's eloquence, intelligence and imagination carry the reader speedily on to the last words of the Conclusion. Its style conforms on the whole to Tocqueville's principles, its structure seems simple and intelligible and it has a new idea on almost every one of its four hundred or so pages. It is not quite without *longueurs*, but on the whole it is as lively as possible, and everyone seriously interested in France, democracy, modern history or the United States can read it with pleasure and profit.

But a second – or third – reading shows that the dazzling first impression is somewhat misleading. The structure, for instance, turns out to be not so much simple as almost non-existent. The 1840 *Démocratie* has a severely lucid and logical framework; the 1835 *Démocratie*, by contrast, seems ramshackle. It consists of four distinct components (not counting the endnotes), written in the following order: the first volume, on the political institutions of the United States (157 pages of the *Oeuvres complètes* edition); chapters 1–9 of the second volume, on American political society (155 pages); chapter 10 of the second volume, on 'what is American without being democratic'[11] (100 pages); and the Introduction, written last (fourteen pages). Tocqueville's scheme, we might say, is to be a political scientist in volume 1 and a sociologist in volume 2, a plan not merely logical but almost inevitable (James Bryce was to do much the same in his *American Commonwealth* fifty years later). But Tocqueville could not really conform to it. The first volume is sufficiently coherent. It opens with a chapter on North American geography (a chapter with some wonderful *chateaubrianesque* word-painting)[12] and three on the history of the 'Anglo-Americans' – their *point de départ*; then it plunges into a laborious description of their political and constitutional system. The sovereignty of the people is identified as the essential principle of American government and society (a thought which recurs throughout the book) and Jared Sparks's account of the township system of New England is exhaustively appropriated. A brief but sufficient account of state government leads to an essay on centralization, where a characteristic Tocquevillean doctrine gets its first airing; the political role of the American courts is well described. Next Tocqueville tackles the federal government. Eccentricities begin to appear. His account of the presidency is unsatisfactory (strange as the fact may seem today, the institution was then too much of a novelty to be easily understood by Europeans), but he devotes many pages to analysing it. He says almost nothing at this point about Congress (and not much elsewhere),* although Joel Poinsett had told him that it was the most important political institution in the country† and, I may add, was the key to understanding the whole political system. This omission is all the stranger because several remarks show that Tocqueville was worried about the possibility of

---

* Some years ago I was asked to write an article about Tocqueville on Congress. The proposal fell through, which is just as well as it would have been difficult to find anything to say.

† See above, p.209.

what he calls 'legislative tyranny'.[13] An excellent account of the federal judiciary, especially the Supreme Court, is not a wholly sufficient compensation. Nothing substantial is said at this point about political parties and their organization, although then as now they were essential to the operation of the system; and although so much space has been devoted to the government of New England villages nothing is said about American cities and their governmental problems, which were growing as fast as the cities themselves.

Some of these blemishes can be put down to unavoidable ignorance (Tocqueville was well aware that he had not been able to investigate everything in ten months) but more was caused by his neurotic refusal to plan his book carefully. As he plunged deeper and deeper into his work he wrote more and more by whim, and revised scantly. By late winter he had finished the first volume, and still thought he might publish it on its own.[14] But he had barely begun to expound what most concerned him, so making a brief but heart-felt excuse ('above all institutions and beyond all technicalities presides a sovereign power, that of the people, which destroys or modifies them as it pleases')[15] he started his book all over again, as it were, devoting nine chapters specifically to popular sovereignty and its consequences. These chapters, loosely connected by theme, are nevertheless almost independent essays. One of them, chapter 5 ('Democratic Government in America') is itself broken up into fifteen mini-essays on such topics as universal suffrage and the payment of public officials. They are fascinating in detail, but the general effect is somewhat higgledy-piggledy. Perhaps it should be borne in mind that Tocqueville was still a fairly inexperienced author. It was Beaumont who had built the main frame of the *Système péniten-tiaire*, and Tocqueville's contributions, mainly in the form of notes, however much they enriched the text, had seriously damaged Beaumont's simple, shapely design.

A deeper truth is that *De la démocratie en Amérique* is the last of its author's American notebooks. Tocqueville there continues the reflections and debates which had preoccupied him increasingly during his tour. Had he so chosen he could have written an excellently tidy text-book on US government, or he could have written up his notes into a wonderful travel book. But what he wanted to do was to settle his own opinion on a dozen or more matters which were, to him, of the greatest importance; he wanted to find out what he really thought of democracy and America, and to persuade as many readers as possible to agree with him. Not surprisingly, then, the book which he produced was *sui generis*: that is a great part of its attraction; but if it has to be categorized, it must be called a political tract. It may have taken Tocqueville hundreds of pages and years of reflection to hammer out his message, but a message he had. It is this which earns him the name of prophet, not his lucky or unlucky guesses at the future.

To expound that message – which contained both analysis and a programme of action – was the purpose of these early chapters of volume 2, the nuclear core of Tocqueville's achievement. It is difficult to summarize them coherently because of the way in which they were compiled. Just as Tocqueville assessed the penitentiary system in terms of its record in America and its possibilities for France, so here he discusses American democracy in itself and in its possible applications. But whereas, thanks to Beaumont, in the *Système pénitentiaire* coherent investigation was reflected in the coherent structure of the book, in the *Démocratie* Tocqueville keeps switching from the pros to the cons and back again and thereby disconcerts his readers, because he states every point so emphatically and never tries to harmonize his discourse. Sometimes (especially when presenting the cons) he is carried away into overstatement. This is particularly apparent when he deals with what, to start with, he calls the omnipotence of the majority in America. The history of the French Revolution and its climax in the Jacobin dictatorship explains why he was so concerned with the threat of legislative tyranny, because it was through the Convention, the revolutionary assembly, that the Jacobins came to power and exercised their dictatorship. Legislative tyranny seemed a real threat, and had been a French preoccupation as far back as 1799 and the Brumaire *coup d'état*, if not earlier. It was inevitable that Tocqueville should discuss it. But a majority in an assembly is not the same thing as a majority of voters at an election, let alone a permanent majority of the citizen body. Unhappily Tocqueville soon lost sight of these distinctions, if he ever saw them, and from writing of the omnipotence of 'the majority' he moves to the possibility of a 'tyranny of the majority' in the United States without drawing breath and then slides into talking as if it were an established and permanent fact.[16] He makes several ringing liberal assertions ('It seems to me that omnipotence is in itself something bad and dangerous ... only God can be all-powerful without danger, because his wisdom and his justice are always equal to his power'), but he also lets fall the famous but preposterous aphorism, 'I know no country where in general there prevails less independence of mind and true freedom of debate than in America.'[17] However often this statement has been quoted by persons anxious to denounce American social conformity, it is absurd, as a comparison of the polemics of the Age of Jackson with the ice age of Metternich or with the press laws of Louis-Philippe quickly makes clear; and the whole drift of this and other passages is repeatedly contradicted by Tocqueville himself, most explicitly towards the end of the book, where he casually shrugs off any great anxiety about majority rule:

> That which is called the Republic in the United States is the peaceful rule of the majority. The majority, once it has had time to discover and organize itself, is the one source of power. But it is not all-powerful. Above it, in the moral universe, stand humanity, justice and reason; in the political world, vested interests. The majority accepts these two restraints, and if it should ever happen to breach them, it is because it has passions, like those of any one man, and because, like him, it can do wrong while knowing the right.[18]

His overall picture of American democracy is warmly enthusiastic as well as penetratingly intelligent; in view of what he says about the American jury, American religion, American lawyers, American education, American local government and political parties, among other things, it is impossible (I would have supposed) to fancy that he really thought such a mature free people, with centuries of experience behind it (as he loved to emphasize) was in danger of tyranny of any kind.* Rather, he saw some form of democracy à l'américaine as the only alternative to dictatorship ('the yoke of a single man') and the only means of preserving liberty.[19] Although he puts the case for

---

* Perhaps this statement needs qualification. When AT discusses race and slavery he does not hesitate to use the word 'tyranny' to characterize American treatment of the Indians and the slaves (OC I i 332–52), and he is right to do so. But he makes little attempt to relate racist tyranny to his theory of tyranny of the majority: that was left to Beaumont in his *Marie*. And see below, p. 273.

pursuing democracy in France very cautiously, it is because, as when
he was recommending the penitentiary system, he wants to persuade
his readers, not dazzle them. Well aware of the enormous obstacles in
his path, he did not want to add to them by incurring charges of exaggeration or Utopian impracticability. He had a Utopia in mind for all that
(he had decided that it was a practical one) and it looked a lot like the
United States. A democracy would never do for those who wanted epic
glory:

> But if it seems useful to you to direct the intellectual and moral
> activity of men towards the material necessities of life, and to use
> them to produce well-being; if reason strikes you as more profitable
> to men than genius; if your object is not to generate heroic virtues but
> peaceful habits; if you prefer to witness vices rather than crimes, and
> fewer great deeds in return for fewer outrages; if, rather than moving
> in a brilliant society, you are content to live in a prosperous one; if,
> finally, the chief object of government is not, in your opinion, to
> raise a whole nation to its greatest strength and glory, but to procure
> for each of the individuals who make it up the greatest possible well-
> being and the least distress; then equalize status and build a demo-
> cratic government.[20]

Why, then, does Tocqueville also devote many pages to what appears
to be anxious denigration of American democracy? A close examination of his text provides the answer. The passages in praise of America
are packed with information and concrete detail; they are persuasive
because of their practicality and knowledge. The passages denouncing
tyranny of the majority and similar bugbears are written in a very
different mode. They profess to be concerned with 'democracy' in
the abstract (notoriously, Tocqueville never satisfactorily defines this
term)[21] and with 'Europe'; but France is the real preoccupation, and
Tocqueville's eloquence is at the service less of political science than
of political rhetoric, as he tries to manipulate the views of those whom
he expected to be his most important readers.

We have seen that after his return from America, and particularly after his resignation from the *parquet*, Tocqueville relapsed into
a sort of legitimism. Even the *Système pénitentiaire* was consistent
with this: prison reform was not a party issue, and had been taken
up by the Bourbons during the Restoration. Not that Tocqueville

had rediscovered his loyalty to the fallen dynasty: he wanted stable government in France, and efforts to bring about a third Restoration could only be disruptive. Perhaps he can best be described as a fellow traveller of legitimism. Loyalty to his family and friends was certainly a motive, and good manners may have been another: living as he did among legitimists he may well have felt constrained to support their protests when they were justified. And in 1834 he was so disgusted with the July Monarchy that he said that Louis-Philippe would make himself a worse tyrant than Napoleon if he got the chance (perhaps he was influenced by the fact that many former imperialists, starting with Talleyrand, had enlisted in the new regime).[22] He could reasonably claim to have re-established his credentials: he had a right to a hearing, the more so as there were many liberal legitimists who vainly hoped to combine free institutions with rule by the elder line of Bourbons. Much of what Tocqueville wrote was directed at their prejudices and anxieties. By taking them seriously he could hope that his radical new views would be taken seriously too.*

Once accepted, this hypothesis explains much else – for example, the fact that his pages on the dangers of democracy are reference-free. He did not need to define his terms carefully because his legitimist readers would share his own sense of their meaning. He could and did denounce what today is called dictatorship without ever specifying Napoleon Bonaparte (nor did he mention Charles X and his failed *coup d'état* in July 1830). Tocqueville was no doubt well aware of the survival of popular Bonapartism and its tactical alliance with republicanism, but Napoleon and Napoleon II were both dead and Napoleon III (then just Prince Louis Napoleon, an exile) did not seem to be much of a threat. Even so, tact was necessary (not least for fear of offending the Left). Tocqueville merely hints at his disdain for conspirators, whether legitimist or republican, contrasting their violent activities with the peaceful campaigns of American political parties, although, at the climax of his argument, he denounces as blind those who suppose that the monarchy of Henri IV and Louis XIV can be restored.[23]

---

* It is tempting to suggest that AT's disdainful arguments in favour of a commercial democracy were consciously set out to beguile his upper-class readers into accepting the political vision of Sieyès as stated, most famously, in his *Qu'est-ce le Tiers État?*, but it cannot even be shown that AT read Sieyès before 1835.

In fact, Tocqueville was so anxious to persuade this sect among his readers that he went a long way towards under-cutting his message, by what he did not say, by what he said, and by the way in which he arranged it. Perhaps he hoped that liberal or republican readers would be so impressed by his depiction of democracy in America, and by the way he used it as a corrective to the errors of France, that they would overlook his elaborately expressed doubts – as indeed they did.

He knew the risks he ran. At the beginning of his chapter 'On Democratic Government in the United States' he remarks: 'I am entering a war-zone. Every word of this chapter may well upset in various ways the parties which divide my country.' Nevertheless, 'I will say all I think';[24] but he was not above using literary guile to make his thoughts acceptable. A man of no party had no choice. But the point nowadays must be to disentangle his message from the envelope in which he delivered it.

To understand what he seems to have been up to it is enough, perhaps, to draw attention to the twin lines of argument which wind their way through volume 2.

The first argument is thoroughly concrete, and already familiar. The theme is America. Tocqueville picks his way from topic to topic, assessing the performance of American government as he goes; always intelligent and instructive, he can sometimes astonish by his perceptiveness. Thus, in discussing political parties, he puts his finger on a very important point. In a huge country there will be a tendency for the various regions (Americans would call them sections) to pull apart into separate nations: 'if civil war comes, it is a conflict between rival peoples rather than between factions.'[25] Great national parties, which oppose each other on general principles, resist this tendency. Here Tocqueville seems to be directly prophetic of what was to happen in the United States a generation later, when the breakdown of the Jacksonian party system was to be followed in a few years by war between the United States and the so-called Confederate States. In chapter 3 he makes as trenchant a case for liberty of the press as anyone ever has, and rams it home, for the instruction of the French, with a masterly explanation of how it works in America: 'It is an axiom of political science in the United States that the only way of neutralizing the influence of newspapers is to multiply their number.' He is mystified that no French government has ever grasped the point.[26] Chapter 4 is a vindication of freedom of association, again as practised in America. He admits that in theory this freedom might have unfortunate results in a nation unused to liberty,* but it has not yet produced any such results in the United States, because Americans have never known any other system: they brought the right of association with them when they migrated from England; 'today, the exercise of the right has become one of their habits and customs' (*moeurs*).[27] And so it goes on. Tocqueville has many reservations, but his drift is indicated in the title that he gives to chapter 6: 'What are the Real Advantages That American Society Derives from Its Democratic Government'.

It will be seen that the questions which, so far, Tocqueville discusses are serious and interesting; his answers are sensible to the point of seeming, nowadays, banal. What is disconcerting is that in the same breath, as it were, he also discusses some silly questions. This is the second line of argument.

The silliness lies rather in Tocqueville's language and logic than in his underlying intention. He rightly sees that an explicit comparison of France and America would he enlightening, indeed necessary for his purposes, and, through many pages, he undertakes one. And there is nothing foolish in, for example, trying to work out whether American government is more or less expensive than French. Unfortunately he frequently seems to think that his business is to compare 'democracy' with 'aristocracy', and defines neither term – for if he were to try he would have to decide what sort of a state France was, and since it was not exactly an aristocracy, and was certainly not a democracy, the whole basis for an ideological comparison would break down (it is a great pity that Tocqueville was not prepared to use the word 'oligarchy' systematically). It was simpler to ask whether democracies or aristocracies were better at conducting foreign policy, or at controlling corruption, or running national administration. The reasoning tends to grow more and more *a priori*, less and less empirical. Forgetting such figures as Cardinal de Richelieu, Superintendent Fouquet and Sir Robert Walpole he finds for France and aristocracy in the matter of public honesty: corrupt

---

* All French governments of the epoch were terrified of a revival of the revolutionary clubs such as the Jacobins and Cordeliers, which had flourished between 1789 and 1794. AT himself was to support the suppression of such clubs under the Second Republic.

American politicians are merely vulgar, and they contaminate the morality of the people, whereas 'there is a certain aristocratic refinement in the depravity of great lords, an air of grandeur which often means that it is not contagious.'[28] M. de Talleyrand must have read this passage with gratification – or amusement. Tocqueville also decides that aristocracies conduct foreign policy better than do democracies, or monarchies for that matter: 'an aristocratic body is a resolute and enlightened statesman who never dies.' This passage caught the eye of John Quincy Adams, and he wrote a dignified protest to the author: 'The eighth President of the United States is now quietly in office – The political *Doctrines* of the several Presidents have been as different as the features of their faces, but the cardinal points of Policy regulating the movements of the Nation in its orbit have been as fixed and steady as those of the Austrian or the Russian Monarchy. I name them because they are the only Governments of Europe, which have for the last half century had any fixity in their systems at all. And even of them, if the reigns of the Emperors Joseph 2, and Paul were taken into the account, their stability would bear no comparison with that of the United States.'[29]

What is curious about this rebuke is that it should have been necessary. Tocqueville knew a great deal about American diplomatic history; he actually quotes George Washington's Farewell Address at length in this very chapter; and he knew well Edward Livingston, Andrew Jackson's Minister Plenipotentiary in France from 1833 to 1835, and formerly Secretary of State. Livingston was indeed the only American informant acknowledged by name in the *Démocratie*. So Tocqueville must have realized that the foreign policy of the United States, as conducted from the days of Benjamin Franklin to those of Jackson, had been singularly consistent, intelligent and successful. He saw the dilemma and solved it by the thought that George Washington, who saved the people from their impulse to involve themselves in the wars of the French Revolution, was really an aristocrat. In the teeth of the record he insisted that democracies can never undertake or persist in great diplomatic designs, maintain necessary secrecy or exercise patience. He did not give any examples of an aristocracy turning in a superior performance, and would have been hard-pressed to find one had he looked at, say, the history of France in the eighteenth century.[30]

This disjuncture between what Tocqueville knew and what he alleged is so odd that it demands explanation.

It must not be supposed that he was insincere. A *gentilhomme* in every fibre, it was easy enough for him to surrender to the instincts of his caste and shake his head over everything that might go wrong in a republic. In the fire and urgency of composition he might well go further than cool reflection would have approved – but having once adopted a position he never withdrew from it. And there was great plausibility in everything he said so long as he kept to generalities and abstractions. Even there he cannot always be acquitted of class bias. For instance, he returned to the subject of centralization, insisting that in the wrong hands (a tyrannous majority) it could be fatal to liberty, while emphasizing that no such threat yet existed in the United States.[31] He was, in fact, a warm admirer of American federalism and local self-government, and his doctrine of decentralization was perhaps the most characteristic part of his message. But today his readers should bear in mind that opposition to centralization became something of a shibboleth among legitimist nobles after 1830. They had lost Paris and the Court, but they had retained great local influence – especially in the west, where they were strongest – and it was natural for them therefore to oppose centralized administration as much as possible. Hervé de Tocqueville, with his belief in strong national government, was behind the times. Not so his son, who may also have been influenced by the cry of 'states' rights' in America.

At least centralization was and is a real issue. Not so tyranny of the majority. Tocqueville could generalize as much as he liked, but when it came to demonstration he was at a stand. Finally he could only instance a wartime lynch-mob in Baltimore in 1812, racial prejudice in Philadelphia, and the allegation that unorthodox writers did not always get the sales and reviews which they deserved.[32] He did not ask himself if riots, racism and philistinism were unknown in European societies, and when he came to list the various devices by which an oppressive majority could be circumvented he did not point out that every one of them was already operative in the United States.

Yet whatever ground Tocqueville conceded to the alarmists (too much for the effectiveness of his pamphlet), his central position was unaffected. He wanted to persuade his countrymen that democracy, as America showed it might be, was worth a try, and that all the alternatives were worse. History has substantially vindicated him (so far) and France, in the later twentieth century, accepted a Tocquevillean republic after trying almost everything else. But the fact that it took the French roughly a century and a quarter to get to that point demonstrates how difficult was the task that Tocqueville had set himself. His non-partisan stance might win him readers, but not adherents. To accept his reasoning would have required the legitimists to abandon their *raison d'être*, loyalty to the House of Bourbon and the memory of the *ancien régime*. Republicans would have had to give up their faith in class war and revolutionary dictatorship, and accept the July Monarchy as a reasonable compromise between parties. As for the Orleanists, who had most to gain from espousing Tocqueville's views, they were both too timid and too narrowly selfish in their class attitudes to do so. The Bonapartists, lurking in the wings, were the party of Caesar; Tocqueville himself drew the line at them. Opposition to Bonapartism was his most unvarying political principle from first to last.

Read today as a pamphlet, the *Démocratie* seems striking chiefly for its good sense and accuracy; but it is far more impressive as a work of analysis, political, historical and sociological. Nothing among Tocqueville's American discoveries exceeded the importance of the *point de départ* as a concept. The more he reflected on it the more he grasped its profound implications. The first Americans reached New England (he never paid much attention to the foundation of Virginia) as religious republicans, and from that everything else flowed. But the *point de départ* could only have been so effective because it was reinforced by other circumstances: by time – the 150 or so years during which the experiment unfolded – and by experience. Tocqueville came to lay great stress on a people's practical experience of government: we have seen him applying the idea to British society. History shaped society, but society also shaped history: the interweaving operation of these forces made a nation. The point seems trite enough today, and the whole mind of the Romantic age can be seen moving towards it in, for example, Scott's novels as well as in Guizot's lectures; but Tocqueville was the first to make it his own, and generate a masterpiece from it.

He distinguished three forces at work: the physical environment, the legal system, and *les moeurs*, of which *les moeurs* was the most important. He was well aware that he was giving this word a new and much-extended meaning. In his American letters and notebooks he mostly used it to refer to sexual morality, but by the time he came to write the *Démocratie* he had much bigger ideas: 'by this word I understand the intellectual and moral tendencies which men bring to the social state.'[33]* This coinage explained to Tocqueville what he had been doing in America. It gave him licence to display all the results of his researches; for example into the political effects of religion in the United States. 'If by this point of my book I have not made the reader aware of the importance which I attach to the practical experience of the Americans, to their habits, to their opinions, in a word to their manners, in sustaining their laws, I have failed in the chief object which I set myself in starting to write.'[33] It would have been a very dull reader who missed the point.

It cannot be denied that Tocqueville's sense of what procedure was necessary for analysing and explaining a society was correct, and the result was a portrait of America which still repays study and, in its day, was the first of its kind; but it led him into a profound difficulty from which he was never wholly able to escape. The more that he studied, reflected, and wrote, the more the Americans appeared a distinct and peculiar people, unlike even their first progenitors, the British. Not that Tocqueville was a believer in American exceptionalism in the vulgar sense: he never succumbed to the delusion that the laws of social evolution were suspended for the benefit of the United States. But if, as his investigations demonstrated conclusively, American institutions and the American political system resulted from that people's *point de départ*, and from their geography, laws and manners, how could they be successfully imitated in France? It was a reasonable question, even if one were not a believer in French exceptionalism (and Tocqueville, if not a rabid nationalist, was at all times a warm patriot). No wonder that he offered only cautious recommendations, as we have seen. 'One

---

* It is a difficult expression to render in English, comprising as it does morals, manners and customs. As used by Tocqueville it is roughly equivalent to the Latin *mos*, *mores* (from which it derives) and this has led social scientists to try to domesticate *mores* (which some pronounce as if it rhymed with *bores*) as an English word. I do not think that they have succeeded, and shall use the word *manners*, originally the exact equivalent of *moeurs*, trying to extend or revive its meaning as Tocqueville extended *moeurs*; though when necessary I shall use the French word instead.

can only hazard opinions,' he said.[34] His opinion, in flat defiance of
the view which he was to state in his Introduction, and which forms
the epigraph of this chapter, was that democracy and the American
political system were not interchangeable terms, but what he had seen
in America had convinced him that the prudent and gradual introduction of democratic institutions, which in this way would become part
of the habits and opinions of the people – in other words, their *moeurs*
– was a real possibility, and he was to spend the rest of his life advocating it; but he could not pretend that he was offering anything more
than a hope. And although he would exert his considerable powers
of persuasion to convert his readers to that hope, he was well aware
that ultimate success or failure lay predominantly with forces outside
his control. The convictions, passions and interests that divided
France were not going to yield immediately to sweet reason. Hence
Tocqueville's doctrine was for long more honoured in Britain and the
United States, where it was not particularly needed (being a rationalization of their actual history and politics) than in France, where it
was.

But he never quite gave up hope. The excesses of the French
Revolution and the Napoleonic dictatorship had shown all too clearly
what the future might hold: a society in which the citizens were equal
in degradation, thrust down below the right level of humanity into
slavery to a single man. America displayed an alternative.

> It is difficult to induce the people to take part in government; it is
> still more difficult to supply them with the experience and the beliefs
> which they lack, but need in order to govern well. The democratic
> will is volatile;* its agents, vulgar; its laws, imperfect. I admit all this.
> But if it is true that soon there will be no middle way between the
> empire of democracy and the yoke of one man, ought we not to try

---

* This sentence well illustrates the difficulties created by Tocqueville's carelessness with the
word *démocratie* and, to some extent, by the French language itself. He wrote: 'Les volontés
de la démocratie sont changeantes.' Here, by *démocratie*, he certainly meant what others might
call, according to taste, *the people, the popular majority, the crowd, the masses* or *the mob*. But *la
démocratie* also connotes democracy as a system of government. Tocqueville ought to have
asked himself whether he was making an observation about public opinion, in which case he
was right but unoriginal, even trivial; or about democratic government, in which case he was
probably wrong. Instead he wrote as if he could have it both ways, and was thus certainly
misleading. Mob rule and democratic government are not the same thing, and democratic
governments are not noticeably volatile.

rather for the former than submit voluntarily to the latter? And if it were necessary to accept complete equality, would it not be better to allow ourselves to be levelled in liberty rather than under a despot?[35]

Tocqueville did not want to turn Frenchmen into Anglo-Americans, even if it were possible. 'My purpose has rather been to demonstrate, using the American example, that their laws and, above all, their manners can permit a democratic people to remain free.' French liberty would and should be different from American: 'I would think it a great misfortune for humanity if liberty had to take the same form in every place.' Yet by careful preparation, during as much time as it took, a people might be trained for liberty, and once so trained, could exercise it. The alternative was universal tyranny, disastrous for noble and *bourgeois*, rich man and pauper.[36]

So ended volume 2, chapter 9, and having reached this point Tocqueville asked himself if there need be a chapter 10. His message about democracy was now as clear, strong and complete as he could make it. On the other hand, this book was as much about America as it was about democracy, and there was still much to say about the country (he had not yet exhausted his notebooks); furthermore his readers would rightly expect it of him. He decided to press on; but in spite of its precise and limited title ('Some Reflections on the Present State and Probable Future of the Three Races Which Inhabit the Territory of the United States') chapter 10 has the appearance of another ragbag. Tocqueville now seems determined to leave nothing out: he writes as if it is more important to report his thoughts and observations than to make them hang together; he apologizes for sometimes repeating himself, but does not seem to know or care that he occasionally contradicts himself;* and few readers are likely to blame him, so deep and wide-ranging and so many are his observations on such topics as race relations, the dangers facing the Union, the Americans as a business people, and so on. 'These matters, which bear on my main subject, are

---

* For instance, he comments perceptively on the way in which, thanks to steamboats, Americans have become frequent travellers and thereby get to know each other: travel homogenizes the nation (OC I i 402). But only a few pages earlier he writes as if each of the states were a distinct people, incapable of blending with the others, and that Americans are patriots for their states, not for the Union (ibid., 384).

not part of it: they are American without being democratic, and it is above all the portrait of democracy which I have attempted.'[37] Away he went.

Throughout the *Démocratie* of 1835 he likes to explain to his readers and to himself what he is up to; it is an endearing trait; but here he gives himself away. His headlong process of composition has let him down, and now he is misleading. 'American without being democratic ...' Nothing could be less true of the topics that he was about to discuss – for example, race relations. It is not too much to say that from colonial times onwards the race question has always been the central difficulty of American democracy, and this was never truer than in Tocqueville's day. The United States was a slave-holding republic, and many are the works of polemic and scholarship which have explored the meaning of that contradiction.* In chapter 10 Tocqueville explores it himself, with all his usual intelligence and more than his usual humanity: it is as if he found it easier to sympathize with slaves than with convicts, even if his analysis was somewhat tainted with what we must call racism, picked up, undoubtedly, from his authorities.[†] But he blunders in not pointing out that here was a supreme example of the way in which manners shape society and politics. Had he integrated his discussion of slavery into the exposition of his theory he would greatly have strengthened both, and he would also have strengthened his case for liberal democracy, since the only cure for the disease of slavery was to free the slaves and concede them equal rights (as was, in the end, so painfully to happen). But Tocqueville had saddled himself with a formula, and did not re-examine it. Scribbling away in his garret for dear life, he had not the temperament nor, he thought, the time (but his deadlines were all self-imposed) for structural revision. Words, sentences, paragraphs might be, and were, gone over again and again; the larger shaping of his treatise never received more than perfunctory attention.

Yet the omission hardly matters. As in the earlier sections, deep recurring preoccupations give the ragbag coherence and link it vitally to the rest of the book. I might even say that Tocqueville has found

---

* See Don E. Fehrenbacher, *The Slaveholding Republic* (Oxford University Press, 2001).

† 'If freedom is denied to the Negroes of the South, they will end by seizing it by violence; if freedom is granted to them, they will not be slow to abuse it' (OC I i 379).

another way of making his case, and is beginning at the beginning for the third time. He was by now incapable of writing about America without bringing in his favourite themes: they bubbled to the surface whatever his topic, and his topics, as I have said, were in themselves democratic, or he made them so. When he thought to write something about American maritime commerce (it would have been a shame to waste the conversations he had had with Mr Schermerhorn during the voyage to America), how did he account for its success? Why, in terms of the American national character:

> Any American, taken at random, will be found to be hot in his desires, enterprising, adventurous, above all an innovator. This spirit stows itself, indeed, in all he does; it is part of his laws, his politics, his religious doctrines, his economic and social theories, his private business; it goes everywhere with him, to the depths of the forests as much as to the hearts of the cities. The same spirit, applied to sea-borne trade, makes the Americans sail faster and sell cheaper than all other merchants ...[38]

It is another example of manners at work, which is why Tocqueville discusses it. It is never predictable what he will talk of next, but certain what he will say. Thus, when he enlarges on one of his favourite themes, the value of free associations spontaneously formed by private citizens, the example he chooses to give is the American political party (and he takes the opportunity to discuss Andrew Jackson's presidential record soberly and elaborately). Chapter 10, in fact, is only superficially an afterthought: whether Tocqueville consciously realized it or not, it brilliantly reinforces his earlier arguments, and much enriches his portrait of democracy.*

After the last chapter comes the first. To anyone reading the *Démocratie* in the order in which Tocqueville wrote it (and however often it has been read before) the Introduction comes as a slight shock,

---

* In fact the only real oddity in chapter 10 is the conclusion, when AT predicts that America, the country of liberty, and Russia, the country of slavery, will dominate the future of the world. This prediction seemed very impressive during the Cold War, but AT's admirers have said little about it since 1990. It should be realized that in 1835 AT was strikingly original only in predicting such a future for the United States; belief in the power and menace of reactionary Russia was almost universal in political circles, and was dispersed only during the Crimean War.

for it is mostly about France and Europe, which are largely lost to sight behind American detail in chapter 10. Tocqueville mentions the United States in his opening sentence and then no more for ten pages (out of fourteen). His subject is instead the great historical transformation which he calls 'the democratic revolution': the transition, taking many generations, from a society dominated by a military nobility, whose wealth was in land, to a society of infinite diversity, in wealth and occupation, where no one caste enjoys dominance, but all share equality of status.* More particularly, he is concerned with the broken and directionless state of France in the wake of the revolutions of 1789 and 1830. If his grand historical scheme is based on Guizot and (somewhat) on Lingard, his view of post-Revolutionary France is all his own. The old order, he says, is gone for good: never again will kings and nobles exercise power in the traditional way (of which he paints, nostalgically, a pretty but unhistorical picture).[39] It is no use gazing back longingly at the receding shore and at the wrecks littered upon it; all eyes should be directed to the cataracts ahead and the question of how to get through them: 'a new political science is needed for a wholly new world.'[40] The Christian world is condemned to democracy, it is God's will; the task must be to secure its benefits rather than succumb to its evils, and Tocqueville's book is designed to show how. He is as elitist as ever. While never in so many words admitting that part of the work of the French Revolution had been to create a new governing class, the notables, to which he himself belonged, he is firm in asserting that the educated classes must seize control of the democratic movement and direct it according to their superior knowledge and understanding, for otherwise the violent and ignorant lower orders will destroy society. There is not much time left; action is urgent; but the rewards may be great:

> I dream of a society where all, regarding the law as their own handiwork, love it and submit to it without difficulty; where, the

* In AT's French, *égalité des conditions*. This is usually translated as 'equality of condition', but this is misleading since nowadays it seems to imply economic equality, which AT knew perfectly well did not exist any longer in America, if it ever had. He used the word in the same sense as Lady Catherine de Bourgh, when she was trying to bully Elizabeth Bennet: 'Who was your mother? Who are your uncles and aunts? Do not imagine me ignorant of their condition.' In context it is perfectly clear what AT was concerned with, but not everyone has always remembered the context.

authority of government being respected as necessary rather than divine, love is felt for the head of state not as a passion but as a calm and rational sentiment. Each citizen having his rights, and being sure of keeping them, a manly, mutual confidence would be established between the classes, and a sort of reciprocal condescension, as far from pride as from humiliation. Educated in their real interests, the people would understand that to profit by the blessings of society it is necessary to pay for them. Free associations among the citizens would replace the power of individual nobles, and the State would be sheltered alike from tyranny and licence ... Changes in the body of society would he regulated and gradual; should there be less distinction than under an aristocracy, there would also be less poverty; enjoyments would be less spectacular, well-being more general; learning and science would diminish, but ignorance be rarer; passions would be less violent and manners gentler; there would be more vice and less crime.[41]

His study of America proves that all this is perfectly possible.

This manifesto* reveals a great deal about Tocqueville. In its rejection of the *ancien régime* it shows his political and historical realism: whatever his sympathies, he could not endorse the reactionary longings of the legitimists. In its prescriptions it shows his hopes for France under the July Monarchy:† hopes which were to be greatly disappointed, but which he did not abandon even after Louis-Philippe's fall. It betrays the limitations of his democratic faith: even after his American journey he could not believe that undiluted government of the people, by the people, could be a success – they needed guidance. The only political issue which he tackles head-on is anti-clericalism: he argues passionately that 'religion' (by which he usually means the Catholic Church) does not need to be supported by political authority, is indeed much better without it for liberty and equality are its true friends; and he also insists that republicanism, if it knew its own interest, would make an ally of religion.[42] Here Tocqueville implicitly criticizes both the Restoration and the July Revolution; and here we can see how deep a mark America made upon his thought.

---

* I use this word deliberately. Tocqueville's Introduction bears much the same relation to the Revolution of 1830 that the *Communist Manifesto* does to the Revolution of 1848. Karl Marx was another author who learned from Guizot.

† See OC I i 324 for a closely parallel passage.

His reference to 'manly, mutual confidence' requires comment (in other passages he writes of 'male virtue'). There is no mystery about what he meant: virtue had been a commonplace of traditional republican thought (which Quentin Skinner wants us to call Neo-Roman) since the Renaissance. In Tocqueville's time the idea had been most strikingly expressed in the *Social Contract* of Jean-Jacques Rousseau and in the portentous canvases of J.-L. David's neo-classical period, in which solemn warriors strike attitudes of devotion to their fatherland; or in Greenough's semi-nude statue of George Washington.* The notion seems to have been that in Utopia citizens and statesmen alike would be animated only and at all times by stern considerations of the public weal, at least when assembled in the forum: all considerations of personal or local interest would be banished. When the personal did intrude it had to be subsumed in the public: Lucretia's rape was to be punished not as a crime against a woman but as an act of tyranny – it was not to be avenged as a matter of family honour. Brutus was to be admired for unflinchingly sentencing his sons to death as conspirators, not blamed for having brought them up badly. It hardly needs saying that the ideal was unworkable: 'nothing straight can ever be built with the crooked timber of humanity' – Isaiah Berlin's advocacy has made Kant's remark a cliché. It was not a cliché which occurred to Tocqueville when writing the 1835 *Démocratie*, or for some years afterwards. He required only the most mythically Neo-Roman behaviour from citizens and their representatives, and was ruthless in condemning any lapses. In short, he was as yet fundamentally mistaken about the nature of politics, which is as natural a dimension of human life as eating, drinking, sex or commerce; a universal process by which human beings adjust to reality – especially the reality of other people – and adjust reality to themselves. It is messy, never wholly successful, and necessarily incomplete. It is the opposite of Utopia, and it may be observed that if it is the difficulty of Utopianism which has made so many Utopians into totalitarians, its impossibility has made many others into democrats. Tocqueville in 1835 had not yet glimpsed this.

---

* Canova's nude statue of Napoleon, on the other hand, has to be regarded as a joke, though definitely not intended as such.

Neither in the *Démocratie* nor anywhere else did he express the slightest political interest in *female* virtue. He seems to have been entirely deaf to any question of women's rights, and in this was manifestly inferior to his great contemporary and friend John Stuart Mill. As usual, Tocqueville was not alone in his obtuseness: Frenchwomen were not to get the vote until 1944; but even in 1835 he could have discussed the issue. It was being debated in America, and Mary Wollstonecraft's *Rights of Women* had been published over forty years previously. Tocqueville's silence on this matter (and on others to be discussed in due course) shows how much he was a creature of his time and place, and how much the limitations of the July Monarchy were his also, though he so often deplored them.

The Introduction, then, summarizes or implies Tocqueville's political creed as well as his historical vision, and shows clearly what he hoped to achieve by his book. He wanted to launch a new kind of liberalism and help to steer it. He was claiming a place not just among France's authors but in her governing elite. The rest of his life would be the story of how his ambition fared.

Up to a point he had calculated shrewdly; the Introduction was certain to fascinate the salons and academies of Paris. Both in the questions it asked ('Where are we?', 'Where are we going?') and in the suggestions it made it spoke to the central preoccupations of the day. But it is surely impossible to feel that it did full justice to the extraordinary masterpiece which Tocqueville had written. The message of the *Démocratie* is indeed superbly summarized in the Introduction, but as important as the book's message was its method, and its findings were perhaps more important than either. The *Démocratie* is the greatest book ever written on the United States. Tocqueville could not make that claim, but his readers have repeatedly made it for him; and that, surely, was an achievement to outstrip any other.

We have no direct evidence as to what Beaumont thought of the manuscript brought to him in August 1834. Since it owed so much to him he is unlikely to have felt disappointed. No doubt he in turn showed his friend the still-incomplete manuscript of his novel, *Marie, ou l'esclavage aux États-Unis*. Tocqueville thought very well of it: he let stand, or now drafted, the puff for *Marie* which still appears in the Introduction to the *Démocratie*. For the rest, he enjoyed his country holiday, staying first with Beaumont's sister, Mme de Sarcé, at her chateau, Gallerande, and then with the rest of the family at Beaumont-la-Chartre. Writing to Marie Mottley he had nothing but praise for the hospitality he was receiving, but both to her and to Kergorlay he expressed astonishment at the pleasure which the Beaumont family took in the petty details which made up the country round – 'a life of potatoes'. He had no idea that before long he himself would be retiring rapturously to the country, but it is possible to think that potatoes already attracted him more than he realized: 'I love to look at fields; at the sight of a fine summer evening in a remote and peaceful countryside; listening to the various sounds which are heard at long intervals, and the silence which follows them, I feel afresh a calm which goes straight to my turbulent heart.' But it would only do for a holiday, he could never live shut in behind hedges, 'I would prefer life's roughest storms to such peaceful-ness.' Perhaps, he thought, he was irritated by a happiness which he could never share: 'I will never be happy, Marie, that is certain. There is no concord in me. With limited abilities I yet feel vast desires; with delicate health, an inexpressible need for action and emotion; with a taste for the good, passions which drive me away from it.' Such men as he could never attain lasting happiness; but at least his love for Marie gave him a constant point of reference. There was his harbour, there his clear horizon, whatever clouds hid the sky overhead. 'Yesterday evening I was happy enough to be at a gathering, I was among people I like in a place which I find agreeable, my mind was at peace, and I was in good health; but I felt that something was missing ... you.'[43]

These tender sentiments left no trace on the bread-and-butter letter which Tocqueville sent to Beaumont's father after his return with Gustave to Paris. He had had his usual bad luck with public transport:

Not having been able to get seats in the Vendôme *diligence*, we were forced to smuggle ourselves onto the roof where, rolled about among the luggage, we passed the most disturbed and chilly night that can be imagined. I have never more clearly realized the advantages of my height.* People have no clear idea, I assure you, of the advantages

* The editors of the *Lettres Choisies* inform us that AT was 1.62 metres tall – say, 5′ 4″.

of being short. While Gustave, with his long legs and arms, was like a semaphore in action, I contrived to nestle down into a small hole where perhaps I would be sleeping still but for a basket of chickens which suddenly interrupted a most pleasant dream by falling onto my nose. I let out a shriek, as you can well believe, but so did two or three of the cocks inside the basket, so I thought it wise to fall silent, in the hope that they would imitate my self-control.[44]

Back in Paris, Tocqueville turned seriously to the business of publication. Weeks ago he had discovered some of the drawbacks of dealing with Gosselin. 'If the said G. had read my manuscript the result of my visit was scarcely flattering to me; for the more I answered his questions about the book the more I saw alarm beginning to run away with him.' He said that on reconsideration he would print only 500 copies, and when challenged gave a typical publisher's explanation: if he printed a thousand copies and the book did not sell, he would be certain of a loss; whereas, if a second impression were required, the cost of reprinting would only somewhat diminish his profit.[45] He talked of publication in November (in the event the book was not put on sale until January). Tocqueville resigned himself to these arrangements; by the end of October he was busy correcting proofs.

If he was relatively tranquil about Gosselin's proceedings, it was perhaps because he had a larger anxiety. He wanted to test the water, and with this in mind circulated copies of his Introduction in his family (he may have felt that Beaumont's verdict was not sufficiently objective). The response was instructive.

Kergorlay, who had had a wretchedly boring, empty summer, jumped at the chance of being useful, and reported enthusiastically: 'The whole, that is, your general ideas, their classification and their development, seems fine to me and hangs together ... to my mind the fundamental ideas are capital ones with both depth and novelty, whether in themselves or in the connections which you make between them.' He made a number of suggestions for small improvements, many of which Tocqueville apparently adopted, and remarked that 'nobility is your style's characteristic' (which must have pleased). He saw no need to tone down any remarks to appease any class of readers, no doubt meaning the legitimists (which must have reassured).[46] Unfortunately Tocqueville's other relations were less encouraging.

They were legitimists to a man, and they did not find his demonstration of the utility of democracy and its compatibility with their beliefs and interests sufficiently persuasive. One wrote: 'It is essential that Alexis take care not to attack the fallen Restoration and its unhappy, discrowned sovereigns. It would even perhaps be wise not to attack Louis-Philippe too strongly. Alexis is at the start of his career; it would be disagreeable if all the government's newspapers were against him.'[47] It is not known who wrote these remarks, perhaps the result of an astute reading between the lines; but perhaps Tocqueville took the hint. There is no overt attack on either Bourbon or Orleans in the *Démocratie*, though plenty of implied criticism.

Perhaps the comment was written by Camille d'Orglandes, member of a Cotentin family that was linked to the Tocquevilles by two marriages (Louis de Rosanbo and Louis de Chateaubriand had both married Orglandes ladies). He certainly wrote a letter (now lost) about the Introduction which Tocqueville thought it necessary to answer at length. He felt that Orglandes had misunderstood the Introduction, so he repeated the argument as emphatically as possible: equality was on the way, it could not be averted, and therefore the political choice lay between democratic government ('by which I do not mean a republic but a social system in which more or less everybody takes part in public business') or between unlimited, because modern, absolutism. In a demoralized country like France there would be no bounds to its tyranny. 'We have seen some fine preliminary sketches of such a regime under Bonaparte, and if L.P. had a free hand, he would show us a yet more perfect version of it.' Both these choices were unattractive, but 'between the two evils, I have chosen the lesser.' It would be difficult but not impossible to make a democratic government succeed; he did not believe that God had willed equality of status simply to lead men into a despotism like that of Claudius or Tiberius. 'It wouldn't be worth the effort.'

This repetition of the Introduction has its own value; still more interesting is the justification which Tocqueville offers for writing his book:

I am not quarrelsome by nature: when an opinion which I don't share seems to me unimportant or when I am not entirely convinced that its opposite is true, I hold my peace. It was thus that I managed to live for a very long time among people who were greatly surprised at last to see me resolutely doing things which they thought had never crossed my mind. So it was not until after full consideration that I decided to write the book which I am about to publish ... [But] it will soon be ten years since I conceived most of the ideas which I have just expounded to you. As I did not find them agreeable, I turned them over again and again, from every point of view, before accepting them. I only went to America to clarify my misgivings. The penitentiary system was only a pretext; I used it as a passport. In the United States, I came across a thousand things which were unworthy of my attention, but I discovered others which brightly illuminated my understanding. I discovered facts of which the knowledge, I thought, was useful. I did not go there with the idea of writing a book,* the idea of a book came upon me there. I think that every man owes society his thoughts as well as his energies. When one sees one's fellows in danger, it is a duty to try to rescue them.

Tocqueville does not know if his book will succeed, do good or do harm (though he hopes not the last); but it had to be written. And he does not regret having written boldly, plainly and frankly: 'if I find it very easy to keep quite quiet, as I have already said to you, once I do speak I always seek the clearest terms in the world's clearest language, which is ours, to express my ideas. It is a habit which, when speaking in public, I have often wanted to shed, but I have never been able to.' [48]

The chief note of this long letter is, surely, self-confidence. Before the event Tocqueville was nervous about legitimist criticism, but when actually confronted by it he merely reiterated his views and defended his style. It remained to be seen what other readers would say, and how he would react to their opinions. Meanwhile, with Beaumont's help, he continued to work on his proofs. In December the finished volumes were distributed to the journals, the author's friends and the bookshops.

---

* This is not strictly accurate. Perhaps what AT meant was that he had not thought of writing *this* book.

CHAPTER THIRTEEN

FAME
1835–1836

*Le livre va jusqu'à présent merveilleusement. Je suis
confondu de son succès; car je craignais sinon une chute, du
moins un accueil froid, en raison du soin qu'avait pris son
auteur de se tenir en dehors de toutes les parties.* *

ALEXIS DE TOCQUEVILLE TO EUGÈNE STOFFELS,
16 FEBRUARY 1835[1]

THE FIRST SIGN of what was to come appeared in the workshops
where *De la démocratie en Amérique* was printed. According to
Beaumont, Tocqueville was much struck by the interest which the
workers took in his book (we should remember that the printers of
Paris had been in the forefront of the July Revolution): 'All, from the
foremen and the proofreaders down to the typesetters, took unusual
care with their work, and seemed passionate for the success of a book
in which each, according to his contribution, felt honoured to have a
concern'.[2] Tocqueville thought that this was a good omen; so did his
publisher. It would be interesting to know what these workers made
of a treatise on the magical topic, democracy, which was so full of
reservations. Probably, like many later readers, they found in it what

---

* Up till now the book has been doing wonderfully. I am bewildered by its success; for I feared,
  if not a failure, at least a chilly welcome, because of the care taken by the author to stand aloof
  from all the parties.

they wanted: perhaps particularly the demonstration that in certain circumstances democracy could be successful.

The tiny knot of family and intimate friends – hardly large enough to be called a coterie – was as enthusiastic as was to be expected. Beaumont made his views plain in his American novel, *Marie*, which he was struggling to complete, and which contained an explicit puff for Tocqueville's book in its Foreword.[3] Eugène Stoffels wrote enthusiastically from Metz before he had finished the first volume to commend the Introduction as the best possible account of the character and evils of the age. Kergorlay, writing from the country, after soliciting Tocqueville's assistance in a project for beating up an insolent commoner (the spirit of the *ancien régime* still lingered at Fosseuse)* said that the only fault he found was a certain dryness in the first volume; for the rest, the style was excellent, the ideas weighty and original, and although they cast Kergorlay himself into a melancholy, their success with others 'who know nothing' would be lasting.[4]

Tocqueville was no doubt gratified by these praises, but his political and intellectual ambitions required a much larger success, and inspired by Mme Ancelot's good advice he set out to ensure it by every means he could think of. The *Démocratie* was notionally published in January, but on 24 December *Le Courrier français* carried a notice by Léon Faucher: 'This book seems destined for great success, taking into account the importance of the subject and the novelty as well as the evidence of its insights. It will come to its readers as a revelation.' Faucher deserves honour as the first commentator to record his favourable opinion, but he soon had company: a steady stream of enthusiastic reviews followed during 1835.[5] Most of them were rewarded with appreciative notes from the author. Early copies were dispatched to Tocqueville's most valued English friends – Lord Radnor, John Bowring and Nassau Senior. Senior acknowledged the gift enthusiastically, and suggested various British periodicals to which the book might be sent. Tocqueville acted on this suggestion at once.[6] It would be some time before copies reached the United States, but there were Americans in Paris who raised interest in it by their letters home.

---

* We hear no more of this affair. AT usually complied with all Kergorlay's requests and commands, but it is hard to imagine him agreeing to this one.

Nevertheless, the great and immediate success of the *Démocratie*, like that of so many books, owed more to word of mouth than to reviews which appeared only gradually and may almost be said to have responded to public opinion rather than to have formed it. The social, intellectual and political elites of France overlapped during the years of constitutional monarchy to an extraordinary extent, and the opinions which mattered were formed in their salons. It was essential for Tocqueville to secure a favourable reception in those daily gatherings where, refreshed by weak tea and light cakes, and under the firm guidance of intelligent hostesses, *le tout Paris* came to its conclusions. If the salons approved so would everyone else, and Paris being the intellectual capital of Europe the word would soon spread to other cities and countries. So Tocqueville sent a presentation copy to Pierre-Paul Royer-Collard, with a suitable letter. He recalled that Royer-Collard had welcomed the *Système pénitentiaire* when it appeared, and said that his gratitude made it obligatory to present this new work, although Tocqueville's admiration for Royer-Collard's character and writings would have been cause enough. Thus flattered, the veteran liberal leader read the book and became enthusiastic. 'There has been nothing like it since Montesquieu' was his verdict, and the *mot* spread rapidly through Paris.[7] (The comparison with Montesquieu is still the one absolutely safe thing to say about Tocqueville.) Rather strangely, Tocqueville does not appear to have sent his book to Guizot, to whom he owed so much: perhaps he already thought that Guizot had become too conservative. He did, however, write to Chateaubriand.

This was difficult but necessary. Chateaubriand and his Tocqueville relations were still on cool terms. Yet for Alexis to ignore a man who was such a close connection, and to whom, as a writer, he owed so much, would be insulting; furthermore, Chateaubriand was the star of Juliette Récamier's salon, the most influential of the day: his patronage would be of the utmost value. So as soon as possible Tocqueville sent him a copy of the *Démocratie*, accompanied by a letter which is a curious mixture of sincere tribute and gross flattery, suggesting that he had little respect for his kinsman's character and penetration:

> When one has the good fortune to encounter in one's own country the greatest writer of the age it becomes a sort of obligation to lay before

him the tribute of one's efforts, a tribute often most unworthy of him in itself, but acceptable because of the feeling behind the offering. And when family ties also attach one to that same man, to whom one is anyway united by patriotic pride, one feels [acute] anxiety not to fail in what, even without them, must have been considered a duty.

So far so good. Tocqueville now feels free to say what is really on his mind:

> Perhaps you will recognize in this work the development, no doubt very incomplete, of one of those great truths of which you have brought a host into the world – and which men now farm out, each finding a single one a sufficient burden. No-one, sir, has handled the approach of Democracy like you. The object of this book is to make known the effects produced by the reign of that same Democracy, the approach of which you tranquilly proclaimed, in that country which has peaceably made it the object of its journey, and where it will undergo its farthest development ... You are not only the man who has best painted the past but also he who has most prophetically foretold the future. Placed at the point of junction between two great revolutions, the one which is finishing and the one which now begins, you have illuminated both aspects of that immense canvas. No-one has described as you have the conquering march of Democracy through the world ...[8]

What is perhaps most striking about this letter is that Chateaubriand's American writings are praised in terms which, ever since, many have applied to Tocqueville himself. And whatever the letter-writer's *arrière-pensée*, no-one should doubt his essential sincerity. He is not only discharging a debt; he is acknowledging the tradition in which he writes.

Chateaubriand made no modest disclaimers in his reply. He ignored Tocqueville's more outrageous compliments and went straight to what he took to be the point:

> Most certainly we are entering the democratic era; the democratic idea is everywhere. It is undermining all thrones, ruining all aristocracies. One can fight it; accidents can stay its development. But whatever one does or whatever one says, it will gain the decisive victory. You cannot imagine, sir, how happy I will be to read your book and how

much I congratulate myself on [our] family ties ... I was already being talked of, a little, when I saw you, a child, at Verneuil. In your turn you will see me decay into childishness; men will speak of you, and I will be forgotten.[9]

When it came to flattery Chateaubriand had nothing to learn, but his enthusiasm for his young follower was genuine. He read the book, praised it to his friends, and induced Mme Récamier to invite Tocqueville to her salon.

This was no little favour. Chateaubriand and Juliette Récamier were each other's last loves: the death of Mme de Staël in 1817 had brought them together, and they were never to be separated. Mme Récamier had long been known as the most attractive woman in France, and now she devoted herself to furthering Chateaubriand's interests – first political, and then, after 1830, literary – above all, to saving him from boredom. She was no longer rich, or young, but she was still charming, and supremely skilled in the arts of society. Although she professed to be living in retirement, in a comfortable apartment in the Abbaye-aux-Bois, near the Luxembourg, all Paris (when invited) flocked to her long drawing-room, with its huge portrait of Mme de Staël at one end and a Louis XVI chimney-piece at the other.[10] The conversation was the best in France, largely because of Mme Récamier's insistence on good manners – she never allowed noisy arguments, or political rant. It was an environment perfectly suited to Tocqueville. Many years later he tried to explain its magic:

> Few traces of her former beauty then remained, but we were all her lovers and her slaves. The talent, labour and skill which she wasted on her salon, would have gained and governed an empire. She was virtuous, if it be virtuous to persuade every one of a dozen men that you wish to favour him, tho' some circumstance always occurs to prevent you doing so. Every friend thought himself preferred. She governed us by little distinctions, by letting one man come 5 minutes before the others, or stay five minutes after, just as Louis XIV raised one courtier to the seventh heaven by giving him the *bougeoir*, and another by leaning on his arm. She said little, but knew what each man's *fort* was, and placed from time to time a *mot* which led him to it. If any thing were peculiarly well said, her face brightened. You saw

that her attention was always active, and always intelligent. And yet I doubt whether she really enjoyed conversation. *Tenir salon* was to her a game, which she played well, and almost always successfully: but she must have sometimes failed, and sometimes have been exhausted by the effort. Her *Salon* was perhaps pleasanter to us than it was to herself.[11]

He was not so sadly perceptive on his first visits. He was invited to hear Chateaubriand read from his unpublished and unfinished *Memoirs*. It was the joyful high point of his first success.

I went. I found a gaggle of celebrities in bud or in bloom. A small, well-chosen salon: Ch. above all, Ampère, Ballanche, Sainte-Beuve, M. de Noailles and the duc de Laval, the same who said ten years ago: '*Saquedié!* I've passed some very agreeable moments with that woman.' M. de Ch. introduced me to everyone there in such a way as to make me great friends among those who did not write and sincere enemies of those who did. But all alike overpowered me with compliments.[12]

After the curtain-raiser, the star performance. Chateaubriand sat with his back to the fireplace; his listeners sat in front of him on chairs arranged in a semi-circle:

It would take too long to tell you what I heard. The first Restoration and the Hundred Days. Some bad taste. More often bitter bile, profundity in the depiction of Napoleon's difficulties on his throne, verve throughout, poetry in full measure, Bonaparte's march on Paris after his return from the isle of Elba as Homer and Tacitus together might have painted it, the battle of Waterloo described in a way that set every nerve on edge, although it contained nothing but the distant rumble of guns. What can I say? I was moved, agitated, really and profoundly shaken and, in expressing extreme admiration, did no more than say what I thought.

He went home treading on air.

He was soon very much at ease in the Abbaye-aux-Bois. A German visitor to Paris saw him there at about this time:

Opposite [Cousin] was a young man with a pale, somewhat sickly face. People were showing him marked deference and attention. His manner had a grace and courtesy which the present generation of the French seem to value less than the previous generation. 'Who is that young man?' I asked my companion, for I was very struck by him. 'It is M. de Tocqueville,' I was told, 'the man who has just published a remarkable book on democracy in the United States. That book had an astonishing fate – it pleased all parties. The liberals and the legitimists praised it, while the *juste milieu** did not attack it. But as few Frenchmen possess powers of observation as delicate as that young man's, few have been able to enjoy the same success. He is greatly liked and run after; every salon wants him.'[13]

He did not make so favourable an impression on another *habitué* of the Récamier salon, the marquis de Custine, who met him there in 1841. Custine, ostracized by polite society for his notorious homosexuality, jealous of the younger man's sudden fame, and unsympathetic to his politics, had not yet purged his spleen in the huge success of his *Letters from Russia*, published two years later. Tocqueville, he said:

is a puny, thin little man, still young: his manner is charming, but he lacks frankness, his mouth looks aged and ill-shaped, his hue is bilious, his expressive countenance would have captivated me had I distrusted him less; but I saw that he spoke with a forked tongue, and that he believes only what will further his aims. Such is the new star on our public horizon as he seemed to me …[14]

Custine's opinion was shared by few. 'Every salon wants him' … He became a member of the informal, fortnightly dining-club presided over by Pierre-Simon Ballanche, philosopher and devotee of Mme Récamier. The other members all belonged to the Récamier–Chateaubriand circle: Faucher, Sainte-Beuve, Ampère, and one or two others. Tocqueville still went to Mme Ancelot; he visited the affected yet golden-hearted Mme de Castellane, the mistress of his cousin Molé – she always kept herself free to receive him at two o'clock when he was in town. He also visited the somewhat shady Mme Le Tissier; the duchesse de Broglie, daughter of Mme de Staël; and, in 1836, Talleyrand's niece by marriage and mistress, the beautiful and brilliant duchesse de Dino, to whom he was presented by Royer-Collard. The

* The nickname ('the happy medium') given to supporters of Louis-Philippe.

old *doctrinaire* was as important a conquest as any hostess. He sent for Tocqueville and told him that the *Démocratie* was the most remarkable work on politics to have appeared for thirty years. He, Chateaubriand and Lamartine were praising it everywhere, Tocqueville told Eugène Stoffels:

> So for the time being I am well-launched, much astonished at what is happening to me and really dizzy with the praises that ring in my ears. There was a woman at the court of Napoleon whom the Emperor took it into his head one day to create a duchess. That evening, as she entered some grand salon and heard herself announced by her new title, she forgot that it referred to her and stood aside to make way for the lady whose name had just been proclaimed. I assure you that something analogous is happening to me.

He knew his limitations, and couldn't believe that he or his book deserved so much fuss.[15]

Before long he went to see his publisher about a second impression. Gosselin, who was sticking to his principle of never reading his authors' books, nevertheless greeted him with a wide smile and said, 'Why, it seems that you have written a masterpiece!' Tocqueville tried hard to be businesslike, but it did not come naturally to him, and Gosselin was still the most cautious of publishers: he issued two more impressions of the *Démocratie* in 1835, but they were no larger than the first. However, he was quite willing to raise the author's royalty per copy from 20 to 25 *sous* (1 franc: roughly tenpence a copy in pre-decimal British currency). He invited Tocqueville and Beaumont to dine with him and with another of his successful authors, the poet-politician Lamartine.[16]

To find out what so impressed the first readers of the *Démocratie* (as distinct from those who merely met the author) it is best to look at the reviews. Tocqueville himself thought that the best of them was that written by John Stuart Mill, published in the October issue of the *London Review*, a Benthamite journal. Mill had several advantages over earlier reviewers. He knew, directly or indirectly, what they had said; as, effectively, the editor of his paper he could give himself as much space as he liked; by the time it appeared he had met Tocqueville, talked long with him, and started a correspondence. But his chief asset was his own keen and earnest intelligence. He was acute, logical, and the complete master of his abilities. Any experienced reviewer must respect the professionalism of his article: the main themes of the *Démocratie* are laid out fully and accurately and with a sword-like brilliance that almost transcends Tocqueville's own style. Mill was a born popularizer; he was also frank and fair. He apologized for having to omit consideration of Tocqueville's arguments about religion and the chapter on the three races; he recommended the study of the entire work 'both to the philosophical statesman and to the general reader'. Tocqueville could not have had a better introduction to the British public, and he wrote gratefully: 'a writer's trade would be too delightful if he encountered many readers of your stamp.'[17]

To the credit of both men, this endorsement did not mean that Mill had agreed with everything that Tocqueville said or did not say; he did not accept the idea of majority tyranny, and in a tart footnote pointed out that American democracy was far from complete: 'the aristocracy of skin, and the aristocracy of sex, retain their privileges.' But in only one respect, and that doubtful, can Mill be said to have misrepresented his author. Throughout his article he treated the *Démocratie* as an entirely liberal, even a radical work: he used it as a weapon against the House of Lords, the Tories and the Whigs. And Tocqueville did not object: whatever his long-range anxieties, he was certainly a friend of democracy in the circumstances of 1835.

Using Mill as a yardstick it can be seen that of all the French reviewers only one, Sainte-Beuve, writing in *Le Temps*, approaches the Englishman for comprehensiveness. In one respect, indeed, he surpasses Mill: he notices that while Tocqueville has confidence in American democracy, he is much less hopeful for Europe and France. He picks up the notion of the *point de départ* and wonders mournfully if it is necessary to emigrate to establish a free and just society; would the Old World ever be capable of establishing a society where the defeated, the injured, the puritan could unite in the pursuit of a peaceful and well-founded liberty? Sainte-Beuve was the most Tocquevillean of all the reviewers.[18]

By the rest, although the level of discussion was commendably intelligent and the enthusiasm great, Tocqueville's book was only fitfully illuminated. The legitimist *Gazette de France* flatly rejected the suggestion that American practices might serve the legitimist cause: 'Our fathers' generation, we must admit, were less grossly imposed on when, in the last century, the English constitution was held up for their admiration. At least in England they kidnapped only sailors and sold only women ...' The reviewer denounced America's racial record at great length, using facts and arguments drawn entirely from the *Démocratie*. He compared the July Monarchy, greatly to its disadvantage, to the American presidency, but 'a true monarchy, representative, legitimate, and national' (i.e. the Bourbons) was preferable to either. The writer summed up his view by remarking that France should imitate the government of the United States when it had no more wars to fight, no more great armies or dangerous neighbours, 'when the French people are filled with respect for the laws, and when the Christian religion, having purified their morals, will have prepared them for liberty – then we will have scant fear of a republic in France, and we will be able to adopt American institutions.'[19] (It will be seen that, consciously or unconsciously, the reviewer has picked up Tocqueville's belief in the supreme importance of manners, however ironically he uses it.) Another conservative journal denounced American democracy as incompatible with the divine principle of hierarchy and lamented the egoism of American society. 'The plea which M. de Tocqueville has written in favour of America seems to us to be the most just and vehement accusation that has ever been brought against her.'[20] Tocqueville's optimistic attempt to convert his own caste to sense and reason through the American example failed immediately.

The legitimists also ignored or rejected his attempt to demonstrate the value of religious freedom to the Church.[21] *Le Semeur*, a Protestant journal which favoured the separation of Church and state, was not so unintelligent: it welcomed Tocqueville as an ally. And Lammenais, to whom Tocqueville sent a presentation copy, wrote to commend his love for humanity and respect for human dignity, traits nowadays so uncommon. But *Le Semeur* had little influence, and Lammenais had quarrelled irrevocably with both the Church and the Pope: neither could be of much use to Tocqueville.[22] Liberals, whether strongly supportive of the July Monarchy or merely acquiescent in it, should have welcomed the *Démocratie* as a philosophical justification of the July Revolution, but its complexity was such that they all found something to question. Guizot and his clique of rigid *doctrinaires* disliked the assertion that the future lay with democracy rather than with the supremacy of the *bourgeoisie*.[23] Salvandy, a semi-perpetual Orleanist minister, denied that the United States was really a democracy – Tocqueville had been taken in, it was really a dictatorship of the majority, which was as bad as any other and contrary to Nature, for the head should rule, not the body (Salvandy was no believer in a wide, let alone universal suffrage). Pellegrino Rossi, a leading Italian liberal who was also a distinguished economist, reviewing the *Démocratie*, predicted that equality would be transient: the day would come when the rich in America would be very rich and the poor very poor; 'it seems to us that M. de Tocqueville has somewhat exaggerated the effects of the laws of inheritance.' Léon Faucher stoutly denied the danger of tyranny of the majority. So did Francisque de Corcelle* in the *Revue des deux mondes*, although his review had been written under the eye of Tocqueville himself; and he rejected Tocqueville's melancholy view of the future, accusing him of exaggeration and self-contradiction.[24]

Clearly, the reviewers of the 1830s kept their independence of mind, even if they were not above borrowing ideas and information liberally from the work which they were reviewing. But what is more striking, nearly two centuries later, is that however patchy may have been their response to Tocqueville's message, they were unanimous in their reaction to the messenger: 'This is one of those books which resist analysis. It contains chapters which are books in themselves. We called M. de Tocqueville the American Blackstone; that is not all we thought; our pen nearly wrote a greater name' (Salvandy); 'the imagination of a young man and the patient observation of maturity' (Rossi); 'His mind is impartial and lofty, and his book may accurately be considered as an historical document worthy of belief; it is neither

---

* C-F-P ('Francisque') Tircuy de Corcelle (1802–92) came from a noble family that was both Burgundian and Norman. A Norman landowner after 1844 he was a neighbour of AT. His father, an émigré who returned to France after Thermidor, supported Napoleon in 1815 and again went into brief exile. Francisque was largely brought up by a pious uncle, but followed his father into the Carbonaro conspiracies of the 1820s. In 1830 he was a close associate of La Fayette, one of whose grand-daughters he married and whose *Memoirs* he was to edit (with C. de Rémusat), but he soon began to move towards the Right. He met AT in about 1835, and they became close friends.

an apology nor a satire' (*Le Bon Sens*, a republican paper); 'a book with which, both for its facts and speculations, all who would understand, or who are called upon to exercise influence over the age, are bound to be familiar' (John Stuart Mill). 'Nothing, absolutely,' wrote an American, 'has been written by a foreigner which approaches to an accurate delineation of our political organization' – except the *Démocratie*. The *National* (once Thiers's paper, now leaning towards republicanism) thought that 'the intelligence which dictated this book on American democracy and the remarkable merits of its execution place the author among [our] superior men, and give him indisputable title to the esteem and gratitude of his fellow citizens. *L'Écho français* spelt out what this meant: 'Such books should open the way to the parliamentary tribune.'[25]

For in that distant epoch the writing of a masterpiece of political thought was deemed to be an excellent qualification for entry to the Chamber of Deputies. It was only necessary to make sure that the reputation of the masterpiece was widely diffused, which, thanks to the practice by which provincial newspapers copied the Parisian journals *in extenso*, happened spontaneously. Tocqueville had hoped for such an outcome, especially in Normandy and the Cotentin, his likeliest parliamentary prospect. His interest in the region was becoming pronounced: probably through family influence he had already (November 1834) been elected to the fellowship of the Société Académique de Cherbourg. It must have been gratifying when a Norman paper, announcing the fact, called the *Démocratie* a masterpiece, and mentioned the *Système pénitentiaire* favourably too.[26] Before long Tocqueville had undertaken to write an article on pauperism for the Cherbourg academy's journal: it would give him a chance to sort out his thoughts on the English Poor Law and its implications.

Winter passed in a swirl of activity. Beaumont finished *Marie* and Gosselin published it. This was an important event in Tocqueville's life, for as he and Beaumont constantly insisted, their books were complementary. *Marie*, indeed, reads like a negative to the *Démocratie*'s positive: it is not a work of political or social anatomy, but is full of the particulars and the living movement which Tocqueville omitted; in fact a reader may almost regret that the two friends abandoned their original plan of joint authorship: together, they might have produced a really comprehensive study of the United States. It had not been possible: their diverging interests pulled them apart, as we have seen, and perhaps it was time that each man faced the challenge of solo authorship. Beaumont had more to learn. He made the great mistake of writing his study of racism and slavery as a novel, while not respecting the form. It was a golden age of fiction: he might have read Stendhal and Balzac; we know that he read Scott and Fenimore Cooper. Nevertheless, in his Foreword to *Marie* he apologizes for writing a novel about a serious subject: he only does so, he says, because he wants to attract frivolous as well as serious readers.[27] As if this insult to the public were not enough, he avows that he is no novelist, and proves it all too well in what follows. Yet *Marie*, for all its obvious failings (Nassau Senior praised it, but said that it had perhaps too much sentimentality (*onction*) for cold English tastes),[28] is still very well worth reading. The idea of a propaganda novel attacking American slavery was a good one, as would be shown triumphantly fifteen years later in *Uncle Tom's Cabin*; and Beaumont packed his book with vivid information – nearly half of it consists of appendices and notes, just like the *Système pénitentiaire*. To anyone who knows Tocqueville and Beaumont's American letters and notebooks, let alone the *Démocratie*, *Marie* appears like an old friend, full of pleasingly familiar material and many new thoughts. The overlap with Tocqueville's preoccupations is marked, and the long note in which Beaumont defines and asserts the actuality of equality in America might have been written in answer to some of Tocqueville's twentieth-century critics, such as Edward Pessen, though in fact he chiefly had British writers of his own day in mind, particularly Thomas Hamilton, whose *Men and Manners in America* had appeared in 1833.[29] Here, and indeed throughout the book, is additional evidence of the substantial identity of Beaumont's views and observations with those of Tocqueville, and mini-essays like those on American women and American sociability so evidently draw on Beaumont's notebooks that the loss of these comes to seem unimportant.[30] Above all, if *Marie* is taken in conjunction with Tocqueville's *Démocratie* and Michel Chevalier's *Lettres sur l'Amérique*, which appeared in book form in 1836, somewhat to Tocqueville's dismay (he disliked any hint of competition),[31] we must agree that readers of these three French writers could form a much fuller, fairer and more accurate picture of Jacksonian America than any British writers of the period, singly or together, came near to supplying.

Marie had nothing like the runaway success of the *Démocratie*, but its merits ensured that it was welcomed and widely read. Beaumont and Tocqueville could each feel that he had hit his target, and each, equally, felt that he was owed a holiday after all his efforts; so on 21 April, four years almost to the day since their departure to America, they set off together again – for England.

The need for a rest (of the energetic kind which Tocqueville always preferred) is on the face of it a sufficient explanation of this journey, but other factors must be mentioned. Tocqueville was always an investigator, and he could not feel that in 1833 he had done more than make a good start on a study of England; and for reasons that are not altogether clear he and Beaumont decided, before leaving Paris, to extend their inquiries to Ireland. Not that Tocqueville intended to write about Britain: he was furious when Gosselin, without his knowledge, told the *Journal des débats* that he did. He did not want to presume on his sudden fame, or to endanger it by publishing superficialities: as he told Comte Molé, who took a kinsman's kindly interest in his affairs, England was much harder to understand than America;[32] but he must have hoped that a British tour would help him in planning the second part of the *Démocratie*, which was already stirring in his mind and had been vaguely promised in the first part.[33] He meant to consolidate his position, but not in a hurry. Beaumont indeed soon began to plan a book on Ireland, but it is doubtful if he did so before getting to that country. He must have wanted to go to Britain largely because he had never been there, even if Tocqueville had the idea first.

Tocqueville discovered that before setting out he needed one other person's consent. Marie Mottley had put up with a great deal in the previous four years. She had allowed her lover to leave her for his long visit to America. She had allowed him to put off making any definite plans for their future while he wrote his book. Now he was proposing to leave her again for several months (over four, as it turned out). It seems (the evidence is scrappy but unambiguous) that she put her foot down. Tocqueville might go, but when he came back he must marry her. In his absence she would receive instruction in the Catholic faith, abjure Protestantism and be received into the Church.

In his heart of hearts Tocqueville may have been glad to have his hand forced at last, and anyway he was running out of excuses: he would be thirty in August and legally free to marry as he chose. But we gather that there were agitated scenes before he gave in, and he left for England in a gloomy frame of mind. He had always enjoyed his bachelor freedom, and he probably did not relish a confrontation with his parents (it is possible that some of his gloom was caused by a scene with them). However, he had no choice: he loved Marie and was by now utterly dependent on her love for him. He must have known that it was the right decision for both of them.[34]

Apparently Tocqueville was not very well when he left for London; the weather which he met there did not make him feel any better. Even at noon, he said, the streets were like nothing so much as the tunnels of a coalmine, lit by a single lantern. London was as expensive as ever – he and Beaumont had to chase about before they could find affordable lodgings in Regent Street; and the British class system obtruded immediately and disagreeably. As he renewed his acquaintanceships and presented his letters of introduction he met the same reception as formerly: 'Much insolence in the antechambers ... great kindness in the drawing-rooms, and prodigious servility on my return to the antechambers.' These experiences and the London fog led him to philosophize ('there is nothing more favourable to philosophy than fog'). Having had some experience of every class, he decided that he did not entirely like any of them. The rich had a certain loftiness of tone and distinction of manners which attracted him, but their way of life – 'the luxury, the pomp, the great possessions, the artificiality' – bored and repelled him. The middle classes lived much more simply, and were more straightforward, but were so vulgar that he couldn't bear to see them very often. That being the case it was fortunate for him that the invitations which rained down all came from the greatest possible names, the cream of the Whig nobility – not only Lord Radnor, but also Lords Holland, Lansdowne, Brougham. They were all as kind as possible, but sunlight, he said, if only the sun would show himself, would do more to cheer him up than all the candles of the grand saloons where he was spending his evenings.[35]

Nevertheless, it was just as well that he had middle-class friends, for it was they who came to the rescue when he fell seriously ill in early

May. Henry Reeve (1813–95) was a promising, rather pushy young man, ostensibly reading for the Bar but also launching a career in journalism. He had met Tocqueville in Paris in March; now he carried off the invalid to Hampstead, where he lived with his mother, and kept him there for two weeks until he recovered.

It is difficult to know what to think about Tocqueville's health, or rather his ill-health at this point. As we have seen, strangers meeting him for the first time thought him sickly, and in some sense he undoubtedly was; but his American journey was that of a man full of energy and zest for life, with a marked taste for outdoor activities – swimming, walking, hunting. His illness in Tennessee was brought about by external conditions, though it must be noted that the robust Beaumont was unaffected. But Tocqueville suffered all his life from what the Abbé Le Sueur used to call gastritis.[36] The attacks were irregular – he could go many months without having any – but, when they did come on, were agonizing. Tocqueville himself seems to have thought that they were caused by too much high living and excitement, which, if correct, would help to explain his London collapse; but we do not know what were his symptoms on that occasion. The doctor brought in by Reeve forbade him to take any exercise but approved of fresh air; he mitigated the rigour of this regime by lending the patient books to read out of doors.[37] There is no hint of any trouble with the lungs, though the appalling atmosphere of the Big Smoke might have made anyone ill.

Tocqueville refused to let Beaumont waste his time and money in nursing him; he made him stay in Regent Street, and only allowed him to come to dinner at Hampstead every second day. In these circumstances Reeve's conversation was a great comfort. The young man, though a very conservative Whig, greatly admired the *Démocratie* and decided to translate it. He worked at the job throughout the summer, and no doubt benefited from the author's advice during the period of illness. By the time Tocqueville was better again they were firm friends.[38]

Tocqueville had by then been in England for nearly a month. Illness or no illness, he had made good use of his time. At first his opportunities were somewhat limited by the grand society in which he was moving. As a result he grew preoccupied with class and class relations:

'The respect given to wealth in England is frightful to observe.' He and Beaumont did not pretend to be rich, but as they were foreigners they were forgiven – there was something piquant in the idea that two such men, without lackeys or carriages, even if they were of ancient families, could produce books of merit. When they broke out of their gilded circle and dined with the family of a City merchant the snobbery was still worse:

> Our hosts were sterling fellows, full of cordiality, but I won't hide from you that they were terribly like Americans. We would have told them so except that throughout dinner they did nothing but make fun of the Americans who, according to them, had no company manners. At the same time our hosts, being great Tories, took pains to make us think that they were on close terms with the aristocracy.

He had noticed the same sort of thing eighteen months before: 'They complain of the distance and chill reserve of the great lords, but how could it be otherwise when the only thought of those they meet is to exploit them for their own ends?'[39] Tocqueville began to doubt his earlier conclusion that there was not going to be a revolution in Britain: surely all that ostentatious wealth, even though it generated so much servility, must also be generating resentment? Surely the peasants must covet the lands monopolized by the gentry and nobility? He was quite cross when a noble lady remarked in his presence that people had been threatening her with revolution all her life and it had never happened ('The same might be said of death,' someone riposted). Tocqueville dismissed the remark as typical of the Whigs and their limitations. They had been gambling with the British constitution for a century and a half and didn't realize that the game was up:

> And the English in general seem to me to have great difficulty in grasping general, undetermined ideas. They judge facts of the day perfectly well, but their tendency and long-term consequences aren't understood. The Whigs seem to me to exhibit this characteristic more than most. More than anybody else they have need of illusions ...

It was perhaps this sort of experience which made him decide that his next book must still be on America. Beaumont could have England, if he wanted it.[40]

Nevertheless Tocqueville remained deeply preoccupied with the question of the fate of the English aristocracy. In a remarkable letter to Comte Molé summing up his views at this point he struggles with the failure of Britain to conform to the pattern of democratic transformation announced in the *Démocratie*;[41] he clings to the prediction that class war will bring about equality of status, as in France and America; but he has had to take into account the economic conditions of Britain as she industralized, and is reduced to predicting that this difference will produce the same result.[42] Class war is class war, whatever the ingredients. But Tocqueville has had to surrender one of his most cherished beliefs, that the hunger for landed property is the essential motor of the age of the democratic revolution.

For this he had Nassau Senior to thank. The economist had taken up the subject in his letter about the *Démocratie*: 'I do not think that in England the wealth of the poor has been sacrificed to that of the rich … [the English labourer] has not landed property, because it is more profitable to him to work for another than to cultivate.' Tocqueville had energetically defended his view, but Senior did not give ground.[43] They renewed the argument on 24 May, if they had not done so before. There was a remarkable witness: the young Cavour:

> I found Mr Senior walking in the garden with M. de Tocqueville and M. Beaumont, discussing the great subject of the Division of Property. An extraordinary thing was the radical Englishman was in favour of large ownership and the legitimist Frenchman of small ownership. Mr Senior thinks that the small proprietor has neither security nor comfort, and that it is much better for him to be in the employ of a large proprietor and have nothing to fear from bad luck or bad seasons. M. Tocqueville refuted his argument very well both on moral and material grounds.
>
> De Tocqueville observed acutely that at the present moment two contrary and up to a certain point incompatible movements were in action: a political-democratic movement and a social-aristocratic one, that is to say, on the one side a general and equal redistribution of political rights amongst a continually increasing number of individuals, and on the other a proportionally increasing concentration of wealth in the hands of a few. This anomaly cannot last long without a grave danger to the State. It will be necessary to bring the political and social forces into harmony. It is the only means of assuring stability.[44]

But it would not do. Whether Tocqueville admitted it or not (and the letter to Molé shows him weakening), the fundamental basis of British economy, society and politics was being transformed. Agricultural land-ownership was no longer the sole key to power, prosperity and survival, whatever was the case in France, and theory would have to take account of the fact.

In the background was Tocqueville's *Mémoire sur le paupérisme*, which he had finished just before leaving France, and which would be published by the Cherbourg academy that autumn.[45] It has been taken very seriously by some recent writers[46] but I find it one of Tocqueville's weakest efforts. For this the hurry in which he wrote is no doubt to blame. Presumably he chose the subject himself (he had already written a strongly Malthusian appendix on 'American Pauperism' for the *Système pénitentiaire*)[47] but when he got to work he quickly discovered that his visit to Salisbury Sessions with Lord Radnor and a reading of the work of Alban de Villeneuve-Bargemont* would not be enough to carry his discussion much further forward. So he wrote for help to Nassau Senior, who sent him copies of his 1833 report on the Poor Law, the Poor Law Amendment Act of 1834, and several other publications on the subject.[48] But even Tocqueville could not digest so much material in three weeks, and the resultant *Mémoire* is a triumph of manner disguising lack of matter. It has three principal faults. First, like his work on prisons, it shows all too clearly the limits of his intellectual and moral sympathies. He had interviewed convicts in America, however unprofitably; there is no evidence that he ever had a conversation with a pauper. To him, unemployment merely demonstrated that 'Man, like all complex organisms, is passionately lazy by nature.'[49] Second, he finds fault with all proposals for dealing with the causes and effects of poverty without having anything better to propose. Finally, and most important for our present concern, he had only the sketchiest knowledge of the history of poor relief in England and did not understand the New Poor Law which Senior and his colleague Edwin Chadwick had devised for their country. So it was

* Alban de Villeneuve-Bargemont, *Économie politique chrétienne, ou recherches sur la nature et les causes du paupérisme en France et en Europe, et sur les moyens de le soulager et de le prévenir* (Paris, 1834). Villeneuve-Bargemont (1784–1850) was a philanthropic legitimist who served as a prefect under the Restoration, like Hervé de Tocqueville.

impossible for him either to accept the new system or to subject it to any of the serious criticisms which it richly deserved.

Some of these inadequacies became obvious, even to Tocqueville, in a year or two: he tried to write a second report on pauperism for Cherbourg, but gave it up as a bad job.[50] But he never gave up his fundamental attitude. He saw, with everyone else, that private charity of the traditional kind could not cope with the perpetual modern problems of over-population and un- or under-employment; he did not believe in any of the new remedies on offer, whether a Poor Law (Senior) or workers' savings-banks (Villeneuve-Bargemont), except as short-term expedients; and the vision to which in his heart he clung was the creation of a society of broadly equal peasant-proprietors, economically secure, in which leadership would be exercised by a class of educated notables like himself.

As a response to the problems of an urbanizing industrializing world this vision is breathtakingly inadequate, but it has to be acknowledged that the society which it imagines has a strong resemblance to the rural France that emerged from the Revolution, what is sometimes called *La France profonde*, the protection of which has been such a leading principle of French government policy both in the twentieth century and (so far) in the twenty-first. Tocqueville, it might almost be said, was anticipating from afar the Common Agricultural Policy.

But there was more to it than the trammels of national experience. When Tocqueville visited England in 1835 he was thinking seriously about his own future. His impending marriage would force his parents to set him up with his own domicile at last, and although he may not have guessed that his mother's death was imminent, and certainly did not know what estate, if any, would be settled on him, he was already reconsidering his disdain for a life of potatoes. He was now getting used to making long, enjoyable visits to his brothers at their chateaux, especially to Édouard's Baugy, near Compiègne – Édouard, whose strongly Christian views on agronomy were substantially the same as his own, and may be presumed to have influenced and been influenced by them.[51] Happiness might well be increased by a country house of his own which he could share with Marie. It was the pattern of his time and his caste. Properly managed, it could secure him a solid base for his political career. And as a leader in a democratic countryside he would be able to vindicate the doctrines of *De la démocratie en Amérique* – no little advantage. No wonder he clung to the persuasion that England was only an exception to the general law of modern development which he had proclaimed – an exception that would fall into line one day, even if it meant another bloody revolution.

Such were his views when a few days after the conversation with Senior he met John Stuart Mill for the first time. Mill, if not yet eminent, was well on his way towards eminence. He had discovered the *Démocratie* with great excitement in April, and written to his agent in Paris: 'Can you tell me anything of Tocqueville? What is his history? And in what estimation is he held in France?' He was just launching the *London Review*, and on 19 May settled that he would notice the *Démocratie* in the third number that autumn, which as we have seen, he did.[52] Apparently he still did not know that Tocqueville was actually in London, but that was soon put right: one of their common acquaintances introduced them on 26 May. It was the meeting of two greatly gifted but very different minds. Mill was incomparably lucid, logical and well-informed; perhaps his greatest quality was his unimpeachable integrity; next to that, his earnest public spirit. Mentally, Tocqueville was much untidier, but he had an imaginative gift which Mill lacked and, recognizing his lack, deeply respected. They got on exceedingly well, but Tocqueville took the lead. Probably because Senior had at last made him see the significance of the Poor Law Amendment Act, which took away control of the workhouses from the country squires and gave it to London-appointed officials, Tocqueville had conceived the idea that the radically, almost chaotically localized English government of tradition was about to be superseded by a centralized system. It was one of his luckier shots, and as usual he ran away with his notion. Mill defended the tendency. English decentralization, he said, was unsystematic, like its begetter, the English mind, and he expected the new forms of local government to be thoroughly independent of central government. But Tocqueville thought that 'the English mind' was really the aristocratic mind, and asked Mill if centralization were not a natural consequence of that great cause of everything, democracy? Mill said that he would need time to think about it.[53]

The conversation was a great success, and was resumed on 29 May, with the MP John Roebuck making a third. These English radicals much impressed Tocqueville. Unlike their French equivalents, they were not revolutionaries, they respected law, property and religion ('there are a great number of passionate sectarians among them') and were more or less educated gentlemen, whereas the French radical was poor, coarse, impudent and profoundly ignorant of political science.[54] Here was new support for an old prejudice. But his liking for Mill went beyond such considerations. He was deeply gratified when Mill pressed him to become a contributor to the *London Review*, essentially on his own terms, but thought that his new friend exaggerated his merits:

> I love liberty by inclination, equality by instinct and reason. These two passions which all men feign I think I really feel within me, and for them I am ready to make great sacrifices. Such are the only advantages that I recognize in myself. They amount rather to the absence of certain vices than to the possession of any unusual qualities.

He wanted to see as much of Mill as possible, and pressed him to come to dinner on 14 June, before Tocqueville went back to France for two or three days (to attend Marie's reception into the Church, though he did not explain this). 'I would gladly arrange to pass two or three hours with you before getting into my coach.' Before long, inevitably, he agreed to write something for Mill's journal (the article on pre-Revolutionary France already mentioned).[55]*

Apparently Tocqueville was not expected at Boulogne, where the ceremony that made Marie a Catholic took place, but the outcome of the sudden impulse which took him there was happy. The clouds of the spring dispersed: Marie realized anew that he loved her, and was restored to happiness and serenity. Alexis too grew calm and gay; he returned to London resolved to enjoy his last days there. The weather was better, and he was as fascinated as ever by the *bizarrerie* of the English scene. Previously he had told Mme Ancelot about running into Byron's daughter Ada at a fashionable party; now he described a banquet given by Lord Brougham for 200 of his intimate friends:

> Don't suppose, Madame, that one goes to such a dinner for the food. Eating is the excuse; orating is the real point of the occasion. After the frugal repast has disappeared, a great silence falls and a kind of

---

* See above, p. 4.

herald, standing on a stool, pompously calls on the guests to charge their glasses, then the host rises and proposes the health of someone or something, which is only an excuse for making a speech about that someone; for mentioning the House of Lords, the Commons, the magistracy, the Army, the Press, the public schools and in short everything of which there was no question five minutes earlier; when the orator has finished, the guests all stand, silently empty their glasses, then wave them under their noses nine times, crying with a very solemn air each time, *Hurrah!* with all the strength that Nature has given to their lungs; that is the first display of enthusiasm. Next they proceed to the second, rapping on the tables; this exercise lasts a long or a short time, depending on the enthusiasm or the fatigue of the diners. The same ceremony is gone through fifteen or twenty times, always with the same silence, the same solemnity and the same imperturbable gravity, it is a matter of State ... all this, dear Madame, in the most civilized and intelligent nation in the world, only a hundred leagues from Paris.[56]

He continued to make friends: one lady, Harriet Grote, the lively wife of George Grote, historian and radical MP, found him 'a most engaging person. Full of intelligence and knowledge, free from boasting and self-sufficiency – of gentle manners, and handsome countenance. In conversing he displays a candid and unprejudiced mind ...'[57] Such was his prestige that he was invited to testify before a parliamentary committee on electoral corruption, and did so on 22 June. That day the committee was chiefly concerned with the secret ballot, a favourite radical proposal; Tocqueville's business was to explain how it worked in France, which he did with notable precision and intelligence (interestingly, he admitted that he had paid no particular attention to the secret ballot while he was in the United States, indeed, that he had paid insufficient attention to elections there).[58]

It was the high point of his visit, and perhaps he had lingered in London on that account; at any rate, he and Beaumont started their journey to Ireland two days later. They had their usual ill-luck with stagecoaches on the way to Coventry, their first stop: 'Ten hours spent on the roof of a *diligence*, with a storm of wind and a flood of rain, were enough to make us regret, in the midst of the world's most civilized country, the American wilderness. From time to time we glowered at the aristocracy of the stagecoach, who were sitting inside, however we did *not* launch a Revolution.'[59] During the next ten days they made their way slowly through the Midlands and Lancashire.

It was a revelation. This was an England they had never seen, and hardly seem to have expected. The people in Birmingham were as hospitable as those in London, but in every other respect were entirely different. They had no leisure of any kind: 'they work as if they were to become rich tonight and die tomorrow.' They were intelligent, but in the American way. The town was a vast slum, like the faubourg Saint-Antoine. The noise of steam and hammers was incessant. 'Everything is black, dirty and dark, although every moment breeds gold and silver.'[60] On 20 June they reached Manchester, which Tocqueville found an even less attractive industrial capital:

> At Birmingham, almost every house is occupied by one family only; at Manchester, part of the population lives in damp cellars, hot, stinking and unhealthy: thirteen or fifteen individuals in each one. At Birmingham that is very rare. At Manchester, stagnant water, streets ill-paved or not paved at all. Too few public privies. These conditions are almost unknown at Birmingham. At Manchester some great capitalists, thousands of poor workers, next to no middle class ... the workers are gathered into factories by the thousand – by two thousand – three. At Birmingham, the workers labour at home or in small workshops alongside their masters. At Manchester, they need women and children above all. At Birmingham, men especially, few women.

Tocqueville was appalled by Manchester, and devoted several pages of his notebook to a description of 'this new Hell', which has become famous. He drove home the contrast between the miserable dwellings of the workers and the bright palaces where they were forced to toil; between Manchester, the factory city, and more civilized places such as Paris ('Nowhere do you hear the sound of horses carrying the rich inhabitant to his home or his recreation'). 'It is in the midst of this infected sewer that the great river of human industry rises and fertilizes the world ... It is there that human intelligence perfects and brutalizes itself, that civilization produces its marvels and that civilized man returns almost to savagery.'[61] Liverpool, where they arrived on 4 or 5 July, was only slightly less disheartening: 'A fine city. The poverty is almost as great as in Manchester, but it is hidden. Fifty thousand poor people live in cellars.'[62]

Tocqueville's response to the Black Country and the cotton towns was that of all humane persons in the nineteenth century. It is to his credit that he felt he had to write down his disgusted impressions. But it is notable that he did not allow them to divert the course of his investigations. Centralization and local government were what he wanted to understand, were what he chiefly asked and wrote about. The spectacle of the Industrial Revolution made little alteration to his thought, although the whole future of humanity was bound up in it.

(What would have happened had he ever met Friedrich Engels?)

He was not so intellectually impervious to the next great sink of human misery that he encountered, in Ireland. England, a complex phenomenon, had perplexed him, but Ireland was another matter. It was England's Sicily. It was a vast display of rural poverty, a subject on which he had been reflecting, off and on, for years. He and Beaumont had discussed Ireland with Mill and Senior while they were in London – Senior had even staged a discussion between himself and John Revans, secretary of the Irish Poor Law Commission, for their benefit. So they were not quite uninstructed and unprepared, but they brought no dogma to their investigation. Yet Ireland managed to surprise them, for it was a country ruined by its aristocracy, it seemed, a possibility which Tocqueville (who should have known better) had envisaged only in Sicily.

They arrived in Dublin from Liverpool on 6 July; Tocqueville was unwell for a day or two, but they were soon hard at work. On 11 July they talked to two intelligent Protestants, who, while analysing the disastrous state of agriculture in Ireland, remarked that 'Here we have all the evils of aristocracy without a single one of its advantages.' The same day they attended a banquet in honour of the Lord-Lieutenant, Lord Mulgrave. A toast was proposed to 'the resident noblemen' and drunk with acclaim. Tocqueville noted that one could only understand this after having been in Ireland for some time (it was his sixth day there). The toast was a jibe at absentee landlords.[63]

This is a good example of Tocqueville's matured powers as an observer. He now knew how to find significance in every encounter, however slight. In contrast with his American procedures, he now listened to everyone with something to say – Protestants, we see, as well as Catholics – which in such a bitterly divided country was essential for the formation of accurate views. Towards the end of his visit he remarked tetchily that it would take three months to understand Ireland, not just three weeks,[64] and he certainly did not see everything – he never got to Ulster, for example. But he seized every opportunity that came his way. He never lost sight of the fact that this was a society in crisis, and the best compliment that may be paid him today is that although he did not know that the crisis would culminate ten years later in the Great Famine, he mentioned most of the factors which brought about that disaster, and his journal may still be read profitably by those trying to understand it.

It helped that Ireland was a Catholic country. A convivial dinner with the Bishop of Ossory reminded him of France: the conversation was 'enthusiastic, superficial, frivolous, often marked by jokes and witticisms' – nothing like an English banquet. Tocqueville was also reminded of France when he and Beaumont found themselves sharing a stagecoach between Kilkenny and Cork with two cheerfully drunk young men who shouted pleasantries at everyone they saw on the road and got laughing rejoinders from men and women alike.[65] But the most valuable thing was that as Frenchmen and Catholics they were welcomed by every bishop and priest they met and given absolutely frank answers to their questions (although it does not seem that discretion was much practised by any Irishman). They all felt at home together. In this way Tocqueville and Beaumont were shown all the woes of Ireland, and could not help noticing how consistent the picture was. Thus the Bishop of Ossory told them:

> Travel into Mayo, you will meet there thousands of men on the point of dying of hunger, literally. The Marquis of Sligo has 70,000 acres of land in the same county, of which he eats the revenue in England. Yet the law does not compel this man to give his fellows any portion of his superfluity. Why are so many people dying of hunger in Mayo? Because the landlords think it in their interest to convert everything to grazing and that, if they can get themselves a little more money, they can laugh at every other consideration.[66]

At length Tocqueville consolidated his notes into a remarkable piece of travel writing describing a day spent with a country priest in his parish. It was a fictionalized account of his experiences, rather like Beaumont's

Marie, only better written; and it faintly recalls the dialogue between the Sicilian and the Neapolitan of 1827:

> I can imagine, I said, that a Protestant lord living in the midst of a hostile population might not be very ready to alleviate public distress, but in Ireland you have a certain number of great Catholic land-owners. Don't they set a better example?
>
> Not at all, replied the priest. Catholics and Protestants oppress the people in much the same manner. From the moment that a Catholic becomes a great landowner, he conceives for the people's needs that selfish contempt which seems natural to aristocrats, and like the others he greedily seizes every chance of enriching himself at the expense of the poor.[67]

Tocqueville intended to draw a parallel portrait of the life of a Protestant clergyman, but never got further than making a few notes. It was the fate of 'Quinze jours dans le désert' all over again.

Nevertheless, the seventy-seven printed pages of the Irish journal are so full of information – about absentee landlords, rural violence, schools, interfaith hostility, poverty, hunger and so on – that it is strange at first sight that Tocqueville never made any use of them. The main reason was that while there was certainly a book to be written about Ireland, Beaumont was the man for the job. Tocqueville was still hesitating about his next literary venture, and still had a lot to say about America. He was as determined as ever not to compete with his friend. Beaumont remembered that one evening in Kilkenny they had a long conversation in which they compared the English and the Irish aristocracies then each made a memorandum. Beaumont's subsequently went into his book; Tocqueville's (entitled 'How Aristocracy can form both one of the Best and one of the Worst of all Governments') was suppressed until after his death, for the same reason which suppressed 'Quinze jours'.[68] It was less of a loss to the world than might appear: in their views of Ireland Tocqueville and Beaumont were, as always, entirely at one (though Beaumont enriched his ideas by paying a second visit in 1837), and Beaumont's book in places reads exactly like Tocqueville in both style and argument.[69]

A second reason for Tocqueville's reticence about Ireland was that he could not entirely concentrate on the subject. Although many documents have been destroyed or lost (particularly Marie Mottley's letters) we find that the course of true love was still not invariably running smooth. From such letters as survive it is clear that Tocqueville wrote regularly to his *fiancée*, amusing her with a detailed chronicle of his journeyings. But at least once he had to write to her in a different strain, when something occurred which drove her to seek reassurance (as she would repeatedly do during the rest of their life together):

> I never could divide the world into more than two parts: on the one side, action, glamour, fame – the outer world; on the other, the heart's sweet affections, the sharing of all opinions, the confiding of all thoughts – there, I see only you, I have never met anyone there but you. You are my only image of all that enchanting side of life. You alone will be that image for ever. Marie, I repeat again what I have said before: we are bound to one another *for life, until death*.[70]

We do not know what had upset her, but it is possible to guess. Among the letters waiting for Tocqueville when he got to Dublin was one, also now lost, from Kergorlay; in his reply Tocqueville recounted the success of his trip to Boulogne, but added ominously, 'if I don't find you at Paris when I get there, please may I at least find a letter from you setting out fully what you have made of the conduct of my family and of Marie since my departure.' Trouble, he evidently feared, was brewing in a fresh quarter: another letter waiting for him was from Édouard and Alexandrine, which for days he could not bring himself to read properly. It was full of anxious affection, but it advised against his marriage to Marie for various reasons, the chief, it appears, being the writers' fear that it would destroy the brothers' friendship. Alexis exerted himself to banish this notion: rather he hoped, he said, that Marie would bind them all together even more closely; but he added, 'I have not made any decision.' This remark would hardly have pleased Marie had it come to her attention; however, it is difficult to believe that it was sincere or realistic.[71]

Perhaps the Kergorlay letter implies that Marie and the Tocqueville family were supposed to get to know each other during the absence of Alexis, but if so there is nothing to indicate that they did: Tocqueville's surviving letters to his parents from Ireland contain no reference to Marie at all. Still, it is clear that he was once more anxious and gloomy when, after attending the annual meeting of the British Association for the Advancement of Science, which that year took place in Dublin, he said goodbye to Beaumont (who was off to Scotland) and headed for France on 15 August. Neither then nor later was he in any mood to write up his Irish researches.

He travelled slowly, partly because of ill-health, partly, no doubt, because of what awaited him in Paris. Tocqueville had a sharp tongue, but he was not quarrelsome and his affections were acute. He was fearfully sea-sick on the way to Cherbourg, so he stayed with Hippolyte at Nacqueville for two nights for fear of gastritis. He was somewhat cheered by his sister-in-law Emilie, who promised him her support, whatever his decision about Marie. When he got back to Paris he found that his cousin Marie de Macmahon, Louis de Rosanbo's daughter, was dying of what sounds like tuberculosis. But he had other business on hand which must have seemed to him even more engrossing.[72]

We catch glimpses of him in Paris and at Baugy; then on 14 October he writes to his cousin Camille d'Orglandes announcing his imminent marriage. It is a curious letter, written only nine days before the contract was to be signed: this suggests that Tocqueville was still afraid of family rows, and anxious to minimize their possibility. Even more curious are the flat lies which he tells about his bride: he says he met her through a family which he had come to know in England (in other words, since 1832), that she is a Catholic (true, but misleading), that she comes of a very honourable family and is roughly his age. He is thus pretending that he is not committing a *mésalliance*; but what can have been the point? D'Orglandes was certain to find out the truth before long, if he did not know it already, unless the whole Tocqueville family was uniting to maintain the fiction. But all this matters less than the fact announced. The contract was signed on 23 October at Marie's apartment in the rue de Belle Chasse. Three days later the religious ceremony was performed at the church of St Thomas d'Aquin. Everyone was there: the whole Tocqueville family, Mrs Belam, Beaumont and Kergorlay. All the amenities were observed, whatever the private thoughts of the witnesses, or the disputes beforehand. Alexis and Marie were beginning their new life with a fair wind.[73]

CHAPTER FOURTEEN

INTO POLITICS
1835–1839

Don't imagine, mon cher ami, *that I am unthinkingly
enthusiastic, or enthusiastic at all, about the life of the
mind. I have always valued action above everything else.*
TOCQUEVILLE TO KERGORLAY, 4 OCTOBER 1837[1]

TO BEGIN WITH they were going to live at 12, rue de Bourgogne,*
in the heart of the faubourg Saint-Germain, but while the furnishings
were being prepared they went to Édouard and Alexandrine at Baugy,
where Tocqueville's high hopes of friendship all round seemed to be
realized. It was one of his amiable traits that he liked to have his friends
round him when he was happy. He loved Baugy and its inhabitants,
and in January had urged Beaumont to join him there: 'They have
put me in the keep ... where they showed me a room for Alexis and
next to it one for Gustave.' Now he renewed the invitation: 'Bring a
gun ... We might be inconvenienced without it.'[2] The tone is still that
of a bachelor, but two weeks later, when he returned to Baugy after
a short visit to Paris (a new edition of the *Système pénitentiaire* was
being prepared), he reported that he found there a nice warm bed and
a most loving reception.[3] Kergorlay wrote, gloomy about himself as

---

* AT moved house in Paris repeatedly between his marriage and his death; he lived always in
 lodgings when not in a hotel or staying with his father. It is perhaps worth remarking that in
 1839 he moved from the Left Bank to the Right, and went back only once.

usual, but glad to have heard from Comte Hervé and Beaumont that the all-important first weeks of marriage had been successful: he also hoped (it turned out, in vain) that Marie would discard any memories of his opposition, for he was now nothing but a wrestler defeated and disarmed. Four hundred *faire part* cards had been sent out; the replies of congratulation poured in, including one from Camille d'Orglandes and several from England. Sarah Austin (Henry Reeve's aunt, and a woman of letters) was acknowledged by a touching avowal: 'how much I wish to present Madame de Tocqueville to you. I hope with her to enjoy two things not easily found united in this world – a busy intellectual and a tranquil calm home-life.' He went on, even more revealingly: 'Such is my dream; and in order to make it a reality, I have had the audacity to choose my wife for myself. Now that the thing is done, a good many people think I acted wisely. But I do not aspire to revolutionize our habits;* many a year will pass by ere marriage, generally speaking, will cease to be anything but an *affaire* [business agreement].' In spite of all that it had cost him to keep himself up to the mark, Tocqueville had triumphed and acted in accordance with his consistent beliefs.† Nothing he ever did was more democratic, modern, or honourable.[4]

The honeymoon at Baugy was, in short, a great success, but after three weeks or so Tocqueville began to feel restless for lack of work. 'I am impatient to be settled in my own home and back in a groove.' He threatened to send some dilatory cabinet-makers a *'thunderous'* letter by the hand of his valet, Jacques.[5] A graver matter soon made such concerns inconsequential. The comtesse de Tocqueville had been in failing health for months. Alexis may not at first have realized it: at any rate, in his surviving letters to her from Ireland he does not (for once) mention her ailments. By December her condition was all too obvious: Camille d'Orglandes was much concerned by her 'deplorable health', adding that Comte Hervé had thought her rather better in the days leading up to Tocqueville's wedding; d'Orglandes hoped, without much confidence, that the improvement had been maintained. But the end came on 9 January 1836. After a month of suffering the last

---

* *Moeurs*, surely, in the original (the letter is extant only in a nineteenth-century translation).
† See above, p. 9.

day was peaceful; Tocqueville described it all to Mme de Grancey, but had much less to say of his own feelings than of his uncle Rosanbo's: 'for he was there, don't worry. He was the same as ever, feeling every-thing and thinking of everybody else as if he were unpreoccupied. His family's fate has been so sad, my dear cousin! Providence struck down the race! His parents died on the scaffold; so did one of his three sisters, then the second died in the bloom of youth, and now the third has gone after twenty years of misery ...' (and Rosanbo had just lost his daughter). Tocqueville wrote to his old colleague, Louis Bouchitté, thanking him for a letter of condolence and affirming his belief in an afterlife, but saying nothing personal about his mother or his loss. He came nearest to it in a letter to John Mill, whose father was dying: 'I have just had the misfortune of losing my mother and I have felt the full extent and all the bitterness of such sorrows.' But he doesn't go into details.[6]

There would be little point in further discussion of Tocqueville's relations with his mother. There seems to be no doubt that he was distressed by her sufferings and sorrowed for his loss; that does not do away with the impression formed of earlier years. How little we know is sharply demonstrated by a surprising passage in a letter to Eugène Stoffels: 'Marie deeply regrets my mother, who was always very good to her.' Is it possible that Louise de Tocqueville, in the end, had not objected to her son's choice of a wife?[7]

Her death was followed by a distribution of some of the family property. Alexis was the chief beneficiary. It is tempting to see a cause and effect here, but it is plain from the marriage contract that such a settlement was pending even before the death of the comtesse. It seems that Alexis and Marie were expected to take possession of the chateau and lands of Tourlaville, just outside Cherbourg; perhaps the death and obsequies actually held things up.[8] Be that as it may, in April, Tocqueville set off to inspect the place. He did not take Marie with him, on the grounds that 'one can't make a woman go travelling at this season' – not, at least, in the Cotentin, where the roads were still dreadful, 'mere lanes, just broad enough to admit a horse and his burden'. Tourlaville, today beautifully restored and meticulously main-tained – it is one of Cherbourg's chief tourist attractions – might have been expected to appeal to him: it had a romantic and sinister history, which in 1604 had culminated in the execution for incest of the young *châtelain* and his sister; but it was nearly derelict, and the demesne buildings were let to a farmer. It would cost 1,000,000 francs to put in order. So after long negotiations Alexis instead took possession of the family's cradle, the château, lands and village of Tocqueville itself; and in the summer of 1837 he began to make it his home.

His choice was not altogether free. The chateau was part of the family patrimony, and no Tocqueville would have dreamed of realizing capital by selling it, if it could be avoided: for one thing, land was much the safest available investment. This attitude was wholly representative of what Tocqueville, idiosyncratically, loved to call his *caste*. As François Furet has explained, a *caste*, in Tocqueville's thought, was not so much a group closed to all who were born outside it as a group deprived of all political power and therefore all the more fiercely determined to preserve its compensatory privileges.[9] After the fall of the Bourbons the legitimist nobles, dislodged from political office and social sway, retired to their chateaux to wait for the better times which never came, although for fifty years they hoped that the peasants at least would always follow the lead of their former masters. Disillusionment was slow in coming, and Tocqueville died before it was complete. Not that he was a supporter of the Bourbons; but during his years in the Cotentin, and especially while he served as deputy and representative, his correspondence constantly shows him playing a role from which he gained deep personal satisfaction: that of the benevolent leader of the countryside, a sort of mini-monarch. It was the possession of the domain of Tocqueville which made this possible, although, in another small demonstration of his fidelity to democratic principle, he always rejected the title of *comte* which went with it (even if many tradesmen insisted on putting *M. le Comte* or *M. le Vicomte* on their bills).[10]

Once installed, Tocqueville developed a strong personal devotion to his chateau. It was a commitment second only to his marriage: André Jardin rightly says that it was 'perhaps the happiest passion of his life.' He liked the feeling of identification with family, provincial and national history that the place gave him, and it may well have strengthened his bond with his father. For Comte Hervé was deeply attached to the scene of his childhood, in spite of the changes which time and farming activity had wrought on it; he was hurt when Hippolyte dismissed it as dreary. He never seems to have contemplated returning to live there himself, but he came on frequent visits to Alexis. And no doubt he encouraged the works of restoration undertaken by Alexis and Marie (especially, at first, by Marie) over the years. It was a family trait: Hervé had devoted himself to the embellishment of Verneuil during his years there, and nowadays the grounds of Nacqueville, Tourlaville and Tocqueville testify to the degree to which his sons followed his example and that of his father, Comte Bernard.[11]

Finally, we must remember the pea-patch of Verneuil. Alexis de Tocqueville was born in Paris and resided there, some of the time, in almost every year of his life; but he never seems to have identified himself as a Parisian, though he had many Parisian attitudes. At Tocqueville he rediscovered the happiness which he had known as a child in the only settled home he had ever had. He greatly enjoyed settling down with Marie in the rue de Bourgogne, but once her efforts had begun to make Tocqueville habitable there was no contest. He became, in the fullest sense, 'Tocqueville of that ilk'.[12]

It is difficult to form an accurate idea of the chateau in Tocqueville's time, or of all the changes which he made there. In 1828 he referred to it as an old ruin, and was still doing so when he went to live there nine years later. The spell of the place was slow to be felt, partly because of building works. It is amusing to watch his attitude altering. In June 1837 (when, admittedly, he was ill) he wrote to Francisque de Corcelle: 'I find our poor *gentilhommière* a thousand times uglier now that I am taking thought for our future guests. It is *abominable*.' If Corcelle came he must prepare to live in the middle of a farmyard. 'Chickens, pigs, turkeys and geese are the objects of recreation which will catch your eye …' A few days later he concedes that the chateau is delightful in summer, though it must be frightful in winter; he and Marie enjoy going for rides together, there are few neighbours to bother them, the tranquillity is marvellous for his work – he feels happier than he has for ages. His contentment is completed, he confesses, by his position in the village. 'I meet absolutely none of those hateful attitudes which divide the upper from the lower classes almost everywhere in France and make the atmosphere so unhealthy for the rich. On the contrary, I enjoy a respect of which I can boast, for it is not accorded on my account, but to the memory of my grandmother.' But then Marie began the work of rebuilding and repairing. It had to be done, but Tocqueville hated to find himself surrounded by workmen, 'a detestable race, noisy, gnawing animals, not at all the right neighbours for a philosopher like me'. He left the business entirely to his wife and shut himself up in the little room which was all that she let him keep. 'You see that I am a model husband.' But when, next summer, the work still went on and he was chased from room to room ('just now we are confined to our bedrooms'), his patience, never his strong point, wore thin. He rejoiced when work had to be suspended for a time because the supply of seasoned timber had run out.[13]

Henry Reeve, visiting in the summer of 1844, was to be struck by the likeness of the chateau to the peelhouses of Teviotdale, and remarked that it had probably been built for similar purposes: 'the Cotentin, lying within eighteen leagues of the Isle of Wight, may be considered as a border district in relation to England.' Nassau Senior has left a good physical description of the chateau, which he visited in 1850 and 1861:

> Creepers in great luxuriance cover the walls up to the first floor windows. The little park consists of from thirty to forty acres, well wooded and traversed by an avenue ... leading from the road to the front of the house. To the west the ground rises to a wild common commanding the sea, the lighthouses of Gatteville, Barfleur, La Hogue, and a green plain covered with woods and hedgerow trees, and studded with church towers and spires of the picturesque forms of the eleventh, twelfth, and thirteenth centuries. It has no grand features, except the sea and the rocky coast of the Cotentin peninsula, but it is full of variety and beauty. I can understand Tocqueville's delight in the house and in the country.

Senior's bedroom, in one of the round towers, had granite walls six feet thick. He does not mention the pond or small lake in the garden south of the house, but otherwise the chateau apparently looked much as it does today.[14]

In one respect only was the chateau defective: it was damp, even in summer, and bad for the health of both husband and wife, especially in winter. According to Marie it killed Alexis in the end. But before that it gave him years and years of as much content as he was capable of.

It was as well that he had such a refuge. There can be no doubt that he needed undisturbed quiet for his writing, unattainable in Paris since he had become famous. It was there that he had finished his promised article for Mill, 'État social et politique de la France avant et depuis 1789', which turned out to be a sketch for his *Ancien Régime*.[15] But for more sustained work he needed country quiet. Originally he found it at Baugy, a chateau much like Tocqueville, but in the end he outstayed his welcome. Between 1836 and 1838 he lived there for months at a time: indeed, in the spring of 1838 Édouard and Alexandrine abandoned their home for Paris, leaving Alexis and Marie in possession. It is difficult to acquit Alexis of inconsideration. It was all very well for him to shut himself up in his turret-room and get on with the second part of his *Démocratie*; Édouard no doubt had daily business; but Marie had nothing to do; she was only a guest, and eventually she and Alexandrine got on each other's nerves. Tocqueville himself noticed what he called Alexandrine's feebleness and indolence, but he loved her affectionate heart. Still, it is no wonder that the breach which had opened between the two women was never really closed, except perhaps during the last illness of Alexis. It was worse with Marie and Emilie. After a visit to Nacqueville in the autumn of 1838 Tocqueville wrote despairingly to Kergorlay that the two would never get on: 'Their good points and their bad are alike opposed to each other.' Besides, Émilie was frivolous and extravagant and a bad influence on Hippolyte, who was extravagant himself, and a bad manager of his finances (Marie was an excellent manager, no doubt in part because she had always had to live on a limited income). The two couples had little to do with each other over the next twenty years, though they lived so near. The bond between the male Tocquevilles – the father and the brothers – was too strong to be broken, but Alexandrine and Émilie joined in mocking Marie, behind her husband's back, for her English accent, English taste and English passion for small dogs (which last was shared by Alexis). Marie went on her way tranquilly, and, once she was in full command of her own house, concentrated on looking after her husband and getting on good terms with his friends. She became particularly close to Beaumont and his wife Clémentine, a granddaughter of La Fayette, whom he married in June 1836.[16]

Soon afterwards, in July, Tocqueville took Marie on a two-month tour to Switzerland by way of Metz and Strasbourg. It might have been a belated wedding-tour, and in some ways assumed that aspect; but the main reason for it was that Marie was unwell, and they hoped that the waters of a Swiss spa might help her. She had always suffered from acute menstrual pains,[17] and Tocqueville may already have begun to fear that the marriage would be childless. At Metz they stayed with Eugène Stoffels, who like his friend had recently married;* and there the two men had lively discussions of the *Démocratie*, its doctrines, and Tocqueville's ideas for its sequel. Tocqueville seems to have been at his most eloquent, but when he had gone his way Stoffels, to his sorrow and surprise, found himself unconvinced, and after at least one sleepless night wrote to say why. As Kergorlay often complained, Stoffels had a solid strain of Germanic common sense, and he knew Tocqueville's character very well. It seemed to him that his friend was letting his ideas run away with him. Tocqueville wanted to rally all decent Frenchmen to him, without regard to party; as to the dynastic question, he was happy to let the people have whichever monarch they voted for; he wanted the communes of France to be self-governing, and to give all their citizens municipal voting rights; he wanted to abolish the Chamber of Peers, replacing it with a second chamber derived vaguely from some American model; he wanted to reduce the army in size and cost; he wanted freedom of the press and an extended jury system. All this amounted to the Republic without the name and, said Stoffels, was at present politically impracticable. Tocqueville might think him too much influenced by fear, prejudice and ignorance; but was it not equally likely that Tocqueville himself was being carried away by an *idée fixe*? Such was the weakness of great men: Napoleon had been ruined by clinging to his 'continental system'. If Tocqueville published a book advocating his programme, everyone would respond like Stoffels, and his brilliant political prospects would be at an end. 'Forgive me, dear Alexis, for all the ideas and expressions in this letter which may have wounded you.' But he had had to write it. He felt like a mother who sees her child running into danger.[18]

Tocqueville replied from Berne. Stoffels had been afraid of angering him (he knew his friend's uncertain temper), but 'I am not yet such

* See above p. 62.

a great man as not to know that one of the best benefits of friend-ship is a friend's sincere and truthful advice.' Stoffels had sketched his proposals accurately, but he thought the disagreement with him was a mere nuance. He himself had for years been appalled by the split between men who especially prized morality, religion and order and those who loved liberty and equality more even than law. He wanted to show that such a confrontation was mistaken and unnecessary. 'Such is my general proposition. You understand it; you share it.' But (he said) he loved liberty more passionately, more sincerely than Stoffels. He loved liberty as much as he loved morality, and was not afraid to sacrifice his peace and quiet to obtain it; but he was 'a liberal of a new kind', not to be confounded with most democrats of the day. Whether he would be able to make a mark with his doctrine only God could say. It was perhaps presumptuous to try.

> Tell me, if you like, that my undertaking is a rash one, too much for my abilities; even that it is a dream, a chimera. But let me at least believe that the enterprise is something fine – great – noble; that it is worth the commitment of a man's time, fortune and life; and that it would be better to fail in it than to succeed in something else. To persuade men that respect for the laws of God and man is the best means of remaining free, and that liberty is the best means of remaining upright and religious cannot, you say, be done. I too am tempted to think so. But the thing is true, all the same, and I will try to say so at all costs.[19]

This affirmation was probably enough to satisfy Stoffels that his friend had not become a dangerous radical, but evidently both men knew that the central, practical point could not be refuted: in that age Tocqueville's programme (which he had, of course, already laid out in the *Démocra-tie*) was never going to rally most Frenchmen. Charles de Rémusat,* who admired Tocqueville and got to know him well after he entered the Chamber of Deputies, made much the same point in his memoirs:

---

* Charles de Rémusat (1797–1875), son of Napoleon I's lord chamberlain; married one of La Fayette's granddaughters, like Gustave de Beaumont and Francisque de Corcelle. Deputy and representative from the Haute Garonne, 1830–51. He was a close associate of Thiers and served as minister of the interior in the Thiers cabinet of 1840. He succeeded Royer-Collard at the Académie Française, 1846. Thiers appointed him foreign minister in 1871. His memoirs, not published until after the Second World War, are an invaluable and agreeably written source for his period.

Tocqueville's great merit was that he was the author of his own opinions ... Thus he had become not only a liberal, but a democrat, that is, he was convinced that the world was going to belong to democracy. It demonstrated great power and intellectual independence in a great-grandson of Malesherbes. But as he disdained legitimism without hating legitimists, as he was untainted by any rancour against the Bourbons and their party, his liberalism, purely the work of his reason, was irreproachable but cold, and only moderately persuasive.[20]

The political career on which Tocqueville was soon to embark would constantly be bedevilled by his inability to relate his programme to the actualities of politics – to the struggle between Left and Right, between what were called the parties of movement and resistance. This was by no means entirely his own fault. Left and Right under the July Monarchy, which excluded all extremes from the parliamentary arena, were confusingly fluid terms. Tocqueville was never able to make an effective choice between them. But although he may have already begun to fear such a fate, it was not yet certain, and anyway he was still primarily a successful author, who did not need to worry about political expediency.

The Swiss journey was no great success. Tocqueville found that as a married man he could not pursue his usual strenuous investigative routine in a foreign country. Marie got no better; in fact the waters of Baden, although recommended by the ladies and doctors of Berne, made her worse. Tocqueville did not find Baden agreeable: there was nothing to it but a deep ravine through which naturally hot water was piped to bath-houses; the air was humid and smelled slightly of sulphur. Tocqueville would have been extremely bored but for the books in his trunk. He read Machiavelli's *History of Florence* and Plato's *Laws*; he was not captivated by either of them. Machiavelli, indeed, he rejected: here was the grandfather of Thiers, quite irreligious and impressed only by success (it is a pity that Tocqueville never read the *Discorsi*). Medieval Florence, in its violence and corruption, was useless to the student of modern democracy. He respected but was puzzled by Plato, who wanted to stop the evolution of music by law and never thought of doing without slaves; and although he strongly advocated aristocratic government, he was an ultra-democrat in social arrangements, wanting all property to be held in common. He too was not usable.[21]

Tocqueville made a brief study of the Swiss political system, and decided that he did not think much of it. He found it inferior to both the American and the British.

> The kingdom of England seems much more republican than the Helvetic republic ... He who travels in the United States feels involuntarily and instinctively so convinced that the institutions, taste for and spirit of liberty are bound up with every custom of the American people that he can't conceive of any government for it except a republic. And in the same way, one can't imagine that the English could possibly live except under a free government ... In those two countries liberty appears to me even stronger in the manners than in the laws. In Switzerland, it seems to me stronger in the laws than in the manners.[22]

This remark is enough to show why, for Tocqueville, the country had as little bearing on his new work as medieval Florence or ancient Athens.

He felt much more enthusiastic when, after getting back to France in early September, he and Marie went to stay with Le Peletier d'Aunay at Mareil, for d'Aunay was a convert to decentralization: 'The more he experiences provincial freedom and the status which it confers on its representatives, the more his love of centralization gives way to a reasoned liking for local independence. Almost all deputies are simultaneously members of the *conseils-généraux*; an excellent thing.' Tocqueville began to think of standing for a *conseil-général* himself, in the election which was about to take place.* He travelled to Nacqueville to see if there was an opening for him in the Cotentin, and he actually drafted an election address. It is charmingly written, but its arguments are sadly thin. It would not do; nor would his candidacy. He sent Marie, in his father's care, to Baugy, and followed her a few days later. It was time he returned to his book.[23]

As he had remarked to Comte Molé more than a year before, he had always intended to follow up his volumes on equality, laws and institutions with a study of the influence of equality on American

---

* Every department had a *conseil-général* (departmental council) to help the work of the prefects. One of the most important reforms of the July Monarchy had been to make them elective, so that they could act to a modest extent as checks on the otherwise all-powerful central administration.

civil society, on ideas and manners. He had begun to jot down preliminary thoughts before his mother's death, but did not do more until the
spring of 1836: he had first to write the article on eighteenth-century
France. By April he was hard at work, groaning about 'that damned
Démocratie' to Henry Reeve, and explaining to John Mill that until it
was complete he could write no more articles. As usual he plunged into
his work mind, heart and soul, and being so emotionally committed
inevitably suffered moments of disagreeable panic, when he thought it
was all worthless: 'A thousand times happier are those who are always
self-satisfied; they are of course intolerable to other people, but to
themselves they are deliciously enjoyable.' His progress was slower
than he would have liked, but by the time he left for Switzerland he
seems to have sketched the whole of what became Book One of the
1840 *Démocratie* – 'The Influence of Democracy on the Life of the
Mind in the United States'.[24]

He arrived at Baugy after his travels on 15 October 1836 and
resumed work two days later. He found it difficult to get back into
harness, and regretted that the long interruption meant that the book
could not possibly be finished by the spring, as he had hoped: it would
not appear for a year, at soonest. He decided that if Marie was healthy
(Baugy, being damp, like Tocqueville, was bad for her rheumatism)
and if his work went well he would stay where he was indefinitely,
'for I must say I dread Paris'. Before long he settled down, and by
November was working a steady seven hours a day; but he seemed
to himself to be making little real progress, partly because he was so
self-consciously trying to do his best (very necessary, since he would
no longer be taking the public by surprise). He missed the stimulus
and advice of both Beaumont and Kergorlay. He tried hard but vainly
to get Mill, who was visiting Paris, to come to Baugy, 'for my subject
is beginning to weigh on my mind like a nightmare on a sleeper's
stomach ... As you know, I never take up my pen with the set intention
of following a system and arriving by brute force at my goal; I give
myself over to the natural movement of ideas, letting myself be led
in good faith from one conclusion to another.' So he had no notion of
when he would finish, and greatly wished to talk over his ideas with
Mill, who unfortunately had returned to England before receiving this
letter. But the work, though difficult, went on cheerfully, or so he told

Reeve: 'I have never worked at anything with so much ardour; I think of my subject all day and night and flatter myself that I have become totally unsociable. I would never have imagined that a subject which I have already handled in so many ways could show so many new aspects.' It is impossible to say exactly how far he got that autumn, but it is reasonable to guess that he wrote most of Book Two, 'The Influence of Democracy on American Attitudes and Opinions'. He had to leave Baugy for Paris in December, and regretted it.[25]

Well he might. He seems to have made comparatively little progress during the next few months, though he read a chunk of the book to Beaumont and Clémentine in January (Clémentine scolded her husband for not being enthusiastic enough). In March he had a long conversation with Kergorlay, who gave him a deeply disturbing account of the state of the French army since the July Revolution. Tocqueville did not wholly believe it, but it was enough to inspire his gloomy pages about democratic armies in Book Three. In late May 1837 he and Marie left for Tocqueville, where he hoped to find the tranquillity he needed to finish what was beginning to seem an interminable task. To some extent he did so, but in June first Marie and then he himself fell ill: in his case it was an attack of his old intestinal trouble which he blamed on Thiers, who had given them an excessively rich dinner at the wrong time of day before they left Paris. Then the Chamber of Deputies was dissolved, a general election was announced, and Tocqueville plunged into the quest for a seat.* He was unsuccessful, but by early December, when the vote took place, the *Démocratie* had been neglected for five months or so. Matters did not immediately improve: in December he had to sacrifice a fortnight to jury-duty in Paris.[26]

By January 1838†, however, he was again hard at work: Beaumont, who was writing his book on Ireland, spoke of them both as being 'plunged in the abyss of literary production', and Tocqueville himself wrote of living like a Benedictine in a monastery as he toiled away. Halfway through Book Three ('The Influence of Democracy on Manners Properly So-called') he began to enlist helpers as assiduously as he had for his first volume. He set his father to research the

---

* Described later in this chapter.
† In which month he became a member of the Institut de France when he was elected to the Académie des Sciences Morales et Politiques.

topic of honour under the *ancien régime*: the result was an essay of the greatest value.[27] He still relied on Beaumont's advice, but it was to be months before they could meet for a real deliberation. Much the most important collaborator at this stage was Kergorlay, who was always available. He was going through a wretched phase: in 1837 he seems to have had, or been on the brink of having, what used to be called a nervous breakdown. Chained by love and duty to his parents, he could seldom leave Fosseuse for long, where, much against his inclination, he struggled to restore a failing estate. His closest friends had all married and he felt that he ought to marry himself, but, apart from his misogyny, he found himself caught in the trap which Tocqueville had evaded: unable or unwilling to marry outside his *caste*, and unable to get behind the barriers of social convention, he bounced like a ball between the various well brought-up young ladies whom his family and friends put forward – Mademoiselle N, Mademoiselle X, Mademoiselle Z. Tocqueville said of one of them that he would willingly have slept with her, but would never have made her his wife. Kergorlay came to an agreement with none of them. He had no intellectual project to satisfy him, and middle age was advancing: he reported, almost deadpan, that he had run into Beaumont at a Parisian wig-maker's. In the circumstances it is small wonder that he clung to his friendship with Tocqueville, and that he required constant reassurance: at this period their letters are full of affirmations that they loved each other as much as ever. Tocqueville could not entirely understand his friend: he remarked that in the Middle Ages Kergorlay would have been thought bewitched, but he was always willing to do what he could for him, and at the moment that meant enlisting his help with the *Démocratie*.[28]

By mid-January, when Kergorlay came to stay, Tocqueville had reached his chapter on ambition in the United States, and, by his own account, was at a stand: 'it was a real intellectual *cul-de-sac*, which [Kergorlay] got me out of in a few hours. That lad has in himself a veritable mine on which he alone cannot and does not know how to draw.'[29] What this meant can be discovered from two remarkable letters which Kergorlay wrote during the next month on the same subject of democratic ambition, and on religion. In the first, he states so many characteristic Tocquevillean themes – France's domination by revolution or the memory of revolution; men's preference for equality of status to political liberty; the possibility of a new despotism rising on democratic foundations – that it is tempting to take literally the remark which Tocqueville makes elsewhere, that Kergorlay was his master. Perhaps the truth is that Kergorlay was repeating ideas which the two men had already discussed, or even originated together. Still more striking is Kergorlay's strictly logical approach: he does just what Tocqueville never does – he makes careful, convincing distinctions, and in so doing demonstrates that it is not anachronistic to object to certain aspects of Tocqueville's procedures. Kergorlay even says, 'the word *democracy* is detestably inapt for the usage we give it and must give it today.' The great question is equality of status, which is poorly indicated by a word which really means government by the people.* He is also doubtful of generalizations covering republics and constitutional monarchies: they are all so various; and he thinks it is historically premature to have any views on large ambitions in democracies. Had Tocqueville followed Kergorlay's advice, his book might have been less ambitious but more convincing.[30]

Kergorlay is equally impressive when answering a now lost letter from Tocqueville on religious doubt. He has a robust way with him:

> Unlike you I don't feel it impossible to live with doubt; I don't know if this is because of my own nature or the consequence of my reasoning on the subject. But what does seem clear to me is that no man can have complete certainty on any subject; and I don't see how that point can seem dubious to you or to any other man who knows how to think. All our faculties are limited; all are very imperfect instruments; how then could they arrive at certain results? I believe that life should be passed in discerning and classifying the different degrees of probability in our various branches of knowledge and that our actions should be the same as they would be if the most probable contentions had been entirely proved.

To act energetically it is necessary to take probabilities for certainties, but too much should not be made of this technique: it is only a blindfold to prevent vertigo when crossing a bridge. He goes on to write a panegyric on philosophical doubt: 'I believe, *mon cher ami*, that

---

* Twenty years later AT himself makes and elaborates this point in his preparatory notes for the unfinished second volume of the *Ancien Régime*. See OC II ii 198–9, and the Pléiade edition, 611–12.

it is necessary to live with our lack of certainty, as if with guests who simply won't leave, and that we must be patient with the drawbacks; we will never get back to blind belief; but it is very doubtful that we have lost by the change.' Possibly Tocqueville would also have profited greatly had he been able to accept this advice.[31]

Perhaps, superficially, he did: it was more than compatible with his reasons for abandoning Catholicism.* But like those reasons it could get no purchase on his innermost life: as he said in reply, 'there are in me powerful instincts which your words cannot calm. It is, I admit, unreasonable to desire more or other than the common destiny of humanity, but such is the involuntary and all-powerful impulse of my soul.'[32] (He had been reading Pascal.) A similar pattern can be seen in his response to Kergorlay's other letter. Tocqueville was grateful for all the help and advice which he received, and readily appropriated ideas and information which he could use, but on some matters he was beyond influence or argument.

By the middle of March he was once more in the state of mind which had marked the writing of the 1835 *Démocratie*.

> I have numberless highs and lows, am now in the seventh heaven, now flat on the floor, unable to see more than three feet in any direction. You must know what it's like, no-one who meddles with writing doesn't, but it happens to me more often than to many others, I think. And I find besides that these painful moments don't bring with them sufficient compensation: I am never completely satisfied and I often despair.

This was his state of mind throughout the spring and summer, and his task seemed never-ending. 'The author's trade is decidedly hard and hateful when practised as we do it,' he wrote to Beaumont in July. 'so, although you may well accuse me of swearing a drunkard's oath, I affirm that after this work I shall study, but write no more, or at least nothing requiring a long haul.' Nevertheless he was drawing near the end. A letter to Édouard two days later shows that he was well-launched on Book Four, 'The Influence of Democratic Ideas and Feelings on Political Society', which was largely to be devoted to centralization. He wrote on through the summer and early autumn

* And see above, pp. 50–51.

and at last, on 10 October, told Beaumont that he had written the last word of the last chapter: 'sing *alleluia*.' But when Beaumont sent his congratulations Tocqueville pulled back: he was now plunged in revision, and had just destroyed the first hundred pages, which would have to be done all over again. Beaumont, in fact, seemed to be nearer publication than he was, and the idea agitated him extremely. He could not bear the thought that *L'Irlande* might be published before he and Beaumont met again and collated their texts, so that they could be sure of appearing as united in word as they were in heart. He couldn't go to Paris before January, he must stay at Tocqueville to finish the revision (in his distress he began to repeat himself). He was working as hard as he possibly could.[33]

This last assertion was undoubtedly true: he desperately wanted to publish that winter, and had already begun negotiations with Gosselin. But by January 1839 it was necessary to return to Paris, and there he fell ill from overwork. On the last day of the month he wrote to Beaumont that unless he recovered soon he would give up the idea of publishing 'in the spring'.[34]

His letters also show that he was passionately anxious for a success, so he should have been encouraged by what happened on 29 January. He told Beaumont:

> I was astonished, confounded, confused and I don't know what else the day before yesterday on seeing M. de Chateaubriand walk in to hear, said he, some of my manuscript. It was necessary to read to him. You can imagine that having made such a move, I don't know why, he was not going to start criticizing. So he was immensely complimentary. I discount three-quarters of what he said, but enough remains to make me hope that his impression, although frightfully exaggerated in his remarks, really was favourable.[35]

Tocqueville always found it difficult to be gracious about Chateaubriand, who was nevertheless genuinely proud of his kinsman. The 1835 *Démocratie* not only showed his influence, it confirmed many of his observations about America; and as Marc Fumaroli has pointed out, the 1840 *Démocratie* was to influence the 'Conclusion' of the *Mémoires d'outre-tombe*.[36] His visit was no doubt prompted by genuine respect, but Mme Récamier or some other friend may have hinted that

Tocqueville needed encouragement. Unfortunately his spirits were so low that the effect was not what was hoped for: 'So at this moment I am like a horse to which, after having tied up its four legs, one applies a lick of the whip.'[37]

A better cure for exhaustion and despondency was at hand. The very next day Tocqueville wrote to Beaumont again with great news: the Chamber was prorogued, and would soon be dissolved: an election was at hand. The horse rallied to the sound of the trumpet. Beaumont must immediately abandon Ireland and come to Paris to make the necessary political contacts, 'for now is the time for our great wager, a wager disastrous to make at this moment, but which it would be still more disastrous to lose.'[38] The *Démocratie* was again thrown aside, and Tocqueville rushed to the hustings. He was in Valognes in little more than a week after writing to Beaumont.

To understand the political scene which Tocqueville now intended to enter, and the situation which gave him his opportunity, it is necessary to go back some years, and to analyse the position of the July Monarchy towards the end of its first decade.

'A popular throne surrounded by republican institutions.' La Fayette's formula had seemed clear and attractive enough when he propounded it, but it proved exceedingly difficult to apply, and in the end its built-in contradictions were to destroy it. But only the most rigid determinist will argue that the July regime was certain to fail, and in its early years it achieved some solid successes, of which the most important were diplomatic. When the powers (including even Russia) realized that Louis-Philippe had no intention of renewing revolutionary war they were perfectly ready to accept him. He never attained such general acceptance at home. One of his first prime ministers, Casimir Périer, had such force of mind and character that he was able to keep the Chamber of Deputies, his colleagues, and, not least, the King in order, but he died in the cholera epidemic of 1832 and no adequate replacement was ever found. The regime remained fragile to the last because except for the reckless Thiers none of its leaders ever admitted the necessity of broadening its support. It was a government of *bourgeois* notables who were not even united among themselves, which in the end was their undoing.

But this danger lay out of sight in 1837, when Tocqueville first stood for the Chamber, and even in 1839, when he stood again. True, some sort of watershed was crossed between the two elections, at least so far as the Cotentin was concerned. In 1837 the contest was dominated by the past. Tocqueville, little more than a carpet-bag candidate, could not shake off the suspicions aroused by his name. His opponents successfully put it about that, as a noble, he must be a secret legitimist, who would revive the *ancien régime* and its abuses if he could; cats must catch mice, they said. It was preposterous, as the voters would have known had they read Tocqueville's article on the *ancien régime*, but then the *London and Westminster Review* did not circulate in the Cotentin. Polydor Le Marois, the sitting deputy, Tocqueville's chief opponent, brought up the matter of the ruined dovecote and warned that Tocqueville would bring back the pigeons.[39] Matters were not helped by the conspicuous legitimism of Comte Hervé and of Hippolyte at Nacqueville. It is no wonder that Alexis lost. But by 1839 the issues had changed in his favour; the 700 or so electors knew him much better, and he was victorious.

It looks simple enough, but nothing about Tocqueville was ever simple. In the first place it must be said that though he had nursed the Cotentin for years, in 1837 he did not neglect the possibility that he might come in for a constituency other than Valognes. There was Cherbourg, strongly disputed between Hippolyte's brother-in-law, the comte de Bricqueville, a Napoleonic veteran, and one H.-A. Quénault, whom Tocqueville regarded as the very embodiment of political corruption: since Bricqueville was in failing health Tocqueville thought of standing in his place. There was the tenth *arrondissement* in Paris, the faubourg Saint-Germain, where Tocqueville was respected on account of the *Démocratie*, and had real support: it was there that Jules Taschereau, a leading journalist, dealt with citizens who asked, 'What are M. de Tocqueville's opinions?' by replying, 'You have read his *Démocratie*?' 'Certainly,' the voter would answer, who had certainly not. 'Well, doesn't that satisfy you?' There was Versailles, where Tocqueville not only wrote two articles, on Algeria, for the local paper, but bought shares in it.[40] All these were places with which he had strong connections, whereas he was hardly known at Valognes. (In the autumn of 1837 he had not even quite finished the business of acquiring his chateau – it dragged out for over two years.) Undoubtedly his candidacy suffered from this, as he well knew; equally undoubtedly, his decision to stake everything on establishing himself in Lower Normandy was, politically, the right one: after 1839 he was never again effectually challenged until Louis Napoleon's *coup d'état* put an end to his political career.

'The department of the Manche is inhabited almost solely by farmers, as everyone knows,' says Tocqueville in the *Souvenirs*. 'There are no large towns; few factories; absolutely no places where workers come together in large numbers, except for Cherbourg.'[41] The land is rich, and under the July Monarchy supported many prosperous peasants, some of whom had the vote. This was eminently true of the beautiful Val de Saire, on the edge of which the chateau of Tocqueville stands: before long its master began to describe himself in documents as 'writer and peasant'. However, his initial support in the *arrondissement* did not come from the peasantry but from the small professional class of lawyers, businessmen and so on, which because of its superior training tended to take the lead in public affairs: it also carried more weight than it was numerically entitled to because the electorate was so tiny (628 in 1837). As Charles H. Pouthas points out, this middle class, like Tocqueville himself, combined its trades and professions with landownership, a combination typical of the July Monarchy; together, all the voters of the *arrondissement* were economically and socially self-sufficient: it amounted to 'a sort of rural democracy'[42] of the type which Tocqueville so often extolled. But as Pouthas does not say, the better-educated elements were particularly susceptible to the attractions of a man like Tocqueville, nationally famous and almost notoriously committed to the values they believed in. His insistence on public probity and the need for deputies to remain virtuously independent of government influence made him a refreshing contrast to Le Marois, who was ready to make any bargain with anybody if it kept him in the Chamber. Yet Tocqueville put himself at the service of any of the Manchois who had business with the central government: he would be a good constituency MP. He was lucky finding in Paul Clamorgan, a lawyer of Valognes, a brilliant political manager – a village Machiavelli, as he admitted himself. He might as well be described as a village Carnot, for he organized all Tocqueville's victories. Between elections he kept Tocqueville informed about all important developments in the constituency; they were in constant touch, and were friends as well as collaborators until Louis Napoleon's seizure of power divided them. Tocqueville's tone in his letters to Clamorgan is distinctly warmer than in those to his other allies.

But Tocqueville did not want to enter the Chamber so that he could be a good constituency MP. The intensity of his ambition was not clear even to so shrewd an observer as Rémusat, but it devoured him.[43] Its ultimate object was perhaps not clear even to himself until he became a minister in 1849, but from the moment that he began to contemplate the Chamber he knew that he wished to shine there, as some sort of paragon of wisdom and virtue. This led him into his first serious political blunder.

In 1837 the prime minister (*président du conseil*) happened to be his cousin Molé, with whom he was on excellent terms. Since Casimir Périer's death there had been a rapid turnover of ministries, and it had become obviously desirable to stabilize the situation. The King lent all his influence to the attempt. In Molé he hoped that he had found a suitable instrument: a man of distinguished family and substantial fortune, who had shown himself more than willing to serve whatever ruler was in power, whether Napoleon, the Bourbons or Louis-Philippe. Molé had replaced Thiers, who had been rashly ready to involve France in the civil war then occurring in Spain. Initially Molé's government had been a partnership with Guizot, now the acknowledged leader of the so-called 'party of resistance', which opposed all concessions to the Left; but the two men having fallen out, the ministry collapsed; in April 1837 Molé formed a new one of which he was the undisputed master. After a successful summer he called an election in the autumn, hoping to strengthen his own following in the Chamber and weaken that of Guizot. He was delighted when he heard that his cousin was to be a candidate, and the Manche prefect took the hint: he advised the voters of Valognes to support Tocqueville. Since there were as yet no modern party organizations in France the national administration, with its array of prefects, sub-prefects, *maires*, *adjoints*, tax-collectors, postmasters and so on was the only effective electoral machine in the country, and Molé must have supposed that he was doing Tocqueville a great favour. But the candidate thought very differently. Just as in writing he was always concerned to be original, so in politics he was always anxious to exhibit his independence. He and Beaumont had agonized for weeks that summer as to whether they should accept the ribbon of the Legion of Honour which had been offered to them, as to many other distinguished men, to mark the marriage of the duc d'Orléans, the heir to the throne (it had taken a firm letter from Royer-Collard to induce Tocqueville to say yes).[44] Tocqueville despised those who allowed themselves to be brought into the Chamber by what he regarded as corrupt means and there voted only as the ministry directed. So when he heard of the prefect's action he wrote to Molé repudiating all official support:

> In other circumstances such a message to the head of the government might appear extraordinary. But I know to whom I am writing; and if the prime minister blames me, I can boldly appeal to M. Molé, whose esteem, if he will allow me to say so, I value more than his support, and before him I am sure to win my case.
>
> You are well aware, sir, that I am not an enemy of the government in general, and particularly not of those who govern at this moment. But I wish to be able to support it intelligently and freely, which I could not do if I let myself be brought in by the government. I am well aware that some men forget, on entering the Chamber, how they got there; but I am not of that sort. I wish to enter as I mean to go on, in an independent position.

He justified his letter by saying that he had used the freedom of a relation and a friend.[45]

Molé was exceedingly surprised by this letter, and answered it at once. His reply, in its plain good sense, was worthy of Bagehot. After repudiating any distinction between Molé the man and Molé the minister he asserted his firm belief in the wisdom of the policies that he was pursuing and in the integrity of his supporters:

> All such assertions seem very flat, I know, to that insincere and popularity-hunting opinion which holds that government (*pouvoir*), whoever wields it, is bound to be the enemy of society. But may I ask if you think you would be any freer of commitments if you came in with the help of the legitimists, the republicans, or any shade of the Left, rather than that of the *juste milieu*? It is necessary to choose; isolation is not independence, and we depend more or less on

those who elect us. The army of the ministry in these elections is not composed only of those who have been brought forward by it or owe their seats to it; it is a party composed, above all, of men who think as we do and believe it is best for the country to support us and beat our enemies. It is among such men, my dear sir, that I would have been happy and proud to number you.

But since it was impossible, he would send out orders that very day to fight Tocqueville's candidacy relentlessly, 'for there can be no neutrality in elections.'[46]

When these letters were published after Tocqueville's death Nassau Senior was moved to ask Beaumont why Tocqueville had refused Molé's support. Beaumont put it down to youth and inexperience. 'Like most young politicians, he thought that he ought to be an independent member, and to vote on every occasion according to his conscience, untrammelled by party considerations. He afterwards found his mistake.'[47] He did not find it out in 1837. He was furious – in part because Molé had patronizingly suggested that when he had more experience he would see things differently – and he hurled off a long, angry reply in which he more or less repudiated Molé's friendship:

> I had flattered myself that whatever our disagreements, the bond which you had sought to forge between us would never break; a bond of affection, of trust, of like opinions and tastes. I see clearly that I must renounce that hope; I do so with profound regret.
>
> I am, *Monsieur le Ministre*, your very humble and most obedient servant, Alexis de Tocqueville.[48]

Tocqueville was no more willing to accept fundamental criticism from the prime minister than from Stoffels or Kergorlay, and loved him much less; but perhaps his rage and his attitude of offended integrity arose from a guilty conscience. At that moment, in mid-September, he was still undecided as to his course, and if he stood for Cherbourg rather than Valognes he would have to be ostentatiously independent – if he was the official Orleanist candidate he would alienate legitimist votes which otherwise, because of his family and reputation, he might well receive, and would need. Nor can he be acquitted of some double-dealing. He had assured Molé that he supported the government although he did not want its backing; yet Beaumont, who was investigating the possibility of a Parisian race for him, clearly regarded him as a supporter of the Left opposition, especially the faction led by Odilon Barrot.[49] Tocqueville did not mean to be treacherous, but it was perhaps just as well for his reputation as an honest man that he was defeated in 1837.

Molé was deeply upset by Tocqueville's second letter, but brought himself to write an affectionate reply in which, while sticking to his guns – he still thought that Tocqueville would have to join a party one day – he insisted that he had always regarded Tocqueville as a son, and even renewed the offer of political support, so long as Tocqueville was not a declared member of the opposition. Tocqueville, no doubt aware that he had gone too far, eagerly clutched at the olive-branch and went so far as to explain his doubts and hesitations, not only as to constituencies, but about entering the race at all. If he did so, he asked only for Molé's benevolent neutrality. He professed entire loyalty to the Orleanist regime:

> I witnessed the Revolution of July with regret, but I am disinclined to start another revolution to destroy the work of the last one; and although I have a great esteem and a real respect for legitimacy, I do not wish to try to re-establish, by disorder, a principle of which the great merit in my eyes is that it forbids disorder. I must add that although I have a deep, burning, sincere love of liberty, I am not the less resolved to resist any free system which is opposed or dangerous to monarchy.[50]

Molé could have asked for no more; but Polydor Le Marois had been at school with Montalivet, the minister of the interior, who insisted that the government support him. In André Jardin's opinion that is probably why Tocqueville lost: he received 210 votes to 247 for Le Marois.[51]

He was not much cast down by his defeat: 'Je suis donc battu, mais je n'ai pas été un instant abattu.'* Although he had repeatedly written to Marie about how much he longed to be back in the quiet of their home, he evidently found that he much enjoyed electioneering. It

---

* Another untranslatable play on words. 'I have been defeated, but never deflated' is the best I can do.

was not so boisterous as in England; it entailed nothing so vulgar as knocking on voters' doors or addressing mass meetings; but he was willing to see anyone who came to meet him, to answer any sincere letter, and to confabulate with his friends. He also kept a sharp eye on the doings of his opponents, issuing private circulars to denounce them when necessary. He began his campaign, in effect, by scolding the *sous-préfet* of Cherbourg for slandering him, and ended it by denouncing the postmaster of Valognes for not circulating his last leaflet in time. He took great pleasure in feeling that he was supported enthusiastically by all the educated, respectable voters. When his father wrote anxiously about his health he brushed the question aside: 'Do believe that commotion is my element, and that it won't kill me, so long as it isn't combined with hours of desk-work as it was last year and so long (as I am firmly resolved) as I avoid all dining-out and evening receptions.'[52]

He admitted to Beaumont that he had been somewhat surprised at his defeat. Apart from the machinations of the government's agents he put it down to Le Marois's vast wealth: 'For three days all the bars in Valognes were crowded at the expense of M. Le Marois, and the peasant electors who had come to vote for me were led to the voting-station half-drunk with cries of *"Point de nobles!"*'* But he remained cheerful. He did not like the look of the new Chamber and was glad not to be part of it. Beaumont too had lost. Tocqueville tried to make him share his own serene reaction. 'I can't tell you with what joy and ardour I shall throw myself again into my studies ... and the future belongs to us, believe me. I have never been more certain of it.' We have seen that he was as good as his word, and Beaumont was equally ready to go back to his desk: 1838 was to be the year of books.[53]

Tocqueville's political optimism was to be vindicated much more rapidly than he expected. In retrospect, 1837 looks like the high point of the July Monarchy. Since 1830 Louis-Philippe's regime had in turn seen off challenges by legitimists, republicans, insurrectionary workers and, in December 1836, an attempted military *coup* by Louis Napoleon Bonaparte (which had partly inspired the pages on military conspiracies in the second *Démocratie*). It had re-established France as a leading

---

* 'No nobles at any price!'

member of the Concert of Europe. True, there was a global economic crisis, affecting Europe, America and China, but it does not seem to have affected the French political situation. The duc d'Orléans had married amid general rejoicing, and Molé's premiership had survived Guizot's defection. It had seemed sensible to the prime minister to call a general election to capitalize, he hoped, on public support by increasing the number of his followers in the Chamber, and by this device Molé did indeed weaken Guizot, though not so much as he had wanted. His victory, however modest, drew a line under the first phase of the July Monarchy, which had shown itself to be stronger than its opponents, and began to wear an air of permanence.

But things did not continue to go so well. If the regime was permanent then ambitious politicians would necessarily seek to dominate it (since they did not expect or want to see it replaced) and they could now, they thought, safely and without much scruple fight each other for power. Molé, personally, was not invulnerable. He could expect no help from the legitimists or the republicans or from the leading men in the Chamber who wanted to replace him. His colleagues were not capable enough to be much help, and the body of his supporters was never quite large or reliable enough to see him through all parliamentary difficulties. With the King's support he was safe enough as long as the opposition was divided, but during 1838 its leaders decided to swallow their personal and ideological differences and unite for the sole purpose of throwing Molé out. Guizot, Thiers and Odilon Barrot formed what was soon notorious as 'the coalition', and their relentless pressure began to wear the government down. Tocqueville and Beaumont, looking up from their desks, were disgusted. 'All I can say is that the enemies of the ministry will end by making me one of its partisans, if it lasts,' said Tocqueville. Such goings-on made him wonder if there was anything in the political world but selfishness 'and if what one takes for beliefs and ideas are any more than walking and talking interests.' He was particularly disgusted by the humbug of the doctrinaires, and his only consolation was Plutarch, 'indiscreet and gossipy', whom he was reading for relaxation, and who showed that things had been no better in antiquity.[54] Anyway, he was unable to affect the situation. At length, after a twelve-day debate on the Address to the Throne in which Molé, as admitted by Guizot in his memoirs, performed prodigies of courage, eloquence and intelligence at the tribune,[55] it became clear that matters could not go on in this way: the ministry's majority was barely in double figures.* Molé decided to go to the country again, and in February 1839 there was a new election.

By this time the opposition had developed a cry, specious but effective, as such things are. What was at stake, they declared, was nothing less than the authority of the Chamber. Molé and Montalivet were merely the King's creatures. They must be ousted, and replaced by patriotic statesmen who owed their power to the Chamber. 'The King rules but does not govern' was their slogan, invented, it was said, by Thiers.[56]

Tocqueville swallowed this claptrap, which shows his relative inexperience; but comments he made suggest a certain scepticism. 'Metaphysical questions about royal and parliamentary prerogatives are of no interest to anyone here that I know of. And I admit to you in a whisper that they don't much interest me either. I see successful or thwarted ambitions making war, but as for principles or even real, powerful political passions, I see absolutely none.'[57] The electors had earthier issues in mind, and the election in Valognes was a repetition of that of 1837, with the important difference that Le Marois, who had double-crossed the government, no longer had its support. Montalivet was out for his blood, with the result that, of all the sitting deputies from the Manche, Le Marois was the only one not re-elected. And Tocqueville was a much stronger candidate than he had been the time before. He was now established and accepted as a permanent resident of his district (it seems to have been about this time that he bought a property in Valognes);[58] far more voters knew him personally; his national distinction left Le Marois nowhere. His election address and circulars were forcefully eloquent; he deserved to win, and did so with 317 votes to 241 for Le Marois.

Election day was Sunday, 2 March. When the result was declared a large crowd insisted on escorting Tocqueville to his inn, the Hôtel du

---

* Parliamentary governments can survive on less, but the lack of institutionalized discipline under the July Monarchy – a whipping-in system – meant that Molé, with such a reduced majority, could never be sure of carrying anything – an intolerable state of affairs for any head of government.

Louvre, cheering all the way. Once there, he addressed them suitably from the balcony, mentioning his gratitude, his patriotism, his independence of the government and of all parties. Finally:

> I am the deputy of the whole *arrondissement* and of all those who live here. Whenever, therefore, one of you has a just request on behalf of a commune or a canton, he may confidently turn to me. Elector or non-elector, someone who has voted for me or against me – he can be sure of my energetic support. I have never doubted that those who today denied me their suffrage were guided in that only by conscience, and I approve all that conscience dictates. I will take away a mind full of remembrance of my friends, but from today, I am happy to state, I have forgotten the names of all my honourable opponents.[59]

Such was the spirit in which he began his parliamentary career. The outlook seemed bright. The only cloud was that *De la démocratie en Amérique* was still unfinished.

CHAPTER FIFTEEN

WRITING DEMOCRACY
1839–1840

Tocqueville m'a tout l'air de s'attacher à la démocratie comme Pascal à la croix: en enrageant. C'est bien pour le talent qui n'est qu'une belle lutte; mais pour la vérité et la plenitude des convictions, cela donne à penser.*

SAINTE-BEUVE, 'NOTES ET PENSÉES'[1]

THE JOY OF VICTORY was swiftly followed by a reaction. It may be remembered that Tocqueville had already been unwell when the election campaign began. Now he collapsed, and retired for a few days to his chateau, where his wife nursed him through a sharp illness: 'I think I would be dead already without Marie's physical and moral support,' he wrote to Édouard. 'I must admit to you that in that aspect my future looks black. I am not sure of the first condition of success, that is, staying alive.' He told Eugène Stoffels, 'I have to acknowledge that I no longer have at my command that iron constitution [*corps de fer*] which you knew in me of old, and which lent itself so readily to all my passions, and to the greatest strivings of my soul.' Matters were not helped by the exhausting flood of letters and visits of congratulation which poured in after his election victory, or by the awful news that

---

* 'To me, Tocqueville has every appearance of devoting himself to democracy as Pascal did to the Cross: rabidly. That is all very well for talent, which is nothing but a noble battle, but when it is a question of truth and full conviction, a pinch of salt is necessary.'

Beaumont had been defeated at Saint-Calais (Sarthe); but a few days restored his vigour, and on 14 March he set off for Paris, by way of Valognes, in good spirits.[2]

It is doubtful if Tocqueville ever really had an iron constitution, whatever he told himself, although he certainly had great vitality, as his recovery from his winter illness in Tennessee demonstrated. His 'gastritis' might leave him alone for months, and then return so savagely as to prostrate him for days, and by the 1850s, according to Nassau Senior, digestion could be so painful to him that he often had to spend an hour suffering by himself after dinner. By 1848 or 1849 he had contracted tuberculosis, which in the end killed him. But even before that calamity he had good reason to worry about his health, and probably had ailments of which we know nothing. The bills for medicines sent in to his address grew steadily longer and more frequent.[3]

Nevertheless, his *début* in the Chamber was highly successful. He fretted beforehand, in characteristic fashion, as to where he should sit: in the eyes of his constituents, he told Corcelle, 'the place where one plants one's behind is of the first importance.'[4] But by the time the new Chamber met, on 4 April, he was safe where he wanted to be, among the deputies of what was called the Centre-Left. The political situation was extremely confused. Molé had lost fifteen supporters, and resigned on 8 March, but no stable ministry could be found to replace him. He remained in place until early April, when he was at last superseded by an avowedly interim cabinet, and then in May by Marshal Soult, who became both prime minister and foreign minister. No-one expected him to last long. He was only brought to power by the need to reassure the citizens after Auguste Blanqui and Armand Barbès staged an unsuccessful insurrection in the streets of Paris. The National Guard had been called out, and Tocqueville served unremarkably in its ranks. But apart from that episode he was not much concerned, this session, with the fate of governments. His chief business, once he had found his way around, was with slavery. He made a fiery speech at the Académie des Sciences Morales et Politiques in which he established himself as an abolitionist, and when the Chamber set up a committee to investigate the subject he was made its *rapporteur*. He worked at his report throughout the summer; it was published in the autumn. He was rightly proud of it. It exhibits many of his most characteristic virtues: it was based on thorough research (Senior sent over several volumes of British parliamentary papers on the theme), eloquently written but coolly argued, and advocated that all slaves should be promptly and simultaneously emancipated in the French Empire. He distributed many copies among his friends.[5] He also made his first speech in the Chamber. A great international crisis was brewing, over the affairs of the eastern Mediterranean, and Tocqueville mounted the tribune to insist that France must take a leading part in any settlement, and that the government must see to it. He was gratified to find that he had made a success, though he was a cold orator. Chateaubriand sent him a letter of congratulations.[6]

He had begun well, but he was not enjoying himself. That autumn he wrote to Corcelle that he regretted being a deputy; he couldn't imagine why he had so longed to be elected; he could do no good. He despised party politics, the politics of low ambition, vulgar camaraderie and envy; revolution would be better than that. Were they never again to see the winds of true political passion arise, when politics might be violent and cruel but would nevertheless be great? He would never, he said, get used to the present state of affairs; never. At the end of the session, in late July, he was glad to escape to Tocqueville and his long-neglected book.[7]

This and other utterances of his parliamentary years show that Tocqueville entered politics with some thoroughly Romantic notions: he had been more influenced by the epic story of the Revolution and Napoleon than he would have liked to admit. (It is hard to believe that in sober mood he would ever have said that he yearned for revolution.) It was immature, but it would not have been dangerous but for the fact that many other Frenchmen had the same attitude. During the last crisis of the Molé ministry Lamartine had proclaimed to the Chamber that '*La France est une nation qui s'ennuie,*' and the *ennui* of peoples, he warned, could easily lead to chaos and ruin. By *ennui* Lamartine meant not only disappointment with the domestic timidity of the July regime, which, whether administratively or legislatively, always ended up by doing less than it might and much less than it should, but restlessness about France's reduced position in Europe. 'You must not believe, gentlemen, that because we are weary of the great upheavals which have rocked the century and ourselves, others too are weary and fear the slightest change. The generations which are rising up round us are not weary; it is their turn to demand action.' All this is strikingly like Tocqueville, and it excited citizens throughout France. Much of the bitter future was foreshadowed in Lamartine's words, and we may think that he and his hearers were deceiving themselves: France was not nearly so eager for a new struggle as they thought; but for the time being such attitudinizing seemed both appealing and sensible.[8]

Summer at Tocqueville, in spite of the everlasting building work, was as agreeable as always. The only disturbance was a terrible thunderstorm on the night of 26 August. Thunder shook the walls of the chateau, lightning flashed round the bedrooms and left behind a strong, unpleasant smell of sulphur; casements were smashed and hundreds of slates on the roof thrown down, but no irreparable damage was done. Tocqueville's chief reaction was pride in Marie's calm courage: 'she was like a very Caesar. There were two or three other women in the house who were unfortunately unable to follow her noble example, and deafened us with their clamour long after all danger was past.'[*] This apart, life was tranquil, and Tocqueville turned with pleasure to revising his slavery report and to putting the finishing touches to the *Démocratie*. J.-J. Ampère, whom Tocqueville had begun to get to know very well and greatly liked, came to stay in September and gave his counsel.[†] Tocqueville ploughed ahead speedily, and on 2 November again reported that he had written the last words. Ten days later he was in Paris, and for the next few months his life was dominated by the business of getting the book into print. Except for an incessant trickle of constituency business his correspondence dwindled almost to nothing, although he was in close touch with Henry Reeve about the English translation, which they contrived should be published simultaneously with the French original, which appeared at last on 24 April 1840.

For months Tocqueville had been fretting about the book's

---

[*] A Plutarchian allusion. When once Caesar tried to put to sea in a fierce storm the captain panicked, but Caesar reassured him: 'Fear nothing. You carry Caesar and his good luck.' (The ship put back to port all the same.)

[†] Jean-Jacques Ampère (1800–1864), son of the great physicist; professor of literature at the Collège de France; the devoted friend of Mme Récamier.

reception, which had earned him a scolding from Royer-Collard: 'You worry too much about success; you will never do anything great and liberating if you always have one eye on the press. You work for the future and, I hope, for posterity. That alone should concern you.'[10] Tocqueville no doubt saw the sense of this, as well as the huge compliment, but he was incapable of taking the advice. 'It's a serious business,' he told Beaumont. '... Although I have so far gone only waist-deep into politics, it's been enough to make enemies of some newspapers which, allied to literary jealousies and the faults of the work, could do me a bad turn.' He was afraid that although the book gained power from being devoted to a single theme, it might also seem monotonous and boring. He worried that Reeve's translation might give him too conservative a colouring, as the translation of the 1835 volumes had done: the criticisms he made of democracy were those of a friend, not a critic: 'it is necessary that your translation preserve that characteristic.' He summed up the whole matter in advance to John Mill, whose approval he was particularly anxious to earn: 'You will bear in mind, while reading the book, that it is written in a country and for a country where, equality having triumphed irreversibly and aristocracy having disappeared entirely, the main task from now on will be to fight the pernicious tendencies of the new order, not to bring that order about. So I often speak hard truths to the new society in America or France, but I speak them as a friend ... In this country equality has all sorts of flatterers, but scarcely any staunch and honest counsellors.' He was somewhat reassured when Reeve, having worked his way through half the proofs, wrote to express his admiration: 'I was particularly impressed by the chapters on the sources of Poetry, the joylessness of democratic peoples, and the one on public works ... you have written the Book of the People for France, as Machiavelli wrote the Book of the Prince for Caesar Borgia.' He was gratified to be one of the first readers.[11]

Yet Tocqueville's anxiety was not unreasonable. The work which he had undertaken was the most ambitious that he ever attempted. He had said from the first that the 1835 *Démocratie* was incomplete, focusing too exclusively on politics, laws and institutions (in this judgement he was surely too harsh). It needed a supplement, either by Gustave de Beaumont or by himself. In the event, each wrote one: Beaumont his

Marie (and, arguably, his *L'Irlande*); Tocqueville, his extension of the *Démocratie* into two further volumes. His subject, he told everybody, was the influence of equality on men's ideas and opinions;[12] indeed, on the whole of human life. It was an impossible task. He struggled with it for four years before achieving what he regarded as a publishable text, and even then the subject was not exhausted, though he was. Failure was inherent in his situation: he was attempting something huge, and altogether new. Not enough research had been done by anyone to supply him with arguments and information: he had to rely wholly on himself and on the comments of his friends. There being only one fully modern democracy in the world, whether one took the word politically or socially, it was difficult to decide what was universally true of the system, and what was merely American, as Tocqueville acknowledged. He tried to meet the point by reading and investigation, but as we have seen he got nothing out of Plato and Machiavelli (perhaps he smiled wryly at Reeve's compliment) or the Swiss constitution. The classical and modern authors that he read, or dipped into, were not much more helpful: Aristotle, Plutarch, Aquinas, Montaigne, Bacon, Descartes, Pascal, La Bruyère, Mme de Sévigné, Saint-Évremond, Montesquieu, Rousseau, Fontenelle, Massillon, Malesherbes, Guizot, Lacordaire, Mignet.[13] (It is an odd list, and some of its items were to be positively injurious to Tocqueville's thought.) He was, in fact, his own best authority, but the water in his well was running low: not much fresh material could be found in his American notebooks, though he still made good use of them from time to time, and of his English ones. It is even half true that he had nothing to say which he had not already put into the 1835 *Démocratie*: the 1840 *Démocratie*, in a sense, is simply a vast elaboration.' So failure was inevitable; but some failures are more valuable than many successes. It was not dishonourable to Tocqueville that he was a pioneer who occasionally lost his way in the forest, or that many others have since followed and improved the trail which he cut.

The 1840 *Démocratie* is much debated. Its merits, its defects and its applicability are, and have always been, the subject of fierce controversy.* But a biographer would endanger the success of his own work

---

* There has been lengthy discussion as to whether the two parts of *De la Démocratie en Amérique*

by entering far into the discussion. Any thorough critique of the book would be so long as to throw the biography out of shape, and might even compromise the entire undertaking. Yet the work was patently a great event in its writer's life, and must be registered as such. The trick is to read it, so far as may be, as autobiographical, and to eschew all other angles of approach. In such a reading even blemishes are valuable, because significant. For good or bad, Tocqueville put the whole of himself into this book. The biographer's task is to show how he did it, and to display him.

He wrote for fame, or at least that was one of his motives. Not that he planned a literary career: he despised the trade. But he meant to use renewed literary success to force his way into the Académie Française as well as the Chamber of Deputies, and to be heard respectfully in both. It was an achievement well within his grasp. He had matured as a writer since 1835. The second *Démocratie* was not to be an inspired hotch-potch like the first. As we have seen, the grand theme was to be analysed under four main headings, and each chapter was to have a logical place in the overall pattern. In practice, Tocqueville remained at the mercy of his method, which he described in several letters. 'It is my custom only to decide the plan and principal ideas, and then to follow the course of my thoughts, quickly or slowly, as they serve me,'[14] but he largely achieved his scheme. And his style was much easier, more like that of his letters than the careful prose of the 1835 *Démocratie*: he wrote personally, as if among friends.

The book was solidly constructed round the antithesis between a theoretical model of 'aristocratic' society and one of 'democracy'. In itself this was a reasonable device for conveying Tocqueville's thought, and it had precedents all the way back to Plato's *Republic*; but it also carried with it certain dangers that Tocqueville did not manage to avoid. It is doubtful that he saw them. Superficially this was because of the philosophical method he chose to employ. The fact that he looked into Francis Bacon suggests that he considered adopting an inductive method, but if so he will have had to conclude that it was impracticable, for lack of data – a problem which he tried

are separate works or not. My own view is that the second part is integrally dependent on the first, indeed is unintelligible without it, so that it ought certainly to be read as a continuation, not a sequel, let alone as an independent treatise.

to conceal from himself, perhaps, as well as his readers, by constant references to 'democratic nations' (meaning France and America) but which nevertheless dogged him throughout his work. He turned to Cartesian deduction instead, and stuck to it all too faithfully. (This decision partly explains a curiosity that has been too little noticed, the fact that the opening chapter is devoted to 'the Philosophical Method of the Americans', which according to Tocqueville was a sort of frontier Cartesianism.[15])It can be argued that since Tocqueville wanted to write about modern democracy and was short of evidence, he had no other choice if he wanted to be scientific rather than just journalistic, but even if so he made a fundamental mistake. Nothing in Descartes or anyone else makes it unnecessary or undesirable for a philosopher to test his deductions against such empirical evidence as he has, rather the contrary; but Tocqueville gives no sign that he has grasped this vital point. Instead he firmly states his premiss at the opening of every chapter – for example, in Book I, chapter XI: 'Democratic nations … will cultivate the arts which serve to make life comfortable, in preference to those which try to make it beautiful';[16] infers his way to one or more conclusions; and then, if he happens to think of a scrap of supporting information, adds it by way of decoration (here, a contrast between the aristocratic art of Raphael and the democratic art of Jacques-Louis David).[17] Taken overall, no procedure could be more unpersuasive, at least to the hostile or the sceptical. For instance, Tocqueville's grand theme in the last section of the book ('the Influence of Democratic Ideas and Feelings on Political Society') is that a democratic society may give rise to a benevolently tyrannical state which will gradually suck the energy and manhood out of its citizens. As an illustration of this tendency he fastens on working men's savings banks (which he had recently discussed in his unfinished 'second Memoir on Pauperism').[18] These were favourite devices among liberal theorists of the period who could not swallow socialism: to encourage saving in the working class was to do something to resist the ill-effects of unemployment and perhaps to buy off unrest. It was insufficient (not many workers could save anything out of their miserable wages) but it was something, and philanthropists took up the idea enthusiastically. But no private group could guarantee the depositors against the risk of losing everything; only the state could do that, so it did, and guaranteed the rate of interest too. This was too much for Tocqueville: here was a flagrant case of undue centralization and interference with the rights of private property and the sacred duty of self-reliance.[19] It did not occur to him that he was making himself ridiculous and undermining his larger argument, since indigence is more likely to sap energy and manhood than savings banks. Nor did he help himself by his shocked denunciation of democratic governments (i.e. the Orleanist regime) for borrowing money rather than supplying their needs by taxation, as happened, he said, in the good old aristocratic times. He should have remembered what brought about the summoning of the Estates-General in 1789, to give but one example.[20]

Methodologically, then, it is easy to fault Tocqueville. But to be content with such criticism would be to miss the deepest point. His problem was psychological as much as, or more than, it was philosophical. He explains himself in a document written in 1841 entitled 'My Instinct, My Opinions'.

> Experience has proved to me that almost all men, and I most assuredly, ultimately rely more or less on our fundamental instincts and that one does nothing well except in conformity to those instincts. So let me ask myself sincerely what are my *fundamental instincts* and my *serious principles*.
>
> I like democratic institutions with my head, but I am aristocratic by instinct, that is to say I despise and fear the mob.
>
> I passionately love liberty, legality, respect for rights, but not democracy. That is what I find in the depth of my soul.
>
> I do not belong to the revolutionary party, or to the conservative party. But, however, and after all, I support the latter more than the former. For I differ from the latter rather about means than about ends, while I differ from the former both about means and ends.
>
> Liberty is the first of my passions. There is the truth.[21]

Tocqueville was uncomfortable in the new era. His instincts collided with his ambition, and he could renounce neither. The 1840 *Démocratie* may be read as his attempt to think his way through to an ideological posture that would resolve his dilemma, which was as much a matter of the emotions as of the intellect. Undoubtedly he hoped to carry his readers with him, but his prime concern was to satisfy himself. In his book he would relieve his feelings, even at the expense of logic and consistency, and having done so would feel able to assert his final doctrine, even if it was not erected on philosophically solid foundations. This explains one of the book's most striking features: that for most of its course it denounces the weaknesses and dangers of democracy, only to end with splendid affirmation. It may have struck Tocqueville that he had gone too far in his tirades (his frequent insistence to his friends that he was also the friend of democracy was quite sincere), but essentially the pattern was dictated by his personal difficulty, as sketched in the 'Instinct and Opinions'. He desperately needed to have it both ways, for otherwise he would either have had to retire to the *bocage*, like his brothers, or sacrifice his sense that he was an honest man.

Almost all the theoretical peculiarities of the book can be explained in this way. Thus, if the problem with Tocqueville's model of 'democracy' was too little empirical evidence, the problem with 'aristocracy' was the reverse: European society had been dominated by aristocracies of various kinds throughout its history, and to elicit their common essence, if there was one, was difficult. But Tocqueville wrote as a Frenchman for Frenchmen: the only aristocracy he bothered with was that of his own country, and his reckless generalizations were derived exclusively from that specimen. The British nobility might have served as a corrective, but to Tocqueville's infatuated eyes it was simply an improved and luckier variant of the French model. Worse, he forgot his own warning in his article for John Stuart Mill, that the pre-revolutionary *noblesse* was far from homogeneous,* and wrote in the *Démocratie* as if it consisted entirely of feudal lords. The essence of the aristocratic centuries, he said, lay in hierarchy and stability: every man knew his place, every man fulfilled his duties, especially the nobility, and no-one contemplated or desired change of any kind. Democratic society was just the opposite, egalitarian and dynamic. Tocqueville succumbed to a danger that he had avoided in the 1835 *Démocratie*: he let himself drift into nostalgia for the lost world, most conspicuously, perhaps, when discussing aristocratic and democratic manners.† Aristocratic manners, he says, vanished at the Revolution, and their light

---

* See above p. 4.
† *Manières*, not *moeurs*. Cf. AT's conversation with Sedgwick, above, p. 256.

touch, their delicacy, have left no trace even in memory. 'We need not attach much importance to this loss, but I may be allowed to regret it.' For:

> If an aristocracy's manners emphatically did not lead to virtue, they sometimes ornamented it. It was emphatically no ordinary spectacle, a large and powerful class, of which all the conventions seemed to reveal at every moment natural loftiness of feelings and ideas, delicacy and decency of taste, urbanity of behaviour. Aristocratic manners induced beautiful illusions about human nature, and although the picture was often deceptive, there was a noble pleasure in looking at it.[22]

Tocqueville does not always give so wistful a picture of 'the aristocratic centuries': in spite of himself, he knew too much. So when, dipping into Mme de Sévigné's letters, he came across evidence of her callous and uncomprehending attitude to the lower orders (when some of them dared to riot against a stamp tax, she thought you could hardly hang too many), he quoted the documents in his book and went on to make intelligent speculations about the improvements in human sympathy that came with democracy.[23] But these insights are hardly sufficient compensation for the misleadingly rosy picture that he generally paints of the *noblesse* in its days of power, a picture which the slightest acquaintance with the historical record (to be found, for example, in Michelet, who was going to receive a presentation copy of Tocqueville's new book[24]) would prove to be false. Tocqueville was not yet systematically interested in that record, or in archives; he was not yet a historian; his aristocracy was as much a deduction from first principles as his democracy. He was so schematic that without intending it he sacrificed the historical vision which had been the mainspring of the 1835 *Démocratie*. His aristocratic society cannot change, by definition; he lays it alongside his conception of democracy, and except for frequent references to the will of God, and one perfunctory passage alluding to revolution,[25] he makes no attempt to show why or how the one condition gave way to the other. He becomes the prisoner of his definition, and by his deliberate blindness to the turbulence of European history in all epochs, other than the latest, makes sure that his concept of aristocracy is quite unreal, for the European nobilities

not only played a full part for good or bad in the process of historical change, they were themselves incessantly altered by it: the French
noblesse of 1789 was not the same as that of 1066. Just as bad, from a
historian's point of view, is Tocqueville's nearly complete elimination
of monarchy from his tableau. He never thinks to ask if the *noblesse*
had not, in large part, been the creation and tool of the monarchy in
every century; nor did he notice that the monarchy had been the chief
architect of centralization in France.*

He was equally imprisoned by his definition of democracy.

As has already been hinted, this term, as used by Tocqueville,
has always given his readers great difficulty.† Even when, in the 1840
Démocratie, he tried hard to be exact and consistent in his usage, he did
not always succeed. But on the whole he wrote as if it were synonym-
ous with equality, and not just a label for popular government. So he
felt free to describe any society where 'equality of status' was coming
to prevail as a democratic one. This in itself plunged him into difficulties: it is far from clear that the senses in which France and America
were democratic (egalitarian) in 1840 (he offers no other instances)
are equivalent. Worse still, he was so desperate for illustration that he
fell into the trap of assuming, indeed asserting, that equality is always
and everywhere the same thing, and when he was hammering home
his message that democracy could lead to a new kind of despotism he
produced the following:

> The Pasha who now reigns in Egypt‡ knows that his countrymen are
> all very ignorant and very equal, and so he has adopted, for their
> governance, the science and intelligence of Europe. The personal
> enlightenment of the sovereign being thus combined with the
> ignorance and *democratic weakness* [emphasis added] of his subjects
> the last degree of centralization has been achieved without difficulty,
> and the monarch has been able to turn his country into his factory and
> its inhabitants into his workmen.[26]

---

* This omission, at least, he made good sixteen years later, in the *Ancien Régime.*
† See p. 271, footnote. The best discussion of his usage may be found in Schleifer, 263–74; and
see Kergorlay's letter, above, p. 326.
‡ Mehemet Ali (1769–1849), much in the news as AT wrote because of his attempt to seize Syria
from the Ottoman Empire.

At which the reader must revolt, and exclaim, with Alice, 'a hill can't be a valley, you know.' In no way could the word 'democracy' be used accurately of Egypt in 1840; Tocqueville's usage shows that something has gone badly wrong with his thought.

His tendency to use the terms 'equality' and 'democracy' interchangeably was made worse by his inability to arrive, any more than he had with 'democracy', at a settled definition of 'equality'. (This difficulty had also arisen in the 1835 *Démocratie*.) When trying to sketch his Utopia, his idea of what the future might and should be like, he clearly envisaged equality in something like its fullest, most modern sense:

> great fortunes will disappear, the number of small ones will increase; desires and gratifications will alike multiply; there will be no more exceptional wealth or irremediable poverty ... Each individual will be weak and isolated while society as a whole will be active, forward-looking and powerful; private citizens will achieve only small things, the State, immensities.[27]

Yet elsewhere the equality which he envisages is clearly no more than the triumph of envy, the state of affairs that will result simply from the abolition of all noble privileges; it is the affair solely of the notables, who will and should continue to rule over the lower classes, by right of property and education, for the good of all. Equality of status, he asserts, is the ardent, insatiable, eternal, invincible passion of democratic nations: 'they will endure poverty, enslavement, barbarism, but they will not endure aristocracy' – by which he meant hereditary power and privilege.[28] To Tocqueville the most palpable trait of the democratic revolution, and its most dangerous achievement, was the abolition of the intermediate bodies (*parlements*, provincial estates, the *noblesse* itself) which, according to Montesquieu, defended the people against despotic kings. This myth, essentially a rationalization of the *régime* of privilege, had been dear to families of the *robe* ever since it was first propounded. Tocqueville in his nostalgic vein still professes to take this thesis seriously, but the shallowness of his commitment to it is shown by the fact that he completely fails to mention the Church in this connection, although Montesquieu explicitly identifies it as one of the most important of the intermediate bodies.[29] Tocqueville never showed any tenderness towards the interests and privileges of the First

Estate, and blamed the 1830 Revolution on its pretensions.[30] What matters is not his Romantic regret for a fancied feudal past, which he repeatedly acknowledged was gone for ever, but his interpretation of post-revolutionary history and politics; for on the accuracy of that would depend not only the fate of his book but success or failure in his political career.

After the 1848 Revolution he would for a time go much further towards republicanism, towards being something like a democrat in the modern sense, than he expected to previously. But the 1840 volumes are dominated by the conviction that democratic politics is the politics of envy and resentment. It is necessary to ask, not only whether Tocqueville was right or wrong in this belief, but why he held it.

He might have been disconcerted had he noticed how many of his countrymen were still firmly committed to inequality of status, attaching the noble *particule* to their names and masquerading as counts and marquises when they could get away with it.* Instead he was influenced by his experience as a candidate in the Manche, when he constantly had to refute allegations that he was nothing but an *aristo*, intent on restoring noble privileges. And indeed, hatred of the *ancien régime* and dread of its revival was to be a major theme in French politics for at least the next generation. To that extent, then, Tocqueville characterized 'democracy' correctly. But even in Orleanist France non-nobles were less preoccupied with the question of the 'aristocracy' than were the nobles (perhaps I should write 'the ex-nobles') themselves. Over time, anti-clericalism was to prove a far more persistent strain in French politics than anti-aristocratism, perhaps because the Church was a far more potent and durable force than the old nobility. It could be argued that this was simply another form of the war on privilege, but that was an argument which Tocqueville never made. Undoubtedly, equality was a cherished and well-understood value, but so was fraternity, and problems such as ill-health, unemployment and not getting enough to eat bulked even larger in the popular imagination (if

---

* The Republic has been established in France for over 130 years, but it is still possible, on payment of a fee and the production of proofs, to get the state to certify your noble status. The College of Arms in London is much less of an anomaly, Britain still being a monarchy, with, at the time of writing (2006), a parliamentary peerage.

the history of food riots is any guide). Nationalism, in various forms, was a central and dangerous passion (1840 was the year when the July Monarchy rashly sponsored the transfer of Napoleon's body from St Helena to the Invalides, thus stimulating the revival of Bonapartism). Above all, the value of liberty was not forgotten or unclaimed. Tocqueville himself was a passionate advocate: 'I would, I think, have loved liberty in any age; but I feel inclined to worship it in the age in which we actually live.'[31] It was the guiding star of his life; but in 1840 he seems to have understood it even less than he did equality. He never seriously asks what it might mean to anyone except people like himself. He seems to conceive of it as merely negative (*not*-dictatorship) and as existing when a man like himself can choose a political career and can read, say or do whatever he wishes. To some extent this works: Tocqueville on freedom of the press, for instance, is always excellent, and his anxiety about the over-mighty State was reasonable. However, he sees liberty as a precious but feeble thing, whereas, as a matter of historical fact, it is more potent than equality itself. His mistake was the one made, even more egregiously, by Isaiah Berlin in a famous discourse:[32] he understood liberty only as a proposition, an abstraction, at best as a legal arrangement: he did not consider it as a process with consequences, always important and sometimes unalterable (he did not follow up his observation, already quoted, that 'he who travels in the United States feels involuntarily and instinctively so convinced that the institutions, taste for and spirit of liberty are bound up with every custom of the American people that he can't conceive of any government for it except a republic').* Delacroix's energetic picture *Liberty Leading the People* is more profoundly wise than anything which Tocqueville wrote on the subject. Liberty can be, and often must be, destructive; but she clears the way for rebuilding, and what is built in liberty endures. This, as Tocqueville sometimes admitted, was what the French Revolution demonstrated, and it was to be proved again in the West in the twentieth century by such dramas as the defeat of fascism, the feminist movement, the civil rights revolution in the United States, and the collapse of communism. But Tocqueville was usually far too nervous of revolution to advocate anything like it.

* See above, p. 322.

This was no incidental weakness. The overpowering impression made by the 1840 *Démocratie* is of intense anxiety. Gone is the buoyancy which, in the first volumes, marked the discussion of painful or worrying topics. Behind the formal analysis in terms of aristocracy and democracy lies another painful dichotomy: between revolution and peaceable reform. In one of the most remarkable chapters in the whole *Démocratie* Tocqueville argues that great revolutions will become rare in democratic times because, equality having been achieved, there will be no need for them, and although men will have greater freedom to undertake radical change, they will desire it less because they will have more to lose; but for all its brilliance* the chapter seems to be the work of an author who is not quite convinced by his own arguments.[33] By now Tocqueville was finding it difficult to say anything good of democracy, as is shown by the two most important ideas put forward in the new volumes. The first was his theory of individualism, perhaps the most purely original notion that he ever formed. It is also one of the most triumphantly perverse, deriving, once more, from nostalgia for 'the aristocratic centuries'. In those happy times, according to Tocqueville, when families enjoyed the same status and lived in the same places for generations, men were equally loyal to their dead ancestors and to their unborn descendants: 'a man ... felt he could already perceive his great-grandsons, and he loved them.' Not so in democratic times, which beget individualism – in other words, the retreat from public life into privacy. Ceaselessly families 'rise from nothing' (a characteristic phrase) and revert to it, so their members have no interest in each other, except for their very nearest; the same is true of classes, which come to resemble each other and then merge. There is no longer any class solidarity. 'Aristocracy formed all citizens into one long chain, leading from the peasant to the king; democracy breaks the chain and leaves each link to fend for itself.'[34]

It would be nice to believe that in this passage Tocqueville is groping

---

* AT refers briefly to the oppressive weight of majority opinion in democratic societies, reminding his readers that he has dealt thoroughly with the subject elsewhere (i.e., in the 1835 *Démocratie*). He also takes the opportunity to point out that another revolution in the United States could only be produced by the racial problem, in other words not by equality but by inequality. It is a pity that he did not say this in 1835 (see OC I ii 263).

(as many modern commentators have suggested) towards a theory of the *anomie* or *cafard* which is often said to be characteristic of modern society; but it is plain that he is simply following another deductive will-o'-the-wisp, or indulging that snobbish prejudice against *bourgeois* society which was to be so constant a theme of advanced thought until the late twentieth century. He gives the game away two chapters later when he explains that the Americans successfully counter individualism by elections and party politics: 'When citizens are forced to concern themselves with public affairs they are of necessity drawn out of the world of private interests and periodically compelled to think of something besides themselves.' Taking part in free elections educates them in the reality and importance to them of general concerns, while someone who wants to become or to remain a representative must gain the respect of his fellow-citizens by taking their local concerns seriously – by 'a long succession of small services rendered, of discreet introductions, a constant practice of benevolence and a well-established reputation for disinterestedness'.[35] (It is easy to see what Tocqueville learned in his first years of parliamentary politics.) These observations are offered as a remedy for those evils painted in the chapter on individualism ('As for me, I hold that, in order to conquer the ills that equality can generate, there is only one effective cure: political liberty),[36] but they read more like a refutation. Besides, whatever may have been true of the aristocratic era, the democratic age has been deeply marked by solidarity: by political parties, trade unions, great business firms, proselytizing churches, and so on; and it could be shown that the history of the family has been much more complex than Tocqueville supposed, if it were necessary to discuss a theory which is so patently fanciful.

His other great idea was the threat of centralization and 'democratic despotism'. Centralization, as we have seen, was a concern that (as so often) he had picked up from others.* He made it one of his most particular concerns because he was the first to see that in a society (call it a democracy) where a popularly chosen government reigned supreme, centralization put such a mighty instrument in the government's hands that it might further the emergence and continuation of

---

* See above, p. 194.

a dictatorship – that 'rule of one man' against which Tocqueville had already sounded a warning in the 1835 *Démocratie,* and to which he was passionately opposed. The history of the twentieth century was to offer all too many proofs that he was right to be concerned, though he did not and could not foresee the precise events and mechanisms which were so horribly to vindicate his warnings. What had given him the idea was the course of the French Revolution, which had culminated in the Napoleonic dictatorship by way of the Jacobins. He also saw that the ascendancy of Paris and the instruments of Napoleonic government had not been affected by either the Restoration or the July Revolution: if anything, France was a more centralized country in 1840 than she had been in 1815. No doubt he was alarmed by the reviving cult of the Emperor, and by Louis Napoleon's second attempt at a *coup,* at Boulogne on 6 August 1840. Bonapartism was to lead, in just over ten years, to the establishment of exactly such a regime as Tocqueville feared – a striking though unwelcome demonstration of his prescience. Unfortunately neither the coming of Napoleon III nor that of the twentieth-century dictators validates what he actually said in his book or his mode of treating the topic.

During the past hundred years, he says, the monarchs of Europe have rebuilt their states so that all the powers and functions once shared with independent bodies are concentrated in their own hands. 'I am very far from condemning this concentration of powers; I merely draw attention to it.'[37] This sentence is worth registering because it is the only point in the whole of the 1840 *Démocratie* at which Tocqueville concedes, to the slightest degree, that there may be some necessity for centralization; elsewhere, and at great length, he assumes that it is simply an evil, and tries to demonstrate its deplorable causes and consequences. Once more he states what seems to him self-evident and makes dramatic inferences, rather than engaging in serious investigation of his topic. He has noticed one of the greatest phenomena of his age, the rise of the modern state, but instead of discussing seriously how it was coming about, to what extent it was necessary, and how it could best be organized and controlled, he bundles the whole subject up under the label 'centralization' and sets out to give his readers a fright. This enterprise does not even have the merit of originality: he had said much the same in 1835, and as has already been pointed out,* decentralization at this date was a shibboleth of the legitimists. Tocqueville's fulminations are not essentially different from those of any other member of his order.

Much the same must be said of the 1840 *Démocratie* as a whole. Tocqueville had told Stoffels that he was a new kind of liberal; on the evidence of his book he might as accurately be described as a new kind of legitimist. He had drifted a long way, perhaps without quite realizing it, from the pro-democratic stance and what he hoped was the scientific impartiality of the 1835 volumes.

That he became uneasily aware of this is shown by the last pages of his book and by the 'Avertissement' or preface that he wrote for its beginning, as he had written the 'Introduction' for the 1835 work, at the last moment. The 'Avertissement' is one of those 'not guilty' pleas which read like confessions. Tocqueville does *not*, he says, consider equality to be the sole cause of everything in the modern world. After listing some other factors, especially those concerning the United States (he could very well have referred his readers to the first *Démocratie*) he goes on:

> I recognize the existence of all these different causes and their power, but my business is not, emphatically, to discuss them. I have not undertaken to show the reason for all our inclinations and ideas; I have only wanted to show how equality has modified them.[38]

He again asserts that the democratic revolution is an irresistible fact against which it would be futile to struggle; that being so, his readers may think it strange that he is so severely critical of the societies which the revolution has brought into being. He answers in the terms of his letters to Reeve and Mill: 'I reply simply that it is because I am emphatically not an opponent of democracy that I have wanted to treat it sincerely. Men never take the truth from their enemies, and their friends seldom give it to them; that is why I have told it.' Few others have done so, or pointed out the looming dangers. Having clearly discerned them, or so he thinks, 'I have not been so cowardly as to keep silent.'

This is surely Philip sober trying to extenuate Philip drunk. Even

---

* See above, p. 268.

the magnificent closing pages of the 1840 *Démocratie* cannot take away the impression made by the rest of the book, which is that despite frequent brilliant flashes of insight and common sense, this is the work of a man who regards the egalitarian phantom which he has conjured up with deep hostility and dread, and wants to rally his caste to control if not defeat it. There is not much difference between this position and that of the parliamentary legitimists who followed Berryer: the only crucial point is that Tocqueville is a legitimist who does not support the Bourbons (he assumed that they were finished), just as he was a Catholic who did not believe in the Church.

What is so curious, biographically, is Tocqueville's inconsistency. The disavowals in the 'Avertissement' were perfectly sincere, and he never disavowed the 1835 *Démocratie* (which itself pointed both ways). It is necessary to try to explain the phenomenon.

It would probably be wrong to blame the company he kept while writing the book. The friend whom he most regularly consulted was Kergorlay, a fervent legitimist; but as we have seen, Tocqueville only took his advice when it suited him, and found him most useful as an auditor on whom he could test the logic and clarity of his ideas.[39, 40] Much the same was true of Beaumont and of Édouard, in whose house so much of the writing was done (and it seems that what Tocqueville wanted most from his advisers was praise and encouragement). It does seem clear from the book itself that Tocqueville expected his readership to consist chiefly of people like himself: public-spirited country gentlemen, for the most part. With such an expectation, it was unlikely that he would criticize his or their presuppositions very searchingly, and nor did he; but much the same might be said of the 1835 *Démocratie*, though that he clearly hoped would be read by liberals of all stripes – even republicans – not to mention Americans.

The truth, I suggest, is simply that the 1840 *Démocratie* was above all a highly personal book. The idea which it conveys most forcibly is that of the writer alone in his eyrie wrestling with his ideas. 'I investigated elsewhere in this work the causes to which one must ascribe the strength of American political institutions. ... Today, as I concern myself with individuals ...' Today! For a moment we catch a glimpse of Tocqueville in the tower-room, settling down to work after breakfast. Much further on, as he tries to ram home the point that nowadays government is getting steadily, dangerously stronger, he writes: 'I attach so much importance to everything that I have just said that I am tormented by the fear of having weakened my argument in trying to make it clear.' Not for Tocqueville any attempt at a sham-objective, 'scientific' prose. He writes as a man speaking to men.[41]

Nor is it solely a question of style. There are more ways than one of being persuasive and eloquent; Tocqueville chooses to write personally because his ideas are themselves personal. One of the first topics which he tackles in Book One, 'The Influence of Democracy on the Life of the Mind in the United States,' is religion. Misled by his method, he makes several mistakes, declaring, for example, that no new religion can arise in democratic society because the citizens will laugh at new prophetic claims (he had not heard of Joseph Smith); but it is not his method which will strike the reader as determining his views. Rather, he seems to fear that in the democratic age his own religious beliefs will be threatened. This he cannot tolerate. 'For my part, I doubt that mankind can ever simultaneously endure complete religious independence and entire political liberty.'[42] Briefly abandoning Cartesianism (and, arguably, thereby contradicting the argument of his first chapter), he asserts that men cannot resolve all their difficulties by going back to first principles every time, so there must always be doctrines laid down as dogmas, and it is preferable that they refer to God rather than to politics, for religious doubt is bound to enervate the soul and weaken the will, thereby preparing citizens for slavery, whereas a reasonable dogmatic religion, even if it cannot guarantee salvation in the next life, will at least be very useful for human happiness and greatness in this one (has he been overdosing on Pascal?) And what should a reasonable religion teach? Why, monotheism, the immortality of the soul and the duty of loving your neighbour. All other religious doctrines, whether the political and legal maxims of the Koran, or the cult of the saints in medieval Christianity, are firmly rejected as unwise and inessential.[43]

It will be seen that very few readers at any time, whether believers or unbelievers, could be satisfied with these teachings, especially as Tocqueville does not make the slightest effort to back them up with evidence. But it was psychologically necessary for Tocqueville himself to maintain them, so he shovels them into his book on democracy. These passages are important because they illustrate the firmly theistic basis of his thought. As a historian or social scientist he usually relied on purely secular analysis and explanation, but when it came to values religion was indispensable. It was part of the foundation of his being, laid down in childhood, even though he had had to jettison so many of the Abbé Le Sueur's teachings. Unfortunately, as we have seen, he was never able to transcend the cultural limitations of his cradle Catholicism. He follows up his chapter on religion and democracy with one on the progress of Catholicism in the United States in which, among other blunders, he fails even to mention Irish migration to America, and another on 'What Draws the Souls of Democratic Peoples towards Pantheism' (by which he apparently meant unitarianism) in which Cartesianism runs amok and a subtle explanation is found for a non-existent phenomenon. He concludes the one chapter with the thought that, because of democracy, 'our descendants will tend more and more to take one of two courses, either by falling away entirely from Christianity, or entering the Roman Church,' and the other by calling all those who still believe in the true greatness of Man to do battle against pantheism.[44] Tocqueville remained unable to sympathize with Protestantism or to sense its continuing vitality. To have done either would have entailed a relativist recognition of the limitations of his own creed which he was far too anxious a soul to dare.

The sense that his book is shaped as much by personal neurosis as by logic and observation becomes overwhelming when we scrutinize his pages on the democratic family.

To assess, fairly, Tocqueville's disquisitions on this subject, it is necessary to understand the world in which he lived and thought, and that is far from easy. The revolutionary era changed the relations between men, women and children, but it is difficult to say to what extent (here is a particular aspect of that debate about continuity and innovation which was to mark so much of Tocqueville's thought). Theodore Zeldin's learned and subtle exploration of the topic leaves the impression that progress, or change of any kind, was glacially slow in coming to family life in France between 1789 and 1945; and the evidence he cites gives the gloomiest idea of French manners in this respect.* Common sense insists that since the French were not conspicuously less successful than other nations in their marriages, liaisons and domestic life generally, his evidence must be flawed. Probably it is, but the weight of his argument cannot be dismissed. It is clear that conventional French opinion on such matters as marriage, sex, children and women was, by modern standards, lamentably unimaginative and probably changed minimally as a result of the Revolution. Tocqueville's views are best studied in the light of this observation. For the most part they were sadly commonplace; that they went beyond the customary in any respect can be attributed to the way he was brought up and, even more, to his experience of America. It is not surprising that when writing of so vastly important a part of human life he gave himself away completely – more completely than in anything else that he published. So would we all, if we were as honest as he was.

His discussion begins with a last return of his *idée fixe* about the laws of inheritance. He has by now completely revised his first assertions. 'So far the Americans have emphatically not dreamed of doing what we have done in France, that is, stripping from fathers one of the principal elements of their power by preventing them from disposing of their goods as they wish after their death. In the United States the testator's right is limitless.'[45] He explains the difference by Napoleon: 'The author of our civil legislation was a man who thought it in his interest to satisfy the democratic passions of his contemporaries in everything that was not directly and immediately hostile to his power.' What is surprising about Tocqueville's attitude to this state of affairs is that now he seems to endorse it. He still thinks that the new laws of inheritance have democratized society, but he approves the result. He paints the prettiest picture of the old order, in which the father had absolute power over his sons, and the eldest son had the right of primogeniture, which he always exercised benevolently in the interests of his family and his younger brothers; but there was always an element of fear in the relations between a father and his sons. Not so in democratic times: the father having lost the power to disinherit his sons

---

* The caution he gives should always be borne in mind: 'the history of domestic relations cannot be written in the same way as the history of international relations and any description of them must be tentative and incomplete' (T. Zeldin, *France 1848–1945*, Oxford, 1973, I, 285).

a sort of equality reigns over the domestic hearth ... In my opinion, as manners and laws grow more democratic the relations between father and son grow more gentle and intimate; rule, authority, appear less often; confidence and affection are often greater, and it seems that the natural bond strengthens as the social tie weakens.

The same is true of brothers: as they no longer need quarrel over the family inheritance they can remain as good friends for life as they were in their childhood. This new model family is so attractive that even conservatives adopt it. 'I have known furious enemies of democracy who allow their children to use the *tutoyer* to them.'[46]

It is surely impossible to read this chapter without thinking of Hervé, Hippolyte, Édouard and Alexis, which provokes two further observations: that Alexis writes as if there were never any women in a family, and that possibly the softening of family relations which he describes was for the Tocquevilles, and perhaps therefore others, less the consequence of revolution than of a particular family tradition: we may remember Chateaubriand's description of Malesherbes *en famille*; or perhaps it reflected the influence of Rousseau: we may remember Bernard de Tocqueville's library.

Alexis by now was more than halfway through his book, and may suddenly have noticed that he had yet to mention half the human race. At any rate his next four chapters all concerned themselves with women. The first, 'On the Education of Girls in the United States', begins with the resounding affirmation that 'There has never been a free society without morals [*moeurs*], and as I said in the first part of this book, morality is Woman's work. Everything which influences women's status, their habits and their opinions, is therefore of great political interest to me.'[47] It hardly needs repeating that Tocqueville had a great interest in the subject of women's education, and strong views. Like many other European visitors to nineteenth-century America he was fascinated by the energy and independence of the young women he met:

> I was often surprised and almost frightened by the sight of the strange dexterity and happy boldness with which American girls knew how to steer their thoughts and words through warm conversation; one

of our philosophers would have stumbled a hundred times on the narrow way which they ran over without mischance or difficulty.

What he meant by this was that these young Americans had none of the prudery and ignorance of well-brought-up French girls, who were shut up for their schooling in convents ('as in the aristocratic era') and were then left to fend for themselves when they entered the world. The Americans had the better system (he put it down to Protestantism). Since danger was inevitable, they thought it best to teach their daughters how to look after themselves. This was not without drawbacks in Tocqueville's opinion: it made women virtuous but cold, rather than tender wives and amiable companions for men. But it was a price worth paying: 'a democratic education is necessary to protect women from the dangers with which democratic institutions and manners surround them.'[48]

Acute readers may already have found something to frown over, and the impression is confirmed in the next three chapters. It emerges that the only point which concerns Tocqueville in the education of women is the need to keep them virgins until they marry and to stop them from committing adultery afterwards. He explicitly attacks 'European' theorists (he meant the Saint-Simonians) who, 'muddling the distinct attributes of the sexes', want to give women the same functions, rights and duties as men: 'It is easy to see that in thus striving to equal the sexes one degrades them both; and that nothing could ever come of such a gross confusion of Nature's work but weak men and unchaste women.'[49] He wastes no time on such notions (and is evidently unaware of the extent to which they were gaining ground both in Britain and America). His business is to use the example of American women to recommend democracy, and the manners of democracy to criticize traditional marriage in France. He had an axe to grind.

Aristocratic marriage, he says, is often a matter of uniting fortunes rather than individuals, 'so it sometimes happens that the groom is brought to it as a schoolboy, the bride being still at nurse.' It is inevitable that in such unions the spouses feel free to look elsewhere for love – 'that follows naturally from the nature of the contract.'[50] A further difficulty is the insistence on marrying only in your own order – misalliances are forbidden. This too leads to adultery – 'in this way Nature compensates secretly for the restrictions imposed by law.'[51] How differently things are done in democratic America! There, young women, educated into solid intelligence and manly habits (*sic*), voluntarily take on the yoke of a marriage which, as described by Tocqueville, sounds more like a prison ('inexorable public opinion in the United States takes care to shut women up in the narrow circle of their domestic duties and forbids them to leave it').[52] This puzzles Tocqueville, as well it might, but he explains it by the fact that there are no class obstacles to stop a woman marrying any man who asks her. She can choose freely, and usually does so only when the strength of mind which her education has given her has ripened with experience: 'there are hardly any early marriages.' Her reason tells her that she must sacrifice her self-will entirely to marital necessity: 'for a woman the springs of happiness lie only in the conjugal home.' This reasoned firmness of character makes her an excellent helpmeet. Tocqueville had been particularly impressed by young wives on the frontier: 'Fever, loneliness, boredom never broke their courage … they seemed simultaneously sad and resolute.'[53] To drive the point home he printed an excerpt from 'Quinze jours dans le désert' as an appendix, and remarked that there was almost no adultery in America – so little that it was not considered an interesting subject for fiction, so there were very few American novels.[54]

There is a great deal more of this kind of thing, but it is needless to give further specimens of these effusions of nineteenth-century male ideology. What is important is to understand why Tocqueville put them in his book. He was vindicating his decision to marry Marie. His view of marriage and the family is an advance inasmuch as he explicitly champions marriages of affection against the cold arranged marriages of the aristocratic past. The advance was limited: 'equality of status will never make men chaste,' he says, and at times he comes perilously close to Proudhon's remark that women can only be house-wives or prostitutes: democracy, he says, by putting an end to philan-dering and idle seduction, will increase the number of prostitutes as well as of chaste wives: 'In the eyes of a lawmaker, prostitution is much less fearsome than *galanterie*' – by which he meant Don Giovan-ni's hobby; in this, as in other aspects of the matter, he is positively Victorian, as André Jardin remarked.[55] What can Marie de Tocqueville have thought of these passages, which give men enormous sexual licence, and women none? (At least she would not be able to say that she hadn't been warned.) But we must not lose sight of the point that, taken together, the passages praising the new laws of inheritance and marriages of affection, which are not afraid of *mésalliance*, can bear only one meaning, at least to those who know the story of Alexis and Marie.

Once this is grasped it becomes obvious that much of the book is written with the same purpose: self-justification. Tocqueville remained a noble to his fingertips, but in the 1830s he had broken with the way of his world to what seemed, to him and to it, a shocking extent. He had taken the oath to Louis-Philippe, he had claimed his *patrimoine* under the Code Napoléon, he had married as unsuitably as possible and, worst of all, he had emerged as the prophet of a democratic future for France. And he wrote his new book at the very time that he was challenging both the legitimists and the regular Orleanists for one of the Norman parliamentary seats. So it came about that much of what he wrote can best be understood as a personal manifesto.

It was not easy for him. For much of the time, as we have seen, he let himself be carried away by nostalgia for the old days and by loyalty to his caste into almost hysterical anxiety about the new era. It is tempting to guess that he was partly moved by guilt about his mother: he started writing the new *Démocratie* almost as soon as she was dead, but it would be straining the evidence to say more than that. Nor does his poor physical health seem to be especially relevant to his performance. All that is clear is that in many respects he passionately disliked the new world into which he was being dragged, and yet he was determined to accept it, not merely because (as he thought) it was God's will, but because he agreed with God. Justice, he thought, was on the side of democracy, and therefore he would be too; although, as he so often asserted, all too correctly, he would be a candid friend, never hesitating to point out faults and dangers.

In the end he rose above all difficulties and inconsistencies and composed the last page of his book, one of the noblest things he ever wrote. It is Tocqueville at his best, both as a man and a thinker. It must be quoted in full:

Now that I have concluded my enterprise ... I am left full of fears and full of hope. I see great dangers, which can be averted; great evils which can be avoided or diminished, and I am more and more confirmed in the faith that to be virtuous and prosperous democratic nations only have to will it.

I am not ignorant that several of my contemporaries have decided that here below nations are never their own masters, and that of necessity they obey I know not what invincible and mindless power arising from previous events, or from their ancestry, or the soil, or the climate.

These are false and cowardly doctrines, which can only produce weak men and pusillanimous nations: Providence has created humanity neither entirely independent, nor wholly enslaved. In very truth, it draws round each man a circle of Fate from which he cannot escape; but within its vast area he is strong and free, and so it is with peoples.

The nations of our time cannot escape equality of status; but it depends on themselves whether that equality will lead them to slavery or liberty, to enlightenment or barbarism, to prosperity or to wretchedness.[56]

Thus, after years of painful thought, Tocqueville expressed the creed he meant to live by – and that indeed he did live by, until his death.

The second *Démocratie* was eagerly awaited by the cultivated public, and Gosselin printed a much larger edition than he had done of the first, though he was not wise enough to risk a cheap edition.[57] No doubt to his disappointment, and certainly to Tocqueville's, the book fell flat, and the edition was still not exhausted by 1848. There were various reasons for this mischance. For an author 1840 was an unlucky year: the real possibility of war with all Europe over the Eastern Question distracted the attention of readers, editors and reviewers. Nor, as Tocqueville was very well aware, was he a new star any longer: the surprise at his emergence had worn off. For that matter, America was no longer so popular with French opinion: there had been too much diplomatic friction since 1835, and first the panic of 1837 and then the depression of 1839 had markedly injured the French economy. But undoubtedly the chief cause lay in the book itself. Its virtues worked against it as much as its weaknesses (perhaps even more). If the public had had any particular expectations, it was of more about America;

instead they were confronted by a book which required them to think about democracy. Rossi, reviewing it in the *Revue des deux mondes*, remarked sardonically that 'Reading M. de Tocqueville's book is not something men of today are used to doing; it demands not merely eyes but also thought. It is no amusement, it is work.'[58] And the general political climate was no longer so sympathetic. The liberal consensus of 1835, to the degree that it had ever existed, was breaking up: opinion was moving either to the Right and a sort of sterile conservatism, or to the Left, where both republicanism and socialism were gaining ground. No longer did Tocqueville seem to be the man of the moment, or his concerns particularly urgent. It did not even help that his book was warmly welcomed in Britain; that country was no more popular than the United States in 1840s France. Tocqueville began to acquire among his countrymen that reputation of being a virtuous bore which was to be so damaging to him posthumously.

The reception of the 1840 *Démocratie* has been so admirably studied by Françoise Mélonio in her *Tocqueville et les Français* that it need not be explored at any length here; but three of the reviews must be glanced at for their importance to Tocqueville himself and to our understanding of him.

The first was unfavourable: Sylvestre de Sacy's article in the *Journal des débats*, which appeared somewhat belatedly on 9 October. The *Débats*, without being a government mouthpiece, was a particularly forceful supporter of the Orleanist settlement as it had evolved since 1830, and was hardly likely to welcome a book so full of apprehension and so anxious to see the further expansion of liberty and democratic institutions. Sacy, who knew Tocqueville, disliked having to criticize him, but did so nevertheless, using the *Démocratie* (which he does not seem to have understood) as a springboard for a vigorous defence of the constitutional monarchy as it was in 1840. Tocqueville was furious, and drafted a blistering letter to Sacy (which it is to be hoped that he sent). Sacy, he said, had missed the central point, '*la pensée mère de l'ouvrage*'.

> I noticed that in our time the new order of society which has produced, and still produces, great benefits, gives birth also to some alarming tendencies. These seedlings, if left to grow freely, seemed to me likely

to produce unending enfeeblement of the mind, sordid manners and, at last, universal slavery ... My object in writing my book was to exhibit the fearful possibilities which are opening before my contemporaries ... and thus to inspire those efforts of the heart and the will which alone can fight them, to teach democracy how to know itself and then to govern and direct itself.[59]

He was seldom so trenchant when calm. Here, in a couple of sentences, he expresses the central concern which drove his investigations (successfully or not) and explains why posterity has argued over them ever since. Few topics are of greater importance to modern humanity.

He had responded in very different fashion a week or two earlier, when J.-J. Ampère sent him the article he had just published in the *Revue de Paris*. It was a review in the form of an open letter to Tocqueville; it was favourable, and in verse. 'Forgive me,' said Ampère, 'I had no time to put it into prose.' His summer had indeed been wretchedly busy: he had had to wage a sustained campaign to win a valuable prize from the Académie des Inscriptions, he had put his brother-in-law in a madhouse and his sister in a home for the psychologically disturbed, and he had had to escort Mme Récamier into Germany, where she was going to visit a spa. Wherever he went the new *Démocratie* went with him, and scraps of verse gradually fused into a poem. For his response was the most imaginative of all: he understood that he was confronted with two myths, that of aristocracy and that of democracy. At one moment he found himself taking a steamboat journey up the Rhine:

I see upon its banks
Ruinous fortresses, to left and right,
So many that the hills bristle with towers
Clinging, it seems, to the black flanks of clouds.
Your book pursues me, I can't put it down,
And where could be a better place to read it?
Those ruins speak of ancient aristocracy,
And what, than steam, can better voice democracy?
Here I compare two ages of the world
Whose secrets yield to your all-piercing eye!
Old Europe stands above, upon the hills,
Colossal – crumbling; lofty – ruinous.
Another lies below: this very boat:
Prosaic, yes, but strong, and bold, and new!

How well he understood, he said, Tocqueville's melancholy contemplation of the Middle Ages, when lord and peasant were bound together in mutual obligations, and men worked, built or wrote for the long future. The olden days would have pleased him too, he said, if everyone could have been born a gentleman. But now was the day of Equality, the daughter of Time and Necessity, and Europeans were like the seabirds that had followed Tocqueville's ship across the Atlantic – lost, weary, battered by the winds; the vigilant pilot was Tocqueville himself, warning of storms. Then followed more than fifty lines, summing up Tocqueville's perceptions and his advice:

> To exorcize the evils of equality
> Cherish, you tell us, cherish liberty!

Ampère's eloquent simplifications swept away all the hesitations, contradictions and digressions of Tocqueville's treatise, and so made his thesis all the more comprehensible and persuasive. No wonder Tocqueville was delighted.[60]

He was gratified by all the praise of Ampère and other friends – Beaumont, Royer-Collard – whether given publicly or privately. But the views he most wanted were those of one Englishman. As soon as his book was published in Paris he sent a copy to John Stuart Mill via Guizot, who was now the French ambassador in London, and followed it up with a letter saying what he had done: 'Consider it as testimony of the great esteem and sincere affection I have for you.' Mill replied at once, saying that he had already bought and read the English translation, but 'I shall have the greatest pleasure in owing to your friendship a copy of the second part of your great work.' He was going to write on it for the October issue of the *Edinburgh Review*, but he did not keep Tocqueville waiting for the main points of his verdict:

> You have changed the face of political philosophy, you have carried
> on the discussions respecting the tendencies of modern society, the
> causes of those tendencies, & the influences of particular forms of
> polity & social order, into a region both of height & of depth which
> no one before you had entered, & all previous argumentation & specu-
> lation in such matters appears but child's play now.[61]

That was handsome, to say the least, but when the article appeared

Tocqueville found that Mill had gone even further: not only did he repeat his opinion of the book's importance ('the beginning of a new era in the scientific study of politics'), but he carefully wove into his assessment of the new volumes a reminder of the interest and value of the old. He also paid Tocqueville the compliment of occasionally disagreeing with him, most significantly when he argued that:

> M. de Tocqueville, then, has at least apparently, confounded the effects of Democracy with the effects of Civilization. He has bound up in one abstract idea the whole of the tendencies of modern commercial society, and given them one name – Democracy; thereby letting it be supposed that he ascribes to equality of conditions, several of the effects naturally arising from the mere progress of national prosperity.

(In slightly differing forms, this point was also made by many French critics, at the time and later, and as we have seen was even uneasily apprehended by Tocqueville himself.) Nevertheless we can see why Tocqueville, in his grateful acknowledgement, said that he was going to bind up the review with a copy of his work. 'Of all the articles written on my book, yours is the *only* one whose author has made himself completely master of my thought, and has known how to exhibit it to the public.' And indeed, Mill's incomparable lucidity of thought and expression sometimes enabled him to understand Tocqueville better than Tocqueville did himself, to state his positions more persuasively, and even, here and there, to foreshadow the future development of Tocqueville's ideas.[62]

Mill's essay was and is a work of first-rate importance, even more so in the story of his own thought than in that of Tocqueville's, and it cannot be fully discussed here. But three last points may be made.

First, Mill devoted much of his space to applying Tocquevillean thought to British society and politics, and by doing so finally established Tocqueville as a major influence on British liberalism.

Second, at various points in his review he displayed his own prophetic sensitivity to the onrush of current history in such a way as unconsciously to demonstrate that new issues were arising, new events impending, which already threatened to make the *Démocratie,* so deeply rooted in the Revolution of July, obsolescent. He was inclined to think that Tocqueville should have used the concept of class more systematically, and have acknowledged that the actual rise of the middle class and the imminent advance of most of the working class were two themes of enormous importance. Evil, he reflected, lay not in the domination of the middle class as such, but in the domination of any class whatever. 'Whenever any variety of human nature becomes preponderant in a community, it imposes upon all the rest of society its own type; forcing all, either to submit to it or to imitate it.' He also felt it necessary to assert that 'Economical and social changes, though among the greatest, are not the only forces which shape the course of our species; ideas are not always the mere signs and effects of social circumstances, they are themselves a power in history.'

Third, it is striking that both Mill and Ampère read Tocqueville in the way that he desired. It is a reading which it is easy to overlook in the proliferation of modern commentary, but it is essential. 'Cherish, you tell us, cherish liberty.' In spite of its sociological* aspirations and its anxious preoccupations, the *Démocratie*, throughout its four volumes, is a profoundly political work, the main thrust of which is to establish that equality had become inevitable and could be so ordered by liberty as to build justice. No-one who has studied Tocqueville can doubt that he made his case, or can fail, in spite of all reservations, to be influenced by it. Mill understood this more clearly than any other of Tocqueville's first readers; understood, therefore, that the book of which he had to give an account was a masterpiece and a classic; and so it still seems in the twenty-first century.

---

* In 1840 the word 'sociology' had only just been coined by Auguste Comte.

1. Alexis de Tocqueville (aged sixteen or seventeen) sits at the table behind his father, Hervé de Tocqueville, 1822.

2. Tocqueville's mother. The inscription reads, in translation: 'Portrait made in July 1794 in the Port-Libre prison by Madame de Maussion who was also held there.'

3. Miniature of Alexis as a youth; artist unknown; possibly made by the same painter at the same time as the portrait of Hervé de Tocqueville.

4. Mary ('Marie') Mottley, *c.* 1830.

5. During the first months of the journey through America
Gustave de Beaumont made many sketches, and worked up
some of them into finished pictures. This one catches very
exactly the look of Lake Oneida. The caption reads: 'View
of South Bay village on the shore of Lake Oneida (from
Frenchman's Island)'. The two top-hatted figures in the
foreground are perhaps meant to be Tocqueville and Beaumont.

6. Gustave de Beaumont, 'Departure of the Indians (the
Choctaw tribe) across the Mississippi supervised by the
United States government ...' dated 24 December 1831.

7. Sketch by Gustave de Beaumont of Alexis de Tocqueville, drawn when they set off for Saginaw on 23 July 1831. Beaumont seems to have planned to use the sketch as a basis for a painting. His notes are hard to read, but they tell us that Tocqueville was wearing a straw hat and grey jacket, riding a bay horse and carrying an Indian pipe.

8. Alexis de Tocqueville as a member of the National Assembly and the constitutional committee. This is the best-known likeness.

9. Théodore Chassériau's portrait of Tocqueville. Chassériau
was a friend whom Tocqueville helped to secure the
commission to paint a mural in the Cour des Comptes.

10. Caricature of Tocqueville as foreign minister by Honoré Daumier. The caption reads: 'Replacing M. Drouyn de Lhuys. May the pince-nez which he always carries in his hand make him see clearly in foreign affairs.'

11. Gustave de Beaumont in ambassadorial dress, 1849.

12. Photograph of the north front of the Château de Toqueville in Alexis's time.

13. Villa Montfleury, Cannes, in 1859, by Gustave de Beaumont.

BOOK TWO

Monsieur de Tocqueville

CHAPTER SIXTEEN

DEPUTY

1839–1847

Que diable allait-il faire dans cette galère?
MOLIÈRE, LES FOURBERIES DE SCAPIN

TALKING TO NASSAU SENIOR in the spring of 1848, a few weeks after the February Revolution, Gustave de Beaumont had his own explanation for that catastrophe. The constitutional monarchy, he thought, had been too British for the French. 'In France we are not good balancers of inconveniences. *Nous sommes trop logiques*. As soon as we see the faults of an institution, *nous la brisons*. In England you calculate; we act on impulse ... Unless we greatly improve, we never shall have any permanent institutions; for as we destroy every institution as soon as we discover its faults, and no one is free from them, nothing can last.'[1] No doubt there was something to be said for this view, but it was hindsight. Tocqueville (and Beaumont too) was quite without such scepticism (or call it cynicism) when he entered parliament. The hopefulness of the years before 1830 had not yet entirely deserted him. 'I had passed the best years of my youth in the midst of a society which seemed to be renewing its prosperity and greatness as it renewed its liberty; there I had conceived the idea of a moderate, disciplined liberty, constrained by its beliefs, manners and laws; the charms of such liberty had captivated me; it had become the passion of my life.'[2] He meant to satisfy his ambition and idealism alike by exercising and strengthening this liberty; by playing a part in the drama of public life. The next eight years severely tested the wisdom of this aspiration.

He was a complete novice, and his service in the Chamber of Deputies is best regarded as a new apprenticeship, or as Henry Adams might have said, a further stage in his education. Great things were expected of him – according to Rémusat he was the last man of superior talent to be elected to the Chamber under the July regime – but he only slowly learned his trade, though he was an assiduous student. The nature of his difficulties is clear: it was largely personal. In the House of Commons, because of the layout of the chamber, a member can always have his party (or some of it) around him and behind him when he speaks, supporting him in difficulty and applauding him in moments of success. A United States Senator speaks from the solitary dignity of his desk, usually to a tiny audience. Tocqueville in the Palais Bourbon had to mount the tribune and short-sightedly face a crowded hemicycle, where friends and enemies blurred into a crowd that he confronted as if on trial for his life. This feeling was demoralizing but not baseless. In a few years' time the revolutionary crowd would again invade the Chamber; meanwhile, without needing to call to mind Robespierre howled down by the Convention or Bonaparte driven out by the Five Hundred, he could not forget the fate of so many of his near relations, destroyed for their political visibility. More important still, his temperamental extremism meant that he suffered agonies of stage-fright: he collapsed physically for two days after almost every speech, such was the intensity of his anxiety. He felt so exposed that in his first two or three orations he seemed to be courting martyrdom, and talked too much about his honour and principles, like an eighteenth-century gentleman issuing a challenge to a duel. Royer-Collard, who had great hopes for Tocqueville and seems to have been the only person who any longer felt free to tell him off, said that he was too self-centred. Tocqueville took the hint, though he could not help smiling as Royer talked incessantly of himself while driving home the point that one must not be egocentric. He loved the old man ('He is the last of the Romans') and followed his advice: by the end of his first term in the Chamber his speeches were becoming much more effective. He had learned how to go straight to the point.[3]

But he was barely increasing his influence on the deputies. It was the story of the Versailles *parquet* all over again. He was not a natural orator in an era when oratory was all-important: he could not dominate a debate by the power of his voice and eye, like Guizot, or dazzle with wit, like Thiers. He prepared his speeches as carefully as he did his books and articles; as a result they read better than they sounded, and his colleagues thought him cold and uninspiring. He agreed, acknowledging that he could not think on his feet: when improvisation was necessary he could only come up with sometimes irrelevant fragments of prepared statements.[4] Nor did he revel in the battle, readily taking blows as well as giving them.

He never spoke more than three or four times in a single session. The chief reason was his bad health. In the first nineteen months after his marriage he had had no stomach attacks at all, but after that they came regularly to hamper him. Everyone who now met him for the first time and left a record commented on his sickly appearance: Rémusat at first thought that the greenish tinge of Tocqueville's face showed him to be a sinister conspirator.[5] He changed his mind, and soon became a firm friend, but that hardly helped Tocqueville: remission from pain became rarer and rarer. The demands of the Chamber did nothing to help him in his quest for physical and psychological stability.

Yet as the career of many a great man has shown, it is not necessary to be wholly healthy or even wholly sane to be a successful politician. Tocqueville's failure to establish himself as a leader of the Chamber arose in part from his physique and in part from his temperament: he had all the nervousness of a beginner, he was morbidly sensitive to criticism and was shy with his new colleagues. But it was due, far more, to his social and political conditioning; even to his fundamental convictions.

According to his friend and ally the liberal deputy Jean-Charles Rivet,* he was intolerant of mediocrity. 'He will not court or talk over or even listen to the common place men who form the rank and file of every assembly: he scarcely knows their names.'[6] Tocqueville himself is even more scathing in what is perhaps the frankest passage of his

---

* Jean-Charles, baron Rivet (1800–1872), formerly a prefect and *conseiller d'état*, entered the Chamber for the Corrèze in 1839. A fierce opponent of Guizot, he was defeated in the elections of 1846. Elected to the National Assembly in 1848, he was again defeated in 1849, and went back to the *conseil d'état* until the *coup* of 1851.

Souvenirs: 'I have always supposed that mediocre men, like those of merit, have noses, mouths and eyes, but I have never been able to fix in my memory the particular form which these features assume in them. I am forever asking the name of strangers whom I see every day, and forgetting them again ... I honour the type, for it manages the world, but it bores me to death.'[7] Beaumont, who was at last elected to the Chamber (for Mamers in the Sarthe) a few months after Tocqueville, says the same thing: 'Very early in his parliamentary life he had found that an independent member, a member who, supporting no party, is supported by no party, is useless. He allowed himself therefore to be considered as a member of the *Gauche* [Left]. But I never could persuade him to be tolerably civil to them. Once, after I had been abusing him for his coldness to them he shook hands with Romorantin,* & then looked towards me for my applause! but I doubt whether he ever shook hands with him again.' No wonder that before long Tocqueville was obliged to accept that he was not going to repeat his triumph as an author. 'The trade of writer and that of orator fight each other,' he concluded gloomily.[8]

Beaumont, personally, was a much greater success in the Chamber, making many friends by his geniality. As he found his feet he showed a tendency to foster his career by associating with Thiers. This did not escape Tocqueville's censorious eye. He had assumed that as politicians he and Beaumont would work together as closely as they had as authors, and complained to Kergorlay of what seemed to be desertion. Kergorlay replied in two letters of splendid forthrightness and penetration. The difficulty, he said, lay in the friends' different characters and inclinations. Beaumont was well launched on a commonplace political career,† while 'it is absolutely impossible to say what your future will be.' This was because of the inflexibility of Tocqueville's moral principles. Kergorlay tried to make himself plain without offence by comparing Tocqueville in this respect to that implacable legitimist, Kergorlay's own father: his air of complete political probity made him intolerable to those who lacked it. As with the old comte, Tocqueville made people uneasy. 'They say to themselves, perhaps one day this man will

---

* A deputy voting with the 'dynastic Left' during the July Monarchy.

† Rémusat, perhaps jealous of Beaumont's growing *rapport* with Thiers, dismissed him as capable only of making a very bad minister of the second rank.

embarrass me greatly, because I have happened to make an *evolution* without getting his agreement first.' This was how Thiers responded to Tocqueville, and Guizot, as inflexible as Tocqueville himself, recognized that he would never be able to bridle him. In these circumstances, said Kergorlay, it was no wonder that Beaumont had to keep a little aloof, but he was still as devoted a friend as ever, and Tocqueville must not be severe.[9] It was good advice, though perhaps unnecessary: most of the time Tocqueville needed Beaumont's friendship too much even to reproach him.

But he did lose his temper spectacularly, almost disastrously, on one occasion. The episode is worth describing because of the light it throws not only on Tocqueville's temperament, but on his political difficulties.

After a few years in the Chamber he found himself to be at the centre of a small group of liberal deputies who, like him, opposed Guizot but did not want to work with Thiers if they could help it. In Tocqueville's opinion Thiers was fundamentally untrustworthy and illiberal, and at bottom cared for nothing but his own advancement.[10] Odilon Barrot, the second most conspicuous leader of the opposition, was much more acceptable, but showed a distressing tendency to work with Thiers (it will be seen that Tocqueville still had no idea of the importance of unity and discipline to an opposition). So Tocqueville and his friends toiled, not entirely without success, to establish themselves as a recognized group, not quite a party (they were too few) and not quite outside the ranks of the 'dynastic Left' which Barrot led. It was a difficult position to explain, so when in the spring of 1844 the chance came to own a newspaper they jumped at it. These were great years for the Parisian press. If the July Revolution had done nothing else, it had demonstrated the power of newspapers, and in spite of the September laws that power flourished and grew under Louis-Philippe. Tocqueville knew this, and valued his connection with *Le Siècle*, which he owed in part to Beaumont. Unfortunately *Le Siècle* was committed to Thiers, and eventually it was made clear to him that unless he toed the party line its columns would be closed to him.[11] The opportunity to have a newspaper of his own – *Le Commerce* – could not have come at a better moment.

Like so many of Tocqueville's ventures during the July Monarchy the enterprise of *Le Commerce* was not a success. It was not his fault: he threw himself into the business wholeheartedly, writing for the paper frequently (if anonymously) and playing a full part on the board of management, which usually followed his lead. But he and his associates could not raise enough capital to support the paper, nor could they find a sufficiently talented journalist to edit it successfully. The paper's somewhat equivocal line, which accurately reflected Tocqueville's political ambiguities, failed to please readers. Circulation declined steadily, and in June 1845 Tocqueville gave it all up as a bad job. He lost at least 4,500 francs over the business – about a quarter of his yearly income.[12]

It was an unfortunate affair, made worse by the breach it opened with Beaumont. The two friends had planned that Beaumont would join *Le Commerce* when a six-month stint on the board of *Le Siècle* came to an end, but before then the two papers had fallen out, very noisily, over a big political issue: the question of whether the monopoly of the *Université* (the secular state educational system established by Napoleon) over secondary education should be maintained, or whether private schools should be officially recognized, which would chiefly benefit those run by the Catholic Church. Thiers and *Le Siècle* supported the *Université*, Tocqueville and *Le Commerce* took the other side, and *Le Siècle* asserted that they did so because Tocqueville was still a secret legitimist. This slander induced Beaumont to resign from its board, but as he too supported the *Université* he felt that he could not after all join *Le Commerce*, as he explained in a public letter to Chambolle, the editor of *Le Siècle*.[13]

Tocqueville's reaction was extraordinary. Instead of being grateful to Beaumont for this display of loyalty he wrote him a long, furious private letter in which he came close to breaking off their friendship. His grievance was that Beaumont's brief expression of agreement with Chambolle over the schools question ('I have always been, and have not ceased to be, on your side') might be taken as endorsing the legitimist slur, or at any rate might reinforce it. 'I have only one vulnerable point. My birth and my family's opinions make it easy to believe that I am allied to the legitimists and the clergy, and as I have not married a grand-daughter of General La Fayette, unlike you, this *point de départ* naturally leads my enemies to attack not only my acts but my intentions, not only my conduct but my honour.' And what had Beaumont done? When all these allegations had been revived, he had simply said that he had to dissociate himself from them because Tocqueville was his oldest friend, not because they were untrue. Yet who knew better than Beaumont what sacrifices Tocqueville had made, what supreme effort of conscience, in order to be accepted as a sincere liberal? (Perhaps Tocqueville remembered the strong language of his own letter of resignation after Beaumont was dismissed from the *parquet*.) 'I would have preferred to be abandoned in the virgin forest ... rather than to be treated so by you ...' And so on.[14]

This childish outburst (it reads even worse in French) deeply hurt Beaumont; in reply he sent a long, sorrowful and devastatingly reasonable letter. Tocqueville seems to have realized quickly that his had been one of those letters best not posted. He wrote again, after a meeting in public where they could do no more than shake hands: 'When I thought of the long, long part of our lives that had gone by in such tender and devoted friendship, when I remembered, my dear Beaumont, all the proofs of affection that I have so often received from you, in place of talking politics I was tempted to fall on your neck and say to you that whatever may happen, I will always love you with all my heart.'[15] Things were patched up, but did not fully return to the old footing until the eve of the February Revolution.

This lamentable business recalls the affair of Tocqueville's boyhood duel, when, it will be remembered, he was said to be completely in the wrong.* More than that, it illustrates his somewhat Byronic attitude to himself and to his political career. His first letter to Beaumont shows that his friend's defection to Thiers still rankled, but the real grievance was the fancied slight to his honour. This, perhaps, reflects the pain which the breach with his family and its traditions had caused him; it had left him excessively touchy. He was consistent: in his dealings with his constituents he reacted fiercely and promptly whenever the legitimist slur was raised. Tocqueville invariably contradicted it as vociferously as possible, which seems to have worked: by 1848 the voters trusted him implicitly. But such extreme sensitivity was less serviceable at Paris. Serious politicians were expected to be teamworkers, not

* See above, p. 56–7.

Promethean *poseurs,* disdainful of other men's interests and difficulties. Some of the deputies began to ironize a trifle about their new colleague's well-advertised virtue.

For if Kergorlay had been correct in observing that Tocqueville was more fastidious morally than most politicians, the latter might never have entered the Chamber had he been quite so austere as he and his friend believed, or stayed there long. As it was, ambition and the need for re-election dominated his calculations as they did those of his fellows, with the usual results. Nothing is clearer than this in the record of his relations with his constituency, the *arrondissement* of Valognes.

He was at first dismayed by the littleness of provincial politics. Nothing could be less like his ideal democracy, where patriotic and educated citizens gravely deliberated over the general good, than life in the Cotentin. He poured out his sorrows in several letters to Royer-Collard (who replied, in effect, 'What did you expect?'). Writing from Tocqueville in August 1840, he laments:

> I came here for a rest and I can't have two quiet days together. There are hundreds of local concerns that I am expected to take up that have to be studied on the spot. The whole business is accompanied by immense dinners, a dangerous pastime for so weak a stomach as mine. I go through with them, however, because in this province it is only at table, just about, that there is a chance of bringing men together and forming an idea of current opinion. I have never known a country where the prime symptom of public life, which is men's frequent coming together, is so little known. There are never meetings of any kind; no places where men can freely exchange their opinions and thoughts on any subject whatever.[16]

A theme repeatedly arising is that his constituents know and care nothing about national politics; all they are concerned with are their own personal interests, and that usually means either jobs or decorations – Tocqueville was always having to write letters soliciting the Legion of Honour for village *maires*. He also had to be ready to adjust his opinions, however conscientiously formed. He voted against the Railway Act of 1842 (which Rémusat called the only important law passed in the last eight years of the July regime)[17] on budgetary grounds, but he soon realized his mistake, and began an unwearying campaign to get a line built to Valognes and Cherbourg. A horrid rumour got about that he was a free-trader, which alarmed the horse-breeders and cattle-raisers whose trade was the backbone of Cotentin agriculture: he issued a strong statement explaining that while he had always been a protectionist in principle (which can hardly have been true of this student of classical economics), on a recent visit to his brother Édouard (who was a member of the national council of agriculture and a notable protectionist pamphleteer) he had learned how *particularly*, how *scientifically* essential it was to protect the stockbreeders of France by raising high tariffs against foreign competition.[18] He found that even his anti-slavery convictions might be inconvenient while Cherbourg depended largely on trade with the sugar colonies, although he maintained them honourably.

No-one can be surprised that Tocqueville gradually turned into a thoroughly down-to-earth politician,* who was rewarded by increasingly large majorities at election time; but it is important to understand what these adjustments (or should they be called evolutions?) tell us about him. In one view, it is clear that he enjoyed the electoral competition much more than he did life in the Chamber: his letters to Paul Clamorgan are full of the relish of battle. After his first re-election, in July 1842, he wrote to Corcelle that the ministry's vigorous campaign against him had backfired, producing:

> one of those generous and independent reactions such as one sometimes finds in the country, but never in the Chamber. All those testimonies of esteem, confidence and sympathy that I received last Sunday will be long in fading from my memory. Truth to tell, they are the only real joys that political life has yet given me.[19]

But if we modify our sense of him, to take in this development, he did not do so himself. For instance, his enemies kept renewing the charge that he was a legitimist in disguise because they had nothing else to attack him with. They dug up his resignation from the *parquet* in 1832, his part in the protest against the duchesse de Berry's imprisonment, and his defence of Kergorlay in 1833. These were paltry and

---

* 'He might profess to despise the arts of the politician, but he had them all. No Tammany boss would have worked harder to see that the votes were there. Without ceasing to think of himself as an aristocrat, he was prepared to stoop to conquer' (Max Beloff, *Times Literary Supplement*, 12 July 1996).

ancient matters which did Tocqueville little harm in the end, but his defence of his conduct, in his election circulars, was less than wholly frank and accurate. He denied that there had been any political significance in his resignation; he pretended that he had put his name to the manifesto about the duchesse merely because he had been professionally consulted; he brushed aside the issue of some of his more indiscreet remarks about Kergorlay as mere courtroom tactics. It will be seen that he was slightly misrepresenting the record – understandably, in the circumstances; and he was entitled to affirm his support for the new monarchy as powerfully as he liked ('sincerely, firmly, loyally, I want to maintain our institutions and the dynasty'), but these were scarcely the words of a man rigidly wedded to the precise truth. Only a few months earlier he had made a note to himself, while preparing a speech, of how much he hated and despised the King.[20]

These little fibs and contradictions illustrate the nature of Tocqueville's central political dilemma under the July Monarchy. On the campaign trail (if so ungenteel and anachronistic an expression is allowed) he was once more the Tocqueville of the travel notebooks, seldom letting philosophical preoccupations get in the way of understanding and relishing the social spectacle. But he could not theorize this attitude, so to say, for it would have meant publicly acknowledging and accepting the necessary second-rateness of democratic politics, and then what would there be to distinguish him from such opportunists as Thiers? Even worse, it would have meant ceding the high moral ground to Guizot.

Tocqueville's attitude to his former professor does not show him at his best; Guizot's to him was comparatively straightforward. Whether as politician or philosophical historian, Guizot's view of his time was cut and dried. He believed in progress, and welcomed what he took to be the main achievement of the French Revolution: the sweeping away of the antiquated clutter of the old order and the establishment of a new order, justified and guaranteed by the power of the notables, the richest, most intelligent and most creative element of society; the natural aristocracy. On the other hand he dreaded mob rule, and his single most conspicuous political principle was that order must be preserved. He was democratic in that he would always welcome into the ruling class men who had acquired the necessary wealth and education: that was what he meant by his famous maxim 'Enrich your-selves, gentlemen!' He thought that with the advance of civilization more and more persons would enter the elite. He was not wrong, but his terror of opening the doors to chaos (he never forgot his father's death in the Reign of Terror) meant that he never did anything to hasten or help the process. He had no interest in economics or percep-tion of economic possibilities. Rémusat noticed that he never spoke on trade, public works or public finance, and left the Chamber when they came up for debate, 'yet he aspired to become first minister!'[21] His most constructive work was done as minister of education during the 1830s.

Guizot greatly admired *De la démocratie en Amérique* and would have welcomed political alliance with the author. Tocqueville was elected to the Académie Française in December 1841 ('for the first time in their lives MM. Thiers, Guizot, Villemain, Molé, Cousin were of the same opinion,' he boasted)[22] and took his *fauteuil* on 21 April following. Guizot was unable to be present on the occasion, but he read the new academician's speech and sent his compliments. 'You deal with the greatest questions and you understand all their greatness. Perhaps nothing is rarer today, for things have grown much more than men, and almost all minds now look at them from below. So I take pleasure in your ideas, even when I do not share them. *Why* don't we think the same? I cannot find any good reason.' He was still perplexed nineteen years later when, at that same Académie, he had to pronounce its memorial tribute to Tocqueville.[23]

It is undeniable that Tocqueville, as a thinker and historian, was of Guizot's school; the differences between them, though important, were only nuances.[24] For that very reason Tocqueville may have wanted to keep his distance: he was never generous in acknowledging his intellectual debts, having a neurotic craving to seem original, and he may even have felt a little jealous of Guizot's literary and political pre-eminence. Temperamentally they were perhaps too much alike: Guizot was notoriously cold and haughty except among his close friends; Tocqueville may have found him unapproachable. But there can be no doubt that the real nature of their alienation was political, and perhaps generational. It was Guizot who asserted that the world belongs to optimists, but he behaved as if he thought that any change was bound to be for the worse, whereas Tocqueville the pessimist was never afraid of action, and always sought to make the best of circumstances, however deplorable they were. He had a much wider range of legislative interests than Guizot, and deplored the complete legislative sterility that settled over the July monarchy in its last years: he must have sympathized with the indignant deputy who asked what the government had achieved, and answered his own question: '*Rien! Rien! Rien!*' He was in the contradictory position of being a democrat who distrusted the people, but his American experience clung to him sufficiently to make it impossible for him to follow Guizot as he crept towards reaction. In a phrase, he found Guizot's policy timid and illiberal, both at home and abroad, and the chief lesson he tried to learn as a deputy was how to drive this criticism home.

At first he was hampered by his inexperience. He arrived in the Chamber shortly before the 1840 crisis over the Eastern question. To eyes that could see, this episode laid bare the contradictions which would have to be resolved if the July Monarchy were to endure. Superficially it was absurd: for a moment it looked as if France and Britain were to go to war over the question of whether Mehemet Ali, the pasha of Egypt, might also rule Syria or not. It was a quarrel of imperialisms: France had taken an interest in Egypt ever since Napoleon's expedition of 1798, and Britain was determined not to let a French client (Mehemet Ali) control the central section of the land route to India. Since the British government had the more vital interest and the greater power, both naval and diplomatic, it prevailed in the dispute, which France had been unwise ever to embark on. She had done so less for reasons of Levantine intrigue than to reassert her standing as a Great Power – a point understood all too well by the whole political nation, including Alexis de Tocqueville. French opinion tenaciously resented the various defeats which the country had endured at British hands since the outbreak of the Seven Years War. In the eighteenth century the quest for revenge had led to the intervention in the American Revolution, which had been a military success but was also the indirect occasion of the French Revolution through the regime-wrecking deficit which it generated. The revolutionary and Napoleonic era had ended with Waterloo and the subsequent peace treaty, another unforgotten humiliation from which the same erroneous lesson was inferred, for the memory of Valmy and Austerlitz suggested that a rebound was still possible. Every nineteenth-century regime, from the Restoration to the Liberal Empire, tried to achieve some stupendous international triumph, by arms or diplomacy or both, which would give it the legitimacy in popular opinion that otherwise eluded it. The other Powers understood this very well, and regarded France as a perpetual threat to peace. This was why Russia, Austria and Prussia rallied to Britain in 1840: not out of love for the British Empire, but from a determination to maintain the Quadruple Alliance which had defeated Napoleon and guaranteed the post-Waterloo settlement. This regrouping inflamed French opinion still further, and French statesmen paid a high price for meddling in Mehemet Ali's insurgency against his overlord, the Sultan. They wanted to avoid both war and, equally, another national humiliation. As a Russian diplomat put it, they tried 'evading' under Soult (first minister 1839–40), 'threatening' (or bluff) under Thiers (1840), and 'begging' under Guizot (foreign minister 1840–48). 'They all failed.'[25]

The crisis was just getting under way when Tocqueville made his first speech in the Chamber. Here, one might have thought, was a splendid chance for a young man to make a name for himself by attacking a policy – aggressive support for the pasha – which was sure to fail. Not a bit of it. Tocqueville took the nationalist line, and warned that failure to stand up for Mehemet Ali might imperil the July Monarchy:

> As for me, I was certainly not summoned to found our new dynasty; I have, emphatically, no particular tie to it, I ask nothing of it, nothing but the greatness and happiness of my country; but I want this monarchy to last; why? because I think this monarchy is ... the only stopping place between us and the great misfortunes into which we would be plunged without it. (*Applause*) So I want this monarchy to last; but I am convinced that it will not last long should the idea take root in the mind of France that we, this nation formerly so strong, so great, which has done such great things, which has involved itself in all the business of the world, will meddle in nothing any more; will put its hand to nothing; that everything will be done without it.[26]

He gave a speech on similar lines sixteen months later when, the Thiers government having fallen (after bringing France to the brink of war with all Europe), the new Soult–Guizot government was trying to liquidate the crisis by accepting the decisions of the other Powers.[27] He explained to Mill that it was necessary to attack the British diplomatic victory because not to do so, after the way in which Lord Palmerston had behaved, would have been to damage, even extinguish, a national feeling which might be needed one day. 'National pride is the greatest passion remaining to us; no doubt it is necessary to regulate and moderate its errors, but it is necessary to take care not to diminish it.'[28]

Unsurprisingly these views did not please his English friends. Mill was distressed, and while conceding that French national feeling must be respected, urged that 'in the name of France & civilization, posterity have a right to expect from such men as you, from the nobler & more enlightened spirits of the time, that you should teach your countrymen better ideas of what it is that constitutes national glory & national importance than the low & grovelling ones which they seem to have at present.' Reeve thought that the speech had inflicted a most severe blow on Tocqueville's reputation in London. Senior wrote:

> The speech which you addressed to the French Chamber wd have been utterly ruinous to any English statesman. What, it wd have been said, to think of going to war merely to prevent our being excluded from taking part in the affairs of Syria & Egypt? Or to show that we are not unable to go to war? Or because, we, being one, are in a business taken up by the 5 powers, required to yield to the opinion of the 4? Now you laid down to the French chamber these three cases as fit causes of war – In the English House, either of Lords or Commons, we shd consider such proposals as scarcely deserving a serious answer.[29]

Guizot would no doubt have agreed with the English view, and if diplomacy were only the calculation of forces all nowadays would agree that he was right: to resort to war or the threat of war as a means of solving domestic difficulties is a highly dangerous game, and a war between Britain and France over Syria would not have made the slightest sense, as many thought at the time (King Louis-Philippe chief among them). Furthermore, the Napoleonic days were gone for good: France was not strong enough to fight a war without allies. Every foreign minister between 1815 and 1851 had to accept this, including

Tocqueville when his turn came. But his political point was equally unanswerable. Guizot became foreign minister in the autumn of 1840, when Louis-Philippe could bear Thiers's bluffing no longer; so in the public mind he was associated with national humiliation, and his extreme unpopularity on this account during the next seven years did indeed weaken the July Monarchy. It did not help that his diplomacy was never conspicuously successful.

It must be allowed that during the Mehemet Ali crisis Tocqueville showed himself to be a nationalist who was not above hankering for cheap diplomatic victories. He learned better during the next few years. But as we have seen, his chief concern was different. The July Monarchy seemed to be the liberals' last chance. If it failed the only alternatives were republicanism or Bonapartism. Tocqueville did not yet take the threat of the latter seriously, but republicanism deeply worried him, for it meant, he thought, nothing but revolution. For this reason he was sincere in the support he proclaimed for the Orleanist monarchy, but he erred in not seeing what was required of him if that support was to be of any use. Louis-Philippe had a claim on his loyalty, though he never really acknowledged it. He seems to have supposed that it was sufficient to assert publicly the necessity of Orleanism without welcoming it or, in any but the most perfunctory sense, adopting it (his haverings about accepting the Legion of Honour will be remembered). As time went on he was given ample reason to oppose the Guizot ministry for its complacent inertia. He had the right to attack the ministry for what he thought to be its corruption and reliance on jobbery, and to try to defeat it. He was entitled to despise Louis-Philippe as a mean and pompous usurper (thereby perhaps doing something to assuage his feeling of guilt for having abandoned the Bourbons). What, as an avowed Orleanist, he was not wise to do was to merge all these criticisms into a single sustained and permanent onslaught. To the extent that he had any influence, his campaign (in which he was at one with most of the opposition) could only weaken the regime which he thought necessary.

It is true that his influence until almost the end was small, largely restricted to a handful of deputies: Corcelle, Armand Dufaure, Victor Lanjuinais, Rivet. And by 1847 he had begun to make the necessary (from an Orleanist point of view) distinctions. His hope was to bring down the minister, not the monarch. It cannot seriously be argued that anything which he did or did not do significantly helped to bring on the revolution of 1848.

Indeed, it was largely Guizot's fault that Tocqueville did not reach an understanding with him. As Beaumont was to observe, Tocqueville was not born for opposition: 'Tocqueville was eminently practical, to the great astonishment, or great annoyance, of those who hoped that the man who excelled in theory would be inadequate in action.'[30] During his years as a deputy he was constantly in demand, whether as committee member or *rapporteur* when policy had to be considered – not merely on his old speciality, prison reform, but on slavery and the slave trade and, above all, on the government of Algeria. He was not his father's son for nothing: in 1842 he was elected to the *conseil-général* of the Manche, and thereafter wrote a string of reports on subjects of local importance, especially on the great project of the Cherbourg railway. He strongly disapproved of the system of electing deputies from *arrondissements*, chiefly because the smaller ones (many had no more than 300 electors each) were so easy for the ministry to manipulate by fear or favour, but also because it would be easier for deputies from a department to co-operate on issues which affected all *arrondissements* if they were elected by the department as a whole. But while the system lasted he threw himself zealously into the work of modernizing the life and institutions of the Manche, whether he was in Paris, Saint-Lô (where the *conseil-général* met) or at Valognes. Yet a sense of frustration grew as he discovered how little he was actually able to achieve, in spite of all his reports.

Beaumont was surely right in thinking that Tocqueville would have made an excellent minister; Guizot's tactical obstinacy and ideological rigidity excluded that possibility, as it did so much that would have been useful to France; but it is worth noting that Tocqueville was on good terms with Duchâtel, the minister of the interior and Guizot's right-hand man (there is a surprisingly friendly sketch of him in the *Souvenirs*, that gallery of acid portraits). Politically, Tocqueville is best described as an active, improving conservative, even if he hung the word 'liberal' round his neck.[31] Were there any reasons other than those already given why he could not work with the conservative government?

Tocqueville, in effect, asked himself this very question in 1850, when he began the *Souvenirs*, and answered it, characteristically, from a very lofty perch. An old idea reappears in a new guise. The period of French history from 1789 to 1830 was, he says, a unity, that of the struggle between the *ancien régime*, dominated by the aristocracy, and the new, emergent order dominated by what he calls 'the middle class'. In 1830 the new order achieved its definitive victory, so that all political power and all the organs of government were taken over by the *bourgeoisie*, to the exclusion of everyone beneath it and all those who had formerly been above it. Tocqueville had the lowest opinion of this new ruling class:

> The particular spirit of the middle class became the general spirit of government; it dominated foreign policy as much as the nation's domestic business: an active, industrious spirit, often shameless, usually well-behaved, bold sometimes from vanity and selfishness, timid by instinct, moderate in everything, except in its taste for material well-being, and mediocre [that favourite word of reproach]; a spirit which, mingled with that of the people or the aristocracy, can achieve marvels, but which on its own will only bring about a government without virtue or greatness. Master of everything as no aristocracy ever has been or perhaps ever will be, the middle class, which must be called the governing class, being entrenched in power and, soon afterwards, in selfishness, took on an air of private enterprise, its members devoting scarcely a thought to public business except as a means of profit for private interests and happily forgetting in its petty prosperity the common people of France.[32]

Having thus set the scene Tocqueville next gives a memorably penetrating and unkind description of Louis-Philippe ('He was the accident which made the illness mortal'), painting him as deplorably middle class, in spite of his illustrious descent, and as therefore a wholly inadequate king.[33]

These unkind remarks force on us several reflections. First, they are not merely inadequate but profoundly inaccurate as an account of the July regime. There was no great sociological shift: the men who ruled France under Louis-Philippe, the notables, were in terms of class, wealth, opinion, origins and careers substantially identical with those who had ruled the country since the XVIII Brumaire or even the fall of Robespierre.* The July settlement had made some minor changes in the *pays légal*, and the voluntary emigration to the interior of most legitimists made more, but still nearly a quarter of the deputies after 1830 were landed proprietors, as against nearly a third under the Restoration.[34] And the *pays légal* was far too small and unrepresentative to be termed a class, or to be said to embody the power of a new class (had it been big enough to do so, the regime would probably have lasted much longer). If the term 'middle class' means anything, it cannot be said that the middle class ruled Orleanist France, or that the ruling class was *bourgeois*. The structure of society was far too complex for such generalizations.[†]

What, then, did Tocqueville mean? In part, I think, he was offering not so much a theory of the July Monarchy as one of the nature of the French Revolution, which he presents as a long-contested but ultimately victorious struggle of the Third Estate against the Second (as usual, he ignores the First Estate, the clergy). By 'middle class' he means the Third Estate: in terms of 1789, the *grande bourgeoisie*. Seen in this light his usage is intelligible, if obsolete, and may serve as a reminder that the social sciences were still in their infancy. (A similar objection might be made to the terminology of the *Communist Manifesto*, although Marx and Engels made a huge intellectual advance by tying the concept of class to that of systems of production.) It must also be said that it suited Tocqueville to present the French Revolution as merely a struggle between estates: he did not go so far as Guizot, who in effect believed that the victory of the Third was the consummation of French history, but his interpretation did enable him, like Guizot, to claim the legacy of the Revolution for himself and his kind, and in its name to resist other claims and ideas. He was not merely snobbish: he began the *Souvenirs* during a period of more than usual bitterness, illness and discouragement. It was a relief to discharge his bile on paper. But the most important point to register is that, as so often, his views were not original; in fact they were, by 1848, commonplace.

---

* Charles X's *coup* in 1830 had been in part an attempt to replace these new men with Ultras. It failed.

† The social structure of France under the July Monarchy is admirably described and analysed by Roger Price in *The French Second Republic* (London, 1972), 5–94.

Louis-Philippe himself, who in the early days of his reign liked to pose as the Citizen-King and to be seen walking about the streets of Paris carrying his umbrella (thereby making a gift to caricaturists), was in part to blame for Tocqueville's impression. Disdain for the *bourgeoisie* was part of the cant of the time: not just the bohemians' disdain for respectability, but a common belief on the Left that Guizot's followers were nothing but sordid scramblers after place. Tocqueville merely uttered this belief with unusual verve, in his speeches as well as in the *Souvenirs*.

Most of the time he had little doubt as to its validity. As deputy he was a constant target of petitioners, and so were his colleagues. Returning to the Chamber in January 1842 for a new session, he felt able to appeal to their common experience:

> I ask all of you, sincerely, from the bottom of my heart – I ask you if, fresh from your constituencies, you have not noticed everywhere – everywhere – not just here and there, but everywhere – that the desire for jobs has become a universal passion, the dominant passion, *la passion-mère* (*Cries of Yes yes!*); that it has crept at the same time into all classes, even the agricultural classes which until now have rejected it, thanks to their energetic and healthy manners ...

(This remark did not go down well in his constituency: he had to assure the voters of Valognes that he had not meant *them*.) The *pays légal*, he said, now tended to think that the best thing about the right to vote was the opportunity it gave to obtain an official salary.[35]

It may be said, flatly, that this picture of the July regime, though it became widely diffused, thanks to Tocqueville and others, was a gross exaggeration if not an outright libel on the French people, and that even to the degree that it was true it lacked the significance which Tocqueville attributed to it. He occasionally had doubts himself. During the autumn of 1842 he began to read Tobias Smollett's *History of England from the Revolution to the Death of George II*[*]and was struck not only by the amazing selfishness, corruption and lack of principle of the political society described, but also by how little it mattered in the end: the free institutions of Britain enabled the nation to achieve

---

[*] Not one of its author's best-known works. AT read it in translation.

prodigies. 'I confess that this reading has led me to wonder if we have not been judging our own time and country with excessive severity,' he wrote to Kergorlay; and he began to realize that struggle, conflict and passion were natural and necessary in free countries.[36] It was an important discovery, but the cry of corruption was far too valuable in the battle with Guizot to be discarded, and Tocqueville maintained it to the end. Had the *Communist Manifesto* been published a year or two sooner than it was he might have seized with delight on its remark that 'The executive of the modern State is but a committee for managing the common affairs of the whole bourgeoisie.' But even if Tocqueville and Marx had agreed on a proposition it might still be untrue; and Marx, if in the *Manifesto* he was not merely indulging in rhetorical exaggeration, quickly modified his position, writing in *The Class Struggles in France* that 'It was not the French bourgeoisie that ruled under Louis-Philippe, but *one faction* of it ... the so-called *finance aristocracy*'; he divided the rest of the population into the industrial bourgeoisie, the petty bourgeoisie, the peasantry and the 'so-called *men of talent*' – a crude but serviceable subclassification.[37]

Tocqueville's critique was an inadequate account of the French Revolution, and it did not get to the bottom of what was wrong with the Orleanist regime. Politically it was and remained a sterile attitude, although by 1844 Tocqueville was gradually moving towards partnership with Odilon Barrot, and was carrying his little group of associates with him. Nor did his efforts in committee bear much fruit: slavery was not abolished, prison reform lagged almost as much as ever, the problem of poverty was completely neglected.[38] Worst of all was the slow erosion of such democratic liberties as the July Revolution had introduced. Tocqueville particularly resented the September laws (liberty of the press and of association being causes very dear to the author of the *Démocratie*). It is not surprising that he frequently felt trapped and oppressed by his life in politics. In 1842 he wrote to Marie from Paris wondering if he was really capable of achieving anything: 'I fear that I am unsuited to this life which I sought, this life of daily effort, this life where I have to be always ready, alert, decisive, fertile in expedients. It is all so removed from my character, which is melancholy, lazy (except when moved by passion), despondent, deep but narrow.'

It is not entirely easy to recognize Tocqueville in this description: he was the most active of men, and the range of his political interests was extraordinary. But he had more than politics on his mind that summer. He did not want Marie to think that he was enjoying himself: 'All my friends dined out today, *mon amie chérie*; I am alone. I have just been for a melancholy walk in the Tuileries. At last I have got back and am writing to you ...' His marriage was in trouble.[39]

Kergorlay was probably the only person besides themselves who knew. On a visit to Paris in February 1841 he had found his two friends bitterly at odds. At some stage Alexis had been casually unfaithful and Marie had found out. They started to quarrel, and did so again and again for the next five years or so. It was a miserable time for both of them.

The fact that quarrelling was possible came as a nasty surprise. Tocqueville's volatility meant that he could never be an easy husband, but Marie must have been well aware of this before she married him. 'She ate,' says Rédier, 'so slowly as to drive her ardent table-companion to despair; one day, when she had not done nibbling at some pie, Alexis got up, took away her plate and threw it on the floor. "Some more pie," she said calmly to the servant.'[40] She could handle that sort of thing; she may even have found it comic. She was usually patient and self-controlled: years later Tocqueville said of her, 'She does not get upset for nothing; she knows how to let tranquil days and lucky circumstances unfold in perfect peace and quiet.' This placidity was one of the things that he most loved in her. But as he also said, Marie thought and felt passionately, and sometimes responded violently to misfortune.[41] She responded violently to her husband's philandering. Kergorlay, who behaved throughout the business with marvellous tact, intelligence and affection, warned her against throwing away the treasure of her unusually close union with her husband because of an injury which was without real importance, since Alexis was devoted to her; but it was long before she could absorb the point.[42] She herself was not a person to do anything lightly, so she found it difficult to believe that Tocqueville's diversions meant little. The episode, and the prospects it opened, hit straight at her insecurity: a childless woman in a foreign land, becoming middle-aged (though she had not yet entered the menopause). She had other sorrows at about this time: the deaths of her father, two uncles, and two brothers, all occurring between 1840 and 1842. It is easy to imagine her state of mind, though we have no first-hand account of it. She could not rise above her troubles, and she found that she could no longer trust her husband, or his passionate avowals of love.

He, for his part, was distressed and bewildered, somewhat like a child being punished for a naughtiness that it does not understand. At one stage he wrote to Kergorlay:

> It is quite clear that there is something in me which cannot satisfy Marie and that she can find no happiness except on one condition which I can't meet except by changing from top to toe, a difficult undertaking. I love her ardently, even passionately, I confide in her unreservedly; I desire her happiness and work for it as much as is in me. For me she is, what I think few women have ever been to a man, the prime cause not only of happiness, but of tranquillity, of all endeavour, almost of life itself, yet all that is not enough for her. She would like not only to command, as a rule, my desires, but to keep them prisoner, to suppress them, so to speak. If she has not that, she has nothing ... There is no hope of making her see reason on the point. The passage of time seems to make her more and more irritable about the episode ...

He began to think that he was going to have to choose between wrecking his marriage and perhaps the life of the creature he loved most in the world, or somehow taming the blind instinct which from time to time drove him crazy. Yet 'How could I manage to stop that sort of boiling of the blood that meeting a woman, whatever she may be, still causes me, as it did twenty years ago?' The difficulty was poisoning his days, even when he and Marie found themselves beginning to be on good terms again.[43]

The next few years were marked by the usual incidentals of such a story. Marie kept on saying that he did not love her; he kept on swearing that he did, putting all his eloquence into his pleas, which may have made her distrust him even more. She wrote spiteful letters, he wrote wounded, reproachful ones, which did not always conceal a desire to have the last word. As might have been predicted, money questions made things worse: when Tocqueville discouraged Marie from joining him in Paris for the short parliamentary session in the summer of 1842, on the grounds that they couldn't afford it, she furiously inferred that he was enjoying himself with other women (not unlikely: at about this time a police spy reported to Guizot that he had seen Tocqueville picking up a woman on the Champs-Elysées).[44] Kergorlay, in whom both confided, did his utmost to reconcile them. And eventually hostilities died away, as their need for each other overbore all other considerations, although Marie continued to feel insecure and Tocqueville to think that he was hard done by.

The full details of this sad, predictable comedy need not be chronicled; but one of its scenes is so revealing not only of Tocqueville's character, but of the most important aspects of his life as a deputy, that it merits description here.

In the spring of 1841 he and Beaumont fulfilled a longstanding scheme and made a journey to Algeria. It was quite in the spirit of their voyages to America and England, for Beaumont hoped to get a book out of it, and Tocqueville to satisfy his curiosity and pursue his political education; but as a variant they took Hippolyte de Tocqueville with them. The trip would not be without its dangers. The conquest of the country was still far from complete; no European was safe without a military escort any distance beyond the principal towns. The documents suggest that the travellers' wives did not approve of the adventure: Tocqueville may have been glad to get away from his for a while. The journey was supposed to last two months. Tocqueville, inevitably, was seasick on the voyage from Toulon (Hippolyte, unused to the sea, was much iller); nevertheless he was all eager attention as they approached Algiers, where to their surprise and joy they were met by Corcelle, who joined the party. Tocqueville was unprepared for what he found on shore: a sampler of all races, costumes and languages, 'Europeans, Asiatics, Arabs, Moors, Kabyles, Negroes, each with their own outlook and all confined here in a place too small to hold them'; a town of labyrinths, where half the houses were in ruins and the other half were being rebuilt. Hammering was incessant. It all reminded Tocqueville, he said, of Cincinnati (perhaps the most unexpected remark he ever made).[45] The weather was agreeable, and all auspices seemed fair. He started with a will to take notes in the old style.

The 1841 Algerian notebook might have been his masterpiece in that line;* not only was he as observant and intelligent as ever but, no doubt because all talk was in French, he was able to reproduce the utterance of the men he interviewed more vividly:

[*Philippeville,†* *30 May.*] Lunch with the commanding officer: he is a colonel.

'Nothing, gentlemen, but force and terror can succeed with these people. The other day, I went on a *razzia.‡* I'm sorry you weren't there. There was this tribe which allowed some men who had just been stealing from us and murdering us to escape through its territory. I must add that I didn't want to go to extremes. After I had killed five or six men, I spared the cattle. There was even a tribesman, one of our friends, from whom they had stolen two mules, I ordered another Arab of whom we had reason to complain to give him two cows. Only terror, gentlemen, works with these people. The other day there was a murder on the highway. An Arab suspect was brought before me. I interrogated him and then I had his head cut off. You will see his head on the Constantine gate. As to your so-called colonists at Philippeville, they are rabble; men who think the Army is here just to make their fortune; thieves who would be nothing without us yet who in spite of that I can hardly get to stand guard-duty. Yesterday, I put in a requisition of their carts and horses to bring in the hay and I announced that the first who refused would be sent until further orders to the *blockhaus* of the Apes (that's a *blockhaus* stuck away on a parched, burnt-over mountain).'

All that was said by a man who had the air of being the best chap in the world. A sailor who was there, and who owned some land, replied vigorously that it was wrong to treat the colonists in this way; that without the colony there was nothing stable or profitable in Africa; that there could be no colony without land and so it would have been better to dispossess the tribes closest at hand in order to put Europeans in their place.

And I, listening mournfully to all this, asked myself what could be the future of a country given over to such men and where would this cascade of violence and injustice end, if not in the revolt of the natives and the ruin of the Europeans?[46]

* The notebooks which he kept during his second journey to Algeria in 1846 have been almost entirely lost.
† Modern Skika.
‡ *Razzia*: the sort of bloody expeditions which, under General Bugeaud, the French used against the natives of Algeria to pre-empt, punish or merely discourage resistance.

It will be seen that Tocqueville had not lost his gift for seizing the essential; unfortunately, where Algeria was concerned, he refused to believe what his intelligence told him. It is clear enough, 170 years after it began, that the French invasion and occupation of Algeria was a catastrophe for all concerned, the evil consequences of which are still being felt; and much of the unwisdom of the enterprise was already evident for those who cared to look (Corcelle was particularly dismayed by the cruelty of the *razzias* and the genocidal language – to use a modern term – of the press in Algiers).[47] But Tocqueville could not or would not make the inferences which leap to the modern eye. He studied, he spoke, he wrote voluminously about Algeria;* he was fiercely critical of misgovernment there, and after his second journey, in 1846, succeeded in driving Bugeaud out of his command;† but he could never admit, even to himself, that the whole adventure was a horrible mistake. On the contrary, he said in the Chamber that however much he disagreed with the Soult–Guizot ministry on other matters, he was happy to collaborate with it on Algerian policy, and this olive-branch cannot be dismissed as merely careerist. Tocqueville, it must be said plainly, was a nineteenth-century French nationalist. He was fascinated by the growth of British rule in India, and thought seriously of writing a book on the subject. He admired the Anglo-Saxons so much that he may reasonably be labelled an Anglophile. But he resented the ascendancy of the British Empire; he opposed the Anglo-French *entente cordiale* which was the central achievement of Louis-Philippe's diplomacy; he wished that Napoleon had won at Waterloo; he was eager to assert French power and independence at every opportunity, and if a colonial empire was the way to restore French primacy, or at any rate to catch up with the British, he would enthusiastically support it. Besides, he accepted the ancient, ruinous argument of Pericles: 'You now hold your empire down by force: it may have been wrong to take it; it is certainly dangerous to let it go.'[48] French prestige was at stake in Algeria, and if necessary hecatombs must be paid for it. Tocqueville should have known better, but the only

---

* Algeria takes up 350 pages in the *Oeuvres complètes*, not counting letters.

† Thomas-Robert Bugeaud de la Piconnerie (1784–1849), duc d'Isly, marshal of France. The leader and commander of the French enterprise in Algeria for most of the July Monarchy. AT deeply disapproved of his methods of war and government.

alternative to Bugeaud's military government which he offered was the equally disastrous policy of colonization, of settling Algeria with Europeans. He knew what a settler society was like, for he had visited and criticized both Ireland and the American South, but he would not admit that France in Algeria was manufacturing her own equivalent of the Irish problem.

It was a matter of the emotions. Every so often common sense, or prophetic insight, broke through: when a choice had to be made he always opposed war, and in his enormous official report on Algeria in 1847 he said that if the original inhabitants of Algeria were treated only as so many obstacles to be driven off or trodden under, if they were to be strangled and smothered rather than educated towards civilization, then Algeria would become, sooner or later, a battleground where the two peoples would fight each other mercilessly, and where one of them would perish: 'God spare us, gentlemen, from such a fate!'[49] But he never acted as if he believed his own perceptions.[50]

Nationalism was the oxygen of nineteenth-century Europe, or perhaps I should say the chronic influenza. The French Revolutionary and Napoleonic wars were largely expressions of French nationalism; nationalism largely shaped the history of all other European countries, and of the United States, from 1815 or earlier, and culminated in the Great War of 1914. A biographical explanation of Tocqueville's attitude may therefore seem superfluous; he shared the assumptions of his generation and could scarcely have avoided doing so. Over time he grew more realistic, although he remained romantically patriotic. But if we are to understand him, we should perhaps remind ourselves that he was still Chateaubriand's kinsman and that he had a deep devotion to the French writers of the seventeenth century. Molière, Pascal, Bossuet, Racine: these characterized his country's greatness, and his deepest wish seems to have been that France should attain that level again. The distance between that wish and international assertiveness may seem wide, but the century of Pascal was also the century of Louis XIV, of whom Tocqueville deeply disapproved, but who probably influenced him, as Napoleon did, more than he ever realized.[51]

His Algerian notebook was cut short when he fell ill. Although he had manfully lied to Marie on the topic, his health had been getting steadily worse from the moment that he arrived in Algeria – the usual intestinal trouble, no doubt. When the party reached Mostaganem it lodged with Bugeaud, who invited his guests to go with him into the interior on a *razzia* against Abd-el-Kadr, the leader of the Algerian resistance. Tocqueville longed to go, and it would have been an exciting experience: the column fought three successful battles before it got back to Mostaganem; it sacked the stronghold of Tackdempt and occupied Mascara.[52] But Tocqueville's friends were sure that he was not fit for such an adventure, and persuaded him to be sensible. Beaumont stayed to look after him while Hippolyte and Corcelle went with the army. Tocqueville resisted his weakness for another two weeks, but at Camp Eddis, outside Philippeville, the day after his lunch with the colonel, he went down with a bad attack of dysentery: he twice lost consciousness and at one point had to be carried on a stretcher; it was days before he was free of the bloody flux. Beaumont nursed him as devotedly as ever. They decided to return to France as soon as Tocqueville was able to travel, and arrived at Toulon early in the morning of 12 June. Tocqueville wrote at once to Marie, telling the whole story, and concluding: 'I am no longer exactly ill, but am still in pain and excessively feeble.' He and Beaumont, he said, would return to Paris in short stages.[53]

It was a miserable story. Perhaps the most striking thing about it today is the nature of Tocqueville's response to his misfortunes. The departure of Hippolyte and Corcelle with Bugeaud made him intensely wretched for days. It was years since he had been so upset. He kept on asking himself if he had done the right thing by staying behind, although his reason and his friends shouted yes! 'Instinct revolts. This is the first time that I ever gave up a scheme that was both silly and dangerous. That worries me. I think one must beware of a common sense which is too inclined to avoid dangers, even useless ones.' Tocqueville was now in his late thirties, but the spoiled child in him was not quite outgrown, nor the rashly eager traveller observed by Beaumont in America: 'Instead of sparing his feeble frame, he seemed at heart to want to submit it to the roughest and even the most dangerous tests.' Tocqueville sadly conceded that dangerous journeys were not for married men in weak health; but he hated the concession.[54]

He displayed his character even more vividly in the letters which he wrote to Marie after his return to France. Even from Algeria he sent letters full of sexual longing and frustration: '*Ma petite amie chérie*, everything in me wants you, my heart, and also I assure you my senses. This burning climate excites them but all the same I have been up to this minute *completely* chaste, I give you my most sacred word of honour. Not only have I not been unfaithful, which is no great merit, given the life I lead, but I have not even succumbed to desire in another way, which is more meritorious. Guess how delightedly I will throw myself into your arms.' But it struck him that she might be menstruating when he got home. She must write at once about her timetable. 'Think of me, love me, because I adore you.'[55]

He was even more emphatic as he and Beaumont inched their way across the Midi. His illness had destroyed the tone of his mind; he fretted about his body: 'It is a machine which needs rest, but unhappily it is in the clutches of a mind which rest murders.' He fretted about Beaumont: nobody, except Marie herself, could have looked after him better, but he must be bitterly disappointed, for the need to nurse Tocqueville had made it impossible to work on his book. Above all he thought of Marie and sex. He meant to spend a day or two staying with his father in Paris, so as not to be a complete wreck when he got home; he still wanted to know when Marie's menses began and ended. '*Mon amie adorée*, how ravishing it will be to fold you in my arms. And won't that moment seem sweet to you? Do you love me as passionately as I suppose and as I love you? ... I must break off to catch the post.'[56]

His health and spirits revived markedly as he went up the Rhone; he reached Paris, and received dramatic news: Lacuée de Cessac, of the Académie Française, was dead, and the obvious candidate to succeed him was Tocqueville, who had yearned for a *fauteuil* ever since his first success as an author. He instantly decided to spend a few extra days in Paris, in order to make the required visits to the available academicians, and hastily informed Marie ('a new *ennui* has befallen me').[57] He did not arrive in Tocqueville until 30 June, when, contrary to his hopes, he met an extremely frosty reception.

Marie had reason on her side. She had been without her husband for over two months, and had had to endure many small annoyances. He had nearly died (she must have been appallingly worried). He had sent her letters boiling with a lover's impatience and then, at the last moment, put off his return in order to linger in Paris. No doubt she thought the worst, but matters were bad enough without that. She did not forgive him for three days.

When she allowed herself to calm down, she must have reflected that, given the circumstances and Tocqueville's character, little less than the knowledge that she was dying would have brought him away from Paris and his academic campaign. Whether the Académie deserved its prestige is a point not worth discussing. Tocqueville hungered for certified fame and merit, and to become an Immortal was an even better mark of status than favourable book-reviews and steady sales. He knew what Malesherbes had said at his reception in 1775 after he had been elected without competition: that the Académie was a tribunal, independent of all authorities, and respected by all authorities:

> which values all talents, which judges all kinds of merit, and in this enlightened century, a century in which every citizen can speak to the entire Nation by means of the press, those who have the gift of teaching men, or of moving them – the Men of Letters, in short – are to our dispersed people what the orators of Rome and Athens were to their peoples assembled.[58] *

This was a mission worth aspiring to. Besides, Cessac's death had created two vacancies in the Institut: he had also been a member of the Académie des Sciences Morales et Politiques. Tocqueville was determined to get this other place for Beaumont. So he remained in Paris and, in both matters, campaigned successfully. It is to be hoped that Marie came to see that it is useless to punish people for misdeeds which they truly cannot help (however, next time Tocqueville went away to Algiers, she accompanied him).

He spent the summer and autumn recuperating slowly at his chateau: it took much longer than he had hoped. In December he was elected to the Académie with twenty votes out of the thirty cast; a week later Beaumont was chosen to replace Cessac at the Sciences Politiques. During the next four months one of Tocqueville's chief preoccupations was the writing of his reception speech.

* This passage – indeed, Malesherbes's entire address – has a clear bearing on Book 3, ch. I, of his descendant's *Ancien Régime*: 'How, towards the middle of the eighteenth century, the men of letters became the chief politicians of the country, and what resulted.'

It was not altogether easy. The custom of the academy required that he speak a eulogy of his predecessor, and Cessac was an unrewarding subject, a general and administrator who devotedly served every *régime* from the old monarchy to the first Restoration. At first Tocqueville thought of humanizing him with personal anecdotes but could think of none, though he had known him at the Sciences Politiques, for he had given only the impression of duty personified. He consulted Thiers (political disputes were not allowed to sully academic relations), who was happy to send Tocqueville a letter to Cessac from Napoleon himself; but it began, 'My dear Cessac, you are a fool,' so that was no good.[59] Royer-Collard had a disobliging and therefore unusable anecdote of Cessac (who became pious in his old age) worrying on his deathbed about his sexual sins, but not at all about having been the official who annually supplied Napoleon with hundreds of thousands of conscripts to destroy in Russia and Germany. But Royer also made the excellent suggestion that Tocqueville should use his oration as an opportunity to pass philosophical judgement on the Empire and its servants, those men of whom Cessac was the type, 'the great citizens of absolute power'.[60] Tocqueville seized this idea gratefully, and carried it out exactly. In this way academic necessity briefly got him back to what posterity must surely regard as his proper business.

It was a supremely elegant performance, which reveals new shades of meaning at each re-reading. Tocqueville did his best for poor Cessac ('he became a Christian as fervent as he was sincere') but could not disguise his opinion that his predecessor was an unimaginative time-server ('he served God as he had done the Emperor)'. Napoleon and his regime were treated candidly:

> He was as great as a man can be without virtue.
> The singularity of his genius justified in the eyes of his contemporaries and as it were legitimated their extreme subservience; the hero hid the despot; and it was possible to think that in obeying him one submitted less to his power than to the man. But after Napoleon had finished with enlightening and animating the new world that he had created, nothing remained of him but his despotism …

The chief interest of the piece is that although Tocqueville keeps himself out of view ('there is something yet more modest than speaking modestly about oneself, and that is to say nothing at all on the subject'), the discourse is a distillation of his profoundest thought. It was a suitable offering to the Académie: the Immortals might as well know what they were getting; but it was also a valuable exercise for Tocqueville himself, a moment when he thought through his past and present work, and intuited where he was going to go next. *De la démocratie en Amérique*, or rather its doctrines, frequently makes itself felt: for instance, in explaining what he took to be the central achievement of the French Revolution, Tocqueville at last gives a sound working definition of *égalité des conditions*:

> the French Revolution had destroyed all that remained of castes and classes; it had abolished every kind of privilege, dissolved private associations, divided goods, diffused knowledge, and built a nation of citizens more like each other in their fortunes and their education than had ever before been seen on Earth ... it guaranteed us for ever against the worst of all tyrannies, that of a class; but at the same time it made our liberty more problematic.

It can be seen that Tocqueville's mind is also moving forwards to the questions that he was to consider in the *Ancien Régime*; and perhaps the most impressive passage is a panegyric on liberty, which foreshadows the *Souvenirs* as well:

> I believe firmly that it rests with our contemporaries to be great as well as prosperous on condition that they remain free. Nothing but liberty can call up in us those powerful feelings in common which carry away and support our souls beyond the ordinary; it alone can bring variety into the uniformity of our condition and the monotony of our manners; it alone can divert our minds from petty concerns, and elevate the goal of our desires.[61]

The elite of France, led by Queen Marie-Amélie, crowded the hall of the Institut under the famous cupola to hear Tocqueville's address and Comte Molé's reply of welcome; everyone was looking forward to a brilliant intellectual tournament. On the whole they were disappointed. As in the Chamber, Tocqueville was better read than heard, and the moment was not quite right for an anti-Napoleonic diatribe: the Emperor's body had been brought back from St Helena and splendidly re-interred in the Invalides only fifteen months before. Many in the audience were frankly bored, and most thought that Molé had the better of the exchange. He too might be labelled a timeserver, and in defending Cessac and Napoleon he was defending himself. He did so with waspish elegance, but today his plea for the regime of Brumaire and the men who served it wears a commonplace air. Even in 1842 there were dissenters: Guizot's verdict has been cited already, and Royer-Collard (not surprisingly) thought Tocqueville's address much the better of the two, as he told the duchesse de Dino – no doubt he also told Tocqueville.

Some time before – after Tocqueville's second speech on the Eastern question – the duchesse had asked Royer what he thought of Tocqueville as a politician. His response had been grudging: 'He has a fund of honest motives which is not adequate for his purposes, and which he imprudently expends, but some remnants of which will always be left to him. I am afraid that in his anxiety to succeed he will wander into impossible paths by an attempt to reconcile irreconcilable elements.' He offered one hand to the Left, said the sage, and another to the Right and would have offered a third hand if he had it. 'Our hermit of the rue d'Enfer displays a considerable spice of malignity beneath his excellent qualities,' commented the duchesse, who liked Tocqueville.[62] But even Royer-Collard would not have accused Tocqueville of gesturing to all sides in his academic address. He had defied the worshippers of Napoleon and the supporters of the *juste milieu* and reaffirmed his commitment to uncompromisable principles of liberty and integrity. He had given meaning to his stance of political independence: we can see why his friends always stuck to him. At the same time we can see why independence turned so quickly into impotent isolation. Royer-Collard understood. He thought that the criticisms in Tocqueville's speech had been too accurate to be popular: 'the Emperor and the Empire have a greater influence over men's minds than I was aware.'[63]

So Tocqueville's political career was doomed to stagnate – until there was a new revolution.

CHAPTER SEVENTEEN

FEBRUARY

1847–48

*Quoiqu'il n'y ait rien de plus clairement établi dans la
législation de Dieu sur les sociétés humaines, que le rapport
nécessaire qui unit les grands mouvements intellectuels
aux grands mouvements politiques, les chefs des nations ne
semblent jamais l'apercevoir que quand on le leur met sous
les yeux.*

ALEXIS DE TOCQUEVILLE[1]*

ALL OVER WESTERN AND CENTRAL EUROPE the harvest
of 1846 failed, destroyed by incessant rain and the potato blight which
had already brought on the Great Famine in Ireland. In France, as so
often before in the country's history, the resultant dearth led to rage
and riot: the price of bread at one moment rose to 90 *centimes* per
kilo, inducing Victor Hugo to remark that '*les jacqueries germent.*'[2] In
the town of Buzençais (Indre) the outbreak of violence was particularly savage: after it had been repressed three of its leaders were guillotined. One of the objects of popular hatred there was a rich man
called Chambert. On the evening of 13 January 1847 his servants were
warned to make themselves scarce next day or they would share their

---

* 'Although nothing is more clearly written in God's law for human society than the necessary
  concordance between great intellectual movements and great political ones, leaders of nations
  never seem to notice the fact until it is thrust before their eyes.'

master's fate. Next day came, and so did the mob: the town and its biggest factory were sacked and Chambert's house was attacked. A man called Venin ('I am the chief brigand') marched into the sitting-room; Chambert's valet bravely knocked him down, but then thought better of it and ran away. Chambert, who had gone for his gun, came back and shot Venin dead. For this he was hunted from room to room and then from house to house; cornered at last, he was beaten to death, crying, 'Mercy, friends!' 'You have no friends,' was the reply; then the rioters went back to the Chambert house to deal with their victim's old mother.

Fortunately for her a devoted servant, Madeleine Blanchet, stood by her. First she tried to get her mistress away to safety; but then, surrounded in the courtyard by a crowd which knocked Mme Chambert down and showed every sign of intending another murder, she turned at bay, shouting, 'You won't kill my mistress without killing me!' and did her best to intercept the blows, although Mme Chambert urged her to escape: 'Be off, my poor girl, let me die here, be off!' Two men were touched by this heroism and helped Blanchet to take Mme Chambert to a place of safety; but the woman's blood was up, she returned to the house, now being looted, to save what she could of the family's posses-sions, and was surprisingly successful. News of her exploits eventually reached the Académie Française, which annually awarded prizes for virtue. It decided to give Blanchet a special one of 5,000 francs and a gold medal. The speaker at the prize-giving (there were seven other awards) was Alexis de Tocqueville.[3]

Tocqueville hated having to deliver this oration, largely because he was expected to moralize at length (in the end he cut fourteen pages of his draft, and confined himself to describing the deeds of the prize-winners); but he told the Blanchet story thrillingly. The whole speech deserves a place of honour among his minor works: it is one of his few encounters with the actualities of life for the French poor. Thus he shows (perhaps without meaning to) how inescapable and crushing was the burden of debt on the working classes. Yet he does not mention what, to a later eye, is the most obvious lesson of the stories he tells: they all illustrate the inanity of the July regime, a government which apparently could not protect the rich and would not help the poor. It had no support among the workers of the towns and did not deserve any: even the Académie's prizes came rather too late to be useful (if welcome), given that the recipients were being rewarded for the virtue of having already saved themselves or others.* Such reflections could have no place at a prize-giving; but only ten weeks previously Tocqueville, serving his term as rotatory director of the Académie and president of the Institut, had made a speech formally congratulating the King on his name-day and expressing the hope that he would long enjoy the glory of reigning by the consent of his intelligent people. In his reply Louis-Philippe, among other banalities, congratulated France on enjoying 'peace, order and liberty'. (It was on this occasion that Rémusat made Tocqueville laugh indecorously by murmuring in his ear that 'the loyal citizen must be suitably moved, but the academician suffers.'[4]) There is no hint that anyone in the charmed circle as yet foresaw trouble.

But the July Monarchy was increasingly unstable. Its founders had tried to do for France what has been done successfully in many other European countries – Belgium, Britain, Denmark, the Netherlands, Norway, Sweden and, above all, Spain, a state with as turbulent a history as its northern neighbour, where the Bourbons have frequently been dislodged, but still reign. The Spanish instance shows not so much that murderous disagreements may destroy monarchies, as that powerful popular consensus can renew them whatever the difficulties. The July Monarchy never won such a consensus, though it had much intelligent support. Disagreement among its leaders helped to bring it down; but so, perhaps, did their agreement. The rationale of the regime was that France should be governed by its wealthiest and best-trained citizens – the notables. Property qualifications for the vote and for eligibility to the Chamber, measured by the amount of tax paid by each individual, were slightly easier than they had been under the Restoration, when the electorate never numbered as many as 100,000 persons. In 1831 that of the new regime comprised 166,583 voters, who by 1847 had increased to 241,000 – but they were still less than 3 per cent of the adult male population, whereas in Britain, after the Great Reform Act, the electorate was, roughly, 10 per cent of adult males,

* 'Is not a Patron, my Lord, one who looks with unconcern on a man struggling for life in the water, and, when he has reached ground, encumbers him with help?' (Samuel Johnson, *Letter to Lord Chesterfield*).

and in the United States every adult white male citizen had the vote. Thus the vast majority of Frenchmen were still barred from any direct share in power, and a growing number actively resented the fact.

Here was a threat to the regime which could never be disarmed. The obvious course would have been to extend the franchise somewhat, but no single small extension would alter the fact that the majority of citizens was excluded. On the other hand a bold extension – a turn perhaps to universal male suffrage – would overthrow the very foundation of the regime, its insistence on what the notables called 'political capacity', on their right, along with the petty oligarchs of town and country, to monopolize power. Politicians who took this view, who in this way were essentially conservative, held office from first to last under Louis-Philippe and refused to contemplate any radical reform (and in 1846 Richard Cobden, the leader of the Anti-Corn Law League, was astonished at the failure of the French opposition to demand more than insignificant changes).[5] The majority of the monarchy's supporters, the so-called party of resistance, would not tolerate any change at all. So the opposing 'party of movement', which never won a majority in the Chamber, was eventually driven to employ tactics which threatened the stability or even the very existence of the regime: in no other way could it hope either to win power or push through any new laws which it might think necessary – laws about schools, the abolition of slavery, prison reform, and so on.

This state of affairs meant that the monarchy came to be largely at the mercy of events. It was constantly jolted by international emergencies, riots, economic crises and attempts on the life of Louis-Philippe ('It is only in hunting me that there is no close season,' he observed),[6] which, cumulatively, left it greatly weakened. It was not helped by its absolute refusal to make concessions. The King would not hear of diplomatic initiatives which might lead to war; Guizot would not (or at any rate did not) countenance any extension of the franchise. To secure their hold on power he and Duchâtel perfected le système Guizot, which seemed to the opposition to be a perversion of the work of the July Revolution. The 1840 ministry (Soult–Guizot) relied on the September press laws and on a system of electoral fraud and corruption which, while not particularly surprising or shocking to anyone with some knowledge of English parliamentary history or American

machine politics, scandalized earnest liberals like Tocqueville. By
1846 the ministry was so practised in its black arts that, in a fatal
triumph which broke all precedents, it won a general election with a
majority of 100 seats. A real organized conservative party seemed at
last to have emerged. But the ministry was as wedded to inertia as
ever, and no countervailing liberal party arose to force it into action:
as Guizot remarked, there were no French Whigs, only a hopelessly
divided opposition which had as one of its components an increasingly vigorous republican faction, although it was illegal to advocate
republicanism. The conservatives began to lapse back into factional-
ism themselves.

In these circumstances the individual traits of the political leaders
counted for little, although as Tocqueville liked to point out they were
collectively as distinguished a generation as France had known. Guizot
was one of the greatest of French parliamentarians; Thiers, for all his
attitudinizing and eccentricities ('In Thiers there were unplumbed
depths of shallowness,' says Douglas Johnson) and the unswerving
egoism which made him so bad a party leader, yet kept the idea of
constitutional opposition alive by his vigour, eloquence and intelligence. Odilon Barrot was a lesser man but a good speaker and a conscientious organizer. The stormy petrel Lamartine was even more egoistic
than Thiers; yet if his inconsistency and opportunism deprived him of
any solid influence in the Chamber, his eloquence and radicalism won
him a great following in the country at large. But all the activity of
these men was a winnowing of the wind. No long-term achievements
seemed possible; politically they all lived from day to day. According to
Tocqueville public opinion generally was sunk in apathy. The victory
of 1846 confirmed Louis-Philippe and Guizot in their fatal compla-
cency, reminiscent of that of Charles X and Polignac.[7]

Tocqueville had no such reason for short-sightedness, and during
the summer of 1847 he began to feel seriously anxious about the future.
Characteristically, he was less perturbed by the economic crisis and by
the increasing illiberalism of the regime, than by the movement of
ideas.

At the end of July he and Marie retired as usual to their chateau.
The only writing which Tocqueville had in hand was an essay on the
history of Cherbourg for a volume edited by Aristide Guilbert: it was

essentially another move in his long and still unsuccessful campaign to bring a railway to the Cotentin. He attended the *conseil-général* and, we may presume, cultivated his constituents. The result was a slowly growing uneasiness about the political outlook. France, he told Nassau Senior, was peaceful and fairly prosperous (this statement was erroneous); but although everything seemed calm, many minds were starting to think that the present system could not last. Tocqueville did not at first agree (what could be put in its place?) but he never stopped saying that for seventeen years the government had been corrupting 'the middle class' – by which, as we have seen, he meant the *pays légal* – turning it into 'a petty, corrupt, vulgar aristocracy' which it was degrading to be governed by. If this opinion became general it might lead to great misfortune, he thought (but he went on propagating it). He wrote to Corcelle:

> I don't know if your neighbourhood resembles mine. Here, people's minds are calm, even apathetic, little concerned with politics, with no marked liking for any idea or any man, but surprisingly given over to a deep, unaggressive contempt for all ministers and administrators, and infested with the unshakeable conviction that everything is for sale or may be got by favour and that political immorality is the general, habitual atmosphere in which the political world moves.*

Nobody wanted to do anything about it, but as Tocqueville pondered these attitudes he began to be alarmed. He did not see how a government with so little support could last much longer: 'for the first time since the Revolution of July I fear that we may yet have to live through some more revolutionary trials.' He did not see when or how it could happen, but a storm would arise sooner or later, unless something happened to revive public morals.[8]

He and his correspondents, Corcelle and Beaumont, were shocked by two great scandals which burst on France that summer: two former Orleanist ministers were sent to prison for having taken bribes, and the duc de Choiseul-Praslin murdered his duchesse (the daughter of Marshal Sébastiani, another ex-minister) in every circumstance of incompetent cruelty. The duc was allowed to kill himself with arsenic

---

* He was to repeat this assertion in his speech of 27 January 1848.

before being brought to trial, which, as everyone noticed, was not what would have happened to a working man. The affair, said Tocqueville, gave him nightmares; worse, as he wrote to Beaumont, 'it is impossible to suppose that this string of criminal, shameful deeds erupting in the midst of the upper classes doesn't demonstrate a profound sickness in national morality and, especially, that it won't weaken the ascendancy of society's summit over its base.' In short, the notables were discrediting themselves. Beaumont, whose family had known and liked the duchesse, quite agreed: 'it is all too clear that the public sensation has only been so great because it has roused in the masses the one revolutionary passion remaining to them; that of equality.' He also denounced Lamartine's *History of the Girondins*, which had just appeared and was selling thousands of copies: 'The book is perfidious in that while it judges severely the crimes of which it paints the most terrible picture, it at the same time always apologizes for the criminals' (Chateaubriand was more succinct: 'The miscreant! He has gilded the guillotine!').[9]*

Events would soon confirm that these various episodes did indeed portend a great crisis, but Tocqueville's apprehensions were aroused even more by his reading. Alerted, perhaps, by the extraordinary success of Étienne Cabet's *Voyage en Icarie*, he began to study socialist authors such as Louis Blanc, François Fourier and Robert Owen. In the autumn of 1847 he wrote a strikingly civil letter to Prosper Enfantin, the Saint-Simonian leader, who had sent him a copy of his latest work:

> There is, throughout your book, a lively awareness of the suffering of the poor and enthusiasm for everything which can equalize the sum of human happiness in this world. I too believe that the drive of the long revolution which our fathers began and of which we will not see the end is towards a greater development of equality on the Earth and a more and more equal sharing of the goods which it produces.

He could not approve of Saint-Simonian methods (his suspicions of that sect largely explain his initially ungenerous attitude to Michel Chevalier), but he was glad to think that he and Enfantin had the same goal, and he signed off with assurances of his most distinguished consideration.[10]

* AT thought the same: see *Souvenirs*, OC XII 94–5.

However much allowance is made for conventional courtesy, Tocqueville's sincerity in this letter need not be doubted: he had said much the same in a letter to Arthur de Gobineau as early as 1843. There had been a shift in Tocqueville's thought: the protean word equality has acquired a meaning which would be acceptable to any modern Christian or Social Democrat. But at about this time he also seems to have read Proudhon, and another word suddenly gained prominence in his vocabulary: property.[11]

What is Property? had been published in 1840 (the same year as the second part of the *Démocratie*) and had created a sensation by its blunt answer to its own question: 'Property is theft.' This dangerous epigram made all property-holders, large or small, shake in their guilty shoes, although at this stage Proudhon, the voice of the French peasantry and *artisanat*, had in mind mainly the property in land which, in spite of the Revolution, still underpinned the ascendancy of the notables: only later was he to attack industrial capitalists, and he never questioned – indeed, he asserted – the right of every citizen to ownership of his dwelling, his cabbage-patch and the tools of his trade. He had been much influenced by the 1835 *Démocratie*, and agreed with Tocqueville on many points – for instance, on decentralization and the dangers of violent revolution. He was quite as great a writer, and is still temptingly quotable, but here it is only necessary to establish that whenever he took up a theme from Tocqueville he pressed it to extremes. For instance: 'humanity, for the last four thousand years, has been going through a process of levelling ... French society, unknown to itself and by the fatality of Providential laws, is every day engaged in demolishing property (for example, by the laws of expropriation, the conversion of bonds, the protection of the labour of women and children).'[12] 'Property is the last of the false gods.'[13]

As a liberal and a landowner, Tocqueville could not be expected to welcome such an unusual disciple.[14] He was no exception to the depressing truth that wealth usually makes its owners timid rather than brave. So it is not surprising that he took fright in a particular way as soon as he sensed that the July Monarchy, dedicated to the protection of property, was in danger. His reaction did not even have the merit of originality. As far back as December 1788, when the Estates-General was about to be summoned, the princes of the blood had warned Louis XVI:

The State is in peril ... soon the rights of property will be attacked, and inequality of wealth will be set up as a matter for reform; already the suppression of feudal rights has been proposed. Can Your Majesty bring yourself to sacrifice and humiliate your brave, ancient and respectable nobility?[15]

Allowing for the abolition of feudal rights, Tocqueville's position sixty years later was no different. He was determined to resist all pernicious new doctrines. He held that property (undefined, as usual) was the last guarantee of ordered, civilized society and must be protected at all costs.[16] He stuck implacably, indeed bloodily, to this doctrine throughout 1848, like so many lesser men. This attitude was the root of the year's tragedy. Frenchmen knew too little of each other. Certainly the notables, Tocqueville among them, projected their own violent hatred and panic onto the urban workers, and in doing so created the very monster which they feared. Tocqueville was not even exceptional in expressing his fear in ideological terms, as if he were resolved to demonstrate the accuracy of the Marxian tenet that ideas are determined by material circumstances, and have no other validity. But not many had his natural genius for historical and political reflection; which explains why his less intellectual colleagues were slow to respond to his message.

In 1847 the emergency had not yet arrived, and Tocqueville's socialist reading, perhaps reinforced by the work he did on his oration on virtue, and by the economic crisis, explains why at this moment his pendulum swung briefly as far to the left as it was ever to go. He took up his pen. It had become increasingly clear, even to many of Guizot's followers, that for all its parliamentary strength the ministry was stagnant, and that France could not afford such inertia. Tocqueville and Dufaure* thought that they saw an opportunity. The King would never again accept Thiers as first minister if he could help it, for fear of being plunged into another dangerous foreign crisis, and Barrot had now signed on as Thiers's junior partner. So Tocqueville's group hoped

---

* Armand Dufaure (1798–1881), lawyer, deputy for Saintes (Charente-Inférieure) 1834–48; minister of public works in the 1839 Soult ministry. He was a forceful orator and a capable politician; he and AT worked more and more closely together during the last years of the July Monarchy.

that if they formed themselves into a new party (they proposed to call themselves the Young Left) with a programme of moderate reform, they could attract enough conservatives – men like the intelligent and energetic Charles-Auguste de Morny* – to destroy Guizot's majority in the Chamber and, if the King saw sense, to take his place. Dufaure asked Tocqueville to draft a manifesto, and during October 1847, while Tocqueville and Marie were visiting Comte Hervé at Clairoix (Oise), where the old man was now living with his acknowledged companion (*dame de compagnie*), Mme Guermarquer, widow of the family agent at Lannion, Alexis got down to work. The document he produced was never used, presumably because events moved too fast; it survives only in revealing fragments.[17] They show Tocqueville struggling with most of the usual problems of his career in the Chamber as he tries to find a way of distinguishing his position clearly from both Guizot and Thiers, and analyses the underlying weakness of the regime in pages which would eventually be inserted, little modified, into the *Souvenirs*; but there are novelties, and they seem clearly to stem from his examination of socialist writings. He sees that the July regime has become identified with the rights and power of the propertied class, and will now be challenged on this ground:

> it is between those who have possessions and those who do not that the struggle of parties will now be waged. The great battlefield will be property and political questions will turn chiefly on greater or lesser modifications of property rights. So we are again going to see great public agitation and great parties.[18]

If socialist doctrines on the point are not to be victorious something will have to be done for the poor and the labouring classes. The poorest should be exempt from taxation; welfare institutions should be set up: savings banks, credit bureaux, free schools, factory acts, charity workshops (*ouvroirs*), a poor law, etc.

> In short, there are three methods for relieving the people: 1. By lifting some of the public dues off them or at least only charging them

---

* Charles-Auguste de Morny (1811–65), illegitimate son of the comte de Flahaut (therefore Talleyrand's grandson) and Hortense de Beauharnais, mother of Louis-Napoleon Bonaparte. At this stage Morny was a supporter of Guizot, but nevertheless believed that reform was necessary.

proportionately to their means. 2. By setting up institutions which will enable them to get out of debt and look after themselves. 3. By direct assistance to the needy.

The current parliamentary parties are united, he says, in their indifference to the plight of the people; unless this changes there will eventually be a grave crisis, though he does not expect it to come soon.[19]

It can hardly be denied that Tocqueville (perhaps belatedly) had put his finger on a real problem and real if limited remedies, but his views do not seem to have found favour with his friends; and anyway the crisis of the regime was about to be touched off by a very different reform programme.

Tocqueville now explicitly accepted the view that the working people, who had carried the July Revolution, had reason to feel cheated of the fruits of victory: this was one of the most important tenets of the republican Left. But Odilon Barrot and his followers of the 'dynastic Left' (Gustave de Beaumont among them) believed that the central issue was electoral and parliamentary reform, meaning that placemen (prefects and other officials) should be barred from election to the Chamber, and that the size of the electorate should be doubled. After the defeat of 1846 it was more than ever difficult to see how this moderate and sensible programme could be carried into law, and the September laws made it formidably difficult to agitate – avowedly political public meetings, for instance, were illegal. So the dynastic Left launched the celebrated 'banquets' campaign in the summer of 1847. This was possible because it was legal for subscribers to meet for public dinners, provided that all non-subscribers were excluded. Barrot went up and down France eating and drinking at crowded feasts, where the diners could propose radical toasts and demand reform. Most of the opposition deputies participated, but there were some conspicuous exceptions: Thiers, for instance; Dufaure; Tocqueville. Although Tocqueville gave Thiers no credit for his abstention, their reasons were the same. The banqueters were appealing to the *pays réel* against the *pays légal*; their agitation was subversive, and if it failed would merely have made them more odious to the King and the conservative majority; if it succeeded in rousing the people anything might happen. Unsurprisingly, this was also Guizot's view.[20]

By December, when the political world reassembled in Paris, it seemed that the banquets had failed: they had come and gone and left no trace. The last of them was supposed to be held in Paris after parliament met, but even that was now doubtful. The only banquet which had roused real enthusiasm was the one honouring Lamartine in July, in Mâcon, his constituency, which had been a tribute to the author of the *Girondins* rather than part of the campaign. Lamartine took advantage of the occasion, and defied a thunderstorm which erupted overhead to make some highly inflammatory remarks. But for the rest, the banquets had chiefly served to advertise the split between the republicans and the dynastic Left. As so often before, the opposition's divisions made it deplorably ineffective.

Attention turned to the opening session of the Chambers. There was a general belief that the ministry was weaker than it seemed on paper: Guizot himself shared it. He was alarmed and angered by the banquets, and by the clamour of the opposition press; he was also worried by the rise of the 'progressive conservatives' – he said, years later, that had they known how to be patient they would soon have attained a majority in the Chamber, 'but impatience and lack of foresight, those two fatal maladies of so many political performers' overwhelmed them. More seriously, Guizot, although he was now prime minister as well as foreign minister (Soult having retired) was tactically constrained, not only by his own rigidity and his belief that he was indispensable, but by the insuperable obstinacy of the King, who was displeased on the one occasion when Guizot hinted that reform might eventually be possible, and threatened to use his veto for the first time if any reform measure were passed by the Chambers.[21] Louis-Philippe, from having been the solution in 1830, had become the central problem. He was brave, intelligent and kindly, but he had an excessive admiration for his own talents. His insistence on ruling France from behind a façade of liberal institutions deceived nobody and pleased few. His weaknesses had grown more pronounced as he aged, especially the compulsive garrulity which made it almost impossible for him to listen to his ministers or anyone else, as Tocqueville discovered on the one occasion that he was given a private audience. 'I want you to talk to me a little about America,' said the King, but Tocqueville knew that this meant he was going to talk on the subject himself, which he did for three-quarters of an hour.[22] In these circumstances it is not surprising that Guizot decided to follow his own reactionary instincts. Like Charles X in similar difficulties, he decided to rally his supporters by carrying the battle to the foe. The King having pledged his unwavering support, Guizot inserted in the Speech from the Throne, which opened the session, a deliberately provocative phrase denouncing the opposition's 'hostile or blind passions'.* The bait was taken, and for the next few weeks fury raged in the Chamber, with Guizot icily (and unwisely) refusing to make the slightest concession and the opposition deputies denouncing him as worse than Polignac. The resemblance was certainly becoming very striking and, to Tocqueville, alarming.

He spoke on 27 January, in what was his most famous and successful speech, although – or perhaps because – it was less formally impressive than some of his other orations. Its power lay in its rhetoric. Tocqueville had two purposes. The first was to play his part in the opposition's grand scheme to pin the accusation of corruption not just to the government as a whole, or to lesser ministers, but for the first time to Guizot himself, his official secretary having been caught in jobbery. Tocqueville did not miss the chance to revel in self-righteous denunciation:

> Never, never would I have believed, while hearing the minister for foreign affairs expound from this tribune with admirably chosen words the moral law of politics, while hearing him hold such language as to make me proud of my country, though I am of the opposition – never, assuredly, would I have believed that what has happened was possible.

It was gratifying to agitate the Chamber with this sort of thing. But he also had something fresher to say. The government, he urged (and he clearly had the whole regime in mind) must mend its ways or it would fall.

> People say that there is no danger because there are no riots; they say that since there is no significant disorder on the surface of society, revolution is far from us. Gentlemen, let me say that I think you are

---

* Nothing more precisely illustrates the difference between nineteenth-century and current parliamentary conventions than the reaction to this phrase, which nowadays would hardly be noticed.

deceiving yourselves ... Look at what is going on among the working classes which today, I admit, are peaceable. It is true that they are not afflicted by political passions, properly so called, to the same extent that they were formerly; but don't you see that their passions, from being political, have turned social? ... Are you not listening to what they say every day among themselves? Don't you hear them repeating incessantly that all those above them are incapable and unworthy of governing? That the present distribution of goods in society is unjust? That the foundations of property are not equitable?

If such opinions continued to spread there would be a mighty revolution sooner or later. The ministry must change its ways. Throughout history governments had fallen when they became unworthy of power.

> Gentlemen, consider the old monarchy. It was stronger than you, stronger in its origins; it relied more surely than you can on tradition, on ancient manners and antique beliefs; it was stronger than you, and yet it tumbled down into the dust. And why did it fall? Do you think it was by accident? Do you think it was the doing of one person, or of the deficit, of the oath in the tennis-court, of La Fayette or Mirabeau? No, gentlemen; there was a deeper, truer cause, and that cause was that the then ruling class had become, by its unconcern, its selfishness, and its vices, incapable and unworthy of governing! ('*Hear hear! Hear hear!*')

He ended by pleading for reform, or if not for that, then for a change of heart in the government; otherwise nothing lay ahead but the abyss.[23]

Tocqueville for once said much that the Chamber wanted to hear, and his success was correspondingly great; but Dufaure told him that it would have been even greater if he had not tried to frighten the house with his talk of revolution: nobody believed it. And Tocqueville, searching his soul eighteen months later, discovered that he had not entirely believed it himself. Who could have expected such a revolution as was actually going to occur? 'I believe I saw more clearly than anyone else the general causes which were driving the July Monarchy to its ruin. I did not imagine the accidents which were going to bring it about. Nevertheless the days which separated us from the catastrophe were rapidly running out.'[24]

Indeed they were. The government's essential mistake was to

drive the opposition to extremes; the mistake of the opposition leaders was to try to draw back at the last minute. Their anguished dithering over the proposed Parisian banquet would be purely comic had its outcome been less serious. Vanity, timidity, ambition and foolishness (Tocqueville was to say of Barrot that he always blended a certain silliness in his faults as well as in his virtues)[25] drove them down the road to a disaster that most did not want. The dynastic opposition could not decide whether it dreaded the government or the people of Paris more; most of the republicans feared to provoke a savage repression. Almost everyone was secretly relieved when the government formally banned the banquet. Barrot proposed to save face by moving a vote of censure on Guizot in the Chamber. It was a last gesture of futility: Guizot treated it with contempt. But meanwhile events had taken the turn which Tocqueville had increasingly feared: the Parisians had gone down into the streets, and many of them meant business.

The banquet had been announced for 22 February, and the news of its cancellation by no means reached everybody. The day dawned in drizzle, later setting into a steady downpour. This was not going to deter the crowds: as Georges Duveau has pointed out, it was the usual weather for great *journées* in French history.[26] Students from the Left Bank, then workers from the *faubourgs* converged on the place de la Concorde and the place de la Madeleine from the morning onwards. There was no great air of crisis, rather of good humour – there were even some cheers for the army as its detachments moved to take up positions from which they could control events – but some street-boys amused themselves by making bonfires of the chairs and kiosks in the Champs Elysées. The Chamber of Deputies postponed debate on Barrot's motion and turned to consideration of a charter for a bank in Bordeaux. Tocqueville was there, and observed that only the two speakers on the subject paid any attention to the order of the day: everyone else was preoccupied with what was going on in the streets. He himself was not yet alarmed: two days previously Duchâtel had assured him that everything was under control. He now repeated the assurance; but Tocqueville noticed that his habitual *tic*, a sort of wriggling of the neck and shoulders, was much worse than usual: 'this small observation made me more thoughtful than anything else [that day].'[27]

Well it might. The next forty-eight hours were dominated by a series of almost inexplicable miscalculations by the government which, more than anything else, brought about the sudden collapse of the monarchy. On the morning of Wednesday, 23 February, the crowds were larger than ever, and more threatening. Tocqueville went down to the Chamber and found his colleagues in the same anxious, distracted mood as the day before; at length they got themselves to the point of asking the cabinet to make a statement on the situation. It was three o'clock; suddenly Guizot, coming from the Tuileries, walked into the Chamber with his usual steady step, mounted the tribune, and holding his head as high as possible – he did not want anyone to detect how deeply he felt humiliated – announced that he and his colleagues had been dismissed.[28]

Louis-Philippe had lost his nerve. He had chosen to rely on the National Guard, rather than the regulars, to restore and maintain order in Paris, and then suddenly discovered what, if he had had competent officers, he should have known long before, that the Guard was not to be relied on: it too, or most of it, hated Guizot and wanted reform. The Queen and his sons insisted that Guizot must go, and in a moment's weakness which he seems almost immediately to have regretted,[29] he acquiesced, and sent for Molé, who was certainly not the man of the hour: precious time was to be lost while he tried and failed to form a cabinet. In short, at a moment of serious crisis the King had deprived France of its government. The crisis immediately began to get worse.

Tocqueville sat in the Chamber and sardonically watched his colleagues' reaction to the thunderbolt. It seemed to him that the conservatives of the majority were dismayed only by the loss of place and profit; that most of the opposition, as they exulted, were thinking chiefly of getting their hands on the loot; and that the leaders of the opposition had suddenly become discreet, thinking that they might soon need the support of the men who had just been dislodged. Dufaure's behaviour to Tocqueville became shifty, as he prepared to break with him in order to get a ministry – which amused rather than angered Tocqueville, since Dufaure's calculations were so transparent. He must also have thought them futile, for that evening, visiting Beaumont, he said that as the National Guard had been allowed to overthrow a ministry all authority was prostrate. Beaumont was not impressed. 'You always take the gloomy view,' he said. 'Let us first enjoy our victory, and worry about the consequences later.' Dining *chez* Lanjuinais, Tocqueville found much the same attitude: still no-one recognized the revolution. He went home early, and then straight to bed, and although he lodged very near the ministry of foreign affairs,* 'did not hear the gunfire which was to shape so many destinies ... I slept without knowing that I had seen the last day of the monarchy of July.'[30]

For early that night some of the demonstrators tried to force their way into the ministry of foreign affairs. They were resisted by the guard. A shot was heard, fired probably by one of the crowd (such an incident must have been almost inevitable in the circumstances). In alarm the guard fired in their turn, with deadly effect: about fifty demonstrators were killed. The word flew through Paris; before long the citizens decided that Louis-Philippe must go; they determined to take control.

In the morning (24 February) Tocqueville was told by his tearful cook that the government was massacring the poor people. He did not believe it, but left the house to gather news and to consult his friends. He could not find Rémusat or Beaumont, who had both been summoned to the Tuileries, where the King was still trying to put a ministry together, Molé having failed.[31] Dufaure too had disappeared, but as Tocqueville walked along the boulevards with Corcelle he saw revolutionary activity on every hand: barricades were rising all about him. He noticed a great contrast with the July Days. Then, Paris had been boiling, so that it had seemed to him like one vast steaming cauldron. Now the insurgents were merely businesslike. 'This time they were not overthrowing a regime, they were letting it fall.'[32] He set out for the Palais Bourbon, and on his way saw further evidence of the feeble bewilderment which had afflicted everyone in authority from the moment it became clear that the National Guard was unreliable. He was at first relieved to find the place de la Concorde occupied by regular troops, commanded by General Bedeau, whom he had got to know during his visit to Algeria in 1846; he supposed that they

---

* AT was now living at 30, rue de la Madeleine; the foreign ministry was a few doors away on the boulevard des Capucines. In a few years the whole area would be drastically remodelled by Haussmann.

were there to protect the Tuileries and the Chamber of Deputies. But Bedeau had received orders not to fight, and not having the sense or the initiative to disobey could think of nothing to do but harangue the insurgents ineffectively. Tocqueville had to warn him to desist, and get back on his horse, or he would be lynched. Minutes later, a few yards away, the crowd massacred a detachment of gendarmes. Tocqueville himself was challenged as he made his way through the crowd: where was he going? 'I replied, to the Chamber, and added, to show that I belonged to the opposition, "*Vive la Réforme*! You know that the Guizot ministry has been thrown out?" "Yes, Monsieur, I know," said his challenger jeeringly, gesturing towards the Tuileries, "but we want more than that."'[33]

Tocqueville reached the Chamber and found everything in disorder: the president, Paul Sauzet, was refusing to open the session. Tocqueville went to reason with him but found him in such a state – pacing to and fro, sitting down, standing up, sitting down again with one foot tucked under his big behind, 'as was his custom in moments of great stress', that it seemed likely he would do more harm than good if he did start proceedings. 'It was very bad luck for the House of Orleans that it had an honest man of this kind in charge of the Chamber on such a day. A bold rascal would have done better.' Worried about the defencelessness of the Chamber, Tocqueville started out for the ministry of the interior to see if anything could be arranged; on his way he met Odilon Barrot and Gustave de Beaumont coming along surrounded by a large crowd. Their hats were jammed down on their heads as far as they would go, their coats were covered in dust, their faces were haggard. It was their moment of triumph – they had been appointed ministers – but they looked as if they were on their way to be hanged. Beaumont whispered to Tocqueville that he had just seen Louis-Philippe abdicate.[34]

Beaumont had had an exceptionally trying morning. He had got to the Tuileries at nine o'clock to be told that a new ministry, led by Thiers and Barrot, had been formed, and that he was part of it. Marshal Bugeaud was to be put in command of all the military forces in Paris, and both decisions were to be published in the *Moniteur*. But that would take time, so Barrot and Beaumont were sent out to spread the good news through the city. They went as far as the Porte Saint-Denis and back, and at first all seemed to be going well: they were welcomed with enthusiastic cries of *Vive la Réforme!* and *Vive Barrot!* and were politely helped past the barricades, Barrot speechifying when he could. Beaumont noticed that the barricades were formidably well-built. But the news of Bugeaud's appointment changed the atmosphere: Bugeaud was bitterly hated by the Parisians for his part in the massacre of the rue Transnonain in 1834. Barrot and Beaumont began to hear cries of *À bas Louis-Philippe! Mort à Louis-Philippe! Plus de Bourbons!* and *Are you sure you haven't been lied to, M. Barrot?*[35]

When Beaumont got back to the Tuileries, at about 11.15, he found that precious time was being wasted. Thiers wanted to withdraw as first minister in favour of Barrot, but Louis-Philippe, who still seemed to have no sense of urgency, threatened instead to recall Guizot, which took Beaumont's breath away. Then the King went out to review his troops, and was booed by part of the National Guard. This appears to have been his moment of truth, and it broke him. Without even looking at the regular troops and the loyal guardsmen he went back into the chateau, and soon, to Beaumont's horror, people began to talk of abdication. Beaumont at this point let himself be distracted by his pressing need for lunch, and when he rose from table he found that the fatal decision had been taken; he was only in time to see the King writing the actual act in the midst of an incessant scrimmage of coming and going. One anxious flunkey* hurried in, asking impatiently if the document was ready: the King replied patiently, 'I can't write faster, you know.' Gunfire could be heard in the distance. Once the act was signed it was given to Marshal Gérard to proclaim; Beaumont went with him to the Palais-Royal, where another gendarmerie post was under fierce attack. General Lamoricière, who was trying to stop the fighting, received two bayonet wounds; Beaumont himself came under fire. He went back to the Tuileries with his brother-in-law, Oscar de La Fayette, and found the great palace utterly deserted – no King, no courtiers, no politicians, no servants, no soldiers. He thought this universal flight as unnecessary as it was unwise, but there was nothing to be

---

* Said by others to have been the duc de Montpensier, Louis-Philippe's youngest son. But if so, surely Beaumont would have recognized him?

done, so he too left and was just beginning to cross the gardens when
Odilon Barrot (who had carefully kept out of sight for the past few
hours) reappeared, with a crowd of cheering supporters. Beaumont
joined him, and they went off to proclaim a Regency at the ministry
of the interior, which was in the rue de Grenelle. Tocqueville met
them just outside the Palais Bourbon. It was about 3.15. He wanted
to know if they were going to do anything to make the Chamber
safe. 'Who cares about the Chamber!' said Beaumont curtly. He
thought that it had ceased to exist, whereas Tocqueville held that, as
the last surviving political institution, it should be strongly supported
if the people were to be recalled to the idea of the rule of law.[36]
Nevertheless he went with his friends to the ministry of the interior,
but such was the noise and confusion that he despaired of doing any
good, and returned to the Chamber, where on his arrival he was told
that Sauzet had opened the session after all and that the duchesse
d'Orléans had just appeared with her young son, the comte de Paris,
in a last attempt to save the July Monarchy by getting the Chamber
to acknowledge her son as King and herself as Regent. On hearing
this Tocqueville ran up the stairs four at a time and rushed into the
Chamber.[37]

The scene that followed was to be described in some of the most
memorable pages of the *Souvenirs*, which will not be paraphrased here.
It need only be said that after gazing at it all for a moment Tocqueville
made his way to his usual seat on the upper benches of the centre left,
'for it has always been my rule that in moments of crisis it is not only
necessary to be present in the assembly that one belongs to, but to
show oneself in the place where everyone is used to seeing one,'[38] and
settled down to watching the death of the monarchy and the rebirth
of the republic. As he had feared, no-one was making the least attempt
to protect the Chamber; at first the crowd came in a trickle, then in a
flood; the duchesse and her party had to be moved from their seats
below the tribune to benches at the back of the hemicycle, or they
would have been crushed (Tocqueville helped them get to their new
position). None of the great orators of the Chamber was present with
the exception of Lamartine in his own accustomed place: waiting in
the wings, so to say. Tocqueville went to him to suggest that he alone
could make himself listened to and restore order; to his astonishment

Lamartine merely replied, without looking at him, 'I will certainly not speak while that woman and that child are present.' Because of his late arrival Tocqueville did not know that a little earlier Lamartine had demanded, from his seat, that the session be suspended while the duchesse was unconstitutionally present; he had already decided that the monarchy could not and should not be saved (a conclusion with which it is hard to disagree). Tocqueville stared for a moment at Lamartine's tall thin figure and trance-like air, and then went back to his place. A little later, after Odilon Barrot, abandoning his futile enterprise at the ministry of the interior, had arrived and made an equally futile appeal on behalf of the duchesse (who then disappeared), Lamartine mounted the tribune and in effect proclaimed the Republic. After a while he began to read out the names of various journalists and politicians who were to form a provisional government (a list concocted earlier by the radical newspaper *Le National*); the crowd by now was enormous and so was the uproar; finally he got agreement to the list and led everyone off to repeat the performance of the Hôtel de Ville, for want, Tocqueville supposed, of any better idea.* A moment later the Chamber was empty. Tocqueville decided to go home. As he left he met a large detachment of the National Guard under Marshal Bugeaud and General Oudinot coming to the rescue – half an hour too late. The July Chamber had dispersed for ever.[39]

Tocqueville had sat through the drama with a calm that surprised himself. He thought it was because there was no real danger; everyone was consciously playing a part. They had all read the *Girondins* or seen *Le Chevalier de Moulin Rouge*, a Dumas play about the great Revolution, and could sing the Girondin chorus; they knew what attitudes to strike. Yet this new revolution was real enough, and seems to have shaken Tocqueville more than he realized, although certainly not more than might have been expected. When he got back to the rue de la Madeleine he told Marie, he says, in a few words – can they really have been few? – what had occurred, and then sat down to be miserable. He was interrupted by Jean-Jacques Ampère, whom he had invited to dinner, though Tocqueville had forgotten. Ampère was full of enthu-

---

* In fact Lamartine had learned that another newspaper, the *Réforme*, was trying to set up a different provisional government at the Hôtel de Ville; when he arrived the two slates were merged.

siasm for the fall of the monarchy; Tocqueville's pent-up wrath and anxiety were suddenly emptied over him:

> I spoke to him with a violence of language that I have often remembered with some shame; only a friendship as sincere as his could have pardoned it. I remember saying to him, among other things, 'You understand nothing about what has happened; you are thinking like a Parisian loafer or a mere poet. You say it is the triumph of liberty; it is liberty's last defeat. I tell you that this people which you admire so naïvely has just shown conclusively that it is incapable and unworthy of living in liberty. Tell me what it has learned from experience? What are the new virtues it has acquired? What are the old vices it has discarded? No, I tell you, it is the same as always: as impatient, as thoughtless, as contemptuous of the law, as easily led by bad example and as reckless as its fathers were. Time hasn't changed it a bit, except that it is now as frivolous about serious matters as it was formerly about trifles.

Ampère was driven to shout back; they ended by agreeing to let the future decide between them – 'that upright and enlightened judge who, however, always arrives too late, alas!' – and Ampère forgave Tocqueville. It is difficult not to suspect that he had been paying for the sins of that other poet, Lamartine, who Tocqueville came to think had turned France upside down merely to amuse himself.[40]

Yet the incident tells us more than the state of Tocqueville's temper. When he assailed 'the people' in his outburst he meant only the Parisians, and the Parisians of the lower orders at that. He had by now conceived a ruthless hostility to them which was to determine his behaviour for the rest of the year. It had deep roots. He had been brought up on the terrible legend of the revolutionary crowd, of which the Commune of Paris had been the embodiment. He had witnessed the July Days in 1830 and several of the riots and insurrections which had marked the life of the July Monarchy. As a prison reformer his concern had never been to understand the causes of crime so much as to discover means of turning criminals into respectable, docile citizens. His ostentatious disdain for material concerns did not help: before long he would compare 1848 unfavourably with 1789: 'Then it was a revolution of hearts and minds, today it is one of the stomach.'[41] (This remark about 1789 was historically far from accurate, as in calmer moments he knew, and his own intestinal troubles should have taught him to take the stomach's problems seriously.) His removal to the countryside after his marriage not only cut him off, for much of the year, from his native city, but infected him with rural prejudice against Paris.

The events of February could hardly have engendered this hostility on their own. Tocqueville had never admired the regime which had been overthrown, and the people had not been the cause of its fall: it had destroyed itself. As these things go, the revolt had been comparatively bloodless, in part because of Louis-Philippe's magnanimous refusal to save his throne by the use of force: he had seen revolution enough in his long life, and would rule by consent or not at all. And as Peter Amann once wittily remarked, 'Postrevolutionary vandalism was hard on Paris street lights but easy on private property and persons.'[42]

But Tocqueville could take no comfort. Physically brave, he was intellectually frightened by the February Revolution, for reasons already given. Like Louis-Philippe, he looked back on France's revolutionary history, but with a very different attitude. It would be necessary, he thought, to teach the frivolous Parisians a lesson. There would have to be war on the streets.

He never wavered from this position. It was scarcely the finest phase of his career. The fact that half of France soon came to agree with him makes the matter worse, if anything.

CHAPTER EIGHTEEN

JUNE
1848

*Les partis ne se connaissent jamais les uns les autres: ils
s'approchent, ils se pressent, ils se saisissent, ils ne se voient
point.**

ALEXIS DE TOCQUEVILLE, *SOUVENIRS*[1]

AN ADVANTAGE OF BEING CYCLOTHYMIC is that while you
are easily plunged into the depths, you are also easily swept up to the
heights. So it was with Tocqueville. On 24 February he went to bed
in despair about the future of his country. The night was disturbed,
since the streets were continually full of happy Parisians singing the
'Marseillaise', shouting their triumph, firing guns and letting off
fireworks in celebration.[2] But next day Tocqueville wrote what can
only be described as his own shout of triumph to Paul Clamorgan. He
boasted about the perspicacity which he had shown in his speech of
27 January – 'I doubt if any politician has ever been a better prophet
or seen his prophecies so completely realized' – and gloried in the
discomfiture of his critics, who had shrugged off his warnings. The
country was now in a terrible state, politically and commercially, but
the question was what to do next. There would have to be a constituent assembly, and while Tocqueville alleged that he had no wish to be

---

* 'Parties never know one another: they get close, they shove, they grapple, they never see.'

one of its members, he would not reject a draft, although the task of representing his country might be dangerous. He urged Clamorgan to report on political attitudes in the Manche immediately; he himself would soon be arriving at Tocqueville. Two days later he wrote again, having just heard that his longstanding rival Léonor Havin* had somehow got himself appointed one of two government commissioners for the department; vigorous action would be necessary to thwart any hostile schemes.[3] That Tocqueville was insincere in his protestations of indifference is also suggested by the prompt publication of a fresh edition, the twelfth, of the *Démocratie*. It carried a new introduction by the author claiming that the February Revolution had confirmed his prediction that the victory of democracy was near at hand and irresistible. The example of the United States, he said, was more instructive than ever. 'The laws of the French Republic can and should be different, in many respects, from those which govern the United States, but the principles underlying the American constitution, those principles of order, of checks and balances, of true liberty, of deep and sincere respect for the laws, are indispensable to all Republics, they should be common to all, and we can predict safely that where they are not to be found the Republic will soon cease to exist.'[4] This introduction repays study as Tocqueville's manifesto for the Second Republic, expressing principles which he maintained throughout its brief and stormy existence; but it may also be read as an early attempt to establish his republican credentials in the eyes of the voters: he was not a *républicain de la veille* (republican of the eve) but a *républicain du lendemain* (of the morrow), and although he rallied to the new system he had to prove his sincerity. It helped him that he had a new publisher, Pagnerre, a staunch *républicain de la veille* who was also a much bolder businessman than Gosselin. Pagnerre brought out the first cheap edition of the *Démocratie*, consisting of 4,000 copies. It sold well: two further printings were called for that same year.[5]

Tocqueville passed the first day of the new order in walking about Paris, observing. The city was as quiet as a Sunday morning,

---

* Léonor-Joseph Havin (1799–1868), whose father had been a member of the Convention, was deputy for Saint-Lô, 1831–48. He belonged to the dynastic Left, and supported AT's candidacy at Valognes in 1839, but the two men, though frequently forced to collaborate, were essentially competitors for leadership in the Manche.

but what struck him most was the evidence of that great historical novelty, working-class victory. 'I did not see a single one of the agents of the former public authorities, not a soldier, not a gendarme, not a policeman. The National Guard itself had disappeared. The people alone bore arms, guarded public places, supervised, ordered, punished.' It all went so well as to constitute, one may think, a wonderful advertisement for Proudhon's anarchism, but Tocqueville did not see it like that. He did not expect the tranquillity to last, and he despised the ideas of the revolutionaries more than ever (Proudhon himself thought that the trouble was they had no ideas: 'there is nothing in their heads.') The general calm did not reassure the propertied classes: their terror was enormous. 'I do not think that it had been so great at any former revolutionary crisis, and I think it can only be compared to that felt by the great cities of the civilized Roman world when they suddenly found themselves in the power of the Vandals and the Goths.' As to the revolutionaries themselves, they had been as much surprised by events as everyone else, yet soon a torrent of impracticable proposals poured forth to bewilder the minds of the people:

> Everybody had plans; some detailed them in the newspapers, others in the posters which soon covered every wall, others simply cried them in the open air. One would offer to destroy the inequality of wealth, another that of education, a third to level the most ancient of inequalities, that between men and women; specifics were offered against poverty, and remedies for the curse of labour which has tormented humanity since its beginning.

Tocqueville had no difficulty in dismissing these wild notions, which he lumped under the single label of socialism, the essential character (he said) and most frightening memory of the February Revolution. The Republic was no longer an end but a means.[6]*

Karl Marx says somewhere that revolutions come in two phases, the beautiful and the ugly. The French Revolution of 1848 certainly

---

* Louis Blanc, the socialist leader, was to say much the same thing: 'the only thing which seemed certain was that Republicanism, as a form of government, was henceforth a settled matter. But this did not suffice to the earnest friends of progress. It was less the laying their hands on a political instrument which they had in view, than the future use which might be made of it.' *1848: Historical Revelations* (London: Chapman & Hall, 1858) 383.

illustrates this aphorism, if indeed it did not suggest it. Tocqueville was to claim that he had always foreseen that things would turn ugly, but the weeks of the beautiful revolution were so full of hope and happiness that they still touch the heart. George Sand, who hurried up from Berry to lend her pen to the cause, noticed, like Tocqueville, that Paris was amazingly quiet immediately after the days of February, but the streets soon came to life again, with some resurrected rituals giving a republican flavour to the usual spectacle:

> Who are these sturdy workmen coming along crowned with garlands, with hatchets, spades or axes under their arms as if they were guns? They are paviours, navvies, woodcutters, types of their trades, with beards prematurely grey and a trusty air, stepping out with sober assurance. Behind them come fifty others, effortlessly shouldering an enormous pine-tree, the green branches of which are looked after by children, who make sure they are not sullied by the dirt of the roadway. It is the Tree of Liberty; the symbol of the Republic is going past.[7]

It will be seen that Tocqueville was not wrong in pointing out a tendency to play-act revolution, but such scenes have their charm. Tocqueville himself was not quite immune to the atmosphere. He found to his surprise that in spite of what he had said to Ampère he was, personally, glad that the July Monarchy had been destroyed. He had supported it as the best available expedient, but he had never loved it, and he had been less and less happy in the parliamentary world, for reasons already explained. Now he seemed to see new possibilities. There was no mistaking the way ahead; true, it was going to be dangerous:

> but my soul is so made that I fear danger less than uncertainty. Besides, I felt that I was still in my prime; I had no children and few needs, and above all I had at home the support, so rare and precious in a time of revolution, of a devoted wife with an acute, steadfast mind and a naturally lofty soul that would be equal to any turn of events, and could rise above any misfortunes. So I decided to throw myself neck and crop into the arena and commit myself to the defence not of such and such a government, but of the laws of society itself, not sparing my fortune, my peace of mind or my person.

When the date of the election was announced he hurried down into

Normandy to present himself to the voters: Clamorgan had told him
that he was certain to win, but his presence was required.[8]

The national situation was extremely difficult. At its centre was the
continuing economic crisis, which Tocqueville characteristically put
down to chimerical notions picked up by the workers from the socialists. Banks were failing left and right, consumption had collapsed, the
Treasury was nearly empty. The only hope of salvation lay in the
elections, and then in the meeting of the National Assembly: but could
it operate freely, confronted, as it would be, with the aroused working
population of Paris? 'In my opinion, it should concede as many political
freedoms as possible, so as to have the right to stand firm on questions
of property and order,' Tocqueville told Clamorgan.[9]

Even before he left Paris he expected the majority of the new
assembly to be moderate, if not conservative: all the doctors, lawyers
and law officers who feared a threat to what Tocqueville called their
'notional property' – that is, their professional privileges and perquisites – would rally to the support of order (another new word becoming
frequent in Tocqueville's writings); but he was unprepared for what he
actually found in Normandy. He wrote to Marie:

> I can hardly convey the singular impression made on me by the sight
> of the countryside and even of the towns which I have just come
> through. I might have been in a different country from the France
> of Paris. People minding their own business, artisans, labourers all
> peaceful – the tranquillity of the fields, unworried peasant faces
> – it all forms such a contrast with what I left behind that I began to
> wonder if it was I, not the placid people I was meeting, who had the
> wrong ideas. The truth is that revolution has as yet shown itself only
> in Paris. Everyone else knows it only by hearsay.[10]

The electoral contest turned out to be the most satisfying that he ever
went through. Initially, in spite of Clamorgan's assurances, he was
uncertain of victory, and one side of him, remembering all too clearly
what things had been like in the Chamber of Deputies, yearned to be
back in private life for good. He paid a flying visit to his chateau and
burst into tears when he got inside: it had been five months since he
was last there, and it felt like years; the contrast between the cherished
pleasures of life at Tocqueville and the general state of the nation was
too much for him.[11] But the battle went well.

Superficially, the challenge was much greater than the last time. The Provisional Government had not only decreed universal male suffrage but had abolished the system of representation by *arrondissement*: the whole department would now vote for all its representatives, as Tocqueville had long wanted. This great increase in the number and dispersion of voters proved no handicap to him in the event: the former deputy from Valognes was well-known throughout the Manche, partly because of his service on the *conseil-général*. He thought that his great strength was that he did not want victory too desperately. The farmers admired a candidate who refused to answer impertinent questionnaires from republican committees: he seemed a man of independent character who would stand up for their interests in Paris. Their confidence in him increased his confidence in himself, and made him speak better than he had ever done in the Chamber: 'today I had moments which would not have been unworthy of a real orator.' He issued an election circular in which he explained why he had ceased to be a royalist – monarchy, he said, was no longer viable in France – and what sort of republican he had become: 'the Republic, to me, is true, sincere, real liberty for everyone, within the limits of the law; it is the government of the country by the country's free majority.' He did not believe in military or Jacobin dictatorship, or in socialism: 'for me the Republic is, above all, the reign of the rights of each man, guaranteed by the will of all; it is profound respect for all types of legitimate property.' He had seen how the United States flourished by following these maxims. He did not believe in a war to revolutionize the whole of Europe. He would happily stand aside if there were another candidate who the voters thought would serve them better, since this was no time for personal ambitions or petty rivalries, for not only liberty but society itself was in danger (this was probably a hit at Havin).[12] All this was just what the Manchois wanted to hear. The men of property, at any rate in the countryside, were closing ranks against the new regime in Paris and its dangerous doctrines.[13]

Tocqueville took pleasure in at least one demagogic stunt. Commissioner Havin, as agent of the new minister of the interior, Ledru-Rollin, was trying by every means to maximize the pro-government vote, which entailed doing as little as possible for Tocqueville, with whom he had quarrelled over the affair of the banquets the previous year. Now there was to be a new banquet at Cherbourg for up to 2,000 persons, presided over by Havin and his colleague Vieillard.* They could not avoid inviting Tocqueville, but they did not give him a place at the official table or ask him to speak. They underrated their man. Modestly he took his place at a side-table, but he saw his chance when someone proposed a toast to the memory of Colonel de Bricqueville, who had died in 1844. Tocqueville went briskly to the speakers' stand to pay his own graceful tribute to Bricqueville, and then, 'since here I am,' he proposed his own toast, 'TO THE UNION OF THE TWO GREATEST REPUBLICS ON THE FACE OF THE EARTH TODAY: THE FRENCH REPUBLIC AND THE REPUBLIC OF THE UNITED STATES OF AMERICA!' After repeating his usual line that France had much to learn from the successful democracy across the Atlantic – 'in America the Republic is not a dictatorship enforced in the name of liberty, it is liberty itself ...' – he went on to demand America's help in resisting British naval dominance: 'the land is free, but the seas are still enslaved.' What was Cherbourg itself, if not a living protest against that slavery (an allusion to the French government's long efforts to turn Cherbourg into a great naval base)? 'So it is first and foremost at Cherbourg that it is proper to propose a toast, TO THE CLOSE UNION OF THE TWO REPUBLICS! And at the same time, TO THE FREEDOM OF THE SEAS!' This claptrap went down extremely well, as he had known it would, and he took pleasure in hearing from Clamorgan that Havin had felt obliged to praise the speech as very adroit; but he was too ashamed of it to reproduce the text in the *Souvenirs*.[14]

After that his election was more or less certain. As usual he had to deny absurd rumours, including one that he was the author of the law against poaching (he denounced it as a relic of the *ancien régime*). He missed Marie and lived for her letters, though when they came they reported that not only she but Jem, his favourite dog, was ill (Jem seems to have been on heat). When the letters did not arrive, or arrived late, he darkly suspected that they had been intercepted by the police (it does not seem to have occurred to him that postal services might suffer during a revolution). He too fell ill, with the usual stomach troubles,

---

* Narcisse Vieillard (1791–1857), former artillery officer; former tutor to Prince Louis Napoleon. Elected deputy for Carentan (Manche) in 1842, as a member of the dynastic Left, he was defeated in 1846 and turned to republicanism. He was appointed a commissioner for the Manche at the same time as Havin.

which cast him into a gloom about his electoral prospects, and he was furious when the elections were put off for two weeks, though the postponement enabled him to return to Paris for a few days. At last it was Easter Sunday, 23 April, election day. Voting was to take place in the *chef-lieu* of every *canton*, so in the morning all the electors of Tocqueville gathered together and formed into double file, in alphabetical order, for the five-kilometre walk to Saint-Pierre-Église.

> I settled to march in the place to which my name assigned me, for I knew that in democratic times and countries it is necessary to be called to the front by the people, and not to put oneself there. At the end of the long file came pack-horses and carts for the handicapped and invalids who wanted to come with us. We left behind only children and women; in all we numbered a hundred and seventy. When we got to the top of the hill overlooking Tocqueville we stopped for a moment. I knew that they wanted me to speak, so I climbed up the far side of a ditch, they stood round me in a circle, and I made such remarks as the situation suggested.

He warned them particularly against being corrupted with food or drink at Saint-Pierre. Then they set off again and all voted at the same time, 'and I have reason to think that they almost all voted for the same candidate', for on arrival at Saint-Pierre, he felt exhausted and rested himself against a pillar, complaining of his weariness as he did so. An old peasant thereupon said to him: 'I am very surprised, Monsieur de Tocqueville, that you should be tired, since we all brought you here in our pockets.'[15]

It was a charming occasion; the same sort of thing happened in a thousand places in France that Easter. The beautiful revolution was not quite finished. The national turn-out was 84 per cent, the highest in French parliamentary history. Tocqueville did outstandingly well, getting 110,704 votes out of the 120,000 cast in the Manche: only the two commissioners came in ahead of him. The Manche sent sixteen representatives to the Assembly, so all in all Tocqueville, who had yet again run without party or official support, might well feel that he had emerged as the leading politician of his department. Even so, with a politician's eye he noticed that his victory had not been quite complete: several communes in his former constituency, Valognes, failed to give him a majority. How was this? Clamorgan assured him that the intrigues of some longstanding opponents explained it, and Tocqueville professed himself satisfied. He was gratified that in Cherbourg what he called 'the lively party' (*le parti vif*) – republicans and socialists – which had opposed him, was defeated.[16] But these details leave the nature of his support unanalysed. Once it is considered, a pattern of great significance emerges.

During the July Monarchy Tocqueville's support had consisted essentially of people like Clamorgan – a rural middle class of farmers, local officials and professional men, all of a certain standing in the world; we may presume (and Tocqueville's statements in the *Souvenirs* imply) that in 1848 he enjoyed the support of such men throughout the department. But there were not enough of these small notables to explain the size of his vote. It can be assumed that to the extent that they were leaders in their neighbourhoods they carried with them other men of their type. But another element was probably at least as important. The legitimists felt freed by the February Revolution. The usurper had fallen, there could be no more question of taking a disloyal oath, and the future of France was once more wholly uncertain. Anything could happen, and the nobles felt it their duty and pleasure to participate in electoral politics again. (So did the Church: when the Assembly met Tocqueville noticed with some surprise that three bishops and more than a dozen other priests, including the great Dominican preacher Lacordaire, had been elected.) Tocqueville was the beneficiary in the Manche. Whatever he called himself, the nobles knew that he was one of them, and was yielding at last to the bidding of his ancestry. On the day of the election he left for Paris as soon as he had voted, but on his way stopped briefly at Valognes. His constituents there crowded round promising to come to his rescue if the Assembly were attacked: they shared his apprehensions. He writes in the *Souvenirs*: 'I blame myself for having at the time seen nothing in these pledges but vain words, for as a matter of fact they did all come, they and many others, as we shall see.' When, on the last of the June Days, they do arrive, he tells us who they are:

> I was moved at recognizing among them many landowners, lawyers, doctors and farmers, who were my friends and neighbours. Almost all the old nobility of the region had taken up arms on this occasion

and joined the column. It was so almost everywhere in France. From the muddiest squireens to the elegant and useless heirs of the greatest houses, all remembered that they had once belonged to a ruling class of warriors, and everywhere they gave an example of promptness and vigour, so great is the vitality of those old aristocratic corps.

For he goes on, helplessly surrendering to myth and nostalgia: 'they were still like themselves even when they had been humbled to the dust, and rose up several times out of the shadow of death before resting there for ever.'[17] This passage gives the game away: Tocqueville is describing a movement of which he himself was part, or even the embodiment.

And what was that movement? Tocqueville does not mention what was probably its most important, because most numerous, element: the peasantry, who were outraged by the Provisional Government's decision to raise the land tax by 45 per cent. This grievance bound them to their lordly neighbours. It was the last straw, and the moment had come for the Vendée, or perhaps one should say the *bocage*, to take its revenge. The June Days were to be as much a collision of sections (to use a nineteenth-century American term) as of classes. The West resolved that the tyranny of Paris must be broken. Tocqueville and his friends did not see in their opponents desperate Frenchmen, taking up arms in June only because 1848 had betrayed them even more completely than 1830, and left them without work or food; they saw only the infidel, Jacobin city which had oppressed them ever since the fall of the Bastille. (Tocqueville, the intellectual, still saw Parisians as the deluded victims of socialist visions, who had to be taught a lesson in sound economics.) All these impulses were already at work during the election. For the Manchois the beautiful revolution was already dead, or rather it had never lived: it had been stillborn.*

The opening of the Constituent Assembly on 4 May was an emotional, joyous occasion, when everyone cheered the Republic, whatever their real views. It also marked the coming of the ugly revolution.

---

* Yet the Manche was not among the most conservative departments in the West. See A.-J. Tudesq, *Les Grands Notables*, map on p. 1069: '*Les représentants du people, Élection d'avril 1848: les conservateurs: Répartition départmentale.*'

The Provisional Government that had been set up in the Hôtel de Ville on 24 February was never more than an unstable, temporary expedient, but it deserves to be remembered with respect because of the many sweeping reforms which it decreed or attempted: for example, it introduced universal male suffrage, limited the working day, abolished slavery in the French empire and imprisonment for debt, and ended capital punishment for purely political offences: there was not to be another Reign of Terror. It was a government of sincere republicans, unlike most of those which followed it until the Franco-Prussian War. Its members were not of one mind ideologically or personally: it was only an uneasy coalition of liberal and radicals, who undoubtedly made mistakes: everyone does. They were defeated by the size and intractability of the problems which they faced, and it is exceedingly unlikely that any government, of any stripe, could have done better. For one thing the February Revolution had been too sudden and too swift: no-one was prepared, either with policies or personnel, to replace Guizot. Government, for months to come, could be nothing but desperate improvisation.

The revolution had made a bad economic situation disastrous. Tocqueville's letters during his election campaign are full of personal money worries, unlike any other period of his correspondence. Writing to Clamorgan in early April he says: 'Paris is like a battlefield covered with the dead or dying. Almost everyone I meet here is either ruined or about to be ruined. [Mme de Tocqueville and I] as yet are suffering only in our income, but the number of families who have lost both income and capital is immense.'[18] Trade was at a standstill. There had been a run on the banks, which had nearly broken the Banque de France; gold coin had disappeared, such paper money as was available rapidly depreciated, and anyway there was not enough of it. In the circumstances it is not surprising that there were ceaseless bankruptcies (Marx lays great stress on these in his *Class Struggles*) and general unemployment. This set of problems alone would have been enough to test any government to the utmost. But there were others.

'The earth is again quaking in Europe' had not been the least accurate warning in Tocqueville's January speech,[19] although in the weeks following there is hardly a reference to any country but France in his papers. Even before the Parisian revolution another had broken

440

out in Naples; by May there had been upheavals throughout Italy, in Austria, in Hungary, in Prussia. Now was the time, it seemed to some, when France could at last tear up the hated treaties of 1815 and march again to the liberation of the nations, especially the Poles. The difficulty was that with most of the country opposed to such a war, with an empty treasury and a quite unprepared army, the enterprise would be no better than a gamble, and if governments beyond the Rhine and the Alps had been broken their armies had not. It seemed sensible, then, to continue the pacific policy of Louis-Philippe, if in somewhat more assertive language, and Lamartine, as foreign minister, did so. When the fanatical Jacobin Delescluze, whom Ledru-Rollin had rashly sent as a commissioner to the Nord, attacked a town just across the Franco-Belgian border in the name of liberating Belgium, Lamartine eagerly disavowed him and apologized to the outraged Belgian government; but unfortunately the enthusiasts for a revolutionary foreign policy were concentrated in Paris, and might at any moment drive Lamartine from office as nothing but a new Guizot.

Still more threatening was the social question. The workers of Paris, having overthrown the July regime, understandably expected to make substantial gains under its successor. They were unemployed, ill-housed, ill-clad and hungry. Their demands were condensed into the slogan 'the right to work', which actually embodied two ideas: a claim for employment and a claim for relief. Neither claim was unreasonable or unattainable: given a little time, energy and intelligence, a useful programme of public works could have been devised for Paris, as happened at Marseille, where the commissioner Émile Ollivier set the unemployed to digging a canal. Louis Blanc, the socialist who had been thrust into the Provisional Government by the workers, had plenty of ideas for effective relief; he was placed in the Luxembourg Palace to preside over a commission which held hearings on the workers' problems. In spite of their desperation (half the businesses of Paris, and therefore the employment which they provided, disappeared in 1848) the workers seem for a long time to have been remarkably patient and good-humoured. They were anxious for help, but as one of their leaders famously told the Provisional Government during its first meeting, 'the people will wait; they will put three months of misery at the service of the Republic.' But fear and hatred, those passions which feel like wisdom, grew steadily more intense in France beyond the capital, and the Parisians themselves were starkly divided. The fact was that in the 1840s Paris was becoming something quite new to the French: a rapidly industrializing city that was also rapidly increasing in population as it drew workers to itself from all over the country. Very few people had any useful ideas as to how this phenomenon might be managed, or how such a city could be decently governed. Meanwhile, it was frightening.

All these problems were connected, and the Provisional Government was defeated by the connection. 'There have been wickeder revolutionaries than those of 1848,' said Tocqueville, 'but I do not think that there have ever been any who were stupider.' He would have done well to include himself in this condemnation. Writing to Nassau Senior he blamed France's troubles as usual on wrong notions of political economy held by most of the population, but his own were no better. He clung to the doctrines which he had picked up in his youth, the commonplaces of the *juste milieu*, and exaggerated them: he was all too sure that if the state interfered in the economic process by alleviating unemployment with a dole, or public works, or by regulating hours of work and wage rates, enterprise would suffer and everyone would be worse off in the end. It is perhaps unfair to point out that ever since Bismarck set out to kill socialism with kindness governments have been interfering in just the ways that Tocqueville dreaded, and in many more besides, yet civilization continues. What is not unfair is to remark that at no point in 1848 did Tocqueville display the slightest fellow-feeling for the workers in their distress, and consequently had no gleam of understanding about them. In this he was entirely at one with most of his fellow parliamentarians. The majority of the Provisional Government and its successor, the Executive Committee, also did not understand. 'Ah, M. Arago, you have never suffered from hunger,' said the insurgents of June to one of its members when he tried to reason with the builders of a barricade. The panic and stony-heartedness of the conservatives – of those who would soon be called 'the Party of Order' – was the chief cause of the disasters which afflicted France that summer.[20]

If Tocqueville was no worse than others, he was no better. Like Marx on the other side he wrote of the great social conflict as if it were entirely a matter of class war. Like any legitimist (and he was very like a legitimist) he denounced the centralization of government as inimical to liberty, but on examination his conception of liberty is almost indistinguishable from his idea of order. The course of events suggests very strongly that the issue was largely the clash between country and town; between the agrarian past and the industrializing future. That year witnessed the last *jacquerie*, or traditional peasant rising, when, after February, railway lines and railway stations were attacked, cotton mills were destroyed and there were risings against the new forest laws in the Pyrenees and the Alps. Tocqueville did not grasp this aspect of what was happening, still less did he suggest ways of handling it. As a practical matter he was now a republican, but he gave scarcely any details about how he thought the republic should work: it was enough to refer enquirers to the United States as depicted in his book. He found it much easier to attack other people's ideas. But his words and deeds give the game away. His ideal society was still a larger version of the Cotentin. Intelligent peasants would defer to educated gentlemen, and both would combine to keep the dangerous towns under control. 'Liberty under law' was the slogan: and the law was the one protecting property.

Tocqueville regarded the opening of what was called the Constituent Assembly (in a characteristic reminiscence of 1789) with thoroughly mixed feelings. He explained himself most fully to Beaumont just before election day. He foresaw little but embarrassment, even danger, in the new parliament, and could not be sure of doing anything useful there. 'However, I would be sorry to see the doors of the Assembly close in my face. I have several reasons. Politics has become our career. Perhaps we were wrong to take it up, but take it up we did. It would grieve me to abandon it just when such great events are occurring, to be dismissed from my country's affairs just when my country is being so sorely tried.' At least they were rid of Thiers, Molé and Guizot* and all that shabby world of party politics; this was some consolation for the inexperience, ignorance and folly of the new government. And there was still his friendship with Beaumont, which experience had

---

* Not for long. Guizot was in exile, but by-elections soon brought Thiers and Molé into the Assembly.

made wiser and more tolerant but no less deep and sincere: it helped him to resist gloomy thoughts.[21]

Not with complete success. He wrote to Clamorgan that a fight between the supporters of the Assembly and 'the violent party' was certain, and palpably he desired it. He even told Mathilde de Kergorlay (in 1846 Louis had got married at last) that unless a great man fell out of the clouds to save them, all France would collapse into anarchy, civil war and general ruin (his prayer would be answered, unacceptably, seven months later).[22]

The Provisional Government could not please everybody, and ended by pleasing nobody. Millions of peasant landowners had been alienated, as we have seen, by the rise in the land-tax (imposed to avert national bankruptcy). The Parisians still claimed the right to work, but a viable system of unemployment relief could not be invented overnight, and the government was ideologically split on the very idea. All it agreed to were the so-called national workshops, which might have worked well, but were never properly supported. Their name, *ateliers nationaux*, recalled, and was meant to recall, Louis Blanc's proposal of *ateliers sociaux* – workers' co-operatives – but otherwise had nothing in common with them. Blanc himself thought the national workshops were appalling: '[they] devoured vast sums of public money in useless labour, sterile and humiliating as being a sort of hypocritical alms-giving, under a flimsy veil.'[23] In Paris, they were little more than refuges where unemployed workers could draw a dole and loaf, which a great many of them resented. The workshops were indeed very expensive and a focus for the anger of taxpayers, who would not accept that, in the workshops or out of them, the men and their families would have to be saved from starvation. And the people, seeing that gains from the revolution were slow in coming, began to feel betrayed: on one occasion Louis Blanc himself was denounced as a traitor to the cause.

The period between February and May was one of almost incessant tumult, of demonstrations and counter-demonstrations (Tocqueville, as a member of the National Guard, shouldered his musket during one of them). Demonstrations were mostly good-tempered and undirected, but they had a tendency to turn into riots, and the government was perpetually afraid of being overthrown: on the eve of one episode

Lamartine burned all his papers. The situation was explosive, and a great deal would depend on the wisdom of the leaders of both sides. George Sand did not help. She was working as a propagandist for Ledru-Rollin in the ministry of the interior, and without his knowledge issued a leaflet saying, in effect, that if the new Assembly did not satisfy the Parisians they should throw it out. This greatly alarmed the conservatives, since it was just what they feared.

George Sand and Tocqueville met on 3 May, as guests of Richard Monckton Milnes, an Englishman well-known to them both, who like many others (including Nassau Senior) had come over to Paris to witness the revolution.* It was his custom to invite guests of all views, often conflicting, to what he called 'breakfast' (someone asked Carlyle what would happen if Christ returned to Earth: 'Monckton Milnes would invite him to breakfast') but was really lunch (*déjeuner*). The practice was popular in London but startling in Paris. It startled Tocqueville, though he seems to have known beforehand that Mme Sand would be of the company. Milnes placed them next to each other, to Tocqueville's dismay:

> I had never spoken to her, I don't think that I had ever seen her (for I had seldom gone into the world of literary adventurers in which she lived) ... I was very prejudiced against Mme Sand, for I loathe women writers, above all those who systematically disguise the weaknesses of their sex, instead of interesting us by displaying their real characteristics; but in spite of that, she pleased me.

And he seems to have pleased her. They were absorbed for an hour in a conversation about politics. Sand was already disillusioned with the revolution, and in two weeks' time would retreat to Berry, where she found that she was regarded as a dangerous communist; but she interested Tocqueville greatly, for 'it was the first time that I had found myself having a direct and easy conversation with someone who could and would tell me what was going on in the camp of our opponents.' She had not yet fully understood what was going to happen.

* Richard Monckton Milnes (1809–85), minor poet, backbench MP (first as a Tory, then as a Whig), first biographer of John Keats. Created Baron Houghton in 1863. Under that title he is remembered as a patron of Swinburne and for his enormous collection of pornography.

Mme Sand painted for me, in great detail and with striking vivacity, the condition of the Parisian workers, their organization, their numbers, their arms, their preparations, their opinions, their passions, their terrible determination. I thought the picture over-drawn; it was not, as the event proved. She herself seemed to me very frightened of a popular victory, and showed a certain solemn pity for what was going to happen to us. 'Try to get your friends, *Monsieur*,' she said to me, 'not to drive the people onto the streets by alarming or irritating them; at the same time, I would like to persuade mine to be patient; for, if battle is joined, you must understand that you will all perish.'

Tocqueville did not find these words encouraging.[24]

The Sibyl had spoken, but not in time. It was too late for individuals to divert the course of events, as Lamartine now discovered. He had been elected to the Assembly by Paris and ten departments with a total of 1,600,000 votes, but his popularity was based on illusions. The Left supported him as the founder, more or less, of the Republic; the Right hoped that he would use his power to crush all revolutionaries. Both sides were disappointed, for Lamartine believed in compromise and conciliation. When the new Assembly decided to replace the Provisional Government with an Executive Committee, rather like the Directory of 1795, he was ready to let Louis Blanc be discarded but insisted on retaining Ledru-Rollin, the leader and epitome of *les républicains de la veille*. This punctured his popularity with the conservatives, the vast majority of the Assembly, who could make no distinction between one sort of radical and another; his standing rapidly declined and was never to recover.

Then, on 15 May, when the Assembly had not yet finished organizing itself, it was invaded by the crowd. It was the turning-point of the 1848 revolution and remains its most mysterious episode. Many at the time (including Tocqueville and Beaumont) believed that the plan was to massacre the representatives, or at the very least to send the Executive Committee packing and replace it with a Committee of Public Safety; some historians nowadays think it was cunningly manipulated by the government to discredit the most radical leaders and contrive a pretext for throwing them into jail.[25] Anything is possible in a revolution. It seems clear that the ministry of the interior had agents in the crowd – it would be surprising had it not; how far they actually

controlled what occurred can only be guessed. The actual events of
the day do not suggest that anyone was in control. However, there is
general agreement on three points. First, the crowd, of 20,000–50,000
people, was in holiday mood. The spring day was as hot as summer.
The demonstrators were unarmed. Their chief concern, on which
they insisted, was Poland. As they approached the Palais Bourbon a
unanimous cry of *Vive la Pologne!* went up, which Tocqueville later
said was the most formidable sound that he had ever heard.[26] To the
Parisians, who believed in France's mission to free the nations, and
to the many Polish exiles in the crowd, the liberation of Poland from
Russian and German rule was a point of honour. It was hardly an
urgent matter: in that Year of Revolutions Poland was one of the few
European countries where nothing much happened. Lamartine and
his colleagues had no intention of provoking a European war about
Poland. The crowd brought along a petition protesting against such
pusillanimity.

Second, none of the leading radicals – not Blanqui, not Barbès, not
Blanc, not Raspail, and certainly not Proudhon, who conspicuously
stayed at home that day – approved of the demonstration; they saw, as
the crowd as yet did not, that the balance of force had for the moment
swung against the Left, and that it was folly to give the conservatives
an excuse for repression. But the people did not realize that the revolution had entered a new phase, in which demonstrations could achieve
nothing. So in the spirit of Ledru-Rollin's immortal explanation, given
a year later ('I am their leader, I must follow them'), Blanqui and Raspail
let themselves be drawn into the march, although they thought that no
good would come of it and were sure that it could not overthrow the
Assembly: as Blanqui explained at his trial the following spring, there
was too large a majority against the socialists for such an enterprise to
succeed, not only in the National Guard and the provinces, but among
most Parisian workers. A government so formed would not have lasted
eight days: 'I say that it would have been absurd to risk our political
future on a throw of the dice when the odds against us were ninety-
nine to one.' Barbès and Blanc agreed.[27]

Third, whatever the demonstrators' intentions, the effect on the
conservatives and moderates, and especially on the conservative
representatives, was as disastrous as Blanqui can possibly have feared.

They had expected trouble ever since a preliminary demonstration two days previously; some of them had come armed to the Assembly. Tocqueville brought a swordstick, which he left propped up in a corridor outside the debating-chamber. The Assembly building was a huge wooden affair, hastily run up in the courtyard of the Palais Bourbon when it was realized that the old Chamber of Deputies was far too small for the new parliament, which had 900 members. Nassau Senior, when he visited it on 19 May, noticed the resemblance of its layout to that of the House of Commons, but also that it was so large that no-one could make himself heard unless there was perfect silence, and even then he had to shout, 'which is fatal to good speaking'.[28] This had some bearing on what occurred on 15 May. At about noon the vast crowd surged across the pont de la Concorde and surrounded the Palais Bourbon. There were troops on duty to control the people, but not enough. Courtais, the commander, agreed that a delegation of twenty-five might enter to present the Polish petition, but when the doors were opened not only the twenty-five but as many of those behind them as possible also pushed in, more, apparently, by an instinctive movement than by design. There were some 2,000 intruders. For the next four hours all was confusion in the chamber. Demonstrators crowded the galleries until they were ready to collapse, and thronged round the representatives on the benches and the floor. The noise, dust and heat were appalling. The President of the Assembly banged his gavel ineffectively; the bolder members of the crowd thought that they would like to make speeches from the tribune, and fought each other to possess it. Raspail read out the petition about Poland. Barbès made a speech demanding war and a special tax on the rich. Blanc made three speeches to the crowd inside and outside the building, urging the demonstrators to behave legally and respectfully and leave the Assembly alone, but all he gained by this was to be carried back into the chamber shoulder-high, in spite of his attempts to escape. Blanqui spoke on Poland and on the workers' poverty, but was pushed aside by another leader, Hüber (apparently an *agent provocateur*), who bellowed out, 'I declare the Assembly dissolved!' Barbès, seeing nothing else for it, proclaimed a new Provisional Government and led off many demonstrators to the Hôtel de Ville (the whole affair had become a parody of 24 February). Suddenly drums were heard and the National

Guard entered the chamber, putting the last of the crowd to flight. Outside, most had long since gone home; Barbès and his followers were easily arrested at the Hôtel de Ville, and in the next few days Blanqui and others were also taken. Many of the radical clubs were closed down by order of the police.[29]

The affair seems almost comical in retrospect, but it is hardly surprising that it terrified the majority of the representatives; it scandalized a great many sincere republicans who believed in parliamentary democracy; and the National Guardsmen who came to the rescue were so angry that Louis Blanc (who was blamed for everything) and Courtais (who was blamed for letting in the demonstrators) would have been lynched had not some of the representatives come to their defence: Tocqueville found himself shouting about Courtais, 'Tear off his epaulettes, but don't kill him!' From now on the cry was, *Il faut en finir!* ('This mustn't go on!') Paris would have to be disciplined. Next day Tocqueville himself said that the whole thing had been got up by Barbès, who, if he had been able to get a proper hearing, would have compelled the Assembly to choose between agreeing to his demands or death on the spot. This baseless assertion shows how powerful pre-existent opinion can be, for on the day itself Tocqueville, sticking to his usual place according to his rule, formed a somewhat different impression of the situation. True, he saw in Blanqui what he wanted to see:

> a man ... the recollection of whom has always since filled me with disgust and horror; he had sunken and withered cheeks, white lips, a sickly, wicked and unclean air, a dirty pallor, the look of a mouldered corpse, no visible linen, an old black frock-coat wrapped tight round his lank and fleshless limbs; he seemed to have been living in a sewer ...*

but for the rest he noticed that even if some of the demonstrators had hidden arms they seemed to have no intention of using them. Many seemed only to want to have a look round, 'for even in our bloodiest riots, there is always a multitude of men, half rascals and half gapers,

---

* Blanqui had only recently emerged from nine years in one of those French prisons which AT had been trying to reform since 1833.

who think that they are at a show.' Fists were shaken at the representatives and insults hurled; but Tocqueville could not help noticing signs of vivacious intelligence among the sweaty and in some cases drunken visitors:

> I heard a man in a worker's blouse, just beside me, saying to his comrade, 'See that vulture over there? I'd like to wring his neck.' Following the indication of his eye and arm, I saw without trouble that he meant Lacordaire, who could be seen sitting in his Dominican habit on the upper benches of the Left. I thought the remark shocking but the comparison admirable, for the long, bony neck of the reverend father, emerging from his white hood, his shaven head surrounded only by tufts of black hair – his narrow face, his hooked nose – his close-set, staring, brilliant eyes – all indeed gave him a look of the bird of prey which the man mentioned; I was much taken with the observation.[30]

Tocqueville had another encounter with the humanity of the invaders when the National Guard finally arrived. As the crowd surged about in all directions he found himself confronting a young man with a sabre in one hand and Tocqueville's swordstick in the other. He was shouting '*Vive l'Assemblée Nationale!*,' which may have emboldened Tocqueville to demand his property:

'That's my stick!'

'It belongs to me.'

'It is so much mine that I know there is a sword inside it.'

'Of course there is, I had it put in two days ago. Who are you?'

Tocqueville told him; the young man doffed his hat and presented the stick to him, saying that while it was his, he was happy to lend it to Tocqueville, who might need it that afternoon: 'I will do myself the honour of collecting it from your home.' Next day Tocqueville found what was certainly his own stick lying in a corner of the Assembly building. The two weapons were so exactly alike that he did not know which it was that he handed over when the supposed thief came to reclaim his property.[31]

The former magistrate reflected that the story would be very instructive to a judge, warning him against jumping to conclusions even in the face of the clearest evidence; but he did not make any other inferences, for instance, that lethal weapons should not be left about in corridors, or that the workers might not really be dangerous. Like his fellow representatives, he was as convinced as ever that the Parisians would only respond to a heavy hand, and like them he wanted revenge for his fright. The road to the disastrous days of June was now open.

He filled the interim with an important task. On 18 May the Assembly chose him among the first for the committee which was to draft the Republic's constitution. It met and laboured throughout the rest of May and during the first two and a half weeks of June.

In the *Souvenirs* Tocqueville gives an extremely scornful account of the committee's proceedings and of his own part in them. He was well aware that something went terribly wrong. His account is acute and convincing at many points. But the committee minutes survive (they were 'very badly composed', according to Tocqueville) and the impression which they leave is not exactly that made by the *Souvenirs*.[32]

Plato went to Syracuse, Madison to Philadelphia: Tocqueville knew that an extraordinary opportunity had come his way, but he did not expect the committee, made up of republicans, socialists, and veterans of the July Chamber like himself to make much of it. The committee, he thought, 'scarcely resembled the men, so certain of their end and so familiar with the means necessary to attain it who, sixty years ago, under Washington's chairmanship, so successfully drew up the American Constitution'. Lack of time, he added, and the pressure of events elsewhere made success even less likely.[33]

Yet anyone who reads both the committee minutes of 1848 and the records of the constitutional convention of 1787 (which Tocqueville never saw) will be struck by the resemblance between them. Just as Madison opened the convention's deliberations by submitting the Virginia Plan, which thereafter supplied the text for discussion, so Cormenin, the committee's chairman,* encouraged by Beaumont (who was also on the committee), submitted a draft constitution for debate. Tocqueville was dismayed by the littleness of his colleagues, most of whom struck him as quite excessively swayed by vanity, political commitments and preoccupations, and narrow interests: but he would have been equally dismayed in 1787 by, for example, the recklessness

---

* Louis de Cormenin (1788–1868), jurist and political pamphleteer, had a distinguished legal career under the constitutional monarchy, when he belonged to the opposition. In 1849 he rallied to Louis Napoleon, and was a member of the *conseil d'état* until his death.

with which the Southern delegates insisted on writing slavery into the US Constitution. Tocqueville mocked his most celebrated colleague, the ex-priest Lammenais, who on discovering that the committee was inclined to argue with his assertions and to go about its business in its own way, walked out in a huff, never to return; but Alexander Hamilton behaved no better at Philadelphia. Tocqueville remarked that most of the committee members were too ignorant and confused to discuss the general principles which could or should have shaped their drafts; 'and those who had formed clearer [notions] were ill at ease in having to expound them.' They did not want to provoke long, fruitless discussion. 'In this way we ambled along to the end, adopting great principles explicitly for reasons of petty detail, and little by little building up the whole machinery of government without properly taking into account the relative strength of the various wheels and the manner in which they would work together.' This was undoubtedly true; the minutes confirm it; and it was disastrous; but it would have happened at Philadelphia too without the firm leadership of James Madison and James Wilson, and as Tocqueville concedes, some parts of the constitution – those dealing with the legal system – being drafted by men who knew their business thoroughly (most members of the committee were, or had been, lawyers) were excellent.[34]

Why, then, was the 1848 constitution, unlike that of 1787, a palpable failure? And why was Tocqueville unable to impose his views? He tried to reply to both these questions in the *Souvenirs*, but was too close to the matter to be objective. The minutes suggest answers.

The committee members may not have been willing or able to discuss political philosophy, but most of them shared the same preconceptions. Thus when the socialist Considérant put forward the proposal that women should be given the vote he said he knew that it would not be accepted, but he may have been surprised when it was not even attacked (was this the episode which led Tocqueville to remark that Considérant 'would have deserved to be sent to a madhouse' had he been sincere?). One of the points on which all agreed was that in the Republic the National Assembly, as representing the sovereign people, would be supreme; yet – or perhaps I should say, therefore – the committee's constant, concentrated preoccupation was how to check it. At first sight this is bewildering. Parliamentarians ought to believe in parliaments, and usually do. As everyone knew, the Assembly was in great danger and might soon be fighting for its life. This made no difference. The committeemen were experienced enough to know that the overwhelming victory of the conservatives in the spring elections might never be repeated; or, at least, that one day 'the Mountain' (as the Left now called itself – another revolutionary reminiscence) might win the majority. Haunted by the usual memories the committee supposed that its prime duty was to make sure that the Assembly could never legally turn into another Convention. Tocqueville's proposal that the legislature be bicameral, in the name of checks and balances, was rejected: as he says, public opinion had pronounced strongly in favour of a single Chamber, not only in Paris, but in nearly every department; but other means of weakening the Assembly were found. On the whole, they coalesced as a single device: strengthening the executive.[35]

Tocqueville observed that most of his colleagues were unable to shake off the past: remembering the failure, fifty years previously, of the Directory, they were determined to have a one-man executive; a president. Tocqueville agreed to this. But he realized that in a country with such a powerful monarchical tradition such an innovation might be extremely dangerous, for it was not innovative enough. Now for the first time he saw clearly the great truth that was to dominate all his later historical writing: that continuity is at least as powerful a force as change. (This is another point which the US Constitution illustrates: in one light it appears only as the charter of a reformed British Empire.) The committee members could not differentiate a president from a king, and a French king at that. At every turn they heaped powers and privileges upon him. Thus, when it was a question of fixing his salary they considered, among other matters, that Paris had always lived in large part off the luxury trades generated by the Court. So they bid up the president's salary to 600,000 francs *per annum* (£24,000), to renew this stimulus. There was to be a presidential court. For a private citizen such a salary would be enormous, but it was inadequate for the splendours envisaged. One of the difficulties of Louis Napoleon's presidency is thus foreshadowed: he was certain to overspend (and did so lavishly). But indeed every detail of the presidency as devised by the committee seems premonitory not of Louis Napoleon Bonaparte the man, but of the office which he was to win and of the way in which, in it, he conducted himself. Executive usurpation, the threat which so unnecessarily exercised Americans in the early nineteenth century, was certain to be an eventuality in France even before it was thought possible that the Bonapartist pretender would be a serious candidate for the presidency. There was no other way in which the office, as designed, could be conducted.

It cannot be said that Tocqueville made any effective resistance to this development; rather, he made it worse. As the great acknowledged authority on the American republic he might have been expected to do better. But by 1848 his claims in this respect were largely hollow. He had not visited the United States for sixteen years and had not written on it for eight. He was neurotically unable to re-read his books, once they had been published; he was dependent, therefore, on memories, or what he thought were memories, of what he had once known. He proposed unsuccessfully that the president be chosen by an absolute majority of an electoral college, failing which he should be chosen by the Assembly. This was an idea taken straight from the US Constitution, as he acknowledges in the *Souvenirs*; but it is not one which any American would have recommended, given the difficulties which it can and has caused from time to time (not least in 2000), and his advocacy shows how little he had kept up with American politics. He actually supported the preposterous clause introduced by Auguste Vivien which made constitutional amendment all but impossible (the amending process in the US Constitution is one of its greatest strengths).* Indeed, if his observations on the point to Nassau Senior, three years later, may be trusted, he strongly approved of it, thinking that it would give the new constitution time to become generally accepted. Worst of all, he and Beaumont pushed through a clause limiting the president to a single term of four years. They too were victims of their own experience: they were afraid that a re-eligible president would try to secure his re-election by large-scale corruption.† They were right, but they were soon to learn that the alternative was worse. Tocqueville in early 1851

---

* Admittedly, this point was easy to overlook in 1848, when the US Constitution had not been amended since before AT was born (and would not be again until after his death).
† It has often occurred to me that AT would regard as corruption almost everything nowadays accepted in the West as legitimate electioneering.

reflected sadly that 'This vote, and the great influence which I brought to bear on it, is my most unpleasant memory of that period.' A year later, and he would have been even more emphatic.[36]

An alternative system was briefly glimpsed, first when Cormenin introduced the clause proposing that the president should be chosen by popular vote, and then again when, to everyone's vast astonishment, Louis Napoleon Bonaparte, the Emperor's nephew, was elected to the Assembly by four departments in the by-elections of 4 June. This gave a frightening glimpse of what the future might hold if Bonaparte became a candidate for the presidency, so the committee reconsidered the question of popular election. Perhaps after all it might be better to have the president chosen by the Assembly? This would in effect have given France a parliamentary government (as eventually emerged under the Third Republic), but thanks to Napoleon I, Charles X and Louis-Philippe the French had scarcely ever known true parliamentary government and were not, that summer, ready to try it. As the committee well knew, the people expected to choose their head of state themselves. The original proposal was confirmed. Tocqueville later supported it vigorously in the Assembly. As he explains, 'I was, I admit, much more desirous of quickly installing a powerful leader of the Republic than of organizing a truly republican constitution. We were then under the divided and indecisive rule of the Executive Committee, socialism was at the gate, and it must not be forgotten that the June Days were at hand.' It was another decision which he regretted later, but meanwhile he and his colleagues adumbrated what looks like a boss-shot at the constitution of the Fifth Republic.[37]

That was its strength: however faulty its details, the constitution of the Second Republic, especially as it was amended before adoption that autumn by the Constituent Assembly, corresponded powerfully to an abiding French political instinct – or habit. The constitutional committee's members, as Tocqueville remarked, had never known anything except monarchy and its traditions, and could do no better than experiment uncertainly with republicanism. He believed, and said repeatedly, that the choice before France was between liberty and equality, but it seemed at least as obvious to his colleagues that the choice was between liberty and equality on the one hand, and power on the other. Assertive nationalism was a permanent feature of French life: we have seen Tocqueville expressing it. The Napoleonic tradition was one of glory as well as dictatorship. It would probably have shaped the Republic's new institutions even if no new Napoleon had been in the field.[38]

Set beside these considerations it hardly seems to matter that Tocqueville (at one in this with Lammenais) from start to finish deplored the fact that the new constitution was going to be as centralized as the old ones. Centralization was the bugbear of others besides himself: of the legitimists and the rest of his constituents. The spring and summer of 1848 saw a successful revolt against Paris, but just as the Parisians of February had been cheated in the moment of their victory, so were the provincials of April and June. The former leaders of the July Monarchy (with exceptions, such as Guizot and the Orleans princes) were about to stage a remarkable comeback, seizing the leadership of the Assembly, which was to be theirs for three years. Their first great success came when, on the constitutional committee, they reasserted the traditions of 1793 and 1799.

Tocqueville could only respond in the bitter pages of the *Souvenirs*. Neither there nor anywhere else did he ask himself why the French majority should submit to a devolution of government which would only shift power from the hands of the central administration to those of reactionary country squires, of village lawyers and small town businessmen. He never met the arguments put forward, for instance, by Thiers when he remarked to Nassau Senior in 1853 that France's centralization was made necessary by her geographical position. 'We are in the midst of hostile neighbours. Paris is not even now three marches from the frontier. We are always in danger of an attack, and have often to make one, if we wish to keep our relative position.' Only a strong centralized government ('a master') could, for instance, manage the necessary conscription. Besides, Thiers did not think much of local government. Quite in the spirit of the *ancien régime* he believed that the ministry of the interior had to exercise strict supervision of all local activities, otherwise there would be appalling waste of taxpayers' money. Tocqueville disdained such considerations, or at any rate never discussed them. Instead he was always ready to tell the few who listened to him that local self-government was the school of virtue and citizenship. The historical record, even in New England, suggests that he was deceiving himself.[39]

He felt that he was ineffective on the constitutional committee, and explained that the heart had gone out of him when he lost the battle for bicameralism.[40] Certainly the minutes do not show him as intervening very often – much less often than, for example, Beaumont. No doubt he was discouraged, but the true reason for his quiescence was that he agreed with his colleagues on most points, and where he did not his disagreements were too speculative to be worth insisting on. As all the committee members knew so well that they did not have to say it, a radical reconstruction of government in France was not on the agenda: 1848 was not 1789. The work of the great Revolution was unassailable. The notables supposed that their job was to reassert their power, and Tocqueville was one of them. What neither he nor anyone else, on or off the committee (except perhaps Lamartine) could conceive was that their essential, urgent, pre-eminent duty was to reconcile the French to each other; to devise a political system which all lawful interests could accept as legitimate and worth supporting, thereby making possible a resurrection of the nation's energy, intelligence and public spirit so that France could master the problems and the dangers, external and internal, which were to confront her so brutally for the next hundred years. Probably it was already too late. Whatever the faults of the new constitution, and they were many, it could have worked, like all constitutions, if the will had been there. Instead it became just one more issue in the battle between the factions.

The preliminary draft was completed on 17 June and delivered to the Assembly two days later. It was immediately sent for scrutiny to the various *bureaux* (committees) whose views it was desirable to know before beginning a full-dress debate. But this was business for later. The immediate preoccupation of the representatives was their long-awaited showdown with the workers of Paris, which began on Thursday, 22 June, when it became clear that the Executive Committee would not retreat from its decision to close the national workshops at once. The *faubourgs*, at the end of their patience, rose in arms, and after four days of bloody battle were defeated by the combined efforts of the National Guard, the regular army and the Garde Mobile,*

---

* The Garde Mobile was a device of the Provisional Government to get the *gamins* (urchins) of Paris off the streets. They were enlisted, put into uniform, paid well and given military training. To everyone's surprise they proved loyal to their paymaster and shot down their

all under the command of General Cavaignac, the minister of war. During the struggle the Executive Committee was forced to resign and the Assembly made Cavaignac temporary dictator. By the end of the fighting 708 government supporters had been killed, including five generals and the Archbishop of Paris, who had been trying to negotiate a truce; there were at least 3,000 dead insurgents (this figure is probably a gross underestimate); and 15,000 arrests. Cannon-fire had battered much of eastern Paris into ruin.

Such, in stark outline, is the story of the June Days. Tocqueville's doings during these events and their preliminaries are only intermittently visible, although his account of all that happened to him during the fighting is precise and vivid:

> [*24 June.*] At the corner of the street, right beside the Château d'Eau, there was a large, tall house under construction; some insurgents, who had no doubt got in through the courtyard at the back, established themselves there without being noticed; suddenly they appeared on the roof and loosed a great volley upon the troops who were filling the boulevard and were far from expecting an enemy posted at such a point, and so near. The noise of the muskets, echoed terrifyingly by the houses opposite, made them expect a similar surprise from that side of the street too. Our column fell immediately into incredible confusion: artillery, infantry, cavalry were immediately mixed in disorder, the soldiers fired in all directions without knowing what they were doing, and fell back in tumult some sixty paces. This retreat was so disordered and impetuous a movement that I was thrown against the walls of the houses facing the rue de Faubourg-du-Temple, knocked down by the cavalry and generally jostled in such a way that I lost my hat and almost my life. It was quite the most serious danger that I incurred during the June Days. It made me realize that all is not heroic in the heroic game of war: I don't doubt that accidents of this type often happen even to the best troops, but nobody boasts of them and they are not mentioned in bulletins.[41]

The pages of the *Souvenirs* which describe the rising contain many passages as dramatic as this, and Tocqueville himself is always vividly present. He was himself both brave and sensible under fire, or the risk of fire, and as inquisitive as ever: he was only present in the rue de

fellow-citizens devotedly.

Faubourg-du-Temple because he wanted to see and understand for himself what was happening.[42] By contrast, his account of how the fight came about is somewhat patchy.

He tells us that he went with pistols in his pocket to the absurd Feast of Concord on 21 May, when the Assembly had to sit through a day-long parade on the Champ de Mars of soldiers and militia who would soon be fighting each other; but he says very little about developments in the Assembly during the next month: he was hard at work in the constitutional committee. Yet they were not without interest.

By then the majority of the representatives, whether monarchists or middle-of-the-road republicans, were incapable of tolerating the workers' movement any longer. This is not to say that the representatives were villains. On the contrary, many, perhaps most, of them agreed with the Parisians' insistence that the Republic must be socially as well as politically democratic, and much time was spent in the first weeks of June in suggesting ways for reviving the economy (which, everyone agreed, would be far the best way of helping the people). Tocqueville alleged that these discussions were inspired by mere fright, but many of the suggestions made bore a strong resemblance to those which he himself had put forward just before the February revolution,* and his friend the comte de Falloux,† whose intransigent leadership played its part in bringing on the final crisis, was to insist in his memoirs that although he wanted the national workshops closed he also wanted repressive measures to be matched with programmes of assistance: the endowment of friendly societies, the improvement of savings banks, protection of child workers, the demolition of slums, and so on. All was benevolence, but it will be noted that none of these measures would have been of much immediate use to the unemployed.[43]

And on one point the majority was unanimous: the national workshops must go. It was an obsession: they must be destroyed so that the propertied classes could be sure that they were in control again, demonstrate their mastery, and sleep peacefully at night. Various

---

* See above, p. 415.

† Frédéric-Alfred-Pierre, comte de Falloux (1811–86), a devoted Catholic and legitimist, entered the Chamber of Deputies in 1847; elected to the assemblies of the Second Republic, he emerged as one of his faction's strongest leaders.

rationalizations were offered. Victor Hugo, who had recently entered the Assembly as a conservative, solemnly warned his colleagues that whereas the July Monarchy had bred idleness in the rich, the Republic, through the workshops, was doing far worse, it was breeding idle habits in the poor: 'this indolence, fatal to civilization, is possible in Turkey, but not in France. Never shall Paris copy Naples; never, never shall she copy Constantinople!' Never, he cried, should the intelligent workers of Paris become *lazzaroni* in peace and janissaries in war! The business class, the *patronat*, dismayed that labour was in short supply although there was so much unemployment, was convinced that if the workshops closed trade would revive. Others, appalled by the number of men enrolled (by June there were about 100,000), said that the cost was intolerable; many saw and said (but not too loudly) that here was a potentially dangerous revolutionary army: had not thousands of them joined the crowd on 15 May? And Tocqueville's belief that the working class was rapidly being corrupted by dangerous socialist fallacies was widely shared. *Il faut en finir*, said the representatives.[44]

So the Assembly heard but did not listen to the pleas of Caussidière, one of the few left-wing leaders still at large. They did not know, he said, the real position of unemployed provincials who, having lost everything, had come to Paris seeking work, men from all sorts of factories and *ateliers*, who had been signed into the national workshops and given nothing to do. As a consequence the boulevards in the evening were clubs of despair; these honest democrats listened bewildered to the chaos of excited oratory, but were clear about one thing: 'Try and give us bread, or we will take our guns and throw ourselves on the bayonets – we will destroy ourselves.' Lamartine and a few others tried to solve the problem by proposing that the state take over and fund all railway construction, which at present was going on much too slowly: this would create useful, well-paid work on a large scale. The plan made some headway in the Assembly, but events cut it short. Weeks before, the Executive Committee had decided that the national workshops would have to be closed, but it could not bring itself to say so or to make any effective preparations for the event. The boulevards grew ever more riotous and the Assembly angrier. At last Falloux forced the Committee's hand: in the name of the labour *bureau*, of which he was chairman, he proposed the immediate closure of the workshops, and prepared a report for the Assembly to debate. The Executive Committee gave in. It published its own decree on 19 June, saying that the men in the national workshops were to be sent to labour on land reclamation in distant provinces. Falloux's report, decreeing the immediate dissolution of the workshops and requiring all workers between the ages of eighteen and twenty-five to join the army or lose the dole, was published on 21 June; civil war broke out on the 23rd.[45]

Tocqueville only sketched these events in the *Souvenirs*. He was not trying to conceal the fact that he stood to the Right even of Falloux on the issue. He was so sure of his ground that he took it for granted. The Parisians, he believed, were bent on destroying the very foundations of society; only force would defeat them; all France beyond Paris agreed with him, and the sooner that battle was joined the better. He devotes a chapter of the *Souvenirs* to his relations with Lamartine in the weeks after the Assembly met, and is brilliantly unkind about the poet in power who was so reluctant to take command of the forces of reaction and so eager to retain some support on the Left. Tocqueville is as unfair as he is unkind, but just as the reader begins to resent the fact he suddenly checks himself and admits that his own judgement was faulty: Lamartine knew better than he did the real danger of the situation and how necessary it was to play for time (and indeed, though Tocqueville does not say so, it was Lamartine who made sure that the forces of order were strong enough to conquer when battle was joined). This characteristic spasm of candour is one of the traits which make the *Souvenirs* so valuable; but it does not get round the fact that on the whole Tocqueville was blindly prejudiced about the situation. He gives himself away when he has to mention Louis Blanc. He concedes that Blanc defended himself ably when he was accused of being behind the 15 May affair, but does not admit that Blanc was innocent, and cannot conceal his regret that he was, for the time being, acquitted; and he sneers vulgarly at what he regards as Blanc's lack of talent.[46]

Il faut en finir. By now the workers too were spoiling for the fight, which was clearly imminent. There was immense agitation as news of the decrees spread through the *faubourgs*. On 22 June a deputation of workers visited Alexandre Marie, a member of the Executive Committee who had been indirectly responsible for the workshops from the first; he received them with threats and insults. The barricades began to go up. Tocqueville and Corcelle walked into the quarter round the Hôtel de Ville to see what was going on. To explore as much ground as possible they separated, and Corcelle found himself constrained to help in building a barricade, but he was so clumsy that the insurgents soon let him go. Returning to the Assembly, Tocqueville found it in a state bordering on panic; it voted itself into continuous session; the Executive Committee delegated all authority over the situation to General Cavaignac. Fighting was already fierce, but Tocqueville did not get home until one in the morning, and as he crossed the Pont-Royal all Paris seemed asleep; all was silent. The tranquillity half persuaded him that there was not going to be another battle, that the Assembly had already triumphed.[47]

Long after daybreak he awoke to the sound of gunfire: the bedroom window was shaking. Marie said that it had been going on for an hour, but she had let him sleep as he would need all his strength that day (she was not a daughter of the Royal Navy for nothing). Tocqueville dressed at once and went to the Assembly, where he stayed until he was sent out with three colleagues (Cormenin was one) to give moral support to the troops. He found time to scribble a note to Marie, urging her to take herself and Comte Hervé to safety at Saint-Germain or Versailles; she did so in such a hurry that she forgot to let Tocqueville know where she would be, or that she had got there safely. It added to the anxieties of a dreadful day, when the insurgency was at its height. Tocqueville wrote to Clamorgan saying that if the Assembly were defeated in Paris it would leave the city and call France to arms. 'I hope that France would hear it, for this is not about political forms, but about property, family, civilization, in short everything that makes life worth living ... But what a war, my friend, what an appalling war!'[48]

The Assembly's victory, though not easy, was never really uncertain. In July 1830 and in February 1848 the Parisian insurgents were opposed only by unpopular and ill-organized governments; they had taken the offensive and achieved speedy success. In June 1848 their foe was capable, resolute and strong, not least in its access to endless reinforcements; and the Parisians stood on the defensive. They had been scandalously treated. Not only would the closure of the workshops apparently deprive them of all public relief, but the able-bodied among them – the chief breadwinners – were now threatened with either years of military service or with transportation to the Second Republic's equivalent of labour-camps. The barricades were erected so that they could stay at home, or at least die fighting. Cavaignac, initially short of troops, took his time about launching his onslaught, which made some of the less courageous representatives hysterical, but he knew what he was doing. The insurgents were challenging him to defeat them, barricade by barricade, house by house: Tocqueville was reminded of the siege of Saragossa in 1808, when for months the Spanish heroically resisted the army of Napoleon. The Parisians might have been even more dangerous and harder to subdue had they relied on sniper fire, which was what demoralized Marmont's men in 1830. As it was, they fought with unexpected skill and tenacity; but Cavaignac was able to defeat them with cannon and cavalry. By the afternoon of 26 June it was all over; order reigned in Paris. Tocqueville left the Assembly for the rue de la Madeleine; as he walked along he could survey the field of victory.[49]

'One would like to discover in his writing some of the accents of pity shown by men like Armand de Melun,'* says André Jardin, but Tocqueville remained implacable. Another sightseer on 26 June was the great Russian socialist Alexander Herzen, who was arrested near the Madeleine by a National Guard officer, who thought he looked a suspicious customer. He was taken off to a police station, surrounded by soldiers.

> The first man we met was a *représentant du peuple* with the silly badge in his button-hole: it was De Tocqueville, the writer on America. I appealed to him and told him what had happened: it was not a joking matter; they kept people in prison without any sort of trial, threw them into the cellars of the Tuileries, and shot them.† De Tocqueville did not even ask who we were; he very politely bowed himself off, delivering himself of the following banality: 'The legislative authority has

---

* Vicomte Armand de Melun (1807–77), member of the Legislative Assembly 1849–51, was the French and Catholic equivalent of the Earl of Shaftesbury. He devoted his life to mitigating the problems of the poor. In 1846 he founded the *Société d'économie charitable*, of which AT was a member.

† Quite true. The regular army behaved decently, but the vengeful National Guard committed many atrocities. Dead bodies were frequently thrown into the Seine.

no right to interfere with the executive.' He might well be a minister under Napoleon III!

(Herzen was released some hours later.)[50]

Tocqueville had no doubts about the necessity of this latest massacre in Paris, and even Lamartine and Louis Blanc accepted that the rising had to be suppressed. It had been provoked, Tocqueville continued to believe, by the Left, and no counter-measures could be too rigorous. Only in personal relations might he relax. When in 1849 his colleague on the constitutional committee Victor Considérant was driven into exile because of his part in the rising of that year, he wrote to Tocqueville for help in protecting some Italian property of their friend, the Princess Belgiojoso.* Tocqueville, who was foreign minister at the time, responded favourably at once, though not without making some severe remarks about the bloodthirsty character of Considérant's political friends. But this mitigation of his attitude, if that is what it was, seems to have been unique.[51]

---

* Princess Christine Trivulzio de Belgiojoso (1808–71), a rich and patriotic Milanese, lived in exile in Paris, where she held a brilliant salon of which AT was an *habitué*. In 1848 she returned to Milan and raised a company of soldiers to fight the Austrians.

CHAPTER NINETEEN

RETROSPECTION

1848–1851

A history is not the less interesting for being incomplete.

A. DE GOBINEAU[1]

THE PARISIANS HAD LOST the battle of June, but as Tocqueville immediately realized it was not clear who, if anybody, had won. The Republican government had swept away the most fervent supporters of the Republic, and done so in such a way as to win itself no new friends. The legitimists and the Orleanists had for the time being sunk their dynastic differences in order to form a new conservative grouping (they saw fit to call themselves 'moderates'), the Committee of the rue de Poitiers, which meant to exploit the Right's strengthened position to impose its own view of society on republican France. Its most prominent leaders were all veterans of the July Monarchy: Berryer, Molé, Broglie, above all Thiers, and it was nakedly the party of the *grands notables*. That was its strength and its weakness: it was not going to vanish, but its chances of regaining power, rather than influence, were poor, at any rate in the short term. It showed wary respect for the governing Republicans but attacked the Left relentlessly, greatly helped in this by the weakness of the Left's remaining leaders: Lamartine was a spent force and Ledru-Rollin was inept. As to the old dynastic Left, to which Tocqueville belonged, it was still an army of generals without soldiers, and events since February had laid bare its essential conservatism: it accepted the Republic in good faith, but otherwise there was little to distinguish it ideologically from the rue de Poitiers. In changed circumstances it still struggled, as it had under Guizot, to establish a position that was both independent and electorally popular: still struggled and still failed. The truly moderate Republicans clung to Cavaignac and his government like drowning men to a life-raft: they had no other asset, and this one soon diminished, since Cavaignac's popularity steadily lessened: to govern is to choose, and Cavaignac's choices regularly alienated more voters than they pleased. There was thus a huge political void in France. It might be filled by a man and a cause, and before the end of the summer it was clear that both were at hand. Louis Napoleon Bonaparte won another by-election, returned to France from exile, and took his seat.

In July Eugène Stoffels wrote to Tocqueville asking for a letter about politics. The reply shows his friend plunged into one of his blackest moods:

> I don't believe in the future ... No longer do I hope – I wouldn't say this to anyone else – no longer do I hope to see the establishment in our country of a government that is at once lawful, strong and liberal. That ideal was the dream of my whole youth, as you know, and also of the days of my prime, which have already gone by.

Then there appeared what was to become a favourite image:

> We are sailing on a stormy, shoreless sea; or at least the shore is so distant, so uncertain that our life and perhaps that of those who come after us will have ended before it is discerned ...
>
> It is not that I expect an uninterrupted train of revolutions. On the contrary, I expect long intervals of order, peace and prosperity; but I do not now expect the establishment of a solid and well-ordered social and political system. How could I? In 1789, in 1815, even in 1830 it was possible to think that France had been attacked by one of those violent illnesses after which the health of society becomes more vigorous and enduring. Today we see that we are afflicted by a chronic infection.

He concluded by saying again that what made the June insurrection so pernicious was that it was inspired by wrong ideas. Not cannon or bayonets, not even dictatorship, could defeat them permanently.[2]

These thoughts and phrases were the germ of a famous passage in the *Souvenirs*[3] and besides forming a powerful example of Tocqueville's prophetic insight show his mind turning back to meditation on the history of France, the theme which was to dominate his thought for the rest of his days, if it had not always done so.

The turn is illustrated quite as unmistakably in the speech that he delivered to the Assembly on 12 September. He had not previously spoken from the tribune of the new parliament, but now four days a week were being devoted to the grand debate on the constitution; it was necessary to make himself felt on the subject, and he planned three major addresses – one of which could not be delivered because of illness. On 12 September the subject was the right to work. The constitutional committee had refused to write this dangerous slogan into the constitution; after much discussion it proposed Article 8 of the preamble:

> The Republic must protect each citizen in his person, his family, his religion, his property, his work and his home ... it must ensure subsistence to the unfortunate, either by finding work for them (as much as its resources permit) or by assuring, where their families cannot, the necessities of life to those who are in no condition to work.[4]

This was not enough for representatives on the Left: they proposed various amendments explicitly guaranteeing the right to work. In practice the language would make no difference: ever since the June Days the government had been doing what it could to relieve unemployment, for example by taking over the job of building and running the railway line from Paris to Lyon. But 'the right to work' was an ideological issue of the highest importance; Tocqueville had gone as far as he was prepared to go in concessions on the point; besides, a month previously there had been a tremendous battle in the Assembly between Proudhon and Thiers, in which Proudhon had advocated what amounted to an emergency tax on the incomes of the rich and Thiers, while tearing the proposal to pieces, had also launched a root-and-branch attack on socialism. Tocqueville too wanted to make a stand: he could not leave the topic to Thiers, whom he mistrusted as much as ever.

His speech was a great success, heckled by the Left (the President had to call its representatives to order) and applauded by the Right; it was printed as a pamphlet as well as in the *Moniteur* (Tocqueville sent some specimens to be distributed in London). His line was that if the right to work was conceded the way would open inexorably to communism or socialism (defined as a form of servitude) and the destruction of property. His tactics were the ones usual in such effusions: a determination to ignore common sense and to frighten his audience with the blackest possible inferences from what, on the face of it, was a fairly harmless proposition, that the Republic 'recognizes the right of every citizen to education, work and relief'.[5] His warnings had their effect: the amendment was rejected; more evidence, perhaps, that Tocqueville's oratory was at last becoming powerful. Of greater interest is the second theme of his speech. He wanted not only to defeat but to discredit the claim for the right to work, and he tried to do so by arguing that it was not a legitimate part of French revolutionary tradition. It was the *ancien régime*, he said, that was like socialism: it aspired to assume total responsibility for the lives of its subjects; the Revolution of 1789 was all about the freedom of the individual. Shamelessly, he quoted Robespierre of all people on the point ('Abandon the former mania of governments for governing too much'), to the astonishment of his hearers (what can his father have thought?) and before that he swung into a passionate eulogy of the great Revolution in highly revealing language:

> Was it by speaking of material interests, of the material needs of men, that the French Revolution did the great things which made it illustrious in the world? ... Do you think that it was by speaking of such things that it was able to arouse, to inspire, a whole generation, setting it in motion, driving it across our frontiers, throwing it into the middle of war's dangers, confronting it with death? No, gentlemen, no, it was by evoking things loftier and lovelier, it was by speaking of the love of country, of the country's honour, it was by speaking of virtue, generosity, disinterestedness, glory, that it did such great things; for, after all, gentlemen, be assured that there is only one secret for making men do great things: it is by appealing to great ideas. (*'Very good! Very good!'*)[6]

And as to property, the great achievement of the Revolution was to distribute it more widely than ever before, making France a nation of

ten million landholders; the very people most threatened by the socialists. To be true to the glorious revolutionary tradition, the February
Revolution must claim not the democratic and social republic, but the
democratic Christian one. What was needed was not the right to work,
but the right to public charity.[7]

This sophistical, almost Jacobinical discourse is interesting as
coming from the future historian of the Revolution; its interpretation
of the spirit of 1789 is explicit, and would underlie all Tocqueville's
future work on the subject. It is full of other Tocquevillean traits – for
instance, the United States is held up as a model democracy where
socialism is never thought of – but perhaps its most striking characteristic is its impudence. This orator, who disliked all revolutions, and the
February Revolution in particular, which he would have stopped if he
could, now tells the men who made it that they had got it all wrong. It
raises doubts about Tocqueville's sincerity, doubts reinforced by the
first half of his next speech, delivered on 5 October, when on behalf
of the constitutional committee he argued in favour of choosing the
president by popular vote, rather than by vote of the Assembly. His
account of a parliament which combined legislative and executive
supremacy could hardly have been more scathing: it would not be like
the revolutionary Convention, he conceded at last, there would be no
repetition of the Reign of Terror, but under such an Assembly 'we
will have a tyrannical, busybody government, a changeable, violent,
thoughtless, scatterbrain government, without traditions, without
wisdom ... and, I must add, a profoundly corrupt and corrupting
government.'[8] The existing Assembly might well have resented these
strictures, but it did not protest, and towards the end of his speech
Tocqueville showed that like many former Orleanists he accepted the
Republic as the best government in the country's circumstances, and
went beyond them in his interpretation of current opinion:

> France is today instinctively, not perhaps in ideology completely, but,
> I repeat, instinctively, deeply, republican. She has achieved equality,
> she worships it. (*'Very good!'*) She distrusts hierarchy, she fears
> authority, she has no superstitious respect for power, she does not
> believe in the hereditary rights of princes. France, in the secret fibres
> of her being, is thoroughly republican.

So why was there hesitation about accepting the Republic? Because the people had reason to fear that it meant socialist anarchy, from which, 'as the honourable M. de Lamartine has said,' it might seek refuge with a phantom – taking a name for a man. (*'Very good, very good!'* said the Assembly again, on registering this anti-Napoleonic thrust.) The Assembly must reassure the people by endorsing the political revolution and repudiating the social one; and it could best do that by burning its boats and making the presidency a guarantee of an ordered future, by adopting the method of popular election. Tocqueville's logic was not impeccable, but these remarks were greeted by such a hubbub of acclamation that the sitting had to be suspended for ten minutes.[9]

These two speeches show the point which Tocqueville had reached by the autumn of 1848; he did not depart from it while the Second Republic lasted. One consequence was that he became a firm supporter of the Cavaignac government (even though he thought it deeply mediocre) and of Cavaignac's candidacy for the presidential election, somewhat to his surprise: as he reminded Beaumont, he had never been a ministerialist before.[10] When Cavaignac, hoping to broaden his support, decided to appoint some ministers from Tocqueville's faction Tocqueville hoped to be among them, but the post he wanted was that of minister of education, for which Cavaignac thought he was much too right wing: he had long ago committed himself to what was called 'freedom to teach' (*liberté d'enseignement*) – in other words, official recognition of Catholic schools and certificates – and secularism, keeping the Church out of the classroom, was already an article of faith among good Republicans such as Cavaignac himself. Besides, Tocqueville that autumn was still clamouring (at least in his letters to Beaumont) for a strong policy of what he called order; he wanted Cavaignac to break completely with the *républicains de la veille* and reach out to the rue de Poitiers; it was even necessary to be reactionary. Cavaignac, who wanted to unite the Republicans, and whose governmental programme was not unlike that of Franklin Roosevelt in 1933 (as F. A. de Luna pointed out long ago), might well feel that Tocqueville was not the man for him, if such remarks came to his ears, as they probably did. Tocqueville accepted the situation, admitting that 'if my name appeared in the new Cabinet it would be a banner of reaction'. He contented himself with his appointment as the French delegate to an international conference due to meet at Brussels to discuss the crisis in Italy. It would mean that he and Beaumont, whom Cavaignac had sent as ambassador to London, would once again be working closely together, and meanwhile he could explore in the archives of the foreign ministry.[11]

Very shortly all these plans and aspirations came to nothing. The Brussels conference never met. The new constitution was promulgated on 12 November: Tocqueville's old friend Mme Ancelot saw it being read out in a muddy public square by Armand Marrast, President of the Assembly,* peering through spectacles while trying to take shelter from the rain under an umbrella. She thought he looked grotesque, 'and the law died under weight of ridicule.'[12] On 10 December the first presidential election in French history was held. With the partial exception of the Bonapartists no-one understood how to fight such a contest. Cavaignac did not campaign and the resultant inertia of the public administration almost amounted, in Tocqueville's opinion, to treason. The rue de Poitiers, as a body, decided to sit out the business, not realizing that it thereby forfeited its claim to leadership.[13] The Left did not see the importance of uniting behind a single candidate, and there was no mechanism – no nominating convention, for example – by which it could do so. But the Bonapartists, who since the spring had single-mindedly been studying how to bring Prince Louis Napoleon forward, were comparatively well-prepared. After his rejection by Cavaignac, Tocqueville, in rage and anxiety, found himself on the sidelines. It was cruel, he said, in such a crisis, 'to have a clear idea of what should be done, to feel in oneself the courage to do it, and to be able to do almost nothing.'[14] He gave up hope of victory for Cavaignac, who had come to epitomize the hated Republic: the 45-centime tax was still being collected (with some difficulty), the countryside was still alienated. But he may have been surprised at the actual results: Louis Napoleon received just over 5.5 million votes, or 74 per cent of the total, while Cavaignac received just under 1.5 million (19.5 per cent); the rest – Ledru-Rollin, Raspail, Lamartine – were nowhere (poor

---

* Armand Marrast (1801–52) was editor of the *National* and a leading Republican under the July Monarchy. In 1848 he was successively Mayor of Paris and President of the National Assembly. He was one of the most active members of the constitutional committee. AT disliked him, and disapproved of him as a centralizer.

Lamartine received only 17,914 votes). Turnout was 75 per cent of the electorate, down from the spring, but the Bonaparte victory could not have been much more convincing. It showed that Prince Louis had not needed the rue de Poitiers, although many of its members had rallied to him as the lesser of two evils (Cavaignac's programme of reform having been too much for them). Tocqueville, just before election day, remarked that 'Prince Louis is simultaneously supported in the provinces by those who want to overthrow the Republic and in Paris by a large body of ultra-republicans'; the exiled Guizot observed that 'it is a great deal to be simultaneously a national glory, a revolutionary guarantee, and a principle of authority.' For the first time in a generation French nationalism, as bound up with the memory of the Emperor, could find legitimate political expression, and the peasants were given a candidate who was at once an assurance that they would keep their gains from the great Revolution and an embodiment of state authority: the name of Napoleon seemed a promise of order, prosperity and prestige. The army deserted Cavaignac for Bonaparte at the polls. In short, a new and formidable political force had arisen. Characteristically, Thiers and his followers failed to recognize it. Sounding like the equally misguided Cicero commenting on Octavian, Thiers remarked of the new president, 'he is a cretin whom we will lead.' No doubt this got straight back to Louis Napoleon.[15]

Even before the election the careerists had begun to join him. Among them was Odilon Barrot, who according to Tocqueville was afraid of ending his long career in irrelevance and liked the idea of playing mentor to 'the little great man'. Rémusat, more brutally, said that Barrot wanted to be remembered as something more than a muddler and windbag. It was through Barrot that Tocqueville first met the prince, who, no doubt by pre-arrangement, gate-crashed a dinner given by Barrot, apparently late in the autumn, for Tocqueville and Rémusat. Rémusat snubbed him (and later decided that he had been wrong to do so); we do not know how Tocqueville behaved (he nowhere refers to the incident), but like Rémusat he refused to be drawn into a political discussion; and later the two of them (who now saw eye to eye on most public matters) agreed that it would be a good thing if all Louis Napoleon's agents were as maladroit as Barrot.[16]

Louis Napoleon took his oath of office before the Constituent

Assembly on 20 December, pledging absolute loyalty to the Republic; it was generally suspected that one day he would forget having done so and make himself Emperor. Meanwhile France had to be governed, as difficult a task as ever. One of the chief problems was the Assembly, which now went some way to justifying Tocqueville's distrust of supreme single chambers. Its work was done, its mandate exhausted; it should have been giving way to a new assembly elected under the constitution, but it clung to power, delaying the new elections for months (they were finally held on 13 May 1849), and even then refusing to dissolve until the very last minute. Hundreds of the representatives knew that they would not get into the Legislative Assembly, which was to have fewer members than the Constituent and in which the Right would be much stronger; but they did not make good use of their last days, exerting themselves chiefly in factious opposition: Ledru-Rollin was constantly proposing impeachments. Confronted by such a body Louis Napoleon found it difficult even to put together a cabinet. (The previous cabinet had left office with Cavaignac.) The legitimists refused to work with him, save for Falloux, who had gone into politics solely to further the interests of the Catholic Church. The Republicans, rightly regarding the president as a rival, also refused to co-operate, and the Orleanists, as we have seen, meant to manipulate him: Thiers and Molé would not take office, but they offered general support in the Assembly – reserving the right to withdraw it when they saw fit. Lamartine, to whom Louis Napoleon made overtures, would only agree to serve if no-one else would – hardly a formula for success. That left the eager Barrot, who took office on the same day as the president himself. Even he was not entirely tractable, but he happened to be the one leading French politician whom Louis Napoleon knew well, and the president had learned patience in his long years of exile, conspiracy and prison. He skilfully used the first months of his term to improve his standing, for example by efficiently and bloodlessly suppressing a street revolt in Paris in late January, and by making frequent visits to the hospitals when cholera returned to France that summer.

Tocqueville played very little part in politics at this time; he was seriously ill in January and February, and only shakily convalescent during March, April and May. The most precise account of his symptoms comes in a letter to Clamorgan of 22 January, in which he says that he has been suffering from a violent *grippe*, which first attacked his chest and then his guts. Perhaps it was indeed influenza: Marie was ill in some way early in January, Tocqueville may very well have caught an infection from her, and such a malady would explain his relapses during February and the lassitude which lasted for weeks. But the possibility cannot be overlooked that this was his first serious attack of tuberculosis: the pattern resembles that of his last illness in 1858–9. By the spring he was somewhat better, but felt desperately in need of a holiday, and in writing to Beaumont he referred to his health as 'that very incomplete condition to which I give the name'.[17]

Next to his physical weakness, his chief concern at this period was the matter of his re-election to the Assembly. His letters to Clamorgan and to other constituents show him delicately evading the traps surrounding him. For although the Manche had not voted for Louis Napoleon quite so overwhelmingly as some other departments, it had given him a majority of 65 per cent, and Tocqueville's emphatic support for Cavaignac had not gone unnoticed. He could have protected himself against any ill consequences by signing up with the rue de Poitiers, but that would have meant repudiating most of the colleagues with whom he had worked since May 1848, and he did not think that he could do so honourably, or disavow his record. Independence, as usual, was his chosen course and, to judge by the result, the wisest one: he was one of only two representatives for the Manche to be re-elected of those who had won in April 1848 (even Havin lost), and he came head of the poll. His position thus became one of unquestionable pre-eminence, and he had got there while scarcely lifting a finger: he did not visit his constituency once during the campaign. To enquiries he answered merely that his record could be judged from his speeches and votes in the Assembly, as recorded in the *Moniteur*.[18] He drafted an election manifesto but decided not to issue it because it would change no opinions. Nevertheless it is of great interest, for it is the clearest possible summary of his political views and actions during the first year of the Second Republic. It shows yet again what a very conservative liberal he was. There were repeated affirmations of his loyal support for the Republic, and in this we can be certain that he was sincere: in February he had written a long private letter to George Grote in which he said that if order and prosperity could be restored France would adjust better to the republican form of government than to any other, 'since at bottom our social organization, our tastes, our instincts, our very vices, are republican'. It was just what he had said in his speech of 5 October, and shows him taking the final step, which he could not do at the time of the *Démocratie*, though the logic of that book pointed unmistakably towards it. But for the rest of the document he gloried in negatives. He had, he said, resisted socialism and the right to work; he had voted in the Assembly for the suppression of political clubs, for the limitation of press freedom, for the imposition of a state of siege in Paris,* and against all measures not based on 'the doctrines of a sound political economy': for example, the nationalization of the railways, a tax on mortgages, shortening the working day, progressive taxation and the abolition of the system by which the middle class could buy their sons out of compulsory military service (although abolition had been strongly supported by his friend General de Lamoricière and by General Cavaignac). He even boasted of his vote with the majority for lifting the parliamentary immunity of Louis Blanc and Marc Caussidière, thus driving them into undeserved exile (once more we seem to hear Guizot's perplexed question, '*Why* don't we think the same?').† Tocqueville concluded by saying that he had believed from the first that the Republic could exist only if it suppressed licence, reformed all abuses of liberty, and set up a strong and generally accepted executive power. He had already said that he trusted Louis Napoleon to respect the Constitution; the implication was that he would be a desirably strong executive.[19]

This assessment was perhaps Louis Napoleon's reward for his attempts to cultivate Tocqueville and his group. Tocqueville had at first thought him honest but very mediocre, but after dining at the Elysée and sitting next to his host throughout the meal he wrote to

---

* This is puzzling. Such was his dislike of military government that he voted against the imposition of the state of siege in June 1848, which in the *Souvenirs* he describes as a mistake (OC XII 161–2). Here he is probably referring to the September vote to extend the state of siege until the end of October.

† See above, p. 383.

Clamorgan that he was less confident in his assertions: 'You know that I am not without a certain skill in reading men. But I cannot yet paint the intellectual portrait of this one. A private education and several years in prison have bestowed on his features and his conversation a discretion which defeats the observer. So I am postponing my conclusions.' In early May the president appointed him to yet another committee for the investigation of French prisons; he interpreted this to Clamorgan (who was relied on to spread the word to the voters) as proof that he was recognized as a loyal supporter of Louis Napoleon and his government. Perhaps Tocqueville already sensed that he was seen as a possible minister; he may even have been sending out signals of his availability. At any rate, these manoeuvres did him no harm. At the election he received 82,404 votes out of 94,481 cast, and in August was elected president of the *conseil-général*.[20]

Tocqueville was not present in the Manche to savour these triumphs. Election day found him in Germany, whither he had gone a few days earlier, ostensibly to improve his health by a much-needed rest.

It seems that he planned a very Tocquevillean rest. He wanted to repeat the exploits of his youth by studying the revolutionary situation in Germany. How his interest in that country originated is not known: perhaps he was influenced by his fellow academician Cousin, who introduced the French to Hegel; or perhaps he read the newspapers and began to realize that Germany was becoming an ever-more important force in Europe. Whatever the reason, she became a preoccupation that lasted the rest of his days. In 1849 he tried to get introductions to leaders in both the liberal and conservative parties, and hoped that he would reach Berlin.[21] But Marie was with him, and was no Beaumont: travel always made her ill, and she collapsed at Bonn. Then urgent letters from Rivet and Beaumont brought Tocqueville back to France on 25 May or thereabouts: he had to leave Marie to fend for herself.

The crisis which recalled him was less an event than a panic among the conservatives. The legislative elections had reduced the number of Cavaignac republicans in the Assembly to eighty, and returned some 500 candidates of the party of order; but this overwhelming victory gave the conservatives little pleasure, for to their terror the Mountain won 150 seats. A century and a half later it looks as if a two-party system were struggling to emerge, but the conservatives, quite irrationally, felt that they were once more staring ruin in the face. Government stock fell by 5 per cent. Characteristically, Odilon Barrot made matters worse by resigning. He said later that he did so because the more conservative Assembly needed a more conservative ministry; but that hardly fits the outcome, which was a more Republican one. It is more probable that Barrot was trying to strengthen his position against both the party of order and the president. The Burgraves, as Thiers and Molé were now known, in ironic allusion to an unsuccessful play of that name by Victor Hugo, still refused to take office,* but they intended to control the cabinet through their command of the majority in the Assembly. Louis Napoleon had not yet shown his hand, but there were indications that he too intended to be master: in a letter to Barrot about the crisis he remarked that the first necessity was to give a clear and energetic lead to the administration: 'We must choose men devoted to my person, from prefects to police inspectors … We must get rid of most of the officials appointed by M. Dufaure.' (This was an allusion to Dufaure's brief service as minister of the interior under Cavaignac.) 'Finally, it is necessary to reawaken everywhere the memory not of the Empire, but of the Emperor …' If Barrot saw anything in this letter, it was only an opportunity to show who was really in charge: no-one could be found to replace him as prime minister, so he agreed to remain, and invited Dufaure to join the government and bring two friends with him: Lanjuinais, and Tocqueville as foreign minister.[22]

What Louis Napoleon made of this development would not become clear for months, but as a parliamentary manoeuvre it was brilliantly successful. Disraeli in 1844 defined 'a sound Conservative government' as 'Tory men and Whig measures';[23] in France in 1849 it was liberal (or Republican) men and conservative measures. Tocqueville was well aware of this; he knew that the remodelled Barrot cabinet could not survive without the support, or at least the toleration, of the Burgraves and their supporters, and sometimes chided Dufaure, that sturdy Republican, for being insufficiently accommodating to their wishes. But the cabinet survived, and indeed, in the Assembly,

---

* AT observed contemptuously that they wanted power, 'but responsibility, no' (OC XII 200).

grew stronger. Tocqueville never forgot its frailty; nor did his wife: when Nassau Senior visited her at the foreign ministry in July she remarked, 'We ourselves have removed nothing from our own house. We are birds of passage in this *hôtel*.' In theory, the ministry was at the mercy of Thiers, and he was so unfriendly to the experiment that he deterred Rémusat from accepting the post of foreign minister. But in practice he could not bring Barrot down for no reason, and Barrot was careful not to give him an excuse. The reshuffle had greatly strengthened the team. Barrot could rely on Dufaure to help him effectively in the day-to-day battle on the floor, and Tocqueville had become a strong parliamentary performer. Falloux, the Catholic and legitimist, regarded himself as Dufaure and Tocqueville's prisoner, but he was a loyal colleague and a capable minister of education. The ministry's programme was unexceptionable. By the autumn Tocqueville might reasonably hope that it would succeed in what he regarded as its main mission: to survive until prosperity returned and the Republic had become generally accepted.[24]

If Tocqueville's appointment to the cabinet was somewhat fortuitous (it was Dufaure whom Barrot needed) his appointment to the foreign ministry was still more so. He had again hoped for the ministry of education, but Falloux, indispensable as the one legitimist in the cabinet, would not move, so he accepted foreign affairs. He took office on 2 June 1849.

He now sat at the desk where Talleyrand, Chateaubriand and Guizot had sat before him, but if he gave the point a moment's attention, or wondered what sort of a revolution it was which promoted Chateaubriand's nephew, he did not say so (although it may have been at this time that he amused himself by looking up Talleyrand's letters to Louis XVIII in the archives). Another man might have felt that he had reached the summit of his career, but Tocqueville had never wanted or expected to become foreign minister. He was far from sure that he would be equal to the challenge. 'I am by nature full of self-distrust,' he was to write, 'and the nine years which I had frittered away so miserably in the last parliaments of the monarchy had much increased this natural weakness.' But he had always hoped for power, and now he found that he actually enjoyed exercising it. The discovery gave him self-confidence, which his oratorical successes since January

1848 had already stimulated: he preferred the National Assembly as an audience to the Chamber of Deputies, though because of the size of the hall he had to scream his way through his speeches, interrupting them from time to time to rest his throat. The foreign ministry crowned this development. It even cured the bad manners resulting from his shyness: he no longer had to seek out politicians and grope for something to say to them; they came to him, full of business, and at last he found it easy to be gracious. He discovered that great questions were not necessarily more difficult to manage than smaller ones and that, if anything, he enjoyed them more: he rose to their challenge. Besides, he was always sure of willing and capable helpers. Of these the most important to him personally was Arthur de Gobineau, a promising young journalist whom he selected for his *chef de cabinet* (head of his private office).* It proved to be a good choice: Gobineau served Tocqueville devotedly.[25]

Tocqueville was excellently qualified for his new position. He had travelled widely, and had a large acquaintance among the notables of half Europe. He had long reflected on modern history and on France's place in the world. In personal relations he was frank, sincere and intelligent, and contributed greatly to the harmony and smooth running of Barrot's unstable cabinet. He worked well with the Assembly, and seems to have made a favourable impression on the statesmen and diplomats he encountered. He threw himself into his work with all his formidable powers of application and understanding. He had at last found ways of deploying his talents as he had hoped to do when he first entered politics. All in all, there is reason to think that had he enjoyed a longer spell in office he might have left as strong a mark as any of his illustrious predecessors; but circumstances were against him, and almost as soon as he had mastered his job, he lost it.

Given his antics at the time of the Mehemet Ali crisis, he might have been expected to do something rash: he was as ardent a nationalist as ever. But he had always been more prudent than his language suggested, and he had no difficulty in adopting the principles which

---

* Arthur de Gobineau (1816–82). Met AT 1842–43, and assisted him in some enquiries into modern (especially German) political philosophy. Worked on the *Commerce* during AT's involvement with that paper, and collaborated with Kergorlay in editing the short-lived *Revue provinciale*, 1848–49.

had governed French foreign policy since 1830, if not since the battle of Waterloo. Never again must France wantonly unite the European Powers against herself. In 1849 it was also supremely necessary to reckon with the short and long-term consequences of the great revolutionary storm which had broken over Europe the year before and had still not entirely subsided. Among the problems which Tocqueville had to deal with were those of German refugees in Switzerland and Hungarian refugees in Turkey,[26] though he was determined to interfere as little as possible in the affairs of central and eastern Europe. But there was no escaping the question of Italy, which dominated Tocqueville's months in office and led, both directly and indirectly, to his fall.

The whole peninsula had been disturbed. In the spring of 1849 Piedmont's renewed challenge to Austria for control of Lombardy had been crushingly defeated at the battle of Novara. Revolution had been suppressed in Naples and Sicily, and in August the Austrians reconquered Venice. All these incidents might well concern, without involving, the French Republic. Instead it plunged into the quagmire of the Roman problem.

The Pope, Pius IX, had been driven from the city in November 1848 and had taken refuge at Gaeta in the Kingdom of Naples. Mazzini had proclaimed the Roman Republic, and Garibaldi had arrived to command its defence. Fatally, in the spring of 1849, the French Assembly authorized the Barrot government to send an expeditionary force to the papal states: Tocqueville voted for the small credit requested. The force sailed under General Oudinot and occupied Civita Vecchia. The declared object of the expedition was left vague, but it could only be either to restore the Pope or to defend the Roman Republic. Either plan was calamitous. It was like the first despatch of American 'military advisers' to South Vietnam: a commitment had been made without any clear perception of the consequences.

Seen in retrospect, the temporal power of the Pope was clearly a medieval anachronism that served no good purpose, religious or otherwise. But Pius IX and his cardinals were intent on its restoration: that is, on the Pope's right and duty to reign as an all but absolute monarch. The temporal power was assumed to be necessary to preserve the papacy and Catholicism itself. The large body of Catholic voters in France agreed. It meant nothing that Rome's priestly government had long been notorious throughout Europe for its inefficiency and oppression, or that the Romans had repudiated it. Pius did not much mind who restored his power provided that it was restored untrammelled, and he was rightly confident that if France, the eldest daughter of the Church, would not do it, then Austria would. He and his secretary of state, Cardinal Antonelli, as unyielding as they were slippery, cared very little for the dilemmas of French statesmen.

Such being the case, the most prudent course for those statesmen would have been to hold aloof from the whole affair, but once the expeditionary force had sailed that was impossible. Tocqueville entered office refusing to take responsibility for the decision to send it, of which he said he thoroughly disapproved, though how he reconciled that with his vote for the expedition is hard to see.[27] But French prestige was now involved, and must be maintained. He did not even object when, on joining the cabinet, he learned that the order to take Rome by force had already been given.

Prestige was the fundamental issue, and not a simple one. The Catholic vote was important, and Tocqueville had no opinion of the Roman republicans: so far as he was concerned they were mere terrorists, like their supporters in Paris, who staged a demonstration on their behalf on 13 June (thanks to the indecisiveness of Ledru-Rollin it turned into a half-hearted rising that was easily suppressed: Ledru fled into exile). But the French state had repeatedly intervened in Italy over the centuries, competing for power and influence there first with Spain and then with Austria; it was the general view that the peninsula could not be abandoned now. After 13 June the Republicans who wanted to go to Garibaldi's assistance did not matter; but Louis Napoleon did. His two uncles, the Emperor Napoleon and the Viceroy Eugène de Beauharnais, had conquered and ruled Italy, and the president had his own ideas of what its future should be: there was no question of a hands-off policy. Tocqueville and the liberals agreed: they took the straightforward nationalist view that France must assert herself in her own sphere of influence if she wanted to remain a Great Power. So they acquiesced in the attack on Rome, although the preamble to the French constitution affirmed that the Republic would never attack another country (still less a sister republic). As Thiers was to say, 'To know that the Austrian flag was flying on the Castle of St Angelo is a humiliation under which no Frenchman could bear to exist.' Tocqueville entirely agreed; but he gave strict orders to Oudinot not to damage any of the great monuments of Rome, and like everyone else he hoped, even assumed, that by taking Rome the French would be in a position to induce the Pope to liberalize his government.[28]

Oudinot entered Rome on 2 July, and handed back government of the city to the Pope. The fallacy in French policy immediately became apparent: Pius would make no important reforms, and did not even thank the French for what they had done. He could not be coerced for fear that he would call in the Austrians – the one outcome which was intolerable to all shades of French opinion. Thoroughly perplexed, the French started quarrelling among themselves, and Tocqueville was in the middle of it. He had sent Corcelle as special envoy to the Pope, but Corcelle, once a *carbonaro* and now a devout Catholic, went over to Pius IX's side and complained incessantly about the minister's attempts to keep him in order, which led Tocqueville to reflect on the limited convenience of having a close friend for an agent ('Corcelle is driving me mad').[29]

At this stage Tocqueville and the president agreed precisely about the policy to be pursued, even if they could not get Corcelle to execute it: pressure on the Pope must be maintained; but conservative opinion was startled when Louis Napoleon deliberately leaked to the press a letter expressing his displeasure with Pius. Thiers, who cared nothing for liberal government in Rome so long as the Austrians were kept out, tried to undermine both president and ministers in the Assembly, and Louis Napoleon was furious with Barrot for not defending him, and especially his letter, effectively. Falloux had just had to resign because of ill-health, and his departure would probably have broken up the ministry anyway, but Louis Napoleon had already decided to have done with it. The Roman wranglings had laid bare fundamental incompatibilities between the president and the ministers. It had become all too clear that these last regarded themselves as answerable, in the last resort, to the Assembly. Louis Napoleon decided that the time had come to show them, and the Assembly too, who was really the master.

Legally he was unassailable: 'The President of the Republic appoints and dismisses ministers,' said the Constitution (Chapter v, section 64), and after reading accounts of cabinet meetings in which his wishes and suggestions were almost routinely snubbed it is easy to sympathize with him.[30] In the Assembly Thiers and the Burgraves, blinded by their years in authority, by personal vanity and by self-interest, believed, and acted upon the belief, that the last word would always rest with them, so long as they were supported by a parliamentary majority; they would always be able to control Louis Napoleon, even without taking office ('the folly of clever men is wonderful,' remarked Tocqueville).[31] President Andrew Jackson of the United States had faced a similar situation in 1831, and had responded similarly, by dismissing his entire cabinet, except for the postmaster-general, and Jackson was not a Bonaparte. Louis Napoleon sent a message to the Assembly on 31 October dismissing the Barrot ministry and naming its successors, who included Barrot's brother – thereafter known as 'Cain'.[32]

In this message Louis Napoleon not only laid down that he must have for ministers men who would do as they were told, 'men who would be as conscious of my responsibilities as of their own, as concerned with action as with words', but added, 'the name of Napoleon is in itself a programme. That is to say: at home – order, authority, religion, the well-being of the people; abroad – national prestige. It is this policy, initiated by my election, which I desire to see triumphant with the support of the Assembly and the people.'[33]

Tocqueville described this message as 'insolent'. He might well take personal umbrage at its thrust, since he had always been careful to work amiably with the president, informing and consulting him on everything. Foreseeing such a reaction Louis Napoleon wrote a private letter to Tocqueville, assuring him of his liking, respect and sympathy; the implication was that there were others in the former cabinet, no doubt including the notoriously uncouth Dufaure, of whom this could not be said. Tocqueville replied gratefully, while admitting that his feelings had been hurt, and visited the Élysée to show that he was reconciled.[34]

But he had no doubt as to what the event meant. The president, he told Beaumont:

wants to govern, and above all to *seem* to govern all by himself. He thought that, little by little, we were casting him into the shade and that the country would in the end lose sight of him. He wanted to display his independence of us and of the National Assembly. That is why he chose the moment when we were most assured of a parliamentary majority and why, instead of choosing new ministers from the leaders of that majority, he has looked to the lowest of the low among the parties for men to serve him.[35]

He thought it was now clear that Louis Napoleon was determined somehow to resurrect the Empire, and had dismissed Barrot and his colleagues because they would never assist, or even tolerate, a *coup d'état*, although he admitted that there had been many secondary reasons why the president might have wanted to get rid of his inconvenient ministers. Unlike most of his friends, Tocqueville did not expect the president to overthrow the Republic immediately. He had studied the man closely since his letter to Clamorgan in the previous spring, and among other things had noticed Louis Napoleon's tendency to take one backward step for every two taken forward. His letters to Beaumont on the affair are venomously exact and penetrating; it is lamentable that he did not complete his portrait of the president in the *Souvenirs*:

> The President is a monomaniac who will only give up the imperial dream with his last breath; he is audacious to the point of imprudence and insanity; but at the same time he is lymphatic and apathetic. He never makes two moves in succession. He has just given his vanity great satisfaction; he thinks he has humiliated the Assembly and all the party leaders and has much improved his standing in the eyes of France. That is enough for him for the moment. He will live off it for some time, until a new prick of the spur rouses him to jump the last ditch.[36]

The crisis was over for the time being, but that did not make it any easier for Tocqueville and his friends to decide what to do next.

At least Gobineau could be provided for: Tocqueville secured a post for him in the French embassy at Berne. This sort of patronage was to become all too common under the Third Republic, and cause serious trouble, but Tocqueville would have been surprised to be told that there was anything objectionable in his conduct. He had enjoyed playing patron to his friends: he had not only sent Corcelle to Naples and Lamoricière to St. Petersburg, but at Louis Napoleon's suggestion had appointed Beaumont to the embassy at Vienna. Now Beaumont resigned and returned to his seat in the Assembly. He regretted having to leave Vienna, and was warm in his thanks to Tocqueville for having sent him there. Tocqueville's response to events was not quite so straightforward. He took a modest satisfaction in his short record as foreign minister: 'I think I did all that there was to be done during my time in power ... I think I made a contribution to enforcing order on 13 June, to maintaining the general peace and to bringing France and England together,' but his dismissal left him at a loss: as he told his niece Denise, 'I don't have the art of immediately substituting a large new mental project for the one that has ended';[37] in fact he seems to have fallen into the same pit of lethargy that swallowed him on his return from America in 1832; but worse was to follow. Marie had been exhausted by her exertions as a minister's wife, and now she succumbed to a particularly prolonged and painful recurrence of her uterine troubles, which did not go away entirely until January. Soon after that, Tocqueville himself fell seriously ill.

Medically, it was the turning-point of his life's history: he was never again to be wholly free of doctors. It is therefore vexing that it is only possible to make a good guess as to the nature of his ailment. He coughed up blood in March and applied for a six-month leave of absence from the Assembly, which was granted on the 26th: as it turned out, he did not return to his duties for more than a year. His doctors (Andral and unnamed colleagues) seem to have taken the gravest view of his illness from the start, though they did not share all their alarms with their highly strung patient (who was to be plagued with untruthful physicians until his life's end). At first they assured him that his lungs were in no way affected, and when he had recovered somewhat told him that they were healed; he seems to have believed them unquestioningly on both occasions. But the doctors were unsparing in their diagnosis of his larynx. It was a serious matter, they said, and the right treatment was a long and comprehensive rest of his throat (perhaps they thought that shouting in the Assembly through long and noisy sessions had done him no good). Through March and April and into May he was under orders to stay at home in the evenings (a rule that he faithfully obeyed, except for one dinner at the Élysée as the president's guest) and was forbidden long conversations: he was allowed to speak but not to talk. Andral may have calculated that if he rested his throat he would also rest his lungs. In March there seem to have been fears for his life, and during April he was still very feeble. Marie fell ill again, perhaps from the strain of nursing him. He wrote in disgust to Monckton Milnes: 'for six months our house has been a den of misery. When the wife gets better the husband falls ill, and *vice versa.*' His chief concern was to be cured of his cures, or at any rate to stop taking his medicines. He was livelier in May, and as soon as Marie was better they were off to Tocqueville. She had already decided that they ought to spend the winter somewhere warm on the Mediterranean: 'if he is not to speak, if he is not to write, if he is not to read or even think about politics, and such are the orders of his physicians what is the use of his staying …?'[38]

It seems all but certain that Tocqueville was beginning to suffer from the tuberculosis that eventually killed him. Beaumont does not appear to have guessed what was wrong until the summer of 1858: he had been over-impressed by his friend's former prowess as a swimmer and a climber of mountains, which seemed to prove that his lungs were among his healthiest organs; but the patient and his wife cannot have been wholly deceived, however brave the faces they assumed.

Even so, Tocqueville was not entirely docile. Nassau Senior visited Paris in May and called on him five times, to be greeted with a torrent of talk: the episode compels the realization that Tocqueville was a chatterbox. Senior did his best to limit the damage by keeping his visits short.[39]

The return to Normandy was welcome to both Tocqueville and Marie. They had not been there together since 1847, and they were happy to be home again. They did not chafe at their enforced quiet: rather, they were glad to use Tocqueville's illness as an excuse to keep bores away. The only drawback was the weather, which was too British for Tocqueville's taste, but he pretended that Marie felt quite at home with rain, wind and cold (they kept fires burning right through August). It was true that she got her health back fairly quickly, while his recovery was slow and incomplete. His throat was still vulnerable: he found that he could not safely read aloud, which was normally one of their chief pleasures.[40]

It was a retreat in every sense, and Tocqueville used the time to take stock – did so, indeed, for the next eleven months. In terms of the outcome, it was the most important period of his life since 1832. He was beginning to feel that he had little political future. Like everyone else, he foresaw a *coup d'état*; the question was, when would it occur? Meanwhile the party of order in the Assembly had made an unholy pact with Louis Napoleon: he agreed to sign a law curtailing universal suffrage in return for a doubling of his salary. This sort of thing led Tocqueville to wonder if there was any point in continuing to struggle for the Republic. He wrote to Beaumont: 'would it not employ our moderation and our acknowledged honesty better to look for the least irregular possible exit from the Constitution, the one most respectful of the national will, and try, if not to save the Republic, at least to save liberty from perishing with it?' This would mean trying to come to an understanding with Louis Napoleon, but Tocqueville was not yet ready to make the attempt. For one thing, politics did not seem so urgent from the Cotentin as they had in Paris; for another, he felt wearily middle-aged. His long-drawn-out convalescence persuaded him that youth had gone for good; perhaps he was even getting old (he was forty-four): 'The truth is that I am less impatient, calmer and infinitely better-tempered than I was formerly. I am richer, as you can tell, in negatives. I am becoming sterile and easy-going ...'[41]

These remarks should be read sceptically. It was not in Tocqueville to do nothing if he had an alternative. As his strength returned he reached for his pen.

> Exiled for the time being from the theatre of action and unable even to give myself to any programme of study, because of the precarious state of my health, I am reduced, here in my solitude, to meditate on myself for a moment, or rather to summon up visions of the recent events in which I was an actor or of which I was a witness. The best use I can make of my leisure seems to me to be to retrace those events, to paint the men I saw taking part in them, and to ascertain and engrave on my memory, if I can, the confused features which form the indistinct physiognomy of this my time.[42]

So begins the *Souvenirs*, his memoir of the revolution of 1848, which he started in July 1850.

Its great value as a historical and biographical source must be clear to any reader of the present book. In spite of its ideological rigidity and many narrative gaps, it forms a document, along with the *Communist Manifesto* (how Tocqueville would have hated that conjunction!), where all serious study of 1848 has to start. That revolution stimulated a flood of memoirs and histories; it is a proof of Tocqueville's powers that his *Souvenirs* stands out from the crowd. No more need be said on this well-established point. Nor is it necessary to measure the *Souvenirs* against Tocqueville's other masterpieces, the *Démocratie* and the *Ancien Régime*. Each is a work of a different *genre*, meeting a distinct need. Each succeeds, as much as books can. Except in point of lucidity and intelligence they are very unlike each other; but palpably they have the same author. The same mind is gracefully at work in all of them. The point, again, is too obvious to be insisted upon. Perhaps all that need he said at last in praise of the *Souvenirs* is that without it Tocqueville's *oeuvre* would be infinitely less fascinating; for only in this book does he take the stage himself.

What cannot be taken for granted is the shape and nature of the book, and how Tocqueville conceived and wrote it. He himself is at first quite explicit about his intentions. He writes, in the tone of a man fighting off temptation:

> these recollections will be my mental recreation, and emphatically not a work of literature. They are set down for myself alone. This screed will be a mirror in which I shall entertain myself by contemplating my contemporaries and myself, and not a canvas for the public. Even my best friends will have absolutely no knowledge of it, for I want to be free to paint without flattery. I want to analyse sincerely what were the secret motives which shaped our actions ... and, having understood, to state them. In short, I want the record of my memories to be sincere and, for that reason, it is necessary that it remain entirely secret.

There can be no doubt that as he went to work Tocqueville meant every word of this declaration, but the pitiless verve of his memoirs shows that he had at least one other motive. He needed to discharge pints of accumulated bile. The eruption of the February Revolution had convinced him that he was living in a world of idiots, which explains the extraordinary sardonic bite of his portraits. His description of his sister-in-law Alexandrine on the morning of 24 February is quite unsoftened by twenty years of friendship:

My sister-in-law had lost her head, as usual. Already she imagined her husband dead and her daughters ravished. [There had been gunfire in the street outside her house all night.] My brother, although one of the staunchest of men, could not think what to do, not being himself, and I never saw more clearly that if a brave wife is an enormous asset during a revolution, a wet hen, even if she has the heart of a dove, is a frightful encumbrance. What annoyed me most was to see that my sister-in-law had no thought for her country in the lamentations which the thought of her family's fate drew from her every second … I admit that she was kind-hearted and even intelligent, but she had somewhat shrunk her mind and chilled her heart by devoting herself rigidly and solely, in a sort of pious selfishness, to *le Bon Dieu*, to her husband, her children, and above all to her health, hardly concerning herself with anybody else; the best woman and the worst citizen that one could conceive of.[43]

Such acid miniatures litter the *Souvenirs*, and while making irresistible reading somewhat alienate us from the author: it is impossible to think that he is fair (his description of Lamartine is one of many which certainly are not) and it is therefore difficult to trust his judgement. Tocqueville came to regret his rancour. He never revised the manuscript, but he realized that it was bound to be published after his death and left strict instructions that until the last of his victims was dead the book might appear only in bowdlerized form. (So faithfully were these instructions obeyed that the complete *Souvenirs* was not published until 1942.) But it had been a tremendous relief to let rip during that wet summer of 1850.

The first part, taking the story as far as the proclamation of the Republic, was poured out during July; true to his first intentions, Tocqueville revealed it to no-one except (presumably) Marie, though he told Ampère that he had something to show him (*'you alone'*) if he came to Tocqueville in August. In the event Ampère did not come. Others did – Comte Hervé, Édouard and his children, Senior, his wife and daughter, Rivet – but none was let into the secret. Senior's journal shows that Tocqueville was in high spirits, talking all the time except, because of doctor's orders, when driving in a carriage; even that rule was broken when he went down to Saint-Lô for the *conseil-général*. The improvement in his health was such that, characteristically, he decided he was as good as cured; but ten days away from home in late August and early September disillusioned him. As president of the *conseil* he had to be very busy and speak frequently; then it was necessary to deliver a speech of welcome when Louis Napoleon came to Cherbourg for a naval review (once more Tocqueville urged the case for the Cherbourg railway). By the time he returned to Tocqueville he was exhausted, and once more his throat was giving trouble; he told Clamorgan that he was now in worse health than he had been when he arrived in Normandy. Marie was ill again. Cold winds blew across the Cotentin; as soon as Marie was well enough to travel they left for Paris, where Tocqueville's doctors renewed the ban on conversation and more or less ordered him to winter in the south. He and Marie left for Italy on 30 October.[44]

Tocqueville had not forgotten the *Souvenirs* amid these other preoccupations. The project was too important to him, and became more so as he wrote. It was the expression of all his disillusionment with politics and of his anxiety, both personal and patriotic, about the future – hence the passionate tone of Part One and the speed with which he wrote. It was an eruption of his feelings – he did not even bother to divide the text into chapters. But the act of composition forced him to change most of his initial assumptions. He was a mature writer at the height of his powers; as an artist, he could not do less than his best; the result was unquestionably a work of literature – it is rather astonishing that he could have supposed for a minute that it would not be. That summer Nassau Senior, who had at times a Boswellian trick of asking useful easy questions, wanted to know which was the golden age of French literature. 'The latter part of the seventeenth century,' was the unhesitating reply. 'Men wrote solely for fame, & they addressed a public small & highly cultivated. French literature was young, the highest posts were vacant: it was comparatively easy to be distinguished. Extravagance was not necessary to attract attention. Style then was the mere vehicle of thought. First of all to be perspicuous, &, being perspicuous, to be concise, was all that they aimed at.'[45] Such was Tocqueville's declaration of faith, but to the reader of the *Souvenirs* it is almost unnecessary – every page proclaims the admirer of Pascal and Molière, de Retz and the duc de Saint-Simon and (from a later period, but still in the great tradition) the *Mémoires d'outre-tombe*, so much of which he had heard read aloud in the author's presence.

The slightly contrived eloquence of the 1835 *Démocratie* is a thing of the past. Tocqueville now writes, as in his letters, but with greater care, with the directness, perspicacity and concision that he admired. He was beginning to compose a masterpiece.

That being so, it was idle to tell himself that he did not expect readers. He was writing a contribution to the history of his times, as Guizot would soon be doing,* and even if he meant to defer its publication indefinitely, it would still have to conform to the standards of science. He had been producing work based on thorough documentary research ever since 1827, and he was not going to change his methods now. As early as 9 July he was writing to Clamorgan asking for help in getting hold of Parisian newspapers from 1848, though he did not say what he wanted them for; and in Paris, during October, he interviewed Odilon Barrot, Rivet and Beaumont in order to get their accounts of 24 February.† He did not explain why, but they were bound to guess. By the time that Tocqueville left for Italy the secret of the *Souvenirs* was not quite so absolute as had originally been intended.[46]

The journey south went tolerably until they put to sea (the party consisted of Alexis, Marie, and at least two servants – a cook, and Tocqueville's valet, Eugène). At Genoa their rather small ship was invaded by a crowd of English travellers, so that there was hardly room to move on the decks or in the saloon. Then between Leghorn and Civita Vecchia one of the worst storms that Tocqueville had ever known broke out. Waves flooded the deck continually and everyone had to take refuge in the saloon. Men, women and children were jammed against each other, according to Tocqueville, like the cargo of a slave-ship. Everyone was seasick.

> But the worst thing was that there was so little air that I really thought that I was going to suffocate. My lungs are not yet as elastic as they were before my illness and I felt that I might stop breathing at any moment. Happily there was a small skylight next to me which I managed to open; that meant that I got several waves in my face, but at least I was allowed to live, which for the moment was all I cared about.

---

* Guizot's *Mémoires pour servir à l'histoire de mon temps* began to appear in 1859. Each chapter was followed by a generous printing of documents.

† GB's memoir of February 1848 confirms the accuracy of AT's notes on his 1850 interview.

The storm subsided at dawn, and they landed at Civita Vecchia, but Marie had suffered so much that Tocqueville thought it unlikely that she would ever again agree to travel by sea. Passing through Rome as quickly as they could (Tocqueville did not want to get involved in the political and diplomatic situation there), they reached Naples on 21 November.[47]

Tocqueville had intended to winter at Palermo, but neither he nor Marie could face another winter voyage, and possibly another storm. For a few weeks they remained at Naples. It was an interesting time to be there. The reaction against revolution was stronger, perhaps, in the Kingdom of the Two Sicilies than anywhere else, and the King, Ferdinand II (otherwise known as King Bomba), was busy conducting palpably rigged trials of the leading Neapolitan liberals, many of them formerly his ministers, before thrusting them into his revolting dungeons for long terms. Mr Gladstone happened to be visiting Naples that winter, and made it his business to attend the trials and inspect the prisons; the result would be the publication in 1851 of two savage pamphlets denouncing the Bourbon regime ('the negation of God erected into a system of government') which gave him a heroic European reputation overnight. Tocqueville met Gladstone, but his response to the Neapolitan scandal was very different, and not only because he was probably tired of visiting prisons. He dismissed the king to Corcelle as a poltroon turned into a tyrant by unnecessary fright; he told Dufaure that the pleasure of beginning to feel well again was in part spoiled by the 'moral maladies' of the country. It was depressing to be in a city where all liberties were either imperilled or actually destroyed, and it was largely the fault of France. 'When the French rise in revolution they immediately plunge Europe into anarchy, and when order is re-established in France all the old abuses spring up again everywhere else. So the peoples, it must be admitted, love us scarcely more than the princes.' The February revolution had been disastrous for Italy; it was frightful to see liberty trodden underfoot and destroyed; Tocqueville decided to avert his eyes and live only for enjoyment. That meant leaving Naples, where the inns were ruinously expensive as well as flea-ridden; and he had nothing but distaste for the Neapolitans themselves: 'what noise! what inconceivable dirt, what rags and tatters, what vermin! You would have to go into the nastiest streets of Algiers to find anything so abominable as what you meet at every turn on the streets of Naples.' Early in December he and Marie moved to a rented house in Sorrento, where they stayed for the next four months.[48]

Sorrento delighted them and their friends – Ampère and the Seniors having soon joined them. Ampère was given a spare bedroom, and the Seniors – Nassau, his wife, and their daughter Minnie – took the first floor of the *palazzo*, the Belvedere Guerracino, of which the Tocquevilles had taken the second. The weather was usually balmy, the views were magnificent, the country round delightful for walking. The air was so clear that it was almost possible to count the houses in Naples, eighteen miles off across the Bay; the neighbourhood of Sorrento, said Senior, seemed gilt: 'whatever was not white with buildings was golden with oranges.' They took trips to Amalfi, Pompeii and Paestum, and Tocqueville climbed Vesuvius again: Mr and Mrs Senior got less than halfway up, but Minnie and Tocqueville went right to the top. He was getting back his old *élan*. Unfortunately Marie was still unwell. She was very seldom able to go out, and when she did she had to ride a donkey. 'It is true that we have a terrace as long as an esplanade, from which we enjoy the best view in Sorrento; it would be an incomparable exercise yard for a prisoner of state; but for someone who is supposed to be at liberty,' said Tocqueville, 'it seems very insufficient.' He worried about getting her safely back to France; meanwhile he picked violets on his walks and gave her a large bunch every time he got home. Another cloud on his spirits was the news from France. He hungered for it, and was deeply grateful for Beaumont's long and regular letters, yet they depressed him. He poured out his thoughts to Senior and Ampère, but it got him nowhere; essentially, France was confronted with a dangerous and insoluble dilemma, and although Tocqueville felt frustratingly useless at Sorrento he would have achieved no more had he been in Paris.[49]

But for much of the time Louis Napoleon and the Assembly were forgotten and the party chatted of whatever came to mind: the Church of England, the problem of poverty, the brilliant simplicity of Voltaire's style ('He had a right to answer, as he did to a lady who talked to him about the beauty of his phrases, *Madame, je n'ai jamais fait une phrase de ma vie*'*), Talleyrand, Napoleon, and ancient Egypt, on which Ampère was something of an expert. Thanks to Senior's journal it is still possible to enter into the agreeable time that they were all having.[50]

Yet although Tocqueville appeared to hold nothing back from his English friends he said nothing to them of what was becoming his deepest preoccupation. He was coming to the conclusion that, whatever happened, his career in politics was ending and that he would be best advised to return to writing full time. He talked the matter over with Ampère, and no doubt Marie, and (by letter) with Beaumont; but his most remarkable expression of his thoughts came in a letter to Kergorlay, written a week or so after the move to Sorrento.

As the two friends sadly acknowledged, their once abundant correspondence, in which they had shared every thought and feeling, had dwindled of late years almost to nothing: now, when they wrote, it was usually to each other's wives. We do not know how often, or how regularly, they had seen each other since Kergorlay's marriage. But the old bond was still strong, and when Tocqueville wanted to discuss his innermost thoughts he still turned first to Louis.

He had always planned a working holiday; he had brought boxes of books with him, there was the *Souvenirs* to attend to, and Sorrento was a perfect place for reading and writing. But he did not at first feel in the vein, and while waiting for inspiration to return he began to think seriously of another project. He started to tell Kergorlay about it:

> For a long time I have been preoccupied, perhaps I ought to say bothered, by the notion of again undertaking a big book. It seems to me that my true value lies above all in works of the mind, that I am worth more in my thoughts than in my deeds, and if I am ever to leave some trace of myself in the world it will be much more by what I write than by a memory of what I have done. The last ten years, which have been so sterile for me in so many ways, have nevertheless given me a truer understanding of human affairs and practical matters without my mind losing its habit of looking at human activities as a totality. So I think I am better suited than I was when I wrote the *Démocratie* to tackle successfully some great topic of political literature. But what topic should I choose?[51]

* 'Madam, I have never coined a phrase in my life.'

The point was crucial: he would have to find something that would interest the reading public and rouse his own enthusiasm, 'for I plunge at once below mediocrity when I don't passionately enjoy what I'm doing.' He had been looking round for such an *idée mère*, in his few moments of leisure, for some years, but now the matter was becoming urgent: he felt that old age was at hand; he must decide. It would have to be a contemporary subject: in the last analysis, it was only questions of the day which interested the public or, even more important, Tocqueville himself. (This remark throws some light on an incident recorded by Senior. He took Tocqueville to call on Carlo Troja, a former Neapolitan prime minister who by some oversight had not been sent to the dungeons. He was now devoting himself to the Dark Ages, '& spent half an hour proving to us the identity of the Daci, the Getae, the Gothi & the Normans – a fact which we had no wish to contest. How happy, said Tocqueville as we left him, a man must be who in these times can interest himself about Dacians & Goths.'[52])

The broad field in which he hoped to find his *idée mère* was easy to identify:

> I have for long had the idea, as I think I have told you, of selecting from that great expanse of time which runs from 1789 to our own days and which I continue to call the French Revolution, the ten years of the Empire, the birth, development, decline and fall of that prodigious enterprise. More and more I have thought and think that I would do well in choosing to paint that epoch. Not only was it great, it was unusual, even unique, and yet so far, at least in my opinion, it has only been presented in false or vulgar colours. Besides, it throws a bright light on the epoch which preceded it.

Tocqueville's first thought was to outdo Thiers, whom he clearly had in mind as the chief dauber of false colours; for one thing, he found Thiers's pretensions to military expertise ridiculous.* But on reflection he modestly doubted if narrative history was quite his *métier*: 'what I have best succeeded at so far is in interpreting events rather than in recounting them'; besides, he didn't want to write a long book; he wanted to put together a volume of reflections and verdicts on the

---

* Thiers's *History of the Consulate and Empire* began to be published in 1845; its last volumes did not appear until 1862.

Empire, on such topics (here he began to list what read like chapter headings) as 'How the Empire Came About'; 'How It was Able to Establish Itself in the Midst of the Society Created by the Revolution'; 'What were the Means That It Made Use Of'; 'What was the *True* Nature of the Man Who Founded It'; 'What Brought About Its Successes, What Its Failures'; 'The Transient and Durable Effects It Had on the History of the World, and in Particular on That of France'. 'It seems to me that there we have the making of a really great book; but the difficulties are immense.' They might have daunted Montesquieu himself. Tocqueville begged Kergorlay to help him with his advice; but he ended proudly:

> I am vain enough to believe that I am more likely than anyone else to bring to such a subject a free spirit, and to write of men and things without passion or reserve. For, as to men, even though they may have lived into our day, I surely neither love nor hate them, and as to the forms of what we call constitutions, laws, dynasties, classes, they have, I will not say value, but existence in my eyes only in their effects; I have no traditions, no partisanship – emphatically – I have no *cause* but that of liberty and human dignity. I am sure of that. And for work of this sort a disposition, a natural tendency of this kind is as useful as it has often been damaging when my business was not that of discussing human affairs but of intervening in them.

Kergorlay replied to this remarkable letter as it deserved – thoughtfully, encouragingly, and at length; but he could not do so before 19 January, and in the meantime Tocqueville had gone back to the *Souvenirs*. Before he did so he had not been able to refrain from dashing down a sketch of what he might say about Napoleon. The note of dispassionate enquiry is not very audible:

> I would like to show ... with what incomparable art he discerned in the most demagogic aspects of the Revolution all that was useful for despotism, and how he brought it to natural birth; starting with his domestic government, I want to contemplate the exertions of that almost divine intelligence, grossly employed in shackling human liberty; that perfected, scientific organization of power, which only the greatest genius during the most enlightened and civilized times could have conceived; and how under the weight of that wonderful machine society was crushed and smothered, becoming sterile, so that

intelligence slowed, the human spirit languished, souls shrank, great men no longer emerged, and against the flat vastness of the horizon, wherever one looked, nothing showed except the colossal figure of the Emperor himself.[53]

It is not just hindsight which shows that Tocqueville's mind was again on the brink of a great leap forward.

Tocqueville underrated his narrative powers. It was not necessary to write like Michelet or Thiers (or, for that matter, Macaulay, whom he was soon to read and admire). The art of narrative, like every other literary form, requires selectivity and imagination; it must be a form of analysis. Tocqueville was fully equal to the challenge, as the *Souvenirs* shows. The second part, which was written at Sorrento between December and March,[54] takes the story of the 1848 Revolution, as he witnessed it, from February to the deliberations of the constitutional committee. It is incomplete: he meant to chronicle the Cavaignac government, but never did so. The fragment, nevertheless, is full of vitality, and sweeps the reader along from set-piece to set-piece: the 1848 elections, 15 May, the June Days, the making of the constitution. It was quoted so extensively in earlier chapters that its merits need not be demonstrated here. Perhaps it is worth remarking that its style still illustrates those virtues which Tocqueville valued in Voltaire and the writers of the seventeenth century: it is brilliantly lucid, direct and unpretentious. Tocqueville was true to his models. Only once did another influence unmistakably assert itself, in the elegiac passage already quoted where Tocqueville saluted the old *noblesse*:

At the very height of the June Days the man died who, in our time, perhaps best conserved the character of our ancient families, M. de Chateaubriand, to whom I was linked by so many family ties and childhood recollections. He had fallen long since into a kind of mute stupor that made us think at times that his mind was extinguished. However, in that state he heard the din of the February Revolution, and wanted to know what was happening. He was told that the monarchy of Louis-Philippe had just been overthrown; he said, 'Well done!' and fell silent. Four months later the roar of the days of June also reached his ears, and again he asked what the noise was. They told him that there was war in Paris and that he was hearing the cannon. He tried in vain to stand, saying, 'I want to go there'; then he fell silent, this time for ever: he died the next day.[55]

It was a leave-taking: of an ancient France, of a man to whom Tocqueville owed much, and of the *chateaubrianesque* style that he used occasionally to emulate. By 1851 he only had one voice: his own.

The first part of the *Souvenirs* was written, as it were, at a sitting. The second was written by fits and starts, and although it flows out of the first with perfect ease, it leaves a somewhat different impression, if only because it covers a much longer period (months instead of days). And Tocqueville opens it with a long, reflective chapter that further slows the pace, but which may be considered the heart of the book – or at least the clearest indication of how the *Souvenirs* relates to work past and work yet to come. It consists of a meditation on the nature and causes of the February Revolution, allegedly recollected from the evening of 24 February, after he got home from the rout of the Chamber of Deputies,* but transparently a piece of literary contrivance. He offers his view of historical causation, not without a side-swipe at mere men of letters that looks forward to the *Ancien Régime*: men who have no political experience and try to reduce everything to grand causes according to their pet theories: 'for my part, I hate these absolute systems, which make all historical events depend on great First Causes ... and which so to say eliminate human beings from the history of the human race.' Such theories, he thinks, are invented simply to gratify their authors' vanity. He names no names (he almost never did), so it is permissible to think that one of the writers he has in mind is the author of *De la démocratie en Amérique*. But he also disparages mere politicians, who can never see anything larger than the hurly-burly in which they live, and here he certainly had Thiers in mind, for this was exactly the criticism he had made of Thiers's history of Napoleon the previous summer, when he casually mentioned to Senior that he hoped one day to write on the subject himself.[56] He himself insists on the difference between 'general' and 'accidental' causes, and applies the distinction to the February Revolution. Among the general causes he places the industrial revolution,

---

* See above, pp. 426–7.

which had filled Paris with discontented workers: this must be one of the earliest uses of the phrase. He surveys the whole course of French history since 1789, and concludes with the image that is recurrent in his writing at this period:

> Will we ever arrive, as current prophets assure us, perhaps as vainly as their predecessors, at a more complete and profound social transformation than our fathers ever wanted or foresaw, and than we ourselves can yet conceive? Or shall we end merely in intermittent anarchy, the chronic and incurable malady well-known to ancient nations? As for me, I cannot say, I do not know when the long voyage will end; I am weary of repeatedly mistaking treacherous fog-banks for the shore, and I often wonder if the *terra firma* which we have been seeking for so long actually exists, or if our destiny is not rather to beat about eternally at sea![57]

And in another passage of familiar thoughts he explains his anxiety for the future of French liberty:

> I had passed the best years of my youth amid a society which seemed to be becoming great and prosperous as it again became free, so I conceived the idea of a temperate, regulated liberty, restrained by religion, manners and law; the charms of that liberty moved me, it became the passion of my whole life; I felt that I could never be consoled for its loss, and now I saw clearly that it would have to be forgone.[58]

This was the heart of his political faith; it was another theme which, inevitably, would figure largely in the *Ancien Régime*.

But he is still the Tocqueville of 1848, as we have met him in his letters and speeches, and in his next chapter, still in reflective vein, he abuses 'socialism' as the essential and fallacious doctrine of the February Revolution – only to astonish us by adding the following thought, almost unique in his work:[59]

> Will socialism remain buried under the contempt which so rightly covers the socialists of 1848? I raise the question without answering it. I do not doubt that the constituent laws of modern society will be much modified in the long run; it has happened already to many of their chief clauses, but will they ever be destroyed and others put in their place? I think it impracticable, but I say no more, because

the more I study society in former times, and the more I learn in detail how society operates now, and when I consider the prodigious diversity that one comes across, not only of laws, but of the principles of laws, and the different forms they have assumed and which the right of property assumes, whatever men say, here on Earth, I am tempted to believe that what we call necessary institutions are often only those to which we are accustomed, and that where the organization of society is concerned, the field of possibility is much vaster than men who live in particular societies ever imagine.[60]

Even Tocqueville could not keep his restless mind in thrall to his prejudices for ever. It is true that this passage had no sequel in the few years left to him; but it makes one wonder what his views would have become had he reached old age. As it is, this is as near as Tocqueville ever got to seeing what is obvious today: that his own political and economic opinions were as ill-founded as those which he so passionately resisted.

At this point it is convenient to take leave of the *Souvenirs*. The later chapters written at Sorrento, describing events from February to June, have been quoted exhaustively in my own earlier chapters and need not be recapitulated. The last describes the deliberations of the constitutional committee, and is notably rougher than the rest. It was an embittering topic, but Tocqueville would probably have revised his treatment were it not for events. He meant to: he made a note to get hold of the committee minutes to refresh his memory.[61] But when he returned to France in April his time was claimed by other matters, and when he resumed work on the book in September he skipped the period between summer 1848 and May 1849 in order to recount his experiences as foreign minister while the memory was still fairly fresh. But because of the events of December 1851, this third part was also left unfinished (he turned decisively to other work) and is the least interesting, because the most conventional, of the three sections: there are so many ministerial memoirs! – and Tocqueville does not always escape the chief danger of the *genre*, that of being too self-justifying. Part Three is notable chiefly for his unfinished portrait of Louis Napoleon.

The book, then, is radically incomplete and unrevised, which, to Tocqueville's own meticulous eyes, was a serious weakness. Today's readers are likely to be more charitable. It is deeply regrettable that he was unable to carry out his complete scheme, but what we have is remarkable: it is Tocqueville's self-portrait. The wit, the eloquence, the deep feeling, the predominant pessimism, the occasional sparks of hope: the characteristics that are to be found in his letters and the records of his conversation are here deployed by the artist. He tries to shed all pretence and to bring out on paper his faults as well as his intelligence, and does so perhaps more successfully even than he realizes. As a historical source the *Souvenirs* is invaluable; as a biographical one unique. It is particularly important in showing Tocqueville at the hinge of his fate: he turns into a historian before our eyes. The *Démocratie* and the *Ancien Régime* were events in the history of Europe. The same cannot be said of the *Souvenirs* but (to speak personally for a moment) of all his works it is the one which I could least spare to oblivion.

CHAPTER TWENTY

DECEMBER

1851–1852

*Even after 1848, tho' the Bourbons were discredited we shd
not have tolerated a Bonaparte, if we had not lost all our
self possession in our terror of the* Rouges. *That terror
created him …*

TOCQUEVILLE, CONVERSATION WITH SENIOR,

9 APRIL, 1857[1]

TOCQUEVILLE AND MARIE left Sorrento on 14 April 1851 and
arrived in Paris on the 30th. All thoughts of literature had to be put
aside. The long political crisis, so faithfully chronicled by Beaumont
in his letters, was approaching its *dénouement*, and Tocqueville could
not stay aloof, though by 1 December he was saying that were it not
for honour he would resign from the Assembly at once.[2]

In March 1848 he had congratulated himself on seeing his way
clear before him. Now, except that he had to earn his parliamentary
salary, nothing was clear. Nothing is very clear in retrospect, either.
The French political world was in a turmoil of disputes about ends
and means, and as Tocqueville said repeatedly, it was impossible to tell
what the future would be, whether in the short or the long term – this,
although the air was thick with threats and warnings of *coups d'état*,
either by the president or the Assembly.

The situation was eventually to be resolved by a presidential *coup* on 2 December, which was itself to be a matter of fierce debate and was a permanent stain on the reputation of Louis Napoleon, partly because of blunders in its execution. Yet it must not be judged, after more than a century and a half, as self-evidently inexcusable. Louis Napoleon had been elected with more than five and a half million votes to fewer than two million for all his rivals combined, and was confident that if he could stand again he would be triumphantly re-elected, not just because there was no convincing competitor, but because of his performance in office and, still more, because he represented stability, for which the citizens deeply longed. When Tocqueville spent three weeks in the Manche that summer he discovered that most of the voters were solidly behind the president. 'He is in office, which is a determining reason for our peasants, who have no enthusiasm for him but say, in the manner you know, of their own accord, "Why change a man who hasn't made any mistakes?"'[3] Under Louis Napoleon, France again had an effective government, and prosperity, at least in the towns, was beginning to return. If Bonaparte had not actually restored France's international prestige, most Frenchmen thought that he had, which did just as well. He had made many official tours (including the visit to Cherbourg), in which he and France got to know each other (very necessary: he had not lived in the country since his childhood). He became generally accepted as a dignified and competent head of state. He had earned a second term, and the constitutional ban on it seemed ridiculous and undemocratic. Somehow or other it must be circumvented or repealed; if it were, the people would certainly approve.

Even if that had been all, repeal would probably not have been possible, since it would require amendments to the constitution, but Tocqueville, who had been studying the president's character closely for two years, was certain that it was not all. Louis Napoleon, he said, was not content to be a mere democratically elected president, however powerful or popular. 'He trusted in his star; he believed firmly that he was the tool of destiny and the necessary man ... I doubt if Charles X himself was ever more infatuated with his own legitimacy than he was with his.'[4] It was perhaps a weakness in Tocqueville that to him a strong monarch always seemed an actual or potential despot, whether Charles X, Louis-Philippe or Louis Napoleon; it does not follow that he was always wrong. He feared and detested Bonapartism. He had warned against the thing, if not the name, in the *Démocratie*.[5] He did not have the vocabulary to do his views justice: the word 'dictator' was not yet current in its full modern sense of brutal and illegitimate power; but he had never forgotten Napoleon I and was correctly convinced that Louis Napoleon meant to emulate him. Louis Napoleon had little taste for liberty and, in Tocqueville's opinion, particularly detested parliaments. He was a danger to France.

But what was the alternative? The Mountain had been driven from power. Almost the only thing which could unite conservatives was the prospect, however dim, of its return. For the rest, factions of Orleanists, legitimists, moderate Republicans and, increasingly, Bonapartists quarrelled carelessly in the Assembly. The dominant group there was still that of Thiers and the resurgent Orleanists who, to judge by their behaviour, had learned nothing and forgotten nothing like the Bourbons before them. Thiers had uttered his famous *mot*, 'the Republic ... is of all governments that which divides us least,' but he did not act as if he meant it, or even understood it: he first said it during the Assembly debate on the *loi Falloux* (which might just as reasonably have been called the *loi Thiers*), the schools measure which by largely handing over primary education to the Church exacerbated and embittered anticlericalism so that it remained one of the most divisive issues in French politics for the next hundred years and more.[6] (It was also at this time that Thiers dismissed the French lower classes as 'the vile multitude' or mob – in the debate on the law of 31 May 1850 which disfranchised three million citizens.)* Thiers and the other Burgraves seem to have regarded the 1848 revolution as a mere unfortunate accident; they did not take the Republic seriously (whereas Tocqueville did: it was his strength). They respected nobody's opinions but their own, failed to take realistic account of the return of Bonapartism, and were incapable of concession or compromise. As a result the Assembly grew more and more isolated and unrepresentative, and therefore steadily feebler, though the representatives did not realize this until too late. Louis Napoleon made a perfectly just point in a speech at Dijon on 11 June

* Because of his illness AT missed both debates. We know that he opposed the law of 31 May, and it is hard to be sure that he approved of the *loi Falloux*. He believed in *liberté d'enseignement*, but the law went much further than that, and one of AT's firmest beliefs was in the separation of Church and state.

1851, when he remarked of the Assembly, 'For three years, it has been noticeable that I have always been supported when it has been a matter of fighting disorder with severity; but when I have wanted to do good … by taking measures to improve the condition of the people, I have met only inertia.'[7] His complaint was contemptuously ignored. The Burgraves intrigued ceaselessly to bring back the Orléans family: they hoped to run the Prince de Joinville, one of Louis-Philippe's sons, for the presidency in 1852. It was widely suspected that they would themselves stage a *coup d'état* if they could get enough support in the army: they had great hopes of General Changarnier, the commander in Paris, until Louis Napoleon dismissed him. Meanwhile they postured as 'the party of order', and hoped to thwart Louis Napoleon's designs, whatever they were, by using the majority in the Assembly; but this turned out to be impossible because the other main component of the majority, the legitimists, detested Orléans far more than Bonaparte, and would not co-operate systematically. Attempts at 'fusion', that is, at uniting behind the last of the Bourbons, the childless 'Henri V' – the comte de Chambord, formerly the duc de Bordeaux – in return for his recognition of Louis-Philippe's grandson, the comte de Paris, as his rightful heir, did not succeed: Chambord would make no concessions. He meant eventually to return to France at God's invitation, not as the result of intrigues in a discredited Assembly (it did not strike him that if such had been the attitude of his great-uncle Louis XVIII there would have been no Restoration in 1814).

Tocqueville could not associate himself with such a crew, not least because, by using their power to disrupt the Republic as much as they could, they threatened a return of what he called anarchy; for his fear of the Mountain was still powerful, though he did not need to insist on it as much as in 1848. A new theme emerges in his writings at this time, a respect for the French people. They had come through the turbulence of the recent past with extraordinary self-discipline, he thought; they had profited from their revolutionary education; but still he did not entirely trust them, or at least not the Parisians. He feared that the elections of 1852, in which the Assembly and the presidency would be renewed, would bring in a Red parliamentary majority, which would once more endanger property. This fear of 1852 was widespread, and seems to have grown stronger as 1851 neared its end.[8]

It was while he was still at Sorrento that Tocqueville decided that the best thing to do in this tangle was to support Louis Napoleon, on conditions. He decided, tentatively, to treat the president's ambition for re-election as legitimate, and to work to have the constitution amended to make a second term legal. On his return to Paris he found that many others had come to the same conclusion: for once he was with the majority. Unfortunately there were many difficulties about this course. The worst was the near-impossibility of amending the constitution at all, let alone in time for the 1852 elections. In their anxiety to protect the Republic against assaults from either Left or Right the constitutional committee had laid it down that revision could only be considered during the last year of an Assembly's term; that for a given amendment to pass, the Assembly had to vote for it three times, at monthly intervals, passing it each time by a three-quarters majority; and that the quorum for such a vote was to be five hundred.[9] It is never easy to get such majorities, especially on important questions, or to keep them together. Even the US Constitution only requires two-thirds majorities, in both chambers, each voting once, to pass amendments.* In the French Assembly of 1851 the task was almost impossible, for the committed Republicans regarded the proposed amendment, legalizing the president's consecutive re-election, as no more than a dodge to resurrect monarchy. Most of Tocqueville's closest associates, among them Dufaure, took this view: they could not overlook the fact that had Cavaignac been elected there would have been no problem. It was the president's Napoleonic ambitions which created the crisis, and it could even be argued that such ambitions justified the one-term rule, which hampered them. Thiers, who had broken entirely with Louis Napoleon, was committed to the Joinville candidacy. However, his influence was not what it had been: many other leading conservatives, including the duc de Broglie (one of the Burgraves) and Montalembert, the leader of the Catholics in the Assembly, supported revision. Naturally Louis Napoleon, whose influence was steadily increasing, did so.

Tocqueville's plan was not quite hopeless, but at first he himself

* It also provides that three-quarters of the states must approve an amendment; but this requirement of federalism had no equivalent in the centralized France of 1851.

was. When Nassau Senior came to Paris early in May Tocqueville told him that it was childish to hope for a legal majority in favour of revision. And there was the related problem of the suffrage 'law of 31 May'. It had been passed in a moment of panic, when the Left had won four by-elections in Paris. The Right had won ten by-elections at the same time, but it was a curious feature of the party of order that it was always less impressed by its victories than by the fact that they were never quite total. So as Émile de Girardin said to Senior, the law replaced universal suffrage with a new version of Guizot's *pays légal*. Tocqueville held that the measure destroyed in advance the legitimacy of any elections held under it: sovereignty of the people meant what it said, and universal suffrage was necessary in a republic. Perhaps surprisingly, this somewhat advanced position became one of his principles.* The law of 31 May would have to be repealed.[10]

Louis Napoleon took a less high-minded view of the matter: 'Do you suppose that after having been elected by six million votes I would want an electoral system which would only give me four million?' He made this remark on 15 May, during an interview at the Elysée to which he had summoned Tocqueville. Tocqueville found it hard to imagine why he had been sent for, but it seems clear enough in retrospect. The Prince-President (as he was now usually called) was a skilful chess-player beginning his end-game. His half-brother, Auguste de Morny, was already convinced that only force could resolve the great political dilemma, but Louis Napoleon, always slow to make up his mind, was even more cautious than usual at this time, if only because a *coup d'état* could all too easily go wrong. He would exhaust all possibilities of a legal re-election before committing himself to other methods. He would give the Assembly a last chance to be sensible; he set about rallying as much support as possible for constitutional revision by constitutional means. He liked Tocqueville, who (according to himself) had always treated him with respect and consideration during his brief ministry, and was conspicuously upright. He now hoped to enlist him for the coming battle, which was not difficult, Tocqueville having already made his choice.[11]

---

* Though he still thought that mere vagabonds and drifters should not have the right to vote. He had not supported universal suffrage under the July Monarchy, but had been much encouraged by the elections of 1848 and 1849 in the Manche.

Tocqueville's chief preoccupation during the interview was to understand his host. 'There is nothing more difficult than to get past the immobile surface of that face and get to the bottom of his mind,' he wrote afterwards; 'one can never gather anything from a conversation with him but *impressions*.' (He was to say much the same in the *Souvenirs*: 'his eyes were dull and opaque like that thick glass used in ships' cabins, which lets in light but through which nothing can be seen.') Tocqueville was perhaps hampered by his own cleverness: the Prince-President seems to have agreed straightforwardly with almost everything that he said, and he gave Tocqueville *impressions* which later events proved to have been wholly accurate. He had very little hope that the Assembly would give him his constitutional revision; he was far from having given up the idea of launching a *coup d'état*, and he was determined to smash the law of 31 May, but wanted to do it at the last minute, 'as a kind of appeal to the people and a blow struck against the Assembly'. Tocqueville was equally frank, and warned the president earnestly against a resort to force, making it plain that he himself would have nothing to do with such an adventure.[12]

Nothing could be done about revision before the end of May, when the Assembly would enter the last year of its term. The weather was frightful. Tocqueville passed the time by trying to clarify his views on paper, but the memorandum which he wrote only shows him recoiling from every likely outcome. It amounted to this, that to stick by the letter of the constitution was impossible, but to violate it was wrong, and might lead to worse still ... He broke off in mid-sentence.[13]

At the beginning of June, through the kindness of Rivet, Tocqueville and Marie moved to a house in a park on the edge of Versailles, the Grille du Grand Montreuil, and liked it so much that they stayed there throughout the summer and autumn. The country surroundings were good for both of them, and Tocqueville found it easy to take the train from Versailles to Paris when he was needed at the Assembly. There, Broglie had introduced a bill proposing to call a new Constituent Assembly to revise the constitution. The bill went through the usual procedures; a committee was set up to report on it, and Tocqueville was a prominent member and, eventually, the *rapporteur*. He spoke up for revision at every opportunity, on the grounds that 'the election of 10 December' had created a situation (meaning the fact that the executive and the legislature could not work together) from which there was no escape except by violence, illegality, or revision. He wanted a new Constituent Assembly to please the legitimists, who still hoped to bring back the comte de Chambord, and the repeal of the 31 May law to please the Republicans. Broglie charged him with inconsistency and Barrot, in his memoirs, with not being sufficiently committed to revision; he answered them both by remarking that it was not enough to support revision theoretically; there had to be a demonstration of practicality by a readiness to make any concessions compatible with honour that would increase the number of supporters. This was good sense, and the fact that he uttered it demonstrated how much he had learned since he first entered politics. As *rapporteur* he showed himself as good as his word, listening patiently to the criticisms of such colleagues as Barrot and Montalembert, and answering them respectfully. He probably changed no views, but the committee was unanimous in accepting his report as the best basis for discussion in the Assembly.[14]

The debate began inauspiciously, for a number of Republicans wanted to record their votes against revision even before hearing the report, which the president of the Assembly refused to allow; there was much hubbub before Tocqueville could get a hearing. No doubt he suffered as usual from stage-fright; he was also anxious about his throat, asking permission to read out only the first, longer and more important of the report's two sections. 'Not long ago I was seriously ill, and I'm afraid that to read out the whole of this work would be too much for me.' Unanimous consent was readily given.[15]

The report that followed was Tocqueville's last parliamentary performance. It was written with all his characteristic lucidity and economical eloquence; it contains much forceful argument. Unfortunately, for all its merits, it could not be equal to the historical moment; it cannot be ranked among its author's best writings; it is only an exercise in practical politics. It is highly illuminating for all that.

He began by saying that he would not beat about the bush, but in a sense the whole speech was an exercise in obfuscation. He flattered his hearers by calling them statesmen, 'not rhetoricians or children', but men who knew the way of the world and were not to be satisfied by words alone; he professed to be laying deep constitutional, even philosophical problems before them; but what he was really trying to do was to rally the so-called party of order to seize its last chance. Unless conservatives of all stripes could unite in the Assembly and agree on a course of action they were doomed to defeat and might as well surrender to the Prince-President at once. Tocqueville's business was to put over this message without actually offending the representatives by stating it. His report thus lacks something of his usual intellectual distinction, and even has an appearance of inconsistency, since in speaking for the majority of the committee (always in the spirit of compromise and concession) Tocqueville not only had to take care to do justice to the views of the minority, but also to the different shades of opinion within the majority itself; nor did he quite resist the temptation to enlarge on his own particular views.

The report failed. After some days of fierce debate, in which Tocqueville, no doubt exhausted by his earlier effort, took no part, a large majority of the Assembly voted for revision, but it fell far short of the constitutionally mandated three-quarters; rigid Republicans, out of principle, and Thiers's Orleanist faction, out of opportunism, voted against it. Marx was to point out ironically that in this way 'the majority of parliament declared against the Constitution, but this Constitution itself declared for the minority and that its vote was binding.' When the news reached Louis Napoleon he admitted to Morny that he was now seriously considering a *coup d'état*: planning for it went on steadily from that moment. The Assembly, having completed its work, prorogued itself for three months, leaving the field to the Prince-President.[16]

Yet this unlucky report must not be neglected.* It throws great light on Tocqueville's politics in 1851, and indeed on French politics of the time in general. For instance, Tocqueville sees fit to attack the system of *scrutin de liste*, by which voters in a department have to chose between batches of candidates (slates, Americans would say). This seems to have been a personal view, though no doubt it was shared – but not by all: not, for instance, by Beaumont. Tocqueville's argument is that it is impossible, in a departmental election, for most of the voters to know anything about more than one or two of the candidates:

---

* At least it won AT his only mention, so far as I know, in all the works of Karl Marx (see *Eighteenth Brumaire*, 101).

With what result? In disturbed regions or times of public excitement extremist parties will impose their choice on the people without
consulting them; in peaceful regions and quiet times the list of representatives will be drawn up in advance by political managers with
private interests and to satisfy personal hatreds and friendships

– either way, the people have to vote blindly. 'The choice, which has
the appearance of being that of the body of citizens, has really been
that of a very small coterie.' (Tocqueville had made it clear to Nassau
Senior a few weeks previously that what he was really afraid of under
the *liste* system was 'a compact minority which concentrates all its
votes on its own candidates' – a minority of Reds.) Tocqueville also
revived the question of indirect election of the president, and made
much of what he thought was American practice: as in the constitutional committee, he praised the electoral college in wildly inaccurate
terms ('the American people only choose the electors, who choose the
President'), which suggest that he had made no study of the subject
since he read *Federalist 68* while sailing down the Mississippi, or at least
since the first publication of the 1835 *Démocratie*.[17]

What these passages together show is that Tocqueville still did not
understand or like modern, democratic political parties. In this he was
far from being alone. The idea of party was a most ancient one: there
were parties of a kind in republican Rome. Tocqueville was well aware
that there were true parties in Britain and in the United States, and in
France there was not only the Mountain but the party of order. It was a
large, amorphous grouping, loosely co-ordinated by the committee of
the rue de Poitiers; it rested firmly on the principle that private property
was sacred and should be defended against all competing claims; it
could count on the financial, physical and electoral support of a durable
majority of Frenchmen (those whose passion for wealth and order, as
Tocqueville said to Clamorgan, had kept Louis-Philippe on the throne
for eighteen years and might yet put Louis Napoleon there); when it
controlled the government it fully justified Marx's famous observation, already quoted, that 'The executive of the modern State is but a
committee for managing the common affairs of the whole bourgeoisie.' Its conduct when it controlled only the Assembly justified another
of his observations, that the Assembly had transformed itself from

being a body of the freely elected representatives of the people into 'the usurpatory parliament of a class'. It was not much of an advertisement for party politics, but Tocqueville's reservations rested on other considerations. He could not accept party discipline at any level – not for himself, not for the electorate, not for parliamentarians. The unvarying right and power to make free individual judgements was very close to what he meant by liberty. He was correct in thinking that *scrutin de liste* implied management by coteries – or, to give them their proper name, disciplined political parties. He was right in saying that direct election of the President of the United States was difficult, if not dangerous, but he did not see that the political parties, not the electoral college, were the intermediate bodies which made the system workable. At bottom, he refused to admit that free, democratic politics is impossible without organized parties, because such parties necessarily rest on the proposition that what matters, first and foremost, is winning power. Power is the object of the game, and each player must be convinced that, whatever else is important or true, his side has a better claim to power than any competitor. 'My party right or wrong' is the slogan, and though no honest citizen can truthfully promise to abide by it always, at every juncture, serious politicians know that they have to abide by it as much as possible. From this necessity flows much else: above all what was to be called, in an extreme case, democratic centralism; more normally, caucus politics – the word deriving from the earliest practitioners, the parties of the United States.[18]

Tocqueville was incapable of accepting such a system. His temperament, his upbringing, his achievement as a writer, his experience as a politician (especially his relationship with his constituents over time), his generation, made it impossible. Of these considerations, it is perhaps his generation that most needs to be stressed here. Caucus politics was making its appearance in France (and was on the brink of maturity in Britain) but its symptoms were scarcely recognized for what they were and were vigorously opposed. The party of order relied for victory on influence from above: ministers, land-owners, industrialists, *patrons* generally; when the opposition, of necessity, tried to create mass organizations the phenomenon was seen as merely one more piece of Red subversion, was outlawed, confronted, repressed and driven underground (the principle of free association was perhaps that which the governments of the Second Republic, including those of Barrot, took most delight in violating). The French propertied classes were outstanding for their ebullitions of panic-stricken selfishness and stupidity. But their ideological position, which Tocqueville fully shared, must be respected, if they themselves cannot be. The classical republican ideal of a free, independent-minded and virtuous citizenry, guided by the likes of Pericles and Cincinnatus, may have been obsolete but was bound to die very hard. Even in Britain there was much hesitation and suspicion about Joseph Chamberlain's restructuring of the Liberal party in the 1870s, and Tocqueville's great successor as a commentator on American politics, James Bryce, wrote his *American Commonwealth* (1888) to warn Britain against machine politics.* In American terms he was a mugwump; Tocqueville was a mugwump *avant la lettre*.

In these considerations may be found the central explanation of Tocqueville's failure as a politician, for it was really the failure of a system; of representative politics as practised in France between 1815 and 1851. To be sure, Tocqueville's temperament did not help: in fact nothing could be more unhelpful than his inability to take a stand without immediately qualifying it almost to the point of complete negation. He was always setting out to cross the floor and then getting stuck halfway. This tendency is very clearly seen in his attitude to Louis Napoleon. But he was not alone in his havering, and at least his havering was a matter of principle, and not of the vanity and cabinet intrigue which largely governed his parliamentary colleagues. The wonder was not that he occasionally despaired, but that occasional flashes of intuition showed him how different, in the long run, things were going to be: too late for him.

A few other details of the report must be mentioned. First, it contains one of Tocqueville's new celebrations of the French (apart from the workers of Paris). He commends their response to the unexpected February Revolution, when much against their will they had to fight: they did it 'with admirable courage and resignation, with a restrained energy and a practical wisdom of which their detractors†

---

* I am grateful to Dr Hugh Tulloch for straightening me out on this point.
† Was AT thinking of himself?

never thought them capable, and which will be an eternal honour to them among mankind'. Alas, he is still thinking of the June Days. He also sets out to frighten his hearers into assent to his proposals. This was not difficult; according to Walter Bagehot, who happened to be vacationing in Paris, the dread of a renewed socialist or anarchist revolution was so strong that trade was almost at a standstill. Tocqueville himself, writing to Marie from Valognes in August, reported that the *bourgeoisie* were ready for anything, turning to Louis Napoleon like a drowning man clutching at a branch. The root cause was the financial crisis: incomes were down by at least 25 per cent, 'the Cotentin is ruined' and the farmers were jibbing at paying their rent. (Tocqueville himself was straitened enough to have given up the idea of moving his household to his chateau for the summer.) Unfortunately for Tocqueville, his alarmism did not frighten the necessary number of representatives into voting for revision, as we have seen.[19]

More interesting and revealing is Tocqueville's advice as to what should be done if the proposal for revision failed. Emphasizing that he spoke for the whole committee, he remarked that with such a vote the constitution would receive a new consecration: a curious tribute to the veto power of the parliamentary minority. 'From the day that we may hope no longer, nothing is to be done but submit ... for the Constitution, as we have already said, is the only legality, is the sole political law that we know, today, in France; there is nothing beyond it but revolution or adventurism. The National Assembly must highly resolve not only to respect the Constitution itself, but to make sure that everyone else respects it.' Any attempt to launch unconstitutional candidacies would be not only inconvenient and irregular, but culpable. It was a call to resist any plot by Louis Napoleon. Unfortunately the *rapporteur* gave no hint as to how this might be done, and he got no help from the floor. As Marx was to say, 'The party of Order proved by its decision on revision that it knew neither how to rule nor how to serve ... neither how to uphold the Constitution nor how to throw it overboard; neither how to co-operate with the President, nor how to break with him.'[20]

Tocqueville can fairly be acquitted of such futility. Had revision been carried, at least the immediate crisis would have been defused: the prospect of Louis Napoleon's legal re-election would presumably have reassured public opinion and the business classes. Nor should Tocqueville's insistence on the obedience due to the constitution be dismissed as simply unpractical. If Louis Napoleon had announced his resolve to respect the law and stand aside in 1852 while making sure that the new elections passed off peacefully it is to be presumed that this too would have restored confidence; and anyway it is very hard to believe that the Red threat was as serious as the Right asserted (this came to be Tocqueville's view). It was hardly a moment when a clear-headed liberal need feel obliged to discard his principles; and the principle involved was of the utmost importance to Tocqueville. He was profoundly convinced that law and liberty went together; in a sense, were the same thing. It was one of Europe's most ancient traditions;[21] Montesquieu had taught it; it was embedded in the history of Le Peletier and Lamoignon. Tocqueville's lifelong passion for liberty (a word which was becoming more and more prominent in his discourse) roused in him an equally passionate desire to teach his countrymen the importance of respect for the law, of government by laws, not men. The constitution might be a defective law, but law it was, and the only guarantor of all the others. To violate it at all was reprehensible; to overthrow it by force would be the worst of crimes.

Yet the problem of what to do remained, growing steadily more intractable. At times Tocqueville seems to have given up the project of revision as a bad job; but at the meeting of the *conseil-général* of the Manche in September he successfully wielded his prestige, skill and authority (once again he had been elected president) to get the *conseil* to declare its support both for revision and for the repeal of the law of 31 May. Probably he was pushing at an open door: almost every other *conseil-général* did the same, that session. It was as if they had constituted themselves as so many colleges of electors, or so many electoral primaries. However it was, the result could not have been more encouraging for Louis Napoleon. Yet Tocqueville, speaking in favour of the revision, tried to make the vote one of confidence in the Assembly. Whatever his private expectations, he made the excellent point that it would only take a shift of fifty votes for the Assembly to approve revision by the required majority, and that the voices of the *conseils* might have the effect of changing fifty minds. His tone when speaking to the councillors is noticeably more authoritative than it was when he addressed the Assembly: almost masterful. He repeated his insistence on the importance of legality: 'What the Assembly wanted to say amounts to this, that from the moment when all regular reform shall have been tried, when legal revision shall have become impossible, everyone, government and citizens alike, must obey, and yield to the law.' In other words, put up with the impasse and hope for the best. It was high-minded, but scarcely hopeful. It is almost as if Tocqueville, by recommending this behaviour, was preparing himself for the world of retirement and internal exile: a world in which, as an ideologist and a writer, he need make no concessions to the deeply unpalatable calculations and compromises of French politics in the age of Louis Napoleon and Thiers. Soon he would no longer have any influence on events; he would have to be content with keeping the flag of idealism flying, like Ibsen's Hilmar Tonnesen, in the hope of leaving a legacy for better days. But it was weary work, and he would be glad to get back to Marie on 10 September.[22]

She had stayed behind at Versailles, as she was still unwell and could not face the upheaval and discomfort of a journey. Tocqueville barely visited his chateau during the *conseil-général*, staying instead with Hippolyte at Nacqueville and then sharing lodgings with him at Saint-Lô, Hippolyte now being a member of the *conseil*. Tocqueville missed his wife, and wrote to her almost every day as in the past; she did the same, to his great satisfaction, though the posts were irregular and Marie was sometimes fractious:

> I have already told you that your letters are my only comfort here. The news they contain, the feelings they express are a great help, for I know nobody with better sense than you have and your affection is the only thing I believe in absolutely in this world and in which I have unreserved confidence. The *only* thing, mark it well. So I allow myself to smile sometimes when I hear you speak of losing my affection. You have it till life, till death. Don't you know that?

Marie was unwell and lonely, which helps to explain her gloom. It was the first occasion since 1847 that they had been separated for any length of time. It was hard on them both.[23]

Back at Versailles, Tocqueville settled down happily to writing the third section of the *Souvenirs*. He decided to skip the year between the

June Days and his appointment as foreign minister: 'it has seemed to me more important, while my memories are still quite fresh, to recount the five months that I passed in government.' He would return to the earlier period if he had time. Perhaps he realized that time was in fact running out. He would not even be able to complete his account of his ministry.

Louis Napoleon and Morny had decided to make no move until the members of the Assembly had returned to Paris: they did not want to have to deal with a multiplicity of centres of resistance in the departments. The Assembly reconvened on 4 November (and the Tocquevilles moved to a flat in the rue de Castellane for the winter). The Prince-President greeted the parliamentarians with a message full of the gloomiest political and economic prognostications for 1852, proposing the repeal of the 31 May law as a remedy. The Assembly, in a last, infatuated, suicidal gesture, rejected the proposal by a majority of six votes. F. A. Simpson's comment cannot be bettered: 'Already by a minority vote it had refused to allow the country to have the new constitution which it desired. Now by the barest possible majority it had refused to restore the one feature in the old constitution which was really popular.' Realizing belatedly that it was utterly defenceless, the Assembly (or rather, the royalist parties there) tried to claim ultimate control of the army, but the motion was rejected: the Republicans would not vote with the royalists. The actual commander-in-chief, the president, paid no attention.* Nor did his troops. Many of them were Republican voters, and anyway army discipline trumped politics. [24]

Beyond the walls of the Assembly nothing seemed to be happening: the wiseacres began to say that nothing would until the New Year. On 1 December the representatives debated a railway line between Lyon and Avignon, rather as the Chamber of Deputies had discussed the Bordeaux bank on 22 February 1848. But the next day, the 2nd, was the day of Austerlitz, and had been chosen by the president as that on which he would at last cross his Rubicon. During the night the army was deployed in and round Paris; proclamations were secretly printed and, at dawn, plastered on every conspicuous wall in the city; every ministry was seized, and at 6.30 a.m. Morny took over as minister of the interior.

---

* Had the motion passed it would merely have accelerated the *coup d'état*.

The Palais Bourbon was surrounded by cavalry and infantry; seventy-eight representatives, generals and journalists (including Thiers, Cavaignac and Changarnier) were roused from their beds and arrested. When, at about ten o'clock, the Prince-President showed himself, riding through Paris with old King Jérôme, his uncle, and the comte de Flahaut, Morny's father, at his side, he was master of the situation, and the news was being flashed by telegraph throughout France.

Up to that point it was a well-planned and neatly executed enterprise, and it seemed that the plotters had thought of everything. The drums of the National Guard had been slashed in the night; the main presidential proclamation emphasized that the *coup* was aimed solely at the Assembly, which was said to be a centre of conspiracy; only governmental newspapers were allowed to appear; and a plebiscite was promised in a fortnight, which would approve (or, in theory, disapprove) a new constitution, under which Louis Napoleon would be president for ten years. But as soon as the news got about some two hundred representatives, Tocqueville and Beaumont among them, hurried to the Palais Bourbon. They could not get in, but the legitimist *maire* of the tenth *arrondissement* (nowadays the sixth) offered them the use of his town hall. So for several hours the National Assembly continued, passing unanimous motions deposing Louis Napoleon and constituting itself an emergency government, and throwing copies of its decrees out of the window to the street (having got in to the *mairie* they could not get out again: the building had been rapidly surrounded by soldiers). Berryer, the portly legitimist leader, harangued the crowd from a balcony, and was received with some warmth – many of the Parisians mistook him for Ledru-Rollin, supposedly returned from exile. The troops were genuinely uncertain what to do, but eventually the representatives were driven from the town hall as they had been from the Palais Bourbon, and this time they were not allowed to go unsupervised. They were herded, two by two, a mournful procession, through the narrow streets of the *quartier* Saint-Germain – presumably by way of the rue de Grenelle and the rue du Bac – until they reached the riverside barracks of the Quai d'Orsay, where they were to be confined until further orders. They did not receive much sympathy from what Rémusat described as a thin and apathetic crowd, though according to Tocqueville there were cries of '*Vive l'Assemblée Nationale!*' evoked, he thought, by compassion for all the distinguished men – 'former ministers, former ambassadors, generals, admirals, great orators, great writers' – forced to trudge through the mud of the streets surrounded by bayonets, like a band of malefactors. He felt intensely humiliated, as his account of the affair shows. [25]

They spent the night in the barracks. Tocqueville recalled, a few weeks later:

> The gayest time … that I ever passed was at the Quai d'Orsay. The elite of France in education in birth, & in talents particularly in the talents of Society – was collected within the walls of that barrack. A long struggle was over, in which our part had not been timidly played, we had done our duty, we had gone thro' some perils, and we had some to encounter, & we were in the high spirits which excitement and danger shared with others, when not too formidable, create. From the Court yard, in which we had been penned for a couple of hours where the Duc de Broglie and I tore our chickens with our hands & teeth, we were transferred to a long sort of gallery or garret, running along the higher part of the building, a spare dormitory for the Soldiers, when the better rooms are filled. Those who chose to take the trouble went below [and] hired *palliases* from the soldiers & carried them up for themselves. I was too idle, & lay on the floor in my cloak. Instead of sleeping we spent the night in shouting from *pallias* to *pallias* anecdotes, repartees jokes, & pleasantries – *C'était un feu roulant, une pluie de bons mots.** Things amused us in that state of excitement which sound flat when repeated. I remember Kerdrel,[†] a man of great humour exciting shouts of laughter by exclaiming with great solemnity, as he looked round the floor, strewed with mattresses & statesmen, & lighted by a couple of tallow candles *Voilà donc où en est reduit ce fameux parti de l'ordre.*[‡] [26]

Such reactions to a situation of such stress are not in the least surprising. But the notes which Tocqueville scribbled to Marie while he was a prisoner add some different shades to the story (and imply, among other things, that the conditions of his captivity were not especially oppressive):

---

* 'It was a rolling cannonade, a rain of epigrams.'
† Presumably Vincent Audren de Kerdrel (1815–99), a legitimist representative from Brittany (Ile-et-Vilaine). He ended as a senator for life under the Third Republic.
‡ 'So this is what the famous Party of Order has sunk to!'

2 December 1851. I do not know whether you have received the letter which I sent to tell you that I was well, that I was in the barracks next to the river across from the Tuileries and that if you should be able to send Eugène to me with a little food and an overcoat, you would give me great pleasure. A.

[3 December 1851]. A gentleman whom I do not know is kind enough to carry this letter to you. I am very well. I have nothing to fear. I have written to you twice to request you to try and send Eugène to me here in order to bring me my greatcoat and my galoshes. If that is possible I shall be most happy. By speaking to the officers, by saying that I am unwell and by giving my name he will be allowed to come to me. I embrace you from the bottom of my heart as you can suppose. A.

The unusually formal language shows that Tocqueville was expecting his notes to be read by the authorities.[27]

And those authorities were somewhat embarrassed by what had happened. The Assembly's demonstration of defiance had been unexpected. It saved the honour of the representatives, but had no other consequence; still, Morny and Louis Napoleon could not overlook it. They gave orders for the immediate demolition of the *salle de carton* where the Assembly had met since 1848, and decided to transfer the prisoners from the barracks to more regular jails – Vincennes, Mont-Valérien, Mazas. Beaumont was sent to Mont-Valérien. Charles de Rémusat was among those sent to Mazas, and was much impressed by what he found there – a whitewashed cell lit by gas, with no bad smells, furnished with a hammock, a table, and a chair. It sounds as if Mazas was one of the prisons which had benefited from Tocqueville's long campaign. Rémusat had been a prison reformer himself in 1836, when he was *sous-secrétaire d'état*, and had introduced cellular carriages for those under arrest, though in 1851 he may not have appreciated the irony when he found himself carried in one. But the officer in charge broke the principle of silence and allowed his captives to keep the doors of their cells open so that they could talk. He said it was not a favour that he granted to his normal clients – convicts, madmen and prostitutes, but he was fairly sure that representatives of the people would not abuse it.[28]

Tocqueville was far too angry to be amused, even in retrospect. He thought it ignominious to be transported in a paddy-waggon and assumed it was a deliberate insult. He was sent not to Mazas but to Vincennes (whither some members of the Assembly had once hoped to send Louis Napoleon). Tocqueville did not have to sample the dungeons there: Vincennnes was a military prison, and the officers treated the representatives as prisoners on parole (Beaumont found the same at Mont-Valérien). Eugène appeared at last, and Tocqueville felt that he was again in touch with Marie, who was taking the affair badly, which deeply worried her husband. 'For mercy's sake I beg you [not to torture and distress yourself]. And in spite of my extreme desire to see you, I engage you not to come here because I am not sure they will let you in.' Tocqueville was offered an order of release by the prefect of police at the intercession of a friend,* but angrily refused it: he would not go free before his colleagues were released. Next day, 4 December, the order came to let them all go, and they made their way back to central Paris as best they could. Within a day or two Louis Napoleon sent his old tutor, Vieillard, whom Tocqueville knew well, to apologize for his arrest, but Tocqueville would not let Vieillard into the house. [29]

There was something farcical about Tocqueville's martyrdom, unpleasant though it was, and although he took some pride in it. There was nothing farcical about various other calamities which resulted from the *coup*. The workers of Paris had no love for the Assembly: they remembered the June Days too clearly, and resented the fact that the representatives, even their own, had drawn generous stipends while they themselves were unemployed and hungry. On the morning of 3 December a handful of Montagnard representatives tried to stimulate the building of barricades in the faubourg Saint-Antoine, but had very limited success. Why, said the workers, should we fight for men who had been paid twenty-five francs a day and did nothing useful to earn them? Angered, Representative Baudin cried, 'You will soon see how one can die for twenty-five francs a day,' and a few moments later he was indeed shot and killed.† There was more fighting next day, 4 December; some of the bourgeoisie were showing, unusually – I might

---

* The brother of the painter Théodore Chassériau, whose admirable portrait of AT had been exhibited in the Salon of 1850.
† His last words are legendary, and it cannot be certain that he uttered them; but his death was real enough.

almost say, uniquely – some sympathy for the insurgents, so they too were shot down on the boulevards. Many bystanders were also killed. Perhaps the soldiers were drunk and got out of hand, but Morny was entirely ruthless. By 5 December resistance in Paris was at an end. That in the provinces was just beginning, but it did not amount to much, even in the Alpine south-east, where it was most serious; a week later order had been restored everywhere, giving Louis Napoleon the chance to pose as its preserver, when he was really its disturber.[30]

France was entering upon a new phase of her history. Tocqueville's political career was at an end. Before it quite finished he made three gestures which between them convey his own verdict on the event and on that career.

Mrs Grote had been spending the autumn in Paris. On 6 December Tocqueville read to her a letter for *The Times* giving his account of the *coup*, and the next day sent it to her. She smuggled it successfully to London, and it was printed (anonymously) on 11 December, becoming part of the great campaign which the Thunderer (inspired by Henry Reeve) was launching against the new dictator. Tocqueville's chief concern was to give an accurate account of what had happened, since Louis Napoleon was trying to silence all hostile voices and to impose his own version of events; but for Tocqueville accuracy entailed denunciation of violence, aggression and defiance of the law. He had almost nothing to say about anything other than the struggle between the president and the Assembly; in fairness to him it should be remembered that, writing on the 5 or 6 of December, he probably had only the vaguest knowledge of much that had occurred. With this reservation it may be said that his account is full and fair. His verdict on the whole affair is worth quoting, though unsurprising: 'Force overturning law, trampling on the liberty of the press and of the person, deriding the popular will, in whose name the Government pretends to act, – France torn from the alliance of free nations to be yoked to the despotic monarchies of the Continent, – such is the result of this *coup d'état*.'[31] He was never going to forgive Louis Napoleon's crime, in part, no doubt, because he himself had been so entirely ineffective in resisting it. Nor could he for long forgive the French, and particularly his own sort, for acquiescing so eagerly in what had happened, and being so ready to sacrifice their country's liberty, dignity and honour in return for material well-being. The salons of Paris were full of self-styled gentlemen and their poor little wifelets (*femmelettes*)* who had been so frightened by the thought of what 1852 might do to their incomes that they welcomed the ignominious new regime with transports of joy. He was disgusted and appalled, but he agreed with his brother Édouard that there was nothing to be done.[32]

He was still a member of the *conseil-général* of the Manche, and when it met in special session in March he was again its president, and the chief author of the latest report about the Cherbourg railway. After the session he resigned. Although publicly he professed otherwise (he wanted to leave open the possibility of returning to the *conseil* if times improved), he did so because he was not going to take the oath to Louis Napoleon that was now required of him, and everyone knew it (including Clamorgan, now a fervent Bonapartist: he and Tocqueville broke off relations, which were never to be resumed). Tocqueville resigned, as he told Beaumont, with deep regret: it was foreclosing the future and becoming an *émigré* of the interior; it was sacrificing his particular, and particularly agreeable, position in the department, one founded on respect for him personally, and independent of political opinions – his sort of democracy. But not to resign would be ridiculous, and anyway his regrets were trifles compared to the general mass of shame and misery generated by the *coup d'état*.[33]

He was extremely bitter about what had happened, and blamed it all on the February Revolution, which had generated socialism and the terror of socialism that had given Louis Napoleon his opportunity. He still did not recognize that his own commitment to obsolescent economic theory, his obsessive cult of property and his fear of revolution made him a part of the problem which he analysed. But as his reference to emigration of the interior suggests, he was aware that after twenty-one years he had fallen into the trap which had engulfed so many of his family and friends after the July Revolution. He had devoted the best years of his youth and maturity to building a free state in France, and now it seemed that he was condemned to ineffectiveness on the sidelines of a despotism. He did not abandon hope, but curiously if logically he now associated that hope with the cause which

---

* English cannot do justice to the venom of this word.

his family had maintained and which he had abandoned: the cause of the Bourbons. Not that he reverted to legitimism of the old school. On the contrary, since the legitimists showed a distressing tendency to slide towards acceptance of Louis Napoleon, he wanted a reconciliation between the pretenders of the elder line and Orleans and an explicit commitment to liberalism by the comte de Chambord, which would make him the rallying-point for all those opposed to the Bonapartes. He wrote a long memorandum for Chambord's eyes pressing liberalism upon him.* It was another exercise in wishful thinking, but Tocqueville never wavered again. His acceptance of the July Monarchy had always been *faute de mieux*, and although he had been a sincere Republican it had never been without anguish; besides, both Louis-Philippe and the Republic had failed; Louis Napoleon was a criminal; who was left but Henri V?[34]

It is to be hoped that his brothers and his father were never so unkind as to say, 'We told you so.'

---

* Chambord received the document and made a polite remark or two, but no more came of it. It found its way into print in November 1871, at a time when the legitimists were desperately trying to get their King to show the small amount of tact and common sense which was all that was then required to bring him back to his throne. Notoriously, Chambord failed them completely.

WRITING HISTORY
1852–1855

Je n'ai jamais désiré le pouvoir, mais la réputation. *
ALEX DE TOCQUEVILLE, 1852[1]

LOUIS NAPOLEON was now the absolute master of France, and
after another year would make himself Emperor (on 2 December
1852), calling himself Napoleon III. The interim was spent in consoli-
dating his regime. The most spectacular and successful means that he
employed was economic; he precipitated a landslide of investment
through which France at last began to catch up with the other industrializing states of Europe (Britain, Belgium and Prussia); but his
programme made little impression on Tocqueville, who saw it only as
a repetition, on a larger scale, of the *friponnerie* (dishonest speculation)
of the July Monarchy. Other aspects of the dictatorship struck him as
much more important, and alarming. The resistance in the Midi had
been brutally defeated, and the thousands of arrests were followed by
sentences of exile, or of penal labour in Algeria or (worst of all) of
transportation to Cayenne in French Guinea, which, as Tocqueville
bitterly remarked, was tantamount to a sentence of death. He was
infuriated by the new press law, the most restrictive since the time
of the first Napoleon (he did not seem to remember that the Second

---

* 'I never wanted power, only fame.'

Republic, even in its early, liberal days, had led the way in censorship). He was also outraged by the affair of the Orleans seizures. The Prince-President felt it necessary to persuade French public opinion that order was threatened from the Right as well as the Left, thus making his rule seem more necessary than ever. To show that there was still an Orleanist as well as a socialist conspiracy he exiled half a dozen leading generals, Tocqueville's friends Lamoricière and Bedeau among them, and also the most conspicuous Orleanist leaders, including Thiers and Rémusat. His master-stroke, however, was a decree in January 1852 by which the private fortune of Louis-Philippe, which in 1830 had been carefully reserved for his family instead of being merged in the estates belonging to the monarchy, was seized outright, and the Orleans princes were required to sell all their other possessions in France within a year. This robbery was too much for Morny, who had been a conspicuous Orleanist until very recently: he resigned from the ministry of the interior. It was also too much for Montalembert, the Catholic leader, who had publicly welcomed the *coup d'état*; but it served Louis Napoleon's turn, for he could pretend that he was depriving conspirators of their financial resources, and he ostentatiously devoted the proceeds of his raid to charity. To Tocqueville the affair was one more proof of the regime's essential criminality.[2]

Tocqueville's detestation of Louis Napoleon after the *coup d'état* had a passion to it which never relented. He resented the exclusion of the *grands notables* from political power (one of Louis Napoleon's chief objects), but his opposition also had other, deeper roots. He had been brought up in a tradition according to which the dictatorship of the first Napoleon was the negation of all that was best in French history and civilization. He thought the new government a travesty of law, liberty and justice: it was a democratic despotism. The earliest years of Louis Napoleon's autocracy were particularly oppressive: Tocqueville could see nothing in them but a resurrection of the police state which had blighted the country during his childhood and led it to disaster. All this was enough to stiffen his resistance, and to it was added his sense of personal failure. But the new Bonapartism had an unforeseeable effect on him which was the strongest factor of all in his opposition: it reminded him of what he really believed in. Liberty was a word that had never been absent from his vocabulary, but during his political career, and especially during the Second Republic, he had tended to confuse it with other things, above all with the protection of landed property and resistance to socialism. Under the Second Empire he was reminded almost daily of the truth. Liberty was the right to think, speak and publish as you chose; the right of free association; the right to take part in the government and politics of your country; the right to call power to account. It was security from arbitrary arrest and imprisonment. It was law and justice for all; it was the hope of progress. It was, in other words, very like the democratic ideals which had informed the first volumes of *De la démocratie en Amérique*. Tocqueville had never become cynical, but the author of the *Souvenirs* was a man on the brink of despair. Paradoxically, the *coup d'état*, by demolishing all the confusions and compromises which had been fostered by the parliamentary system, demonstrated to Tocqueville not only political reality, but his true faith. It revealed an unbridgeable gulf between him and Louis Napoleon. The discovery was to inform all the work of his last years.

He was lucky in having work to turn to, even though it would be long before he could bring it into focus. Those parliamentary liberals who had thus far survived from the July Monarchy were politically extinguished by the Second Empire, except for the indestructible Thiers and a small number of the close associates whom he protected; and even Thiers, after he was allowed to return from exile in August 1852, had to devote most of his time for the next decade to completing his Napoleonic history. Dufaure's political career was to revive briefly in the early years of the Third Republic, but until then he worked as a barrister. Death cut down most of the others. Tocqueville himself was the first to go, in 1859; Beaumont followed in 1866, Lanjuinais and Lamartine in 1869; Broglie in 1870. Odilon Barrot lasted until 1873, but never returned to public life. If these men were to find renewed fulfilment in such time as was left to them they would need to take deliberate action, as did Duvergier de Hauranne, who wrote a ten-volume history of French parliamentary government, or Guizot, who devoted himself to his memoirs and the affairs of French Protestantism.

Beaumont was especially to be pitied. In the last months of the Second Republic his world collapsed about him. His little daughter Alix died; so did his father and his father-in-law, George Washington de La Fayette, who left his affairs in such a mess that Beaumont reported gloomily to Tocqueville that while his children might eventually benefit from the La Fayette inheritance he and Clémentine never would. The loss of his parliamentary career and salary was simply the last misfortune. In January 1852 he felt forced to retire to Beaumont-la-Chartre and live with the utmost economy so as to avoid further debt and, most important of all, save enough to help his sons when it was time to launch their careers. He went to Paris only when it was absolutely necessary, and otherwise passed his days either in trying to comfort Clémentine, who took Alix's death very hard, or at his desk, chewing his pen and trying to think of something to write about. The tone of his letters is brave but unmistakably depressed. He felt quite at a loss.[3]

The same could not be said of Tocqueville. His creative energies had always been much greater than Beaumont's, and as we have seen he had been thinking for more than a year of returning full-time to literature. He thought he knew exactly what he wanted to write. The French Revolution was to be his theme, the first Napoleon's part in it his subject. He had always been fascinated by the Emperor, like so many of his generation; he still considered that he was the embodiment of the Revolution and the builder of modern France, for good or ill. Difficulties about these notions would soon emerge, but for the time being Tocqueville was happy enough to plunge into the Bibliothèque Nationale, emerging only to visit the Archives Nationales, where everyone was helpful, and the archives of the foreign ministry, where they were not. It was only when he lifted his head from his books and papers that the thought of his country's condition plunged him again into gloom.[4]

He soon filled a notebook, in his usual way, with information, ideas and extracts; unfortunately for him and us he lost it that summer, but there is other evidence of how his thoughts were moving. That winter, it was Tocqueville's turn to act as president of the Académie des Sciences Morales et Politiques, and with much lamentation ('that damned academical discourse') he prepared an elegant presidential address, to be delivered on 6 December. The *coup d'état* meant that it had to be postponed until 3 April, and heavily revised: in its original version it had not only proclaimed the rights of intellectual and academic freedom against the interferences of government (*pouvoir*), it had held up Napoleon I as a horrid warning, as the greatest enemy of the Académie itself, which he had actually closed down (it had been reopened by Guizot in 1832). After consulting Beaumont, Tocqueville decided that in the circumstances this passage was dangerously provocative: it might draw the new Bonaparte's unfriendly attention to the Académie.* Tocqueville suppressed the passage (and thereby made his *discours* somewhat insipid) but the draft survives, and shows that he was again taking up the themes of his acceptance speech to the Académie Francaise, delivered ten years previously almost to the day: he was demonstrating that his account of the First Empire, when written, would not err on the side of leniency.[5]

For the rest, his speech was primarily a defence of political science (what nowadays would be called political theory) as distinct from the empirical, rule-of-thumb art of government. He admitted, indeed he asserted, that to excel in the theory of politics was not to be sure of success in the arena. Illustrious authors, he said, succeeded in politics rather in spite of their ability than because of it; he hinted at Guizot and mentioned Montesquieu: it was probably a good thing that Montesquieu had confined himself to commentary; he might otherwise have become not an outstanding publicist but a failed minister, 'something all too common'. His auditors can hardly have missed the ironic allusion to the speaker himself. Perhaps they laughed.[6] But the most significant passage came a few paragraphs later, where Tocqueville said he was astonished that in France, of all countries, he should have to define, defend and assert the importance of political science, for where had it achieved more?

> Look around you, look at our monuments and ruins. Who raised the first and made the second? Who changed the appearance of things to such an extent that if your grandfathers could be reborn they would recognize neither the laws, nor the manners, nor the ideas, nor the attire, nor the customs they were used to; scarcely the language which they spoke? Who produced the French Revolution, in short, the greatest event in history?

---

* This was a reasonable fear. Four years later the imperial government arbitrarily appointed ten extra members to the Académie, to keep it in order. This was in flat defiance of the academy's constitution. The intruders were known to the other members as 'the garrison'.

Answer, the political scientists, 'who sowed in the minds of our fathers all the seeds of novelty from which suddenly sprouted so many political institutions and civil laws unknown to former times'.[7] In hindsight this passage shows clearly enough which way Tocqueville's mind was tending.

His work in the libraries went well, but before he could make further progress his life, he felt, would have to change completely. On the day that he delivered his *discours* he wrote to Mrs Grote that he was longing to get away from Paris, for since it was impossible to fight the government a man like him could only preserve his self-respect in silence, solitude, and work, conditions hard to secure in the capital. He expressed himself even more forcibly to Beaumont:

> I can't tell you the disgust, contempt and weariness caused me by the miserable, unproductive little combinations and agitations which still prevail here in what remains of the political world and which, fortunately without leading to any other action, produce a tangled skein of small intrigue ... I sigh for my avenue of oaks and for the company of my cows.

He was beginning to feel uncomfortable in polite society. When he uttered the word liberty he was met with the astonishment that greeted the former *émigrés* in 1814 who wanted to bring back the *ancien régime*: 'Where have you been, my dear fellow? You're drivelling!' He told Mrs Grote that he would stay in the country as long as he could manage without the scholarly resources of Paris, though he would probably have to return at the end of autumn.[8]

This attitude was never going to change: his opinion of the life of potatoes was completely reversed. Another reason for burying himself at Tocqueville was financial. The loss of his parliamentary salary (9,000 francs a year) was not so serious a matter to him as it was to Beaumont, but he felt it, and the large part of his income which was derived from his land in the Cotentin was affected by the bad weather and poor harvests of the early 1850s. Paris was shockingly expensive, and now there was no need to maintain a permanent residence there. Then, although he felt quite well at the moment, he and Marie never seemed to be really healthy in the city any more. They decided on a complete *déménagement*. They would give up their apartment, distribute some of its contents between their chateau and Comte Hervé's flat in the place de la Madeleine, and store or sell the rest. When they had to revisit Paris they would stay with the comte or hire lodgings. It was an epoch in their lives.

The move was long, exhausting and exasperating. In the middle of it Marie had to go off to spend a few days with her aunt at Chamarande, since it was far from clear when they would see each other again (Mrs Belam, in her late eighties, had recently been making her will). Tocqueville wrote to his wife daily, as always, now, when they were apart, and we get a wonderful glimpse of his marital attitude from his letters:

> I have at last received your letter of yesterday, my darling, and it has taken a weight off my shoulders ... What weather we had here! The rain did me more harm than if I'd been out in it. It made me worried and impatient. I told myself that you were, perhaps, the only woman in France who, though unwell, would prefer the risk of walking a league through mud and rain to hiring a horse-drawn cab. Such behaviour is so contrary to your character and intelligence that when I catch you doing it I always think it must be somebody else. Thank God, you were more lucky than wise.[9]

(Marie was always afraid that horses would bolt.)

Tocqueville did not enjoy being cooped up, day and night, in one small room while the clearing and the packing went on, but eventually all was well. Marie came back and then set off for Tocqueville while her husband travelled more circuitously by way of Beaumont-la-Chartre, where he made a short stay that cheered up Beaumont enormously:

> if you value the knowledge that you have done a good deed, know that you have never done a better, or one more deeply felt by those for whom you laboured. Without making the least disturbance in our peaceful solitude, you stimulated and enlivened it; for the first time in two years I saw my poor wife return to life with her old vivacity of mind and feeling, which had been almost extinguished. Her resurrection guaranteed mine.

Tocqueville replied in equally good spirits from his chateau, where he was enjoying himself arranging his books. He was careful to give Beaumont all the information he would need about stage-coaches when in due course he paid a visit in his turn.[10]

Alexis was always happy at Tocqueville, even when, as now, the builders had to be called in. The house had not been occupied since the summer of 1850, and scarcely for two years before that, and the ground floor was now uninhabitable: damp had rotted all the woodwork in the main salon. Tocqueville and Marie decided to cut two large new windows to let in the sunlight and thus, they hoped, keep the room dry. At first, it seems, he found it hard to adjust to his severance from the life of Paris: he besought his friends to send him news; but he meant to stay where he was for as long as possible. It was no great sacrifice. Before long he plunged into his work.[11]

He found that he was in for a prolonged struggle with his materials and his ideas. His conception of his book was both clear and cloudy. It originated in his repeated observation that the great Revolution had never ended; this, he thought, was a theme worthy of his ambitions. As he wrote to Mme de Circourt two months later:

> I think there is still much to say on the French Revolution as a great movement: what caused it, what it produced, what was its tendency, where it is taking us. I think that we are well placed to see this vast subject as a whole, to assess it, to judge it; we are sufficiently near it to see it distinctly and to understand, by a sort of internal reaction, still felt in our minds and hearts, the thoughts and feelings which filled the hearts and minds of those who launched that terrible adventure into the world, yet far enough off for it not to be impossible to appraise their deeds and discern what their efforts really achieved. That is the work which I wish to undertake. But I don't yet know from what angle to approach it, nor how to steer myself on the ocean of the French Revolution ...[12]

At first he took the easy course of writing up the notes on Napoleon which he had made in Paris (it was at this point that he discovered the loss of his notebook). With speed and certainty he sketched two chapters on the *coup d'état* of 18 Brumaire, an VII (1799), or rather on the conditions which made it possible. As he explained in a letter to Kergorlay, he found it natural to turn to this theme because, in spite of great dissimilarities, there were great resemblances between 1799 and the era which he had just lived through. A lesser man would have been more than content with what he achieved. The chapters were written with all the verve and wit of the abandoned *Souvenirs*, and culminated in a brilliant picture of a weary and demoralized country looking inevitably for salvation to the army, the one remaining vigorous and successful national institution.

> All the letters of the day say the same thing: *the present situation can't last* ... The nation, despairing, full at the same time of fear and feebleness, looked about listlessly for someone to come to the rescue. Who would it be? Some thought of Pichegru, others of Moreau, others of Bernadotte.
>
> 'Retired to the countryside, to the deepest Bourbonnais,' says M. Fiévée in his *Memoirs*, 'I noticed only one thing which reminded me of politics: the peasants whom I met in the fields, the vineyards and the woods all accosted me to ask if there was any news of General Bonaparte and why he had not returned to France.'

The end of chapter two. Thrilling! Who could fail to turn the page to chapter three? Only it was never written.[13]

Tocqueville had several immediate excuses for going no further. With Brumaire he had plunged into the middle of things. This was no way to start a book. And if he went on as he had begun he might well find himself writing the sort of narrative history that he was determined to avoid, brilliantly though he could do it: he refused to compete with Thiers. Analysis was the thing. These reasons for breaking off seemed plausible; but there were deeper, more convincing motives.

Ten years before he had publicly asserted that Napoleon was as great as a man could be without virtue; in the suppressed part of his academic address he had called him the great enemy of liberty. Such views, if driven home in his book, might lead to trouble with the new authorities, and Tocqueville, I guess, did not want to find that he had written a second unpublishable book. Yet it would be worse if he found himself forced to praise Bonaparte, and he knew that if he were honest he would have to do so, though not unreservedly. Tocqueville was no more unresponsive than any other nineteenth-century Frenchman to the legend of the Emperor* and knew that he would find much to admire in Napoleon's achievements, especially during the Consulate. Imperialists would seize on his eulogies and ignore his reservations,

---

* So admirably analysed and described by Sudhir Hazareesingh in *The Legend of Napoleon* (London: Granta Books, 2004). See also Pieter Geyl, *Napoleon For and Against* (London, 1949).

and nothing was farther from Tocqueville's wishes than to reinforce Bonapartism.

On the contrary, the two chapters which he drafted were a terrible indictment of the French people for letting themselves arrive at the point where they were ready to support the dictatorship of a Napoleon. He went much further than he had indicated to Kergorlay, and as he said to Beaumont wrote with plenty of impetus 'because what I had to convey were almost our contemporary feelings'.[14] His account of France in 1799 is an allegory, and not an obscure one, of France in 1851. For instance:

> the Jacobin Club reopened. The members once more displayed the old badges, the old language, the old slogans, for parties change very little: it is a remarkable fact that they show themselves more unbending in their ideas and practices than are, individually, any of the men of whom they are composed. The Jacobins reappeared just as they had been during the Terror, without being able to revive it. The only effect was to drive the nation still more hurriedly away from liberty, by the fear which they inspired.

Or this:

> What most demoralizes men living through long revolutions is less the mistakes or even the crimes which they commit in the ardour of their faith and passion than the contempt which they sometimes end in feeling for that same faith and passion when, weary, disenchanted, disappointed, they turn at last against themselves and decide that they were adolescent in their hopes, ridiculous in their enthusiasm, and more ridiculous still in their devotion. Broken by such a fall, the strongest souls cannot recover. Men are crushed by it, to the extent that not only can they no longer attain great virtue, they seem to have become almost incapable of great wickedness either.[15]

Writing at full speed, Tocqueville was discharging all the spleen which would otherwise have gone into the *Souvenirs*, had he undertaken to finish that work. Indeed, the chapters on Brumaire may be read as the *Souvenirs*' completion, that book's matter being too discouraging to handle directly.

For that very reason the chapters are somewhat untrustworthy history. Tocqueville's account of the last months of the Directory seems accurate enough, but once its message has been decoded a reader is bound to wonder if the narrator is really reliable. Tocqueville was probably not conscious of this, but the vengeful impulse which drove him to write was soon exhausted; having scarified the French for being ready to submit to a tyrant he had no more to say on the point. And as he pondered the records, questions of a quite different type began to occur to him. The central argument of his Brumaire chapters was that although the French had come to reject the Republic, because of its many failures, they were still fervently loyal to the Revolution, because of what it had done for them. But what was that? Everyone said that the peasants had got much richer, but exactly how much richer? And how much had the Revolution changed the structure of French society? As against what was generally thought, Tocqueville was coming to believe that under the *ancien régime* France was already, overwhelmingly, a country of small peasant proprietors, which would seem to suggest that the changes made by the Revolution, when it seized and distributed the lands of the Church and the émigrés, were marginal. How could he find solid information on these points?[16]

He put these questions to Kergorlay by letter, and as usual got a thoughtful and helpful response, though Kergorlay was far from sure that the questions were answerable. Statistics were needed to make an estimate of pecuniary gains from the Revolution, and where were they to be found? Historians had simply not made the right enquiries; in fact, 'I think that nothing is more unknown to the France of today than what the France of yesterday was administratively, pecuniarily, materially.' As to the question of the distribution of land before the Revolution, answering it would require interminable research. Kergorlay had under his eye documents which enabled him to say that Tocqueville's theory was correct so far as Fosseuse and its neighbouring communes were concerned: the same peasant families owned the land then as now; 'but how can one generalize from this one study?' Kergorlay, old friend though he was, did not quite know his man. 'An army of Benedictines would be needed to reveal that unknown period, quite as much as for the darkest epochs of the Middle Ages; and you have better things to do than become one of those indefatigable researchers; besides there would only be one of you.' This was not the way to put Tocqueville off; he loved archival research, and Kergorlay's remarks had shown

him a way to exercise his talents in a vast field, much as Royer-Collard
had shown him how to exploit the necessity of making a speech about
Lacuée de Cessac.* Kergorlay had referred in passing to Valognes and
the archives of the Manche as possible mines of information, so two
weeks later Tocqueville wrote to Zacharie Gallemand, a landowner at
Valognes who had always been a staunch political supporter, for help
in estimating the actual benefits that came from the abolition of feudal
dues on the famous night of 4 August 1789:

> Being unemployed in the present time, I am trying to live usefully in
> the past and the direction of the great work which I have undertaken
> is leading me to make a very detailed examination and, if possible,
> one that is more precise than any made so far, of the state of French
> society at the moment when the Revolution transformed it ... It
> occurred to me that you could perhaps indicate some sources which I
> might investigate for our area [*pays*] and this hope leads me to write
> to you ... The importance of the subject is my excuse.

Gallemand wrote back most helpfully, and also suggested that
Tocqueville get in touch with the Manche archivist, François Dubosc,
which he did; but Dubosc's reply, when it came in late November, was
not particularly encouraging: the archives were as yet entirely unsorted.
By that time Tocqueville had drawn up a programme of what needed
doing that would do credit to a student nowadays planning one of those
formidable French doctoral theses. All forms of profit would have to
be investigated – the purchase of confiscated lands at knock-down
prices; the payment of debts and rents in depreciated currency; the rise
in wages (Birette, the agent at Tocqueville, assured him that the price
of labour had shot up in the Cotentin in the last years of the Empire,
as able-bodied men were conscripted to the army); the abolition of
feudal dues and of certain taxes; the non-payment of taxes. He read
every relevant book that he could lay his hands on, and made extensive
notes. Napoleon, as a topic, began to gather dust.[17]

It is possible to regret this. The period of the Consulate was a subject
that seems admirably suited to Tocqueville's strengths, including his
talent for pen-portraits, and unlikely to suffer from his weaknesses.

* See above, p. 402.

True, Thiers had already published several thick volumes on the topic, but Tocqueville might reasonably have regarded this as a challenge which had to be answered, since Thiers was an ardent centralizer. But Tocqueville was not a professor, or, any longer, a politician. He was a Romantic, who could only write successfully when his feelings were deeply engaged; and it is easy to see why he was uninspired by the topic of the creation of the Napoleonic state. He could not celebrate it, as he had celebrated that other exemplar of the new order, the United States; instead he found himself drawn to studying the ruin of the old order.

He had a happy summer, clouded only by the death of Eugène Stoffels in July. Tocqueville was distressed, partly because he liked Stoffels so much, and partly because he was the first of his intimate friends to die. But it could not be helped, and for the rest Tocqueville enjoyed his studies so much that he came somewhat to resent any inter-ruption, however agreeable otherwise, even visits from Kergorlay and Beaumont. Ampère came to stay for several weeks, but that was different: he could be assigned a tower-room to get on with his own work, while Tocqueville studied in the room below. He wrote to Freslon:*

> You would laugh if you could see the man who has written so much on democracy surrounded by works on feudal law and bent over *terriers* and other dusty registers which enumerate all the rights of certain lordships and note the monies that they were still producing at the end of the eighteenth century. The tedium of these studies, joined to all the reasons I had already not to love the *ancien régime*, will end by making me a real revolutionary.[18]

Tocqueville in his tower was far from being without access to primary sources, but the Parisian archives drew him, and in October he and Marie set off for the place de la Madeleine. On arrival Tocqueville again fell seriously ill, this time with pleurisy. He put it down to the appalling weather they met on their journey, which had begun by giving him rheumatism in his shoulder and side; he was relieved that,

---

* Alexandre Freslon (1808–67). Lawyer, journalist, Republican politician. A member of the National Assembly, 1848–9; minister of education for two months under Cavaignac, 1848. Friend of AT and opponent of the Second Empire.

according to his doctors, his lungs were unaffected by this new malady. It is difficult to share his confidence in their verdict, for although his tuberculosis appears to have been in remission it is quite possible that it caused the pleurisy, and anyway Dr Andral's treatment was decidedly antique. He believed in counter-irritants, so he blistered Tocqueville four times and kept the wound raw between treatments; the patient was in constant pain for three weeks or so. He was assured that the treatment was necessary to root out the illness and all its consequences, and was grateful that he was not blistered a fifth time; but it is hardly surprising that his convalescence was long and slow. As late as 17 December he had not found the strength to return to his work. Then, in the last week of December, just as his recovery began (Andral said it would take five or six months) Marie succumbed to *une grippe abominable* (presumably influenza) and had to take to her bed. 'My wife and I have the habit of being always ill, one after another.'[19]

So began the winter, and so it continued. Tocqueville was never really well, and in January he had one of his stomach attacks – the worst, he told Beaumont, for twelve years – that is, since 1841, when he went down with dysentery in Algeria. His spirits were also lowered by the state of politics, which seeped dismally into everything, even family life. He had already had a painful dispute with Édouard the year before, and now Hippolyte, whose political course since 1830 had been extremely erratic,* having rallied to the Empire tried to justify himself in a letter to his brother. He received a frosty reply: Hippolyte's recent behaviour was as foreign to Alexis 'as all the chief actions of your life have been since you were twenty', which actions he then listed unforgivingly, though ending with assurances of brotherly devotion. He was as unrelenting with everyone else. He was severe when Rémusat, 'that delicate and charming mind', now returned from exile, sought to prove that the detested regime was solidly founded and that those who expected its downfall were fools. He could see no merit or intelligence in the imperial government, and was glad to think that Louis Napoleon made a great mistake when he married Eugenia de Montijo on 30 January; he was bitterly amused to think that this,

---

* A long footnote in the 'Correspondance familiale', OC XIV 288 n.3, gives full details of Hippolyte's eccentricities.

of all things, was what would alienate him from the faubourg Saint-Germain: 'To violate humanity and the laws may be overlooked, but a *mésalliance*! Fie!' Nor did the clear propensity of the British and their government to accept the situation and work with Louis Napoleon escape his censure; in fact it became one of his chief complaints over the next few years, until the end of the Crimean War. Read today his letters plentifully demonstrate that he was politically consistent and high-principled, but the constant reaffirmation of his attitude becomes wearisome, and as his principles were sometimes only prejudices his judgement suffered. He became convinced that one day before long Louis Napoleon would go to war with Britain, and repeatedly told his British friends so, whereas such a war was something that the Emperor was determined to avoid. Unlike Tocqueville, he remembered the lesson of Trafalgar and Waterloo.[20]

Not all the distractions of Paris were medical or political. Tocqueville had become friendly with the family of Edward V. Childe,* Americans living in Paris. Mrs Childe, the sister of Robert E. Lee, presided over a salon full of brilliant men and women, among them Prosper Mérimée, Alfred de Vigny and Tocqueville himself. In March 1853 her elder daughter Florence, aged fifteen, ran away with a Polish diplomat, Prince Soltyk. Because of this Mrs Childe became the victim of spiteful Parisian tongues. Tocqueville was furious, and seized a chance of displaying his loyalty to his friends. The guilty couple had taken refuge in Geneva, and Mr Childe decided to go there to get his daughter back. Tocqueville gave him a letter of introduction to his old friend the publicist Auguste de la Rive, who contrived to dissuade the angry father from a wild scheme of re-abduction and got Soltyk to agree to marry the girl. Tocqueville did not think much of her: according to him she was ungrateful as well as morally feeble, but he was glad that he and La Rive had done what they could for the worthy parents.[21]

None of these concerns was allowed to keep Tocqueville away from his research for long. As his health falteringly recovered he pursued two lines of enquiry, both inspired by his wish to discover why in 1789

---

* Edward Vernon Childe (1804–61), of Boston; he was for a decade or so the Parisian correspondent of several New York newspapers. He returned to America in 1856, after his wife's death; from there he wrote a valuable series of letters to AT.

revolution began in France rather than anywhere else. The first, and as it turned out the less fruitful, was inspired by his experience of 1848. In that year revolution had been an international phenomenon: why had the same not been true of 1789? Was Germany (for instance) so different from France? He decided to learn German, and sought out German correspondents. He wrote to Christian von Bunsen, equally distinguished as a historian and a diplomat,* that he wanted to study the European response to the French Revolution from the fall of the Bastille to the fall of the monarchy:

> Unfortunately, and much to my regret, I do not know Germany. So far I have lived exclusively in the English world. I imagine that during the last sixty years the Germans must have published memoirs, collections of letters or diplomatic documents which bring to light what I want to discover. I do not know of them, and in consequence cannot procure them. And the French Revolution must from its beginning have given birth, either deliberately or incidentally, to writings which reflect general public opinion. My semi-ignorance of German and my almost complete ignorance of Germany (which is happily not incurable) deprive me of this necessary information.

So he turned to Bunsen for advice, which was courteously given and scrupulously followed, though not at once. Tocqueville soon began to carry out his resolution of learning German, and decided that in a year's time, when he hoped to have mastered the language, he would make a long visit to Germany.[22]

As if this project were not enough, Tocqueville continued his second line of enquiry, that of investigating through archives the nature of French society and government on the eve of the Revolution. When his health permitted he went to the archives of Paris, stored in the Hôtel de Ville, where he could find the records of the pre-revolutionary government of the region (*généralité*), the Île-de-France. Unfortunately they were more meagre than he had expected. He made a note:

> These files contain few documents anterior to 1787 and, beginning at

---

* Christian von Bunsen (1791–1860) was the Prussian ambassador in London 1842–54; he and AT had many English friends in common, notably Mrs Grote, who was the initial link between them. Bunsen highly approved of Tocqueville's plan, and as a sign of respect sent him his book on the Church under the emperor Commodus. AT did not at once find time to read it.

that date, the old administrative system was profoundly modified and there began the transitional and rather uninteresting period which separates the administrative *ancien régime* from the system set up under the Consulate which rules us still.

(This must be the most dismissive remark ever made about France between 1787 and 1799.) He could not see his way forward. 'I am lost in an ocean of research,' he wrote to Beaumont, 'where fatigue and discouragement keep seeking me out.' He was not just discouraged about himself, but about the whole human race and its history. The only reason for working was to avoid feeling exiled in his own country.[23]

No doubt his dismal state of health had much to do with his despondency; and Marie was if anything worse. She was undergoing her menopause, as well as her usual ailments, and for the next two years seems to have been at best a semi-invalid for most of the time. She and Tocqueville could only explain their debility in terms of variations of the climate. They needed a bolt-hole, somewhere they could vegetate in the sun until Nature restored them. Their chateau was too damp and draughty, Paris, apart from any other consideration, far too expensive. Beaumont suggested they look for a refuge nearby: he wanted them to buy a villa at Auteuil or Passy, even (he hinted) if it meant selling Tocqueville; at any rate they should stop their perpetual house-moving, bad in itself for health.[24]

Alexis and Marie decided that it would be too difficult and expensive to find what they wanted near Paris; they chose instead the Loire valley, and set Beaumont to finding a house for them. He jumped at the chance of making himself useful; and before long discovered Les Trésorières, near Tours, which was to let for a year – just what they wanted. Facing south, it was full of sunshine, and sheltered from the north wind by hills. It had never been let before, so the furniture was in tolerable condition; it had a small park, a kitchen garden, stables and a coach-house; and next door lived a famous physician, Dr Bretonneau. The only drawback was that there was no view.[25] After a few days' hesitation Tocqueville and Marie decided to accept Beaumont's recommendation, and installed themselves at Les Trésorières on 1 June. The short journey by train from Paris exhausted them both, which showed how right they were to retreat to the countryside; they liked the house at sight. Their pleasure was much diminished when the servants' rooms turned out to be full of bedbugs. Tocqueville saw this as the latest in a succession of unforeseen misfortunes which had beset him for a year. 'Who could have imagined beforehand that a house which its owner had just been living in could be infested in this way?' Fortunately a vigorous campaign routed the enemy, and Tocqueville began to settle in.[26]

Les Trésorières lay in the village of Saint-Cyr on the north bank of the Loire, some four kilometres from the centre of Tours. Tours itself is a beautiful town, somewhat like Metz or even a smaller, quieter Paris. It is not clear what Tocqueville expected to find there. He was determined not to waste his time making acquaintances, and did not do so (though he made an exception for the archbishop, who was invited to dinner). Before leaving Paris he told Senior that he might do some work in the cathedral library, but it soon struck him that Tours also contained the departmental archives of the Indre-et-Loire. One misty morning, very soon after his arrival at Saint-Cyr, he set off along the river and presented himself at the prefecture. It was perhaps the single most fortunate moment in his entire career as a writer.[27]

Tours, like Metz, had been the centre of one of the great *généralités* of the *ancien régime*, and its records of that era, unlike those at Saint-Lô, had just been put in order by the departmental archivist. Charles de Grandmaison, an earnest and energetic young man (1824–1903) had only been *en poste* for a year or so.[28] He was a man of the Loire: born at Poitiers, he died in Touraine, and spent his life devotedly tending the records in his care. But he had been trained at Paris, in the École des Chartes, and his first job had been in the department of manuscripts at the Bibliothèque Nationale, where he had taken note of Tocqueville's visits and his conversations with the keeper of manuscripts. He immediately recognized his small, weary-looking visitor, with his quiet air of distinction, and put himself at his service. Tocqueville explained that he was investigating the causes of the French Revolution, and with that in mind wanted to study the administrative records of Tours from the reign of Louis XI onwards. Grandmaison soon convinced him that even if the roots of the Revolution went down that far it was impossible for a newcomer to historical manuscripts to make much of the documents: years of training were necessary. Tocqueville did not need much convincing, and agreed that it would be wise to confine himself to the last phase of the *ancien régime*, that is, to the eighteenth century, which he had already begun to investigate (though Louis XI eventually put in two or three fleeting appearances in the *Ancien Régime*).[29] He promised to return next day, and when he did Grandmaison noticed that he had brought with him an official black morocco-bound portfolio, the one useful relic of his brief ministry. Grandmaison had a selection of documents waiting for him, and he set happily to work.

A day or two later Grandmaison noticed that the usually undisturbed quiet of the archives was being broken by a number of persons who came to gape at the celebrated visitor. He asked Tocqueville if he would like to share the archivist's own office. It was small, and rather cramped for two, but it was private, and looked onto the prefect's kitchen-garden. Tocqueville gratefully accepted: perhaps he was reminded of the garret in which he wrote the 1835 *Démocratie*; at any rate, he worked in Grandmaison's office for the rest of his time in Tours, at an old battered desk which in future years was in Grandmaison's eyes the most valuable piece of furniture in the room. Tocqueville took to visiting the archives almost every day; it is not surprising that he and Grandmaison began to become friends as soon as Tocqueville was sure that he was not dealing with a Bonapartist stooge. For his part Grandmaison succumbed to Tocqueville's charm, his kindness, and his brilliant conversation. Tocqueville made a point of chatting to him for fifteen minutes or so every day, and readily discussed the documents with him. Forty years later Grandmaison remembered Tocqueville's sonorous and musical voice,* his pure and elegant diction, his sober but expressive gestures, above all his slightly malicious smile and the brightness of his eye.[30]

Guided by Grandmaison, Tocqueville plunged into the official correspondence of the old *intendants*, agents of the Crown who in the eighteenth century governed most of France. They were the forerunners of the nineteenth-century prefects, and Tocqueville had been brought up in prefectures. He had been a minister. The

---

* Grandmaison is unique among witnesses in characterizing AT's voice.

documents were exactly to his taste. Before long he was writing to Freslon:

> At Tours I have found not buried treasure, but a deposit as precious, to further my undertaking (I think, by the way, that one would make the same discovery in the archives of every prefecture which was formerly the seat of a *généralité*). It is a collection of papers which will give to any student a clear idea of the ways in which all the various business of public administration was conducted ...

At this stage he thought that he was merely doing the preliminary work for a single chapter, but before long he began to realize that he was amassing material which would make half a book, at least. As he was eventually to say in the foreword to the *Ancien Régime*:

> In a country where the public administration has become all-powerful, few ideas, desires or grievances arise which do not, sooner or later, come naked to its attention. Visitors to its archives will acquire not only a very precise idea of its procedures, the whole country will be revealed. A foreigner who today was shown all the confidential correspondence which fills the files of the ministry of the interior and the prefectures would soon know more about us than we do ourselves ... I have discovered the *ancien régime* still alive in its ideas, its passions, its prejudices, its practices ... I have in this way acquired many insights into that old society which its contemporaries did not have, for I had before my eyes that which was never shown them.

This was a discovery that Tocqueville could not keep to himself. For a while the Revolution, like Napoleon previously, began to recede as a topic.[31]

To safeguard his health Tocqueville passed only his mornings at the archives. He devoted his afternoons to the study of German, which he did not enjoy but thought indispensable for his current project; in the end he acquired a sound reading knowledge of a tongue which he found deeply unsympathetic. He hired a tutor in German, and it was no doubt a help that Marie knew the language well. In the evenings, after dinner, they read to each other. Tocqueville was especially fond of travel books.[32]

It was a quiet life which suited them both. By October Tocqueville could report to Beaumont that they were well, and that Marie was in better spirits than she had been for years. They continued to have nothing to do with the locals, except for Grandmaison, who came to dinner several times, but a steady stream of visitors from afar descended on Saint-Cyr: Comte Hervé, Ampère (who stayed for several weeks), Kergorlay, Guerry, Beaumont, Corcelle and so on – mostly summer visitors. Less welcome was Mrs Grote, who came in the winter, just when Tocqueville was beginning to write. She was blithely demanding. She stayed in Tours for ten days or so in February, and although she was fobbed off with the Hôtel de l'Univers (recently built to take advantage of the new custom generated by the railway) she had to be visited or entertained to a meal every day. Tocqueville lamented at length to Beaumont: 'The obligation to entertain Mrs Grote is not a light obligation and besides we have become so fond of our own little ways that the intrusion into our life of people whom we greatly like but who are not, after all, intimate friends, vexes us somewhat, my wife above all.' There was no knowing how long she would stay, or what she would do next: Tocqueville tried to deter her from descending on Beaumont by saying that because of building works there would be no room for her at Beaumont-la-Chartre. This letter would have cruelly mortified Mrs Grote had she read it, for she was devoted to Alexis, and he was never slow to flatter her. (In general he did not think it necessary to be sincere to women, except his wife, and his letters to them always overflowed with elaborate compliments.[33])

An even more tiresome attention was of a different nature. Arthur de Gobineau, Tocqueville's former *chef de cabinet*, sent him the first two volumes, just published, of his *Essay on the Inequality of the Human Races*. Comte Hervé brought them to Saint-Cyr, and Tocqueville read them during October. It was a distressing experience. Tocqueville had real affection for Gobineau, who had furthermore often made himself useful as a research assistant, but he could not hide from himself or the author that the *Essay* was a sad disappointment to him (and the final two volumes, which came out in 1856, were no better). It was, in fact, one of the most mortally mischievous books published in the whole nineteenth century. Gobineau's formal education was fragmentary and incomplete; his attitude to the world was that of an extremely opinionated autodidact. He had good German and had picked up some philology (just then an extremely fashionable study) and learned some Sanskrit; this led him to conceive a myth which explained the fact – quite certain, in his opinion – that the whole of humanity was degenerate. Once there had been a clear division between the three human races – white, yellow and black – of which one, the white, was pre-eminent for intelligence, beauty, strength and wisdom, and was responsible for all the great achievements of civilization. But, fatally, the great race had interbred with its inferiors, and after three thousand years was largely indistinguishable from them. Things had got particularly bad in the last five hundred years, and were going to get worse: civilization and humanity itself were dying. Already the human population everywhere was shrinking. Man had no more than five or six thousand years left.[34]

This nonsense had the great advantage, from Gobineau's point of view – that of a *bourgeois* passing himself off as a noble whose inheritance had been lost during the French Revolution* – of explaining his misfortunes and foretelling the ruin of his enemies. As J.-J. Chevallier puts it, it was 'intellectual revenge and psychological compensation masquerading as a philosophy of history'. To Tocqueville it had two crucial disadvantages: it was not credible, and its possible consequences were appalling. He told Beaumont that Gobineau wrote like a horse-dealer rather than a statesman (the simile came naturally to a man from the Cotentin): 'I believe absolutely none of it.' He was not quite so frank to the author himself. Gobineau had always insisted that his findings were entirely scientific, and Tocqueville never chose to challenge him on that score. Probably he realized from the first that Gobineau was unpersuadable: he had a gift for assuming and relentlessly defending indefensible positions. Before long he would be claiming to have deciphered the cuneiform inscriptions of Nineveh and to have proved that they were Persian, not Assyrian. But as a moralist and politician Tocqueville protested incessantly against the probable consequences of Gobineau's doctrines. They were fatalist, and he was against all forms of determinism, whether deriving from Augustine, the Calvinists, the Jansenists or from Gobineau's theory of race, for they all ended in the cramping or the complete abolition

---

* Gobineau did not have a genuine claim either to the noble *particule*, '*de*', which his family had appropriated, or to the title of *comte*, which he assumed after the death of an uncle in 1855.

of human liberty. He thought all such doctrines probably false and certainly pernicious. In whose interest could it be to persuade backward or enslaved peoples that, being what they were, they could have no hope of bettering their condition, changing their manners or reforming their government?

> Do you not see that your doctrine leads naturally to all the evils to which permanent inequality gives birth, to pride, violence, contempt of one's fellows, tyranny and degradation in all its forms? ... Courage, energy, uprightness, foresight, common sense are the true reasons for the prosperity of empires as for that of families and, in short, the destiny of Man, whether as an individual or a nation, is what he wishes to make it.[35]

For the time being, though the correspondence continued, the debate was suspended, not to be resumed until after the publication of the *Ancien Régime*. One day, unforeseen by Tocqueville, it would be important to the world; in 1853 it was simply part of the background to an author's struggles. Tocqueville read books and documents, he made notes, he sorted his notes; but his problem that autumn seems to have been something like writer's block. His temperament still swerved up and down, and when it was down he suffered grievous self-doubt, in spite of the excellence of the Brumaire chapters written the year before. In September he announced that he would 'go into winter quarters' on 15 October and force himself to write at least the all-important first chapter. On 19 October he told Kergorlay that he would begin writing in December. Four days later, writing to Rivet, he was more optimistic, and expected to start in ten days' time; but when the ten days were up he was only promising to start the following week; he simultaneously worried to Freslon that a good book might be impossible, and then what would he do? '*Vivre pour vivre* has never been possible for me.' Two weeks later he was still, he said, standing on the edge of the big ditch; and writing to Mrs Grote on 22 November, almost exactly two months after his first letter to Freslon, all he could say was that he could feel the writer's itch coming upon him ... Eventually he started.[36]

By the end of May, when he and Marie left Saint-Cyr, he seems to have drafted most of what became *L'Ancien Régime et la Révolution*.[37]

He had put aside his notes for the time being and plunged ahead; when it came to the point he wrote very fast. The whole draft would eventually be revised, most of it heavily; but the first five chapters, which eventually appeared as Book One, were only to be lightly altered, and because of their character need to be considered separately from the rest of the work. It is therefore convenient to examine them at this point in the story.

They take up only eighteen pages of the *Oeuvres complètes* edition. The writing is so simple, its discourse so trenchant, Tocqueville makes it all seem so easy, that its importance may well be overlooked, especially as Book One has (apparently) so tenuous a connection to Book Two (which was not divided into Books Two and Three until the second edition). But easy it was not.

Tocqueville laboured anxiously at his style. Sometimes, he told Mrs Grote, he was hung up for days together, 'having the thoughts, yet not hitting off the "phrases" in a way to satisfy his critical ear ...'. Beaumont was to tell Senior, 'I have known him recast a sentence 20 times over.' But it is doubtful if this perfectionist tinkering achieved very much. Tocqueville always struck off elegant and lucid first drafts that usually needed little polishing (his obituary of Le Peletier d'Aunay, dashed down at the family's request in 1855, reads excellently). His only serious problem with Book One was the risk of redundancy. It was essential that he include nothing that was not strictly pertinent to his theme.[38]

Book One's striking difference from the rest of the *Ancien Régime* arose because it was meant as overture to the larger work, the great book on the Revolution which he did not live to finish, of which the *Ancien Régime* was meant to be no more than the first volume. As Tocqueville told his favourite nephew Hubert in March, he planned not so much a history, or a series of philosophical observations, as a blending of the two. He meant to follow the French Revolution from epoch to epoch, from its beginning to the fall of the Empire, paying more attention to the general movement of events than to particular incidents. (The *Ancien Régime* as published illustrates this technique.[39]) It was necessary to find a way of making these points to his readers so that they would know what to expect. Book One is Tocqueville's attempt to do so. It reads like an expansion and rephrasing of the project that

he sketched in his letter to Mme de Circourt eighteen months earlier.*
He insists that it is now possible to understand the origins and nature
of the Revolution far better than did contemporaries, such as Edmund
Burke.[40] He makes several firm remarks contradicting past and current
assumptions about the Revolution: 'the first and last objective of the
Revolution was not, as has been generally believed, to destroy the
power of religion and weaken that of the State'; rather, where the
State was concerned, it was to sweep away all the institutions of the
Middle Ages – parliaments, orders, privileges, local self-government
– the old constitution of Europe – and replace them with a much more
modern, powerful, centralized system. For the rest, he mostly asked
searching questions: what did Europeans of the day think of the Revolution? Why was it launched? Why did it break out in France rather
than elsewhere? Why did it take one course in France and others in
other countries? The time had come, said Tocqueville, to answer these
questions and he thought he could do so.[41]

No-one, after reading Book One, could be in any doubt as to
what Tocqueville was about, but he sacrificed much in achieving this
lucidity. He gives a few unsourced quotations, mostly from Burke, and
makes a few allusions to events, but there is nothing in his exposition
which can accurately be called evidence or argument. It is all assertion.
Perhaps that is why Tocqueville eventually denounced these five small
chapters as the most mediocre and least original part of his whole
book. 'At least it has the merit of being short.' His technique occasionally led him astray. For instance, one of his themes is that the Revolution attacked the Church, not religion; religion was something planted
in the hearts of the people, and after unjust ecclesiastical privilege
had been swept away it revived: religion, even Catholicism, is in no
way incompatible with democracy. This was a theme first sounded
in the *Démocratie*; it had not gained in plausibility in the twenty years
between the two books; but like Tocqueville's other sweeping statements it was presented without evidence, and seemed no less plausible;
in that company, its element of wishful thinking was disguised from the
author, if not from his readers. And taken as a whole the five chapters
were little more than a summary of some of Tocqueville's favourite

* See above, p. 531.

notions. They have the charm of his conversation; they are scarcely scholarly. Perhaps it does not matter. They open the book superbly, which no doubt explains why Tocqueville let them stand. He wanted readers, and this was a good way to get them.[42]

Tocqueville and Marie gave up Les Trésorières on 28 May 1854, when their lease expired. As a medical experiment their sojourn had been only moderately successful. Tocqueville believed that Marie's health was restored, but he himself had had several bad stomach attacks during the year and left Tours no better than when he arrived. The place had had attractions (not only the archives) of which the nearness of the Beaumonts was the most important. Tocqueville wrote to Gustave two days before he left Saint-Cyr:

> My wife said to me this very morning, as we chatted before getting up (I idle somewhat at that moment of the day) that the only consolation she had in leaving the neighbourhood of such good friends as you two was the thought that Time and all the good and bad fortune which it has delivered in its flow have only strengthened the ties of our friendship, while for so many other people it is the great unbinder [*délieur*].

Tocqueville added a telling observation about Clémentine and Marie to this glimpse of his marital life: 'We enjoyed the company of Madame de Beaumont more than ever. Her society is not only attractive to my wife, but singularly good for her. There are some people I greatly love but yet from whose company I scarcely ever see her emerge other than upset and cross.' (Tocqueville was no doubt thinking of his brothers and their wives.)

> When she leaves Madame de Beaumont she seems serene and happy with everybody, notably with me, which I find very agreeable. It must be that your wife, as well as having that natural kindness which sets her apart from so many others, has some delicate art which can easily manage a mind that does not willingly adapt to the views of other people.[43]

This letter throws some light on the state of the Tocqueville marriage, which now had to endure a testing five months. Tocqueville was bent, with all the energetic determination of his character, on his proposed visit to Germany. Marie was not as sure: another cholera epidemic was spreading across western Europe, and she had reason to fear that her health would not be equal to such a journey. She would have preferred to spend the summer at Tocqueville. But her husband was so ardent for the voyage that he convinced himself that Marie was quite well and (except when he was actually suffering from stomach aches) that he was himself fit again. His eagerness was of long standing, and he needed a holiday after his months of toil. He gave many other reasons, all connected with the French Revolution and the *ancien régime*, but he had gone as eagerly to Germany in 1849, when they did not apply. His zest for travel was still alive, and we must surely suspect that his intuition told him that the nation on the far side of the Rhine was more than ever worth a French statesman's attention. Tocqueville had long believed, with most of his countrymen who thought about such matters, that the real danger to France came from Russia, with which, in that very year, war broke out. Under the Second Republic, as he says in the *Souvenirs*, he favoured the unification of Germany so that it could assist the West in resisting the Tsar.* It is hard to believe that he did not have such considerations somewhere in mind as he planned his visit to Bonn, Dresden and Berlin.[44]

The journey was an almost complete failure. They reached Bonn on 19 June, having travelled by way of Brussels, where they met the exiled Lamoricière. Along the way Marie's forebodings were all too thoroughly justified: her old uterine affliction returned, and for the first six weeks of their stay (they took a furnished flat with a view across lawns to the Rhine) she led the life of a semi-invalid. Tocqueville's research and scholarly contacts in Bonn went well, though he still could not hold a conversation in German and formed the decided impression that most German professors were pedants. A pleasant change was afforded by two new English acquaintances, George Cornewall Lewis and his wife, Lady Theresa Villiers.† Lewis was a coming man in British public life,

---

* A. J. P. Taylor poured scorn on this calculation in *The Struggle for Mastery in Europe* (Oxford, 1954), 34; but then he was fanatically anti-German.

† George Cornewall Lewis (1806–63), politician and polymathic author. Poor law commissioner, 1834–46. Married Lady Theresa (sister of the Earl of Clarendon), 1844. Editor of the *Edinburgh Review*, 1850–55. Chancellor of the Exchequer, 1855–8. Home Secretary, 1859–61; Secretary of War, 1861–3. Baronet in succession to his father, 1855. He was the sort of earnest, erudite man to whom AT was often attracted. His best-known remark was, 'Life would be

and Tocqueville held forth to him unguardedly on the horrors of Louis Napoleon's despotism: 'His govt is far more oppressive & interfering than the govt of his uncle.' He explained the legend of Napoleon in Balzacian terms: 'in every village there was some vieux soldat who cd relate the wars of the empire – who remembered its glories & triumphs – who had forgotten its misery & disasters – & who converted it into a sort of mythical tale. Every such man was the center of a little circle of listeners & admirers – & his accounts constituted nearly all that the country people knew of the Past.'[45] The Lewises and the Tocquevilles decidedly took to each other, and thenceforward Lewis was reckoned among Tocqueville's most valuable English friends.

But the Lewises left Bonn and disaster struck. Marie had a severe rheumatic attack which completely robbed her of the use of her right hand and arm. All thoughts of Dresden and Berlin had to be abandoned. On medical advice they went instead to the spa of Wildbad in the Black Forest, so that Marie could take a course of hot baths there.[46]

It is to be hoped that the volatile Tocqueville did not make matters even more difficult for them both by losing his temper, but however much he loved his wife the strain on his patience was severe. Marie's condition deteriorated: Tocqueville had to dress her and cut up food for her. Her treatment was worryingly expensive. They knew nobody at Wildbad, and nobody spoke French. Tocqueville thought the place a sunless hole, all too aptly named ('*le bain sauvage*'). Two or three grand hotels lay in a wilderness of pine trees and mountains, and society was entirely made up of the hunchbacked, the twisted, the one-armed, the crippled and the legless: 'I begin to believe that a man with the use of two legs and two arms is an exception among the human race.' Worst of all, his work was at a standstill. For lack of anything else to do he began to study a collection of the laws of the duchy of Württemberg; characteristically, he eventually found them so interesting that they figure in a long note to the *Ancien Régime*, but it was a meagre amusement. Eventually the devoted Ampère found his way to them and did his best to cheer them up during the last week of their ordeal; but Marie's hand got very little better, and it was a defeated party which trailed slowly back to France in late September.[47]

tolerable were it not for its amusements.'

They crossed the frontier at Valenciennes, where they were searched and every printed paper, whatever its nature, was confiscated. 'I recognized my country.' Tocqueville reflected that patriotism had little to do with the soil of the fatherland. 'I have just passed three months in a country which, compared to ours, can be called a land of liberty, and the thought of again breathing the air of France enslaved and so content with its enslavement depressed me.' The events of the next six months did nothing to cheer him. The cholera epidemic continued. The Crimean War, which had started well, was sinking into a winter stalemate at Sevastopol, and news of the suffering of the allied armies was beginning to circulate. British military mismanagement was not only discrediting that country's aristocracy and destroying its military reputation but damaging the credit of liberalism. Tocqueville could not forgive the British for making an alliance with Napoleon III. He could not forgive his countrymen either.

> I find with pleasure as time goes by that my heart is not one of those which are allured by victory, and that I get more devoted to my cause the more I see it conquered and abandoned. I feel less and less able to associate with those who are its enemies, or are even just indifferent to it, the more that luck appears to overwhelm the new regime with its favours and thus to justify it in the eyes of the mob.[48]

Such was the ground-bass of Tocqueville's correspondence during the winter. The descant was more positive. Marie, Ampère and he went straight from Valenciennes to stay with Comte Hervé in his little house at Clairoix near Compiègne, but it was too damp for Marie and her rheumatism, so after Ampère's departure they took a house that was even smaller, a sort of miniature Trésorières, and underfurnished (the comte lent them some sticks), but was at least warm, dry and sunny. It was their sixth change of residence (not counting hotels) in six months, but now for a time their gypsying ceased. They were supposed to move to Paris in January – then in February – then in March – but somehow there was always a reason for not doing so when the time came. Marie's health began to improve steadily, if not without setbacks (Tocqueville marvelled at her patience). Alexis made a short visit to Paris to collect his books and working papers.[49]

He had not looked at his Tours notes for five months, and had made plenty more during his stay in Germany, so the first thing to do was to reduce them all to order.[50] He sorted them into seventeen separate files, and then compiled an index under eleven distinct headings, which together summed up the subject he meant to explore, so accurately that today they are recognizable as an anatomy of the book which he finally wrote;* then he went through them all, using his index to find and make useful extracts. It must have been extremely laborious, and in view of the sparseness of his citation in the finished work may seem to have been unnecessary, but it served the double purpose of reacquainting him with his material and of convincing him that he had thoroughly mastered his subject – very useful psychologically, for he was going to have fits of anxiety about the whole thing right up to publication day. Only when the whole process was complete did he take out his draft chapters and rewrite them thoroughly in the light of his documentation, quoting memoirs, letters, *cahiers de doléances*, monographs and official papers to clinch his arguments. By April, when at last he and Marie moved to Paris, he had given seventeen chapters – those which now form Books One and Two – more or less their final form.

It will be seen that Tocqueville's latest hermitage was as productive for him as any of the others. His father and Mme Guermarquer went back to the place de la Madeleine in January; after that Tocqueville had no distractions of any sort. The weather was unkind: in mid-February a blizzard blanketed France, and winter did not wholly relax its grip until May. Tocqueville and Marie found that the only room in their house which was really sunny in such conditions was his study: they lived there by day and night (nothing is said about how their servants managed). Tocqueville was attacked by *grippe* at the end of January, to his desperate disappointment, for he had been working 'with a *flaming* ardour'; besides, confined to his room, he missed the open air, where he liked to spend as much time as possible, even in winter, and not being able to work transformed his refuge into a prison. But he made a swift recovery and was even well enough to make a second short visit

* 'England, Germany; Municipal and Provincial Administration, Taxes, Taille, Capitation, Public Charges; Provincial Institutions, Bourgeoisie, People; Nobility, Seigneurs, Feudal Rights; Unclassifiable; Administration, Centralization, Intendants; Bookselling, Press; Great Council, King's Council; Justice, Parliament; Church, Clergy; *Maréchaussée* [mounted police].' See Gannet, *Tocqueville*, 213 n.42.

to Paris in mid-February, from which he was heartily glad to return to his '*chères paperasses*' (though he was beginning to tire of Compiègne itself). Then came the blizzard. Tocqueville walked every day for an hour in the snow-buried forest and remembered the even whiter woods of Tennessee nearly twenty-five years earlier. The chief difference in the scene, he sadly reflected, lay in himself: twenty-five years made a revolution in any man's life. But (he thought, more cheerfully) if he had to start again he would do nothing differently, bar various small stupidities; and above all (he told Beaumont) he had kept the friend with whom he had hunted parrots at Memphis. His single worry now was about his father. The comte too had caught the *grippe*, and though he recovered, it did not seem to be to full health. Tocqueville was forced to reflect on Hervé's great age, and also on his character: 'You can't imagine what a tender, loveable old man he is. He has never shown more affection to his children than during the last few years nor a more charming good humour to everybody.' At least he showed no immediate signs of dying.[51]

By the end of March it was time to leave Compiègne. When he could bring himself to write Tocqueville worked in long, concentrated bursts, which eventually exhausted him; now, as at Tours ten months earlier, he had to pause. One symptom was that he was finding what became Book Three, chapter 1, on the position of the men of letters in eighteenth-century France, extremely difficult. Back in Paris, where the demands of his social and academic life instantly resumed, it was no easier. He decided to put off further work on his manuscript until he went to Tocqueville in June. But in the twelve chapters of Book Two which he had finished he had written what André Jardin justly calls the essential part of his book – 'the vast picture of France on the eve of 1789'.[52]

CHAPTER TWENTY-TWO

WRITING REVOLUTION

1855–1856

Then none was for a party;
  Then all were for the state;
Then the great man helped the poor
  And the poor man loved the great;
Then lands were fairly portioned;
  Then spoils were fairly sold:
The Romans were like brothers
  In the brave days of old.

LORD MACAULAY, *LAYS OF ANCIENT ROME*

EVEN IF TOCQUEVILLE had growing reservations about Parisian life (after a few months in the country he defined the obligations of society as the duty imposed by civilization to bore and be bored[1]) he could still be stimulated by it, and his return to the city in April came at an exciting moment: the Emperor had apparently decided to bring the Institut, now the only centre of audible opposition in France, to heel. He proposed some radical alterations to its statutes, which would have the effect of ending the academicians' independence. Naturally they were highly indignant, and Tocqueville threw himself joyfully into their campaign of resistance, which before long succeeded. But he did not give up research: he went regularly to the Archives Nationales. He and Marie lodged for seven weeks at 37, rue de Fleurus, their *pied-à-*

terre near the Luxembourg, which their smart friends thought fearfully out of the way.* Tocqueville did not care: money saved by living in such a way could go towards necessary repairs and improvements to his chateau. In late May Marie went to visit Mrs Belam at Chamarande. Tocqueville returned to civilization, as he put it – he moved in with his father at the place de la Madeleine. He missed Marie, and when she wrote to say that she had had an attack of some kind and lost the use of her voice he panicked, having perhaps become chronically anxious about her health as a result of her years of invalidism: not only did he decide to join her at Chamarande as soon as he could, he wrote a letter to Mrs Belam's servant 'recommending' that if Mme de Tocqueville grew worse she was to let him know at once. Mrs Belam was now a very old woman, and no doubt Tocqueville felt that he could not rely on her. Fortunately Marie soon recovered. She was still anxious about her inheritance, for Mrs Belam, a recent convert to Catholicism, had become excessively devoted to her curé. Tocqueville told her not to worry: 'I certainly didn't marry you for your money.' If necessary he was even prepared to take Mrs Belam into his household, for 'you have never been so precious to me, and while I can keep you I don't think I have the right to complain of anything at all.' He admitted that he had hesitated twenty years earlier, but today he would take the same decision with greater love and absolute certainty.[2]

At the beginning of June they went to Tocqueville. Marie travelled there directly, but as before Tocqueville made a detour by way of Beaumont-la-Chartre, where he was warmly welcomed. He read the new chapters of his book to his host and hostess, who were warmly enthusiastic, but Tocqueville unjustly suspected them of being too much influenced by friendship. He had one of his stomach attacks, perhaps brought on by anxiety.[3]

At home again he was happier than he had been for a year. Even before he reached the chateau he had slipped back into his role as the great man of the district: when he passed through Valognes he was careful to call on all the proper people, lest they should think that he was dropping them now that he was no longer a politician in need

---

* This view might have surprised Gertrude Stein, who lived at 27, rue de Fleurus sixty years later.

of their votes. He was received, he said, with friendly warmth, 'but with Norman prudence, that is to say nobody mentioned what was on everybody's mind – politics.' His spirits shot up as he got back into the carriage and rolled on towards Tocqueville. It was beautiful weather, and he was delighted to see his house again, though the grounds were now terribly overgrown with young trees which would have to be cut down. He and Marie were both well – 'God send that we remain so! Health, good weather and home nowadays seem to me quite sufficient for human happiness. I was not always so moderate in my desires. But in just compensation age, which has robbed me of so much, has at least given me the art I once lacked completely, of contenting myself with my circumstances.' It was wonderful to be back, after wandering about for three years from place to place, none of which entirely suited them.[4]

Settling in had its cares, but Tocqueville found everything charming. The house was soon full of workmen building a new chimney to heat both his study and bedroom, but he did not much mind. He was more interested in playing the country squire. There was an outbreak of smallpox in the village, and he had everyone vaccinated – poor Marie's body reacted badly. He listened to his neighbours' talk, and found them only moderately concerned with the war, now entering its second year: 'they fear above all the rise in expenditure, and when they have time they moan about the loss of their sons, gone for soldiers, but at bottom they are so much delighted at selling their beasts and their corn so dear that everything else is lost in their joy.' He began to see how country-dwellers sank into their own form of gross materialism: he hoped to resist the infection. He was fascinated by the letters from the army which illiterate peasants brought to him to read out.

This correspondence should be read in order to understand the singular character of the French peasant. It is strange to see the ease with which these men become accustomed to the risks of military life, to danger and death, and yet how their hearts cling to their fields and to the occupations of country life. The horrors of war are described with simplicity, and almost with enjoyment. But in the midst of these accounts one finds such remarks as: 'What crops do you intend to sow in such a field next year?' 'How is the mare?' 'Has the cow a fine calf?' &c. No minds can be more versatile and at the same time more constant. I have always thought that, after all, the peasantry is superior to all other classes in France.

This sympathy, which if not new was at least now better-informed, was to leave a profound mark on the *Ancien Régime*.[5]

Not that the book was moving again, or would do so for months. By now the nature of Tocqueville's creativity must be clear. He worked in short, passionate bursts with extraordinary speed and thoroughness, but took a long time to screw himself up to performance point. Tocqueville at Tocqueville in 1855 was just like Tocqueville at Tours in 1853. On 4 August he told Corcelle that he was getting back to work but had not yet *entered into it*, 'as Pascal puts it'. He got out his chapter on the political influence of men of letters in the mid eighteenth century (what eventually became Book Three, chapter 1), which had already caused him trouble, and was not encouraged when Marie read it and told him that it was flat and over-subtle – 'which appears to me correct, unfortunately'. When Ampère and Lanjuinais came to stay he read them some of his draft, 'and they did not appear dissatisfied,' but still he could not find the energy to make a push and finish. It was not that he was lacking in mental vigour: that summer he began his rather solemnly high-minded correspondence with Sophie Swetchine,* and his letters to his father show him acting informally as the comte's agent for his lands in the Cotentin (in November, as a winter of dearth approaches, we find him trying to get the curé and the *maire* of the commune to work together on poor relief, and suggesting that Comte Hervé increase the size of his regular dole of bread). Simply, authorial inspiration did not come. In September he said that his torpor prevented him from working. In October he blamed the incessant rain, which kept him indoors: 'no-one can work well in prison.' In early November it was his usual stomach trouble: 'for there is a close bond between the stomach and the head.' Suddenly he stops making excuses, stops even mentioning his book (except to say that he is nervous about publication) until on 27 December he reports to Ampère that he

---

* Sophie Petrovna Soimonova (1782–1857), of a noble Russian family, married, 1799, General Nicholas Swetchine. In 1815, she converted to Catholicism. In 1816–17, the Swetchines settled in Paris. They got to know all the most aristocratic French Catholics; Mme Swetchine became a sort of unofficial religious director to many of them, including Montalembert and Falloux.

has reached the last chapter ('How the Revolution broke out spontaneously from the conditions depicted'), but there is still an enormous amount of checking to be done: 'How ridiculous it would be if, after taking so much time to write this volume, I let errors remain because I was in a hurry!' He began to look forward to travelling to Paris to see to publication, although he was still tormented by his insides (which seem to have been particularly distressing that winter). Finally, in the first week of February, he set off. He left Marie behind planting hedges and shrubberies. She was in better health than she had been for years, had even got back her old dash and gaiety, and so (like a true Englishwoman, we may think) was wearing herself out in the garden.[6]

❧

L'Ancien Régime et la Révolution, as the world has had it since the second edition, consists of a Foreword, three Books, and substantial endnotes. This is the only simple statement that can accurately be made about an amazingly rich and complex work.

The book which Tocqueville carried with him to Paris was incomplete. He had drafted and revised its twenty-five chapters, but had not yet added the endnotes, written the Foreword or supplied the finishing touches. Nevertheless, his great contribution to the endless debate about the French Revolution was in place.

The complexity begins with the consideration of Tocqueville's intentions. As is clear from his correspondence with Kergorlay, and still more from the article which Kergorlay published after his death, his literary ambitions were now of the loftiest. He was a mature writer at the height of his powers, and he aspired to an achievement which would put him on the same level as the French writers he most admired, particularly those of the seventeenth century. Kergorlay, who was always spurring Tocqueville on to loftier achievement, praised the *Ancien Régime* highly, but it was only after his friend's death that he was ready to say unambiguously (after quoting Tocqueville's *tour de force* on the French national character, a sentence of Proustian length), 'this man was a great writer,' and to compare him to Montesquieu, Massillon, Pascal, Rousseau, Fénelon, Voltaire and Maistre, not to his disadvantage. Kergorlay would only concede to critics that Tocqueville's prose, though dazzlingly lucid, was so packed with thought that it resisted superficial readers – a reservation that would surely have pleased Tocqueville, and still seems just. There can be no doubt that his prose had grown more laconic, as he and Kergorlay liked to say, since the second *Démocratie*; severe yet flexible, simple but ironic, and always going straight to the point. He took endless pains with his style, and erected a monument of French literature. It was his second masterpiece and, with its predecessor, was going to keep his name alive indefinitely by its emotional and intellectual command of its material. Had Tocqueville survived to complete his grand design as he completed that of the *Démocratie* the two works would have palpably complemented each other, and together have made up a sweeping survey of politics in the modern world; revolution in France was a topic nicely matching democracy in America. Only his death defeated him.[7]

Yet style, as Tocqueville perfectly understood, cannot be divorced from structure and subject-matter, and his mastery had not yet purged some old failings. Behind the magnificent façade lurked all too much jerrybuilding; or (if the image is too harsh) lacunae and incoherences as characteristic as his fine prose. This is not a question of the sort of correction with which later scholarship pursues a pioneer. Rather it is a matter of faults in the original design, blemishes which need never have appeared, which a biographer must try to explain. They seem to arise from the book's duality. As Richard Herr was to put it, Tocqueville proposed to write a history that was also a political tract.[8] On the one hand he wanted to bring home to his readers what he believed to be the truth, that the *ancien régime*, quite as much as the Revolution, had created modern French society; the Revolution was only a furious accelerator, sweeping away obsolete or inconvenient laws, customs and institutions more ruthlessly than any ministers of the old monarchy would have dared to contemplate, though their labours tended in the same direction. He also intended to blend this history with a critique of the new order, especially as it was operating under Louis Napoleon, and with an explicit affirmation of his own political creed: his love of liberty as he understood it, and his fierce patriotism. Advanced historical scholarship was to be combined with political pamphleteering. Tocqueville meant these two aspects of his book to reinforce each other; it is necessary to ask if they did or did not do so.

As history, the *Ancien Régime* was undeniably a triumph. Tocqueville did not live to show the revolutionary assemblies at work, or to do more than allude to the crowning achievements of Napoleon; but he said quite enough to transform the historiography of the Revolution for good. He restored a sense of the continuity of French history, which is why the chief initial reaction of his first readers seems to have been surprise. They had for long assumed that the pre-revolutionary past had no relevance whatever to the nineteenth-century present. And it was not only Tocqueville's conclusions which mattered, as he was well aware. He paraded his research as an example of the right way to tackle modern history, as medieval history had already been triumphantly studied (can he have been thinking of Michelet?). In his attempt to depict France in the eighteenth century he was palpably influenced by the early chapters of Macaulay's *History of England*, a book which he read with relish in 1853, though he imitated neither Macaulay's parliamentary prolixity nor his confidence in progress (he thought, rather, that he was dealing with two immense historical disasters, the *ancien régime* and the Revolution). He was not the first French historian to plunge into modern archives: Thiers, for instance, boasted of having read 'and re-read' 30,000 letters by Napoleon, but he made a very different use of the material, as Tocqueville pointed out when discussing the *History of Consulate and Empire*: '[I] expected more from so good a speaker & so admirable a converser. It is too long & too detailed. What do we care whether the Duke of Dalmatia marched on a given point by one path or another?' Thiers was not a philosophic historian; he did not investigate the causes, 'intrinsic & extrinsic', which formed Napoleon. No-one could make such a criticism of Tocqueville on the Revolution; and his example has been followed ever since by those seriously investigating the subject.[9]

And as a tract the *Ancien Régime* was as successful, at least in France, as the *Démocratie* had been. It sold in what were large numbers for such a book; it was widely reviewed and heatedly discussed, as Françoise Mélonio has shown in her study, though she also seems to show that one of the reasons was that people had largely forgotten what the *Démocratie* said, so that the old message seemed new. Tocqueville was gratified: he began to hope that the French were stirring again: 'for a book so full of the desire for liberty as mine to be in such demand, that desire cannot be as dead as many believe and some hope.' Indeed, events up to 1871 were going to demonstrate the plausibility of Tocqueville's sketch of the volatile French national character, and the Third Republic was to establish a fairly liberal regime, though without ending *friponnerie* or generating much of the virtuous, manly spirit that Tocqueville had hoped for. After that he and his books gradually faded from view and from memory; and even today, after the great revival of interest in the late twentieth century, it is hard for anyone but the deeply committed to read the *Ancien Régime* for its political ideas. It seems to be largely a sermon for another day. But such is the fate of tracts.[10]

It is when the historical and the political themes are studied together that difficulties arise. Modern undergraduates reading history are constantly warned against the vice of 'presentism' – that is, of assuming that the past was just the same as the present, or supposing that the only interesting thing about ancestors is how they opened the way for their descendants. Tocqueville would have found that error hard to avoid in any circumstances, since his mission was to demonstrate the continuity of French history.

> In 1789 the French made the greatest effort ever undertaken by any nation to cut the thread of their destiny in two, as it were, and by a gulf to separate themselves as they had been from what they wanted to be henceforward ... I have always thought that they were much less successful in this unusual enterprise than has been believed abroad, and than at first they believed themselves.

In consequence he was always alert for evidence that the French had not greatly changed, and what we look for we tend to find. 'As I proceeded with these studies, I was astonished to recognize in the France of the period, at every turn, many traits familiar to our own time.'* Beyond that, it was perhaps inevitable that the attempt to combine a tract in favour of liberty with a monograph on the old order should breed historical error. His sketch of France, the revolutionary nation, since 1789, is scarcely history – it is a kind of meta-history. All too characteristically, Tocqueville assumes what he needs to demonstrate. *Liberté,*

---

* He might have cited the continuity of penal policy from the *ancien régime*, through the Revolution and into the nineteenth century to illustrate the point (see above, p. 228–29), but this did not occur to him.

égalité, fraternité: did the French ever consciously choose between them, as he asserts? They disliked the horrors of civil war, Parisian dictatorship, foreign invasion, famine and unemployment, and acted accordingly: but these are choices of a different kind. Tocqueville offered prophetic assertion rather than documented analysis; and if we are to take seriously the question of the temporary defeat of liberty in mid-nineteenth-century France we will, among other things, be obliged to make searching enquiry of Tocqueville and his like. Many ruinous political disputes (for instance, in the last years of Louis-Philippe) were touched off by rivalry among the *grands notables*, who showed so little interest in sharing power with those outside the magic circle, or indeed beyond their own particular coteries; and it was elite stupidity and selfishness, as much as any other cause, which wrecked the Second Republic and let in Louis Napoleon. As we have seen, Tocqueville himself was not quite blameless. It was not overlooked by many readers (certainly not by Bonapartists) that to some extent the *Ancien Régime* was the embittered utterance of a bad loser.[11]

And Tocqueville's main assertion was that centralization, the antithesis of free government, had been the achievement of the *ancien régime*; the Bourbons had thereby opened the road for the Committee of Public Safety and the Bonapartes (Louis-Philippe no longer figured very high on Tocqueville's list of villains). Over the centuries local liberties, and local capacity for liberty, independence and self-government, were steadily undermined and suppressed by Parisian authorities; royal despotism was so powerful a force that not only did it rob the French of any taste for liberty, it destroyed all the institutions and laws which constituted the social and political order, so that when it weakened the state collapsed immediately into revolution; in some respects the activities of the royal government could even themselves be called revolutionary, so destructive were they; and yet, when the dust settled, the *ancien régime* could be seen to have reconstituted itself in splendour, and not only because of Napoleon Bonaparte. It was the only sort of government which the French were fit for. Such is what Sudhir Hazareesingh has recently called 'the Tocquevillian Myth', and he vigorously repudiates its validity for France in the later nineteenth century, whether under the Second Empire or the Third Republic, insisting that recent research has demonstrated 'the energetic and creative nature of local civic life before 1880, whether in terms of village and communal politics; peasant politicization; municipal theory and practice; political socialization through religion; associational activity; and the reconstruction of local memory and local heritages'. For the eighteenth century Peter Jones has established that the government of the old monarchy 'was less a centralising than a bureaucraticising force'; that the towns and villages of rural France enjoyed considerable autonomy until deep into the Revolution; that it was the Jacobins and Napoleon who established the rigid centralized administration which Tocqueville deplored. Tocqueville, it may be argued, mistook the fatal flaw of the *ancien régime*. It was not despotism but inefficiency.[12]

If this judgement is correct, it suggests a crushing verdict: perhaps the *Ancien Régime* is obsolete. Yet that does not seem fair, or even plausible. For some reason readers in the twenty-first century still concern themselves with Tocqueville's little book. What is that reason?

Something must be allowed for the abiding allure of his subject. So long as Western civilization values the study of the past (and there are few signs that it is ceasing to do so), the French Revolution will be read and written about, for its drama, its complexity, for the moral and political passions which it embodies. It was one of the greatest events, or series of events, in history, and so long as this is understood it will be strenuously debated. Tocqueville's voice makes itself heard in that debate, whatever his factual blunders, because his point of view was that of an extremely intelligent, well-informed and passionately concerned observer; indeed, a participant, if we accept his view that the Revolution continued throughout his lifetime. He is himself, as it were, one of the consequences of the Revolution, and should be studied as such. Besides, nineteenth-century France is worth studying in its own right, and to understand it, it is necessary to understand Tocqueville, and to understand Tocqueville it is necessary to understand all his works, including the *Ancien Régime*. So much seems incontestable.

But as Tocqueville's biographer I am forced to believe that the secret of the *Ancien Régime*'s continuing vitality lies in the fascination of Tocqueville himself, even if the old observation that every book is a concealed autobiography is rejected. If we also set aside academic rules and consider the *Ancien Régime* solely as a work of literature by a great author then the things which professors object to (I am one myself) can be seen for what, essentially, they are: simply features of the landscape, characteristics that contribute to a reader's interest and pleasure, traits that reveal the man himself, in all his weakness and strength. And a man like Tocqueville enlarges our sense of human possibility and of the meaning of human lives in everything he writes. He does this through his intellectual and artistic gifts, and through his passionate sincerity. So the accuracy of his conclusions is of limited importance, so long as he is not wilfully perverse, which Tocqueville never was. Let us attempt a reading of the *Ancien Régime* in this light.

Tocqueville's ambition for the success of his book was intense: he wrote to his father in November 1855: 'I passionately desire to finish my great work; I hope God will allow me to do so.' To him, the *Ancien Régime* was primarily a political work, a blow struck for liberty, and in due course he was to express surprise that his English reviewers did not discuss it as such – Albion letting him down again. He wanted, above all, to appeal to the common reader: for this reason he refused to include any documentary footnotes (to the irritation of historians to this day), quoted from his masses of material as sparingly as possible in his main text, and was often quite unspecific in his allusions to 'an intendant', 'a marquis', and so on. It was almost as if he preferred to fire off blanks rather than bullets. Scholarly considerations must take second place to evangelizing.[13]

Not that he disavowed his labours of research: he was proud of them, and indeed, as Robert Gannett has shown, exaggerated them.[14] It is usually a safe maxim that nothing is ever done for the first time, but Tocqueville's research into the archives of the old order and the interpretation which he put on his results really do seem to have been unprecedented.* Driven, as we have seen, by his own enquiring mind and the questions that it raised, and assisted at the crucial moment by Grandmaison, he had discovered the enormous value of administrative records for understanding pre-revolutionary France and the Revolution itself. It was a great achievement, but the cause of liberty was what mattered.

---

* Rémusat scrupulously examined this very point in his review of the *Ancien Régime* in the *Revue des deux mondes*, 1 August 1856.

This priority will come as no surprise to readers of Tocqueville's letters. He had wavered, ever since the *coup d'état*, between hope and fear for the future of France. Understandably he exaggerated the extent of Louis Napoleon's tyranny; he felt horribly isolated in his views; but surely liberty might yet revive? He launched his blow.

> Is any man born with a soul so base as to prefer to depend on the whims of someone like himself rather than to obey laws which he has helped to establish, if his nation appears to have the virtue necessary to make a right use of liberty? I believe that there are certainly none. Despots themselves do not deny the excellence of liberty; only they want to keep it all to themselves. They do not think that anyone else is entirely worthy of it.[15]

Here, as in his occasional barbed references to the Emperor Augustus, a nephew of an uncle, Tocqueville is commenting severely on Napoleon III in a way to which no censor could object (though it would not have saved him under Napoleon I, who exiled Mme de Staël and silenced Chateaubriand). In the Foreword and in his concluding chapter he put forward his view that in 1789 the French wanted both liberty and equality, but under the pressure of events had had to choose between them, and chose equality, as they did again and again afterwards. Tocqueville exerted himself to persuade the French that they had been wrong: only liberty, he says, can effectively fight the vices of egalitarian societies, where nothing matters but money:

> Democratic societies which are not free ones can be rich, refined, cultivated, even magnificent, powerful from the mere weight of their homogeneous mass; one can find there much private merit – good family men, honest businessmen, most worthy landowners; one will even find good Christians, for the fatherland of such is not in this world and the glory of their religion is to breed them amidst the greatest corruption of manners and under the worst of governments: the Roman Empire in extreme decadence was full of them; but what one will never see in such societies, I dare to assert, are great citizens, nor, above all, a great people, and I am not afraid to affirm that the general level of hearts and minds will never cease to decline while equality and despotism are partners.[16]

So much for the Second Empire. Tocqueville does not entirely despair of his countrymen: 'On several occasions since the beginning of the Revolution, right up to the present, we have seen the passion for liberty die out, then be born again, then again die out, and again be born; so it will be for a long time yet,' while the passion for equality will never flag. But the French nation is so extraordinary, more extraordinary than the events of its history, so full of contradictions that it is impossible to know what it will do next:

> disobedient by nature, and yet adjusting better to the arbitrary, even violent rule of a prince than to the free and lawful government of its leading citizens; today the declared enemy of all obedience, tomorrow abandoning itself to slavery with an enthusiasm that nations better endowed for the condition can never attain; led by a thread when no-one resists, ungovernable as soon as someone gives the example of resistance; fooling, therefore, all its masters, who fear it either too much or too little; never so free that one need despair of enslaving it, never so enslaved that it cannot break its yoke ...

This is perhaps the most sustained piece of rhetoric in all Tocqueville's writings (it is part of the sentence which Kergorlay admired so much) and is perhaps best read and enjoyed as such; but at the time it was written it was meant as a signal of hope; as a rallying-cry.[17]

What are we to make of all this? Perhaps we should begin by registering the striking similarity, even identity, of thought and language, in detail and in general, between the *Ancien Régime* and *De la démocratie en Amérique*. Sometimes similarity verges on self-plagiarism: 'I admit that in studying our old society in all its parts I have never entirely lost sight of the new one.'* Tocqueville himself was well aware of the likeness, and drew attention to it in the Foreword, where he found it necessary to recapitulate the vision of the course of French and European history that he had set out in the Introduction to the *Démocratie* in 1835. He claimed, accurately, to have been consistent over twenty years, which is all the more striking when we learn that he had been neurotically unable to re-read the *Démocratie*, even to make necessary revisions, since its first appearance.[18]

---

* OC II i 75; cf. OC I i 12: 'I admit that in America I have seen more than America; I have sought there the image of democracy itself ...'

There are some notable changes. Whereas the emphasis in the *Démocratie* was on equality, in the *Ancien Régime*, as must already be clear, it is upon liberty. This is unsurprising: by 1856 Tocqueville had behind him a long experience of what it meant to be deprived of it. He does not exactly explain what he means by liberty; as usual, he assumes that his readers know what he is talking about, and as a matter of fact they do, or should do: he means the liberty under law which he had expounded and defended in the *Démocratie*, the *Souvenirs*, and a dozen other places. He is still an elitist, believing in the superior wisdom of 'leading citizens', and we know from other documents that he has despaired of universal suffrage, which Louis Napoleon, the democratic despot, found so useful; his ideology has changed very little since his youth. As in 1835 and 1840 we can see what he wanted and why he wanted it, and need not deny him our sympathy.

Yet there is one especially important difference. In 1835 the tone is buoyant; democracy is on the march, young Tocqueville is not afraid of the future or especially enamoured of the past. In the *Ancien Régime* his mood is quite other:

> Already, among the shadows of our future, we can see three very clear truths. The first is that all the men of our time are caught up by an unknown power which they may hope to regulate or moderate, but not to overcome, which gently but speedily drives them towards the destruction of aristocracy; the second, that of all human societies those which will have the greatest difficulty in escaping absolute government for long will be, precisely, those in which aristocracy is no more and cannot be revived; the third and last is that nowhere can despotism produce more pernicious effects than in such societies.

This is a preoccupation which we can also find in Tocqueville's letters and conversations at this period: 'the loss of our aristocracy is a misfortune from which we have not even begun to recover,' he told Nassau Senior in 1854. It recurs throughout the *Ancien Régime*. In the *Démocratie* he had not regarded the consequences of the nobility's fall so gloomily, although 'aristocracy' was discussed at great length.* But by 1856 M. de Tocqueville took no pleasure in democracy, and surrendered to historical nostalgia.[19]

---

* See above, pp. 349–51.

Nostalgia for what, exactly? What did he mean by 'the loss of our aristocracy'? These are questions which have to be answered at several different levels, and they bring us to the heart of the matter.

By 1856 the *noblesse* had long since recovered from the demographic and economic shocks of the renunciation of privilege, the emigration, and the Reign of Terror. As Tocqueville's own career amply demonstrates, nobles were still conspicuous in politics, business, society and the life of the mind. He can hardly have been regretting feudal privilege (which he condemned mercilessly in the *Ancien Régime*), or the Assembly of Notables of 1787, or the Chamber of Peers which was destroyed in 1848. It is true that by their own folly (as well as that of Charles X) the legitimists had lost national political power in 1830, but as Tocqueville knew perfectly well they had retained much of their influence in the countryside (he had done so himself), and anyway not all nobles were legitimists (as, again, he himself proved). Furthermore, if the word 'aristocracy' is taken to mean government by the rich, well-educated and well-born, without regard to antique snobberies, France was thoroughly subordinated to such an elite until long after Tocqueville's time (even, some would say, up to the present). If, as is most likely, he was referring to the *ancien régime* itself, he must have meant a period before the seventeenth century, for he always insisted that it was Richelieu and Louis XIV who broke the power of the *noblesse*; but it is hard to see what there is to regret in the *noblesse* of the Fronde and the Wars of Religion.

Like so much else in the *Ancien Régime*, Tocqueville's mythmaking went back to the *Démocratie*. Had he not said in its Introduction: 'When royal power, supported by aristocracy, peaceably governed the peoples of Europe, society, in the midst of its distresses, enjoyed several types of happiness which it is difficult to imagine or value nowadays'? He also remembered Montesquieu, who in the *Esprit des lois* had insisted on the importance of 'intermediate bodies' to make a true monarchy: he was thinking chiefly of the French *parlements*, of which he was by birth an ornament, but also of the *noblesse* generally and of the clergy. Their function was to protect law and liberty, without which monarchy was mere despotism: 'no monarch, no nobility; no nobility, no monarch.' As we may remember, Tocqueville in his youth had hoped that the Restoration's Chamber of Peers would become such an intermediate body, and had an idealized view of the House of Lords.* His great ancestor, Malesherbes, had used the very language of Montesquieu when remonstrating to Louis XV in 1770: Frenchmen, he said, were not slaves, but all the intermediate bodies were either powerless or abolished, there was only one counsellor left, the nation itself.† Like Malesherbes, *le président* Rosanbo, Tocqueville's grand-father, had honoured the *parlements* as the vanguard of resistance to royal tyranny. Tocqueville wrote full in the tradition of his mother's family (the tradition of the Tocquevilles, nobles of the sword, was as we have seen somewhat different). Above all, however, Tocqueville in the *Ancien Régime* was determined to make the case for liberty against the Second Empire, and eighteenth-century polemics, which on the one hand constantly scrutinized the Bourbon monarchy for signs of despotism, and on the other championed the *parlements*, made it easy for him. He did not test his assumptions so rigorously as a historian should. It was just too convenient to use poor Louis XVI as a stand-in for Napoleon III, even though Tocqueville knew, indeed insisted, that Louis was a reforming king ('that good and unlucky prince').[20] Besides, his reforms only made things worse.

Similar considerations explain the onslaught on centralization in Book Two. It was an ancient theme: it had been an issue in 1789, it had then been a favourite grievance of the legitimists, and had figured conspicuously in the *Démocratie*. But in the *Ancien Régime* Tocqueville handled it with an eloquent ferocity that made the subject his own for ever. There can be no doubt of his passionate sincerity, but as we have seen already the case he makes is not a scholarly one. It is political. As with the *parlements*, he was not really concerned to be judicious and fair. He does not condescend to answer such arguments as Thiers made to Nassau Senior in 1853‡; he was so hostile to centralization that he refused to grant even rationality, let alone good intentions, to the royal government. He makes absolutely no allowances for the kings. All of them, according to him, from Philippe le Bel to Louis XV, laboured to extend their power over the French, apparently for

---

* See above, pp. 82, 243–4.
† AT does not mention Malesherbes in the *Ancien Régime*, but he quoted this passage in his article on the *ancien régime* in 1836: see OC II ii 63–4.
‡ See above, p. 455.

no reason except egotistical satisfaction. No king or minister is given credit for statesmanship, patriotism, prudence, vision or common sense; no room is found to mention any crises which they might have had to meet, such as foreign invasion, famine, insurrection or civil war. Tocqueville could not avoid mentioning, eventually, the deficit and bankruptcy which brought on the final crisis of the old order (though he did so only in passing), but nowhere did he consider what seems an obvious point, that it was France's aspirations to international preponderance, at least as much as anything else, that fatally overstrained the regime: Choiseul rebuilt the navy, Vergennes plunged the country into the War of American Independence, Louis XVI sank a fortune (almost literally) into building a naval base at Cherbourg, and all these policies were popular.* Tocqueville gave the forty kings no credit for creating France. Only Louis XVI got a kind word, because of his reforming zeal.[21] No admissions were to be made of which Louis Napoleon might take advantage. The 'Tocquevillian Myth' was in part a response to the Bonapartist dictatorship. Tocqueville hoped to rally opinion in resistance, and in preparation for whatever regime succeeded (he had no faith in Louis Napoleon's durability). It cannot be said that his attitude was soundly historical; but it had the strongest possible foundations in the political experience of his entire life.

He was not the only man of his time to believe the myth, and he did not even make it up; but he believed it religiously, because, as a historian and political writer, he had in the end only one subject, announced in the opening pages of the *Démocratie* as the advance of equality, but really the fall of the *noblesse*. That this should preoccupy him is not surprising: it preoccupied many of his politically active fellow nobles, and indeed may be said to have preoccupied their opponents, who wanted to secure their own victory. The slightly obsessive quality of Tocqueville's concern reflected his character; he brought passion and commitment to whatever he undertook. The *ancien régime*, then, seems his preordained topic, so much so that it seems likely that his gradual turn from Napoleon to the Revolution, and from the Revolution to the eighteenth century, was driven not only by what François Furet calls 'the logic of all histori-

---

* In his introduction to the *Ancien Régime* Georges Lefebvre gently rebuked AT by remarking that for a historian and sociologist 'not to have taken sufficient account of war in the experience of the French is a surprising lacuna' (OC II i 30).

cal work, which is to proceed backward in time in search of origins',[22] and by the incidents of research, but by a deep impulse of which he was not at first conscious himself. He was one of a defeated class, and could not forget or pardon the defeat. He yearned for his birthright, by which, he felt, he was entitled to be part of the government of France. He had never thought much of equality as a principle; since the 1848 Revolution he could see nothing in it but the instinct of envy, as he told Senior as early as 1850: 'it is a wish that no one should be better off than oneself.' The Revolution of 1789 destroyed the regime of privilege,

> But it could not destroy the social distinctions which depend upon manners. It could not enable the bourgeois to feel himself the equal of the *gentilhomme*. It could not deprive the noble of his superior manners, of his self-confidence, of the respect paid to his birth, or of many other advantages incident to his position. These things excite the envy of the bourgeois ... The great majority of the French consists of course of the low-born & the poor and the *égalité* which they fight for is the destruction of the advantages of birth & wealth.[23]

The French Revolution was many things, but all too clearly it had come to interest Tocqueville mainly, at times even exclusively, because it was a convulsion in which the ancient *noblesse* was broken, swept aside and replaced by a new ruling elite. Tocqueville's family had maintained a solid footing in the new world, and he himself had done better than that; his reason and conscience suggested to him that in most ways democracy was an improvement on aristocracy; but he could never get over a sort of heartache for what had been lost.

When we recollect the *Démocratie* Tocqueville's observations to Senior seem to show a sad narrowing and impoverishment of thought. His opinion that envy lay at the bottom of the challenge to the *noblesse* can be discerned in the *Ancien Régime*; but his hankering for what had been, or might have been, expressed itself there not only in the very structure and argument of the book, but in some revealing details. For instance, one of his set-pieces is an evocation of the time when all went well in France between the orders. They collaborated, he alleged, in administering the country and in resisting royal encroachments:

So we see, in Auvergne, the three Orders passing most important laws in common and arranging for their execution under the supervision of commissioners chosen from each of them. The same thing happened at the same period in Champagne. Everyone has heard of the celebrated pact by which the nobles and *bourgeois* of a large number of towns came together, at the beginning of the same [fourteenth] century, to defend the liberties of the nation and the privileges of the provinces against royal encroachment. At that moment in our history several episodes occurred which might have happened in England. Nothing like them was to occur in the following centuries.[24]

The Golden Age is always in the past, but Tocqueville was fortunate in being able to give a date to it: scientific history has never been able to do so. Utopia is similarly elusive, yet Tocqueville discerned it across the Channel. The allusion to England in the passage just quoted was not fortuitous. There, Tocqueville argued earlier in the same chapter, was a country where the feudal nobility had evolved, not into a selfish caste, but into a true aristocracy, which still governed the country. 'Nobles and commoners there co-operated in business, entered the same professions and, which is most significant of all, married into each others' families. Daughters of the greatest lords could marry new men without shame ...'[25] The typology is familiar: it had informed his visits to England twenty years previously, and he saw no reason to change it.

It might be supposed that this medley of fiction and wishful thinking would inexorably lead to a work of bad history. The extraordinary thing is that in *Ancien Régime* it did not do so. Perhaps the reason was that Tocqueville had spent his entire intellectual and political career in the struggle to accept and build upon the work of the Revolution; and he was too intelligent and too honest intellectually to surrender to his prejudices. It may even be argued that his hatred of what had happened to France gave him his framework for interpreting it. He could argue for the essential continuity of French history in the eighteenth and nineteenth centuries, over the gulf of the Revolution, because for him the break had come much earlier, when the monarchy disempowered the *noblesse* and crushed local liberties. This liberated him to analyse the old order for the worm-eaten relic that it was, and show the inexorability of the Revolution's coming. As I have already remarked, his account was not complete, but it was extensive, powerful, and convincing: the work of a great historian.

His account of the peasantry under the old order has always been much admired, and owed a great deal to his experience as a landowner and politician in the Cotentin. It was not only as a joke that he once described himself on a census form as a 'writer and peasant'. He lived among the farmers of Normandy as neighbour, landlord and (for many years) as deputy, and knew them intimately. He shared their concerns, but he never became one of them. He was their friend, but judged them dispassionately and acutely. When, therefore, he met them (or rather their ancestors) in the records of the *ancien régime* he instantly recognized them, and was able to write about them persuasively. He used their hopes and difficulties as the perfect means for conveying just what was wrong with the old order. After listing the oppressive feudal dues to which the *noblesse* and the laws subjected the peasantry, he goes on:

> Please picture to yourself the peasant of the eighteenth century, or rather, the one you know today, for he is always the same: his status has changed, but not his outlook. See him as the documents which I have cited depict him, so passionately in love with the land that he devotes all his savings to buying it and buys it at any price. Yet to acquire it he must first pay a fee, not to the government, but to other landowners of the neighbourhood, strangers as much as he is himself to the conduct of public business, and almost as powerless. At last he gets possession of it; he plants it with his heart as well as his corn. This little corner of earth which in all the vast world is his very own fills his spirit with pride and independence. Then those same neighbours descend on him to drag him from his fields and make him work somewhere else for nothing. If he wants to protect his crops against their deer, the same people prevent him; and they wait for him at the river-crossing to exact a toll. He meets them again at the market-place, where they sell him the right to sell his own produce; and when, home again, he wants to use the rest of his corn, that corn which he has watched and tended himself, he cannot do so until he has sent it for grinding to the mill and to be baked in the oven of these same men. Part of the income from his little estate goes to pay rent, a rent which is never resigned and cannot be bought out.[26]

Great historians do not just record or explain the past; they awaken it, and their readers. This passage shows how Tocqueville was equal to the challenge, as can also be demonstrated by comparing his book with almost any recent study of merit on the same subject. For one example (taken not quite at random): William Doyle's *Oxford History of the French Revolution* opens with a chapter, 'France under Louis XVI', which covers exactly the same ground as the *Ancien Régime*. Readers of the older book will feel at home at once, which in itself says a lot for Tocqueville. But there are great differences between the two texts, and at first sight they seem all in Professor Doyle's favour. His picture of the old order is in every respect fuller, more detailed and more nuanced than Tocqueville's, and on the whole is even more damning; still more impressive is the depth of learning which underlies every paragraph. Doyle draws on a century and a half of research into his subject, as well as his own investigations; furthermore, the premises from which historians now go to work on such a topic have shifted irreversibly. Doyle starts his chapter with geographical description and economic analysis; it would scarcely occur to him, or to anyone else nowadays, to do otherwise. Some may see in this an example of the long reach of Karl Marx's historical materialism, but the influence of Fernand Braudel and his school is probably much greater. There are limits to what can be done in forty pages, but within that restriction Doyle has come close to achieving total history in a fashion that Tocqueville could never have conceived: in his time the work had simply not yet been done, the theories not yet propounded; he himself was a pioneer in both respects. For those who need up-to-date history (students with exams to sit, above all) there can be no contest: Doyle is the man.

Yet it can be argued that Tocqueville and Doyle complement each other. Both are well aware of the absolutely central importance of the peasantry to any account of the *ancien régime* (they made up 80 per cent of the French population). Both understand the misery in which most peasants lived, though Tocqueville, characteristically, attributes it above all to bad laws and customs, whereas Doyle displays a wider range of factors, beginning with the rapid growth of population that was outstripping available resources. Both describe a rural society that was on the brink of collapse. Doyle is more scientific, but it is Tocqueville who makes the reader care.[27]

He is particularly good on the ways in which the government and the privileged classes unjustly burdened the unprivileged:

I have handled many of the militia rolls for a large number of parishes drawn up in 1789; I could see who were exempt from the draw in each one of them: here a gentleman's domestic, there the porter of an abbey; a third is only the valet of a *bourgeois*, it is true, but that *bourgeois* 'lives nobly'.* Only prosperity brings exemption; when a farmer appears annually on the list of a parish's most highly taxed inhabitants, his sons have the privilege of being exempt from the militia; allegedly, for the encouragement of agriculture. The Economists,† strong supporters of equality in everything else, are not at all shocked by this privilege; they merely suggest that it be extended to other deserving classes, that is to say, that the burden of the poorest and most friendless peasants become even heavier. 'The pitiful pay of the soldier,' says one of them, 'and the manner in which he is bedded, clothed, fed, his entire subordination to military discipline, would make it too cruel to recruit any but men from the lowest levels of the people.'

Tocqueville does his utmost to list all the sufferings of the country people under the *ancien régime*, so that their ultimate rebellion may be fully comprehensible; although, admittedly, he changes his tune when he refers to the actual uprising of 1789. Then the peasants are denounced for their cupidity, envy and hatred.[28]

Yet after reading such passages we too feel like revolutionaries; Tocqueville has made himself the voice of the countryside; when we read him we come close to the revolutionary mentality of 1789; we understand the Great Fear, not in its illusions about bandits and an aristocratic plot, but in its sense that an opportunity had come which must be seized: an opportunity to break an intolerable system of social oppression, the one so carefully described by Tocqueville. He works on our emotions, as Doyle does not.

Similar points might be made about other passages in the *Ancien Régime*, all amounting to this, that here we have the living stuff of history. Using the archives, Tocqueville, with steely precision, shows how the monstrous machine of the French state in its ceaseless search for revenue, weighed ever more heavily on the poorer elements in society without succeeding in any large enterprise: the French were plunged into servitude, but nobody profited. The demonstration is so

---

* A term of art, meaning that one was rich enough (whatever one's other disqualifications) to aspire to join the *noblesse*.

† Better known nowadays as the Physiocrats; writers frequently criticized by AT.

unlike most of Tocqueville's other writing that some additional explanation, beyond research, literary genius and a home in the country, seems called for. Perhaps it is worth recollecting that Tocqueville had travelled in Sicily and Ireland; he may even have been influenced by memories of rural poverty in Wiltshire in 1833. However it was, he wrote for once from the point of view of the disadvantaged, not that of the 'enlightened classes'.

His sociology of the old order has many flaws. He almost entirely overlooks the rural poor, the throngs of beggars and landless labourers. In spite of his interest in religion and his insistence that the Revolution was a quasi-religious movement, resembling the Reformation, he has little to say about the First Estate, the Church, although its importance as part of the *ancien régime* and as an issue in the Revolution can hardly be overstated: he mentions its role as an oppressor of the peasantry through feudal dues, and not much else. He has little to say about the artisan class, and not much about the middle class, in spite of their gigantic part in the Revolution (this reflects that disdain for the *bourgeoisie* which was such an unhappy aspect of his character). Surprisingly, his description of the *noblesse* is inferior to that in his 1836 article. The nobility was the only category of Frenchmen, peasants apart, which Tocqueville really knew and understood. Perhaps he knew it too well, and did not feel the need to research it (he appears to have made no use of the family archives to which he had access – the Tocqueville, Rosanbo and Chateaubriand papers). He makes too many rash generalizations: for instance, that as a body the nobles were getting poorer.[29] He has plenty to say about them, but the total effect is curiously vague: they never come to life as individuals as, for all his hostility, the *intendants* whom he quotes so plentifully do.[30]

These failings are regrettable, but were more or less unavoidable in a pioneering work. Much more important is the success of his grand design. In Book Two he establishes what may be called his frame of reference, showing clearly, eloquently and knowledgeably the *ancien régime* in all its complications of oppression and obsolescence. Then in Book Three he turns explicitly from the ultimate causes of the Revolution to its occasions, to the circumstances and events which settled its time and place of outbreak, and its character.[31] In Book Three's first seven chapters he lists these secondary causes: the influence of the politically inexperienced writers of the French Enlightenment; the unforeseen consequences of the growth of national prosperity and of the royal government's constant meddling with the laws and adminis-tration of France; and so on. It is easy enough to make such lists and not especially difficult to settle their relative importance, at least to the writer's satisfaction; but Tocqueville's genius was to convey the way in which they operated together, so that the reader can share the helpless bewilderment of the citizens which by 1788 at latest had made the Revolution unavoidable, for a government which is collapsing uncon-trollably has to be replaced. One of the themes which Tocqueville emphasizes and re-emphasizes is that having had no experience of free politics, or indeed of politics at all, the French had neither the knowledge nor the prudence which might have enabled them to avoid catastrophe. Here he was bringing his own political experience to bear, and it is interesting to see that among the necessary free institutions which the French lacked he lists at last well-led and organized political parties.[32] His experience also makes itself felt in the eighth chapter, when he summarizes the argument of his book, stresses the importance of the *ancien régime* to our understanding both of the Revolution and of nineteenth-century France, and sketches the country's post-1789 history. His conclusion is mournful:

> The Old Order had effectively incorporated a whole ensemble of modern institutions, recently set up, which, being in no way hostile to equality, could easily take their place in the new society, while yet offering conspicuous facilities to despotism. They were excavated from the ruins of all the other institutions, and re-established. They had formerly given birth to habits, passions and ideas which tended to make men docile and divided; now they were revived and exploited. Centralization too was restored from its ruin; and as, at the same time that it was rebuilt, everything which formerly could have limited it was left demolished, we saw emerge, as it were from the very guts of a nation that had just overthrown its royalty a sudden new power that was more extensive, more intrusive, more absolute than any ever exercised by our kings ... The dictator fell, but all that was most solid in his work remained standing; his government died, his administra-tion lived, and whenever since then oppression has been attacked, the attackers have settled for putting a head of Liberty on servile shoulders.[33]

But Tocqueville did not quite despair: in the great tirade on the character of the French which I have already quoted he plainly warned Napoleon III not to take their submission for granted, and elsewhere in the book he praised liberty for its moral and practical value in language whose very eloquence shows that he did not despair of carrying conviction: men who value liberty only for its material benefits, he said, never keep it long.

> In every epoch that which has so so strongly bound the hearts of certain men to it has been its own attraction, its own charm, independent of its material benefits; it is the pleasure of being able to speak, act and breathe without constraint, under the government of God and the laws alone. All who seek to gain from liberty something other than itself are born to be slaves.[34]

At moments like this Tocqueville speaks to every age.

But as a historian (to the degree that his roles can be distinguished) his message is somewhat more complex, and is summed up in this, the last chapter of his book, as it was stated on his opening page. In 1789 the French tried to make a clean sweep of their past, and to found a new state and society shaped solely by their sense of what was right and rational. Tocqueville's message, which makes itself urgently felt as he nears his conclusion, is that this was not done, because it was impossible; and he might well congratulate himself for having stated it convincingly. His task was not quite complete: it would next be necessary to write a study of the Revolution and of Napoleon to show how the old order was resurrected, and how the twin desires for equality and freedom shaped the new society. In his closing sentences he demonstrated that he knew this very well:

> So here I am come to the threshold of that memorable revolution; I will not cross it just yet: soon, perhaps, I will be able to do so. If so, I will no longer be considering its causes, I will be studying the thing in itself, and I will dare to judge the society which came out of it.[35]

Surely these are the words of a man in complete command of his talent and of his ideas.

Yet when he got to Paris he discovered that there was still much work to be done. First he had to find a publisher. He was helped by Ampère's friend and colleague Louis de Loménie,* who introduced him to Michel Lévy, a publisher much patronized by liberals under the Second Empire (Ampère made use of him). On 16 February Tocqueville signed a contract,[36] and immediately began to worry about the book's title. Ampère suggested *Causes of the Revolution*, which would have plainly indicated Tocqueville's main theme and have hinted at the possibility of further volumes on the course of the Revolution and its consequences. He liked Tocqueville's proposed *La Révolution* as a title for the whole work, commenting approvingly, 'you are going to write the philosophical history of the Revolution.' Lévy wanted to call the book *La Révolution Française*, which Tocqueville was half-inclined to agree to: as a title it was imprecise and hardly new, but then it was also short and unpretentious. Beaumont had nothing better to offer, but Reeve, who was now in constant correspondence with Tocqueville about the English translation, thought that the title ought to indicate more precisely what the book was actually about – 'the *sources* of the Revolution'. There, indeed, was the difficulty. Tocqueville had never wanted to publish a study of the *ancien régime* for its own sake, and as we have seen, Book One, as conceived and published, reads like the opening of a work quite different from that in which it actually appeared. But the fact had to be faced: not only had Tocqueville written a book on the *ancien régime* and how it had precipi-tated the Revolution, he had done so in a startlingly new fashion: that was its interest and its merit. So someone (can it have been Marie, who returned to Paris late in February?) suggested a title, *L'Ancien Régime et la Révolution française*, which the publisher liked. So did Mignet (himself a historian of the Revolution) but Beaumont and Rivet did not. Tocqueville would have dithered still, but meanwhile Lévy began to advertise the book under the new title.† Tocqueville accepted the

---

* Louis de Loménie (1815–78) was related to Loménie de Brienne, one of the last prime ministers of the *ancien régime*, and was married to a great-niece of Mme Récamier. He was Ampère's successor at the Collège de France, a student of the eighteenth century and a biographer of Beaumarchais and Mirabeau. No doubt Ampère advised AT to seek him out. In 1859 he was to publish, in the *Revue des deux mondes*, one of the best of all the obituary tributes to Tocqueville.

† At some stage the word *française* was dropped, probably by AT, who always thought of the

fait accompli, which did have the merit of naming the book's two chief concerns. The discussion had lasted the best part of a month.[37]

Long before then Tocqueville had delivered the manuscript to Lévy, whose printers promptly rejected it as illegible. It had to be re-copied, we are not told by whom (again, perhaps, Marie), and while that was happening Tocqueville rewrote chapter 10 of Book Two ('How the Destruction of Political Liberty and the Separation between the Classes Caused Almost All the Diseases of Which the Old Order Died'). He also began to multiply the endnotes.

He had always had a weakness for appendices, large and small, from the *Système pénitentiaire* onwards, but now his pen ran away with him. In the *Oeuvres complètes* the main text of the *Ancien Régime* runs to 162 pages, the appendix on the government of Languedoc, as an example of a *pays d'état*, to five; the notes (in markedly smaller type) to fifty-six. Only Book Two is substantially longer (ninety-one pages) and it would be far less impressive without its annotation. The notes, in fact, are an essential part of the book, which can only be appraised properly if they are taken into account. All of them are weighty, and some (the Languedoc appendix, for example, and the analysis of the *cahiers* of the nobility) are long essays.

Undoubtedly, with better planning or exhaustive revision much of the material in these notes could have been incorporated in the body of the text; but even if Tocqueville now felt that he had pruned his chapters too much he was understandably unwilling to rewrite them yet again, and anyway there was his commitment to Lévy to consider. Many of the notes were too substantial to have been incorporated in any circumstances. It hardly mattered. Tocqueville was not writing a textbook; the notes as they stand are a further expression of their author's mind and taste, thereby adding to the book's attraction.

It was a different matter with the Foreword. Tocqueville, once printing was under way, gave a set of proofs to Loménie. Loménie made one devastating criticism: Tocqueville had said too little about liberty in his account of the old order and the Revolution.

> ... one might suppose from his book that he allotted little significance
> to the spirit of liberty in the revolution, although he must have been

Revolution as a European phenomenon, like the old order which it destroyed.

aware that the constitution of '91, the direct expression of the spirit of 1789, was as liberal as it was democratic, even that it was too liberal, for, in excessively weakening the powers of the executive, it broke too sharply with the already ancient habits of centralization, which he had been the first to discern and describe so well.

Tocqueville took this criticism nobly. He said that he was going to deal with 'the spirit of '89' in his next volume, but Loménie objected ('not supposing, alas, that his prediction would be so correct') that it was impossible to say when that volume would appear, and meanwhile Tocqueville's comparative silence about liberty might mislead, especially as he said so much about equality. He might at least put something about his further plans in the Foreword; indeed, said Loménie, warming to his task, the Foreword as it stood was too short and dry: 'if many people never read prefaces, equally there were many who read nothing else, especially when the book was a very serious one.' Tocqueville was much upset by these remarks, but after he had left Loménie he decided that they were just, and rewrote not only the Foreword but the Conclusion; so it is to Loménie that we owe some of the *Ancien Régime*'s most eloquent pages. Loménie himself thought them splendid, but was even more impressed by his friend's modesty and sincerity.[38]

Three weeks after Tocqueville arrived there, the Congress which was formally to end the Crimean War met in Paris. He paid little attention. He did not believe that this was the last of Louis Napoleon's wars, and made one of those remarks which sometimes sharply remind us that he was a nineteenth-century French nationalist: Russia, he thought, would be humiliated rather than enfeebled, whatever terms she had to accept, and was still a danger; 'I firmly believe that a third campaign would have left her in a far weaker state.' But it was his own campaign which preoccupied him. Nassau Senior arrived in Paris on 7 May, and ten days later complained that Tocqueville had been scarcely visible; but they had dined together on the 17th. 'Tocqueville is full of his book, which is to appear in about a week.* His days and nights are devoted to correcting the proofs and to writing notes, which he

---

* In fact, the book did not appear for a month.

thought would be trifling, but which grow in length and importance.' His spirits were uncertain that spring. Before leaving Normandy he told Mme Swetchine that his intellectual isolation from most of his contemporaries might injure the chances of the book, 'for long experience has taught me that a book's success comes much more from the thoughts that a reader brings to it than from those which the writer expresses.' Arrived in Paris, he missed Marie acutely, which, coupled with anxiety, gave him at least one sleepless night: 'You will understand that my head was full of black thoughts during this insomnia, and how much I wanted you there to comfort me ... I told myself that the ideas in my book were such as to please nobody; that the legitimists would only find there a terribly severe picture of the *ancien régime* and royalty; the devout, such as Corcelle, little sympathy for the Church; the revolutionaries, little liking for the fustian of the Revolution.' The proofs, when they came, tormented him; but he sent a set, in batches, to Beaumont as well as to Loménie, which, Beaumont and Clémentine being as always delighted with what they read, was chiefly good for his morale. That was not the end of Beaumont's usefulness. At Tocqueville's suggestion he wrote an article praising the *Ancien Régime* (a puff preliminary) which, after Tocqueville revised it ('Your friendship said things about me which I really could not allow') was published in the *Journal des débats* over the editor's signature.[39]

June arrived and publication day was imminent. Then came an urgent message: Hervé de Tocqueville was dying at Clairoix. Alexis left Paris at once.

CHAPTER TWENTY-THREE

RETREATING
1856–1858

Je crois qu'on peut se perfectionner toute sa vie. *
ALEXIS DE TOCQUEVILLE, 1856[1]

COMTE HERVÉ'S STRENGTH had been failing for the past year, which because of his great age necessarily made his family apprehensive, but neither he nor they had expected him to die immediately. He was looking forward to paying a last visit to the chateau at Tocqueville, and Alexis had just written him a letter full of the scheme, with assurances that Mme Guermarquer would be particularly welcome. After Alexis and Marie reached Clairoix, on 8 June, he seemed to rally, and next morning talked cheerfully of revisiting the scene of his childhood ('he had no idea of his danger'), but an hour later he died. A religious service was held at Clairoix, but the comte was buried next to his first wife in the Rosanbo plot in the Picpus graveyard at Paris, a spot reserved for families of the victims of the Terror, or at least the noble ones. Nearby were (and are) the two mass-graves where many bodies of the guillotined had been flung.[2]

Tocqueville was prostrated by this loss, the effect of which was made worse by the almost simultaneous deaths of Louis de Kergorlay's father and Mrs Childe, to whom he was deeply devoted. He did

---

* 'I believe that one can improve oneself all one's life.'

not get his spirits back for more than a month. He resolved to leave Paris, 'cette ville maudite', as soon as possible.[3] He was a man of intense feelings, and these blows struck deep.* He filled his letters with his grief for his father and with praise of him; but as when Abbé Le Sueur died had nothing particular to say. Indeed his lamentations were almost exactly the same as those which he poured out for the abbé. Posterity (or at any rate biographers) would give much for a memoir of Hervé by Alexis, or even a sketch of one in a letter, since so many documents have gone astray: only two letters from father to son have survived, and only two dozen or so from son to father after the journey to America, and those not always on the most interesting subjects: there is nothing, for example, about the two little books on eighteenth-century French history which Hervé published in 1847 and 1850.[4] But Alexis felt no impulse to reflect on his father's long and varied life, or to list his achievements. As when Le Sueur died he could think of nothing but his own need, his own loss, and memorializing would have brought no consolation. 'He and my dear Marie, I have to say, were the only creatures tying me to life and I shudder to the bottom of my soul when I consider that now there is only one of them.' Again and again, in his letters, he returns to the theme of Hervé's boundless indulgence to his children, superficially a curious emphasis, considering how thoroughly respectable all the Tocquevilles were, at least in middle age. What did Hervé have to indulge? Political differences, perhaps. But the anxious child in Alexis had never died; his father's abundant, uncritical affection was just what he craved. Emotionally he was unprepared for the event, and in spite of his doubts could turn for comfort only to the pious rituals of the Catholic Church; besides, his more devout correspondents expected it of him.

> I saw in my father, and have seen only in him, religion completely present in the least actions of life and in every last minute of the day … 'Your father,' said his confessor to me on the night before he died, 'sent for me in the hope of consolation; and I came in the certainty of finding in him continual edification.'

* His distress about M. de Kergorlay was complicated by the fact that for some years past the comte had refused to receive him, for political reasons (it is not clear what). But his concern for Louis was straightforward (see AT to Louis, 22 March 1854, 16 June 1856, OC XIII ii 282–3, 297).

Tocqueville saw in this conclusive proof of the value of religion, but still could not believe in the Catholic creed. Who could, alas, unless God took a hand?[5]

Hervé left his affairs in excellent order, so Alexis and Marie were soon able to escape to their peaceful refuge in the Cotentin; but even that did not immediately bring comfort. 'When I got here I recognized, not for the first time, that we see places through ourselves, not in themselves.' He was quite unable to go back to work. But he had to admit that he could not help taking an interest in the fate of the book which he had just published; so much of an interest, in fact, that it gradually brought him back to equilibrium.[6]

The *Ancien Régime* came out a week to the day after Hervé's death, on 16 June. Tocqueville would have stopped it if he could, as a tribute to his father, but as he had sold it to the publisher it was no longer his property; he could do nothing. Instead he was forced to enjoy a prodigious success, equalling, if not surpassing, that of the first *Démocratie*.[7]

Letters from friends and colleagues poured in: Beaumont, Kergorlay, Mme Swetchine, Guizot, Mignet, Freslon, Duvergier d'Hauranne. The press was not so prompt, but the appearance of the book was widely announced, and reviews came out steadily from June to September. The English translation (by Henry Reeve and Lucie Duff Gordon) appeared almost simultaneously with the French original, and was well received; the *Allgemeine Zeitung*, to which Tocqueville and Beaumont jointly subscribed,* included what Tocqueville ungratefully called 'an interminable and very faithful analysis of my book', which at least spread the news across the Rhine. Best of all for the author's morale were the sales. The first impression of the *Ancien Régime* was of 2,200 copies: Lévy was a much bolder publisher than Gosselin, whose first printing of the *Démocratie*, it will be remembered, was of only 500 copies, and his boldness was justified: the edition was exhausted by the end of July, and the second edition by the following spring. Tocqueville wrote to Kergorlay: 'Materially speaking, the book's success is far greater than

---

* It is impossible for anyone who has not actually read the Tocqueville–Beaumont correspondence to imagine how much time, paper and ink the two friends had to devote to the business of keeping up their subscriptions and making sure that the copies of the journal arrived. It makes one unusually grateful for the invention of the telephone.

that of the *Démocratie*. For the three first editions of the *Démocratie* did not in total amount to more copies than the first edition which we have just sold out.'[8] A third edition sold as briskly. 'Lévy is enchanted and so am I. It has produced a nice round sum in royalties for me, every penny of which I am spending on my property here. When' (he asked Beaumont) 'are you going to come and see how my ideas have been transformed into a garden, flowerbeds and meadows?'[9]

Tocqueville took his success and his reviews (even the critical ones) with dignity and sense. For one thing, he was so immutably convinced that he was at odds with his time and that France under the Second Empire was hopelessly money-grubbing and frivolous, that both its praise and its blame could be heavily discounted. He confessed to Mme Swetchine that the pleasure of favourable reviews soon evaporated, whereas the least criticism irked him for ages; but he only deigned to reply to one specimen. Léon Plée, in the *Siècle*, now the leading republican newspaper (and edited by Tocqueville's old rival, Léonor Havin), welcomed Tocqueville's harsh portrayal of the old order, but attacked his view of the Revolution. 'M. de Tocqueville is no friend of the Revolution, nor a eulogist of its actors, nor an admirer of its deeds; he has scarcely any sympathy even for the populace which was forced to make it.' Tocqueville was understandably stung by this, and wrote a private letter of protest to the reviewer:

> How, sir, could you make a remark casting doubt on my sympathy for the common people when a large part of my work is, precisely, devoted to showing in a newer, truer, more vivid light the particular sort of oppression which they suffered, and also their miseries, and how the evil education instilled in them by the royal government and the upper classes explains their violence?

He was also irritated by a review which showed, in his opinion, that its author, Lamartine, had not actually read the *Ancien Régime*, since the book said what the poet accused it of not saying. Tocqueville called Lamartine an ingrate, 'for I am perhaps the only member of the Académie who still shakes hands with him.'[10]

It is easy to see why Tocqueville was annoyed: Lamartine accused him of presenting the Revolution as an accident, which is a mistake no careful reader could possibly have made. There are other errors in his review. But he had certainly read the book thoroughly by May 1857, when he talked of it at length to Nassau Senior in a flood of brilliance, and although Tocqueville might still have objected to his views (which had not much changed) his eloquence makes it clear that the difference between them was narrow but crucial: Lamartine was still in love with the Revolution:

> It was an insurrection against the slavery, not of the body, but of the mind. It was an attempt by France, which personifies modern civilisation, to break out of the feudal and religious prison in which she had lived for ten centuries, and to begin a new life, with new ideas, new objects, new habits, new means, new hopes, and, *as was inevitable* [emphasis supplied], new dangers and new calamities.

Whereas Tocqueville thought that the necessary transformation of France could and should have been achieved without 'new dangers and new calamities'; he did not consider them as inevitable. Nevertheless he devoted himself to explaining how they came about: that is, to the actual causes of actual events.[11]

By 1856 it was not hard to get to the Left of Tocqueville on the subject of revolution; what is a little surprising is to find Guizot taking much the same line as Lamartine, though with greater subtlety. He wrote to Tocqueville congratulating him warmly on the book, but continuing:

> I fear that you present our revolution too exclusively as political. If I am not mistaken, it aspired to reform not just society but human ideas of all matters in this world and beyond this world. It wanted to make Man the master of all things as of himself. It substituted faith in Man for faith in God. That was its philosophy, and it was its philosophy which shaped its politics. It sacrificed its politics without much regret so long as its philosophy was fulfilled and dominant. You describe admirably the sad phenomenon of the nation's easy acquiescence in the revolutionary despotism that Man set up. That I think was its true cause.

And he went on to say what he thought was Tocqueville's essential position, in the *Ancien Régime* as in the *Démocratie*:

> You paint and judge modern democracy as a conquered aristocrat convinced that his conqueror is right. Perhaps you dwell too habitually

on the historical aristocracy which is quite definitely conquered, and not enough on the natural aristocracy which can never be conquered for long and always in the end resumes its rights. Perhaps, if you had more steadily made this distinction, you would have felt more comfortable, while accepting democracy, in attacking what was illegitimate and anti-social in its victory.[12]

The differences between the three writer-politicians are clear and important, but a century and a half later perhaps their agreements are more striking, and throw more light on the success of Tocqueville's book. All agreed that the French Revolution was the greatest event in modern, perhaps in all, history; all accepted 'the principles of '89', the cause of liberty and equality; the lives of all had been dominated by the effects of the Revolution, good and ill; all believed that the work of the Revolution was irreversible. In these points they were at one with French public opinion. Tocqueville, in his hatred of the Second Empire, imagined himself to be more at odds with his fellow citizens (who were forever approving it in plebiscites) than he was. He foresaw that the regime would eventually be destroyed by the Emperor's taste for military adventures, but not that before then it would steadily evolve in a liberal direction (an evolution of which the triumph of the *Ancien Régime* was perhaps the first omen). The French reading public was as convinced as Tocqueville himself that the Revolution was something which had to be understood, and recognized the book as a great help. It eagerly responded to the appeal for liberty in the main text, for the French wanted liberty as well as equality and security, and did not let themselves be discouraged by M. de Tocqueville's gloomy outlook, much though they disliked it; and they had an inextinguishable pride in their country. In Tocqueville's chapter on the peasantry they found one of the roots of that love of *la France profonde* which has been one of the main notes of French patriotism ever since. And if they conceded that things had often gone wrong, the *Ancien Régime* went far towards explaining how and why. Beaumont, who was indefatigable in gathering news about the book's reception and passing it on to Tocqueville, overheard in Tours an Englishman praising it to his companion: 'that book explains very well how France today can be so content with its present government.' This was indeed Tocqueville's message, and the French could grasp it quite as well as the English.[13]

One who did so was Louis de Kergorlay; his verdict was particularly valued by Tocqueville, in part because Kergorlay could be relied on to see things exactly as he did himself.

> Your book gave me the greatest pleasure, the greatest sorrow; you will understand; it is excellent, but at the same time written in a tongue which our contemporaries can scarcely understand … How right you were when you said to me recently that you felt completely isolated even among your closest friends.* I am in exactly the same case.

But in discussing the book Kergorlay soon moved away from its matter to its manner. As we know, Kergorlay understood, as no-one else seems to have done, how intense was Tocqueville's literary ambition. After several pages of praise – he thought that the new book was quite as good as the *Démocratie* and in some respects better, 'for one finds there the more complete experience of a politician and practical knowledge of actual humanity' – he mentioned that he had noticed various small inelegances of detail, probably the result of the haste with which the book was produced. In his reply, after thanking Kergorlay warmly for the pleasure which his letter caused him, Tocqueville begged to be told of every blunder; which Kergorlay undertook to do, though he found it strange to be correcting a member of the Académie Française, which had the responsibility of prescribing good French. He read the book a second and then a third time, and his corrections, with a few suggested by Corcelle, were adopted in the third impression of the *Ancien Régime* (not having arrived in time for the second). It ill becomes an Englishman to pronounce on the point, but they do not seem to amount to much, and Kergorlay's one general criticism – that Tocqueville tried too hard to make everything as clear as possible, forgetting that readers liked to use their intelligence occasionally – seems misguided; Mme Swetchine's praise of the 'incomparable beauty' of Tocqueville's language seems much better justified – but then, she was not French either. Tocqueville accepted his friend's strictures with striking humility. Perhaps humility is not quite the right word: 'thrown back into the life of letters, I have more

---

* Presumably AT meant his brothers and their wives; he can scarcely have had in mind Beaumont or Ampère or Kergorlay himself.

reason than ever to make myself as distinguished as possible.' So he begged Kergorlay to be really thorough in his observations. 'I know that between my style and that of the greatest writers is some kind of obstacle which I must cross if I am to move out of the crowd into their ranks.' Kergorlay did his excellent best to help; among other things he, who had once recommended immersion in Pascal, Montesquieu and Rousseau, now advised a course of Voltaire.[14]

Much less welcome comments came from Arthur de Gobineau, who was having a difficult time as a member of a special French diplomatic mission to Persia. The third and fourth volumes of his *Essai* on race had been published that spring, and copies had been sent to Tocqueville, apparently in the hope that he would lecture on them to the Académie des Sciences Morales et Politiques. This Tocqueville refused to do, because of his mourning for his father and because he disagreed so entirely with Gobineau's immoral ideas about human decadence. In explaining this he allowed himself what looks like a pun: 'my mind is so *toqué**in this respect that the very reasons which you give me to make your ideas acceptable drive me further and further into opposition.' Gobineau had defended himself by saying that he was no more immoral than a doctor who tells his patient that his disease is mortal.

> I reply that if the act is not immoral in itself, it can only produce immoral or pernicious consequences. If my doctor came to me one morning to say, 'My dear sir, I have the honour to announce that you have a mortal illness, and as it affects your very constitution, I have the advantage of being able to add that there is absolutely no chance of saving you in any way,' I would first be tempted to knock the fellow down.

Then, he thought, he would hide himself under the blankets to await the promised end, or follow the example of the refugees from the plague in Boccaccio, eating, drinking and making merry.[†] (Perhaps this passage should be borne in mind when considering Tocqueville's actual dealings with doctors.) He tried to comfort Gobineau for the

---

* Crazy, addled.

† It might be interesting to know exactly when AT read Gobineau's latest volumes. In the Foreword to the *Ancien Régime* he compares himself to a physician (OC II i 73).

small success of his *Essai* in France by explaining that nobody there read books any more, blandly overlooking his own success with the *Ancien Régime*. Gobineau, he thought, might have better luck in Germany (as unhappily he did, when his book fell into the hands of the anti-semitic circle round Richard Wagner).[15]

It must be admitted that this letter was provocative. After reading the *Ancien Régime* Gobineau counterattacked. He avowed himself an extreme reactionary (if reactionary is not too weak a word): everything had begun to go wrong, he thought, in the reign of Philippe le Bel (1285–1314), when the King and his lawyers began the destruction of feudal liberty, of all things 'the most calumniated and the worst understood'. He was delighted to find confirmation of these ideas in Tocqueville. 'You have admirably shown that the French Revolution invented nothing.' But what, then, could Tocqueville find to admire in the men of '89, the members of the Constituent Assembly? All they had done was to open the door to violence and to all the atrocities of democracy. They had cried 'tyranny!' when there was no tyranny, and had exerted themselves only to do badly what many centuries had been quietly preparing. 'You think that we can mitigate the evil which they did by referring to "generous mistakes".* Why generous?' Gobineau hated the Montagnards, but he despised the Constituents.

Then he struck at Tocqueville's throat by denying that parliaments were really free institutions, and that the French would ever be fit for liberty. They were a people who always had the same government, whether under a republic, a parliamentary monarchy or an empire. For they piously preserved an immoderate love for the involvement of the State in all their affairs, for the gendarmerie, for the tax-collector, for the road-surveyor, they had no understanding of local self-government and valued absolute centralization unreservedly. Did Tocqueville remember the time when they worked together at the foreign ministry? Europe was in flames, yet Tocqueville had had to find time to deal with tiresome parliamentary questions before being partially disavowed by the majority in the Assembly and forced out of office. 'What did the liberty or honour of the country gain from such

---

* I cannot find this precise phrase in the *Ancien Régime*. Presumably Gobineau is referring to Book Three, chapter 8, where AT writes of 1789 as a time of inexperience but of generosity, enthusiasm, etc. (OC II i 247).

a form of government?' Anarchy from time to time and despotism always – such was the fate of France, and Gobineau preferred the despotism of the embroidered coat to that of the deputy's black one or to that of the working-man's blouse.[16]

Part caricature of Tocqueville's ideas, part contradiction, this was a formidable challenge. Tocqueville rose to it in a magnificent letter which is one of the most important things he ever wrote.

Gobineau had asserted that, in spite of Tocqueville's suspicions to the contrary, he had become a committed believer in Christianity. Tocqueville accepted this, but seized the opportunity of arguing forcibly that Gobineau's racial theories were logically and doctrinally incompatible with that religion.

> Christianity evidently tends to make all men brothers and equals. Your doctrine makes them cousins at best whose common father is only heavenly; here below there are only conquerors and the conquered, masters and slaves by right of birth, so no wonder your teachings are approved, cited, commented upon by whom? By owners of Negroes who favour eternal servitude based on radical racial difference.

(Gobineau's *Essai* had been welcomed in the southern United States.)

> I know that there are at present in the south of the United States Christian priests, perhaps good ones (even if they are slaveholders) who preach from their pulpits doctrines which are doubtless analogous to yours.

But the mass of more disinterested Christians would never feel the least sympathy for Gobineau's views. Tocqueville congratulated Gobineau on his new-found faith, but regretted that not everybody who sought it could find it (a month later he would be enlarging on this palpable reference to himself in his great letter to Mme Swetchine).[17]

Moving on to politics, Tocqueville declined further debate. He and Gobineau belonged to diametrically opposed schools: what could argument between them achieve? But Tocqueville set out his creed: he made the most precise and explicit statement of his political beliefs that he ever uttered.

> You consider the men of our time to be big children, very degenerate

and very badly brought-up. And in consequence you think it proper to guide them by show, by noise, by much tinsel, fine embroidery and gaudy uniforms which, very often, are only liveries. I think like you that our contemporaries are quite badly brought-up, which is the main cause of their misery and weakness; but I believe that a better education could correct the evil which a bad education created; I believe that it is impermissible to abandon the undertaking. I believe that we can yet turn all men to account by an intelligent appeal to their natural honesty and common sense. The fact is, I want to treat them as adults. Perhaps I am wrong. But I follow the course marked out by my principles and, what is more, enjoy a deep and noble pleasure in following it. You deeply despise the human race, at least our part of it; you think it not only fallen but incapable of ever rising again ... For my part, as I feel neither the right nor the wish to entertain such opinions of my species and my country, I think it is not necessary to despair of them. In my opinion, human societies, like individuals, amount to something only in liberty. I have always said that liberty may be more difficult to establish and maintain in democratic societies like ours than in certain aristocratic societies which came before us, but I will never be so rash as to think that it may be impossible. And God forbid that my mind should ever be crossed by the thought that it is necessary to despair of success ... You will allow me to have less confidence in your teaching than in the goodness and justice of God.[18]

In this way Tocqueville confronted what can nowadays be recognized as an early sketch of fascism. Gobineau gave up: 'You have replied with six pages of irony to my reasoning. So I infer that you don't want to debate ...'[19] He did not try again.

The rest of Tocqueville's correspondence during his autumn, winter and spring in the Cotentin contains much equally interesting material. John Stuart Mill wrote, after a silence of thirteen years (and a prompting by George Grote), to thank Tocqueville for a copy of the *Ancien Régime* and to praise the book in a way which showed that he understood his author as well as ever: 'I cannot say enough to express my deep sympathy with the noble love of liberty that dominates your work and makes of it one continual protest against the depressing regime that your great country, the world's right eye, is reduced to enduring at the moment.' Tocqueville was immensely pleased, and replied at once: 'there is no-one whose opinion matters to me so much as yours ... Until I had your approval, I could not feel certain that I had done well.' Tocqueville was already contemplating a visit to England in the spring, and hoped that they would meet then.[20]

Another voice from the past was more painful. Madame François Begin, the former Rosalie Malye, Tocqueville's first love, had fallen on hard times, and wrote to Kergorlay asking him to approach Tocqueville on her behalf: she seems to have wanted a cash loan.* Tocqueville writhed for two days over the question of what to do. He was quite willing to help Rosalie, indeed felt a moral obligation to do so; the difficulty was Marie. If she knew about the business she would be furiously jealous of the past, and would be angrily suspicious of any renewal of the friendship, even on the most respectable terms. At the moment she had no suspicions of any kind, and Tocqueville felt it would be imprudent to rouse her. He had no right to upset her – his first obligation was to her happiness. He tried to think of a way of helping Rosalie secretly, but since Marie was in charge of their finances there is no reason to think that he succeeded. We hear no more of Mme Begin.[21]

The episode suggests various questions. A few months later Tocqueville sketched his wife's character to Mme Swetchine, to whom he nowadays wrote in his most informal, confidential fashion. He was now working seriously on the sequel to the *Ancien Régime* but was feeling '*unhinged*, as one would say in English'. There was nothing surprising in that: 'A vaguely restless soul and the incoherent activity of desire have always been a chronic malady with me.' He was lucky to live with a woman who could mitigate 'this great ridiculous misery'. But she could not heal him completely. 'She creates round herself a serenity which at moments also comes to me, but which always soon eludes me and abandons me to a causeless, impotent agitation which often makes my soul spin like a wheel out of gear.'[22] Tocqueville is trying to be frank; he has already told Mme Swetchine that Marie feels and thinks 'passionately and violently.' But he cannot quite bring himself to say that her capacity for making scenes has cowed him; that

---

* AT refers to the lady only as 'Mme B.', but Jean-Alain Lesourd is surely right to identify her as 'probably' Rosalie Malye. We know of no other woman whose story fits the facts.

she is a soothing, well-behaved companion as long as she has her own way in everything – which is impossible.

Much though Tocqueville enjoyed life in the country, and much though he disparaged Paris, he had to spend part of the year there for the sake of his work, and in view of the lively picture painted by Nassau Senior of his life in Paris in the spring of 1857 (for example), it is impossible not to feel that he liked living among his friends again, for short periods at least. The trouble was that Marie did not. 'Contact with the world, above all with *our* world,' Tocqueville told Beaumont, 'she finds irritating and disagreeable.' Contact with her husband's family was worse. She and Émilie had not spoken to each other for ten years. In the autumn of 1856, perhaps because of Comte Hervé's death (Alexis disliked the prospect of the family drifting apart), an attempt was made at reconciliation: he and Marie visited Nacqueville for four days. The occasion was a total failure, for which Tocqueville did not blame his wife. His respect for Comte Hippolyte's character and judgement was much less than his affection, and he thought that his marriage to Émilie had been bad for both of them. Men with weak characters, he told Beaumont in the spring, should not marry vulgar women who hid in the hearts under their silk and lace only vanity and a limitless love of money. 'The Belisle family was always worthless. I'm sure you have been convinced of this as long as I have.'[23]

The quarrel reinforces our sense of Marie's insecurity. After twenty years of marriage she still needed constant emotional reassurance, and though she had lived in the most polished society of France all that time, she seems still to have felt snubbed by its members. Her predicament is illustrated by one of Monckton Milnes's anecdotes about his visits to the Tocqueville chateau. At lunch a tactless guest held forth about the horror of misalliances. Tocqueville took his wife's hand, kissed it, and said, 'I married for love and by God! it has been a success!' It was a fine gesture, but if Marie had often to endure such slights it is no wonder that she became unsociable. She was devoted to Gustave and Clémentine de Beaumont, and everyone loved Ampère, but otherwise she seems to have felt comfortable only with her country neighbours and with English people such as Mme de Lamartine and the two Lagden sisters who looked after Prosper Mérimée's domestic life. Then there was her health, which so often seemed worse than her husband's. All in all, the impression must be that at this period she needed support as much as she gave it, and that she might well not be equal to a serious crisis.[24]

During the winter of 1856–7, after a long bout of his usual procrastination, Tocqueville again took up work on the French Revolution. He faced renewed difficulties. At one level he knew just what was necessary: he had to repeat the documentary triumph of the *Ancien Régime*. Just as his immersion in the archives of Tours had brought the eighteenth century to life for him, so now he hoped to discover the soul of the Revolution by plunging into 'a mass of newspapers, pamphlets and unpublished papers' such as he could find in the archives of Paris. But whereas he had arrived in Tours with various testable hypotheses and a clear idea of the questions he wanted to ask, he was now without an *idée mère*, to use his favourite phrase. The vast abundance of available documentation daunted him. His thoughts turned again to Napoleon and the project of setting him squarely in the revolutionary context. He considered examining the record of the Constituent Assembly, but nothing was settled when he arrived in Paris at the end of March, except that the trip to England was now a definite intention.[25]

Tocqueville had learned of the immense collection of French Revolution pamphlets in the British Museum, and with his characteristic hunger for primary sources thought that he might find the inspiration which he wanted there. But as there was no shortage of such sources in France it may be guessed that his old impulse for travel was stirring again. His many English friends had for years been urging him to visit them, and he was curious to see the country again. He would travel alone, or at least only with Auguste, his valet.* Marie was a stout English patriot, but she had not visited her native land for at least thirty years, and there is no evidence that she wanted to do so now. Journeys always made her ill, and she remembered the horrors of her voyage to Naples: she would not risk the Straits of Dover. She went instead to spend the summer with her aunt at Chamarande. Tocqueville joined her there for a few weeks before setting off to spend the last days of June and most of July across the Channel.

---

* Eugène had apparently left his service some years earlier.

This last visit to England has seldom or never received from scholars the attention it deserves, except from Seymour Drescher, who perceptively calls it 'in a sense the last public act of his life'. Yet the journey itself and Tocqueville's responses are so amply documented that his character emerges before us as in a final flowering: as vividly as in the travel diaries of his youth, which his letters to Marie from London much resemble.[26] He was as bright-eyed and observant as ever; he could still discover significance in the slightest encounter. He wanted to find out what changes had occurred in the twenty-two years since his last visit; to his surprise there were few, or rather, only one. The signs of demagogy and revolution which he had detected here and there in 1835 had completely disappeared. 'In appearance, at least, aristocratic institutions there are stronger and less challenged than in my youth. England is still the only country anywhere which can give the idea of the European *ancien régime*, reformed and perfected.' He still did not believe that this state of affairs would last for ever: there was still too great a gulf between the rich and the poor. He took to walking back from the British Museum to his hotel in Albemarle Street, his day's work being done, through the working-class lanes and alleys which lay behind the splendid main roads. Conditions seemed worse than those in the poor quarters of Paris, and if the cleanliness of some Londoners was admirable, the dirt of the others was abominable. 'You can't imagine what happens to linen, faces and hair from the coal-smuts that rain from the sky and against which only incessant care can protect you.' He thought that nobodies in England fell further into squalor than those anywhere else. But he did not allow these observations to diminish his pleasure when he went down to visit Lord Radnor at Coleshill, one of his Wiltshire estates:

> No-one in the country is more respected or leads a life more packed with benevolent and useful activity. What a noble, honourable, happy and enviable old age! His household is like himself. He lives in a fine country-house, surrounded by a fine park; everything conveys peaceful grandeur; absolutely no vain luxury, but an attention to the least details that contribute to the peace and comfort of life. The servants look smart but lack that air of gilded flunkeydom which has so often shocked me in the great houses of England ... But what is most remarkable in this house is the master himself; he is in good

health in spite of the seventy-eight years which he alludes to with serenity; he takes a lively interest in the affairs of his country though he no longer wants to take part in them; he is always busy with everything that can be useful to the people living round him; in everything he sets a good example; he is surrounded by his children, various friends, and universal admiration.

Here was what Tocqueville had been looking for all his life: a properly functioning aristocracy. It was an Utopia realized.[27]

But if England had not changed, the visitor had. On the day of his arrival, as his train hurried through Kent,* Tocqueville, as before, noticed how well-kept and prosperous the country looked; but it did not seem so far ahead of France as it had in 1835; French agriculture was beginning to catch up. Of all the new acquaintances he made the one he liked best – the one who became a friend – was old Lord Hatherton,† a retired politician and devoted farmer, who carried Tocqueville into Staffordshire to see his lands round Teddesley. The visitor's raptures surpassed even what he had felt at Coleshill:

> I admit that complicated machines, even the steam-plough, while interesting me, did not give me much to think about. But the way in which they pile up manure, how they treat it, how they make use of it – all bears on our concerns. The way they use the liquid struck me as ingenious. Unhappily, in this as in all things of this kind, my mind was interested, fascinated by the sight; but I find it difficult to remember what I saw clearly enough to profit. I admired the dwelling of my lords the pigs. It is swept clean every day and the manure removed and I am sure that there isn't a single sty which isn't cleaner than Madame Bono's house.

(Madame Bono was a neighbour at Tocqueville.) This interest in pigs was no passing fancy. He showed it at Coleshill, and Lord Radnor thereupon promised him the present of a pair to improve the breed in the Cotentin; when a few weeks later they arrived at Tocqueville they

---

* No more stagecoaches. But as always happens with such novelties, AT had long come to take this one for granted. He made great use of it during his English visit, and complained bitterly when Marie's letters, which should have reached him by train in twenty-four hours, took forty-eight.

† Edward John Littleton (1791–1863), a great landed proprietor of Worcestershire and Staffordshire. MP, 1812–35; Chief Secretary to Ireland, 1833–5; created Baron Hatherton, 1835. He kept a valuable diary, most of it still unpublished.

were the wonder of the village. Tocqueville was also much interested in iron fencing, and Hatherton gave him, as a parting present from Teddesley, a pocketful of Italian rye-grass seed, directions as to its use, and 'an implement for pulling up thistle roots'. Tocqueville was warmly grateful.[28]

He would never be more than a dilettante farmer, however enthusiastic; but his real business in England did not go nearly so well as his agricultural enquiries.

The Croker collections of French revolutionary material in the British Museum were indeed vast, vaster than he expected: '48,479 books, pamphlets, and sets of volumes of periodicals'.[29] Unfortunately they were quite uncatalogued (and would so remain, rather shockingly, until the late twentieth century) and were therefore, for Tocqueville, in his short visit,* essentially useless. He did not know what to ask for, and there was no Grandmaison to bring him likely specimens. Eventually he gave up, telling Marie that the Museum was a '*humbug!*'. He wrote a dignified letter to Anthony Panizzi, the chief librarian, explaining his difficulties, while thanking the staff for their great helpfulness. He was unaware that all the points which he made had been anticipated twenty years earlier by Thomas Carlyle, which had led to a fearsome quarrel with Panizzi. But even if the collections had been in a more usable condition it is doubtful how they would have served Tocqueville. He was still searching for ideas rather than information, and for those he had to rely on himself, whichever library he worked in. The point is illustrated by what happened when he transferred his researches to the State Paper Office (first incarnation of the National Archives). There, thanks to Lord Clarendon, the Foreign Secretary, he enjoyed the privilege of reading Foreign Office files which related to the first years of the Revolution, which were otherwise closed to the public. He found them fascinating, and copies were sent after him to France (another privilege). He could easily have made an important article out of them for one of the reviews; but they did not much assist his efforts to plan a second volume of his history.[30]

He was spasmodically homesick, and wrote to Marie almost every

---

* The round reading-room had just been opened, so that AT was one of its first users. Another was Karl Marx.

day to say how much he missed his house and her. But it is possible to be homesick and yet to enjoy yourself, especially if you have a mercurial temperament. Invitations rained on him from the first, and he was the star of so many parties that Senior named him the lion of the season. Thinking of his stomach, Tocqueville took precautions: he treated fashionable London as he used to treat Saint-Lô during meetings of the *conseil-général*, refusing all dinner invitations (including one from the Prime Minister, Lord Palmerston), instead taking solitary evening meals at the Athenaeum, where he again enjoyed temporary member-ship, as in 1835: what he called 'this magnificent palace' suited him admirably, and he spent as much time there as he could. But for the rest it was breakfast-parties and lunch-parties, morning calls and evening calls, and occasional dashes into the country to spend a night with the Grotes at their house ('History Hut') near Slough.[31]

The breakfasts need explaining. These were essentially mid-morning meals, halfway between what the French call *petit déjeuner* and *déjeuner*, much valued for the leisurely conversation they made possible. They were particularly popular with the London set where Tocqueville found himself, though Lord Hatherton asked his diary:

> Why are not these breakfasts more common? At the one or two hours given to them one really enjoys Society – which one never gets at a dinner. Yet there are not 12 regular attenders at breakfasts – & but six habitual givers of them – Landsdowne, Senior, M. Milnes & ourselves are the only ones I hear of.

Such occasions suited Tocqueville perfectly. Although he read and wrote English easily, he found that his spoken English had grown rusty;* but his company made no difficulty about talking French. This did not always work: it was a great moment for Tocqueville when he met Macaulay at a breakfast given by Lord Stanhope, as he much admired the *History of England*, but he could not suppress a flash of his malicious humour:

> No author ever resembled his books more; he graciously compli-mented me by wanting to speak French and the toilsome way in which

---

* This discovery surely serves to refute Rédier's allegation that English was the language of AT's household.

hot and vivid thought emerged through the chill embarrassments of a foreign tongue was very agreeable to see.

When a few days later Macaulay gave a breakfast himself his guests divided into two groups as they walked about his lawn, one speaking English with Macaulay, the other French with Tocqueville. Among the second group was Lord Stanley, a future Foreign Secretary and heir of the Earl of Derby, the leader of the Conservative party. Tocqueville was induced to talk about the United States, and Stanley carefully recorded his remarks in his diary. They well illustrate the extent to which Tocqueville was keeping up with American affairs:

> He thinks disunion not probable. The impulse of the moment, which at present tends towards disunion, is less strong in America than it would be in a like case in France: and the interest of both North and south is against a rupture. He thought the South stronger than is usually supposed – the slaveowners had all at stake – local national-ity, personal interest, even personal safety: while their opponents are fighting for a principle which does not directly concern them. But parties had never before been so violent: slavery used to be excused, palliated, represented as an inevitable evil, inherited from former times & for which the present age was not to blame: this was a few years ago the language of the slaveholders: now they identified them-selves with the practice, boasted of it, sought to extend its arena.[32]

Tocqueville's charm, his perfect manners and the distinction of his conversation go a long way to explaining his success in London, and the recent publication of the *Ancien Régime* takes us further. The liberty praised in the book seemed to be English liberty; the model which the French so disastrously (according to Tocqueville) failed to follow, was Britain. Certainly these last considerations explain why Prince Albert insisted on meeting Tocqueville, who duly visited Buck-ingham Palace one Sunday morning and talked to the Prince for an hour. Unfortunately there is no record of exactly what was said, but Tocqueville was more impressed by Albert than by any other royalty he ever met: 'You are lucky to have such a man so near the throne,' he told Lady Theresa Lewis. It was a civilized occasion, but it is reason-able to suspect a political *arrière-pensée* on the part of the host.[33]

At the time of Tocqueville's arrival in London the Whigs were enjoying what proved to be their Indian Summer. The Crimean War had ended in victory, and news of the Indian Mutiny was only just beginning to arrive; Tocqueville's friends and acquaintances were splendidly self-confident. He did not meet everyone who mattered politically – not Disraeli, not Gladstone, who between them were to be the gravediggers of Whiggery ten years later, though he had known both in the past;* not John Mill: perhaps George Grote warned him that since his marriage Mill had become all but unapproachable even to his oldest friends.† Tocqueville's contacts were all with a particular coterie of Whig peers and intellectuals. They welcomed him as a brother.

He was not taken in by their amiability. He met the duchess of Argyll, who pressingly invited him to lunch; he got her to invite Senior too, who was eager to go, but when Tocqueville had to cry off because of a previous engagement she ruthlessly told Senior that he was no longer wanted. This sort of thing led to a splendidly Tocquevillean reflection, notable for its unexpected conclusion:

[*To Marie, 2 July*] As you know, there is still a sort of free-masonry throughout Europe between members of the former upper classes which means that they understand each other with the merest hint … I sometimes amuse myself here by chatting to some of the great ladies I meet who treat me as one of their own and I am surprised to find in them precisely the same vanities, the same prejudices which wrecked the French aristocracy. You should hear them go on about people who don't belong to their natural society and how boring it is to have to receive people like the Reeves or the Seniors or even the Grotes. It always makes me think of the wife of our *sous-préfet* and her complaints about having to receive Madame de Varennes. The same exclusive spirit, the same natural idiocy. So why do they receive so affably all these people whom they consider their inferiors? Because they are afraid. Because they are living in a country where you have to reckon with everybody, and above all with those who speak, write and act. From which I infer that it is more than ever necessary to cry

---

* AT twice called on Gladstone, who unluckily was out on both occasions.

† Mill's frightful wife despised AT as a specimen of what she called 'the gentility class … weak in moral, narrow in intellect, timid, infinitely conceited, and gossiping. There are very few men in this country who can seem other than more or less respectable puppets to us' (see Packe, *Mill*, 338). When it came to infinite conceit Harriet Mill knew what she was talking about.

vive la liberté, which exalts and strengthens great minds and forces small ones to conceal their weaknesses and their grievances.[34]

Whatever the views of the ladies, their husbands, several of whom were ministers, saw in Tocqueville not only a sympathetic *aristo* but a former deputy and minister who might soon return to power: they did not believe in the durability of the Second Empire. Nor did they foresee Tocqueville's early death, though Lord Hatherton spotted that his health was bad and commented on his 'very narrow flat chest.' As an avowed friend of England, he was well worth cultivating; they may have thought it their duty to do so.[35]

If their attentions had an official tinge, Tocqueville was quite ready to exploit it, whether by gaining access to secret archives or by furthering the career of Marie's brother, Joseph Mottley, RN, a commander on half-pay who for years had been hoping for promotion. Marie had urged Tocqueville to do something for Joe, and Tocqueville was quite willing to try (he liked his brother-in-law) though he had little hope of success. But he discovered that Joe was quite right in asserting that 'interest' was the key, the only key ('this must be "Entre nous"'). He visited Joe at Dulwich, where he lived with his mother and sisters: this, so far as we know, was the only time that Tocqueville met his mother-in-law, who immediately concerned herself with his health. Twice he gave Joe dinner – Joe took the precaution of reminding him that he had only the simplest taste in food, a mere joint, or 'your own Athenaeum dinner, for instance – I think far preferable to Soyer's* entire machinery in the art of stuffing. You know how you were vexed on a former occasion'. Then he took up Joe's cause with the First Lord of the Admiralty, Sir Charles Wood.† Sir Charles had never heard of Commander Mottley, but he made enquiries, and less than a fortnight later Joe wrote rapturously to Tocqueville, just returned to France, that he had been promoted to post-captain on half-pay. The *ancien régime* still ruled the Queen's Navy. Joe tried to prove his gratitude by helping in the troublesome business of transporting to France a new carriage (a phaeton) which Tocqueville

* Soyer was the celebrated French chef at the Reform Club.
† Sir Charles Wood (1800–1885), first viscount Halifax (1866), was a distinguished politician, almost continuously in the cabinet from 1846 to 1874; best remembered for his work as Secretary of State for India, 1859–66.

had bought from a coach-maker in Croydon. This extravagance is one of several signs that thanks to his inheritance from his father, and no doubt in part to the sales of the *Ancien Régime*, Tocqueville was feeling much more affluent than formerly.[36]

Sir Charles performed another service: he offered Tocqueville the use of a naval vessel to carry him home to Cherbourg. The offer was gladly accepted. All Tocqueville had to do was to travel to Portsmouth, dine with the admiral in command there, and board a small steamer; the next day (21 July) he saw before him the hill above Tocqueville and could almost believe that he also saw the smoke from his own chimneys. He disembarked at Cherbourg; soon he arrived at his front door. He was grateful and delighted. The Imperial government showed its sense of the significance of this British kindness by forbidding all mention of it in the newspapers.[37]

Tocqueville had enjoyed his English visit, and enjoyed the memory of it (his letters were full of the subject for weeks afterwards) but he was glad to be at home again, even if at first the place seemed oddly shrunken. The heat-wave which had at first afflicted him in London was the presage of a summer and autumn of almost perfect weather, which went on far longer than could be foreseen. Relations and friends filled the chateau during August and September, although Ampère, the visitor most desired, first postponed his arrival and then decided that he could not come at all. He had formed a platonic attachment to an unattainable woman (as once to Mme Récamier), the invalid Mme Louise Guillemin, who lived with her parents in Italy (she was separated from her husband). Tocqueville could not quite conceal a certain vexation in the otherwise magnanimous letter which he wrote to Ampère about this disappointment, a vexation amplified on account of Loménie, who with his wife had been specially invited to Tocqueville to give Ampère pleasure.[38] The party made the best of it, however, and it is clear from Loménie's later account that they all enjoyed themselves. Loménie carried away a touching impression of Tocqueville's democratic delicacy towards his fellow villagers:

> There was formerly in the choir of the village church at Tocqueville a notably splendid pew, reserved from time immemorial for the lord of the chateau, which had gone through all the most revolutionary

periods without being suppressed. This pew, which shocked nobody in the commune, nevertheless took up much space, and it was enough that it could become a grievance for Alexis de Tocqueville to decide to remove it. On the other hand, as he did not want ... the villagers ... to see in this either a confession of weakness or a bid for popularity, he waited patiently until a general repair of the church was undertaken; then one fine day, following this general repair, they saw that the lord's pew had been suppressed and replaced by a much more modest one, placed at the edge of the choir, aligned with and next to that of the *maire* and the municipal council.[39]

The visitors were agreeable, but when they departed Tocqueville and Marie enjoyed their solitude. Tocqueville amused himself with his farm. He was proud to think that his English pigs might improve the Norman breed: 'When one can't render great services to one's country, one can be a public benefactor in small things.'[40] He kept up an intermittent agricultural correspondence with Lord Hatherton and spent all his afternoons in the open air, looking after his land, with greater and greater pleasure. There were only two serious blemishes in this charming life. One was Marie's 'facial rheumatism', which caused her continual anguish. The other was Tocqueville's new book.

It made very slow progress. After more than a year – that is, by autumn 1858 – it would consist of no more than seven roughly drafted chapters and file upon file of notes. The trouble was still not shortage of materials. Tocqueville's friend Taschereau, now in charge of the Bibliothèque Nationale, made an exception to the rules in his favour, just like Lord Clarendon in London, and sent him all the books and documents he asked for. In the spring, when they were digested, he would travel to Paris for more, planning to stay there for several months. But the old problem remained: he only had a cloudy idea of where he was going. He told Freslon that the chapters which he had sketched were not yet fit to be shown; the sketches survive, and certainly do not compare with the Brumaire chapters of 1852, or with the *Ancien Régime* itself.* Sources were not enough: he was still no

---

* After AT's death Beaumont, as editor of his works, after many misgivings published a heavily corrected version of the seven rough chapters which gave a most misleading impression of the state of AT's drafts. See the excellent account by André Jardin in his 'Note critique', OC II ii 7–12.

Baconian inductionist. As a Cartesian he needed an *idée mère* to give shape and point to his researches, and he was still without one. He was still determined to avoid mere narrative, a resolution that would be difficult to stick to once he started to tackle the events of 1789; and he had no clear alternative. He spent every morning at his desk, but the months went by without much to show for his labours. Neither chronologically, nor in terms of historical argument, did he get much beyond the point he had reached at the end of the *Ancien Régime*.

Given time, Tocqueville, with all his ability and ambition, would have found his way successfully forward; but he was not to be given time. The obstacles in his path therefore assumed a sinister importance. One of his problems was that by burying himself in the Cotentin for so long he cut himself off from a form of intellectual stimulus that was most necessary to him. As the history of all his previous books demonstrates, he required the stimulus of other men's ideas, other men's criticisms, to set his creative impulses free, and they had to be men whom he loved and trusted without reserve, men of whose sympathy he could be certain. But Ampère had failed him, and Beaumont, immersed in his own farm and family responsibilities, put off his next visit to Tocqueville until there was a good railway link, which would not exist until August 1858. It does not seem to have occurred to Tocqueville to solve the problem by visiting Beaumont-la-Chartre, or Kergorlay at Fosseuse. Anyway, he was feeling disillusioned about Kergorlay, as he told Beaumont: 'since he became no more than the husband of his wife and the passive agent of ideas and feelings which are so different from those which are natural to him, there is no-one but you to whom I can talk open-heartedly, feeling *at home* [English in the original] both in heart and mind.' This observation seems grossly unfair to Kergorlay, but was sincerely meant: at this time Tocqueville largely let his correspondence with his oldest friend drop, and it was left to Kergorlay himself to suggest a meeting in Paris in the spring for the purposes of discussion. Meanwhile Tocqueville trod water. He was not exactly apathetic about his project – he enjoyed the labour of research too much for that – but he was not caught up in the business of composition with the intensity of earlier times.[41]

The truth, probably, is that Tocqueville, in his writing career, had been seized imaginatively by comparatively few topics, and the French Revolution proper had never been one of them. The causes of the Revolution, and its various sequels (Brumaire, 1830, 1848) – yes; but the great central drama itself did not set his fingers itching for a pen. He was not conscious of this distinction. He toiled on conscientiously, reminding himself of what Chateaubriand had once remarked to him: 'they say that you have to wait for inspiration in order to write; but if I waited for it I'd never write anything.' 'If such a great writer lacked inspiration, a scribbler like myself may be consoled for never experiencing it.' But whatever was the case with Chateaubriand, Tocqueville needed to be obsessed with his subject, and the deliberations of the Constituent Assembly simply did not have that effect on him.[42]

Two or three years earlier he had thought of writing a life of Malesherbes, which his Montboissier cousins, Mesdames de Pisieux and de Grancey, did their best to encourage. He would have been well-placed to begin it, for the muniments room at Tocqueville contained one of the most important collections of Malesherbes papers; but nothing came of the idea.[43] It is difficult not to think that he would have been well-advised to return to his original idea, and tackle the great Napoleon. Had he done so he would have fulfilled Chateaubriand's oblique prophecy, his remark that Tacitus had been born under Nero.* The first Emperor had never lost his allure for Tocqueville, who, as late as 1856, was telling himself that 'My purpose is to paint the true picture of a man more extraordinary than great who up to now does not seem to me to have been drawn either faithfully or in depth.' His particular concern was to be with the opportunities that Napoleon found in the doings and opinions of his time, and with the means that he employed; 'but what I want to paint above all, as to him and because of him, is the great Revolution in which he played so leading a role.'[44] The task was certainly not beyond him, but he did not pursue it, most probably because he felt that he had committed himself with the French public to tackling the Revolution directly, before writing anything else. He would have got back to Napoleon eventually; given time.

It would have been a brilliant performance, exploiting all his talents.

* See above, p. 28.

We get a hint of what was possible in a letter to his favourite nephew, Hubert de Tocqueville. Hubert was making a promising beginning in diplomacy as a junior attaché at the French embassy in Berlin, and Alexis asked him to tell him as much as he could about Germany. When Hubert did so he got a reply in which his uncle's musings seem to foreshadow European history for the next sixty years, as well as showing clearly why he thought that Napoleon was extraordinary rather than great. 'I came back from Germany three and a half years ago convinced that our neighbours across the Rhine were our most irreconcilable enemies'; and for that he blamed the First Empire:

> It was the long, exhausting, and above all contemptuous oppression exercised in Germany by the Empire which united the whole country against us, and lit against us in the hearts of the German people passions which survived and will survive for a long time yet the causes which gave them birth. Fifty years ago we always found in Germany a population very willing to value our policies. Today we will never find a true ally there, whatever we do; and we are forced either to deliver ourselves into the hands of England, which will accept us only on condition that we leave them free to spread over the whole habitable globe, or to Russia, an alliance which always brings with it the risk of a general war. We have made our worst enemies out of our natural allies.[45]

Tocqueville's allusion to the 'contemptuous' attitude of the Napoleonic regime to the Germans resembles his nearly simultaneous analysis of British rule in India (a topic which had long fascinated him). The course of the Indian Mutiny deeply concerned both Tocqueville and his wife during the summer and autumn of 1857: Marie said it stopped her sleeping (her husband: 'I did not know that she had kept so English a heart').[46] Alexis was fairly confident that the British would prevail, and thought that their defeat would be disastrous for the liberal cause in Europe; but as he developed his views in his letters to England he made it clear that though he recognized its importance, and indeed talked of European expansion as the spreading of civilization, he had no great opinion of imperialism's virtue or of its permanent success. Reeve wanted to establish a European population in India; Tocqueville thought this a bad idea:

A race which is inferior physically or by education can certainly put up with the *government* of a superior race ... Foreign government only wounds its feeble feelings of nationality; foreign settlers injure, or seem to injure in a thousand ways the private interests which are precious to all mankind ... I don't doubt that in Algeria the Arabs and the Cabyles are more irritated by the presence of our settlers than by our soldiers.*

This was to Hatherton; to Reeve himself Tocqueville went further. India, he said, could only be retained with the consent, even if merely tacit, of the Indians; but the British were unlikely to retain it for long, being the least amiable of the European nations: 'The most cunning in exploiting to their profit the resources of every country, the least affable, the most disposed to keep themselves to themselves and (I can say this because the fault is so intimately connected to great merits) the haughtiest.' To know them, in short, was to dislike them (not that Tocqueville put it like that). The Sepoy rising had been the revolt of those Indians who knew the British best and had been best treated by them. It was not at all a rising against oppression; 'it was the revolt of Barbarism against Pride.'[47]

It is the same point as the one which he made against the Napoleonic empire; together, the two analyses show that his mind was as lively as ever, so long as it was not labouring over the meeting of the Estates General, and so long as he was healthy. Then in late January 1858, he contracted influenza, which afflicted him seriously for six weeks. He referred to it repeatedly as only a trifling illness, but he would never again be wholly well.

He went to Paris as planned at the end of March; the idea was that he would research there for three months or so, while Marie kept her aunt company at Chamarande; he would join her at the weekends in the small apartment which they were renting in the chateau there. Unfortunately the new owner of the chateau – Persigny, one of Louis Napoleon's closest associates – decided to overhaul the building so thoroughly that it became, for a time, uninhabitable; Marie had to stay at Tocqueville, where her husband would rejoin her at the beginning of May. He did not much enjoy his stay in Paris. He

---

* This seems to show that AT had changed his views on Algeria since 1848.

disliked living in a hotel, and his attitude to his work fluctuated. At times he worked contentedly in the Bibliothèque Impériale, as the Nationale was then called, and the fascination of his studies was as strong as ever; but on the whole he felt that he was making no real progress. Using a favourite image, he told Marie that he was lost in an ocean of paper with no shore in sight; at times he felt like giving up the whole thing. 'Happily Nature which made me sensitive and in consequence excessively volatile at the same time gave me a streak of tenacity which drives me to complete my undertakings in spite of every discouragement.'[48] And no doubt he was sincere when he told his wife that he found the obligatory social round wearisome (though it was also the sort of thing that she liked to hear). It was not quite without its pleasures. Nassau Senior brought his wife and daughter on their annual spring visit to Paris, and they stayed in Tocqueville's hotel, the Bedford, rue de l'Arcade. He spent several evenings with them and talked as well as ever (though he assured Marie that he was avoiding serious conversations with Senior, in order to spare his throat).[49] He broached a familiar subject, the insipidity of young Frenchwomen:

> When a young lady comes out I know beforehand how her mother & her aunts will describe her. 'She has simple tastes. She is pious. She likes the country, she likes reading, she doesn't like dancing, she doesn't like society, she goes out only to please her mother.' I try sometimes to escape from these generalities, but there is nothing behind them.
>
> SENIOR: And how long does this simple, pious, retiring character last?
>
> TOCQUEVILLE: Till the orange flowers of her wedding chaplet are withered. In three months she goes to the *messe d'une heure*.
>
> SENIOR: What is the *messe d'une heure*?
>
> TOCQUEVILLE: A priest must celebrate Mass fasting; & in strictness, ought to do so before noon. But to accommodate fashionable ladies, who cannot rise by noon, priests are found who will starve all the morning, & say mass in the afternoon. It is an irregular proceeding tho' winked at by the Ecclesiastical authorities. Still to attend it is rather discreditable: it is a middle term between the highly meritori-

ous practice of going to early Mass, & the scandalous one of never going at all.[50]

People who give pleasure with such talk usually receive it also, and there is no reason to suppose that Tocqueville was an exception.

But nor can there be any doubt that he was unwell, which sapped his energy and his enjoyment of life. He longed for the Cotentin, and for Marie. He loved getting long letters from her, though he knew that writing them made her ill (rheumatism, presumably): 'I ought to forbid you to do it. But don't expect me to find the courage.' The pain of loneliness never left him, yet he could endure it. But another theme creeps into his correspondence, then gradually, during the rest of the year, becomes dominant. On 14 April he assures Marie that his health is improving. His throat is giving less trouble – this is the first time he mentions that it has been affected – although a 'je ne sais quoi' grips him at the base of his neck and makes speaking a little uncomfortable. 'It was almost nothing, but it was something.' But a few days later he laments the change in himself; now he has every courtesy and assistance from librarians and archivists, but when he was writing the *Démocratie* he had something better – youth, ardour, faith in a cause, hope for the future, and Marie's company. A week or so after that he acknowledges his sheer lack of strength: he is not ill, but neither is he well. He still has the soul of a thirty-year-old, but is physically as frail as a nonagenarian.[51]

He was very glad to be back at Tocqueville in early May, but even there he could not settle down to work. He was restless and worried, he told Beaumont: 'Why? Truthfully, it would be impossible to say. The likeliest reason I can find is that I continue to be *me*'; but among secondary causes the most important was his ill-health. He was not yet defeated, though he was making no progress with his work: he read Theodore Sedgwick's new book on judicial practice in the United States and liked it so much that he wrote a report on it for the Académie des Sciences Morales et Politiques* which was published that autumn,

---

* It was the last piece of writing that AT published. In it he concentrates on explaining the unfamiliar practice of judicial supremacy with all the masterly lucidity of the 1835 *Démocratie*. Modern editions would do well to include it as an appendix. It was perhaps fitting that Tocqueville's last public word should be on the subject which first made his name.

and displays undiminished powers. But in mid-June he coughed up some blood – the same symptom which had heralded the terrible illness of 1850. He made light of it to Beaumont; but he thought he should perhaps consult Dr Bretonneau – only Bretonneau never answered letters.[52]

Beaumont was always quick to take alarm about Tocqueville's illnesses (he had seen so many of them) and to worry about him; a hint was enough. On this occasion he read between the lines and did his best to reassure the invalid, attributing his sickness to the particularly savage influenza of 1858 (which may indeed have triggered the recurrence of Tocqueville's disease), expressing confidence that country life and summer weather would cure him, and reminding him of how many crises he had survived in the past. He wished he could pass on some of his own robust good health. He tried to infuse his friend with some of his own buoyancy. This was very necessary. In letters to other friends Tocqueville was frank about the gravity of the crisis. It made all work difficult; he could hardly speak. He called his affliction bronchitis, since it chiefly affected his windpipe, and that was the word which his doctors used; but in retrospect it is clear that he was actually suffering from tuberculosis of the pharynx or the larynx. The symptoms came and went: his body had been living with the disease for many years, and had to some extent adjusted to it; but there was not going to be another remission. He made some apparent recovery in July and August, but he knew that it was only partial. He told Beaumont that he had lost his *élan*: 'The verve I had at Tours has been put out.'[53]

In the circumstances it is perhaps surprising that he pressed so many of his friends, both French and English, to visit the chateau in August, when the Emperor would be officially opening the railway to Cherbourg and celebrating the completion of the great naval base there; there was to be a grand review of the French fleet and a visiting British naval squadron. Queen Victoria was coming. Tocqueville, as unrelenting as ever in his opposition to the regime, boycotted the proceedings,* but he could not resist the allure of the great naval

---

* He was furious when the press reported that 'Madame de Tocqueville' had danced a quadrille with the Emperor at Cherbourg. The lady in question was not Marie but AT's sister-in-law Émilie, who should have been referred to as 'the comtesse de Tocqueville'. AT blamed both her and the newspapers for the blunder (see OC XI 409).

spectacle, which he and his guests – Beaumont and Clémentine among them – watched from the cliffs at Fermanville. The guns fired salutes all day, and the smell of gunpowder reached as far as Tocqueville itself. A few days later Marie fell ill with 'bronchitis', lost her voice and took to her bed, but the visitors kept on coming. Monckton Milnes invited himself and a parliamentary colleague (Lord John Russell's nephew Arthur); Tocqueville did not want them at all, but welcomed them effusively just the same; his only revenge was to take advantage of Milnes's gluttony and stuff him (he said) like a turkey, so that after dinner he put his feet up on one armchair and went to sleep in another. The English left on 13 August and were immediately succeeded by Tocqueville's niece, Denise de Blic, her husband, and three of their children, who stayed for a fortnight. Tocqueville had rather dreaded this, but in the event the children captivated him and he was sorry when they left. The Corcelles came, as did W. R. Greg, an English acquaintance;* so did Pierre Gossin, an agricultural scientist whose work Tocqueville admired. Marie recovered, and Tocqueville was in generally good spirits. He wrote several letters full of vigour that summer, among them one to Pierre Freslon which included a long account of Royer-Collard (Freslon was going to write an article about him). Tocqueville insisted on the essential consistency and integrity displayed by the great *doctrinaire* during his long career, and part of what he said reads like a summary of his own public life, whether as writer or politician:

> Throughout his life M. Royer-Collard firmly believed that one could and should distinguish between the liberal spirit and the revolutionary one. He passionately desired the destruction of the *ancien régime* and always had a horror of its revival. He ardently desired the abolition of privilege, the equality of political rights, men's freedom and dignity. He always detested that spirit of recklessness, violence, tyranny and demagogy which remains typical of the revolutionary spirit throughout the world. He believed firmly that one could overthrow the *ancien régime* without obeying that spirit. He aspired to bring forth from the revolution something other than the revolutionary spirit! He never thought that it was necessary to destroy the old French society in its entirety; only to break whatever stood in the

* William Rathbone Greg (1809–81), political writer and civil servant.

way of the modern mind, of well-balanced liberty, of the equality of rights, of the opening of all careers and all opportunities to the aspirations of all men. Once the Revolution had occurred, he always wanted to shape our institutions according to this ideal, and to renew, so far as was possible and desirable, the past in the present.

Given this lively mental tone and Tocqueville's good manners it is perhaps small surprise that Milnes, while expressing concern for Marie as he left, had not detected that his host was himself seriously ill.[54]

Such was his case, nevertheless. Early in September he was caught in rain and a sea-fog as he showed Gossin round the farms of Tocqueville and immediately lost his voice again; no doubt the tuberculosis made him vulnerable to any little accident. After a week he decided to go to Paris to consult the doctors there: he had no faith in his Cotentin doctor, André Collin. But at least Collin does not seem to have done him any harm, whereas the Parisian consultants, Andral and Charruau, after diagnosing a light bronchial infection, decided to torture him with vesicatories, painful applications to the skin which were supposed to do him good as counter-irritants. They also told him to drink large quantities of a Pyrenean mineral-water which was supposed to soothe his throat. He went back to Tocqueville to undergo the treatment and found it so painful and ineffective that after a fortnight he returned to Paris for another consultation. Marie was to follow him when she could (as usual there were building works at the chateau which had to be supervised); they had already decided to spend the winter in the warm south. Mme Guermarquer looked after him until Marie arrived, and for the first few days he had the company of his brother Édouard. He wrote anxious letters urging his wife to take care of herself. He himself coughed incessantly, particularly at night.[55]

Marie's arrival was constantly expected and as constantly postponed: she did not reach Paris until 16 October, more than two weeks after her husband. Meanwhile he depended on her letters, though they did not always cheer him. She was ill herself, extremely busy, and having seen Tocqueville recover in the past, thought he would do so this time, and seems to have hinted that he was making too much fuss. Tocqueville insisted that he was quite calm, though she could hardly expect him to be gay; nor were his fears exaggerated: if he was melancholy it was because he feared that from now on his life would be a matter of excessive weakness and tiresome precautions, if he wanted to last. It was almost worse when Marie's letters evoked his house and garden: they brought tears to his eyes:

> I hope that next year we will walk together down the long avenue and see at its end the setting sun lighting the lawn. How have we come to surrender our hearts to mere exterior, insentient objects? It is because, for us, they live. They represent the last of our youth, the best days of our prime, and the inexpressible sweetness of these latest years, the happiest, after all, of my whole life; and their charm has been your doing.[56]

In spite of his general weakness he occasionally had one of the bursts of energy which characterize consumptives; when he went walking in the Bois de Boulogne his pace was so quick that his cab-driver refused to believe that he was an invalid.[57]

He had at first hoped to join Ampère in Rome, but Dr Andral advised against the climate of that city, and he did not think it worthwhile or kind to drag Marie over the Alps just to winter in, say, Pisa.[58] Instead he decided to go to Cannes, which had the advantage of being only half the distance, and in France. Tocqueville spent most of October on the business of hiring a house there, and in trying to inform himself about the place, which was only beginning to be known as a holiday resort. He was not enamoured of the project, but he told himself and Freslon that he might work better at Cannes than at home:

> The trouble with my retreat at Tocqueville, which is so dear to me ... is to be too agreeable. It is not great emotions which render the mind unproductive; they are like a wind which blows about the flame of thought. It is little agreeable occupations which snuff it out; they distract the mind and prevent it from settling down. You see that I am trying to gild the pill.[59]

Marie arrived on 16 October, fretful and weary, but she had come. Then Tocqueville's trusted valet, Auguste, fell seriously ill and had to retire; a manservant to take with them instead had to be found at a moment's notice. Tocqueville was apprehensive about the journey: Marie was exhausted and he himself was nothing to boast of. 'I'm not coughing much, but nor do I digest much.' Nevertheless, they could not defy the doctors' advice. On 28 October they left Paris. Louis de Chateaubriand went to the station to see them off.[60]

CHAPTER TWENTY-FOUR

CANNES

1858–1859

Si j'étais chargé de classer les misères humaines, je le ferais
dans cet ordre:
1. les maladies
2. la mort
3. le doute.

ALEXIS DE TOCQUEVILLE, 1831[1]

TOCQUEVILLE WAS SO WEAK that he could only travel in short
stages. The night of 28 October was spent at Dijon, that of the 29th at
Lyon. The weather turned hostile. Snowstorms blasted France, from
Paris southwards. Alexis and Marie reached Aix-en-Provence on 31
October; they had been followed down the Rhône by a cold and violent
wind, worse than any they had known in the Cotentin; Tocqueville
from his railway carriage observed the angry river flooding its bridges.
From Aix it took them three days to get to Cannes, ninety miles off,
since the railway did not yet go beyond Toulon and they had to travel
in what Tocqueville called a *voiturin* – an uncomfortable hired coach
into which crowded the invalid, his wife, their servants and all the
luggage. No wonder that it could only crawl across country, or that
Tocqueville arrived at Cannes in a state of collapse. Snow, wind and ice
had pursued him even beyond Fréjus. He could have gone no further
and could think only of his bed. Marie was in little better case.[2]

It is a measure of how Tocqueville's health had deteriorated that whereas, in his youth, he had recovered rapidly from his even worse winter journey through Tennessee, it was now to be weeks before he threw off the effects of his journey to Cannes, to the extent that he ever did; and as for Marie, she was not to be restored to full health that winter. Tocqueville's stomach and throat were as troublesome as ever, and by a sinister coincidence Marie too had a throat infection which made it impossible for her to speak for weeks at a time – she had to write what she wanted to say on a slate.* For ten days the unseasonal cold continued, Tocqueville could not set foot out of doors, and the balmy climate of the Riviera remained only a legend. He also complained that the servants were good for nothing: they had been useless on the journey, and Auguste's replacement was a booby.[3]

Bad though the situation was, it was not quite without alleviation. Before leaving Paris Tocqueville had written to Dr Sève, of Cannes, who had been warmly recommended to him, and the physician showed himself from the very first to be attentive and intelligent. He had great experience of patients with lung and bronchial complaints, for Cannes was becoming a favourite resort for such invalids (that was why Tocqueville had thought of it in the first place). His efforts were soon supplemented by those of Dr Maure, of Grasse, formerly a member of the Chamber of Deputies and a friend of Thiers: it was Thiers who, hearing of Tocqueville's plight, sent Maure to him. The house at Cannes, the villa Montfleury, was large and comfortable, and when the weather improved Tocqueville was able to take pleasure in the olive, lemon and orange groves which surrounded it, and in its splendid views of the sea and the mountains. Best of all was the arrival of Hippolyte. No-one in the family had realized, at the time that Alexis left Paris, how ill he was and how unfit to travel – he had not fully realized it himself; but as soon as letters arrived from Cannes they took alarm. Hippolyte left home at once to join his brother, and thereafter Alexis was never to be without the support of his relations and closest friends. In spite of everything, he was in fairly good heart. He wrote to Beaumont that it would be months before he could resume work on his book;

---

* It is natural to speculate that she may have caught AT's tuberculosis of the larynx, but the doctors were eventually satisfied that she only had an uncommonly persistent bronchitis.

Dr Sève told him not to go out, not to speak, not to receive visitors and, above all, not to be bored or melancholy. Confronted with these inconsistent instructions he found that he badly needed light reading: could Beaumont send him some memoirs of the Revolution – Madame Campan,* for instance. 'Take care of those legs of a twenty-year-old which you say you have got back, even if you only use them to hunt hares. As for me, I am more modest. I only ask God to give me back the legs of fifty.'[4]

It was a vain prayer. The last five months of Tocqueville's life can easily be summarized: every long and painful period of recuperation was followed by days or weeks of acute suffering until at last there was no recovery. Tocqueville's essential problem was severe tuberculosis of the right lung (the tuberculosis in his throat was a secondary infection) and in the age before antibiotics he could only enter another period of remission if the lesions in his lung were closed by scarring (*cicatrisation*): in the language of medicine, were fibrosed. It did not happen: perhaps the disease had gone too far before he reached Cannes. Dr Sève did not despair for many weeks: as the chief physician in a supposedly therapeutic seaside resort he had a vested interest in optimism; but Dr Maure seems to have written off Tocqueville's chances from the first. This disagreement in prognosis made little practical difference: Maure said nothing to alarm the patient and his advice was the same as Sève's. The two of them rejected the heroic treatments of the Parisian doctors and recommended the quietest possible life to allow the supposedly beneficial climate to work its magic. They also looked after Marie: it was largely to relieve her that nuns (Sisters of the Congregation of Our Lady of Good Counsel) were brought in to nurse Alexis. Originally they were Soeur Théophile and Soeur Valérie; later Soeur Théophile, exhausted, was replaced by Soeur Gertrude. The experience was a dreadful one for everybody, and it would not be worth dwelling on were it not so revealing of everybody's character, above all that of Tocqueville himself.[5]

As he felt his strength and appetite reviving during November and December he grew more cheerful, especially when at last the sun came out. His chief worry was Marie, who had lost, he said, half her weight

* Mme Campan was Marie Antoinette's first lady of the bedchamber.

since they left Paris. He would never have thought that anyone could lose weight so fast. She was exhausted physically and morally, 'which I never thought to see'. She was his sole providence, and had had to take on too much responsibility during the journey south. The two new servants ('I hardly know their names') were still useless, and even after a month Marie was no better. Tocqueville saw that it was distress about his illness that was laying her low. He did not realize how much cause she had for anxiety, but his mood about himself fluctuated widely. At times he made light of things: 'I sleep, I eat, I go for walks and I cough ...' But he admitted to Corcelle that his throat complaint, though much better, was still afflicting him, 'and there is no trivial illness where a necessary organ is concerned'. He went still further with Beaumont:

> I cough infinitely less, but still, I cough, and it forces me to spit abominably. From time to time little threads of blood are mingled in the spit which frighten me abominably, but seem to have no importance in the doctor's eyes. He always says, and says it more and more often, that I'll leave here completely cured. Decidedly, I hope so too.

His worst affliction was the ban on speaking.. 'I had never believed that it was so necessary for me, and so agreeable, to speak.' It would have been hard for anyone, but was perhaps particularly so for the vivacious Tocqueville.[6]

He was deeply touched by the eagerness of his friends to help him. Both Corcelle and Beaumont offered to go to Cannes. Gratefully, he refused them, but assured Beaumont that he would be sent for if it was useful, let alone necessary. To whom else should he turn, if not to the first and best of his friends? He had not forgotten Kergorlay, but Louis had troubles of his own: a twenty-year-old niece died that December, and his wife had a difficult accouchement; the baby died in January. But it was true that Tocqueville no longer felt so close to him: he actually remarked in a letter that since Kergorlay had become a successful businessman he seemed to attach little importance to his intellectual exchanges with Alexis (Kergorlay vehemently repudiated this allegation).[7]

Most of all, Tocqueville was grateful to his brothers. Once he complained to Beaumont of their heartlessness in letting him leave Paris, and in not dreaming, even for a moment, of accompanying him on his terrible journey, though they knew how ill he was, but he soon repented of this libel. Hippolyte was indispensable, whether in going for the doctor at a crisis or keeping order in the household; most of all, in supporting the spirits of Alexis and Marie by his resolute cheerfulness. Sometimes of an evening he and Marie would sit playing cards while Alexis dozed beside them. At other times, since reading by lamplight hurt Tocqueville's eyes, he was read to:

> I have discovered in Cannes a sort of seminarian, who comes to pass some of the evening with us, reading aloud. This future Levite is a thorough poltroon. As the roads which lead to our house are deserted at night he never fails, though he is nineteen years old, to bring his mamma with him, who knits in the antechamber while her son renders good French prose into Provençal for us.

Tocqueville had not lost his ironic eye. It did not even spare his brother: Alexis observed that Hippolyte consoled himself for the dreadful boredom of evenings at the villa (which he never missed) by spending his days calling on some Bonapartist notables who were staying in Cannes – a senator, a deputy, even an imperial chamberlain. 'My poor Hippolyte!' said the unreconciled liberal. 'What a poor character, but what a heart of gold!'[8]

On the whole the impression left by the letters of these weeks is of a stubborn determination to keep up appearances; as if Tocqueville and the life that he was leading were almost normal. He wrote many letters (of which at least twenty-seven survive), and filled them with remarks about his usual interests. Many of them display his warm-hearted concern for young people: he wrote to his nephew Hubert, to young Edward Childe, and to Corcelle about his daughter Marthe. More than a year before she had received an offer of marriage from a young man called Adolphe de Chambrun, a lawyer of excellent family; he had been accepted, but then the Corcelle parents, using their powers under the civil code, although Marthe was in her late twenties, broke it off; according to Tocqueville, who was furious, they had let themselves be influenced by a notoriously small-minded family lawyer, who had convinced them that Chambrun did not have much money and had no useful connections. Tocqueville thought well of the young man (who before long would be established as a legal counsel to the French embassy in Washington, where he became a friend of Abraham

Lincoln) and used all his influence to patch things up. At first he could not understand why Marthe did not assert herself: perhaps she did not really love Chambrun? Then he had a private interview with her; she reassured him, and he was more ardent in her cause than ever: he was determined that she should not be the victim of her French upbringing of the sort which he disliked so much. It was a great happiness to him at Cannes to receive the news that the wedding date had finally been fixed. His efforts to keep Francisque up to the mark, and to stop him frightening off the groom by endless fussing, had succeeded.[9]

His letters from Cannes also show him trying to stay in touch with the affairs of the world; he was particularly interested in a great quarrel that broke out between Montalembert and the imperial government. But he was vexed by a press report that Hippolyte had gone to Cannes because Alexis was suffering from a dangerous illness. He wrote to his friends in all directions contradicting what he called a false rumour: to Beaumont, to Corcelle, to Ampère in Italy, to Paris, to Normandy, to England. He told Senior, 'I am just now an invalid who takes his daily walks of two hours in the mountains after eating an excellent breakfast.' But he did not pretend to be well. He might say that the 'false rumour' had made him question for the first time freedom of the press; but after writing fifty denials he was driven, he said, to wonder if after all the rumour really was wrong. Perhaps his intuition was beginning to try to tell him the truth; certainly, as he confessed to Beaumont, he was occasionally frightened. Meanwhile, behind his back, his brothers and his doctors were sending grim if not yet desperate letters to each other. Hippolyte had realized, almost from the first, that his brother's lung was the real danger; but nobody told the patient.[10]

Then everything went wrong once more. January was the worst month that Tocqueville had ever endured. Suddenly (he said afterwards that it was like being struck by lightning) he started to cough up blood again, and did so repeatedly for ten days. As if that, his gastritis and his laryngitis were not trouble enough, he began to suffer painfully from a bladder complaint (presumably an infection which his weakened system could not resist or throw off). Almost as bad for its effect on his spirits was the treatment imposed on him: fearfully weak, he lay in his bedroom forbidden to move, read or speak. The doctors were afraid that the slightest emotion might excite him dangerously; except for the two Sisters, only Marie was allowed into his room. Tocqueville was obedient: whenever Hippolyte presented himself at the door, which he did every day, he was waved away. Ill herself, Marie could not speak; for company, most of the time, Tocqueville only had the nuns. These had given an undertaking (probably at Hippolyte's instance, who was perhaps relaying Tocqueville's own request) not to talk to the patient about religion; but one Sunday, Soeur Théophile later reported, he asked them to recite the prayers of the Mass in his presence:

> Each Sunday he renewed his request and once it happened that at the end of the prayers he needed attention of some kind. When the Sister had looked after him he said: 'And now, Sister, be so kind as to finish saying the Mass prayers.' 'They were finished, *Monsieur.*' 'Not so, Sister, you did not read me that fine passage from St John's Gospel which begins with these words: In the beginning was the Word …' So they read it to him.[11]

In this way Tocqueville's reconciliation to the Catholic Church began. He had always believed in a recognizably Christian god; it was natural that he now found comfort in a ritual which had been an essential part of his happy childhood. True, he had long ago renounced as unfounded the claims of the Church; but now, lonely and fearful of death, and with little else to think about, he seems to have begun to reconsider his position. His doubt had never been intellectually radical: it was a difficulty for him rather than the foundation of a new outlook; he was no philosopher, and Pascal was his favourite author. The surprise, perhaps, is that he ever left the Church rather than that he returned to it. His scepticism had always been ideological, even political, rather than systematic; a matter of the temperament and the emotions, as he had made plain to Mme Swetchine. Now his emotions were tugging him a different way. He did not consciously acknowledge that he was a dying man, but his illness may have told him at least that it was time to seek God's comfort and mercy. He must at some stage have considered Pascal's famous bet, but it is unlikely that it weighed with him: he was too sincere for such cynicism.*

---

* In my view, only a mathematician (which AT was not) could have thought of such a proposition, or found it enticing.

The process was drawn out. The local curé, Abbé Gabriel, called regularly at the villa Montfleury, but when at last the nuns induced Tocqueville to receive him he was hardly more gracious than he was to Hippolyte: he made what the Sister thought was a disdainful gesture, and did not speak. But by this stage (presumably the third week in January) he was recovering slightly; thinking it over that night he bitterly regretted his discourtesy, and the next time that the Abbé called he was allowed a brief conversation. Gabriel noted Tocqueville's prostration, and as he went out suggested to the nuns that they should tactfully lead him to realize his danger (evidently with a view to a conversion).[12]

Tocqueville did not need the nuns' counsel: he later spoke of himself as having been 'plunged into the abyss of Death'; sometimes the abyss was so black that he wanted to cry like a child. One of the tortures of that infinitely tedious and alarming time was the thought of his unfinished book. Striking his forehead he said to the Sisters, 'Oh! If you only knew all that there is in there and how much I want to be cured so as to do my work.' He barely ate or slept, and was to tell Beaumont that at one point he almost lost hope: 'the spitting of blood frightened me as much as it failed to trouble my doctors.' But then, round about 20 January, he began to gain ground, to the almost incredulous joy of his friends. The blood-spitting stopped, the bladder became much less troublesome, his appetite returned, his strength increased. By the beginning of February he was writing letters again, and complaining that he had been receiving none: the blundering Corcelle had told everybody that letters would be bad for him, whereas they were in fact his consolation, and the one intellectual pleasure that he was allowed.[13]

This resurgence lasted for about seven weeks. It was never more than superficial. On 5 February he made his first venture outdoors – 'like a lizard into the sunshine' – and by the end of the month was boasting to Édouard that he had walked for two hours without the least fatigue. Earlier, he had reported that his doctors were more and more pleased with the state of his chest (his first acknowledgement that it was a problem), but it is probable that it was at this time that they began systematically to deceive him. He was still extremely feeble, needing and exacting constant attention. But as in December he maintained appearances bravely, if with less success than before. He continued to keep Corcelle up to the mark about his daughter's marriage, and at times his mind leapt into brilliant action. Curiously, for a penitent, he began to read Gibbon's *Autobiography*, in short snatches to spare his eyes, and was soon absorbed:

> [*To Pierre Freslon, 23 February*] Are you not of my opinion, that there is nothing more fascinating than memoirs, above all those of celebrated men, provided that they are at least a little truthful? I always think that I am going to discover the secret of the wonderful machines which produce such wonderful work (I admit that I am often disappointed). This specimen is evidently very sincere. But it only teaches what a prodigious thing a man can make of himself if he possesses an extraordinary memory and passes forty years in the comfort and repose that a high social position and an independent fortune bestow, always working, reading everything ever printed about an almost limitless subject, remembering it all, then, quietly, unhurriedly, collating all these texts, and discovering that he has written, almost without intending to, one of the greatest works of modern literature. And what is profoundly personal is that the same man ... endowed with this extraordinary power, of a kind which usually rules out most others, is, when he starts to write, concise, vigorous, full of life.
>
> But what am I doing, running on about Gibbon?[14]

Another intellectual treasure that came his way was Mill's *Liberty*, published that month, of which the author sent him a copy. Tocqueville was delighted with the attention, and acknowledged it at once. He said he was sure that Mill had given the subject an original turn, and that the book manifested the rare vigour of his intelligence. 'Nor do I doubt for a moment that in the field of liberty we will always march forward shoulder to shoulder.' He hoped that a rumour which had reached him of the death of Harriet Mill was untrue;* if not, he offered his sincerest sympathy. He looked forward to reading the book, but there is no evidence that he ever did so – not surprising, given the state of his health, but deeply regrettable, for if he had he would have seen his own influence stamped deep on almost every page of Mill's masterpiece.[15]

---

* He could have verified the rumour by reading *Liberty*'s famous dedication. Harriet Mill had died at Avignon in November.

Tocqueville was still alive, but the sufferings of January had profoundly changed both his consciousness and his behaviour. He was more and more aware of his dependence on his brothers (Édouard had now come to stay at Nice) and bitterly regretted his frequent surliness towards them. He hoped that they would blame the disease, not the patient. He thought tenderly of his distant friends: of Beaumont, the first person to whom he wrote after beginning to get some strength back ('Who should I write to, if not you, before anybody else?'); of Kergorlay, whose child had just died; of his sister-in-law Émilie. Hippolyte had been writing to her every day, and she had been passing on news of Alexis to his friends in Paris. Past frictions were forgotten: he wrote to her with affectionate confidence in her concern for him, and filled most of his letter with praise of Hippolyte:

> People prate of their fine feelings, but what is more difficult and less common is to come, in the depths of winter, to bury oneself in a hole almost three hundred leagues away from the centre of the world, and to stay there for three months looking after a brother made often bad-tempered and always boring by illness ... This deed of my excellent brother will never be forgotten, I tell you from my heart.

But there was still a cloud: Marie was getting no better, which distressed and surprised him.[16]

Then on 28 February Hippolyte at last went home. He had been expected to stay for one month; he had stayed for over three and a half; it was time that he rejoined his wife and attended to his own affairs. Besides, Alexis seemed better; with Édouard close at hand, Hippolyte must have thought he could be spared. This was a miscalculation. In his thought for friends at a distance Alexis overlooked the needs of someone closer at hand. On 3 March he wrote a cheerfully confident account of himself to Ampère; but that very evening he and Marie had a showdown (considering that Tocqueville could speak only in a whisper, and that Marie was not supposed to talk at all, it is difficult to see how they managed it, but they did). The next day Tocqueville wrote to Beaumont:

> *Mon cher ami*, I don't think I have ever said anything which has cost me so much as what I am going to say to you now: I beg you to come

to me. We are alone here. Hippolyte has flown; Édouard, who is at Nice, is on the point of doing the same.* So here we are, sinking into solitude, just when our strength is returning, when intellectual and physical activity is reviving. If ever you could do us good, it is now. Nevertheless, I would not uproot you from the delightful life you lead, to dump you into the sort of cistern where we are living, but for a reason which I can mention only to you, but which will show the *urgency* of this relief: my wife's state of mind *frightens* me, *mon ami*. She is unwell, more unwell than she has been for a month; she has palpably arrived at the end of her physical and *moral* strength; palpably, this state of mind engenders in her soul ideas, feelings, sorrows and fears, which could end by taking her mind I don't know where. You know Marie. She is reason personified, until the moment when she suddenly lets go the reins. Furthermore, our servants ... are semi-invalids which leads to a slackness in their service just when their ardour and zeal ought to be multiplied a hundredfold. So what can I say to you, old fellow, except COME. COME as quickly as possible. *You alone* can lead us back to the field. Your gaiety, your courage, your liveliness, your complete knowledge of us and our affairs, will make easy for you what nobody else could manage. Come. I know that I am asking an *immense* proof of friendship from you. I know; but I know to whom I speak ... Come. May Madame de Beaumont pardon us, or rather I am sure that she has pardoned us already. I embrace you from the bottom of my heart. A. de Tocqueville.[17]

Light is thrown on this extraordinary letter (which is unlike anything else in the Tocqueville archives) by the letter which Marie sent to Clémentine de Beaumont by the same post. It is painful to read, but it does not suggest that the writer is losing her mind:

My husband has written to yours, my very dear Clémentine, this morning. It is a great sacrifice that we ask of him, we hesitated for a long time before doing so, but our excessive misery has made us egoists and it seems to us that there is no salvation without him ... my poor invalid is better, but still so frail that, night and day, I can't stop worrying, I can't convince myself that what the doctors say is true, that he will be cured by the month of May. As for me, I will never be able to get back to a tolerable state of mind, I am so desperate. I have never seen such suffering. The doctors say that they have never seen

* In fact, Édouard stayed to the end.

anyone so ill. Not only does he have a terrible illness, he has 3 or 4 others less terrible but a thousand times less bearable. Nothing can make good what has happened. So I am so deeply discouraged that nothing can help me, all the time I think how what has happened can happen again, my heart breaks all over again each time the thought comes to me and alas! it never leaves me. I cannot speak at all, for three weeks I got back the partial use of my voice, but new distress has violently revived my throat ailment ... If I see your husband's face I think that I shall once more have some satisfaction on this Earth, but then how frightful it will be when he goes away again. Still, he will do so much good to Alexis now when he has so much need of the distraction of friendly conversation that I am *convinced* that if there is anything which can cure him it will be a few days spent with his best friend ... One of the Sisters of Mercy [Soeur Théophile] who came here from Nice to look after Alexis went home today not being able to take any more, the other one stays but I am *already worried* that I have only one. For the last two months* we have had the Sisters, until then I was the sick-nurse and I grew so exhausted that I was good for nothing. I, four servants, two Sisters, scarcely sufficed to look after him, my household was in revolt, discontented, grumbling, and I unable to speak, always in need of nursing myself, yet not daring to ask even for what was strictly necessary, and which was worst of all, my heart broken in pieces. At length Providence seemed to take pity on us, but his coughing kills me ... I dare write no more, for all I can do is complain ...[18]

Two things must be said about these documents. First, Tocqueville was deeply worried about Marie, and she was deeply worried about him. Second, Marie gives much the more concrete picture of their difficulties, and among other things she hints (with too much reason) that Tocqueville was a very troublesome patient. And while he saw that she was suffering, he did not grasp that it was her well-founded fear that he was dying, or that he would live only as an invalid, which was making her so ill. He had again managed to persuade himself that he was recovering, and that all he needed was company.

Beaumont responded at once to the appeal, and arrived on 11 March. Before then Soeur Gertrude replaced Soeur Théophile, and Monsignor Dupanloup, Bishop of Orleans, who was visiting the Riviera, paid a

---

* It was actually three.

call. Dupanloup was one of the few prelates of the Second Empire of whom Tocqueville approved: he was a member of the Académie Française and did not truckle to Napoleon III.* As much to the point, it was he who, as a young man, had reconciled Talleyrand to the Church. There can be no doubt as to what his welcome to the villa Montfleury at this juncture signified, but we do not know what he and Tocqueville said to each other. Afterwards Dupanloup told Abbé Gabriel of his 'concern about this soul', and thereby strengthened Gabriel's determination; but apparently the curé did not think that the time had yet come to push the matter. However, he called regularly to enquire after the invalid.[19]

Beaumont had not known quite what to expect at Cannes. He had been afraid of what he called 'Catastrophe' for weeks, but he and Clémentine had not quite been able to suppress an unworthy suspicion that Tocqueville's desperate appeal was 'a sort of compliment of friendship'. Such thoughts vanished the moment that he saw Tocqueville. The patient was unable to speak for a few moments, struggling with sobs and tears of joy. He told Beaumont that he had been dying of sorrow and loneliness, and that by coming Beaumont had saved his life; then he did dissolve into tears. As for Marie, she needed looking after as much as her husband. With her ready agreement Beaumont took charge of the stricken household, and rashly promised that he would stay as long as he could be useful, though he had no idea of how long that would be. He approved of the nuns. They were good-mannered and intelligent, and their nursing was skilful: 'without them I don't know what would become of the poor invalid.' He interviewed the doctors.

Their views were appalling. They thought that Tocqueville had a chance of survival – but no more than a chance. He was much better than he had been six weeks before, when, as Beaumont rightly inferred, he had been at death's door, but that was not saying very much. He was a difficult patient to treat. If he had had a less delicate constitution (said the doctors) and steadier nerves, and if all his organs were not so worn out, Nature might have helped him to recover. Instead, he was the

---

* Félix Antoine Philibert Dupanloup (1812–78), Bishop of Orleans 1849, received into the Académie 1854.

victim of his stomach ('always his weak point,' Beaumont reflected), which was upset by every medicine (we know that he was occasionally given laudanum, presumably as a tranquillizer and sleeping draught). Yet only by eating could he regain some strength: 'it is a terrible complication.' He was no longer spitting blood, but he coughed all the time and brought up pus, in which Dr Maure had twice discovered tubercular cells. He expected the blood-spitting to recur, which would terrify the patient. Tocqueville had a perpetual slight fever, and his pulse-rate was 95–100 to the minute, 70 per minute being normal. He was not told that his rate was abnormal, or that he was feverish.[20]

Beaumont's position was extremely difficult. He did not tell even Marie how worried he was, and he was always careful to maintain a cheerful air with Tocqueville. He read aloud, and passed on all the news he could gather from his strolls into Cannes, or from occasional visitors. Lord Brougham, who had first made Cannes fashionable, came to call. Tocqueville was too weak to see him, but he and Beaumont had a long conversation about politics (France was on the brink of war with Austria), which Beaumont afterwards relayed. But these were the merest palliatives. Beaumont's description of the daily round is as sad as possible. Life was dominated by the fact that neither husband nor wife had been allowed to speak properly for months – Beaumont could not imagine how they could bear it. The morning was taken up with medical attentions: Tocqueville's back was covered with leeches. The doctor visited. After lunch the patient took little walks, which gave him great pleasure; Beaumont thought this was a sign of returning strength, until he noticed that Tocqueville was wrapped up in two or three cloaks, although the weather was delightfully sunny, walked like a man of ninety, and never spoke a word. At three o'clock the postman arrived with letters and newspapers, and sometimes Tocqueville felt strong enough to receive visitors. Dinner was at six o'clock, and until then there was an appearance of life in the house; 'but in the evening, the place is a tomb'. Tocqueville was too tired even to be able to listen to reading, and kept on falling asleep, though he struggled to stay awake for fear of having a bad night. Beaumont did what he could to make things livelier, but he felt that he was struggling against impossibility. There was something about their silence which cut off Marie and Alexis from contact with the world, even their most loving friends.

Marie began to talk, to Beaumont if not to her husband, which suggests the degree to which her illness was psychological; or perhaps, rather, the degree of her desperation. She had thought of a scheme for hiring a doctor to live permanently in the household. Beaumont approved of the idea, since it seemed clear that at best Tocqueville would never again be well enough to do without constant medical attention; besides, such a doctor would be good for Marie too. He wrote to Dr Andral in Paris for help in the matter. She complained, not quite fairly, about the Tocqueville family: Hippolyte had retired from the fight, Édouard (who had a sick wife to consider) did not visit very often, and neither of his sons had shown the least concern for their poor uncle's condition. A few days later Marie poured out to Beaumont everything she was thinking and feeling. She was absolutely discouraged, beaten down and exhausted, and worst of all

a little *detached* from her poor husband, whose *condition* has exacted from her more effort than she can make; she spoke to me despairingly of her desire *to be dead*; it is her daily wish; she sees that her husband ardently wishes to live; all her own desire is to see an end to her life, which is crushing her and which she wishes no more of, to the profit of her husband's life on which he sets such a value. Exhausted as she is, she yet sees clearly that she is only in the middle of a terrifying traverse … she quite understands that she will never be able to cross another such abyss, in which she judges sanely …

I have to say something very cruel: her only chance of life is for her husband to die now; a prolongation of his life, which all in all is most likely, will not definitively save him, I very much fear, and will end by devouring her. That is a horrible thing to say to you, but I tell you all I think, and I must say that her too *personal* disposition has separated her a little from him. 'He is killing me,' she said. 'He loves me, but it is not for myself, it is for himself,' and while allowing for the exaggeration produced by her great nervous distress, I think that this thought is all too present in the soul of this poor woman, who just now is *destroyed*. For the rest, she continues to see to all her tasks and duties admirably, and with unlimited devotion; but it is too much like a Religious duty. I said to her whatever I could to bring her back to gentler thoughts, which are also nearer the truth: for, after all, what woman has ever been so passionately loved for herself, and has received more blazing testimony of the fact? I think I did her good;

and yesterday, on seeing her outlook entirely changed, Alexis said to me tenderly that I had saved his wife's life after having saved his.[21]

Beaumont's observations about Marie are full of interest, but most of his attention was necessarily given to her husband. In his letters to Clémentine we can watch his hope, of which he never had much, dwindle to despair. As early as 17 March he was saying, 'Every day I am more dissatisfied with what I see ... Consumption is rightly so called; for every day his strength wastes away, without any equivalent gain.' From the time of Beaumont's arrival Tocqueville declined anew. His cough never left him, but his appetite did, to his astonishment: 'he would be less surprised if he knew that he has a very strong, continuous fever; they are still managing to deceive him, but can they do so for long? Yesterday he gave me a harangue (in a whisper, of course) against his doctor, in whom, he says, he only half believes.' Spring began with fine weather on 21 March, but when Beaumont asked Dr Maure how hopeful he might reasonably be, Maure replied that Tocqueville was like a man who bets his last twenty francs on a lottery in the hope of winning a chateau, at odds of a thousand to one. This comparison made Beaumont tremble. The evenings, he said, were as diabolical as ever, and it was difficult to find suitable reading-matter. Insipid books put Tocqueville to sleep, which endangered his night's rest; novels of the slightest interest disturbed him to the point of insomnia. They could discuss *Madame Bovary* because Tocqueville had read it already; it was not going to give him nightmares*.

Beaumont tried to make him understand what Marie was enduring.

> I said to him, very gently, nevertheless in a manner meant to make an impression: *mon cher ami*, do you know what's wrong with your poor wife? She can do nothing more, and all that she needs is that you should let her rest. I tried to make him understand that even from the point of view of his own interest, he ought to let her have a little peace and so allow her, during her hours off, to replenish her strength, and get some reserve of energy for the days of *great crisis*, which *could recur*, but our poor friend has been spoilt all his life, spoilt

---

* *Madame Bovary* was published in December 1856 and made even more of a sensation than the *Ancien Régime*; the imperial government prosecuted it unsuccessfully in 1857.

by her; the poor woman devoted herself entirely to that, almost to the moment when she came to the end of all her strength, physical and moral. He made a momentary effort to follow the advice I gave him, of which he could not mistake the justice and the grounds; and then he soon returned to the bent of his character, and asked of his poor wife that she continue this way of life and those efforts of which she is no longer capable.

Beaumont was afraid that she would collapse (22 March).

The future looked grim, but Tocqueville continued hopeful, and talked of his second volume. With that in mind he asked Beaumont to read him the memoirs of Comte Miot, a Napoleonic official. Beaumont thought them to be of the greatest interest, showing clearly the character of the Bonapartes, the Corsican clan which had battened on France. 'My God!' cried Tocqueville as he listened, 'what a punishment that family has earned!'

But it was one of the last flickers of his mind. Beaumont did not think that he would ever again be equal to the demands of authorship, even if he made some sort of recovery. He struggled to be hopeful: on 24 March he reported that Tocqueville was a little better, but the next day he started coughing up blood once more. Beaumont asked Dr Maure if the patient had some years still before him; 'Some months,' was the reply. Next day Tocqueville brought up 'small spittings' of blood which, the doctor told Beaumont, certainly came from the chest; but he persuaded Tocqueville that it was a nose-bleed. Nevertheless Tocqueville was frightened. In his fever and his feebleness his manhood was melting away; his feelings were those of a terrified child.

Next day he was calmer, but the doctors were still abusing his confidence with their lies. Beaumont wondered how long he would remain their dupe, and began to worry about his own position. He did not need to explain to his wife that he could not interfere with the doctors' treatment: had he done so they would probably have retired from the case. But he did not like being a party to the deception, and began to wonder if he might not be of more use to Tocqueville if he went to Paris in search of the *secrétaire-médecin* suggested by Marie. At Cannes he felt as if he were only a third Sister of Good Counsel. On 28 March Tocqueville was no longer bringing up blood, but he seemed a little weaker than the day before. He was no longer asking how he was: it seemed to Beaumont that he was living in a complete illusion, 'but I very much fear that it can't last much longer'. Beaumont began to share Marie's irritation about Tocqueville's relations, or at least about Édouard. His presence at Nice, said Beaumont, was almost no help; he and Alexandrine thought only of themselves. Beaumont regretted Hippolyte, who though muddleheaded was much more reliable. This was not altogether fair to Édouard, who turned up on 30 March to stay the night. He was shocked to see how much worse Alexis had become since his last visit, and on 4 April moved into the villa Mont-fleury with his wife. It was just as well; Alexis was glad of his presence, and Beaumont was at the end of his tether. The catastrophe was now certain, and the thought of it robbed him of all courage: 'There are moments when my strength deserts me; sometimes I even think that my health – always very good, however – will collapse' (3 April). He was needed at home, but he could not think of abandoning Marie to solitude. It was for her that he stayed; he could do no more for Alexis; 'I consider our poor friend as finished.' He was now being sustained on laudanum (4 April).

Édouard's arrival, which pleased Marie as well as Alexis, changed Beaumont's calculations. He could no longer overcome his disgust with Dr Maure, who was now telling Tocqueville that he was cured, except for his 'accidental' digestive upset, while telling Beaumont that Tocqueville was in the last stage of phthisis, that his lung was nothing but one large wound and he would be lucky to last more than a week. Beaumont could no longer bear to be a part of this perform-ance, 'which shows how easily poor honesty can be deceived until the supreme moment when it has such need of truth'. Tocqueville thought that his lungs and throat were completely cured. Marie too did not see how near the end was. At least she herself was better. Furthermore, Beaumont was now of very little use to the patient, who fell asleep when read to and had been handed over almost entirely to the care of the nuns. He decided to return to his wife, with the goodwill of both Alexis and Marie. He would, he wrote, look for a *secrétaire-médecin* as he passed through Paris; and although, as he said in what proved to be his last letter to Tocqueville, he went through that city like a bullet, he did carry out his mission, and a young doctor called Thadée Dujardin-Beaumetz (found, according to Jardin, by Corcelle)[22] arrived at the villa Montfleury on 10 April. Beaumont also alerted Hippolyte, Kergorlay and Hubert to the desperate state of Alexis; they left at once for Cannes, and arrived on the 9th. Meanwhile Beaumont reached his home and was warmly welcomed, but he could not stay there; after writing his letter to Tocqueville – he made it as long, interesting and cheerful as he could – he fidgeted back to Paris on the excuse of an election at the Institut, but probably because he wanted to be sure of getting prompt news. He may not have been really reconciled to his desertion of the sinking ship.[23]

But although Tocqueville was dying, he had not wholly lost his ability to respond to events and shape what life was left to him. As Beaumont reported, he was delighted to get the news that the plans for the Corcelle–Chambrun wedding had been settled; as late as 9 April he was able to write a short but vigorous letter to Ampère, welcoming the news that he was coming to Cannes;[24] and before then he had taken the decisive step in his reconciliation with the Church.

Beaumont does not say so in his letters to Clémentine, but a draft passage he wrote in 1860 for his 'Notice' of Tocqueville states that Marie had for some time been trying to induce Tocqueville to make his confession.[25] At first he refused, on the grounds that there were too many dogmas of the Catholic Church in which he did not believe, but before Beaumont left Cannes he had consented, and made his confession to Abbé Gabriel, which the curé deemed quite sufficient; but Tocqueville, not being sure, insisted on making a much more detailed confession to Marie herself the next day.* He looked forward to receiving communion at Easter, but it was exceptionally late that year (24 April) and Gabriel doubted if he would last that long. At this point Édouard (according to himself) took a hand, suggesting to the curé that in view of his brother's increasingly rapid decline the time had come for a final push. Perhaps this was why Marie (who Beaumont had thought to be getting better) asked if Mass might be celebrated at the villa, as she was too unwell to get to the church. The curé turned to Alexis: 'And you, *monsieur le comte*, when will it be your turn?' Tocqueville appears to have had what John Lukacs calls a 'Jansenist'

---

* 'Confession' is the word GB uses, but even if AT did indeed pour out to Marie all his concerns, doubts and regrets, his avowal had no ecclesiastical significance.

scruple:[26] he said that he was not yet ready, and asked to be confessed again. But next day, 6 April, as the ceremony went forward in his presence and Marie communicated, he accepted Gabriel's assurance that he was ready, and received communion lying on his chaise-longue. Édouard, Soeur Valérie and Soeur Gertrude were also present, and according to the nuns Alexis insisted to them that he was acting of his own accord and with full conviction.[27]

It has been difficult for many scholars and controversialists to accept this turn of events, given Tocqueville's lifelong scepticism and the mild anti-clericalism of his later years, and the documents are hard (but not impossible) to reconcile with each other.[28] Nevertheless, the story which they tell is clear and certain; the spiritual and psychological processes involved are wholly intelligible. One point, on which Beaumont, Gabriel and the nuns all agree, should perhaps be emphasized: Tocqueville did not, and was not required to, give his express assent to any of the Church doctrines which he had rejected for so long. It was enough that he now accepted the Church's authority and discipline. He repented; he confessed; he received absolution and communion; his reward was reassurance and, as he apparently told Beaumont, the great happiness of knowing that his union with Marie was now complete.[29] This reading is essentially the conclusion that André Jardin arrived at. But as he also remarked, 'we will not be so bold as to assume any certainty about his last thoughts. There are intimate reaches of the spirit that compel one to silence.'[30]

While all this was happening Ampère, who had not seen Tocqueville for nearly four years, wrote to say that he would like to visit Cannes, and set out before Tocqueville's joyful reply reached him. Deceived by Tocqueville's optimistic letters, Ampère had no idea that he was travelling towards a dying man; rather he was afraid that Tocqueville was on the point of going home without having seen him. Nothing could have been more mistaken, though Tocqueville continued bizarrely hopeful to the last. He told Hubert that he regretted not having devoted more of his life to the interests of religion: 'if God restores my health, I have decided to consecrate myself more ardently to that cause.' It was clear to everyone else that the end was near. Dr Dujardin-Beaumetz later reported to Corcelle that Tocqueville suffered appallingly when the mistral began to blow. On 15 April he had two frightful attacks which nearly suffocated him. He felt a little better in the morning, but then endured another attack which was followed by so deep a tranquillity that the doctor foresaw that the next crisis would be final: Tocqueville's body was mustering its last resources, which would not be enough. Marie did not leave his side all day. According to Dujardin-Beaumetz he listened to 'a short reading': according to the nuns Bishop Dupanloup arrived, and Mass was again celebrated in the sick-chamber, though Tocqueville was too weak to do more than recite the *Salve Regina*. That evening (16 April), at a quarter past seven, watched by his wife, by Louis de Kergorlay, his kinsman and oldest friend, and by the rest of the family present at Cannes, Alexis de Tocqueville died.[31]

EPILOGUE

AMPÈRE ARRIVED IN CANNES on 17 April (soon followed by Corcelle): too late for Alexis, but in time to do what could be done to comfort and help Marie, and to accompany her on her mournful journey back to the Cotentin. For a moment it seemed that her grief, coming on top of her long debility, would kill her, but in a few days she rallied. A funeral service was held at Cannes: Lord Brougham attended as the representative of the Institut, breaking his rule of never going to funerals; but there was never a question of burying Alexis anywhere but in the spot that he had chosen in the churchyard at Tocqueville.[1] The cortège went northwards slowly, which gave Louis de Chateaubriand time to arrange for a lying in state in the crypt of the Madeleine (only a stone's throw from Tocqueville's birthplace). At last the body reached home; interment took place on 10 May, attended by a huge crowd.[2] After that Marie began the struggle of widowhood. She mourned her husband desperately, and her grief soon led to a certain change in her avowed attitude to him and his memory. She wrote lamenting to Monckton Milnes: 'So much perfection to be called away! the friend of all, lamented by all, so useful to all, and I so useless, so worn out, to be left!' If she still had any mixed feelings about Tocqueville, she kept them to herself.[3]

She was a woman of strong character as well as strong feelings. Soon after the funeral she faced the question of what to do about

Tocqueville's huge archive of unpublished material. She called Beaumont in aid, and in this way Beaumont, whom Tocqueville had so repeatedly urged to take up some new literary task after he left public life, found himself committed, for the rest of his days, to act as his dead friend's editor. It was congenial work and he carried it out very capably, though by the standards of the nineteenth rather than the twenty-first century. He was an honourable editor; Marie, by contrast, pushed the prerogatives of a widow to their limit. She seems to have destroyed every letter which she ever wrote to Alexis, and apparently set out to destroy all those which he had written to her, after copying out passages in which he assured her of his undying love. Her last illness and death in 1864 put an end to this lamentable, if understandable, undertaking.

The death of Tocqueville was a public event. News of his danger had seeped out of Cannes long beforehand, and indeed several French newspapers (and, in London, *The Times*) had announced his end before it occurred. When it came it was suitably acknowledged with paragraphs and obituaries in the press, but it appears to have been somewhat overshadowed by the outbreak of war with Austria.[4] In the winter of 1860–61 there was a dramatic change. Beaumont brought out two volumes of Tocqueville's remains, which contained Beaumont's long biographical 'Notice', various unpublished minor works, including 'Quinze jours dans le désert' and the two Brumaire chapters, and nearly 300 letters to various correspondents, including Kergorlay, Eugène Stoffels, and Beaumont himself. The volumes had a great success. Sainte-Beuve, then at the height of his critical authority, praised them highly in two articles marked, undeniably, by streaks of his characteristic malice, and by his take-it-or-leave-it style, but stating unequivocally that Tocqueville was one of the great writers of the age: Sainte-Beuve particularly liked 'Quinze jours dans le désert' and the modesty displayed in the letters to Kergorlay.[5] (All this was the more magnanimous as, in life, the two academicians had been sharply divided by politics: Sainte-Beuve was a firm Bonapartist.) Lévy, the publisher, was so encouraged by the volumes' reception that he commissioned Beaumont to bring out a 'complete works', which turned out to be nothing of the kind, but did include a further volume of letters, one of miscellaneous writings ('Mélanges') and new editions of the *Démocratie* and the *Ancien Régime*.[6] (The *Souvenirs* was held back, an unexploded bomb.)

But Sainte-Beuve was not so gracious when he commented on Père Lacordaire's reception at the Académie Française as successor to Tocqueville. Lacordaire's election created a stir, partly because he was the first friar ever admitted among the Immortals, but chiefly because it was the outcome of an unnatural alliance between liberals and Catholics against Napoleon III's Italian policy. Fireworks were expected: priestly eloquence in defence of Pius IX and defiance of the Emperor; the hall of the Institut was packed for the occasion (even the Empress and other Bonaparte ladies attended). Lacordaire disappointed them all; he made no reference to imperial policy, and said very little about the Pope. His style was ill-suited to the Académie, and his tribute to Tocqueville, though sincere and intelligent, was flat. Only in his somewhat unctuous reference to Tocqueville's piety at death did he strike a new note, and unfortunately it involved him in seeming to say that on the brink of eternity Tocqueville's lifetime achievements were unimportant.[7] Guizot, who responded on behalf of the Académie, was much more successful. He had not lost the gift of commanding an audience, and this one (according to Kergorlay, who was present) hung on his lips as he plastered Lacordaire with compliments and in his turn praised Tocqueville's memory. But he could not resist surveying the long controversy between himself and Tocqueville about the course of modern history, or of taking the opportunity of having the last word. The applause fell away, Kergorlay reported to Marie. Guizot's argument was the same as Molé's in 1837, as Sainte-Beuve pointed out: Tocqueville only disagreed with him because of his political inexperience. In veiled language Sainte-Beuve retorted on Tocqueville's behalf that the truth, rather, was that Guizot himself never learned, but clung obstinately to his first mistakes, and never let experience or criticism or patriotism change his mind.[8]

Read today, these polemics only drive home the fact that Tocqueville was dead and buried. As Françoise Mélonio has pointed out, neither Lacordaire nor Guizot took account of the fact that, as they spoke, the American Union which Tocqueville had described was breaking up in rebellion and civil war, a mistake which Tocqueville would certainly not have made.[9] Essentially, these were the opening exchanges in the debate about Tocqueville, now living only in his writings, that has gone on intermittently to the present day.

Later that year a very different meeting evoked Tocqueville's personality, if not his work, much more vividly. In August some of his closest friends assembled, as Marie's guests, at the chateau. Ampère was there, Gustave and Clémentine de Beaumont, Nassau and Minnie Senior. All was as it had been before. They walked about the countryside; Beaumont and his ten-year-old son Paul bathed in the sea; they talked about Italy, France, America; and Senior as usual made notes of what was said. Gradually reminiscences of their lost friend and host came to dominate their conversations. Beaumont defended Tocqueville's record in the politics of the July Monarchy and on the Constitutional Committee in 1848; Guizot would not have been pleased by his comments. And when, at Senior's suggestion, they passed an evening listening to Ampère reading Molière's *Misanthrope*, a play which Tocqueville had loved, their discussion afterwards evoked Alexis and his world as nothing more direct could have done.[10]

AMPÈRE: The tradition of the stage is that Célimène was Molière's wife.

MINNIE: She is made too young. A girl of twenty has not her wit, or her knowledge of the world.

AMPÈRE: The change of a word in two or three places would alter that. The feeblest characters are, as usual, the good ones, Philinte and Eliante. Alceste is a grand mixture, perhaps the only one on the French stage, of the comic and the tragic, for in many of the scenes he rises far above comedy. His love is real impetuous passion. Talma delighted in playing him.

SENIOR: The desert into which he retires was I suppose a distant country-house: just such a place as Tocqueville.

BEAUMONT: As Tocqueville fifty years ago, without roads, ten days' journey from Paris, and depending for society on Valognes.

MARIE: As Tocqueville when my mother-in-law first married. She spent in it a month, and could never be induced to see it again.

SENIOR: Whom did Célimène marry?

AMPÈRE: Of course, Alceste. Probably five years afterwards. By that time he must have got tired of his desert, and she of her coquetry.

SENIOR: We know that Molière was always in love with his wife, notwithstanding her *légèreté*. What makes me think the tradition that Célimène was Mademoiselle Molière true, is that Molière was certainly in love with Célimène. She is made as engaging as possible, and her worst faults do not rise above foibles. Her satire is good-natured. Arsinoë is her foil, introduced to show what real evil-speaking is.

AMPÈRE: All the women are in love with Alcèste, and they care about no-one else. Célimène's satire of the others is scarcely good-natured. It is clear at least that they did not think so.

MINNIE: If Célimène became Madame Alcèste he probably led her a life with his jealousy.

CLÉMENTINE: Of course he was jealous, for he was violently in love. There can scarcely be violent love without jealousy.

MARIE: At least until people are married. If a lover is cool enough to be without jealousy, he ought to pretend it.

Pour en trouver ainsi, elle avait ses raisons.[11]*

FINIS

---

* 'She had her reasons for thinking so.'

NOTES

1. *Noblesse*

1. Rédier, 16–17.
2. AT to Hervé de Tocqueville, 1 July 1841, OC XIV 223. For further particulars of AT's ancestry see Rédier, 17–20, and Simon.
3. Yale, Beinecke Library: Tocqueville Papers A I e, 'Catalogue des Livres de la Bibliothèque du château de Tocqueville', compiled in 1818. A total of 542 volumes are listed, and it is evident that most of them were acquired in Bernard de Tocqueville's time. The books on 'art militaire' are explicitly stated to have been his 'Bibliothèque militaire *portative*'.
4. The main source for the history of the Tocqueville family in the eighteenth century is the unpublished memoirs of Hervé de Tocqueville, now deposited in the Archive Départementale de la Manche, in Saint-Lô, sous-série 1J. A small portion of the memoirs was published in the *Contemporain*, janvier 1867, as 'Épisodes de la Terreur' (reprinted 1901). I make such extensive use of this most valuable document that there seems to be little point in giving references for particular statements. (For a further account of the memoirs, see the Bibliography.) For my account of the château de Tocqueville, see Leberruyer.
5. For what follows I am chiefly indebted to Ford and to Chaussinand-Nogaret.
6. Nassau Senior, *Journal*, Saturday, 17 August 1850. Senior, one of AT's closest English friends, kept a journal of his conversations with AT and other eminent men from 1848 until shortly before his death in 1864. It is a most valuable source, which was published, with various abridgements and editorial manipulations, in 1872 (ed. M. C. M. Simpson, *Correspondence and Conversations of Alexis de Tocqueville with Nassau W. Senior*, 2 vols.) and then, more fully and accurately, as vol. VI ii of the *Oeuvres complètes* (eds. Hugh Brogan and Anne P. Kerr, 1991). Unfortunately it was there published in French translation. All my citations in the current work are made from the manuscript (National Library of Wales, Aberystwyth), unless otherwise indicated, in the interest of absolute scholarly accuracy.

7. ibid., Tuesday, 22 October 1849.

8. 'État sociale et politique de la France avant et depuis 1789' (published in the *London and Westminster Review*, tr. John Stuart Mill, 1836), OC II i 38.

9. Rédier, 21. She entitled her memoir 'Petit recueil ou abrégé de la vie et de la mort de l'homme le plus vertueux, du meilleur et, je peux dire, du plus chéri des époux. Dédié a la reconnaissance'.

10. Chaussinand-Nogaret, 69.

11. AT to Mme Swetchine, 10 September 1856, OC XV ii 292–3.

12. Grosclaude, 734–5, quotes two letters of the time from Mme de Montboissier, Louise de Rosanbo's *émigrée* aunt, which show both that the marriage was arranged in some haste and that Hervé was not a familiar member of his bride's circle: Mme de Montboissier has forgotten his name.

13. AT to Hubert de Tocqueville, 23 February 1857, OC XIV 329.

14. AT to Hubert de Tocqueville, 4 April 1857, ibid. 330.

15. Allison, 126, is my only authority for this statement; I cannot find any confirmation in Grosclaude.

16. OC II, *L'Ancien Régime et la Révolution*, i, 63–4.

17. Chateaubriand, *Mémoires*, vol. I, 288.

18. Painter, 138.

19. Chateaubriand, *Mémoires*, I, 354.

20. ibid., 521, 541–3.

21. Grosclaude, 706, 711.

22. ibid., 718.

23. ibid., 721.

24. Allison, 162.

25. Grosclaude, 738.

26. ibid., 747.

27. Hampson, 18.

28. Richard Monckton Milnes, 'Commonplace Book', vol. 1844–5, Trinity College Library, Cambridge.

2. *Royalists*

1. As in chapter 1, so here: unattributed information is taken from HT's memoirs.

2. For further details of HT's struggle over the family inheritance, see Jardin, *Tocqueville*, 14.

3. Jardin, ibid., 16; Rédier, 31–2, gets the date of HT's appointment badly wrong, but wisely remarks of the comte's reasons for taking it, 'it was in the manner of the time.'

4. AT to Édouard de Tocqueville, 2 September 1840, OC XIV 214.

5. Jardin, *Tocqueville*, 14; Rédier, 31; Louis de Kergorlay to AT, 4 August 1833, OC XIII i 331; for Le Sueur, see below, 46.

6. Louise de Tocqueville to AT, 'Samedi', [1815 or earlier], Saint-Lô AT 315; AT to Louise de Tocqueville, 19 June 1831, OC XIV 104; AT to comtesse de Grancy, Paris, 11 January 1836, OC(B) VII 145.

7. AT to Francisque de Corcelle, 18 June 1856, OC XV 162.

8. AT to Lady Theresa Lewis, 6 May 1857. I have used the translation in MLR II 376–9.

9. Quoted in Jordan, vii.

10. Senior, *Journal*, Saturday, 25 August 1850.

11. HT, *Memoirs*.
12. Senior, *Journal*, 25 August 1850.
13. Chateaubriand, *Mémoires*, I, 74–5, and n.10.
14. ibid., 56.
15. ibid., 958–9.
16. Jardin, *Tocqueville*, 221: 'under his grave exterior there was still something left of Abbé Lesueur's spoiled, capricious pet'.
17. Rédier, 36.
18. AT to Édouard de Tocqueville, 10 September 1831, OC XIV 133.
19. AT to Henry Reeve, Paris, 14 June 1856, OC VI I 183.
20. OC V I 199.
21. For this information, and for my whole account of the Restoration, I am deeply indebted to G. Berthier de Sauvigny.
22. Here I differ from Jardin, *Tocqueville*, 16, who thinks that HT may well have taken part in clandestine activities, at least as far as keeping in touch with the exiled comte d'Artois. HT makes no mention of any such activities in his memoirs, and his account of a conversation with Chateaubriand (Archives de la Manche, Fonds Hervé de Tocqueville, série J.52 p. 109) implies fairly clearly that although he knew that there was much royalist intrigue, he had no hand in it.
23. Chateaubriand, *De Buonaparte et des Bourbons*, 18–19; Rédier, 34; Berthier de Sauvigny, 15.
24. Boigne, I, 236.
25. Boigne, ibid., 248; Chateaubriand, *Mémoires*, I 237.
26. Chateaubriand, ibid., 1341–2, n.1.
27. AT to Abbé Le Sueur, April 1814, OC XIV 39–41.

3. *A Sentimental Education*

1. OC (8) V 469.
2. HT, *Memoirs*. As before, I will not usually give any references for matter derived from this manuscript.
3. See Berthier de Sauvigny, 42–74; Jardin, *Tocqueville*, 16.
4. Richardson, 54.
5. Jardin, *Tocqueville*, 19; Rédier, 37.
6. Jardin, ibid., 20, seems to think that HT protests too much: it was the situation, not his colleagues and superiors, which defeated him.
7. Richardson, 208 (and elsewhere); Jardin, *Tocqueville*, 20–27.
8. HT, *Memoirs*; AT to Le Sueur, [Metz, 27 July] 1817, OC XIV 42–3. This letter ends with the words 'Mamma is much better,' which may be thought to imply that Mme de Tocqueville managed to make at least one visit to Metz (perhaps for AT's birthday). If she did, the visit was not a success, and she was soon back in Dijon.
9. AT to Le Sueur, [Metz], 6 July [1817], OC XIV 42–42. The editors of the *Correspondance familiale*, André Jardin and Jean-Louis Benoit, state categorically that AT did not enter the school until 1821, but the letters of 6 and 27 July 1817 seem to contradict this assertion, unless they are given a very strained interpretation.
10. Guizot, vol. i 144.
11. Jardin, *Tocqueville*, 58 n.2.

12. AT to Louis de Kergorlay, Versailles, 27 March 1828, OC XIII i 133.

13. Le Sueur to Édouard de Tocqueville, [Paris], 2 August 1821, Yale: Beinecke.

14. Le Sueur to AT, Paris, 16 April 1820, Saint-Lô.

15. Le Sueur to AT, Paris, 27 April 1820, Saint-Lô.

16. AT to Eugène Stoffels, 22 October [1823], OC(B) V 411. GB misdates the letter to 1822.

17. Le Sueur to Édouard de Tocqueville, 14 September 1822, Yale: Beinecke.

18. Le Sueur to Édouard de Tocqueville, 16 September 1822, Yale: for Kergorlay's letters see OC XIII i 41–54; for Mme de Blangy, see Henry Reeve, *Edinburgh Review*, CXIII, 432–3.

19. AT to Sophie Swetchine, 26 February 1857, OC XV ii 315.

20. AT to Charles Stoffels, Philadelphia, 22 October 1831, OC (B) VII 82.

21. The best complete treatment of AT's religious views is Goldstein, from which I hope I have learned much.

22. AT, notebooks, October 1831, OC V I 183. AT said the same thing in much the same words in the letter to Charles Stoffels of 22 October 1831 (LC 240), for which this memo is no doubt the preparatory jotting; AT, *cahier portatif* no. 3, [October] 1831, OC V i 183; AT to Ernest de Chabrol, Philadelphia, 19 November 1831, Yale: Beinecke.

23. AT to Chabrol, ibid.

24. Jardin, *Tocqueville*, 44–6.

25. Le Sueur to AT, 16 July 1822, GWP copy, Yale: Beinecke.

26. Bertier de Sauvigny, 316; Jardin, *Tocqueville*, 63.

27. AT to Sophie Swetchine, Tocqueville, 26 February 1857, OC XV ii 315.

28. Goldstein, 5–11, contains a particularly sensitive and careful discussion of AT's religious beliefs, especially of the question of whether he can reasonably be called a Christian.

29. *De la démocratie en Amérique*, OC I i 310–13.

30. AT to E. Stoffels, Paris, 22 October 1823, OC(B) V 411.

31. See Jardin, *Tocqueville*, 33.

32. AT to Lord Radnor, London, [3] May 1835, OC VI iii 40.

33. Source mislaid.

34. Jardin, *Tocqueville*, 58–9.

35. Kergorlay to AT, Paris, 16 May 1823. We do not have AT's reply. Kergorlay kept very few of his friend's letters at this period.

36. Jardin, *Tocqueville*, 59.

37. Kergorlay to AT, 13 August 1822, OC XIII i 56.

38. Kergorlay to AT, 16 May 1823, OC XIII i 56.

39. AT to Hubert de Tocqueville, Saint-Cyr, 12 January 1854, OC XIV 291–2.

40. AT to E. Stoffels, Paris, 7 August 1823, OC(B) V 410; Stoffels to AT, [Metz], 26 August 1823, PT.

41. E. Stoffels to AT, Metz, 22 April 1824, PT.

42. These three letters from Kergorlay to AT are in OC XIII i 81–7.

43. Kergorlay to AT, Metz, 14 January 1827, ibid., 94.

44. Kergorlay to AT, Metz, 21 July 1828, ibid., 141.

45. AT to Kergorlay, Versailles, 7 September 1828, ibid., 143.

46. AT to Kergorlay, Strasbourg, 16 July 1836, ibid., 380–81.

4. *First Flight*

1. Le Sueur to AT, Paris, 1 January 1823, Saint-Lô.

2. AT to Kergorlay [Amiens, 1824], OC XIII i 69–72.
3. OC(B) V 297 n.2.
4. AT to Kergorlay, [Amiens], 'Ce 29 [1824]', OC XIII i 72–4. This letter, like its predecessor, exists only in defective copies, which has necessitated a small amount of editing, indicated by square brackets. At this period £1 sterling was worth twenty-four French francs. It is not quite clear whether AT's calculations refer to expenses for both travellers, or for only one. If the latter, then the total cost would be rather higher.
5. Gustave de Beaumont, 'Notice sur Alexis de Tocqueville', OC(B) V 25.
6. Mougin to AT, Metz, 7 January 1824, Saint-Lô: AT 268, and [? 5 April 1826], Jardin, Tocqueville, 61. Jardin gives no date for the second letter, which I have not seen in the original.
7. 'Thèse de Licence de Droit Français d'Alexis de Tocqueville: De l'action en nullité ou en rescission', OC XVI 33–7.
8. Beaumont, 'Notice', OC(B) V 4.
9. AT to Édouard de Tocqueville, Versailles, 5 July 1827, OC XIV 45.
10. See OC(B) V, 4–6, 127–59, reprinted in OC V i, Voyages en Sicile et aux États-Unis 37–54, except for the passage about Rome. The only English version is that in MLR. AT gave the MS to Eugène Stoffels; Beaumont borrowed it from the Stoffels family for his edition of Tocqueville's works, and presumably returned it when he had done with it. It has not been seen since.
11. Sainte-Beuve, Causeries du lundi (Paris: Garnier, 4th edition) XV, 95; Senior, Journal, 20 May 1857 and 26 April 1858; GB to his wife Clémentine, 22 March 1859, Yale: 'il l'a lu & en porte absolument le même jugement que nous: de l'intérêt, de talent, et l'immoralité même.'
12. Jardin, Tocqueville, 60.
13. AT to Kergorlay, Tocqueville, 4 September 1837, OC XIII i 472.
14. Bertier de Sauvigny, 354.
15. Beaumont, 'Notice', OC(B) V 5–6.
16. ibid.
17. I am not the first to point out the likeness: see Henry Reeve, 'Introductory Notice'.
18. AT to Kergorlay, Rome, 20 January 1827, OC XIII i 96. This shard is the only surviving letter to any correspondent from AT's Italian journey.
19. AT to Édouard and Alexandrine de Tocqueville, Versailles, 15 March 1830, OC XIV 55.

5. Pupillage

1. Jardin, Tocqueville, 30.
2. ibid.
3. Rédier, 41–2.
4. Jardin, Tocqueville, 31.
5. See Beaumont's heavy hints, 'Notice sur Alexis de Tocqueville', OC(B) V 7.
6. AT to Édouard de Tocqueville, 5 July 1827, OC XIV 47; AT to Kergorlay, 23 July 1827, OC XIII i 107.
7. AT to GB, 1828 or 1829, OC VIII i 73.
8. For all this, see Jardin, Tocqueville, 79–81.
9. Beaumont, 'Notice', OC(B) V 8.
10. AT to GB, 8 May 1830, OC VIII i 98.

11. AT to Kergorlay, 23 November 1827, OC XIII i 118.
12. Jardin, *Tocqueville*, 32.
13. AT to GB, 18 March 1829, OC VIII i 77.
14. AT to GB, 30 August, 15 September and 19 September 1829, OC VIII i 80–87.
15. 'Affaire Montagnac contre La Guérivière', February 1828, OC XVI 48.
16. See OC I i 210–11.
17. See OC XVI 37–76, *passim*.
18. See above, 65–6.
19. AT to P.-P. Royer-Collard, 6 December 1836, OC XI 29.
20. AT, 'Notes sur la Révolution Française de Thiers', OC XVI 537–40; AT to Camille d'Orglandes, 29 November 1834, LC 311: 'It will soon be ten years since I conceived most of the ideas which I have [just] laid before you. As they were not agreeable to me, I [resisted] them at every point before admitting their truth.' The dates do not precisely match, but 'il y a bientôt dix ans' is not very exact, and it is difficult to believe that AT had progressed very far in his thought before he read Thiers.
21. Jardin, *Tocqueville*, 33.
22. AT to Kergorlay, 7 July 1828, OC XIII i 139.
23. AT to GB, 6 October 1828, OC VIII i 49–50.
24. Jardin, *Tocqueville*, 60; AT: 'Conversations assez curieux … avec M. Guizot et Boinvilliers', OC XVI 402.
25. AT to GB, 6 October 1828, OC VIII i 49–71, *passim*.
26. AT to his father, 'this Thursday' [1828?], OC XIV 48–9.
27. 'Introduction', OC XVI 9.
28. AT to GB, 6 October 1828 (`Lingard' letter), OC VIII i 57.
29. ibid., 54–6.
30. Johnson, 322.
31. Kergorlay to AT, 19 April 1829, OC XIII i 167.
32. Guizot, vol. I, i 27.
33. See Johnson, 22–3.
34. AT to GB, 30 August 1829, OC VIII i 80–81.
35. `Séance du 9 Mai 1829: tableau du règne de Charlemagne, une des rédactions les plus soignées', OC XVI 450.
36. `Séance du 6 décembre 1829', ibid., 482–3.
37. ibid., 449, 472, 479.
38. AT to GB, 25 October 1829, OC VIII i 93.
39. AT to GB, 5 October 1828, ibid., 48–9.
40. ibid., 48.
41. AT to GB, 8 May 1830, ibid., 99–101 and n.3. Beaumont was by far the more smitten of the two young men. In his vastly amusing memoir of the July Revolution (unpublished: Yale, Beinecke) he describes how Amélie gave him much-desired rest and recreation during the crisis.
42. In, for example, his letter to Chabrol of 9 June 1831.
43. AT to GB, 15 September 1829, OC VIII i 83–4.
44. OC VI iii 37 n.2, 58 n.4, 59 n.2.
45. Mansel, 144–9, 468–9 n.50.

46. See Jardin, *Tocqueville*, 49. A portrait dated 1849 is preserved in the Tocqueville collection in the Beinecke Library, Yale. For another, see Manzini, 25.
47. AT to GB, 8 May 1830, OC VIII i 99–101; Kergorlay to AT, 21 August 1829, OC XIII i 177. It is not certain that Marie had moved to Saint-Cloud.
48. Rédier, 123–4.
49. Cobb, 2.
50. Kergorlay to AT, 14 January 1837, OC XIII ii 439; AT to Kergorlay, 26 January 1837, ibid., 445–6.
51. AT, OC XII 149–50.
52. AT to Marie, n.d., XIV 379–80. The original of this letter is lost. On the existing copy someone has written 'D'Amérique', but this is a mistake: AT uses the *tutoyer*, which he never did to Marie before their marriage, and the letter has in other respects a strongly conjugal air. Its true date is probably 1837, or later.

6. *July*

1. AT's report to the Procureur-Général, Versailles, 7 May 1829, OC XVI 77–81.
2. Pinkney, 262. See also Hazareesingh, *The Legend of Napoleon*, especially 122–50.
3. AT to Édouard and Alexandrine de Tocqueville, 8 August 1829, OC XIV 51.
4. Guizot, I 342.
5. See OC VIII i 84 n.5.
6. Chateaubriand, *Mémoires*, II 2185.
7. OC XIV 51 n.2.
8. See AT to GB, 19 September 1829, OC VIII i 85–6; Jardin, *Tocqueville*, 78.
9. AT to GB, 4 October 1829, OC VIII i 85–6; Jardin, 78.
10. AT to his mother, 8 October 1829, OC XIV 52.
11. AT to his mother, 28 October 1829, ibid., 53–4.
12. AT to GB, 25 October 1829, OC VIII i 91–2.
13. AT to E. Stoffels, Valognes, 7 March 1839, OC(B) V 441.
14. Pierson, 24 n.
15. Guizot, I 343.
16. René Rémond, *The Right Wing in France*, 88–9.
17. Guizot, I 349.
18. AT to E. and A. de Tocqueville, 18 March 1830, OC XIV 55–8; Bertier de Sauvigny, 428–9; Boigne, iii 207.
19. AT to E and A. de Tocqueville, 24 March 1830, OC XIV 59.
20. AT to E. and A. de Tocqueville, 18 March 1830, OC XIV 58.
21. AT to E. and A. de Tocqueville, 24 March 1830, ibid. 60.
22. ibid.
23. Kergorlay to AT, Toulon, 6 May 1830, OC XIII 184–5.
24. AT to E. and A. de Tocqueville, 24 March 1830, OC XIV 60.
25. AT to E. and A. de Tocqueville, Paris, 6 April 1830, ibid., 61–4.
26. AT to E. and A. de Tocqueville, 29 April 1830, ibid., 65.
27. AT to E. and A. de Tocqueville, Versailles, 6 May 1830, ibid., 67–8.
28. AT to Lord Radnor, London, May 1835, OC VI iii 40.
29. OX XVI 511–12, 515–16.
30. ibid., 513–34.

31. ibid., 525–7.
32. 'Conversations assez curieuses de moi-même avec MM. Guizot et Boinvilliers', ibid., 403.
33. 'La Vérité, 1830, un mois avant la Révolution du 28 Juillet', ibid., 400–402. AT later annotated this essay, 'Très médiocre [his favourite dismissive word] mais curieux à cause de la date.'
34. ibid., 404–5.
35. AT to his mother, Nacqueville, 29 June 1830, OC XIV 69–71.
36. Kergorlay to AT, Torre-Chica, 22 June 1830, ibid., 198–201.
37. Kergorlay to AT, Algiers, 8 July 1830, ibid., 198–201.
38. Bertier de Sauvigny, 442.
39. ibid., 386–7, 443–4; Pinkney, 42–3, 75–81.
40. Boigne, III 229; Bertier de Sauvigny, 445–6; Pinkney, 81–93; Mansel, 242.
41. Boigne, III 232–3, 238.
42. For my account of the July Days I have relied chiefly on Pinkney, Bertier de Sauvigny, Mansel and Pilbeam.
43. Boigne, III 244.
44. Bertier de Sauvigny, 448.
45. Pinkney, 127–9.
46. Bertier de Sauvigny, 449.
47. Howarth, 146.
48. Pinkney, 163.
49. HT to AT, Paris, 27 July 1830, OC XIV 71; AT to Marie, [Versailles], 29 and 30 July, OC XV 375–6; *Souvenirs*, OC XII 86 n. 1. In this note (a passage which AT marked for deletion and which, accordingly, does not appear in the *Lettres choisies* edition) he misdates his encounter with the royal *cortège*: it was not on 30 July, as he says, but on the 31st.

7. *Upheaval*

1. OC VIII i 90.
2. Boigne, IV 4; Chateaubriand, *Mémoires*, 2293.
3. AT to Marie, 30 July 1830, OC XIV 375–6.
4. Beaumont, 'Notice sur Alexis de Tocqueville', OC(B) V 14–15.
5. See AT to Marie, 'Lundi matin, 17 août 1830', OC XIV 37?–77. This date is incorrect: as the editor points out, 17 August 1830 was a Tuesday. It is surely most likely that Tocqueville, full of emotion, mistook the day of the month, not that of the week; and in his letter to Hippolyte of 18 August he says he took the oath 'the day before yesterday'.
6. ibid.
7. AT to Hippolyte de Tocqueville, Versailles, 18 August 1830, OC XIV 71–2.
8. Henrion to AT, 25 September and 25 October 1830; AT to Henrion, 17 October 1830, Yale: Beinecke. The copyist, Bonnel, mistook Henrion for Kergorlay, which in turn misled Pierson (29–30). The letters are unsigned. Eventually André Jardin made the correct attribution.
9. Jardin, *Tocqueville*, 88.
10. Beaumont, 'Notice', OC(B) V 15.
11. The matter has been thoroughly investigated by Pierson (197–205), by Jardin (119–21) and by Mélonio in her edition of the *Voyages*, 1359–60.
12. *Voyage au lac Oneida*, OC V i 338.

13. Rémond, *Les États-Unis*. I have drawn heavily on Rémond for information and ideas about everything bearing on his subject.

14. Jardin, *Tocqueville*, 93; AT, 20 July 1831, OC V i 223.

15. Rédier, 92–3.

16. Rémond, *Les États-Unis*, 255–6.

17. Chateaubriand, *Voyages en Amérique*, 872–3.

18. Michel Chevalier, *passim*; Taylor; Chateaubriand, *Voyages en Amérique*, 874; and see F. J. Turner, 'The Significance of the Frontier in American History'.

19. Chateaubriand, ibid., 871–3.

20. Rémond, *Les États-Unis*, 481–507.

21. Chateaubriand, *Mémoires*, 2312–15.

22. '… l'accueillit avec transport.' Beaumont, 'Notice', 16.

23. AT to Marie, Versailles, 23 August [1830?], 'six heures du matin', OC XIV 378. This letter exists only in a fragment copied from the original, no doubt years later, by Marie. If it was really written from Versailles then the year as copied – 1831 – must be wrong: in August 1831 AT was in America.

24. AT to Marie, Le Ménil, Monday morning, 1830, OC XIV 377–8.

25. E. de Chabrol to AT, 4 May 1831, Yale: Beinecke.

26. Beaumont, 'Notice', 15.

27. AT to his father, 'Thursday [1828?]', OC XIV 48. The book may have been John Howard's classic *State of the Prisons in England and Wales*, first published in 1777, the founding text of modern penology, or, perhaps more probably, Dumont's translation of Bentham's writings on pains and penalties, published in 1829. At least we know that AT had read both authors by the end of October 1830 (see OC IV i 52 n.1).

28. 'Note sur le système pénitentiaire', OC IV i 67.

29. Michelle Perrot, 'Introduction', ibid., 11–12.

30. Hervé de Tocqueville, 'Note sur la Maison Centrale de Détention de Poissy', ibid., ii 299–302.

31. 'Visite à la Maison Centrale de Poissy le 26 Septembre 1830', ibid., i 453–61. This *aide-mémoire*, later drawn upon for the 'Note sur le système pénitentiaire', is in GB's hand, but it exactly expresses AT's attitude.

32. 'Note', ibid., 53.

33. AT to C. Stoffels, 26 August and 4 October 1830, Jardin, *Tocqueville*, 89; AT to E. Stoffels, 21 February 1831, OC(B) V 41–3.

34. AT to GB, 14 March 1831, OC VIII i 106.

35. Pierson, 32.

36. ibid., 38–9.

37. ibid., 36.

38. Charles Lucas, Inspecteur Général des prisons du Royaume, to AT and GB, March 1831, OC IV i 462–3.

39. Pierson, 37–8.

40. ibid., 43.

8. *A Voyage Out*

1. AT to his mother, on board the ship *Le Havre*, 26 April 1831, OC XIV 75. The notably ample sources for this chapter consist of Tocqueville and Beaumont's letters home (OC

XIV, LA); their travel notes – although GB's do not survive in any quantity (OC V i, LA); SP (OC IV i–ii); DA (OC I i–ii); OC(B) VI, VII; the Yale archive; and Pierson.

2. AT to his mother, 26 April 1831, OC XIV 77.

3. AT, notes on shipboard conversations, Yale. These notes were omitted from OC V i but included in the Gallimard edition of the *Voyages* (see pp. 197–98).

4. GB to his father, 25 April 1831, LA 27–8.

5. GB to his mother, 14 May 1831, LA 36.

6. AT to his mother, New York, 14 May 1831, OC XIV 81–2.

7. AT to Édouard de Tocqueville, 28 May 1831, OC XIV 92.

8. AT, notebooks, 13 May 1831, OC V i 292.

9. ibid., 1 June 1831, OC V i 220.

10. AT to his mother, 15 May 1831, OX XIV 84; AT, notebooks, 'Premières Impressions', OC V i 294.

11. GB to his father, 16 May 1831, LA 43.

12. GB to his brother Jules, 26 May 1831, LA 52.

13. AT to Le Sueur, 28 May 1831; AT to Mme de Grancey, New York, 10 October 1831, OC(B) VII 71.

14. AT to his father, Sing-Sing, 3 June 1831, OC XIV 101.

15. Kergorlay to AT, 12 April 1831, OC XIII i 220.

16. GB to Jules, 26 May 1831, LA 47.

17. AT to Le Sueur, 28 May 1831, 97; GB to AT, Sing-Sing, May 1831, OC VIII i 107–8.

18. AT, notebooks, Sing-Sing, 3 June 1831, OC XIV 100.

19. AT to his father, Sing-Sing, 3 June 1831, OC XIV 100.

20. See Hall, vol. I, 49–51. For Edward Livingston's influence on AT's penal thought, see LA 49 n.1.

21. AT, notebooks, 7 June 1831, OC V i 59–60.

22. AT to Chabrol, New York, 9 June 1831, Rédier, 97–101; see also Pierson, 129–131.

23. AT to Alexandrine de Tocqueville, New York, 20 June 1831, OC XIV 108–9.

24. AT to Édouard, New York, 20 June 1831, Yale: Beinecke.

25. LA 42 n.1.

26. AT to Kergorlay, OC XIII i 225–38. The OC, following the manuscript, gives the place and date of this letter as Yonkers, 29 June 1831, but this is a mistake – AT's, no doubt: he and GB did not leave New York city until 30 June. Pierson's detailed discussion of this letter (Pierson, 152–67) is still very valuable.

27. See LA 76 n.4. Colwell's was one of the American names which defeated AT and GB: they spelt it Calwell.

28. AT to his father, Albany, 4 July 1831, OC XIV 113; GB to Jules, 4 July 1931; AT, notebooks, 11 July 1831, OC V i 162.

29. See GB to his father, 16 May 1831, LA 40.

30. AT to Chabrol, Auburn, 16 July 1831, Yale: Beinecke; LC 40.

31. GB to his sister Eugénie, 17 July 1831, LA 90–92.

32. AT to his mother, Auburn, 17 July 1831, OC XIV 116–17.

33. DA, OC I ii 36; notebooks, Auburn, 13 July 1831, OC V 231.

34. AT to his mother, Auburn, 17 July 1831, OC XIV 117.

35. Hall, I 136. Another passage which AT seems to have exploited may be found at 145–8, where Hall describes and discusses the psychology of the settlers.

36. AT, notebooks, 7 July 1831, OC V i 162.

37. ibid.; *Voyage au Lac Oneida*, OC V i 336–41.

38. There is an excellent account of Lynds and the Auburn system in Lewis. There is a good article on Lynds in the old *Dictionary of American Biography*, XI 527. The editors of its replacement, *American Biography*, did not see fit to include him.

39. See SP, OC i 342–5. It is noteworthy that AT and GB cut from this record Lynds's remark that he retired from Sing-Sing after one year in charge because 'I thought I had done enough for the public good.' They knew it was untrue.

40. See Lewis, 63.

41. For the full record of their conversation with Lynds, see OC V i 63–7; for a highly revealing anecdote about him, see OC IV i 345 n.1.

42. AT to Chabrol, Auburn, 16 July 1831, Yale: Beinecke.

43. ibid.; GB to his mother, Canandaigua, [17 July?] 1831, LA 98–9.

44. AT to Le Sueur, New York, 30 June 1831, OC XIV 110.

45. AT, notebooks, OC V i 223.

46. ibid., 19 July 1831, 163.

47. ibid., 21–22 July 1831, 164–5; AT, 'Quinze Jours dans le désert', ibid., 348–9.

48. Richard White, *The Middle Ground: Indians, empires and republics in the Great Lakes Region 1650–1815* (Cambridge University Press, 1991).

49. GB to his father, 1 August 1831, LA 104.

50. AT, 'Quinze jours', OC V i 349.

51. See illustrations to the present work.

52. Sainte-Beuve, *Causeries du lundi*, XV 98.

53. ibid., 98–9.

54. 'Quinze jours', OC V i 349.

55. GB to his brother Achille, on the *Superior*, Lake Michigan, 11 August 1831, LA 121.

56. ibid., 121–2.

57. AT, 'Conversation avec Mr Mullon', 7 August 1831, OC V i 72; GB to Achille, LA 119.

58. AT, notebooks, 3 August 1831, OC V i 173; AT to Mme de Grancey, 10 October 1831, OC(B) VII 241.

59. AT, notebooks, 6 August 1831, OC V i 174–5, 75–6.

60. AT to his father, on Lakes Erie, Huron and Michigan, 14 August 1831, OC XIV 124.

61. AT, notebooks, 3 August 1831, OC V i 175.

62. AT to his mother, on Lake Ontario, 21 August 1831, OC XIV 126–8. It is necessary to read between AT's lines: he does not explicitly mention the Vendée, no doubt from caution.

63. ibid.; AT, draft letter to Dalmassy, August 1831, Yale: Beinecke; GB to his father, Lake Ontario on board the *Great Britain*, 21 August 1831, LA 128–30.

64. See *Ancien Régime*, OC II i 286–7, 'Comment c'est en Canada qu'on pouvait mieux juger la centralisation administrative de l'Ancien Régime'.

65. AT, notebooks, OC V i 210–13; AT to Le Sueur, Albany, 7 September 1831, OC XIV 129–30; GB to his father, 5 September 1831, LA 139, 142.

66. Le Peletier d'Aunay to AT, Paris, August 1831, Yale: Beinecke.

9. *A Republic Observed*

1. AT to Édouard, Boston 10 September 1831, OC XIV 134.

2. AT to his mother, Boston, 27 September 1831, ibid., 136.

3. AT to the comtesse de Grancey, New York, 10 October 1831, OC(B) VII 70. Mme de Grancey was a close cousin, a granddaughter of Mme de Montboissier; AT to Édouard, 10 September 1831, OC XIV 135.

4. AT to E. V. Childe, Tocqueville, 12 December 1856, OC VII 184; GB to Jules de Beaumont, Boston, 16 September 1831, LA 144; AT, notebooks, 20 September 1831, OC V i 227.

5. GB to Jules de Beaumont, Boston, 16 September 1831, LA 150.

6. AT, notebooks, 17 September 1831, OC V i 249; ibid., 19 September 1831, 88.

7. GB, 'Fragments du journal', 29 September 1831, LA 152–4; AT, notebooks, 29 September 1831, OC V i 95; ibid., 96; Herbert B. Adams, 43–4. This essay includes Sparks's answers to a questionnaire left with him by AT in October 1831, and some further questions ('Vous voyez, Monsieur, que je suis incorrigible') in a letter from Cincinnati of 2 December (OC VII 35–9).

8. GB to Jules de Beaumont, 16 September 1831, LA 147.

9. AT, notebooks, 17 September 1831, OC V i 240–41; ibid., 1 October 1831, 97.

10. ibid., 20 September 1831, 88–9, 89–90; ibid., 30 September 1831, 178.

11. ibid., 30 September 1831.

12. ibid., 20 September 1831, 89–90; ibid., 22 September 1831, 92; conversation with Francis Lieber; ibid., 28 September 1831, 94; ibid., 2 October 1831, 101–2; ibid., 18 September 1831, 86; ibid., 30 September 1831, 179.

13. ibid., 27 September 1831, 246.

14. ibid., 1 October 1831, 98–9. As to corporal punishment, Adams was misinformed: women slaves were frequently whipped.

15. AT, notebooks, 18 September 1831, OC V i 87–8.

16. AT to his mother, 27 September 1831, OC XIV 137.

17. GB to Félicie de Beaumont, Philadelphia, 26 October 1831, LA 168.

18. For further details see Pierson, 446–8.

19. AT, notebooks, conversation with Mr Vaughan and Judge Coxe, Philadelphia, 13 October 1831, OC V i 103.

20. For a discussion of this important point see Foucault, 244–56.

21. See Pierson, 471–3.

22. See GB, 'Notice sur Alexis de Tocqueville', OC(B) V 18–19; Pierson, 463–4; OC IV i 576. GB states explicitly that AT conducted all the interviews, although half the surviving rough notes of the meetings are in GB's handwriting.

23. 'Enquête sur le pénitencier de Philadelphie', OC IV i 333, 334.

24. ibid., 335.

25. ibid., 331.

26. ibid., 336–8.

27. AT, notebooks, 5 October 1831, OC V i 103.

28. ibid., 28 October 1831, 185.

29. AT to Édouard, Washington, 20 January 1832, OC XIV 165.

30. Adams, 8.

31. AT to Hervé de Tocqueville, Hartford, 7 October 1831, OC XIV 138–9.

32. ibid., 138, n. 3. See also Bertier de Sauvigny, 417–18.

33. Pierson, 408.

34. AT to Alexandrine de Tocqueville, Philadelphia, 18 October 1831, OC XIV 14.

35. AT, notebooks, 25 October 1831, OC V i 247; Pierson, 513–14.

36. GB to Félicie de Beaumont, Philadelphia, 26 October 1831, LA 170.

37. AT, notebooks, Baltimore, 29 October 1831, OC V i 185–6.

38. ibid., 4 November 1831, 247; ibid., 3 November 1831, 242.

39. ibid., 187.

40. The clearest evidence on this matter is GB's letter to his brother Achille, Philadelphia, 8 November 1831, LA 175–6, where he says that he will publish his Baltimore observations on slavery, 'not very favourable', in the 'great work which is going to immortalize me'.

41. GB to his father, Philadelphia, 17 November 1831, LA 180; AT to Chabrol, Philadelphia, 26 October, Yale. For cajeput oil, see LA 170–71, n. 3.

42. GB to his father, Philadelphia, 17 November 1831, LA 180–81; AT to E. Stoffels, Philadelphia, 18 October, OC(B) V 422; AT to his mother, Philadelphia, 24 October, OC XIV 143.

43. GB to Eugénie de Beaumont, Cincinnati, 1 December 1831, LA 187; AT to Édouard, on board the *Fourth of July*, 26 November 1831, OC XIV 145.

44. AT said nothing of the adventure to his family until he was about to leave America (see p. 213). He wrote a full account to Marie Mottley, now lost. There is a short paragraph on the subject in his letter to Chabrol, 'on board the *Fourth of July* on the Ohio', 26–8 November 1831, Yale, and a fuller description in a surviving fragment of GB's journal (see 'Notice', OC(B) V 228–9, and LA 200–201). Pierson (546 n.) challenges, perhaps too severely, the authenticity of the journal as we have it, stigmatizing it as 'a clumsy amateur fake … constructed, either several weeks, or many years, after the events that it described'. He points out various blunders in the dates, but then GB was often careless about dates, as is shown elsewhere, and, as an editor, frequently tampered with the genuine documents that he printed. But fake or not, there seems to be no good reason for doubting the general accuracy of the account. It is to some extent confirmed by AT's letter to Chabrol, and by a passage in GB's book *Marie* (see Pierson, 547).

45. AT, notebooks, 2 December 1831, OC V i 128.

46. ibid., 127.

47. ibid., 124–32; Ratcliffe, 210–11.

48. AT, notebooks, 30 November 1831, OC V i 278.

49. ibid., Philadelphia, 20 November 1831, 123–4; ibid., Boston, 1 October 1831, 98; ibid., [Cincinnati], 2 December 1831, 125, 284; ibid., 3 December 1831, 131.

50. GB to Jules de Beaumont, on the Ohio, 4 December 1831, LA 191–5; AT to Chabrol, Louisville (*sic*, but written on the steamboat), 6 December 1831, Yale; AT to his father, 20 December 1831, OC XIV 154–5.

51. At this point we have to rely on GB's erratic dating.

52. GB, 'Journal', LA 201.

53. ibid., 201–2; GB to his mother, Sandy Bridge, 15 December 1831, ibid., 196; DA, OC I ii 60; AT to his mother, 'sur le Mississippi', 25 December 1831, OC XIV 158.

54. AT to his mother, 25 December 1831, OC XIV 158.

55. ibid., 161.

56. Pierson, 619–20, quoting P. L. White's translation of a document, '24 Heures à New-Orléans', the original of which has been lost; AT to his mother, 25 December 1831, OC XIV 161; AT, notebooks, 27 December 1831, OC V i 275; 31 December 1831, ibid., 261–6.

57. Pierson, 635.

58. AT to Chabrol, on Chesapeake Bay, 16 January 1832, Pierson 636; AT to Alexandrine, on Chesapeake Bay, 16 January 1832, OC XIV 163.

59. AT, notebooks, 12 January 1832, OC V i 201–2. The Pléiade edition (Paris: Gallimard, 1991) supplies an important missing word, vol. I, 190–91.

60. AT, notebooks, Pléiade edition, I, 191–2 (the better transcription of a difficult MS), OC V i 202–3.

61. Pierson, 643–4.

62. AT, notebooks, conversation with Mr Poinsett, 13, 14 and 15 January 1832, OC V i 205.

63. AT to E. V. Childe, [Paris], 2 April 1857, OC VII 193.

64. LA 209–10 n. 2.

65. GB to his mother, Washington, 20 January 1832, LA 210; AT to his father, Washington, 24 January, OC XIV 166–7, copied from the version published by GB in OC(B) VII 110 and, unfortunately, abridged by him. See also H. Brogan, 'Tocqueville and the American Presidency', *Journal of American Studies*, XV 3, December 1981, 357–75.

66. AT to his father, Washington, 24 January 1832, OC XIV 167; AT to Édouard, Washington, 20 January 1832, OC XIV 165.

67. GB to his mother, Washington, 20 January 1832, LA 209; AT to Chabrol, Washington, 24 January 1832, Yale: Beinecke.

68. AT to Chabrol, Chesapeake Bay, 16 January 1832, Yale: Beinecke.

69. GB to his mother, Washington, 20 January 1832, LA 208; AT to Joel Poinsett, [Washington], 1 February 1832, OC VII 45; AT to Édouard, Washington, 20 January 1832, and New York, 9 February 1832, OC XIV 165 and 168; AT to GB, Paris, 4 April 1832, OC VIII i 111.

10. *Writing Prisons*

1. Pierson, 678.

2. AT to GB, Paris, 4–6 April 1832, OC VIII i 112.

3. AT to E. Stoffels, 22 April 1832, OC(B) V 423–4.

4. Louis Chevalier, xiv, 4.

5. Morris, 15.

6. Louis Chevalier, 17.

7. AT to GB, Paris, 4–6 April 1832, OC VIII i 111–14.

8. AT to GB, Saint-Germain, 10 April 1832, OC VIII i 114–16; GB to Secrétaire-Général, ministère du commerce et des travaux publics, Paris, 12 April 1832, Yale; ministère du commerce to GB, Paris, 10 May 1832, Yale: Beinecke.

9. AT to Mme de Kergorlay, Saint-Germain, 'ce lundi matin' [16 April 1832], OC XIII i 249–50.

10. OC IV i 20.

11. AT to Marie, Marseille, 18 May 1832, XIV 380; AT to Mme de Kergorlay, [end of May], OC XIII i 251–2.

12. AT to Marie, Marseille, 18 May 1832, XIV 380; 'Notice', OC(B) V 36.

13. Jardin, *Tocqueville*, 179–81; 'Sophia Dawes', *Oxford* DNB, vol. XV, 530–31; Bowen.

14. AT to the procureur-général, Toulon, 21 May 1832, OC(B) V 36–7.

15. Jardin, *Tocqueville*, 181.

16. AT, 'Description du bagne de Toulon', May 1832, OC IV ii 45–61.

17. AT to Mme de Kergorlay, Marseille, [?25 May] 1832, XIII i 251–4; Mme de Kergorlay to the editor, *Gazette du Midi*, Marseille, 31 May 1832, ibid., 275–8 n.9.

18. GB to AT, Paris, 17 May [1832], OC VIII i 116–18; AT, 'Examen du livre de M. de Blosseville, De la question des colonies pénales', Gap, 31 May 1832, OC IV ii 62–3; AT to Marie, Lyon, 3 June 1832, OC XIV 383; AT, [*Notes sur les prisons de Genève et Lausanne*], 5–8 June 1832, OC IV ii 64–75.

19. Louis Chevalier, 21.

20. GB, 'Visite de la prison de La Roquette (7 août 1832)', OC IV i 464–5; AT, 'Maison de refuge de la rue de l'Oursine', 'Maison de Saint-Lazare', 'Maison de correction de l'Hôtel de Bazencourt', ibid., ii 76–83.

21. Kergorlay to AT, Marseille, 23 June–20 August 1832; Aix [-en-Provence], 12 September–30 October 1832, OC XIII i 256–301.

22. OC IV i 445.

23. GB, 'Notice', OC(B) I 26–7.

24. AT to F. Mignet, Paris, 26 June 1841, Yale: Beinecke.

25. OC IV i 22–3.

26. ibid., 240, 562 n. 4. Mme Perrot points out that in his draft AT refers throughout to 'Buonaparte' rather than to 'Napoleon'.

27. See OC IV i 208–12.

28. ibid., 206.

29. ibid., 253–4, 256–9.

30. ibid., 218–19, 232; IV ii 39.

31. Michelle Perrot quotes Bentham on architecture in OC IV i 558, and on music, 559; she quotes AT on music, from an unpublished MS, 559.

32. OC IV i 187, 188 n. 1.

33. AT to minister [of the interior?], Philadelphia, 14 July 1831, OC IV ii 37.

34. Foucault, 228, 234, 236–7.

35. ibid., 75–7, 84–9; OC IV i 244.

36. OC IV i 193.

37. Foucault, 90, quoting Rousseau, *Social Contract*, book IV, chapter 5.

38. Foucault, 108.

39. ibid., 119–20.

40. ibid., 115–16.

41. See Ignatieff.

42. ibid., ch. 5, 'Whigs, Jacobins and the Bastille: the Penitentiary under Attack', 114–42.

43. Foucault, 117; OC IV i 560, 173 n. 1; Charles Dickens, *American Notes* (London: Hazell, Watson & Viney, n.d.), 83–93; also *Letters*, ed. Graham Storey *et al.* (Oxford, 1974) vol. III, 110–11, 123–5.

44. AT to Chabrol, Philadelphia, 18 October 1831, Yale: Beinecke.

45. See OC IV i 444–8; Chevalier, VIII.

46. Everitt, 123; Kergorlay to AT, 28 January 1833, OC XIII i 316.

47. e.g., OC IV i 247.

48. ibid., 245.

49. ibid., 205, 235.

50. ibid., 25.

51. L. Sérurier to AT and GB, Washington, 17 May 1832, OC VII 25–6.

52. C. Lucas to GB and AT, Paris, March 1831, OC IV i 462–3; see above p. 147.
53. OC IV i 327.

11. *Between Books*

1. Chateaubriand, *Mémoires*, vol. II, 2517–32; Jardin, *Tocqueville*, 181–5; Kergorlay to AT, Montbrison, 7 February 1833, OC XIII i 319 and n. 2.
2. Boigne, vol. IV, 85–100.
3. OC XIII i 297–300; Kergorlay to AT, 30 October 1832, ibid., 318–19; Kergorlay to AT, 7 February 1833; ibid., 320; Kergorlay to AT, n.d. [*c.* 7 March 1833].
4. OC XIII i 321–7; AT, 'Discours prononcé en faveur de M. Louis de Kergorlay le 9 mars 1833, devant la cour d'assises de Montbrison, par M. Alexis de Tocqueville, avocat à la Cour Royale de Paris'; Jardin, *Tocqueville*, 188.
5. Yale: Beinecke, AT to Chabrol, New York, 18 May 1831, ibid.; AT to Chabrol, 18 October and 26 October 1831.
6. AT to [Louis de Chateaubriand?], Philadelphia, 8 November 1831, wrongly identified by the copyist, Doysié, as a letter to Louis de Kergorlay, Yale: Beinecke; AT to Marie, Toulon, 3 May [1841], OC XIV 416; Kergorlay to AT, 12 September 1832, OC XIII i 282–3.
7. See Kergorlay to AT, Paris, 4 August 1833, OC XIII i 331.
8. For AT and Mrs Belam see OC VI iii 37–8; his difference with Kergorlay is documented in OC XIII i 331–9, in three letters.
9. Jardin, *Tocqueville*, 200; Schleifer, 5.
10. e.g. Schleifer, 5.
11. AT to the comtesse de Pisieux, [July?] 1833, Yale: Beinecke.
12. AT to Marie, three letters, July–August 1833, ibid., 171–2; AT to his mother, Southampton, 7 August 1833, AT to Mrs Belam, [London], [4–5 September] 1833, OC VI iii 37.
13. See Drescher, *Tocqueville and England*, 35–6.
14. AT to GB, London, 13 August 1833, OC VIII i 24–5; AT to Marie, London, 14 August 1833, OC XIV 388–9; AT to his father, 24 August 1833, ibid., 173.
15. OC V ii 11–12; AT to Marie, London, 14 August 1833, OC XIV 388–9.
16. OC V ii 14–17.
17. AT to his father, London, 24 August 1833, OC XIV 173; GB to AT, Paris, 7 August 1833; AT to GB, London, 13 August; GB to AT, Beaumont-la-Chartre, 24 August 1833, OC VIII i 119–30.
18. AT to his father, London, 24 August 1833, OC XIV 173–74; CCT I iii, 'Preface'.
19. OC V ii 25–6, 'Bulwer' (août 1833), 29–31, 'Aristocratie [21 août]', 31–2, 'Centralisation (24 août 1833), 33, 'Police', 35, 'Uniformité [24 août]'. Lawrence Stone devoted years of research and a long monograph to refuting AT's observations, but the debate continues. (See Stone and Stone.)
20. 'William Pleydell-Bouverie, third earl of Radnor (1779–1869)', Oxford DNB VI 872–3; AT to his father, London, 24 August 1833, OC XIV 173–74.
21. AT to Marie, Oxford, 27 August 1833, OC XIV 389–91.
22. OC V ii 17–20.
23. AT to Marie, Bath [but finished at Longford Castle], 30 August 1833, OC XIV 391–4.
24. ibid., 394.

25. ibid., 391; OC V ii 20–23, 'une séance de la Justice de Paix', 26–8, 'Conversation avec Lord Radnor'. AT slightly enhanced these notes when he used them in his 'Mémoire sur paupérisme' (OC XVI 134–6).

26. AT to Elizabeth Belam, [n.p., 4–5 September 1833], OC VI iii 38.

27. See Drescher, *Tocqueville and England*, 35–53, for a thorough discussion of AT's response to England in 1833.

28. 'Dernières impressions sur l'Angleterre', OC V ii 36–43.

12. *Writing America*

1. 'Introduction', OC I i 12.

2. AT to Beaumont, Paris, 1 November 1833, OC VIII i 136.

3. 'Notice sur Alexis de Tocqueville', OC(B) V 37.

4. ibid., 37–8; AT to Kergorlay, [Paris, 11 November 1833], OC XIII i 344; Theodore Sedgwick, *Diary*, 28 November–2 December 1833, Massachusetts Historical Society.

5. Schleifer, 293, n.19.

6. ibid., 7.

7. F. J. Lippitt, R. I., Tiverton, 24 July 1897, Yale: Beinecke.

8. Sedgwick, *Diary*.

9. Schleifer, 10; I infer the date of completion from AT's letters, particularly AT to Beaumont, 14 July 1834, when he looks forward to carrying his gun and his finished manuscript to Beaumont-la-Chartre in mid-August (OC VIII i 142). J.-L. Benoît says flatly that he finished on 14 August 1834 (OC XIV 395 n.1).

10. AT to Beaumont, Paris, 5, 14 July 1834, OC VIII i 139–43; Ancelot, 79; AT to Marie Mottley, Beaumont-la-Chartre, 23 August 1834, OC XIV 395 n.1; AT to Charles Stoffels, Baugy, 31 July 1834, LC 302.

11. OC I i 331.

12. See, for example, OC I i 20–21, on the West Indies as first discovered by Europeans: 'Cà et là se montrent de petites îles perfumeés', etc.

13. See e.g. OC I i 157 (when he first uses the phrase 'despotism of the majority', but, at this stage, has only 'the legislative body' in mind).

14. AT to Nassau Senior, [Paris], 24 March 1834, CCT i 1–2.

15. OC I i 176.

16. See ibid., 261–72.

17. ibid., 263, 266.

18. ibid., 413.

19. ibid., 329.

20. ibid., 256.

21. See Schleifer, 10–12.

22. AT to Camille d'Orglandes, [29 November 1834], LC 310.

23. OC I i 199, 329.

24. ibid., 203.

25. ibid., 178.

26. ibid., 190.

27. ibid., 197.

28. ibid., 230.

29. Ibid., 240; John Quincy Adams to AT, Quincy, 12 June 1837, Massachusetts Historical Society (typed copy at Yale: Beinecke). AT's reply is in OC VII 67–9.

30. OC I i 236–40.

31. ibid., 273–4.

32. ibid., 266.

33. ibid., 319 n. 8.

34. ibid., 323.

35. ibid., 329.

36. ibid., 330.

37. ibid., 331.

38. ibid., 422.

39. ibid., 6–7.

40. ibid., 5.

41. ibid., 7.

42. ibid., 9–10.

43. AT to Kergorlay, Paris, 21 September 1834, OC XIII i 356; AT to Marie Mottley, Beaumont-la-Chartre, 23 August 1834, OC XIV 394–6.

44. AT to comte Jules de Beaumont, Paris, 18 September 1834, LC 306–7.

45. AT to GB, Paris, 14 July 1834, OC VIII 140–41.

46. Kergorlay to AT, [October] 1834, OC XIII 365.

47. 'Observations critiques', Yale: Beinecke, CIII 6.

48. AT to Camille d'Orglandes, [29 November 1834], LC 309–13.

13. *Fame*

1. AT to Eugène Stoffels, Paris, 16 February 1835, OC(B) V 426.

2. GB, 'Notice sur Alexis de Tocqueville', 39.

3. See GB, *Marie*, 2.

4. E. Stoffels to AT, Metz, 26 January 1835, Saint-Lô: AT 2357; Kergorlay to AT, Fosseuse, 24 January 1835, OC XIII i 370–72.

5. The Beinecke Library, Yale, Tocqueville-Beaumont Collection C XI a, holds the following reviews, apparently AT's own collection of clippings: *Courrier Français*, 24 December 1834; *Gazette de France*, 3 and 13 February 1835; *Le Bon Sens*, 5 and 9 February 1835; *L'Écho Francais*, 11 February 1835; *Gazette du Berri*, 21 February 1835; *Le Semeur*, 25 February 1835; *Journal des débâts*, 25 March and 2 May 1835; *Le Temps*, 7 April 1835; *Jo. général de l'instruction publique*, 21 May 1835; *Revue des deux mondes*, 31 May 1835; *Le National*, 7 June 1835; *Moniteur du commerce*, 27 December 1835. Jardin, *Tocqueville*, 215–18, gives additionally *Revue européenne*, 1 April 1835; *Revue républicaine*, 10 May 1835; *Constitutionnel*, 18 May 1835; *L'Ami de la religion et du roi*, 25 and 29 August 1835, 8 September 1835; *L'Européen*, 25 November and 25 December 1835. There were probably others.

6. Senior to AT, Lincoln's Inn, 17 February 1835, VI ii 66–7; Saint-Lô: AT 364 (bills for the shipping costs).

7. AT to Royer-Collard, Paris, [16 or 23 January 1835], OC XI 9; GB, 'Notice', 39.

8. AT to François-René de Chateaubriand, [December 1834], Saint-Lô: AT 614. This MS is only an incomplete draft of the final letter, but it is clear from Chateaubriand's reply

that the letter sent was not significantly different. I suppose it may have been slightly less unctuous.

9. Chateaubriand to AT, 11 January [1835], Saint-Lô: AT 1294. I owe M. André Tarniou warm thanks for helping me to decipher this document.

10. Lehmann, 179–95, gives much the best modern account of Mme Récamier's salon.

11. Senior, *Journal*, 20 April 1858.

12. AT to GB, [Paris], 1 April 1835, OC VIII i 132–3.

13. Éduard Gans, *Revue de Paris*, 7 February 1836, 237–42: see OC VII 285 n. 4.

14. Custine, 420–21.

15. Laughton, i 48, 62; AT to E. Stoffels, [Paris], 16 February 1835, OC(B) V 426–7.

16. AT to GB, [Paris], 1 April 1835, OC VIII i 132–3; Mélonio, 20.

17. Mill, 'De Tocqueville on Democracy in America', 47–90; AT to J. S. Mill, 'Au château de Baugy', 3 December 1835, OC VI i 303.

18. Sainte-Beuve, 'Alexis de Tocqueville: *De la démocratie en Amérique*'. *Le Temps*, Tuesday, 7 April 1835, reprinted in *Premiers Lundis*, II 277–90 (nouvelle édition, Paris, 1894).

19. *La Gazette de France* (feuilleton), 3 and 13 February 1835.

20. 'L.M.', *Moniteur du commerce*, Sunday, 27 December 1835.

21. See Jardin, *Tocqueville*, on *L'Ami de la religion et du roi*, 215.

22. *Le Semeur*, 25 February 1835; Lammenais to AT, 9 February 1835, Saint-Lô: AT 1755.

23. See Mélonio, 34. Mme Mélonio gives much the most thorough account of the reception of DA 1835, 27–54.

24. Salvandy, *Journal des Débâts*, 2 May 1835; Léon Faucher, *Le Courrier français*, 24 December 1834; Rossi, *Journal Général de l'Instruction publique*, 21 March 1835; Corcelle, *Revue des deux mondes*, 31 May 1835, 739–61.

25. *Le Bon Sens, Journal de la démocratie*, 5 February 1835; Mill, '*De Tocqueville on Democracy in America*'; *London and Paris Courier*, 14 January 1836; *Le National de 1834*, 7 January 1835; *L'Écho français*, 11 February 1835.

26. See unidentified and undated clipping in the Yale archive, C XI a.

27. GB, *Marie*, 1–2.

28. Senior to AT, 5 March 1835, OC VI ii 72.

29. GB, *Marie*, 366–71; Edward Pessen, 'Tocqueville's Misreading of America, America's Misreading of Tocqueville', *Tocqueville Review*, 1982, IV, i, 5–22 (and in other works).

30. GB, *Marie*, 363–5 (sociability), 337–9 (women), 269–91 (religion).

31. Michel Chevalier; for AT's attitude, see AT to GB, Baugy, 3 December 1836, OC VIII i 176.

32. AT to Mathieu Molé, Paris, August 1835, OC(B) VII 134–5.

33. OC I i 12.

34. This paragraph is all too conjectural, but it rests on the known sequence of events.

35. AT to Molé, Paris, August 1835, OC(B) VIII 134–5; AT to Virginie Ancelot, London, 28 April 1835, LC 320; AT to Hervé de Tocqueville, London, 29 April 1835, OC XIV 175.

36. Le Sueur to [Hervé?] and AT, [Paris], 29 September 1828, Saint-Lô: AT 278.

37. AT to Alexandrine de Tocqueville, Hampstead, 22 May 1835, OC XIV 179–81; AT to Herbert Norman Evans (his doctor), same date, OC VI iii 43.

38. For Reeve's first meeting with AT and his book see Laughton, i, 42–50.

39. AT to Marie Mottley, London, 5 May 1835, OC XIV 397.

40. AT, notebooks: 'Whigs', 22 May 1835, OC V ii 51–2; AT to Hervé de Tocqueville, London, 7 May 1835, OC XIV 178–9.

41. For this theme see Drescher, *Tocqueville and England, passim*, and especially 35–62.

42. AT to Molé, London, 19 May 1835, LC 325–30.

43. Senior to AT, Lincoln's Inn, 17 February 1835; AT to Senior, Paris, 21 February 1835, OC VI ii 66–71; see also CCT I 5–8.

44. Camillo di Cavour, 24 March 1835, quoted in Levy, 14; for the original, see Cavour, *Diario Inedito con note autobiografiche* (Rome, 1888), 173.

45. AT, 'Mémoire sur le paupérisme', *Mémoires de la Société Académique de Cherbourg*, 1835, 293–344, and OC XVI 117–39.

46. See, for example, Himmelfarb, 147–52; Drolet, 135–47.

47. OC IV i 319–22.

48. AT to Senior, [Paris], 14 March 1835; Senior to AT, 18 March 1835, OC VI ii 73–5; see also CCT I 11–12.

49. OC XVI 128.

50. 'Second Mémoire sur le paupérisme', [1837], OC XVI 140–57.

51. I owe this point to Michael Drolet, to whom my thanks. Édouard published half a dozen works on agricultural policy between 1836 and 1866, with such titles as 'De l'intervention de l'esprit chrétien dans l'enseignement professionel de l'agriculture'.

52. J. S. Mill to Joseph Blanco White, 15 April 1835, to Aristide Guilbert, 8 May, and to Blanco White, 19 May 1835, *Earlier Letters* i 259–63. Mill mentions his first meeting with AT in an unpublished letter to Guilbert, 5 June 1835 (Yale: Sterling) but says only '[I] like him exceedingly and I mean if possible to persuade him to write for the review.'

53. AT, notebooks, 'Conversation with John Mill', 26 May 1835, OC V ii 53–4.

54. AT, notebooks, 'Conversation with J. A. Roebuck and J. S. Mill', 29 May 1835, ibid., 56–8.

55. AT to J. S. Mill, [London, 13 June 1835], OC VI i 293–4.

56. AT to Kergorlay, Dublin, 6 July 1835, OC XIII i 377; to Virginie Ancelot, London, 19 June 1835, Ancelot 84–5.

57. Quoted in Packe, 202.

58. AT, parliamentary testimony, 'Enquêtes sur la corruption électorale', 22 June 1835, OC XVI 88–111: a translation of the official report of the committee, *Parliamentary Papers*, 19 February 1835–September 1835, VIII, 230–41. It is noteworthy that AT gave his evidence in French.

59. AT to J. S. Mill, Coventry, Thursday morning, [25 June 1835], OC VI i 291.

60. AT, notebooks, [Birmingham, 25–30 June 1835], OC VI ii 67.

61. ibid., Manchester, 2 July 1835, 78–82.

62. ibid., Liverpool, 4 or 5 July 1835, 84–5.

63. AT to GB, Nacqueville, 26 August 1835, OC VIII i 154; AT, notebooks, conversation with Mr Kelly and Mr Wilson, 11 July 1835, OC V ii 99; ibid., 105.

64. AT to Hervé de Tocqueville, Dublin, 16 July 1835, OC XIV 184.

65. AT, notebooks, 26 July 1835, 'Dinner with the Bishop of Kilkenny' (here and elsewhere AT got the name of the diocese wrong), OC V ii 129; ibid., 27 July 1835, 'Journey from Kilkenny to Cork', OC V ii 135.

66. ibid., 26 July 1835, OC V ii 128–9.

67. ibid., 'A Catholic Priest and a Protestant Minister in Ireland', begun at Cork, 28 July 1835, OC V ii 136–51.

68. OC(B) VIII 402 n. 1; AT, notebooks, OC V ii 131–4; GB, *L'Irlande*, I, ch. 2, 'Une mauvaise aristocratie est la cause première de tous les maux de l'Irlande'. 211–20.

69. This is most noticeably true of the preface, *L'Irlande*, i–xx.

70. AT to Marie Mottley, [1835], OC XIV 399.

71. AT to Kergorlay, Dublin, 6 July 1835, OC XIII i 378; AT to Édouard and Alexandrine de Tocqueville, Dublin, 12 July 1835, OC XIV 181–3.

72. AT to GB, Nacqueville, 26 August 1835, OC VIII i 153–5; AT to Mme de Grancey, Paris, 22 September 1835, OC(B) VII 136–7, 140–41.

73. AT to Camille d'Orglandes, [Paris], 14 October 1835, LC 342–4; marriage contract, Saint-Lô: AT 3516.

14. *Into Politics*

1. OC XIII i 479.

2. AT to GB, [Baugy], Monday morning, [12 January 1835], OC VIII i 150; to GB, Baugy, Saturday morning, [31 October 1835], ibid., 155.

3. AT to GB, Baugy, 15 November 1835, ibid., 156.

4. Kergorlay to AT, Paris, 7 November 1835, OC XIII i 378–9; Camille d'Orglandes to AT, 6 December 1835, Saint-Lô: AT 2098; AT to Sarah Austin, Baugy, 26 November 1835, in Ross, 121; reprinted, OC VI iii 49.

5. AT to GB, Baugy, 15 November 1835, OC VIII i 157.

6. Camille d'Orglandes to AT, [6 December 1835], Saint-Lô: AT 2098; AT to comtesse de Grancey, 11 January 1836, OC(B) VII 144–5; to Louis Bouchitté, 15 January 1836, ibid., 146–7; to J. S. Mill, Paris, 10 February 1836, OC VI i 307.

7. AT to E. Stoffels, Paris, 11 January 1836, OC(B) VI 430–31. Jardin says that the comtesse did not attend the church wedding (Jardin, *Tocqueville*, 229).

8. See marriage contract, article 4, Saint-Lô: AT 378; AT to Henry Reeve, Cherbourg, 17 April 1836, OC VI i 29; Senior, *Journal*, 18 August 1850. See also H. Reeve, 'Introductory Notice', I, xiii–xiv, although Reeve confuses Tourlaville and Tocqueville.

9. F. Furet, 'De Tocqueville and the problem of the French Revolution', 153–5. I take this, the earliest opportunity, of saying that this indispensable essay contains the most brilliant and persuasive reading of AT's *Ancien Régime* yet published.

10. Many of AT's bills are preserved at Saint-Lô. In a curious way they seem to bring him closer to us than do many of the other documents.

11. Jardin, *Tocqueville*, 231; Hervé de Tocqueville, *Mémoires*.

12. D. W. Brogan, *Tocqueville: French Personalities and Problems* (London, 1946), 204.

13. AT to GB, Tocqueville, 5 October 1828, OC VIII i 49; to Reeve, Tocqueville, 10 June 1837, VI i 39; to Corcelle, 10 June 1837, XV 77–8; to Royer-Collard, Tocqueville, 29 June 1837, XI 34; to Corcelle, Tocqueville, 25 June 1838, XI i 100; to Édouard de Tocqueville, Tocqueville, 10 July 1838, OC XIV 200.

14. Reeve to his mother, Tocqueville, 20 August 1844, Laughton, I, 167–8; Senior, *Journal*, 11 August 1861.

15. See OC II i 31–66. Mill translated it himself, and it was published in what had become the *London and Westminster Review*, April 1836.

16. AT to Kergorlay, Tocqueville, 5 July 1838, OC XIII ii 35; to Kergorlay, Nacqueville, 9 October 1838, ibid., 47; Rédier, 124–5.

17. AT to Kergorlay, Baden, 5 August 1836, OC XIII i 387.

18. E. Stoffels to AT, Metz, 16 July 1836, Yale: Beinecke, CI c.

19. AT to E. Stoffels, Berne, 24 July 1836, OC(B) V 431–5; see also LC 352–5.

20. Rémusat, IV, 44–5.

21. AT to Kergorlay, Baden, 5 August 1836, OC XIII i 387; to GB, Interlaken, 8 September 1836, ibid., 164; to Royer-Collard, 25 August 1836, OC XI 18–19; 'Notes sur Machiavel', Baden, 1 August 1836, OC XVI 541–50; 'Analyse de Platon', [August 1836], ibid., 555–7 (the editor of this volume, Françoise Mélonio, dates this document '1836–1837?', but to me it seems clearly to belong to the weeks in Baden).

22. AT, 'Remarques sur l'histoire Suisse', Berne, 15 August 1836, OC V ii 175–7.

23. AT to GB, Mareil, 22 September 1836, OC VIII i 167; AT, 'A MM. les Electeurs des Cantons de Beaumont et des Pieux', [October 1836], OC X 729–30.

24. AT to Louis-Mathieu, Comte Molé, Paris, August 1835, OC(B) VII 136; to Reeve, Cherbourg, 17 April 1836, OC VI i 29; to J. S. Mill, Paris, 10 April 1836, ibid., 309; to Louis Bouchitté, Baugy, 26 May 1836, OC(B) VII 149.

25. Schleifer, 24; AT to GB, Baugy, 16 October 1836, OC VIII i 171; to J. S. Mill, 19 November 1836, VI i 314; to Reeve, 21 November 1836, ibid., 35; to GB, [3 December] 1836, VIII i 176.

26. GB to AT, 13 January 1837, OC VIII i 178; DA (Pléiade edition), 1163–4.

27. GB to AT, 15 January 1838, OC VIII i 275; AT to Paul Clamorgan, Baugy, 12 January 1838, X 89–90; Hervé de Tocqueville to AT, 17 January 1838, Yale: Beinecke CVI: see also OC III 238–49 ('De l'honneur aux États-Unis et dans les sociétés démocratiques'), DA (Pléiade) I 1150–53.

28. AT to Kergorlay, Tocqueville, 5 July 1838, OC XIII ii 35; Kergorlay to AT, 16 August 1836, ibid., 396–7.

29. AT to GB, Baugy, 18 January 1838, OC VIII i 279.

30. AT to Kergorlay, Tocqueville, 4 September 1837, OC XIII i 472; Kergorlay to AT, 6 [February] 1838, ibid. ii 14–18.

31. Kergorlay to AT, 2 March 1838, ibid., 19–24.

32. AT to Kergorlay, Baugy, 2 March 1838, ibid., 28.

33. AT to Corcelle, Baugy, 19 March 1838, OC XV i 97; to GB, Tocqueville, 8 July 1838, OC VIII i 310; to Édouard de Tocqueville, Tocqueville, 10 July 1838, OC XIV 199–200; to GB, Tocqueville, 19 October 1838, 5 November 1838, OC VIII i 321, 325–7.

34. AT to Corcelle, Tocqueville, 20 December 1838, OC XV i 106–7; to GB, [Paris], Thursday morning, [31 January 1839], OC VIII i 337.

35. ibid., 337–8.

36. Fumaroli, 735, 750.

37. AT to GB, 31 January 1839, OC VIII i 337.

38. AT to GB, [Paris], Friday morning, [1 February 1839], ibid., 338–9.

39. Reeve, 'Introductory Notice', xxiv; Senior, *Journal*, 17 August 1850.

40. GB to AT, 7 October 1837, OC VIII i 239; AT, 'Deux lettres sur l'Algérie', III i 129–53.

41. AT, *Souvenirs*, OC XII 106.

42. Pouthas, 25.

43. Rémusat, IV, 45.

44. Royer-Collard to AT, 15 June 1837, OC XI 32–3.

45. AT to Molé, Tocqueville, 12 September 1837, OC(B) VI 73–5.

46. Molé to AT, 14 September 1837, ibid., 75–8.

47. Senior, *Journal*, 18 August 1861. Senior gets the year of the business wrong – he puts 1835 for 1837.
48. AT to Molé, 18 September 1837, LC 390–93.
49. See GB to AT, Paris, [22 September 1837], OC VIII i 280–88.
50. AT to Molé, Tocqueville, 23 September 1837, OC(B) VI 79–80, LC 393 n.181.
51. Jardin, *Tocqueville*, 292.
52. AT to GB, Tocqueville, 12 November 1837, OC VIII i 262; to Hervé de Tocqueville, 30 October 1837, OC XIV 198.
53. AT to GB, Tocqueville, 12 November 1837, OC VIII i 262–4.
54. AT to GB, Baugy, 22 April 1838, ibid., 291–2.
55. Guizot, IV, 288.
56. Jardin and Tudesq, 125.
57. See Senior, *Journal*, 18 August 1861; AT to Corcelle, Tocqueville, 20 December 1838, OC XV i 105.
58. See OC III ii 51 n.3.
59. AT, ['Allocution à la suite de son élection le 2 mars 1839'], OC III ii 56–7; AT to E. Stoffels, Valognes, 7 March 1839, OC(B) V 439.

15. *Writing Democracy*

1. Sainte-Beuve, *Causeries du lundi*, XI, 459.
2. AT to Édouard de Tocqueville, 11 March 1839, OC XIV 205; AT to E. Stoffels, Valognes, 7 March 1839, OC(B) V 440.
3. See Saint-Lô, 'Vie courante et voyages', AT 365–6.
4. AT to Corcelle, Tocqueville, 10 March 1839, OC XV i 125.
5. AT, 'Rapport fait au nom de la commission chargée d'examiner la proposition de M. de Tracy, relative aux esclaves de colonies', OC III i 41–78.
6. AT to Édouard de Tocqueville, 3 July 1859, OC XIV 209; Marcel, 315 n.1; Chateaubriand to AT, 7 July 1839.
7. AT to Corcelle, Tocqueville, 19 October 1839, OC XV i 139.
8. Alphonse de Lamartine, speech in the Chamber of Deputies, 10 January 1839. I have used the account in Whitehouse, II, 62–5.
9. AT to Léon Faucher, Tocqueville, 1 September 1839, OC XI 85; to Corcelle, [Tocqueville, 4 September 1839], OC XI i 134–5.
10. Royer-Collard to AT, 28 October 1839, OC XI 89.
11. AT to GB, Tocqueville, 23 October 1839, OC XIII i 390; AT to Royer-Collard, Tocqueville, 21 October 1839, OC XI 86; AT to J. S. Mill, 11, rue de Castellane, Paris, 14 November 1839, OC VI i 326–7; Reeve to AT, 22 February 1840, ibid., 54–5.
12. AT to Mill, 14 November 1839, OC VI 326–7.
13. See Schleifer, 26.
14. AT to Reeve, 2 March 1838, OC VI i 42.
15. OC I ii 11–15.
16. ibid., 53.
17. ibid., 57.
18. AT, 'Second mémoire sur le paupérisme', OC XVI 148–57.
19. OC I ii 313–14.
20. ibid., 313.

21. Rédier, 45–9. Rédier gives the date as November 1841.
22. OC I ii 277–8.
23. ibid., 173–5.
24. Jules Michelet to AT, 27 April 1840, Saint-Lô: AT 1979.
25. OC I ii 258.
26. ibid., 307.
27. ibid., 336–7.
28. ibid., 104.
29. *Esprit des lois*, book II, ch. 4.
30. See AT to Lord Radnor, London, May 1835, OC VI iii 38–43.
31. OC I ii 328.
32. Isaiah Berlin, 'Two Concepts of Liberty'.
33. OC I ii 258–69.
34. ibid., 105–6.
35. ibid., 109–11.
36. ibid., 112.
37. ibid., 310.
38. ibid., 7. AT always planned to include the 'Avertissement', and first drafted it in 1836. For this first draft and his subsequent revisions see the Pléiade edition, 1084–6.
39. OC I ii 8.
40. See AT to Kergorlay, 10 November 1836, OC XVIII i 418; Schleifer, 25–6. Eduardo Nolla, in his invaluable critical edition of the *Démocratie*, seems to show that Kergorlay's substantive influence was greatest in the chapter on democratic ambition: see Nolla (ed.), *De la démocratie en Amérique* (Paris: Vrin, 1990), II, 203.
41. OC I ii 149, 319.
42. ibid., 29.
43. ibid., 27–30.
44. ibid., 35–8.
45. ibid., 201 n.1.
46. ibid., 200–205, ch. VII: 'Influence of Democracy on the Family'.
47. ibid., 206.
48. ibid., 207–8.
49. ibid., 219.
50. ibid., 214.
51. ibid., 213.
52. ibid., 209.
53. ibid., 210–11.
54. ibid., 212 n.1.
55. ibid., 215–16; Jardin, *Tocqueville*, 249.
56. OC I ii 339.
57. Mélonio, 66. The book is an indispensable study of the reception of AT's writings in his own country. Crook, 166–98, is excellent on the reception of DA in Britain. Curiously, in spite of the avalanche of American monographs on AT in the last fifty years or so, there seems to be no comparable study of his reception in the United States. Phillips Bradley devotes a few useful pages to the subject in his edition of *Democracy in America* (2 vols., New York: Knopf, 1945), I xl–lii.

58. Mélonio, 70.

59. AT to Sylvestre de Sacy, [1840], Jardin, 272–3: I have made my own translation of this document.

60. Ampère to AT, 24 September 1840, OC XI 136–44. The poem was published in the *Revue de Paris*, 20 September 1840, without the satirical section on AT's 'honest electors' who are destroying his digestion with their long banquets and 'antique abundance'.

61. AT to J. S. Mill, Paris, 3 May 1840, Mill to AT, 11 May 1840, OC VI i 327–9.

62. Mill, 'De Tocqueville on Democracy in America [II]'; Crook, 176–86, is especially illuminating on Mill and Tocqueville.

16. *Deputy*

1. Senior, *Journal*, 20 May 1848, JFI I 110.

2. *Souvenirs*, OC XII 86, LC 800.

3. Rémusat, III, 262–3; AT to Marie, December 1841, OC XIV 444. To see the difference, compare AT's speech of 30 November 1840, on the Eastern question (OC III ii 288–301), with that on the right of search, 20 May 1842 (ibid., 325–33).

4. AT to Marie, [Paris, 19 August 1842], OC XIV 471.

5. Custine, 426–7; Rémusat, IV 44–5.

6. Senior, *Journal*, 21 August 1850.

7. OC XII 103, LC 815–16.

8. Senior, *Journal*, 21 August 1850; OC XII 102, LC 815.

9. Kergorlay to AT, 27 July and August 1840, OC XIII ii 72–5.

10. AT to Odilon Barrot, 16 September 1842.

11. Jardin, *Tocqueville*, 388.

12. ibid., 391. Jardin's lucid account of the *Commerce* episode (388–96) is admirably detailed.

13. GB to Chambolle, 5 December 1844, OC VIII 546–7; AT to GB, 9 December 1844, ibid., 548–50.

14. AT to GB, 13 or 20 December 1844, ibid., 555.

15. AT to Royer-Collard, Tocqueville, 15 August 1840, OC XI 89–90.

16. Rémusat, IV, 12–14.

17. AT to Paul Clamorgan, Paris, 17 December 1841, OC X 203–4. Here we see Clamorgan used as a sort of press officer: he was expected to make sure that AT's statements got effective public circulation.

18. AT to Corcelle, Tocqueville, 14 July 1842, OC XV i 156.

19. AT, 'Allocution de Tocqueville après l'élection du 9 juillet 1842', OC III ii 77; 'Notes pour un Discours', ibid., 208.

20. Rémusat, IV, 14.

21. AT to J.-F. Hervieu, [Paris], 8 January 1842, OC X 208.

22. Guizot to AT, 26 April 1842, Saint Lô: AT 1064; Guizot, 'Reply to Lacordaire', 24 January 1861, OC XVI 332–45.

23. See Johnson, 83–7, for an excellent discussion of the subject; see also Siedentop, *passim*, though I do not altogether agree with some of Dr Siedentop's views.

24. Bury and Tombs, 79.

25. AT, 'Premier Discours sur la question d'Orient', 20 July 1839, OC III ii 265.

26. AT, 'Second Discours sur la question d'Orient', 30 November 1840, OC III ii 288–301.

27. AT to J. S. Mill, Paris, 18 December 1840, OC VI i 331.

28. J. S. Mill to AT, 9 August 1842, OC VI i 337; Henry Reeve to C. C. Greville, Christmas Day 1841, Laughton, i, 143; Nassau Senior to AT, 27 February 1841, OC VI ii 91.

29. GB, 'Notice sur Alexis de Tocqueville', OC(B) V 65.

30. OC XII 45–6, LC 762. The best discussion of AT's political programme, if it may be given the name, is in Drescher, *Dilemmas*; valuable, if less comprehensive, is Drolet.

31. OC XII 30–31, LC 750–51.

32. OC XII 31–4, LC 751–4.

33. Collingham has a particularly lucid and informative discussion of the changes in politics brought about by the July Revolution.

34. AT, 'Discussion de l'adresse', *Séance du 18 Janvier 1842*, OC III ii 201; AT to Clamorgan, Paris, 14 March 1842, OC X 216 and n.2.

35. AT to Kergorlay, Tocqueville, 25 October 1842, OC XIII ii 108–9.

36. Karl Marx, *The Class Struggles in France 1848 to 1850* (Moscow, 1968), 28.

37. Drescher, *Dilemmas*, is admirable on the obstacles in the way of social reform under the July Monarchy.

38. AT to Marie, Paris, 8–9 August 1842, OC XIV 463–4.

39. Rédier, 124.

40. AT to Sophie Swetchine, Tocqueville, 11 February 1857, OC XV ii 309.

41. Kergorlay to Marie, 7 March 1841, OC XIII ii 81.

42. AT to Kergorlay, [Tocqueville], 27 September 1843, ibid., 121.

43. Information from Françoise Mélonio.

44. AT to Marie, Algiers, 9 May 1841, OC XIV 418–19; OC V ii 191.

45. OC V ii 216–17.

46. OC III i 294 and nn.1, 2.

47. Thucydides, *Peloponnesian War*, tr. Rex Warner (London, Penguin, 1954), book II, 132.

48. AT, 'Rapport fait sur le Projet de Loi relative aux Crédits Extraordinaires demandés pour l'Algérie', 24 May 1847, OC III i 329.

49. The best discussion of this topic is Richter, to which I am much indebted. Also very valuable is André Jardin, 'Tocqueville et l'Algérie'. Both papers were written at the time of France's defeat in the Algerian War, to their advantage.

50. See AT, 'Travail sur l'Algérie (Octobre 1841)', OC III i 213–14.

51. H. d'Ideville, *Memoirs of Marshal Bugeaud*, tr. Charlotte M. Yonge (London, 1884), II, 19–23.

52. AT to Marie, Toulon, 12 June 1841, OC XIV 435.

53. AT to Marie, Algiers, 22 May 1841, ibid., 425; GB, 'Notice', 25; AT to Marie, Montaganem, 17 May 1841, OC XIV 424–5.

54. AT to Marie, Algiers, 22–4 May 1841, OC XIV 429.

55. AT to Marie, Toulon, 12 June 1841, OC XIV 435; AT to Marie, Marseille, 13 June 1841, ibid., 437; AT to Marie, Avignon, 14 June 1841, ibid., 439.

56. AT to Marie, Paris, 21 June 1841, ibid., 440.

57. Quoted in Fumaroli, 740.

58. Dorothée de Dino, iii, 122.

59. OC XVI 231–2 n.1, quoting a memorandum by AT of a conversation with Royer-Collard on 8 January 1842.

60. AT, 'Discours', 21 April 1842, OC XVI 251–69.

61. Dino, II, 316.

62. ibid., III, 133.

17. *February*

1. From AT's speech on his entry to the Académie Française, 21 April 1842, OC XVI 255.
2. Guillemin, 53.
3. For all this see OC XVI 288–303, 22 July 1847.
4. AT to GB, [?17] July 1847, OC VIII i 605; OC XII 34.
5. Whitehouse, *Lamartine* II, 174.
6. Howarth, 307.
7. OC XII 35; Johnson, 192.
8. AT to Nassau Senior, Tocqueville, 25 August 1847, OC VI ii 99; AT to Corcelle, Tocqueville, 29 September 1847, OC XI i 239.
9. AT to Corcelle, Tocqueville, 27 August 1847, OC XV 234–6; AT to GB, 23 August 1847, OC VIII i 608; GB to AT, 30 August 1847, ibid., 612; Whitehouse, II, 465.
10. AT to Prosper Enfantin, [Tocqueville], 10 November 1847, LC 591–2. The editors of the LC point out that this letter is known to us only through a draft in AT's papers.
11. AT never names Proudhon, but to me it is inconceivable that he did not read *What is Property?* and it is Proudhonian doctrine that he attacks in his speeches; AT to Gobineau, Tocqueville, 5 September 1843, OC IX 46–7, mentions the Saint-Simonians.
12. Letter to Paul Ackermann, quoted in Woodcock, *Proudhon*, 58.
13. *De la célébration du dimanche*, quoted in Woodcock, *Anarchism*, 112–13.
14. Proudhon's debt to AT has been no secret for the best part of a century: see Mayer, 147–8; Lambetti, 206 n.91; Mélonio, 41–2, 222–3; but so far as I know it has never received the sort of detailed examination and exposition which the subject deserves.
15. Quoted in Lefebvre, 50.
16. See OC XII 96.
17. OC III ii 731–44: 'Note'; 'Question financière'; 'De la classe moyenne et du peuple'; ['Fragments pour une politique sociale'].
18. OC III ii 736–7, 740–41. Readers of the *Démocratie* will remember that in 1835 AT thought that the days of great political parties based on distinct principles were over.
19. OC III ii 743–4.
20. OC XII 43; Guizot, VIII, 534.
21. Collingham, 401.
22. OC XII 32–3.
23. OC III ii 745–58.
24. OC XII 41.
25. ibid., 43.
26. Duveau, 5.
27. OC XII 51.
28. ibid., 53.
29. Guizot, VIII, 589.
30. OC XII 57.
31. GB wrote a memoir of 24 February, now in the Beinecke Library, Yale. It is a vividly written supplement to AT's *Souvenirs*, and ought to be published.
32. OC XII 61.
33. ibid., 65–6.
34. ibid., 68.
35. GB, '24 February'.

36. ibid.; OC XII 68–9. These independent reminiscences confirm each other with beautiful precision at this point.
37. OC XII 69–70.
38. ibid., 70.
39. ibid., 77–8. Bugeaud was certainly present, but AT, who detested him, either failed to see the marshal or failed to remember that he had. He always denied that Bugeaud had been there. See Senior, *Journal*, 27 October 1849; Bugeaud, II 305–6.
40. OC XII 86–9; 125–6.
41. AT to Bouchitté, Paris, 1 May 1848, OC(B) VII 235–6.
42. Amann, 939.

18. *June*

1. OC XII 150.
2. Falloux, I, 270; OC XII 90.
3. AT to Clamorgan, [Paris], 25 and 27 February 1848, OC X 444–7.
4. OC I i xliv.
5. Mélonio, 67.
6. OC XII 93, 95; Woodcock, *Proudhon*, 118.
7. Sand, 8.
8. AT to Clamorgan, Paris, 11 March 1848, OC X 453.
9. AT to Clamorgan, Paris, 7 March 1848, ibid., 450.
10. AT to MT, [Valognes, 14 March 1848], OC XIV 507.
11. AT to MT, Tocqueville, 20 March 1848, ibid., 515.
12. AT to MT, Sunday, 26 March 1848, ibid., 523; AT, [*Circulaire électorale*], OC III iii 39–42.
13. AT to MT, Tocqueville, 20 March 1848, OC XIV 516.
14. AT, 'Banquet populaire de Cherbourg', 19 March 1848, OC III iii 43–6; AT to Marie, 20 March 1848, OC XIV 517; OC XII 111–12: he alleges that he can't remember what he said. He attributes his success to the fact that he was improvising: 'For it can't be said too often that speeches are made to be heard and not read.'
15. OC XII 114; Loménie, 421.
16. AT to Clamorgan, 2 May 1848, OC X 459–60.
17. OC XII 177.
18. AT to Clamorgan [Paris, 7 April 1848], OC X 456.
19. OC III ii 757.
20. OC XII 115; AT to Senior, Paris, 10 April 1848, OC VI ii 101.
21. AT to GB, Tocqueville, 22 April 1848, OC VIII ii 12–13.
22. AT to Clamorgan, [Paris], 2 May 1848, OC X 460; AT to Mathilde de Kergorlay, April–May 1848, OC XIII ii 220.
23. Blanc, 417.
24. OC XII 149–50; see also James Pope-Hennessy, *Monckton Milnes: the Years of Promise, 1809–1851* (London, 1949), 283–5.
25. See Senior, *Journal*, 16 May 1848 (conversation with AT), 20 May 1848 (conversation with GB); Guillemin, 333–52; Agulhon, 52–3, seems to give a qualified assent to Guillemin's thesis.
26. Senior, *Journal*, 16 May 1848.
27. Guillemin, 336; Blanc, 391–2.

28. Senior, ibid., 19 May 1848.
29. OC XII 141; Blanc, 391–7; Quentin-Bauchart, 11–18.
30. Senior, ibid., 16 May 1848; OC XII 135–7, 141.
31. OC XII 140 n.1.
32. ibid., 184. For the committee minutes see OC III iii 55–158.
33. OC XII 180.
34. ibid., 184, 191; see Max Farrand (ed.), *The Records of the Federal Convention of 1787*, new edn., 4 vols. (Yale, 1966), *passim*.
35. OC XII 180, 185.
36. ibid., 189–90.
37. OC XII 189.
38. ibid., 180.
39. Senior, *Journal*, 20 May 1853: see CTG I 184–7; OC XII 180–82.
40. OC XII 189.
41. ibid., 173–4.
42. ibid., 171.
43. Falloux, I, 331–2, 334.
44. ibid., 335–6; Quentin-Bauchart, 29–30; de Luna, 136; Guillemin, 381 n.
45. De Luna, 136–7.
46. OC XII 156. It is not clear whether, in this passage, AT is referring to Louis Blanc's speech in his own defence on 15 May, when he was nearly shouted down, or to that of 31 May, when the law officers asked the Assembly for leave to prosecute him (Blanc, 400, 404); his acquittal took place on 3 June; William Fortescue, *Alphonse de Lamartine* (London and New York, 1983), 184–5.
47. OC XII 156.
48. AT to Marie, [National Assembly], 24 and 25 June 1848, OC XIV 541–2; AT to Clamorgan, 24 June 1848, OC X 468–9.
49. AT to Z. Gallemand, 25 June 1848, OC X 470.
50. Jardin, *Tocqueville*, 416; Alexander Herzen, *My Life and Thoughts*, tr. Constance Garnett (London, 1924), III, 23–4.
51. OC XII 219; LC 929 n.15.

19. *Retrospection*

1. Arthur de Gobineau to AT, 8 September 1843, OC IX 56.
2. AT to Eugène Stoffels, Paris, 21 July 1848, LC 635.
3. OC XII 86–7.
4. Duguit and Monnier, 234 ('Constitution du 4 novembre 1848').
5. OC III iii 167 n.2.
6. ibid., 172.
7. ibid., 180.
8. ibid., 215.
9. ibid., 221–2. André Jardin proposes a small emendation of the French text at one point (p. 221: '*instincts*' for '*intérêts*'): I have adopted it.
10. AT to GB, [Paris], 27 August 1848, OC VIII ii 32.
11. AT to GB, Paris, 24 September 1848, ibid., 53; to Clamorgan, Paris, 17 October 1848, OC X 484; de Luna, 405 n.17.

12. Ancelot, 156; AT to GB, [Paris, 23 October] 1848, OC VIII ii 76.

13. De Luna, 373.

14. AT to GB, [23 October] 1848, OC VIII ii 76.

15. De Luna, 382, 391; AT to GB, Paris, 8 December 1848, OC VIII ii 117. Cicero remarked of Octavian in 43 BC: 'Laudandum, ornandum, tollendum', translated by Anthony Everitt as 'The young man must get praises, honours and the push' (*Cicero*, 301). Within months Cicero was murdered, abandoned by Octavian to his enemies.

16. AT to GB, Paris, 27 October 1848, OC VIII ii 80; Rémusat, 374–6.

17. AT to Clamorgan, Paris, 22 January 1849, OC X 504; to GB, Bonn, 11 May 1849, OC VIII ii 128.

18. See, for example, AT to P.-M. Dudouy, [Paris, April 1849], OC X 528.

19. AT to George Grote, Paris, 27 February 1849, OC VI iii 117–19; AT, 'Projet de circulaire électorale', May 1849, OC III iii 257–61.

20. AF to J.-F. Hervieu, 19 January 1849, OC X 502; to Clamorgan, Paris, 16 March 1849, ibid., 519; Jardin, 'Introduction', OC III iii 24.

21. He filled at least one notebook with his German observations (see OC XII 280) but it is lost.

22. See Rivet to AT, OC XII 280–81 n.2; Barrot, II, 274; Dansette, 277.

23. Benjamin Disraeli, *Coningsby* (1844), ch. VI.

24. OC XII 199–206; Senior, *Journal*, 27 July 1849 (CCT I 65–6): Senior had begun a journal of his foreign journeys and conversations in 1848, and kept it up for the rest of his life, an invaluable source for AT's last ten years; Falloux, I, 467–80.

25. Senior, *Journal*, 17 April 1858, CCT II 193; 23 October 1849, CCT I 69–70; OC XII 234–6.

26. For these and other matters of the kind see OC XII 244–6, and Jardin, *Tocqueville*, 444–6.

27. See Senior, *Journal*, 17 February 1851 (CCT i 231–2) and Jardin, *Tocqueville*, 438.

28. Senior, *Journal*, 31 March 1852 (CTG I 53).

29. AT to GB, Paris, 12 October 1849, OC VIII ii 200.

30. See, for example, AT's letters to Corcelle and Beaumont at this time, *passim*.

31. Senior, *Journal*, 29 January 1851 (CCT I 195).

32. Falloux, I, 557.

33. Corley, 87.

34. AT to Corcelle, Paris, 2 November 1849, OC XI ii 14; Jardin, *Tocqueville*, 449–50.

35. AT to GB, Paris, 4 November 1849, OC VIII ii 232.

36. ibid., 233.

37. GB to AT, 4 January 1850, OC VIII ii 263; AT to Reeve, Paris, 15 November 1849, OC VI i 109; AT to Denise de Blic, Paris, 10 November 1849, OC XIV 252.

38. AT to Corcelle, 1 August 1850, OC XV ii 28; Jardin, *Tocqueville*, 451; AT to Reeve, Paris, March 1850, OC VI i 112; AT to K. de Circourt, 31 March and 5 April 1850; Senior, *Journal*, 14 May 1850 (CCT I 80). For the doctors' inconsistent verdicts see AT to E. Stoffels, Paris, 28 April 1850, OC(B) V 460, and AT to Mathilde de Kergorlay, 9 October 1850, OC XIII ii 228. Anne P. Kerr sensibly suggests that although the crisis broke out in March, AT had probably begun to feel unwell in February (OC XVIII 31 n.6).

39. GB, 'Notice sur Alexis de Tocqueville', OC(B) V 112; Senior, *Journal*, May 1850, *passim* (CCT I 73–94).

40. AT to Corcelle, Tocqueville, 7 June 1850, OC XV ii 23.

41. AT to GB, Tocqueville, 14 June 1850, OC VIII ii 274–6.
42. OC XII 29.
43. ibid., 61–2.
44. AT to Ampère, Tocqueville, 26 July 1850, OC XI 187; Senior, *Journal*, August 1850 (CCT I 99–144); AT to Clamorgan, 17 September 1850 (two letters) and 28 October 1850, OC X 546–50.
45. Senior, *Journal*, 26 August 1850 (CCT I 141).
46. AT to Clamorgan, Tocqueville, 9 July 1850, OC X 545; OC XII 267–76.
47. AT to Corcelle, Dijon, 1 November 1850, OC XV ii 34; AT to GB, Naples, 24 November 1850, OC VIII ii 326–7.
48. AT to Corcelle, Naples, 28 November 1850; AT to Armand Dufaure, Sorrento, 22 December 1850, LC 705–7; AT to GB, Naples, 24 December 1850, OC VIII ii 328.
49. Senior, *Journal*, 11 December 1850 (not in CCT); 25 January 1851 (CCT I 178–82); AT to GB, Sorrento, 26 February 1851, OC VIII ii 377–8; Ampère, 'Appendice', OC XI 444.
50. Senior, *Journal*, December 1850–February 1851, *passim* (CCT I 178–243).
51. AT to Kergorlay, Sorrento, 15 December 1850, OC XIII ii 229–34.
52. Senior, *Journal*, 13 December 1850 (JFI ii 6).
53. Kergorlay to AT, 19 January 1851, OC XIII ii 234–8; AT, 'Sorrente, Décembre 1850 – Napoléon', OC II ii 301.
54. AT noted on the cover of the manuscript that it was written at Sorrento 'by fits and starts' between November and March. This must be a slip: he did not settle in Sorrento until December, and the letter to Kergorlay of 15 December makes it plain that he did not immediately take up his task.
55. OC XII 177–8. In fact Chateaubriand died a week after the fighting ceased, on 4 July 1848. AT has sharpened the rhetorical effect by inaccuracy.
56. OC XII 83–4; Senior, *Journal*, 19 August 1850 (CCT I 112–14).
57. OC XII 87.
58. ibid., 86.
59. The one exception is AT to Harriet Grote, Tocqueville, [25] June 1850, OC VI iii 135, where AT casts the same idea in the form of a general reflection on historical change. Written five or six months before the passage in the *Souvenirs*, the letter illustrates the steadiness with which he clung to his ideas, and shows that what he says in the *Souvenirs* was no mere passing thought.
60. OC XII 96–7.
61. ibid., 179.

20. December

1. Senior, *Journal*, 10 April 1857 (CCT II 158).
2. AT to Hervé de Tocqueville, Paris, 1 December 1851, OC XIV 266.
3. AT to Marie, [Saint-Lô, 4 September 1851], ibid., 563.
4. OC XII 212; see also AT to Senior, Versailles, 27 July 1851, OC VI ii 133.
5. See OC I ii 273–6 and 322–7, 'Quelle espèce de despotisme les nations démocratiques ont à craindre'.
6. See Bury and Toombs, 120–23.
7. Dansette, 321–2.

8. AT to GB, Versailles, 14 September 1851, OC VIII ii 407, comments on the people's horror of the unknown, as he has just found it at the *conseil-général* of the Manche.

9. See Duguit and Monnier, 246: 'Constitution du 4 Novembre 1848, chapitre XI'.

10. Senior, *Journal*, 8, 14 and 18 May 1851 (CCT I 249–56; 18 May conversation misdated); Bury and Toombs, 124.

11. See Morny to Mme de Flahaut, 23 February 1851, Kerry, 86; AT, 'Conversation que j'ai eue avec le Président de la République le 15 mai 1851', OC III iii 422; OC XII 211.

12. OC II iii 421–2. André Jardin questions AT's sincerity in these remarks, thinking them too much like the *rhodomantades* of General Cavaignac, but they are consistent with everything else that he was saying at the time. For instance, the day before the interview he told Nassau Senior that if the president tried to achieve revision without the consent of the Assembly, 'he will find himself in Vincennes.' Senior, *Journal*, 14 May 1851 (CCT I 252).

13. AT, 'Note sur le Projet de Révision (Mai 1851)', OC III iii 417–19.

14. AT, 'Procès-verbaux de la commission chargée d'examiner les propositions relatives à révision de la constitution …', OC III iii 423–4.

15. AT, 'Rapport fait par M. de Tocqueville, au nom de la Commission …', OC III iii 433–53. The section of the report read out by AT is about 5,000 words long.

16. Karl Marx, *The Eighteenth Brumaire of Louis Bonaparte* (Moscow: Books for Socialism, n.d.), 101; Dansette, 324.

17. Senior, *Journal*, 18 May 1851 (CCT I 255, misdated); OC III iii 436, 441–2.

18. AT to Clamorgan, [Paris], 28 June 1851, OC X 555; Karl Marx and Friedrich Engels, *Manifesto of the Communist Party* (London: Penguin, 1967), 82; Marx, *Brumaire*, 113.

19. Walter Bagehot, IV, 31–2; AT to Marie, Valognes, [23 August 1851], OC XIV 554–5; AT to Gobineau, [Versailles], 6 August 1851, OC IX 190.

20. AT, 'Rapport', OC III iii 448; Marx, *Brumaire*, 102.

21. See Southern, 'Liberty', 112–16.

22. AT, 'Intervention dans la discussion sur la révision de la constitution au Conseil-Général, 28 août 1851', OC X 718; Henrik Ibsen, *Pillars of the Community*.

23. AT to Clamorgan, Versailles, 27 September 1851, OC X 558; to Marie, [Saint-Lô, 31 August 1851], OC XIV 559.

24. Simpson, 121.

25. Rémusat, III, 483; AT to Mrs Grote, [8 December 1851], OC VI i 125: this letter enclosed another, to the editor of *The Times* (see p. 521).

26. Senior, *Journal*, 31 December 1851 (CCT II 9–10).

27. OC XIV 565–6.

28. Rémusat, III 484–5.

29. ibid., 489; AT, to the editor of *The Times*, published 11 December 1851 (MLR II 176–92. The French original being lost, a retranslation from the English version was made for the *Oeuvres complètes*, VI i 119–29); OC XIV 271 n.3; Jardin, *Tocqueville*, 467.

30. Maurice Aguilhon, 143–44; Corley, 107–8; René Arnaud, 113–21.

31. MLR II 190.

32. AT to Édouard de Tocqueville, [7 December 1851], OC XIV 271–2. Édouard had written begging him to do nothing rash – just as Hervé had done in 1830 (see pp. 126).

33. AT, 'A Messieurs les Électeurs du Canton de Montebourg', 29 April 1852, OC X 725–6; AT to GB, Paris, 1 May 1852, OC VIII iii 44–5.

34. See AT to Rémusat, 22 March 1852, LC 1030–36.

21. *Writing History*

1. AT to HT, Tocqueville, 24 July 1852, OC XIV 283.
2. AT to GB, Paris, 1 February 1852, OC VIII iii 18–21; AT to E. Lieber, Tocqueville, 4 August 1852, OC VII 143–5; Senior, *Journal*, 17 May 1853 (CCT II 36–9).
3. See GB to AT, 9 March 1852, OC VIII iii 32–5.
4. AT to GB, Paris, 7 March 1852, 22 April, OC VIII iii 32, 41.
5. AT, 'Discours prononcé à la séance publique annuelle de l'Académie des Sciences Morales et Politiques du 3 Avril 1852 …', OC XVI 229–42. See GB to AT, 1 April 1852, OC VIII iii 36. The suppressed passage was eventually published at the very end of the Beaumont edition of AT's works: see OC(B) IX 643–5. The MS is lost. See also AT to Mrs Phillimore, 20 June 1852, OC VI iii 148, and n.2.
6. OC XVI 231.
7. ibid., 233.
8. AT to Mrs Grote, Paris, 3 April 1853, OC VI iii 145–6; to GB, Paris, 7 April 1852, OC VIII iii 39; to GB, Paris, 22 April 1852, ibid., 40.
9. AT to Marie, Paris, [1 May 1852], OC XIV 573.
10. GB to AT, 11 June [1852], OC VIII iii 49; AT to GB, Tocqueville, 15 June 1852, ibid., 51.
11. AT to Mathilde de Kergorlay, Tocqueville, 20 July 1852, OC XIII ii 241–2.
12. AT to Mme de Circourt, Tocqueville, 18 September 1852, OC XVIII 85.
13. AT to Kergorlay, Tocqueville, 22 July 1852, OC XIII ii 244; AT, 'Comment la nation en cessant d'être républicain était restée révolutionnaire', OC II ii 292. AT in his haste misquotes Fiévée, who actually says that he retired to Champagne.
14. AT to GB, [Tocqueville], 24 August 1852, OC VIII iii 71.
15. OC II ii 271, 276.
16. AT to Kergorlay, Tocqueville, 22 July 1852, OC XIII ii 244–5.
17. Kergorlay to AT, 2 August 1852, ibid., 246–8; AT to Z. Gallemand, [Tocqueville, 20 August 1852], OC X 566; ibid., 568 n.2, 569 n.1; OC II ii 293–8.
18. AT to Kergorlay, Tocqueville, 22 July 1852, OC XIII ii 243; to Édouard de Tocqueville, [Tocqueville], 17 September 1852, OC XIV 285; AT to Freslon, Tocqueville, 7 September 1852, LC 1052–3.
19. Ampère to Marie, 14 October 1852, OC XI 213; AT to Senior, Paris, 13 November 1852, OC VI ii 155; to Corcelle, Paris, 21 November 1852, 17 November 1852, 1 January 1853, OC XV ii 62, 65, 68.
20. AT to GB, Paris, 24 January 1853, OC VIII iii 83–4; to Hippolyte, end of December 1852, OC XIV 88; to GB, Paris, 24 January 1853, OC VIII iii 85; see Senior, *Journal*, 23 December 1851, and after that the 'Correspondance Anglaise' *passim* (OC VI i–iii).
21. See AT to La Rive, Paris, 20 March 1853, OC VII 329–30; La Rive to AT, 26 March 1853, ibid., 330 n.3; AT to La Rive, [Paris], 29 March 1853, ibid., 330–31.
22. AT to C. von Bunsen, Paris, 2 January 1853, OC VII 328–9; Bunsen to AT, 21 April 1853, cited in ibid., 329 n.4; *L'Ancien Régime et la Révolution: fragments et notes inédites*, OC II ii 243–65; AT to Bunsen, Paris, 23 May 1853, OC VII 332–3.
23. OC II ii 15; AT to GB, Paris, 23 March 1853, OC VIII iii 95–6.
24. AT to GB, Paris, 2 May 1853, ibid., 118; GB to AT, 9 February 1853, ibid., 87.
25. AT to GB, [Paris], 8 April 1853, ibid., 102; GB to AT, 19 April 1853, ibid., 111.
26. AT to GB, Les Trésorières, 4 June 1853, ibid., 128–9; 15 June, ibid., 131–2.

27. Senior, *Journal*, 9 May 1853 (CCT ii 36); Charles de Grandmaison, 'Alexis de Tocqueville en Touraine: préparation du livre sur l'Ancien Régime juin 1853–avril 1854, notes et souvenirs intimes' (Paris, 1893).

28. My entire account of AT in the archives at Tours is drawn from Grandmaison, *passim*.

29. OC II i 115, 152, 156.

30. Grandmaison, 5.

31. AT to Freslon, Saint-Cyr near Tours, 9 June 1853, OC (B) VI 207–8; *L'Ancien Régime et la Révolution*, 'Avant-propos', OC II i 70–71.

32. AT to Kergorlay, Saint-Cyr, 28 July 1853, OC XIII ii 256; AT to Mme de Circourt, Saint-Cyr, 2 September 1853, OC XVIII 103.

33. AT to GB, Saint-Cyr, 27 October 1853, OC VIII iii 160; 16 February 1854, ibid., 188–9.

34. For this account of Gobineau's thought I have relied on Biddiss; J.-J. Chevallier's introduction to OC IX; John Lukacs (ed. and tr.), *Tocqueville: 'The European Revolution' and Correspondence with Gobineau* (Garden City, NY, 1959), especially 179–87.

35. Chevallier, OC IX 18; AT to GB, Saint-Cyr, 3 November 1853, OC VIII iii 164; to Gobineau, Saint-Cyr, 17 November 1853, OC IX 203.

36. AT to Freslon, Saint-Cyr, 23 September 1853, OC(B) VI 233–4; AT to Kergorlay, [Saint-Cyr], 19 October 1853, OC XIII ii 268; to Rivet, Saint-Cyr, 23 October 1853 OC(B) VI 235–6; to GB, Saint-Cyr, 3 November 1853, OC VIII iii 164–5; to Freslon, Saint-Cyr, 3 November 1853, OC(B) VI 238; to Ampère, Saint-Cyr, 18 November 1853, OC XI 227; to Mrs Grote, Saint-Cyr, 22 November 1853, OC VI iii 161–2.

37. For what immediately follows, and indeed for much else in this chapter, I am largely indebted to Robert T. Gannett Jr's very valuable book *Tocqueville Unveiled*.

38. Mrs Grote, 'Notes relating to St. Cyr', CCT II 48; Senior, *Journal*, 1 June 1860 (CGT II 351); AT, 'Nécrologie de M. Le Peletier d'Aunay', [6 April 1855], OC XVI 413–19.

39. AT to Hubert de Tocqueville, Saint-Cyr, 7 March 1854, OC XIV 295.

40. Gannett, 61–77, is particularly illuminating on the use which AT made of Burke as an antagonist and (surreptitiously) as a model.

41. AT, *Ancien Régime*, title of chapter 2, Book 1, OC II I 83–6; ibid., chapter 5, Book 1, 95–6, where AT, ever anxious to be understood, repeats all his main points from his first four chapters.

42. AT to GB, Paris, 33, place de la Ville-l'Évêque, 17 March 1856, OC VIII iii 379.

43. AT to Theodore Sedgwick, Bonn, 17 July 1854, OC VII 156; to GB, Saint-Cyr, 27 May 1854, OC VIII iii 216.

44. AT to Ampère, Saint-Cyr, 31 March 1854, OC XI 236–7; OC XII 249;

45. D.A. Smith, 'A Conversation with Tocqueville, 1854', *Tocqueville Review*, vol. 10 (1989–90), 239–43, transcribes the entry in George Cornewall Lewis's diary for 7 August 1854.

46. AT to Ampère, Bonn, 21 June 1854, 5 and 21 August, OC XI 245–52, *passim*.

47. AT to Adolphe de Circourt, Wildbad, 1 September 1854, OC XVIII 199; to Ampère, Wildbad, 6 September 1854, OC XI 254; to George Cornewall Lewis, Wildbad, 19 September 1854, OC VI iii 170; OC II i 265–6.

48. AT to Corcelle, Clairoix par Compiègne (Oise), 2 October 1854, OC XV ii 120; to GB, Clairoix, 1 October 1854, OC VIII iii 240; to Corcelle, Clairoix, 23 October 1854, OC XV ii 122.

49. AT to Corcelle, Clairoix, 23 October 1854, OC XV ii 122; to GB, Clairoix, 26 October 1854, OC VIII iii 244–6.

50. The information in this paragraph is drawn almost entirely from Gannett, 138–41, 212–13, nn.25–48.

51. AT to Circourt, Compiègne, 26 January 1855, OC XVIII 234; to Ampère, Tuesday, [16? 23? January] 1855, OC XI 271; to Corcelle, 13 February 1855, OC XV ii 136; to GB, Compiègne, 8 March 1855, ibid., 281.

52. OC VIII iii 262 n.1.

22. *Writing Revolution*

1. AT to Circourt, Tocqueville, 8 November 1855, OC XVIII 282.

2. AT to GB, Paris, 23 April 1855, OC VIII iii 303; 25 May, ibid., 315; AT to Marie, [Paris, 26 May 1855], OC XIV 585; [27 May 1855], ibid., 586–7; AT to Madeleine [27 May 1855], ibid., 587.

3. GB to AT, 18 January 1855, OC VIII iii 319–20; AT to GB, Beaufossé, 20 June 1855, ibid., 320–22; AT to Ampère, Tocqueville, 4 July 1855, OC XI 287.

4. AT to GB, Tocqueville, 1 July 1855, OC VIII iii 324; AT to Senior, Tocqueville, 30 June 1855, CCT II 124.

5. AT to Ampère, Tocqueville, 12 July 1855, OC XI 289; to Corcelle, Tocqueville, 6 July 1855, OC XV ii 138; to Senior, Tocqueville, 25 July 1855, OC VI ii 182–3.

6. AT to Corcelle, Tocqueville, 4 August 1855, OC XI ii 143; ARP 1060; AT to GB, Tocqueville, 28 August 1855, OC VIII iii 336–7; to HT, Tocqueville, 25 November 1855, OC XIV 318; to Circourt, Tocqueville, 4 September 1855, OC XVIII 259; to Corcelle, Tocqueville, 16 October 1855 and 3 November 1855, OC XI ii 152, 153; to Ampère, Tocqueville, 27 December 1855, OC XI 304; to Circourt, Tocqueville, 2 January 1856, OC XVIII 297; to Hubert de Tocqueville, Tocqueville, 3 January 1856, OC XIV 322; to GB, Tocqueville, 7 January 1856, OC VIII iii 359; to Ampère, Tocqueville, 1 February 1856, OC XI 308.

7. See OC XIII ii, 1853–6, *passim*; Kergorlay, 'Essai littéraire sur Alexis de Tocqueville', *Le Correspondant*, April 1861, OC XIII ii 351–67; and, especially, Kergorlay to AT, 7 July and 22 August 1856, 298–307.

8. Herr, 107–19.

9. AT, *L'Ancien Régime et la Révolution*, OC II i 69; AT to Senior, Saint-Cyr, 2 July 1853, OC VI ii 162; Thiers, I, v; Senior, *Journal*, 19 August 1850 (CCT I 112).

10. Mélonio, 97–107; AT to Mrs Austin, Tocqueville, 29 August 1856, OC VI i 192.

11. OC II i 69, 71. See Herr, 114–17, for an interesting Bonapartist view of the *Ancien Régime*.

12. Hazareesingh, 13–14; Jones.

13. AT to HT, [Tocqueville, 5 November 1855], OC XIV 314.

14. Gannett, 143–4.

15. OC II i 75–6.

16. ibid., 75.

17. ibid., 249.

18. AT to GB, Paris, 22 February 1856, OC VIII iii 374.

19. OC II i 73–4; Senior, *Journal*, 10 April 1854 (CCT II 83).

20. OC I i 6; Montesquieu, *De l'esprit des lois*, Book II, chapter 4; OC II i 220.

21. OC II i 166.

22. Furet, in Furet and Ozouf.

23. Senior, *Journal*, 22 May 1850 (CCT I 92–3). This conversation is especially interesting since it shows how early AT formed some of the ideas which underpin the *Ancien Régime*, and how closely they were linked to his fear of socialism: 'Socialism & Communism are the same feelings logically carried out.'

24. OC II i 150.

25. ibid., 148.

26. OC II i 106.

27. Doyle, 1–43.

28. OC II i 184–5, 230.

29. ibid., 144–5.

30. For the *intendants* see ibid., Book 2, *passim* (especially the author's notes).

31. ibid., 193.

32. ibid., 245.

33. ibid., 248.

34. ibid., 217.

35. ibid., 250.

36. AT to Ampère, Paris, 17 February 1856, OC XI 309.

37. Ampère to AT, 16 February 1856, ibid., 309; AT to GB, Paris, 17 February 1856, 6 and 17 March 1856, OC VIII iii 370, 375, 379; Reeve to AT, 4 March 1856, OC VI i 165.

38. All this from Loménie, 425.

39. AT to Reeve, Tocqueville, 25 January 1856, OC VI i 157; Senior, *Journal*, 18 May 1856 (CCT II 132–3, misdated); AT to Mme Swetchine, Tocqueville, 7 January 1856, OC XV ii 269; AT to Marie, [Paris], February 1856, OC XIV 594; AT and GB, correspondence, February–June 1856, *passim*, OC VIII 370–412.

23. *Retreating*

1. AT to Kergorlay, 21 September 1856, OC XIII ii 315.

2. AT to HT, 28 May 1856, OC XIV 324–5; to Mme Swetchine, 12 June 1856, OC XV ii 273; to Kergorlay, 12 June 1856, OC XIII ii 296.

3. AT to Edward Vernon Childe, Paris, [?18] June 1856, OC VII 170.

4. See OC XIV, *Correspondance familiale*, *Table de destinaires*. Hervé's books were *Histoire philosophique du règne de Louis XV* (1847) and *Coup d'oeil sur le règne de Louis XVI* (1850). Excerpts translated into English have been published in Palmer.

5. AT to Corcelle, [Paris], 18 June 1856, OC XV ii 162–3. AT's emphasis on his father's religiosity must be taken more or less at face value, but it suggests that Hervé's outlook changed markedly over the years.

6. AT to Corcelle, ibid., 163; to Mme Swetchine, Tocqueville, 1 July 1856, ibid., 275.

7. AT to Reeve, Paris, 14 June 1856, OC VI i 183.

8. GB to AT, 25 January 1856, OC VIII iii 417; AT to GB, Tocqueville, 5 September 1856, ibid., 432.

9. AT to Kergorlay, [September] 1856, OC XIII ii 312; to GB, 27 March 1857, OC VIII iii 469.

10. AT to GB, 27 March 1857, OC VIII iii 469; to Mme Swetchine, 22 July 1856, OC XV ii 281; Léon Plée, *Le Siècle*, 18, 19, 21 and 27 July 1856: see LC 1185; AT to Plée, Tocqueville, 31 July 1856, ibid., 1186; to Ampère, Tocqueville, 21 October 1856, OC XI 351; to Corcelle, Tocqueville, 13 November 1856, OC XV ii 184.

11. Senior, *Journal*, 8 May 1857; Guizot to AT, 30 June 1856 (Saint-Lô: AT 1668). In this letter Guizot first sketches the ideas that he was to elaborate in his 1861 address to the Académie Française.

12. Mélonio, 100.

13. GB to AT, 19 November 1856, OC VIII iii 449.

14. Kergorlay to AT, 7 July 1856, OC XIII ii 298–9; 22 August 1856, ibid., 305; Mme Swetchine to AT, 13 August 1856, OC XV ii 287; AT to Kergorlay, Tocqueville, 22 and 28 August 1856, OC XIII 305, 308–9; Kergorlay to AT, 1 September 1856, ibid., 311. For a list of Kergorlay's improvements, see OC II i 325–33.

15. AT to Gobineau, Tocqueville, 30 July 1856, OC IX 265–9.

16. Gobineau to AT, 29 November 1856, ibid., 269–75.

17. AT to Gobineau, Tocqueville, 24 January 1857, ibid., 277–8; to Mme Swetchine, Tocqueville, 11 February 1857, OC XV ii 313–16.

18. AT to Gobineau, Tocqueville, 24 January 1857, OC IX 280–81.

19. Gobineau to AT, 20 May 1857, ibid., 281.

20. Harriet Grote to AT, 14 November 1856, Saint-Lô: AT 1648 (wrongly catalogued as from George Grote); J. S. Mill to AT, 15 December 1856, and AT to Mill, [Tocqueville], 19 December 1856, OC VI i 349–51.

21. AT to Kergorlay, Tocqueville, 28 August 1856, OC XIII ii 307–8.

22. AT to Mme Swetchine, Tocqueville, 11 February 1857, OC xv ii 309.

23. Senior, *Journal*, April–May 1857 (CCT II 157–87); AT to GB, Tocqueville, 10 October 1856, OC VIII iii 440; 6 April 1857, ibid., 478.

24. Monckton Milnes, 'Alexis de Tocqueville', *Quarterly Review*, vol. 110 (1861), 527; AT to Marie, [Paris, 26 May 1855], OC XIV 584, and n. 4.

25. AT to Corcelle, Tocqueville, 11 October 1856, OC XV ii 178; AT, 'Idée originaire, sentiment général et primitif du sujet', OC II ii 29; *Tâtonnements* (Nov. et Déc. 56), ibid., 173–4.

26. Drescher, *Tocqueville and England*, 191–2. The main sources for this episode are AT's letters to Marie from 19 June to 17 July 1857, OC XIV 596–626 (the letter of 17 July is badly misdated by the editor, p. 625); the journal of George Ticknor; the Hatherton diary; various letters exchanged with English friends, published in OC VI, all three volumes; and various letters from English men and women, preserved at Saint-Lô.

27. AT to Mme de Pisieux, Tocqueville, 21 September 1857, LC 1263.

28. AT to Marie, London, 20 [June 1857], OC XIV 598; [London, 2 July 1857], ibid., 613–14; Teddesley, 11 July 1857, ibid., 620–21; [Coleshill], Thursday, [16 July 1857], 624; to Radnor, Tocqueville, 19 August 1857, OC VI iii 265–6; diary of Lord Hatherton, 13 July 1857, Staffordshire Record Office D 260/M/F/5/26/72.

29. Brodhurst, 138.

30. AT to Marie, London, 1 July 1857, OC XIV 611; AT to Panizzi, Coleshill, 17 July 1857, OC VI iii 247–8; to Clarendon, [Tocqueville], 21 July 1857, ibid., 250–51; to W. Noel Sainsbury, [Tocqueville, 19 August 1857], ibid., 267–8; AT–Reeve letters, OC VI i 232–45 *passim*.

31. AT to Marie, [London, 21–2 June 1857], OC XIV 599–601; Ticknor, Ticknor to W. H. Prescott, London, 13 July 1857, II, 366.

32. Hatherton diary, 25 June 1857; AT to Marie, 20 June 1857, OC XIV 598; [25 June 1857], ibid., 605; Ticknor, II, 366, for an amusing corroboration of AT's description of

Macaulay, and 362–5, for AT in London; Lord Stanley, 'Breakfast with De Tocqueville 6 July 1857', Derby MSS Liverpool Record Office 920 DER 46/2. For a general account of AT's relations with Americans in his last years see Hugh Brogan, 'Alexis de Tocqueville and the Coming of the American Civil War', 91–112.

33. See OC VI i 353 for AT's effusive comments on the Prince, and for Albert's modestly sceptical reaction to the praise, which was forwarded to him by Lord Clarendon.

34. AT to Marie, [London], 2 July 1857, OC XIV 614.

35. Hatherton diary, 25 June 1857.

36. AT to Marie, [London], 3 July 1857, OC XIV 615–16; J. M. Mottley to AT, 1 July 1857, Saint-Lô: AT 2061 (misdated in the catalogue); to AT, 7 July 1857, Saint-Lô: AT 2061 (misdated in the catalogue); to AT, 7 July 1857, Saint-Lô: AT 2063; AT to Marie [London], 10 July 1857, OC XIV 618–19; J. M. Mottley to AT, 22 July and 18 August 1857, Saint-Lô: AT 2064–5; bill to AT from Messrs Lenny & Co., 10 August 1857, for a 'new Single Body Pony Basket Phaeton, with driving Seat in front for One, painted Blue', Saint-Lô: AT 366. AT paid for this vehicle in September with a draft on his British bank, Barings.

37. AT to Reeve, Tocqueville, 2 August 1857, OC VI i 228–9.

38. AT to Ampère, Tocqueville, 21 November 1857, OC XI 395–7; Loménie to Ampère, 15 September 1857, ibid., 390–91, n.1.

39. Loménie, 420–21.

40. AT to Mme de Pisieux, Tocqueville, 21 September 1857, OC(B) VII 462.

41. AT to GB, Tocqueville, 2 January 1858, OC VIII iii 527; Kergorlay to AT, 15 March 1858, OC XIII ii 334.

42. AT to Freslon, Tocqueville, 12 January 1858, OC(B) VII 478.

43. AT to Mme de Pisieux, Tocqueville, 24 July 1855, OC(B) VII 369–70; to Mme de Grancey, Tocqueville, 15 November 1857, ibid., 466–7; Grosclaude, 776–7.

44. AT, 'Idée originaire'. This was 'to be re-read occasionally to keep me on the high road of my thought, 1856'. The date is in the manuscript, and unquestioned by either of its editors, André Jardin (OC II ii 29) and Françoise Mélonio (ARP 1130); otherwise I would feel great difficulty in accepting it.

45. AT to Hubert de Tocqueville, Tocqueville, 7 February 1858, OC(B) VII 481–3.

46. AT to Reeve, [Tocqueville], 22 September 1857, OC VI i 236.

47. AT to Hatherton, Tocqueville, 6 March 1858, OC VI iii 289–90; to Reeve, Tocqueville, 30 January 1858, OC VI i 254–5. I am reminded of E. M. Forster's remark, two generations later, that the British Empire would be the first in history to be lost simply because of bad manners.

48. AT to Marie, Sunday morning, [April 1858], OC XIV 637. AT seldom or never put proper dates on his letters to his wife, which has often led his editors into error. Specifically, the dates conjectured in OC XIV for his April 1858 letters seem to me palpably inaccurate (I do not rely on them), but it is difficult to suggest convincing alternatives.

49. ibid., 639.

50. Senior, *Journal*, 20 April 1858. I have lightly edited this passage for readability.

51. AT to Marie, [Paris], Thursday morning, [? 14 April 1858], OC XIV 633 (this date suggested by the editors of vol. XIV seems correct); AT to Marie, Sunday morning, 18 [April, 1858], ibid., 638; to Marie, Wednesday morning, [April 1858; Jardin and Benoît suggest 5 May, but by then AT was back at Tocqueville], ibid., 647.

52. AT to GB, Tocqueville, 21 May 1858, OC VIII iii 570; AT, 'Rapport sur un ouvrage de M. Th. Sedgwick', OC XVI 243–7; AT to GB, Tocqueville, 17 June 1858, OC VIII iii 576.

53. GB to AT, 19 June 1858, OC VIII iii 578; AT to Mme de Circourt, Tocqueville, 23 June 1858, OC XVIII 478; to Senior, Tocqueville, 30 June 1858, OC VI ii 213 (CCT II 211); to GB, Tocqueville, 4 July 1858, OC VIII iii 583.

54. AT to GB, [Tocqueville], Thursday, 12 August 1858, OC VIII iii 593; to Ampère, Tocqueville, 30 August 1858, OC XI 409; to Freslon, 8 July 1858, OC(B) VI 444; Milnes to his wife, 10 August 1858, and to Marie de Tocqueville, 25 May 1859, OC VI iii 300 n.1.

55. AT to Hubert de Tocqueville, Tocqueville, 9 September 1858; to Marie, Paris, Monday, [13 September 1858], OC XIV 652 and n.2; to Marie, Paris, September–October 1858, OC XIV 654–62 passim.

56. AT to Édouard de Tocqueville, [Paris], Monday morning, [18 October 1858], OC XIV 355; to Marie, [Paris], Friday morning, [?1 October 1858], ibid., 657; to Marie, [Paris], Monday morning, [4 October 1858], ibid., 662.

57. AT to Marie, [Paris], Wednesday morning, [6 October 1858], ibid., 667.

58. AT to Ampère, Paris, 6 October 1858, OC XI 411; to GB, Paris, 23 October 1858, OC VIII iii 600.

59. AT to Freslon, Paris, 11 October 1858, OC(B) VI 459.

60. AT to Marie, [Paris], Wednesday morning, [6 October 1857], OC XIV 667; to GB, Paris, 23 October 1858, OC VIII iii 600.

24. Cannes

1. AT to Charles Stoffels, 22 October 1831; see p. 50.

2. AT to Édouard de Tocqueville, Aix [en Provence], 1 November 1858, and Cannes, 6 November 1858, OC XIV 356–7; to GB, Cannes, 11 November 1858, OC VIII iii 603; to Adolphe de Circourt, Cannes, 8 November 1858, OC XVIII 502.

3. AT to Édouard, Cannes, 13 November 1858, OC XIV 358. During the winter Auguste returned but was still too ill to be useful.

4. AT to Édouard, ibid.; Hippolyte de Tocqueville to Émilie, Cannes, 17 November 1858, Saint-Lô: AT 317; AT to GB, Cannes, 11 November 1858, OC VIII iii 604–5.

5. Lukacs, 157–8. This article was the first work to put our knowledge of AT's end on a sound footing, and my debt to it is enormous.

6. AT to Corcelle, Cannes, 22 November 1858, OC XV ii 234; to GB, Cannes, 23 November 1858, OC VIII iii 606–07; to Eugénie de Grancey, Cannes, 27 December 1858, LC 1327; to GB, Cannes, 24 December 1858, OC VIII iii 611.

7. AT to GB, Cannes, 24 December 1858, OC VIII iii 611; AT to Kergorlay, Cannes, 29 November 1858, OC XIII ii 343–4; Kergorlay to AT, 25 December 1858, ibid., 345–6.

8. AT to GB, Cannes, 3, 7 and 24 December 1858, OC VIII iii 607–13; to Ampère, Cannes, 5 December 1858, OC XI 415.

9. GB to AT, 23 June 1858, OC VIII iii 582–3; AT to Corcelle, [Tocqueville], 21 September 1858, OC XV ii 227–8; ibid., 228–43 passim; AT to GB, Tocqueville, 4 July 1858, OC VIII iii 584.

10. AT to Senior, Cannes, 12 December 1858, CCT II 216; to Circourt, Cannes, 19 December 1858, OC XVIII 513; to Ampère, Cannes, 30 December 1858, OC XI 417–18; Hippolyte to Édouard, 18 November 1858, Saint-Lô: AT 318. The Tocqueville archive also holds

two versions of a letter written by Dr Sève to Édouard in late November. Sève tries to be reassuring, but his message is gloomy (Saint-Lô: AT 319, 320).

11. AT to Émilie de Tocqueville, Cannes, 23 February 1859, OC XIV 366; GB to Clémentine, 21 January 1859, Yale: Beinecke (GB was repeating what he had been told by Édouard); Lukacs, 166, quoting documents prepared by the Sisters apparently to assist Lacordaire when, as AT's successor in the Académie Française, he was preparing the *éloge* which he delivered at his reception on 24 January 1861.

12. Lukacs, 168; Baunard, 349–52. Baunard was given a full account by Abbé Gabriel of his dealings with AT soon after the event, and noted them down at once. There are some unimportant discrepancies with the nuns' report. I have assumed that the curé gave an accurate account of his own experience, and that the nuns did the same of theirs, and in this way reconciled their testimony.

13. Lukacs, 166; AT to Edward Lee Childe, Cannes, 8 February 1859, OC VII 246; to Lanjuinais, Cannes, February 1859, LC 1328; to GB, Cannes, 15 February 1859, OC VIII iii 614–15; to Corcelle, Cannes, 5 February 1859, OC XV ii 240.

14. AT to Corcelle, 9 February 1859, OC XV ii 240; to Édouard de Tocqueville, Cannes, [6 February and] 27 February 1859, OC XIV 364, 367; to Freslon, Cannes, 23 February 1859, LC 1329.

15. AT to John Stuart Mill, Cannes, 9 February 1859, OC VI i 351–2.

16. AT to Édouard, 6 February 1859, OC XIV 364; to Édouard, Thursday morning, [Cannes, 17 February 1859], OC XIV 365–6; to GB, [Cannes], 3 February 1859, OC VIII iii 613–14; to Kergorlay, Cannes, 5 February 1859, OC XIII ii 346–7; to Émilie de Tocqueville, Cannes, 23 February 1859, OC XIV 366–7; to GB, Cannes, 15 February 1859, OC XIV 366–7.

17. AT to Ampère, Cannes, 3 March 1859, OC XI 419–21; AT to GB, Cannes, 4 March 1859, OC VIII iii 615–16.

18. Marie to Clémentine de Beaumont, Cannes, 4 March 1859, Yale: Beinecke, CI b; Lukacs, 158.

19. Lukacs, 166–7; Baunard, 349–52.

20. GB to Clémentine, 12 March 1859, Yale: Beinecke, DIV r. While at Cannes GB wrote to his wife almost every day, and sometimes twice. The result was what amounts to a detailed diary of AT's last illness. Held at Yale, it makes distressing reading. Yale: Beinecke also holds five drawings of the villa Montfleury and its neighbourhood made by GB at Cannes.

21. GB to Clémentine, 21 March 1859, Yale: Beinecke.

22. Jardin, *Tocqueville*, 531.

23. GB to Clémentine, 4 April 1859 (two letters), Yale: Beinecke; GB to AT, La Chartre-sur-le-Loir (Sarthe), 13 April 1859, OC VIII iii 616–19; GB to Clémentine, [Paris], 16 April 1859, ibid., 619 n.9, original at Yale: Beinecke.

24. AT to Ampère, Cannes, 9 April 1859, OC XI 423–44.

25. See OC IX 13–14 n.5; Jardin, *Tocqueville*, 529. This important statement seems to have been suppressed at Marie's insistence: she did not ever want to take the world into her confidence about the intimacies of her marriage.

26. Édouard de Tocqueville, 'Les Derniers Moments d'Alexis de Tocqueville', 21 July 1866, *La France*; Lukacs, 169–70.

27. Lukacs, 167, 167–8 n.36.

28. The chief difficulty lies in allowing for the different points of view of our informants: the nuns, Beaumont, Édouard, the Abbé Gabriel and Dr Dujardin-Beaumetz; but careful reading reveals very substantial agreement not merely about the events of these weeks, but about their significance. The remaining problem is to know what to make of various uncorroborated statements: for instance, that Dupanloup conducted a Mass in AT's room, and that AT discussed with GB receiving communion after he had done so. Since GB left Cannes on 5 April at the latest, and AT took communion on the 6th, this assertion is inexplicable, unless AT wrote GB a letter which is now lost.
29. OC IX 13–14 n.5; Jardin, *Tocqueville*, 529.
30. Jardin, *Tocqueville*, 532.
31. Ampère to AT, 30 March 1859, OC XI 422–3; Jardin, *Tocqueville*, 531–2.

Epilogue
1. See Loménie, 428.
2. Jardin, *Tocqueville*, 533.
3. Marie to R. Monckton Milnes, Tocqueville, 1 June (1859), Trinity College, Cambridge: Milnes papers.
4. Mélonio, 113, 241 n. 5; *The Times*, 11 April 1859.
5. Sainte-Beuve, *Causeries de lundi*, 93–121.
6. See Mélonio, 120–22.
7. 'Discours de M. Lacordaire prenant place au siège de M. de Tocqueville', 24 January 1861, OC XVI 326.
8. Réponse de M. Guizot', ibid., 332–45; Sainte Beuve, *Causeries*, 127–9.
9. See Mélonio, 116; Hugh Brogan, 'Tocqueville and the Coming of the American Civil War', 108–9.
10. Senior, *Journal*, 12–20, August 1861 (CCT II 220–80). Edited for readability.
11. Adapted from *Le Misanthrope*, Act I, scene 2: 'Pour les trouver ainsi, vous avez vos raisons', which AT misquotes in the *Souvenirs*: see OC XII 83.

BIBLIOGRAPHY

I. Abbreviations

This list explains the abbreviations used in the footnotes and endnotes. For full details of the books and archives mentioned see sections II and III of this bibliography.

ARP	Alexis de Tocqueville, *L'Ancien Régime*, Pléiade edition.
AT	Alexis de Tocqueville.
CCT	Nassau W. Senior, *Correspondence and Conversations with Alexis de Tocqueville*.
DA	Alexis de Tocqueville, *De la démocratie en Amérique*.
CTG	Nassau W. Senior, *Conversations with M. Thiers, M. Guizot, etc.*
GB	Gustave de Beaumont.
HT	Hervé de Tocqueville.
JFI	Nassau W. Senior, *Journals kept in France and Italy*.
LA	Gustave de Beaumont, *Lettres d'Amérique*.
LC	Alexis de Tocqueville, *Lettres Choisies*.
MLR	*Memoir, Letters, and Remains of Alexis de Tocqueville*.
OC	*Oeuvres complètes d'Alexis de Tocqueville*.
OC(B)	*Oeuvres et correspondance d'Alexis de Tocqueville*, edited by Gustave de Beaumont.
Saint-Lô	Saint-Lô, Manche, Departmental Archives, papers of Alexis de Tocqueville.
Senior, *Journal*	Nassau W. Senior, manuscript journal, National Library of Wales.
SP	Alexis de Tocqueville, *Système pénitentiaire*.
Yale: Beinecke	Tocqueville–Beaumont MSS collection, Beinecke Library, Yale University.
Yale: Stirling	Rare Books Room, Stirling Library, Yale University.

II. Primary Sources in Print and Manuscript

The most valuable source for the study of Tocqueville's life and works is undoubtedly the edition of his *Oeuvres, papiers et correspondances* (OC) which began publication in 1951. It is unfortunately still (in 2006) incomplete: we await three final volumes of Tocqueville's *correspondence générale*; and the constituent volumes are somewhat uneven in quality; but as a whole the edition is a noble monument to Tocqueville's memory. Without it the flowering of Tocqueville studies of the last thirty years or so would have been impossible. Its make-up is as follows:

OC I   *De la démocratie en Amérique*, 2 vols. (Paris, 1951), edited by J. P. Mayer, with an introduction by Harold Laski. Revised edition 1960.

OC II   *L'Ancien Régime et la Révolution*, 2 vols. (Paris, 1951): vol. 1 edited by J. P. Mayer; vol. 2, *Fragments et notes inédites sur la Révolution*, edited by André Jardin, with an introduction by Georges Lefebvre.

OC III   *Écrits et discours politiques*, 3 vols. (Paris, 1962, 1985, 1990), edited by André Jardin: vol. 1 introduced by J.-J. Chevallier and André Jardin, vols. 2 and 3 by André Jardin.

OC IV   *Écrits sur le système pénitentiaire en France et à l'étranger*, 2 vols. (Paris, 1984), edited by Michelle Perrot.

OC V i   *Voyages en Sicile et aux Etats-Unis* (Paris, 1957), edited by J. P. Mayer.

OC V ii   *Voyages en Angleterre, Irlande, Suisse et Algérie* (Paris, 1958), edited by J. P. Mayer and André Jardin.

OC VI   *Correspondance anglaise*, 3 vols: vol. I, *Correspondance avec Henry Reeve et John Stuart Mill* (Paris, 1954), edited by J. P. Mayer and Gustave Rudier, with an introduction by J.P. Mayer; vol. II, *Correspondance et conversations d'Alexis de Tocqueville et Nassau William Senior* (Paris, 1991), edited by Hugh Brogan and Anne R. Kerr, translated by B. M. Wicks-Boisson, with a preface by Eric Roll and an introduction by Hugh Brogan; vol. III (Paris, 2003), edited by Anne P. Kerr.

OC VII   *Correspondance étrangère: Amérique, Europe continentale* (Paris, 1986), edited by Françoise Mélonio, Lise Queffélec and Anthony Pleasance.

OC VIII   *Correspondance d'Alexis de Tocqueville et de Gustave de Beaumont*, 3 vols. (Paris, 1967), edited by André Jardin.

OC IX   *Correspondance d'Alexis de Tocqueville et d'Arthur de Gobineau* (Paris, 1959), edited by M. Degros, with an introduction by J.-J. Chevallier.

OC X   *Correspondance et écrits locaux* (Paris, 1995), edited by Lise Queffélec-Dumasy, with a preface by André-Jean Tudesq.

OC XI   *Correspondance d'Alexis de Tocqueville avec P.-P. Royer-Collard et avec J.-J. Ampère* (Paris, 1970), edited by André Jardin.

OC XII   *Souvenirs* (Paris, 1964), edited by Luc Monnier.

OC XIII   *Correspondance d'Alexis de Tocqueville et de Louis de Kergorlay*, 2 vols. (Paris, 1977), edited by André Jardin, with an introduction and notes by Jean-Alain Lesourd.

OC XIV   *Correspondance familiale* (Paris, 1998), edited by Jean-Louis Benoît and André Jardin, with a preface by Jean-Louis Benoît.

OC XV   *Correspondance d'Alexis de Tocqueville et de Francisque de Corcelle; Correspondance d'Alexis de Tocqueville et de Madame Swetchine*, 2 vols. (Paris, 1983), edited by Pierre Gibert.

OC XVI   *Mélanges* (Paris, 1989), edited by Françoise Mélonio.

OC XVII   *Correspondance générale*, 3 vols. (not yet published).

OC XVIII *Correspondance d'Alexis de Tocqueville avec Adolphe de Circourt et avec Madame de Circourt* (Paris, 1983), edited by Anne P. Kerr.

The deficiencies of the OC mean that scholars still have to refer to OC(B) from time to time: *Oeuvres complètes d'Alexis de Tocqueville*, 9 vols. (Paris, 1861–6), edited by Gustave de Beaumont; of these volumes the most useful – indeed, one might say, at this time of day the only useful ones – are V–VII, especially vol. V, which contains Beaumont's 'Notice', the first biography of Tocqueville. Some of the other gaps in the OC are filled by *Lettres choisies* (LC) (Paris: Gallimard, 2003), edited by Françoise Mélonio and Laurence Guellec; it also includes an up-to-date edition of the *Souvenirs*. The best edition of the *Démocratie* is Eduardo Nolla, 2 vols. (Paris: Vrin, 1990). The three-volume selection of Tocqueville's *Oeuvres* published in the Bibliothèque de la Pléiade (Paris: Gallimard, 1991–2004), edited by André Jardin, Françoise Mélonio et al., contains the best currently available edition of the *Ancien Régime*; as a whole, the selection is probably the most convenient presentation of Tocqueville's writings now on the market, though it contains no letters and none of the prison texts.

Abundantly though Tocqueville has been printed, scholarship must also still turn to the manuscript sources, which fortunately are mostly available in no more than two archival collections: the Tocqueville–Beaumont collection at the Beinecke Library, Yale University, and the *Papiers Tocqueville* accessible on microfilm at the Archives Départementales de la Manche, Saint-Lô, Manche. The Beinecke collection centres on Tocqueville as the author of the *Démocratie* (it contains the book's working manuscript); the *Papiers Tocqueville* is particularly valuable for his political career. But each archive has its auxiliary treasures. The Beinecke holds a large number of unpublished papers of Gustave de Beaumont, valuable both to the student of Tocqueville and to historians of nineteenth-century France and Ireland; at Saint-Lô may be found the manuscript memoirs of Hervé de Tocqueville. As a guide to all the main locations of Tocqueville documents, the catalogue to the Tocqueville papers prepared by Vanessa Gendrin (Université de Haute-Alsace, 2002) is invaluable.

Archival investigation never ceases; but I need add only that I have also consulted the manuscript of Nassau Senior's *Journal*, at the National Library of Wales; the Hatherton MSS, Staffordshire Public Record Office; and the papers of Monckton Milnes in the Library of Trinity College, Cambridge. A few other repositories are mentioned here and there in my notes.

III. Other printed works

The titles listed below for my readers' convenience are exclusively those of books and articles cited in this biography: I have not attempted to mention all the books which I have consulted, or which have influenced me; still less, to construct a general Tocquevillean bibliography. I must also remark that although most of these works are secondary, some of them contain documents which are not yet available elsewhere: for example, the memoirs of Virginie Ancelot.

Adams, Herbert B., *Jared Sparks and Alexis de Tocqueville* (Baltimore, 1898)

Agulhon, Maurice, *The Republican Experiment 1848–1852*, tr. Janet Lloyd (Cambridge, 1983)

Allison, John M. S., *Malesherbes: defender and reformer of the French monarchy, 1721–94* (Yale, 1938)

Amann, Peter, 'The Changing Outlines of 1848', *American Historical Review*, July 1963, 939

Ancelot, Virginie, *Un Salon de Paris 1824 à 1864* (Paris, 1866)

Arnaud, René, *Le 2 décembre* (Paris, 1967)

Bagehot, Walter, 'Letters on the French Coup d'État of 1851', *Collected Works* (London, 1968), ed. Norman St John Stevas, vol. IV

Barrot, Odilon, *Mémoires posthumes*, 2 vols. (Paris, 1875)

Baunard, Louis, *La Foi et ses victoires*, 2 vols. (Paris, 1882 and 1884)

Beaumont, Gustave de, *Marie, ou l'esclavage aux États-Unis*, 4th edn (Paris, 1840)

— *L'Irlande* (Paris, 1839)

Berthier de Sauvigny, G., *La Restauration*, new edn (Paris, 1955)

Blanc, Louis, *1848: historical revelations presented to Lord Normanby* (London, 1858)

Boigne, Comtesse de, *Memoirs*, 4 vols. (London, 1907–12), tr. Charles Nicoullaud

Bowen, Marjorie, *The Scandal of Sophie Dawes* (London, 1937)

Brodhurst, Audrey C., 'The French Revolution Collections in the British Library', *British Library Journal*, vol. 2., no. 2, autumn 1976

Brogan, D. W., 'Tocqueville', *French Personalities and Problems* (London, 1946)

Brogan, Hugh, 'Tocqueville and the American Presidency', *Journal of American Studies*, XV, 3, December 1981, 357–75

— 'Alexis de Tocqueville and the Coming of the American Civil War', *Americana: essays in memory of Marcus Cunliffe*, ed. John White and Brian Holden Reid (Hull, 1998), 91–112

Bugeaud, Marshal Thomas-Robert, *Memoirs*, ed. H. d'Ideville, tr. and abridged by Charlotte M. Yonge, 2 vols. (London, 1884)

Bury, J. R. T., and Toombs, R. R., *Thiers: a political life* (London, 1986)

Chateaubriand, François-René de, *De Buonaparte et des Bourbons, Oeuvres complètes*, vol. VII (Paris, n.d.)

— *Voyages en Amérique* (Paris, Bibliothèque de la Pléiade, 1969)

— *Mémoires d'outre-tombe*, ed. Jean-Paul Clément (Paris, 1997)

Chaussinand-Nogaret, Guy, *The French Nobility in the Eighteenth Century: from feudalism to enlightenment*, tr. William Doyle (Cambridge, 1985)

Chevalier, Louis, *Le Choléra: la première épidémie du XIXe Siècle* (La Roche-sur-Yon, 1958)

Chevalier, Michel, *Lettres sur l'Amérique du Nord* (Paris, 1836)

Cobb, Richard, *Promenades* (Oxford, 1980)

Collingham, H. A. C., *The July Monarchy: a political history of France 1830–1848* (London and New York, 1988)

Corley, T. A. B., *Democratic Despot* (London, 1961)

Crook, David Paul, *American Democracy in English Politics 1815–1850* (Oxford, 1965)

Custine, Astolphe de, *Lettres à Varnhagen d'Ense* (Brussels, 1870)

Dansette, Adrien, *Louis-Napoléon à la conquête du pouvoir* (Paris, 1961)

De Luna, F. A., *The French Republic under Cavaignac* (Oxford, 1969)

Dino, Dorothée, duchesse de, *Memoirs*, ed. and tr. Princesse Radziwill (New York and London, 1909), 4 vols.

Doyle, William, *The Oxford History of the French Revolution* (Oxford, 1989)

Drescher, Seymour, *Tocqueville and England* (Harvard, 1964)

— *Dilemmas of Democracy: Tocqueville and modernization* (University of Pittsburgh, 1968)

Drolet, Michael, *Tocqueville, Democracy and Social Reform* (London, 2003)

Duguit, Léon, and Monnier, Henry (eds.), *Les Constitutions et les principales lois politiques de la France depuis 1789* (Paris, 1925)

Duveau, Georges, *1848: the making of a revolution*, tr. Anne Carter, with an introduction by
    George Rudé (London, 1967)
Everitt, Anthony, *Cicero* (London, 2001)
Falloux, Alfred, comte de, *Mémoires d'un royaliste* (Paris, 1888)
Ford, Franklin L., *Robe and Sword: the regrouping of the French aristocracy* (Harvard, 1962)
Foucault, Michel, *Discipline and Punish* (London, 1979)
Fumaroli, Marc, *Chateaubriand: poésie et terreur* (Paris, 2003)
Furet, François, 'De Tocqueville and the problem of the French Revolution', *Interpreting the
    French Revolution*, tr. Elburg Foster (Cambridge, 1981)
— 'Tocqueville', in F. Furet and Mona Ozouf, *A Critical Dictionary of the French Revolution*,
    tr. Alan S. Kahan, 2 vols. (Chicago, 1998 and 2001)
Gannett, Robert T., Jr., *Tocqueville Unveiled: the historian and his sources for 'The Old Régime
    and the Revolution'* (Chicago, 2003)
Gobineau, Arthur de, *Selected Political Writings*, ed. Michael D. Biddiss (London, 1970)
Goldstein, Doris S., *Trial of Faith: religion and politics in Tocqueville's thought* (New York/
    Oxford/Amsterdam, 1975)
Grosclaude, Pierre, *Malesherbes, temoin et interprète de son temps* (Paris, 1962)
Guillemin, Henri, *La Première Résurrection de la République* (Paris, 1967)
Guizot, François, *Mémoires pour servir à l'histoire de mon temps*, 8 vols. (Paris 1858–64)
Hall, Basil, *Travels in North America in the Years 1827 and 1828* (Edinburgh, 1828: photographic
    reprint, Graz, 1965)
Hampson, Norman, *The Terror in the French Revolution* (London, 1981)
Hazareesingh, Sudhir, *The Legend of Napoleon* (London, 2004)
— *The Saint-Napoléon: celebrations of sovereignty in nineteenth-century France* (Harvard, 2004)
Herr, Richard, *Tocqueville and the Old Régime* (Princeton, 1962)
Himmelfarb, Gertrude, *The Idea of Poverty* (New York, 1984)
Howarth, T. E. B., *Citizen-King: the life of Louis-Philippe, King of the French* (London, 1961)
Ignatieff, Michael, *A Just Measure of Pain: the penitentiary in the Industrial Revolution 1750–
    1850* (London, 1978)
Jardin, André, 'Tocqueville et l'Algérie', *Revue des travaux de l'Académie des Sciences Morales
    et Politiques*, 4ᵉ série, 1962 (1ᵉʳ semestre)
— *Tocqueville: a biography*, tr. Lydia Davis and Robert Hemenway (London, 1988)
Jardin, André, and Tudesq, André-Jean, *Restoration and Reaction 1815–1848* (Cambridge, 1983)
Johnson, Douglas, *Guizot: aspects of French history 1787–1874* (London, 1963)
Jones, Peter, *Liberty and Locality in Revolutionary France: six villages compared, 1760–1820*
    (Cambridge, 2003)
Jordan, David P., *The King's Trial* (Berkeley, 1979)
Kerry, Earl of, *The Secret of the Coup d'État* (London, 1924)
Lacordaire, Dominique, and Guizot, François, *Discours de réception à l'Académie Française et
    réponse*, OC XVI 312–45 (Paris, 1989)
Lambetti, Jean-Claude, *Tocqueville et les deux démocraties* (Paris, 1983)
Laughton, J. K. (ed.), *Memoirs of the Life and Correspondence of Henry Reeve*, 2 vols.
    (London, 1898)
Leberruyer, Pierre, *Alexis de Tocqueville* (Saint-Lô, n.d.)
Lefebvre, Georges, *The Coming of the French Revolution*, tr. R. R. Palmer (New York, 1957)
Lehmann, A. G., *Sainte-Beuve: a portrait of the critic, 1804–1842* (Oxford, 1962)

Levy, S. Leon, *Nassau Senior: the prophet of modern capitalism* (Boston, 1943)

Lewis, W. David, *From Newgate to Dannemora: the rise of the penitentiary in New York, 1796–1848* (New York, 1965)

Loménie, Louis de, 'Publicistes modernes de la France: Alexis de Tocqueville', *Revue des deux mondes*, tome 21, seconde période (1 mai 1859), 402–28

Lukacs, John, 'The Last Days of Alexis de Tocqueville', *Catholic Historical Review*, vol. L, no. 2, July 1964, 157–8

Mansel, Philip, *Paris between Two Empires* (London, 2001)

Manzini, Charlotte, *Qui êtes-vous Monsieur de Tocqueville?*, (Saint-Lô, 2005)

Marcel, R. Pierre, *Essai Politique sur Alexis de Tocqueville* (Paris, 1910)

Mayer, J. P., *Prophet of the Mass Age: a study of Alexis de Tocqueville* (London, 1939)

Mélonio, Françoise, *Tocqueville and the French*, tr. Beth G. Raps (University of Virginia, 1998)

Mill, John Stuart, 'De Tocqueville on Democracy in America', *London Review*, October 1835; in *Collected Works* (University of Toronto, 1977), XVIII, 47–90

— 'De Tocqueville on Democracy in America [II]', *Edinburgh Review*, October 1840; in *Collected Works* XVIII, 153–204

— *Earlier Letters 1817–1848*, ed. Francis E. Mineka, 4 vols. (Toronto, 1963)

Morris, R. J., *Cholera 1832: the social response to an epidemic* (London, 1976)

Packe, Michael St John, *The Life of John Stuart Mill* (London, 1954)

Painter, George D., *Chateaubriand, a Biography*: volume one, *The Longed-For Tempests* (London, 1977)

Palmer, R. R., *The Two Tocquevilles: father and son* (Princeton, 1987)

Pessen, Edward, 'Tocqueville', *Tocqueville Review*, 1982, IV I 5–22

Pierson, George W., *Tocqueville and Beaumont in America* (New York, 1938)

Pilbeam, Pamela, *The 1830 Revolution in France* (Basingstoke, 1991)

Pinkney, David H., *The French Revolution of 1830* (Princeton, 1972)

Pouthas, Charles H., 'A. de Tocqueville, Représentant de la Manche (1837–1851)', *Alexis de Tocqueville: Livre du Centenaire 1859–1959* (Paris, 1960)

Quentin-Bauchart, *La Deuxième République et le Second Empire: mémoires posthumes* (Paris, 1901)

Ratcliffe, D. J., *The Politics of Long Division: the birth of the second party system in Ohio, 1818–1828* (Columbus, Ohio, 2000)

Rédier, Antoine, *Comme Disait M. de Tocqueville* … (Paris, 1925)

Reeve, Henry, 'Introductory Notice', *Democracy in America*, 4th edn, 2 vols. (London, 1875)

— *Memoirs of the Life and Correspondence of Henry Reeve*, ed. J. K. Laughton, 2 vols. (London, 1898)

Rémond, René, *Les États-Unis devant l'opinion française, 1815–1852*, 2 vols. (Paris, 1962)

— *The Right Wing in France: from 1815 to De Gaulle* (Philadelphia, 1966)

Rémusat, Charles de, *Mémoires de ma vie*, ed. Charles H. Pouthas, 4 vols. (Paris, 1962)

Richardson, Nicholas, *The French Prefectoral Corps 1814–1830* (Cambridge, 1966)

Richter, Melvin, 'Tocqueville on Algeria', *Review of Politics*, vol. 25, no. 3, July 1963, 362–98

Ross, Janet, *Three Generations of Englishwomen* (London, 1888)

Sainte-Beuve, C.-A., 'Alexis de Tocqueville: De la démocratie en Amérique', *Le Temps*, 7 April 1835, reprinted in *Premiers lundis* (nouvelle édition, Paris, 1894), II 277–90

— 'Alexis de Tocqueville', *Causeries du lundi* (4th edn, Paris, n.d.), XV 93–129

— 'Notes et pensées', *Causeries du lundi*, XI 459

Sand, George, *Souvenirs de 1848* (Paris, 1850)

Schleifer, James T., *The Making of Tocqueville's 'Democracy in America'* (Chapel Hill, 1980)

Siedentop, Larry, *Tocqueville* (Oxford, 1994)

Simon, G. A., *Histoire généalogique des Clerel, seigneurs de Rampan, Tocqueville, etc. (1066–1954)* (Caen, 1954)

Simpson, F. A., *Louis Napoleon and the Recovery of France* (London, 1951 edn)

Southern, R. W., *The Making of the Middle Ages* (London, Grey Arrow edn, 1959)

Stone, Lawrence and Jeanne C. F., *An Open Elite? England, 1540–1880* (Oxford, 1984)

Taylor, George R., *The Transportation Revolution* (New York, 1951)

Thiers, Louis-Adolphe, *History of the Consulate and Empire of France*, tr. D. F. Campbell and John Stebbing (London, 1893), vol. 1

Ticknor, George, *Life, Letters, and Journals*, 2 vols. (London, 1876)

Tocqueville, Édouard de, 'Lettre sur les derniers moments d'Alexis de Tocqueville', *La France*, 14 juillet 1866

Tocqueville, Hervé de, *Histoire philosophique du règne de Louis XV* (Paris, 1847)

— *Coup d'oeil sur le règne de Louis XVI* (Paris, 1850)

White, Richard, *The Middle Ground*: *Indians, empires and republics in the Great Lakes region 1650–1815* (Cambridge, 1991)

Whitehouse, H. Remsen, *The Life of Lamartine*, 2 vols. (London, 1918)

Woodcock, George, *Proudhon* (London, 1956)

— *Anarchism* (Cleveland and New York, 1962)

IV. List of illustrations

1. Unknown artist, *Hervé de Tocqueville*, 1822; 2. Tocqueville's mother, 1794; 3. Unknown artist, miniature of Tocqueville as a youth; 4. Unknown artist, Mary ('Marie') Mottley, c. 1830; 5. Gustave de Beaumont, 'Lake Oneida', 1831; 6. Gustave de Beaumont, 'Departure of the Indians across the Mississippi', 1831; 7. Gustave de Beaumont, 'Alexis de Tocqueville', 1831; 8. Léon Noel, lithograph of Tocqueville, 1848; 9. Théodore Chassériau, portrait of Tocqueville, 1850; 10. Honoré Daumier, caricature of Tocqueville; 11. Lithograph of Gustave de Beaumont, 1849; 12. Contemporary photograph of the Château de Tocqueville; 13. Gustave de Beaumont, 'Villa Montfleury, Cannes', 1859.

Endpapers: Anonymous cartoon of the newly elected members of the Legislative Assembly trooping across the pont de la Concorde, 1849. Tocqueville is visible just behind the front file; Thiers waves his hand at the rear.

Picture credits: Beinecke Rare Book and Manuscript Library, Yale University, 5, 6, 7, 8, 13; Mary Evans Picture Library, 10; Comte d'Hérouville/photo Archives départementales de la Manche, 1, 2, 3, 12; Mrs George W. Pierson, 4; Versailles, châteaux de Versailles et de Trianon, © Photo RMN/© Daniel Arnaudet: 9.

ACKNOWLEDGEMENTS

IN RECENT YEARS, seeing me so preoccupied with Tocqueville, some of my friends took to asking me if I liked him. I found the question difficult to answer, but my considered reply must be that Tocqueville is himself one of my oldest and dearest friends (I have known him for nearly fifty years), and although I use a friend's privilege to be frank about what I take to be his weaknesses, no-one else had better do the same in my presence. At the same time, I don't expect to have the last word. Debate about his life and work will not cease: both are inexhaustible topics, and definitive biography is impossible.

To acknowledge my great and small debts to the many individuals and institutions that have helped me over the years is, I find, to sketch my intellectual autobiography. I began to study Tocqueville when I was an undergraduate reading history at St John's College, Cambridge, in 1958 or thereabouts, and in the next sixteen years (and occasionally since) received everything I asked for in the way of encouragement and assistance from that body; above all when I was elected a research Fellow (Title A) in the spring of 1963. To win election I had submitted two or three draft chapters of a biography of Tocqueville (of which two or three sentences survive in the present work); the idea was that I would devote the period of my fellowship to the job of finishing it. This, finally, I have done; I hope the present Master and Fellows will feel that it at last justifies their predecessors' confidence in me all those years ago.

When my father, Professor Sir Denis Brogan, discovered that I was seriously interested in Tocqueville he made over to me his collection of early editions and secondary works, which has proved invaluable ever since; but I owe his memory thanks for much more than that, and never considered dedicating my book to anyone else. I wish he were alive to read it. In his time he was Tocqueville's true successor as the interpreter of America and France.

In 1962 I was awarded a Harkness Fellowship thanks, in large part, to the recommendation of my then employers, Donald Tyerman, editor of the *Economist*, and John Midgley, the foreign editor. My chief purpose in going to the United States as a Harkness Fellow was of course to get to know that country, but I also wanted very much to improve my qualifications as a Tocquevillean, and I am still grateful to the *Economist* and to the Commonwealth Fund for giving me the opportunity. With the Brookings Institution as my first base I studied democracy in America; then I transferred to Yale, with its outstanding holdings of Tocquevilleana, and worked happily in the Sterling and Beinecke Libraries (the Beinecke opened its doors for the first time during my residence at Yale) until March 1964. I met with unfailing kindness there. Silliman College gave me splendid accommodation; Professor George W. Pierson, the greatest Tocqueville scholar of his generation, supervised my research; my friend Marjorie Wynne and all the other librarians at the Beinecke were as helpful as possible.

Professor Pierson introduced me to André Jardin when he visited the Beinecke: M. Jardin was also all kindness, and I would owe much to him in the years to come. And it was Pierson who, when I returned to England, put me in touch with J. P. Mayer, then the director of the *Oeuvres complètes* project. This encounter was particularly fortunate for me, as Mayer needed someone to re-edit Nassau Senior's corres- pondence and conversations with Tocqueville; he gave me the job and, eventually, Anne P. Kerr as my co-editor: without her meticu- lous scholarship I doubt if I could have finished my task satisfactorily (neither she, nor Mayer, nor I was satisfied with the form in which the Senior material was eventually published, but that was not our fault).

In about 1970 I was approached by Fontana/Collins with a proposal that I should write a short volume on Tocqueville for the then-cele- brated Modern Masters series. I was happy to agree, as I had already begun to feel the need to present a preliminary report, so to say, of my Tocqueville findings. The book appeared in 1973, but not as a Modern Master: the series editor was not yet willing to include a nineteenth-century thinker in his stable, though in the end he published a volume on Karl Marx. But my little book sold reasonably, by my standards, and as I had hoped made me concentrate. So far as the present volume is concerned, it was a valuable rehearsal.

In 1974 I moved from Cambridge to Colchester, to the new University of Essex and its even newer History Department, where I have worked ever since, and where I have always received the encouragement and assistance (often in the form of study leave and research funding) that I have needed. But times were hard for a Tocqueville biographer: the family archives were still closed to researchers except those working on the *Oeuvres complètes* who needed access, and there was little I could achieve except an occasional article (and an occasional return visit to Yale). I turned to other work, but never renounced my Tocqueville project; and eventually I began to feel that Time was no longer on my side. By the year 2000 I had decided that if my book was ever to be written, or rather finished (quite a heap of preliminary drafts had accumulated), I would have to get moving; and then I learned from Françoise Mélonio that the Tocqueville family papers were now available to be studied in the Archives Départmentales of the Manche, at Saint-Lô. Permission had to be obtained, but it was promptly and graciously forthcoming from M. le comte Guy d'Hérouville. I went to Saint-Lô twice, and the British Academy gave me a generous grant to make a final visit, lasting a month, to Yale. I gratefully acknowledge this assistance, and must also record my debt to the late Professor Douglas Johnson, and to Professor Geoffrey Crossick, who were my referees. I was received at Yale as generously as ever, and the visits to Saint-Lô were delightful (especially as the hotel where I stayed boasted a Restaurant Tocqueville). I offer warm thanks to M. Gilles Désiré Dit Gosset and his staff at the Archives.

That was in 2003, and it has been hard slog ever since. If the result in any way justifies so much investment by so many people, it will also perhaps justify the faith in me shown by many other friends and colleagues. Too many on the list are now dead: to those already mentioned I must add the name of Sir Harry Hinsley, who taught me so much when I was an undergraduate, and later did more than anyone else to get my career as a scholar launched.

Among the living, Geraldine de Berly and Judge Jim Fahey gained me access to Auburn State Penitentiary, New York, where I made a most profitable visit. Dr Peter Chapman was at all times ready with advice on Tocqueville's illnesses. William Doyle and Douglas Johnson advised me on certain passages sent to them for comment. Thanks to the researches of Sheila Le Sueur several important details of Marie's life have been verified. I must also acknowledge assistance and encouragement received over the decades from Michael Biddiss, Patrick Brogan, Josette Brogan, Nigel Cochrane, Seymour Drescher, Michael Drolet, John B. Fox Jr, Shirley Hazzard, Nick Joll, Nicholas Jolley, Jeremy Krikler, Sheila Le Sueur, Heinz Lubasz, Françoise Mélonio, Roger Mettam, Munroe Price, Lucy Riall, Melvin Richter, Arthur Schlesinger Jr, James T. Schleifer, Larry Siedentop, Jill Steinberg, Jonathan Steinberg, the late Graham Storey, André Tarniou, J. R. Vincent, Matthew Woollard, the Staffordshire Record Office, and Janice L. Wood, archivist, of the Devon Record Office.

Three other individuals have been invaluable to me: Anne P. Kerr, who has always been available to advise me and to discuss Tocqueville with me, and whose erudition in nineteenth-century French history has taught me much; John Lukacs, who read my MS for Yale University Press and produced a long list of excellent comments and suggestions; and Hugh Tulloch, who also read the MS, and over the years has always been willing to fall in with any scheme of Tocquevillean research where his involvement would help: on visits, for example, to Cherbourg, Metz, Compiègne, Sorrento and Paris, Paris, Paris. I offer all of them my warmest thanks.

Finally I must thank Peter Carson of Profile Books, my publisher, and Mark Handsley, my copy-editor. I and my book owe a great deal to their eye for detail. They must not be blamed for any blemishes which remain after their hard work. The author put them there in the first place, and his is the fault if they are still there at the last.

HUGH BROGAN
Wivenhoe, 29 July 2006.

INDEX